March 2–4, 2015
San Antonio, Texas, USA

I0047355

**Association for
Computing Machinery**

Advancing Computing as a Science & Profession

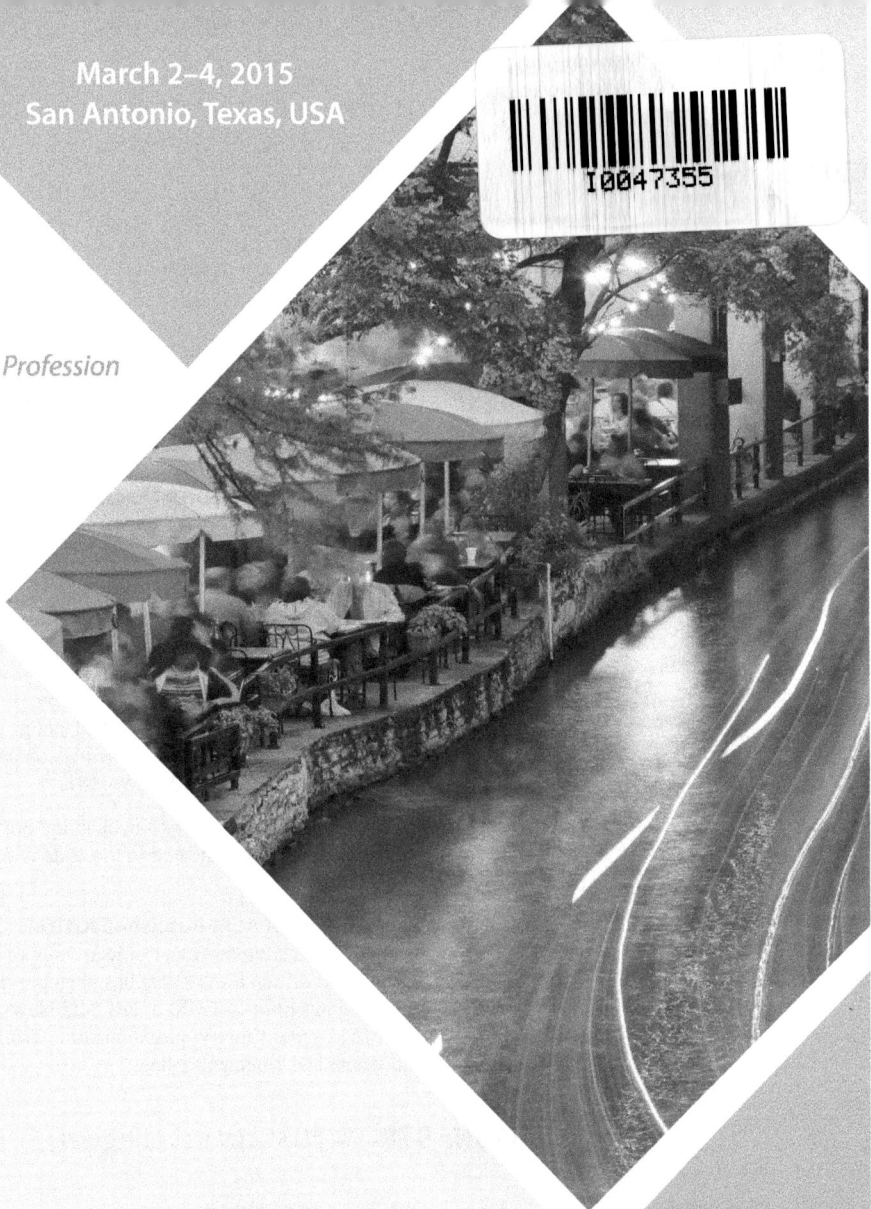

CODASPY'15

Proceedings of the 5th ACM Conference on

Data and Application Security and Privacy

Sponsored by:
ACM SIGSAC

Supported by:
**The Institute of Cyber Security (UTSA)
and CERIAS & Cyber Center (Purdue University)**

Association for Computing Machinery

Advancing Computing as a Science & Profession

The Association for Computing Machinery
2 Penn Plaza, Suite 701
New York, New York 10121-0701

Notice to Past Authors of ACM-Published Articles
ACM intends to create a complete electronic archive of all articles and/or other material previously published by ACM. If you have written a work that has been previously published by ACM in any journal or conference proceedings prior to 1978, or any SIG Newsletter at any time, and you do NOT want this work to appear in the ACM Digital Library, please inform permissions@acm.org, stating the title of the work, the author(s), and where and when published.

ISBN: 978-1-4503-3191-3 (Digital)

ISBN: 978-1-4503-3510-2 (Print)

Additional copies may be ordered prepaid from:

ACM Order Department
PO Box 30777
New York, NY 10087-0777, USA

Phone: 1-800-342-6626 (USA and Canada)
+1-212-626-0500 (Global)
Fax: +1-212-944-1318
E-mail: acmhelp@acm.org
Hours of Operation: 8:30 am – 4:30 pm ET

Printed in the USA

Foreword

It is our great pleasure to welcome you to the fifth edition of the *ACM Conference on Data and Application Security and Privacy (CODASPY 2015)*, which follows the successful four editions held in February/March 2011, 2012, 2013 and 2014. This conference series has been founded to foster novel and exciting research in this arena and to help generate new directions for further research and development. The initial concept came up in a conversation between the two co-founders when both happened to be at the same meeting. This was followed by discussions with a number of fellow cyber security researchers. Their enthusiastic encouragement persuaded the co-founders to move ahead with the always daunting task of creating a high-quality conference.

Data and applications that manipulate data are crucial assets in today's information age. With the increasing drive towards availability of data and services anytime and anywhere, security and privacy risks have increased. Vast amounts of privacy-sensitive data are being collected today by organizations for a variety of reasons. Unauthorized disclosure, modification, usage or denial of access to these data and corresponding services may result in high human and financial costs. New applications such as social networking and social computing provide value by aggregating input from numerous individual users and the mobile devices they carry and computing new information of benefit to society and individuals. To achieve efficiency and effectiveness in traditional domains such as healthcare there is a drive to make these records electronic and highly available. The need for organizations to share information effectively is underscored by rapid innovations in the business world that require close collaboration across traditional boundaries. Security and privacy in these and other arenas can be meaningfully achieved only in context of the application domain. Data and applications security and privacy has rapidly expanded as a research field with many important challenges to be addressed.

In response to the call for papers of CODASPY 2015 a total of 91 papers were submitted from Asia, Australia, Europe, and North America (87 were eventually reviewed). The program committee selected 19 full-length research papers (21% of acceptance rate). These papers cover a variety of topics, including privacy of outsourced data, novel privacy techniques and applications, and access control and security of smart appliances and mobile devices. The program committee also selected 8 short papers for presentation. The program also includes a poster paper session presenting exciting work in progress, as well as a panel session led by Bhavani Thuraisingham on Big Data Security and Privacy. The program is complemented by keynote speeches by William Horne and Günter Karjoth. This year for the first time there will be a co-located workshop on Security and Privacy Analytics (IWSPA15).

The organization of a conference like CODASPY requires the collaboration of many individuals. First of all, we would like to thank the authors for submitting to the conference and the keynote speakers for graciously accepting our invitation. We express our gratitude to the program committee members and external reviewers for their efforts in reviewing the papers, engaging in active online discussion during the selection process and providing valuable feedback to authors. We also would like to thank Gabriel Ghinita (the workshop chair), Adam Lee (the poster paper track chair), and the committee of the poster track for their excellent job. Our special thanks go to our local arrangements chair, Suzanne Tanaka, and to our Web master and publicity chair, Ram Krishnan. Finally, we would like to thank our sponsor, ACM SIGSAC, for their support of this conference.

We hope that you will find this program interesting and that the conference will provide you with a valuable opportunity to interact with other researchers and practitioners from institutions around the world. Enjoy!

Jaehong Park	**Anna Squicciarini**
CODASPY'15 General Chair	*CODASPY'15 Program Chair*
University of Texas at San Antonio,	*Pennsylvania State University,*
USA	*USA*

Table of Contents

Session: Cloud and BigData Security
Session Chair: Elisa Bertino *(Purdue University)*

Session: Software Security
Session Chair: Murat Kantarcioglu *(The University of Texas at Dallas)*

Keynote Address 2

Session Chair: Ravi Sandhu *(University of Texas at San Antonio)*

Short Papers 1

Session Chair: Bruno Crispo *(University of Trento)*

Panel Session

Session Chair: Bhavani Thuraisingham *(The University of Texas at Dallas)*

Short Papers 2

Session Chair: Ram Krishnan *(University of Texas at San Antonio)*

Session: Privacy Preserving Techniques

Session Chair: Li Xiong *(Emory University)*

CODASPY 2015 Conference Organization

General Chair: Jaehong Park, *University of Texas at San Antonio, USA*

Program Chair: Anna Squicciarini, *The Pennsylvania State University, USA*

Poster Chair: Adam J. Lee, *University of Pittsburgh, USA*

Workshop Chair: Gabriel Ghinita, *University of Massachusetts, Boston, USA*

Local Arrangements Chair: Suzanne Tanaka, *University of Texas at San Antonio, USA*

Publicity/Web Chair: Ram Krishnan, *University of Texas at San Antonio, USA*

Program Committee: Gail-Joon Ahn, *Arizona State University, USA*
Elisa Bertino, *Purdue University, USA*
Barbara Carminati, *University of Insubria, Italy*
William Enck, *North Carolina State University, USA*
Elena Ferrari, *University of Insubria, Italy*
Philip W. L. Fong, *University of Calgary, Canada*
Debin Gao, *Singapore Management University, Singapore*
Gabriel Ghinita, *University of Massachusetts, Boston, USA*
Hannes Hartenstein, *KIT, Germany*
James Joshi, *University of Pittsburgh, USA*
Murat Kantarcioglu, *University of Texas at Dallas, USA*
Guenter Karjoth, *Lucerne University of Applied Sciences, Switzerland*
Ram Krishnan, *University of Texas at San Antonio, USA*
Ashish Kundu, *IBM T J Watson Research Center, USA*
Adam J. Lee, *University of Pittsburgh, USA*
Qi Li, *ETH, Switzerland*
Peng Liu, *The Pennsylvania State University, USA*
Fabio Martinelli, *IIT-CNR, Italy*
Balaji Palanisamy, *University of Pittsburgh, USA*
Jun Pang, *University of Luxembourg, Luxembourg*
Günther Pernul, *Universität Regensburg, Germany*
Alexander Pretschner, *Technische Universität München, Germany*
Indrajit Ray, *Colorado State University, USA*
Ahmad-Reza Sadeghi, *Technical University Darmstadt, Germany*
Ravi Sandhu, *University of Texas at San Antonio, USA*
Seung-Hyun Seo, *Korea University, Korea*
Mohamed Shehab, *University of North Carolina at Charlotte, USA*
Hassan Takabi, *University of North Texas, USA*
Mahesh Tripunitara, *The University of Waterloo, Canada*
Vijay Varadharajan, *Macquarie University, Australia*
Danfeng Yao, *Virginia Tech, USA*
Chuan Yue, *University of Colorado Colorado Springs, USA*
Xinwen Zhang, *Samsung, USA*
Sencun Zhu, *The Pennsylvania State University, USA*

CODASPY 2015 Conference Sponsor & Supporters

Sponsor:

Supporters:

DBMask: Fine-Grained Access Control on Encrypted Relational Databases

Muhammad I. Sarfraz[§1], Mohamed Nabeel[*2], Jianneng Cao[#3], Elisa Bertino[§4]

§Purdue University, USA
[1]msarfraz,[4]bertino@purdue.edu

*Oracle, USA
[2]nabeel.mohamed.nabeel@oracle.com

#The Institute for Infocomm Research, Singapore
[3]caojn@i2r.a-star.edu.sg

ABSTRACT

For efficient data management and economic benefits, organizations are increasingly moving towards the paradigm of "database as a service" by which their data are managed by a database management system (DBMS) hosted in a public cloud. However, data are the most valuable asset in an organization, and inappropriate data disclosure puts the organization's business at risk. Therefore, data are usually encrypted in order to preserve their confidentiality. Past research has extensively investigated query processing on encrypted data. However, a naive encryption scheme negates the benefits provided by the use of a DBMS. In particular, past research efforts have not adequately addressed flexible cryptographically enforced access control on encrypted data at different granularity levels which is critical for data sharing among different users and applications. In this paper, we propose DBMask, a novel solution that supports fine-grained cryptographically enforced access control, including column, row and cell level access control, when evaluating SQL queries on encrypted data. Our solution does not require modifications to the database engine, and thus maximizes the reuse of the existing DBMS infrastructures. Our experiments evaluate the performance and the functionality of an encrypted database and results show that our solution is efficient and scalable to large datasets.

Categories and Subject Descriptors

D.4.6 [**Security and Protection**]: *Access controls, Cryptographic controls*

Keywords

Encrypted Query Processing; Attribute-based Group Key Management; Database-as-a-Service

CODASPY'15, March 02 - 04 2015, San Antonio, TX, USA.
Copyright © 2015 ACM 978-1-4503-3191-3/15/03:.$15.00.
http://dx.doi.org/10.1145/2699026.2699101.

1. INTRODUCTION

The advances of Internet technology and the increasing demand for cost-effective and efficient data management have prompted the emergence of cloud storage servers, such as Rackspace, Amazon EC2, and Microsoft Azure. These third party clouds provide reliable data storage and efficient query processing services able to scale to large data volumes. By outsourcing data to the cloud, organizations save the cost of building and maintaining a private database system and have to pay only for the services they actually use. Therefore, organizations are increasingly interested in the paradigm of "database as a service". However in order to protect data from inappropriate disclosure either by the cloud or external attackers, the data are usually encrypted before being outsourced to the cloud. The use of encryption raises issues related to the efficient processing of queries on encrypted data. In order to address such issues, past research has extensively investigated various techniques, such as bucketization [13, 14] and secure indexing [10, 27]. However, these techniques do not differentiate among authorized users of the data and thus do not support flexible access control with different units of access control granularity. This is inconsistent with the data sharing requirements of most real-world applications.

Our work is inspired by the CryptDB project [20], which is the first research effort that has systematically investigated access control for SQL queries on encrypted relational data. The CryptDB architecture assumes a proxy between the users and the cloud server. Authorized users log into the proxy by entering passwords, from which the proxy derives secret keys. Given a plaintext query submitted by a user, the proxy first checks if the query is authorized according to the access control policies. If this is the case, the proxy encrypts the query (i.e., encrypts table/column names and the constants in the query) by the corresponding secret key derived from the user's password. The encrypted query is then forwarded to the cloud, which runs the query over encrypted data and returns the result to the proxy. The proxy then decrypts the query result and returns it to the user.

CryptDB [20] however suffers from the following limitations. The first limitation is the onions of encryption. An onion is a multiple layers of encryptions. Each layer is applied for a specific query operation or purpose, and the encryption layers from the external layer to the most internal layer are increasingly weaker. Consider an onion for equality matching. In this case, depending on the expected queries, there would be three layers in CryptDB: the inner most layer is an adapted deterministic encryption for equality join, the middle one is a classic deterministic encryption for equality selection, and the outer most one is a random encryption to assure the maximum security. Given a query equality join, the proxy transmits the secret keys to the cloud server, so that the server can peel off the first two layers (i.e., random encryption and deterministic encryption) and run the join operation. Therefore, it is easy to see that the support of query operations is at the cost of multiple decryptions of entire columns. In addition, although onions offer multiple levels of security, the security level decreases over time when the outer layers are removed. Hence, the real security level an onion can guarantee is the protection offered by the inner most encryption. Furthermore, to support diverse operations, multiple onions need to be generated (e.g., an *order* onion is necessary if range queries are to be supported). The second limitation is that the the row/cell level access control mechanism is not cryptographically enforced. Instead, CryptDB always encrypts a column using a single key and utilizes a proxy based reference monitor to enforce row level access control. When the access control is not fully enforced using cryptography, the system is susceptible to bypass and SQL injection attacks. For example, a malicious user may trick the database to return more rows than they have access to. The risk of such attacks can be reduced by utilizing cryptographic enforcement since malicious users are unable to decrypt the result. The third limitation is that the row/cell level access control policies are difficult to manage and less expressive compared to attribute based access control policies. CryptDB uses 'speaks for' relationships to specify row level access control policies. Since the policies in such a scheme are specified at user level, each user is associated with many 'speaks for' relationships and the management of policies becomes difficult. Further, CryptDB fails to process queries on the cloud server over data items encrypted with different keys for different users based on access control policy since the ciphertexts are encrypted with different keys even though the users are authorized. The forth limitation is that CryptDB is unable to execute queries that cannot be processed entirely on the server. For example, it does not support queries requiring both comparison and computation on the same column.

To address the limitations of CryptDB, in this paper we propose DBMask, a novel solution that supports cryptographically enforced fine-grained access control when evaluating SQL queries on encrypted relational databases. Our solution does not require modifications to the database engine, and thus maximizes the reuse of the existing database management systems (DBMS) infrastructures. Our novel contributions include:

- A novel approach to support relational query operators by adding a comparison friendly encrypted column per column. Different algorithms such as order preserving encryption [6], symmetric key based searcheable encryption [25] and so on can be plugged in, depending on column data types and the security requirements.

- An approach based on an expressive attribute-based group key management scheme [24, 17, 16] to cryptographically enforce access control policies on outsourced databases at the granularity level of a table, a column, a row as well as a cell. Under our approach, different portions of data are encrypted by different keys according to the access control policies, so that only authorized users receive the keys to decrypt the data they are authorized for access.

- A new architecture to execute encrypted queries over an encrypted databased hosted on an untrusted cloud as a service.

The paper is organized as follows. Section 2 discusses related work. Section 3 provides an overview of our solution and the adversarial model. Section 4 introduces a fine-grained access control model and discusses its enforcement. Section 5 describes the key cryptographic constructs for SQL query operators and briefly analyzes the security of each construct. Section 6 describes the evaluation of encrypted queries over an encrypted database in the cloud. Section 7 reports experimental results. Finally, Section 8 outlines conclusions and future work.

2. RELATED WORK

In this section, we compare related work with our approach. Some of the techniques used in DBMask are built on prior work from the cryptographic community.

In theory, it is possible to utilize fully homomorphic encryption [12] to perform any arbitrary operation that a relational database requires. However, current implementations of fully homomorphic encryption are very inefficient and are not suitable for practical applications [11]. With the increasing utilization of cloud computing services, recent research efforts [7] have developed privacy preserving access control systems by combining oblivious transfer and anonymous credentials. The goal of such work has similarities to ours but we identify the following limitations. Each transfer protocol allows one to access only one record from the database, whereas our approach does not have any limitation on the number of records that can be accessed at once since we separate the access control from query processing. Another drawback is that the size of the encrypted database is not constant with respect to the original database size. Redundant encryption of the same record is required to support access control policies involving disjunctions. By contrast, in our approach the encryption is independent of the policies.

While attribute based encryption (ABE) based approaches [5] support expressive policies, they cannot handle revocations efficiently. Yu et al. [28] proposed an approach based on ABE utilizing PRE (Proxy Re-Encryption) to address the revocation problem of ABE. While such approach solves the revocation problem to some extent, it does not preserve the privacy of the identity attributes as in our approach. Further, these approaches mostly focus on non-relational data such as documents, whereas DBMask is optimized for relational data. Samanthula et al. [21] propose an approach that relies on homomorphic encryption and PRE to handle user revocations without requiring re-encryption of relational data and also supports expressive policies. However, such approach incurs a heavy cost on the end user as all processing is done at the client side since the server does not perform secure query processing. Techniques for efficient query processing over encrypted data have also been investigated. Hacigümüs et al. [13] proposed a pioneering approach that makes it possible to perform as much query processing as possible at the remote database server without decrypting the data and then performing the remaining query processing at the client site. Such approach uses a bucketization technique to execute approximate queries at the remote database server and then execute the original query over the approximate result set returned by the remote server. Asghar et al. [2] proposed a multi-user scheme that supports searches of keywords or conjuctions of keywords on untrusted servers while enforcing authorizations at table/column level. While DBMask utilizes split processing between the cloud server and the proxy for complex queries, DBMask is different in that it performs an exact query execution whenever possible and it enforces row/cell level access control utilizing the attribute based group key management (AB-GKM) scheme [17, 16], whereas the above approaches do not support fine-grained access control of the relational data.

The idea of using specialized encryption techniques such as order preserving encryption [6] and additive homomorphic encryption [18] to perform different relational operations has been introduced in CryptDB [20]. The same idea is extended to support more complex analytical queries in MONOMI [26]. As mentioned in Section 1, while these techniques lay the foundation for systematic query processing and access control, they suffer from several limitations. Similar approaches that utilize trusted hardware instead of an external proxy have also been proposed [3, 1]. Such approaches improve performance as sensitive queries are processed inside the trusted module on decrypted data. However, they require special expensive hardware modules as well as modifications to the existing database query processor.

3. OVERVIEW

In this section, we provide an overview of our system architecture and the adversarial model.

3.1 System architecture

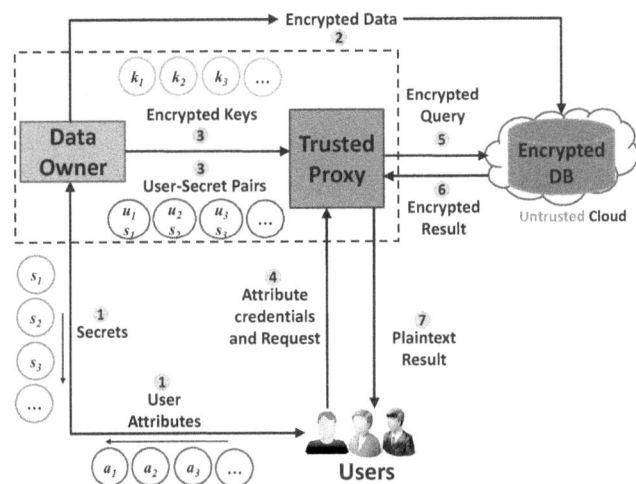

Figure 1: The system architecture

Our system includes four entities: *data owner*, *data user*, *proxy*, and *data server*. Their interactions are illustrated in the system architecture in Figure 1. The data owner uses different secret keys to encrypt different portions of data, according to the access control policies. The encrypted data are uploaded to the data server. A data user with authenticated identity attributes can verify itself to the proxy. The successful attribute based verification of the user to the proxy allows the proxy to either derive or obtain one or multiple secret keys required to encrypt the user query. Given a plaintext query submitted by the user, the proxy uses these keys to rewrite the query into an encrypted query, which can then be executed on the encrypted data in the data server. The encrypted query results are returned from the data server to the proxy, which decrypts the results using the secrets established at the time of verification and forwards them to the data user. Notice that during the query processing stage, the data server learns neither the query being executed nor the result set of the query.

3.2 Adversary model

The data owner remains offline after it uploads the encrypted data to data server. We assume that the data owner is fully trusted.

However, all the three remaining entities might be compromised. For each of them, we discuss the possible violations of data confidentiality, and how to address them.

The data server is assumed to be honest-but-curious. It does not attempt to *actively* attack the encrypted data, e.g., by altering the query answers or changing the encrypted data but instead is *passive*. The server will never be given the key by which the ciphertext can be decrypted to obtain the plaintext. Still, to support query processing, we develop techniques which allow the server to efficiently evaluate SQL queries on encrypted data (see Section 6). In addition, the server itself may be compromised by external attackers. In such a case, the data confidentiality is still preserved, since the attackers cannot decrypt the data. The attackers might also change the query answers and/or the encrypted data (e.g., by swapping the attribute values of any two tuples). However, such active attacks are out of the scope of this work.

The proxy is a trusted third party. All the secret keys, which are generated by the data owner and stored at the proxy, are encrypted. Our key management scheme (see Section 5) requires that these encrypted secret keys cannot be decrypted by the proxy alone. Instead, they can only be decrypted by the proxy with the help of authorized data users. An attack that has compromised the proxy can access the keys of logged-in users. Consequently, it can also access the data, authorized to those users. However, the secret keys of all the inactive users remain secure. In our model, the data owner does not outsource the data encryption operation to the proxy, although it is trusted. This is to avoid a "single point of failure". Otherwise, if the proxy is compromised at the pre-processing stage (i.e., the stage of generating the keys to encrypt data), then the whole system is compromised.

Users are not trusted in our system and the proxy establishes trust via certified identity attributes issued by the data owner. Our system does not store at the user side any secret key, which can be used to decrypt the data. Otherwise, the problem of key distribution would be raised, and data would need to be re-encrypted in case a user is compromised. Instead, our key management scheme assures that the proxy is able to derive the secret keys only by collaboration with the authorized data user. Such a procedure can be seen as a function: $k \leftarrow f(As)$, where k is the secret key, As is the set of user's attributes, and f is a function representing the collaboration between the proxy and the user. Now suppose that the user is compromised (i.e., its attributes are disclosed). To prevent unauthorized data access, the data owner can update the attributes to As', so as to prevent attackers with As from posing as the authorized user any longer. Such a strategy makes it possible for the key k and the data to remain unchanged.

4. ACCESS CONTROL MODEL

In this section, we describe our access control model in detail.

4.1 Attribute based access control

We utilize the attribute based access control (ABAC) model which has the following characteristics.

- Users have a set of identity attributes that describe properties of users. For example, organizational role(s), seniority, age and so on.

- Data is associated with ABAC policies that specify conditions over identity attributes.

- A user whose identity attributes satisfy the ABAC policy associated with a data item is allowed to access the data item.

Access can be controlled at different granularity levels such as column level, row level, and cell level. Each column, row, or cell, depending on the desired level of access control, has an associated ABAC policy. In the case of column and cell level access control, the policy attachment is performed by adding an additional column for each column in the table and in the case of row level access control, the policy attachment is performed by adding a single additional column in the table (Please refer to Section 6.3 and 6.4 for explanation on policy attachment at different granularities of access control). Upon receiving an SQL query from a user for table T, the proxy needs to determine the ABAC policies attached to T satisfied by the users attributes and restrict the query to only those columns, rows or cells depending on the granularity level by adding a predicate to the user query. Such a predicate "encodes" the satisfied ABAC policies as shown by example queries in Section 6. We focus on cell level access control to propose our basic ABAC model. In the basic model, each cell in a database table is attached an ABAC policy. We formally define our model as follows:

DEFINITION 4.1. **Attribute Condition**.
An attribute condition cond is an expression of the form:
"$name_A$ op l", where $name_A$ is the name of an identity attribute A, op is a comparison operator such as $=, <, >, \leq, \geq, \neq$, and l is a value that can be assumed by attribute A.

DEFINITION 4.2. **ABAC Policy**.
Let T be a table. An ABAC access control policy (ACP for short) defined over T is a tuple (s, o) where: o denotes a set of cells in T and s is a Boolean expression over a set of attribute conditions that must be satisfied in order to access o.

DEFINITION 4.3. **Group**.
We define a group G as a set of users which satisfy a specific conjunction of attribute conditions in an ABAC policy.

The idea of groups is similar to user-role assignment in role based access control (RBAC), but in our approach, the assignment is performed automatically based on identity attributes. Given the set of ABAC policies specified by the data owner, the following steps are taken to identify groups:

- Convert each ABAC ACP into disjunctive normal form (DNF). Note that this conversion can be done in polynomial time.

- For each distinct disjunctive clause, create a group.

Example: Consider the following two ACPs defined over the attribute conditions C_1, C_2 and C_3: $ACP_1 = C_1 \wedge (C_2 \vee C_3)$ and $ACP_2 = C_2$. Then the corresponding policies in DNF are as follows: $ACP_1 = (C_1 \wedge C_2) \vee (C_1 \wedge C_3)$ and $ACP_2 = C_2$.

In this example, there are three groups G_1, G_2, G_3 of users satisfying the attribute conditions $C_1 \wedge C_2$, $C_1 \wedge C_3$, and C_2 respectively. We exploit the hierarchical relationship among groups in order to support hierarchical key derivation and improve the performance and efficiency of key management. We introduce the concept of Group Poset as follows to achieve this objective.

DEFINITION 4.4. **Group Poset**.
A group poset is defined as the partially ordered set (poset) of groups where the binary relationship is $\subseteq$.

4.2 Assigning group labels and hierarchical access control

We label the cells using descriptive group names where each cell may have multiple groups associated with it. If there is an ordering relationship between two groups associated with a cell, we discard the more privileged group and assign only the less privileged group. When the proxy decides the group(s) that a user belongs to, it selects the most privileged groups. The idea is that a user in the more privileged group can become a member of the less privileged group by following the hierarchical relationship in the group poset. Note that the group label assignment indirectly attaches an ABAC policy to a cell as described at the beginning of this section.

Hierarchical key encryption techniques reduce the number of keys to be managed. However, a major drawback is that assigning keys to each node and giving them to users beforehand makes it difficult to handle dynamics of adding and revoking users. We address this drawback while utilizing the benefits of hierarchical model by proposing a hybrid approach combining broadcast and hierarchical key management. We utilize a recently proposed expressive scheme called AB-GKM (attribute based GKM) [17, 16] as the broadcast GKM scheme which is described in Section 5.1. Instead of directly assigning keys to each node in the hierarchy, we assign a AB-GKM instance to each node and authorized users can derive the key using the key derivation algorithm of AB-GKM. An AB-GKM instance is attached to a node only if there is at least one user who cannot derive the key of the node by following the hierarchical relationship.

5. CRYPTOGRAPHIC CONSTRUCTS

In this section, we describe the cryptographic constructs used in our approach for secure query evaluation over encrypted data.

5.1 Key management

Broadcast Group Key Management (BGKM) schemes [8, 4, 24] are a special type of GKM scheme whereby the rekey operation is performed with a single broadcast without requiring private communication channels. Unlike conventional GKM schemes, BGKM schemes do not give subscribers private keys. Instead subscribers are given a secret which is combined with public information to obtain the actual private keys. Such schemes have the advantage of requiring a private communication only once for the initial secret sharing. The subsequent rekeying operations are performed using one broadcast message. Further, in such schemes achieving forward and backward security requires only to change the public information and does not affect the secrets given to existing subscribers. However, BGKM schemes do not support group membership policies over a set of attributes. In their basic form, they can only support 1-*out-of-n* threshold policies by which a group member possessing 1 attribute out of the possible n attributes is able to derive the group key. The recently proposed attribute based GKM (AB-GKM) scheme [17, 16] provides all the benefits of BGKM schemes and also supports attribute based access control policies (ACPs).

Users are required to show their identity attributes to the data owner to obtain secrets using the AB-GKM scheme. In order to hide the identity attributes from the data owner while allowing only valid users to obtain secrets, we utilize the oblivious commitment based envelope (OCBE) protocols [15] which are based on Pedersen commitments [19] [1] and zero knowledge proof of knowledge

---
[1] Pedersen commitment is a cryptographic commitment allows a user to commit to a value while keeping it hidden and preserving the user's ability to reveal the committed value later.

techniques [22]. We omit the technical details of the OCBE protocols due to the page limit. The OCBE protocols between the data owner and users provide the following guarantees in DBMask.

- The data owner does not learn the identity attributes of users as their identities are hidden inside Pedersen commitments.

- A user can obtain a valid secret for an identity attribute from the data owner only if the identity attribute is not fake. The data owner sends the secrets to the user in an encrypted message and the user can decrypt the message only if the user has a valid identity attribute.

The idea behind the AB-GKM scheme is as follows. A separate BGKM instance for each attribute condition is constructed. The ACP is embedded in an access structure $\mathcal{T}$. $\mathcal{T}$ is a tree with the internal nodes representing threshold gates and the leaves representing BGKM instances for the attributes. $\mathcal{T}$ can represent any monotonic policy. The goal of the access tree is to allow deriving the group key for only the subscribers whose attributes satisfy the access structure $\mathcal{T}$. Each threshold gate in the tree is described by its child nodes and a threshold value. The threshold value t_x of a node x specifies the number of child nodes that should be satisfied in order to satisfy the node. Each threshold gate is modeled as a Shamir secret sharing polynomial [23] whose degree equals to one less than the threshold value. The root of the tree contains the group key and all the intermediate values are derived in a top-down fashion. A subscriber who satisfies the access tree derives the group key in a bottom-up fashion.

We only provide the abstract algorithms of the AB-GKM scheme. The AB-GKM scheme consists of five algorithms: **Setup**, **SecGen**, **KeyGen**, **KeyDer** and **ReKey**. The **Setup** algorithm takes the security parameter ℓ, the maximum group size N, and the number of attribute conditions N_a as input, and initializes the system. The **SecGen** algorithm gives a user$_j$, $1 \leq j \leq N$, a set of secrets for each commitment com$_i \in \gamma$, $1 \leq i \leq m$. The **KeyGen** algorithm takes the access control policy ACP as the input and outputs a symmetric key K, a set of public information tuples **PI**, and an access tree $\mathcal{T}$. Given the set of identity attributes β, the set of public information tuples **PI**, and the access tree $\mathcal{T}$, the **KeyDer** algorithm outputs the symmetric K only if the identity attributes in β satisfy the access structure $\mathcal{T}$. The **ReKey** algorithm is similar to the **KeyGen** algorithm. It is executed whenever the dynamics in the system change, that is, whenever subscribers join and leave or ACPs change.

Brief security analysis: An adversary, who has compromised the cloud server, cannot infer the keys used to encrypt the data from the public information stored in the cloud server as the AB-GKM scheme is key hiding even against computationally unbounded adversaries. If an adversary has compromised the proxy, the AB-GKM secrets of the users who are currently online are compromised as the proxy derives these secrets using users' passwords and encrypted secrets. Since the data owner performs the setup and key generation operations of the AB-GKM scheme, such an attack does not allow the attacker to infer the secret information stored at the data owner. If such an attack is detected, the proxy can invalidate the existing secrets of the online users and request the data owner to generate new set of secrets using the AB-GKM scheme for the users without changing the underlying keys used to encrypt/decrypt the data. Since the secrets at the time of compromise and after regeneration are different, it is cryptographically hard for the adversary to derive the underlying encryption/decryption keys from the invalid secrets. Notice that, unlike a traditional key management scheme, since the underlying encryption/decryption keys are not required to be changed, such a compromise does not require to re-encrypt the data stored in the cloud.

5.2 SQL-aware comparison

DBMask provides support for both numerical and keyword comparison and is designed so that any comparison friendly numerical or keyword encryption scheme can be utilized to perform relational operations over encrypted data. In the case of numerical matching, we use two variants of AES and Boldyreva et al.'s [6] schemes to support privacy preserving comparison without requiring the decryption of numerical values. We refer to these approaches as privacy preserving numerical comparison (PPNC). For the purpose of reference to individual schemes, we refer to them as PPNC-SEM, PPNC-DET and PPNC-OPE. PPNC-SEM provides the maximum security guarantee among the PPNC schemes and is constructed using AES together with a blinding factor where a simple blinding factor would be,

$$g^r \text{ where } g \text{ is a generator and } r \in \mathbb{Z}_p$$

Since the goal is to reveal equality, the values are unblinded at the time of comparison by providing the unblinding factor (g^{-r}) to the data server where the server unblinds on the fly. PPNC-DET has a weaker security guarantee than PPNC-SEM as it is deterministic encryption and is constructed using 128-bit block AES. PPNC-OPE is Boldyreva et al.'s scheme and has the weakest security guarantee among the PPNC schemes as it is an order-preserving encryption and the encrypted values reveal order of the plaintext. Like numerical comparison, one can utilize any encrypted keyword comparison technique [25, 9]. We refer to this approach as privacy preserving keyword comparison (PPKC). We adopt the keyword search technique proposed in [25] (PPKC-SEM) as it is better suited to relational data and its implementation is available. We provide an abstract description of how these comparison schemes are used in DBMask.

The above approaches can be summarized into four algorithms namely, **Setup**, **EncVal**, **GenTrapdoor** and **Compare**, which we use for comparison in our cloud based database system. The **Setup** algorithm takes as input a set of parameters P and initializes the underlying encryption scheme required for computations. Given a numerical or a keyword value x, the **EncVal** algorithm produces an encrypted value e_x that hides the actual value, but allows one to perform comparisons using the trapdoor value. Given an input (numerical or keyword) value t, the **GenTrapdoor** algorithm produces an encrypted value e_t, called the trapdoor, that is used with its corresponding encrypted value to perform comparisons. Given an encrypted value e_x for x and a trapdoor value e_t for t, the **Compare** algorithm compares the encrypted and trapdoor value and outputs the result.

Brief security analysis: An adversary, who has compromised the cloud server, cannot infer the plaintext values of the encrypted values except what is inherently revealed by the underlying encryption schemes since the private key is not stored at the cloud server. If an adversary has compromised both the proxy and the cloud server, the adversary cannot directly infer the plaintext values using the private information stored at the proxy since the private information used at the data owner to generate the encrypted value and the private information used at the proxy to generate trapdoors is different and it is cryptographically hard to derive one from the other. The adversary may however do a brute force attack by repeatedly executing comparison operations to infer the plaintext values of the encrypted values in the cloud server. Detection and prevention of such an attack is beyond the scope of this paper.

5.3 Computing joins

In order to perform equality join, the joining columns have to be encrypted with the same key so the server can see matching values between two columns. Although the columns using either PPNC or PPKC scheme are encrypted with the same key in our approach, they cannot be matched since values are semantically secure. One way to support join would be to update one of the columns in the join operation at runtime to reflect its trapdoor values and then perform the join operation, but this has high computational and bandwidth complexity as it requires either downloading the encrypted values to the proxy, creating trapdoors and uploading to the database server or keeping a mapping between the encrypted values and trapdoors at the proxy and uploading it to database server prior to join operation. In order to efficiently perform join, we use two schemes namely JOIN-SEM and JOIN-DET with varying security guarantees. JOIN-SEM introduces a new column and stores the blinded trapdoor values corresponding to the comparison friendly PPNC or PPKC encrypted values in this column. The blinding mechanism of trapdoor values and the process of equality matching is as explained earlier in Section 5.2. JOIN-DET encrypts every column able to participate in join with a deterministic encryption scheme prior to uploading to the server and a mapping between joining columns and their respective tables is kept at the proxy. JOIN-SEM provides better security guarantees that JOIN-DET.

Brief security analysis: An adversary, who has compromised either the cloud server or the proxy cannot infer the plaintext values of the encrypted values as the the private key is not stored at the cloud server or the proxy but may repeatedly execute comparison operations to infer the plaintext values of the encrypted values in the cloud server.

6. SECURE QUERY EVALUATION OVER ENCRYPTED DATA

In this section, we provide a detailed description of our privacy preserving query processing scheme for encrypted databases in a public cloud. As mentioned in Section 3, our system consists of four entities: data owner, proxy, cloud and users. Our system undergoes the following phases: system initialization, user registration, data encryption and upload, and data querying and retrieval. We now explain each phase in detail.

6.1 System initialization

The data owner runs the Setup algorithm of the underlying cryptographic constructs, that is, AB-GKM.Setup, PPNC.Setup and PPKC.Setup [2]. The data owner makes available the public security parameters to the proxy so that the proxy can generate trapdoors during data querying and retrieval phase. The data owner also converts the ACPs into DNF and groups users satisfying the same disjunctive clauses. As mentioned in Section 4, these groups are used to construct the Group poset to perform hierarchical key derivation along with the AB-GKM based key management.

6.2 User registration

Users first get their identity attributes certified by a trusted identity provider. These certified identity attributes are cryptographic commitments that hide the actual identity attribute value but still

---

bind the value to users. Users register their certified identity attributes with the data owner using the OCBE protocol. The data owner executes the AB-GKM.SecGen algorithm to generate secrets for the identity attributes and gives the encrypted secrets to users. Users can decrypt and obtain the secrets only if they presented valid certified identity attributes. The data owner maintains a database of user-secret values. When a user or an identity attribute is revoked, the corresponding association(s) from the user-secret database is (are) deleted. The user-secret database is also stored at the proxy with the secrets encrypted using a password only each user possesses. Each user has a different password encrypting her own secrets. Every time the user-secret database changes, the data owner synchronizes its changes with the proxy.

6.3 Data encryption and upload

In our solution, each cell in an original table is expanded into either three if JOIN-DET is used as the scheme to perform join operation or four if JOIN-SEM is used to perform join. The first cell is encrypted for fine-grained access control, the second cell is encrypted for privacy-preserving matching ,the third cell represents the assigned group labels and the fourth cell if exists stores blinded trapdoor value for join operation. We denote the column resulting from the encryption for fine-grained access control as *data-col*, the one resulting from the encryption for privacy-preserving matching as *match-col*, the one with associated group names as *label-col* and the one resulting from storing blinded trapdoor as *trap-col*.

Example: Consider the example shown in Section 4 and suppose that C_1, C_2 and C_3 are conditions defined as as follows. C_1 = "level > 3", C_2 = "role = doctor" and C_3 = "role = nurse". Therefore, ACP_1 is satisfied by all users whose level is greater than 3 and who are either doctors or nurses. ACP_2 is satisfied by all doctors.

Table 1: Assignment Table

Table	Columns	Condition	Groups
Patient	ID, Age, Diagnosis	Age < 40	G_1
Patient	Age	Age > 30	G_2
Patient	Age, Diagnosis	Age < 40 **AND** Diagnosis = 'Asthma'	G_3

Let us first discuss the creation of label-col. Suppose that the above ACPs are applied over a set of cells that satisfy the conditions shown in Table 1 and each cell is assigned one or more group labels as shown in Table 2. If two groups are connected in the group poset, only the label of less privileged group is assigned to the cell e.g. the *Age* value in row 4 is satisfied by both G_1 and G_3 but only assigned label of less privileged group, G_3. Note that the table and column names in the assignment table stored on the untrusted server are anonymized and the values encrypted.

Table 2: Patient Table

ID	ID-grp	Age	Age-grp	Diag	Diag-grp
1	G_1	35	G_1,G_2	HIV	G_1
2	G_1	30	G_1	Cancer	G_1
3	G_1	40	G_2	Asthma	G_1
4	G_1	38	G_2,G_3	Asthma	G_3

Now, let us discuss the creation of data-col. Given a cell in the original table, its encryption in the corresponding data-col is generated by a secret key derived from the AB-GKM scheme [17, 16]. The set of groups associated with a cell decide the key under which

---

[2] We use the dot notation to refer to an algorithm of a specific cryptographic construct. For example, AB-GKM.Setup refers to the Setup algorithm of AB-GKM scheme.

the cell is encrypted. For each group G_i, a group secret key K_i is generated by executing the AB-GKM.KeyGen algorithm. In order to avoid multiple encryptions (i.e., one group secret key for one encryption) in the case where a cell is associated with multiple groups, the AB-GKM.KeyGen algorithm is again executed to generate a master group key K using the group keys K_i's as secret attributes to the algorithm e.g. the *Age* value in row 1 is encrypted with a master key k_{12} generated from the AB-GKM instance having k_1 and k_2 as input secrets with public information corresponding to this master key as PI_{12}. As a consequence, if a user belongs to any of the groups assigned to the cell, the user can access the cell by executing the AB-GKM.KeyDer algorithm twice. The first execution generates the group key and second derives the master key. Public information to derive the key is stored in a separate table called *PubInfo*.

Table 3: PubInfo Table

Groups	G_1	G_2	G_3	G_1, G_2	G_2, G_3
PI	PI_1	PI_2	PI_3	PI_{12}	PI_{23}

Now, let us consider the creation of match-col. Given a cell in the original table, its encryption in the match-col is generated as follows. Our scheme supports both numerical matching and keyword search for strings. If the cell is of numerical type, the PPNC.EncVal algorithm is used to encrypt the cell value. If the cell is of type string, the PPKC.EncVal algorithm is used to perform the encryption. Table 4 shows the final table with both encrypted data-col's where $E_k(x)$ refers to the semantically secure encryption of the value x using the symmetric key k and comparison friendly match-col's, where $comp_n$ and $comp_k$ refer to PPNC.EncVal and PPKC.EncVal respectively.

Now, let us consider the creation of the trap-col. Given a cell in the original table, its value in the trap-col is generated by the PPNC.GenTrapDoor*blinding factor* or PPKC.GenTrapDoor*blinding factor* depending on the data type. The blinding factor is as explained in Section 5.2.

6.4 Data querying and retrieval

Processing a query over encrypted data is a *filtering-refining* procedure. The general algorithm for processing queries on encrypted data is shown in Algorithm 1 and the details are as follows. An authorized user sends a plaintext SQL query to the proxy, as if the outsourced database were unencrypted. In other words, encryption and decryption of the data in the database is transparent to users. The proxy parses the query and generates an abstract syntax tree of the query.

The query is first filtered (Lines 7-13) by removing clauses, aggregate functions, and predicates with aggregate functions that cannot be computed on the server. The PART function (Lines 15-17) then adds the columns referenced by filtered clauses or aggregate functions to the projections of the filtered query. The query is then rewritten for the cloud (Lines 19-21) by the REWRITE function by which each column to be included in the query result (i.e., column following the SELECT keyword in the query) is replaced by its corresponding "data-col" and each predicate in the WHERE clause is replaced with a user defined function (UDF). For each numerical matching predicate, the UDF includes the trapdoor value computed by the proxy using PPNC.GenTrapdoor algorithm and invokes the PPNC.Compare algorithm. Similarly, for each keyword matching predicate, the UDF includes the trapdoor value computed by the proxy using PPKC.GenTrapdoor algorithm and invokes the PPKC.Compare algorithm. The REWRITE function then adds a predicate to the WHERE clause that determines the group(s) of the

user requesting the query before the rewritten query is sent to the cloud server.

Algorithm 1 Pseudo-code for SECUREQUERYPLAN

```
 1: Input:      Q, abstract syntax tree (AST) for the query
 2:              M, metadata of the target table(s)
 3:              G, group(s) a user is member of
 4: Output:     P, a query plan for Q
 5: FilterQ ← Q
 6: ProxyFilters ← []
 7: for f in FilterQ do
 8:     f′ ←FILTER(f, FilterQ)
 9:     for f′ ≠ Nil do
10:         Remove f from FilterQ
11:         Add f′ to ProxyFilters
12:     end for
13: end for
14: for p in ProxyFilters do
15:     if PART(p) in FilterQ.relations then
16:         Add PART(p) to FilterQ.projections
17:     end if
18: end for
19: for c in s.where_clause ‖ s.select_clause do
20:     REWRITE(c, s, M, G)
21: end for
22: P ← SERVERSQL(FilterQ)
23: P ← DECRYPT(P)
24: if ProxyFilters ≠ [] then
25:     P ← PROXYSQL(P, ProxyFilters, Q)
26: end if
27: return P
```

The cloud executes the rewritten encrypted query over the encrypted database and filters the tuples that do not satisfy the predicates in the query before sending back the encrypted result set to the proxy (Line 22). The proxy generates the necessary keys for decrypting the result set using the AB-GKM.KeyDer algorithm with the public information[3] and the user secrets as well as the hierarchical key derivation (Line 23).

If the proxy has removed some clauses and/or aggregate functions (e.g., SUM) from the original query in the query filtering step, it populates an in-memory database with the decrypted result set and refines the query result according to the constraints in the clauses and/or aggregate functions by running the original query (Line 24-26). If no term from the query is removed, the decrypted result set is the final result and the proxy sends the final plaintext result back to the user.

We now illustrate query processing in DBMask through example queries. The queries reflect two scenarios. The first scenario which we refer to as DBMask-SEC provides maximum security and uses PPNC-SEM scheme for numerical comparison, PPKC-SEM scheme for keyword search, JOIN-SEM for computing joins and the label columns reflecting group information are encrypted. The second scenario which we refer to as DBMask-PER provides best performance and uses PPNC-OPE schem for numerical comparison, PPKC-SEM scheme for keyword search, JOIN-DET scheme for computing joins and the label columns are in plaintext.

A user having the attributes "role = doctor" and "level = 4" executes Query 1 through the proxy server.

---

[3]The public information (i.e., PI) is stored at the cloud server and retrieved together with the query.

Table 4: Encrypted Patient Table - Cell Level Access Control with JOIN-SEM

ID-enc	ID-com	ID-trap	ID-grp	Age-enc	Age-com	Age-trap	Age-grp	Diag-enc	Diag-com	Diag-trap	Diag-grp
$E_{k_1}(1)$	$comp_n(1)$	$comp'_n(1)$	G_1	$E_{k_{12}}(35)$	$comp_n(35)$	$comp'_n(35)$	G_1,G_2	$E_{k_1}(HIV)$	$comp_k(HIV)$	$comp'_k(H..)$	G_1
$E_{k_1}(2)$	$comp_n(2)$	$comp'_n(2)$	G_1	$E_{k_1}(30)$	$comp_n(30)$	$comp'_n(30)$	G_1	$E_{k_1}(Cancer)$	$comp_k(Cancer)$	$comp'_k(Ca..)$	G_1
$E_{k_1}(3)$	$comp_n(3)$	$comp'_n(2)$	G_1	$E_{k_2}(40)$	$comp_n(40)$	$comp'_n(40)$	G_2	$E_{k_1}(Asthma)$	$comp_k(Asthma)$	$comp'_k(As..)$	G_1
$E_{k_1}(4)$	$comp_n(4)$	$comp'_n(4)$	G_1	$E_{k_{23}}(38)$	$comp_n(38)$	$comp'_n(38)$	G_2,G_3	$E_{k_3}(Asthma)$	$comp_k(Asthma)$	$comp'_k(As..)$	G_3

Table 5: Encrypted Patient Table - Row Level Access Control with JOIN-DET

ID-enc	ID-com	Age-enc	Age-com	Diag-enc	Diag-com	Groups
$E_{k_1}(1)$	$comp_n(1)$	$E_{k_1}(35)$	$comp_n(35)$	$E_{k_1}(HIV)$	$comp_k(HIV)$	G_1
$E_{k_{12}}(2)$	$comp_n(2)$	$E_{k_{12}}(30)$	$comp_n(30)$	$E_{k_{12}}(Cancer)$	$comp_k(Cancer)$	G_1,G_2
$E_{k_{23}}(3)$	$comp_n(3)$	$E_{k_{23}}(40)$	$comp_n(40)$	$E_{k_{23}}(Asthma)$	$comp_k(Asthma)$	G_2,G_3
$E_{k_1}(4)$	$comp_n(4)$	$E_{k_1}(38)$	$comp_n(38)$	$E_{k_1}(Asthma)$	$comp_k(Asthma)$	G_1

Query 1:

SELECT	*ID, Age, Diag*
FROM	*Patient*
WHERE	*Age* > 35 **AND** *Diag* **LIKE** 'Asthma'
ORDER BY	*Age* **ASC**

The proxy determines that the user is a member of groups G_1 and G_3. It thus re-writes the query as Query 2 if the underlying scenario is DBMask-SEC or as Query 3 if the underlying scenario is DBMask-PER and submits to the cloud server. Notice that the 'ORDER BY' clause is removed from Query 2. The reason being that the cloud server does not have sufficient information to order the query results.

Query 2:

SELECT	*ID-enc, ID-grp, Age-enc, Age-grp,* *Diag-enc, Diag-grp*
FROM	*Patient*
WHERE	UDF_Compare_Num(*Age-com,* PPNC.GenTrapdoor(35), '>') **AND** UDF_Compare_Str(*Diag-com,* PPKC.GenTrapdoor('Asthma') **AND** UDF_Compare_Str(*ID-grp,* PPKC.GenTrapdoor('G_1')) **OR** UDF_Compare_Str(*ID-grp,* PPKC.GenTrapdoor('G_3')) **AND** UDF_Compare_Str(*Age-grp,* PPKC.GenTrapdoor('G_1')) **OR** UDF_Compare_Str(*Age-grp,* PPKC.GenTrapdoor('G_3')) **AND** UDF_Compare_Str(*Diag-grp,* PPKC.GenTrapdoor('G_1')) **OR** UDF_Compare_Str(*Diag-grp,* PPKC.GenTrapdoor('G_3'))

UDF_Compare_Num is a user defined function that invokes the PPNC.Compare algorithm and UDF_Compare_Str is a user defined function that invokes the PPKC.Compare algorithm. The cloud server returns the encrypted row 4 to the proxy. In order to decrypt the resultset, the proxy requires the keys k_1 to decrypt *ID-enc* column value, k_{23} to decrypt *Age-enc* column value and k_3 to decrypt *Diag-enc* column value. The proxy derives the key k_1 for the higher privileged group G_1 using the AB-GKM scheme. In order to generate k_3, instead of executing another AB-GKM key derivation algorithm, the proxy utilizes the hierarchical key derivation to derive k_3 from k_1. To derive key k_{23}, the proxy uses k_3 and PI_{23} to derive k_{23}. The proxy then uses k_1, k_3 and k_{23} to decrypt the resultset and sends the resultset to the user. In the case of Query 2, the proxy orders the plaintext resultset using its in-memory database before sending the final resultset to the user.

Query 3:

SELECT	*ID-enc, ID-grp, Age-enc, Age-grp,* *Diag-enc, Diag-grp*
FROM	*Patient*
WHERE	UDF_Compare_Num(*Age-com,* PPNC.GenTrapdoor(35), '>') **AND** UDF_Compare_Str(*Diag-com,* PPKC.GenTrapdoor('Asthma')) **AND** (*ID-grp* **LIKE** '%G_1%' **OR** *ID-grp* **LIKE** '%G_3%') **AND** (*Age-grp* **LIKE** '%G_1%' **OR** *Age-grp* **LIKE** '%G_3%') **AND** (*Diag-grp* **LIKE** '%G_1%' **OR** *Diag-grp* **LIKE** '%G_3%')
ORDER BY	*Age-com* **ASC**

A user having the attribute "role = doctor" executes Query 4 through the proxy server. The proxy determines that the user is a member of the group G_3, re-writes the query and submits it to the cloud server. The rewritten query is Query 5 if the underlying scenario is DBMask-SEC and Query 6 if the underlying scenario is DBMask-PER. Note that Query 5 performs join by unblinding the trapdoor column on the fly. The blinding and/or unblinding mechanism of trapdoor values and the process of equality matching is as explained earlier in Section 5.2. In Query 6, the joining columns use the equality mechanism of the DBMS and not a manually implemented UDF since the columns are encrypted using a deterministic encryption scheme. The proxy receives and decrypts the encrypted result set using the mechanism explained above and sends the plaintext result back to the user.

Query 4:

SELECT	*p.Age, d.Description*
FROM	*Patient p, Diagnosis d*
WHERE	*p.ID = d.PatientID*

Query 5:

SELECT	*p.Age-enc, p.Age-grp, d.Description-enc,* *d.Description-grp*
FROM	*Patient p, Diagnosis d*
WHERE	UDF_Compare_Num(*p.ID-trap,* *unblinding factor* * d.PatientID-trap,'=') **AND** UDF_Compare_Str(*p.Age-grp,* PPKC.GenTrapdoor('G_3')) **AND** UDF_Compare_Str(*d.Description-grp,* PPKC.GenTrapdoor('G_3'))

Query 6:

SELECT	*p.Age-enc, p.Age-grp, d.Description-enc,*
	d.Description-grp
FROM	*Patient p, Diagnosis d*
WHERE	*p.ID-com = d.PatientID-com*
	AND (*p.Age-grp* **LIKE** '%G_3%')
	AND (*d.Description-grp* **LIKE** '%G_3%')

Table 5 shows the *Patient* table enforcing row level access control. Row level access control is a special case in our scheme where there is only a single additional *label-col* in the table to assign group labels i.e. *Groups*. Query 7 shows the transformation of Query 1 issued by the same user under DBMask-PER scenario. The cloud server returns encrypted rows 3 and 4 to the proxy. The decryption mechanism of the returned results is as explained above.

Query 7:

SELECT	*ID-enc, Age-enc, Diag-enc, Groups*
FROM	*Patient*
WHERE	UDF_Compare_Num(*Age-com*,
	PPNC.GenTrapdoor(35), '>') **AND**
	UDF_Compare_Str(*Diag-com*,
	PPKC.GenTrapdoor('Asthma')
	AND (*Groups* **LIKE** '%G_1%' **OR**
	Groups **LIKE** '%G_3%')
ORDER BY	*Age-com* **ASC**

6.5 Handling user dynamics

When users are added or revoked, or attributes of existing users change, the user dynamics of the system change. This requires changing the underlying constructs. Since DBMask utilizes AB-GKM, these changes are performed transparently to other users in the system. When a new identity attribute for a user is added to the system, the data owner simply adds the corresponding secret to the user-secret database. Similarly, when an existing attribute for a user is revoked from the system, the data owner simply removes the corresponding secret from the user-secret database. In either scenario, the data owner recomputes the affected public information tuples and requires both the proxy server and the cloud server to update the data. Notice that unlike traditional symmetric key based systems, DBMask does not need to re-key existing users and they can continue to use their existing secrets. Since no re-keying is performed, the encrypted data in the database remains the same even after such changes. Therefore, DBMask can handle very large datasets even when the user dynamics change.

Example: Assume that a user having the attribute "role = doctor" is added to the system. This affects only the group G_2. The data owner executes AB-GKM.Re-Key operation with the same symmetric key k_2 as the group key to generate the new public information PI'_2. The proxy and the cloud server are updated with the new secret and the new public information respectively. Notice that this change affects neither the secrets issued to other users nor the public information related to other groups which the new user is not a member.

7. EXPERIMENTS

This section evaluates the performance overhead and the functionality of our prototype implementation. We implemented DB-Mask in C++ on top of Postgres 9.1 while not modifying the internals of the database itself as all functionality on the server side is implemented using UDF's. We use the memory storage engine of MySQL as the in-memory database at the proxy to store the contents of a query when the execution of a query cannot be com-

pleted entirely on the server. The cryptographic operations are supported by using the NTL library[4] while the access control policies expressed as boolean expressions are converted into DNF using the boolstuff library[5]. The 'data-col' in each table is constructed with 128-bit block size AES in CBC mode while the 'match-col' is encrypted with 128 bit key using the underlying PPNC or PPKC schemes. The experimental setup is run on 3.40 GHz Intel i7-3770 8 core processors with 8 GB of RAM in Ubuntu 12.04 environment. We compare the performance of our prototype by running a TPC-C query workload utilizing only a single group under row-level control to evaluate only the encryption/decryption and comparison schemes. The experiment on a web based scientific application called Computational Research Infrastructure for Science (CRIS) is done to analyze the access control functionality of our prototype. The experimental results below show a low runtime overhead with a 33% loss in throughput in comparison to unmodified Postgres. The access control functionality deployed by our prototype on CRIS ensures that a logged-in user is only able to retrieve data it has access to and there is no unauthorized access with a modest overhead on performance.

7.1 TPC-C

The TPC-C workload queries consist of comparison predicates $(=, <, >)$, other predicates such as DISTINCT and COUNT, aggregates such as SUM and MAX and sort operation ORDER BY. In total, the workload contains 53% Select, 4% Delete, 30% Update and 13% Insert statements. The performance of TPC-C query workload with transactions enabled is compared by running the workload on an unmodified Postgres server against running the workload through the proxy of CryptDB and the proxy of our prototype DBMask under two different scenarios as explained earlier in Section 6.4, namely DBMask-SEC and DBMask-PER. We study the performance of the TPC-C workload by evaluating two different metrics: the server throughput for different SQL queries and the interval between issuing a query and receiving the results.

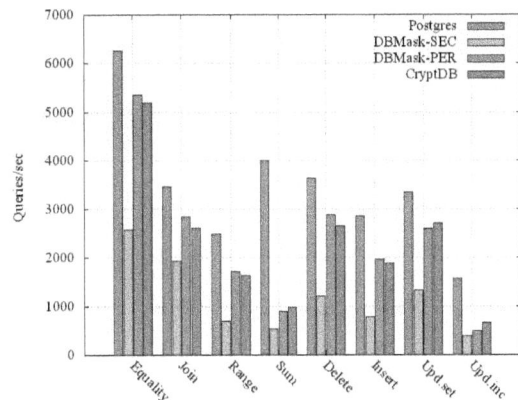

Figure 2: Throughput from TPC-C workload running under Postgres, DBMask, and CryptDB

Figure 2 shows the server throughput. The results show that in comparison to running an unencrypted trace of TPC-C workload on Postgres, there is an overall loss of throughput by: 34% for CryptDB, 33% for DBMask with underlying scenario as DBMask-PER and 68% for DBMask with underlying scenario as DBMask-SEC. DBMask outperforms CryptDB in most cases. CryptDB per-

---

[4]http://www.shoup.net/ntl/

[5]http://sarrazip.com/dev/boolstuff.html

forms best for Upd.inc operations where data is incremented before being updated and Sum operations since such operations cannot be performed on the server by DBMask. The data to be updated is first fetched from the server, updated at the proxy and sent back to the server. The same applies to Sum operations. In general, DBMask provides support for processing a greater range of queries by supporting split execution between proxy and server. We consider a throughput of 33% for encrypted query processing to be modest considering the gains in confidentiality and privacy. DBMask-PER provides better performance over DBMask-SEC as DBMask-PER provides indexing support for equality operations whereas DBMask-SEC does not, computes range operations on the server whereas DBMask-SEC first filters the results at the server before performing the range operation at the proxy, and uses the DBMS equality mechanism for join operations and matching group labels whereas DBMask-SEC uses user-defined functions for equality matching.

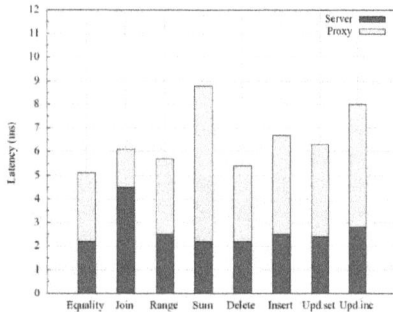

Figure 3: Server and proxy latency

To assess latency, we measure the processing time of the same type of queries used above by studying the intervals at each stage of processing, namely at server and proxy. Fig 3 shows server and proxy latency for several query operations with DBMask-PER as the underlying scenario. We observe that there is an overall increase by 44% on the server side. The proxy adds on average 4.3 ms to the interval of which 24% is utilized in encryption/decryption and the most (67%) is spent in query rewriting, parsing and processing. A Select Sum statement returned a latency of 0.91 ms on an unmodified Postgres database and a latency of 8.8 ms with DBMask primarily due to further processing of the query at the proxy.

Figure 4: Server data transferred between proxy and server

To assess the bandwidth utilization incurred by split execution of queries between proxy and server by DBMask, we evaluate the average data transferred from the server to the proxy. Fig 4 shows average data transferred for those queries that cannot be processed entirely on the server by DBMask. In the worst case, the data transferred is 2.8x in comparison to data transferred from server when plaintext queries are executed entirely on the server. This does not significantly increase the bandwidth requirements between the proxy and the server.

Table 6: Server space for TPC-C Workload

System	Size (GB)	Relative to plaintext
Plaintext	1.2	-
CryptDB	5.4	4.5x
DBMask-PER	3.8	3.2x

Table 6 shows the amount of disk space used on the server by plaintext database, DBMask and CryptDB. DBMask increases the amount of data stored by 3.2 times and hence would not result in significant increase to storage cost. This is also relatively small in comparison to the space overhead imposed by CryptDB (4.5x).

7.2 CRIS

CRIS is a web based application supporting an easy to use system for managing and sharing scientific data. The data in the form of projects, experiments and jobs residing in CRIS is of sensitive nature and hence must be protected from unauthorized usage. To test the functionality of DBMask, we select a workspace which acts as a container for all activities and data to be managed by a single group of scientists consisting of 19 users. We define four ACPbased on six attribute conditions over user identity attributes that capture the access control requirements of this particular workspace in CRIS. The users based on the mechanism explained in Section 3 are arranged into groups and each group is assigned a randomly chosen secret using AB-GKM. To evaluate the performance overhead imposed by DBMask and study the influence of access control, we run plaintext queries on Postgres and compare it to running queries on DBMask at different granularities of access control namely column level, row level and cell level. CRIS database has 87 tables with 298 columns in total.

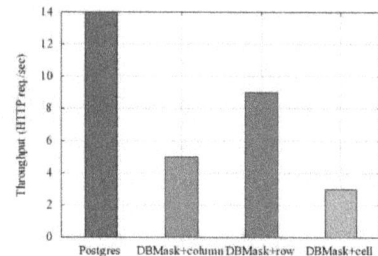

Figure 5: Throughput comparison of Sylvie's Workspace at row level access control

Figure 5 shows the effect on throughput by running CRIS on Postgres in comparison to DBMask with the underlying scenario DBMask-PER. Each HTTP request by a logged in user consists of multiple queries in order to allow a user to create, read, update and/or delete a project(s), experiment(s) or job(s). The results show that there is a loss of throughput by 64% for column level, 36% for row level and 79% for cell level access control with DBMask and a logged in user is only able to access objects it is permitted. We consider this to be a reasonable overhead considering the gains in confidentiality and privacy. The finer granularity of row level over column level results in better performance as row level consumes less disk space and is able to take advantage of indexing to speed table scans. Our scheme is best suited for row level access control.

8. CONCLUSION

In this paper, we proposed DBMask, a novel solution that supports cryptographically enforced fine-grained access control, including row level and cell level access control, when evaluating SQL queries on encrypted relational data. Similar to CryptDB [20] and MONOMI [26], DBMask does not require modification to the database engine, and thus maximizes the reuse of existing DBMS infrastructures. However, unlike CryptDB and MONOMI, the level of security provided by the encryption techniques in DBMask does not change with time as DBMask does not perform any intermediate decryptions in the cloud database. DBMask introduces the idea of splitting fine-grained access control and predicate matching per each cell. Hence, DBMask can perform access control and predicate matching at the time of query processing by simply adding predicates to the query being executed. The choice of predicate matching technique used is configurable so that different techniques can be plugged in depending on the requirements. Unlike existing systems, DBMask can efficiently handle large databases even when user dynamics change. Our experimental results show that our solution is efficient and overhead due to encryption and access control is low.

As future work, we plan to extend DBMask to expand the supported relational operations as well as further optimize the supported relational operations. We also plan to investigate the feasibility of moving some of the proxy functionality into the cloud as a trusted component where the cloud service provider has access to neither the encryption keys nor the internal processing.

9. ACKNOWLEDGMENT

The work reported in this paper has been partially supported by the Purdue Cyber Center and by the National Science Foundation under grant CNS-1111512.

10. REFERENCES

[1] A. Arasu, S. Blanas, K. Eguro, M. Joglekar, R. Kaushik, D. Kossmann, R. Ramamurthy, P. Upadhyaya, and R. Venkatesan. Secure database-as-a-service with cipherbase. In *SIGMOD 2013*, pages 1033–1036, New York, NY, USA. ACM.

[2] M. R. Asghar, G. Russello, B. Crispo, and M. Ion. Supporting complex queries and access policies for multi-user encrypted databases. In *CCSW 2013*, pages 77–88. ACM.

[3] S. Bajaj and R. Sion. Trusteddb: A trusted hardware based database with privacy and data confidentiality. In *SIGMOD 2011*, pages 205–216, New York, NY, USA. ACM.

[4] S. Berkovits. How to broadcast a secret. In *EUROCRYPT 1991*, pages 535–541.

[5] J. Bethencourt, A. Sahai, and B. Waters. Ciphertext-policy attribute-based encryption. In *SP 2007*, pages 321–334, Washington, DC, USA. IEEE Computer Society.

[6] A. Boldyreva, N. Chenette, and A. O'Neill. Order-preserving encryption revisited: Improved security analysis and alternative solutions. In *CRYPTO 2011*, volume 6841 of *Lecture Notes in Computer Science*, pages 578–595. Springer Berlin Heidelberg, 2011.

[7] J. Camenisch, M. Dubovitskaya, and G. Neven. Oblivious transfer with access control. In *CCS 2009*, pages 131–140, New York, NY, USA. ACM.

[8] G. Chiou and W. Chen. Secure broadcasting using the secure lock. *IEEE TSE*, 15(8):929–934, Aug 1989.

[9] R. Curtmola, J. Garay, S. Kamara, and R. Ostrovsky. Searchable symmetric encryption: Improved definitions and efficient constructions. In *CCS 2006*, pages 79–88, New York, NY, USA. ACM.

[10] E. Damiani, S. D. C. di Vimercati, S. Jajodia, S. Paraboschi, and P. Samarati. Balancing confidentiality and efficiency in untrusted relational dbmss. In *CCS*, pages 93–102, 2003.

[11] M. Dijk, C. Gentry, S. Halevi, and V. Vaikuntanathan. Fully homomorphic encryption over the integers. In H. Gilbert, editor, *EUROCRYPT 2010*, volume 6110 of *Lecture Notes in Computer Science*, pages 24–43. Springer Berlin Heidelberg.

[12] C. Gentry. Fully homomorphic encryption using ideal lattices. In *STOC 2009*, pages 169–178, New York, NY, USA. ACM.

[13] H. Hacigümüs, B. R. Iyer, C. Li, and S. Mehrotra. Executing sql over encrypted data in the database-service-provider model. In *SIGMOD 2002*, pages 216–227.

[14] B. Hore, S. Mehrotra, and G. Tsudik. A privacy-preserving index for range queries. In *VLDB 2004*, pages 720–731.

[15] J. Li and N. Li. OACerts: Oblivious attribute certificates. *IEEE TDSC*, 3(4):340–352, 2006.

[16] M. Nabeel and E. Bertino. Poster. towards attribute based group key management. In *CCS 2011*, pages 821–824.

[17] M. Nabeel and E. Bertino. Attribute based group key management. *To Appear in Transactions on Data Privacy*, 2014.

[18] P. Paillier. Public-key cryptosystems based on composite degree residuosity classes. In *EUROCRYPT 1999*, pages 223–238.

[19] T. Pedersen. Non-interactive and information-theoretic secure verifiable secret sharing. In *CRYPTO 1992*, pages 129–140, London, UK. Springer-Verlag.

[20] R. A. Popa, C. M. S. Redfield, N. Zeldovich, and H. Balakrishnan. Cryptdb: protecting confidentiality with encrypted query processing. In *SOSP 2011*, pages 85–100.

[21] B. K. Samanthula, G. Howser, Y. Elmehdwi, and S. Madria. An efficient and secure data sharing framework using homomorphic encryption in the cloud. In *CLOUD-I 2012*, pages 8–16. ACM, 2012.

[22] C. Schnorr. Efficient identification and signatures for smart cards. In *CRYPTO 1989*, pages 239–252, New York, NY, USA. Springer-Verlag New York, Inc.

[23] A. Shamir. How to share a secret. *The Communication of ACM*, 22:612–613, November 1979.

[24] N. Shang, M. Nabeel, F. Paci, and E. Bertino. A privacy-preserving approach to policy-based content dissemination. In *ICDE 2010*, pages 944–955.

[25] D. X. Song, D. Wagner, and A. Perrig. Practical techniques for searches on encrypted data. In *SP 2000*, pages 44–55.

[26] S. Tu, M. F. Kaashoek, S. Madden, and N. Zeldovich. Processing analytical queries over encrypted data. In *PVLDB 2013*, pages 289–300. VLDB Endowment.

[27] S. Wang, D. Agrawal, and A. El Abbadi. A comprehensive framework for secure query processing on relational data in the cloud. In *SDM 2011*, pages 52–69.

[28] S. Yu, C. Wang, K. Ren, and W. Lou. Attribute based data sharing with attribute revocation. In *ASIACCS 2010*, pages 261–270, New York, NY, USA. ACM.

Differentially-Private Mining of Moderately-Frequent High-Confidence Association Rules

Mihai Maruseac
University of Massachusetts, Boston
Boston, MA 02125
mmarusea@cs.umb.edu

Gabriel Ghinita
University of Massachusetts, Boston
Boston, MA 02125
Gabriel.Ghinita@umb.edu

ABSTRACT

Association rule mining allows discovering of patterns in large data repositories, and benefits diverse application domains such as healthcare, marketing, social studies, etc. However, mining datasets that contain data about individuals may cause significant privacy breaches, and disclose sensitive information about one's health status, political orientation or alternative lifestyle. Recent research addressed the privacy threats that arise when mining sensitive data, and several techniques allow data mining with differential privacy guarantees. However, existing methods only discover rules that have very large support, i.e., occur in a large fraction of the dataset transactions (typically, more than 50%). This is a serious limitation, as numerous high-quality rules do not reach such high frequencies (e.g., rules about rare diseases, or luxury merchandise).

In this paper, we propose a method that focuses on mining high-quality association rules with moderate and low frequencies. We employ a novel technique for rule extraction that combines the exponential mechanism of differential privacy with reservoir sampling. The proposed algorithm allows us to directly mine association rules, without the need to compute noisy supports for large numbers of itemsets. We provide a privacy analysis of the proposed method, and we perform an extensive experimental evaluation which shows that our technique is able to sample low- and moderate-support rules with high precision.

Categories and Subject Descriptors

H.2.0 [**Database Management**]: Security, integrity, and protection

General Terms

Security, Experimentation

1. INTRODUCTION

Association rule mining (ARM) [6, 25, 29] is a popular and widely-studied method to discover useful correlations among items in a data repository. ARM is an indispensable tool in numerous application domains, such as market analysis, medical research, cyberdefense, etc. In the case of market-basked data, ARM can help

identify customers' shopping patterns and improve shopping experience and/or increase sales. In the healthcare domain, ARM can help identify correlations between medical conditions and symptoms, and assist in early diagnosis or finding effective treatments.

ARM is tightly related with the *Frequent Itemset Mining (FIM)* problem which aims at discovering sets of items (in data mining terminology *itemsets*) that appear frequently in a dataset. Formally, let $\mathbf{I} = \{i_1, i_2, \cdots, i_n\}$ be a set of n items and let $\mathcal{D} = [t_1, t_2, \cdots, t_t]$ be a dataset of t transactions, where each transaction comprises of a set of items, i.e., $t_i \subseteq \mathbf{I}$. The *support* of an itemset $X \subseteq \mathbf{I}$, denoted by $\sigma(X)$, is the number[1] of transactions t_i that include X (i.e., $X \subseteq t_i$). Given threshold σ_0, FIM finds itemsets X such that $\sigma(X) \geq \sigma_0$, called σ_0-frequent items.

An *association rule* r is an implication of the form $X \rightarrow Y$, where $X, Y \subseteq \mathbf{I}$ are itemsets, which captures the likelihood that a transaction that contains X also contains Y. The strength of an association rule is measured by its *confidence*, defined as $c(X \rightarrow Y) = \frac{\sigma(X \cup Y)}{\sigma(X)}$. The support of the rule, defined as $\sigma(X \cup Y)$, is an indicator of the statistical significance of the rule. Typically, for a rule to be representative, its frequency must exceed a *minimum support threshold*.

Although ARM has numerous benefits, mining results may disclose sensitive details about individuals included in the dataset. For instance, with some background knowledge on the items purchased by Alice (a super-market customer) in a given day, an adversary may be able to narrow down Alice's transaction to a small set, and learn about other items, potentially sensitive, that she may have bought. This threat has been first identified more than a decade ago [31, 16], and numerous solutions have been proposed since [35, 15, 8], culminating with the state-of-the-art and provably secure techniques for differentially-private data mining [23, 34].

Differential privacy (DP) [9, 10] is a powerful semantic privacy model that transforms a dataset in a way that bounds the probability of an adversary of learning whether a particular individual is present in the dataset or not. To achieve this goal, DP provides a data access interface that allows only statistical queries, e.g., *"how many transactions contain a specific itemset?"*, and the result of each query is additively perturbed with random noise according to the *Laplace mechanism* [10].

Existing state-of-the-art DP-compliant mining techniques [23, 34] follow a FIM-centric approach: first, they compute the noisy supports for a large number of itemsets, and then they attempt to identify high-confidence association rules based on the itemset supports. However, this method only works well for rules with very large supports. For lower-support itemsets, the amount of noise added by the Laplace mechanism becomes significant compared

---

[1] Some authors define support as ratio (or percentage) of transaction count to the dataset cardinality, with values between 0 and 1.

to the actual values, leading to large errors in the computation of confidence. In fact, to avoid large errors, the state-of-the-art *PrivBasis* technique [23] does not even compute itemset supports for moderate- and low-frequency itemsets. As we show later in Section 6, for some datasets *PrivBasis* discards itemsets and corresponding association rules that occur in fewer than 50% of all transactions.

While mining rules with very large supports is important, we argue that the inability of existing techniques to privately extract high-confidence rules with moderate or low support is a serious drawback. For instance, in a medical database, there may be relatively rare symptoms or conditions that occur in less than 10% of the patients, yet treating these patients is a very important goal that cannot be neglected. In the cybersecurity domain, searching network and system logs for signs of intrusion must account for low-frequency events, because attacks tend to occur rarely relative to legitimate traffic. Finally, in market research applications, there may be relatively few luxury product purchases that account for a large proportion of revenues, hence learning attributes of customers that are likely to purchase such items is an important objective.

We propose an approach that focuses on privately mining *high-confidence rules (HCR)* that do not have very large supports. As opposed to existing techniques that are centered on solving the FIM problem [23, 34], we directly sample high-confidence rules using the exponential mechanism of DP [28], without having to first compute supports for large numbers of itemsets. Our technique is guided by a novel representation of the association rule space, coupled with an integration of the exponential mechanism with reservoir sampling [18]. Our representation allows us to precisely identify valuable rules within a broad range of supports.

Our specific contributions are:

- We identify an important drawback of existing differentially-private data mining techniques, namely their inability to extract high-confidence rules that have moderate and low support.

- We devise a novel representation of the association rule space and an algorithm that extracts directly high-confidence rules using the exponential mechanism and reservoir sampling.

- We provide a privacy analysis of the proposed technique for differentially-private association rule mining.

- We perform an extensive experimental evaluation which shows that the proposed technique is accurate, and clearly outperforms the state-of-the-art in finding association rules with low and moderate supports.

The rest of the paper is organized as follows: Section 2 provides background information on differential privacy and reservoir sampling. Section 3 introduces the proposed technique for representing and weighting association rules, followed by the complete algorithm for privately sampling rules in Section 4. We provide a privacy analysis of our method in Section 5, followed by an extensive experimental evaluation in Section 6. We survey related work in Section 7, and conclude in Section 8.

2. BACKGROUND

2.1 Differential Privacy

Differential privacy (DP) [9, 10] addresses the limitation of syntactic privacy models (e.g., k-anonymity [30], ℓ-diversity [26], t-closeness [22]) which are vulnerable against background knowledge attacks. DP is a semantic model which argues that one should minimize the risk of disclosure that arises from an individual's participation in a dataset.

Two datasets $\mathcal{D}$ and $\mathcal{D}'$ are said to be *siblings* if they differ in a single transaction, i.e., $\mathcal{D}' = \mathcal{D} \cup \{t\}$ or $\mathcal{D}' = \mathcal{D} \setminus \{t\}$. An algorithm $\mathcal{A}$ is said to satisfy differential privacy with parameter ϵ (called *privacy budget*) if the following condition is satisfied [9]:

DEFINITION 1 (ϵ-INDISTINGUISHABILITY). *Consider algorithm $\mathcal{A}$ that produces output $\mathcal{O}$ and let $\epsilon > 0$ be an arbitrarily-small real constant. Algorithm $\mathcal{A}$ satisfies ϵ-indistinguishability if for every pair of sibling datasets $\mathcal{D}, \mathcal{D}'$ it holds that*

$$\left| \ln \frac{Pr[\mathcal{A}(\mathcal{D}) = \mathcal{O}]}{Pr[\mathcal{A}(\mathcal{D}') = \mathcal{O}]} \right| \leq \epsilon \qquad (1)$$

In other words, an attacker is not able to learn, with significant probability, whether output $\mathcal{O}$ was obtained by executing $\mathcal{A}$ on input $\mathcal{D}$ or $\mathcal{D}'$. To date, two prominent techniques have been proposed to achieve ϵ-indistinguishability [10, 28]: the *Laplace mechanism* (and the closely related geometric mechanism for integer-valued data) and the *exponential mechanism*. Both mechanisms are closely related to the concept of *sensitivity*:

DEFINITION 2 (L_1-SENSITIVITY [10]). *Given any two sibling datasets $\mathcal{D}$, $\mathcal{D}'$ and a set of real-valued functions $\mathcal{F} = \{f_1, \ldots, f_m\}$, the L_1-sensitivity of $\mathcal{F}$ is measured as $\Delta_{\mathcal{F}} = \max_{\forall \mathcal{D}, \mathcal{D}'} \sum_{i=1}^{m} |f_i(\mathcal{D}) - f_i(\mathcal{D}')|$.*

The *Laplace mechanism* is used to publish the results to a set of statistical queries. A statistical query set $\mathcal{Q} = \{Q_1, \ldots, Q_m\}$ is the equivalent of a set of real-valued functions, hence the sensitivity definition immediately extends to such queries. According to [10], to achieve DP with parameter ϵ it is sufficient to add to each query result random noise generated according to a Laplace distribution with mean $\Delta_{\mathcal{Q}}/\epsilon$. For COUNT queries that do not overlap in the data domain (e.g., finding the frequency of each item $i_j, 1 \leq j \leq n$ in the transaction set), the sensitivity is 1.

The *exponential mechanism* has been introduced in [28], and is concerned with algorithms that produce generic outputs, as opposed to numbers. A *quality function* q associates each possible element o in the algorithm's output domain to a weight $q(o)$. The higher the weight for o, the more likely the item is to be selected as output. Specifically, the exponential mechanism samples randomly as output one element from the output domain, such that the probability of outputting an element o is proportional to $\exp(\frac{q(o) \times \epsilon}{2 \times \Delta_q})$.

An important property of differentially-private algorithms is *sequential composability* [28]. Specifically, if two algorithms $\mathcal{A}_1$ and $\mathcal{A}_2$ executing in isolation on dataset $\mathcal{D}$ achieve DP with privacy parameters ϵ_1 and ϵ_2 respectively, then executing both $\mathcal{A}_1$ and $\mathcal{A}_2$ on $\mathcal{D}$ achieves DP with parameter $(\epsilon_1 + \epsilon_2)$.

2.2 Reservoir Sampling

Many applications require the extraction of a sample of size k_{sample} randomly chosen from a set of elements. If each item has the same chance to be drawn, then we have the classical problem of *uniform sampling*. However, in the general case each element has a weight associated to it, and the selection probability of each element is proportional with its weight. The naïve approach to implement *weighted random sampling (WRS)* is to perform two passes through the data: in the first pass we sum all the weights to generate a cumulative distribution of the sample space, whereas in the second pass we select an element based on its relative weight to the total weight. This procedure is repeated k_{sample} times, each time with one less item in the set.

However, in some applications, the number of items is either too large, or not readily available beforehand, e.g., streaming data. In such cases, traversing the set of elements two times is either not feasible, or not possible. To solve this problem, Knuth [17] developed a set of algorithms which pass only once through the dataset, and use auxiliary memory to materialize a sample of elements that represent a valid sample at any moment through the algorithm's execution. The auxiliary memory of size k_{sample} elements is called *reservoir*. Reservoir-sampling techniques are concerned with computing the probabilities to replace an item in the reservoir with a new one from the set (or stream) of new elements, such that each element has the same probability to be present in the sample (i.e., uniform sampling).

The work in [18] adapts Knuth's approach to weighted random sampling. To achieve WRS, the work in [18] changes the distribution probability of the auxiliary variable used to keep an element in the reservoir. In the case of WRS, the distribution is represented as an exponential distribution with parameter depending on the weight of the item, as given by (2) where v_i is the auxiliary value associated with element i and w_i is the weight of the element. U_i is a random variable distributed according to the uniform distribution in $[0, 1]$ – for each item i the algorithms select a new variable U_i.

$$v_i = -\frac{\ln U_i}{w_i} \qquad (2)$$

At each moment in the algorithm's execution, the reservoir contains the k_{sample} elements for which the auxiliary variable v is the lowest. In Section 4 we show how to combine reservoir sampling with the exponential mechanism of differential privacy to solve efficiently the problem of privately determining high confidence rules.

3. PRIVACY-PRESERVING HCR MINING

3.1 Problem Representation

To model the private high-confidence rule (HCR) mining problem, we employ a representation of association rules in the Cartesian space given by the support domains of the rules and the rules' antecedents. That is, each rule $r = X \to Y$ is represented as a two-dimensional point with coordinates (x, y) where $x = \sigma(X)$ is the support of antecedent X and $y = \sigma(r)$ is the support of the entire rule, as illustrated in Figure 1(a). Note that, this mapping is not injective, as several rules may be represented by the same point, if their support and confidence values coincide.

Given that for any itemsets X and Y it holds that

$$0 \leq sup(X \cup Y) \leq sup(X) \leq t$$

all rules can be represented as points in the first octant as shown in Figure 1(a). The confidence of a rule equals the slope of the line passing through the origin and the point corresponding to the rule.

Using this representation, we can see that existing approaches for privacy-preserving association rule mining [23, 34] are only able to extract very high-support rules, situated in the region marked with hatching in Figure 1(b). Note that, doing so finds only a limited set of rules, and numerous high-quality rules that may only have moderate support are neglected. In contrast, out approach aims at extracting rules with moderate and low supports as well[2], illustrated by the hatched region in Figure 1(c).

---

[2]In our method, we still consider a small minimum support threshold, mainly to filter out rules with extremely low support that are not statistically significant, and are situated around the origin of the Cartesian space. We provide more details about this threshold in Section 4. Nevertheless, our algorithm considers rules with supports situated in a large fraction of the antecedent support domain.

Denote by $\mathcal{R}_\mathbf{I}$ the set of all association rules that can be generated using items from $\mathbf{I} = \{i_1, i_2, \cdots, i_n\}$. The private HCR problem that we are solving is formally defined as follows:

PROBLEM 1. *Given a transaction dataset $\mathcal{D} = [t_1, t_2, \cdots, t_t]$ with t transactions containing items from $\mathbf{I} = \{i_1, i_2, \cdots, i_n\}$, a confidence threshold $c_0 \in [0, 1)$ and a value $k \in \mathbb{N}$, construct under differential privacy with budget ϵ a set $\mathcal{R}_k \subset \mathcal{R}_\mathbf{I}$ of association rules, such that $|\mathcal{R}_k| = k$ and $\forall r \in \mathcal{R}_k$ it holds that $c(r) \geq c_0$.*

Since there might be more than k rules passing the confidence threshold, there are multiple solutions to this problem for the same values of k and c_0. Furthermore, due to the noise introduced by differential privacy, not all extracted rules will actually meet the confidence threshold requirement. To characterize the accuracy of a solution to the above problem, we use as metric *precision*, which measures how many of the extracted rules do indeed have confidence larger than c_0. The precision metric has values in the interval $[0, 1]$, with 1 the ideal value.

3.2 Exponential Mechanism for HCR

The main limitation of existing private mining algorithms [23, 34] is that the search is guided by noisy itemset support values. If one attempts to mine all frequent itemsets of a certain length l, then the resulting sensitivity is $\binom{n}{l}$ which may grow very large even for moderate l values. Doing so will either require a large amount of privacy budget, or will add too much noise to the supports, rendering the data unusable (e.g., confidence values may exceed 1 or may even become negative). To work around this problem, the solutions from [23, 34] rely on either truncating the transactions, or using small values of l (i.e., counting only short itemsets, $l \leq 2$ [23]). However, neither approach is suitable for the HCR problem. Specifically, truncating transactions at length l might split an itemset $X = \{i_1, i_2, \cdots i_{l+1}\}$ even though the rule $i_1, i_2, \cdots i_l \to i_{l+1}$ might have confidence 1. Thus, such a rule is lost.

Private HCR extraction based on noisy itemset supports has a more fundamental problem due to the large impact that added noise may have when computing ratios. Consider for instance a rule $X \to Y$ where $\sigma(X) = 4000$ and $\sigma(X \cup Y) = 1000$, thus the actual confidence is $c(X \to Y) = 0.25$. Assume the threshold value is $c_0 = 0.5$. If the added noise has mean 1000, the noisy count values may reach $\sigma_{noisy}(X) = 3000$ and $\sigma_{noisy}(X \cup Y) = 2000$. As a result, the confidence value $c_{noisy}(X \to Y) = 0.67$ will exceed the threshold c_0, and the rule will be incorrectly identified as HCR.

We consider a different approach, which does not rely on computing noisy itemset counts with the Laplace mechanism. Instead, we employ the exponential mechanism [28] described in Section 2.1 to directly extract high confidence rules. Specifically, we associate each rule r with a quality function q and a weight $\exp\left(\frac{\epsilon \times q}{2 \Delta q}\right)$. Then, we sample k rules *without replacement* such that the sampling probability is always proportional to the weight.

There are two fundamental aspects to consider in our approach. First, we must define an appropriate quality function to determine the sampling weights in the exponential mechanism. Second, the exponential mechanism must compute the quality function value for each candidate rule, and this process becomes computationally intractable due to the very large number of candidate rules (exponential in the number of itemsets n). To this extent, we must devise an effective sampling strategy such that the performance overhead of the proposed approach is tractable in practice. In the rest of this section, we address the former aspect, whereas the latter is the focus of Section 4.

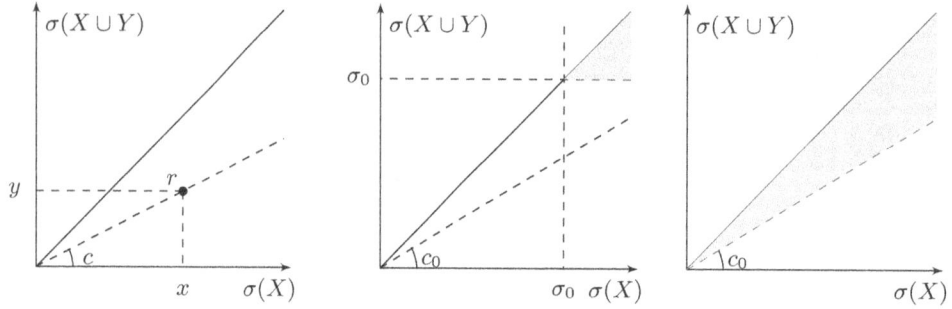

(a) Representation of a rule r with confidence c in the Cartesian space. x is the support of the antecedent and y is the support of the rule.

(b) Existing techniques (e.g., *PrivBasis*) extract only rules with very high frequency (shaded area).

(c) Our technique extracts rules with a broad range of supports, including moderate- and low-support rules.

Figure 1: Representation of rules in the Cartesian space of antecedent and rule support domains

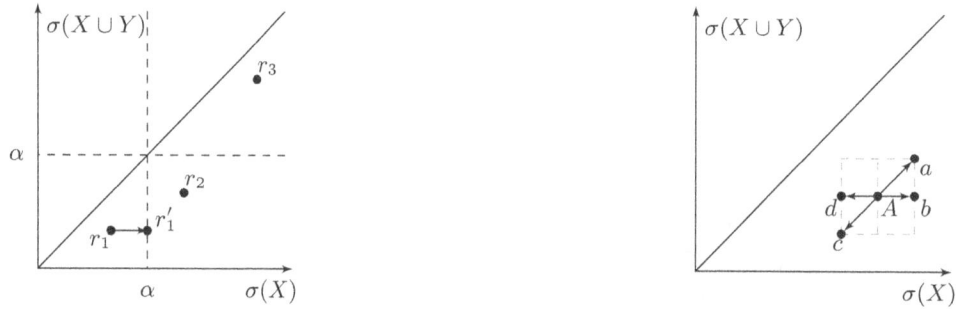

Figure 2: Transformation of a rule under the quality function: rules for which the support of the antecedent is lower than α (r_1) are transformed in rules with a lower confidence but the support of the antecedent exactly α (i.e., r_1'). For all other rules (r_2, r_3), the quality function q_α is the same as the confidence

Figure 3: The four possible locations where a rule r situated at point A in dataset $\mathcal{D}$ can be found in the sibling dataset $\mathcal{D}'$

3.2.1 Quality Function and Sensitivity Computation

An intuitive choice is to link the quality function used in the exponential mechanism to the confidence value. However, simply setting the function to be equal to confidence is not a good approach. Consider, for example, a dataset $\mathcal{D}$ in which an itemset X appears in exactly one transaction t. The transaction t may or may not contain other items not included in X. In this case, $\sigma(X) = 1$ and since $\sigma(X \cup Y) \leq \sigma(X)$, it results that either $c(X \to Y) = 1$ (if $Y \subset t$), or $c(X \to Y) = 0$ (if $Y \not\subset t$). However, in a sibling dataset $\mathcal{D}'$ which is obtained from $\mathcal{D}$ by removing transaction t, we have $\sigma(X) = 0$ which causes $\sigma(X \cup Y)$ to be 0, and thus the value of the confidence is not defined. Thus, the sensitivity of the quality function is also not defined. Since we need to sample across all possible rules, the situation described above will occur frequently in practice.

To address this problem, we employ a quality function which depends on a *sanity bound* parameter $\alpha > 0$, and is defined as follows:

$$q_\alpha(X \to Y) = \frac{\sigma(X \cup Y)}{\max\{\alpha, \sigma(X)\}} \qquad (3)$$

For rules of the form $X \to Y$ for which $\sigma(X) \geq \alpha$, the value of the quality function $q_\alpha(X \to Y)$ is equal to the confidence of the rule, i.e., $c(X \to Y)$. From (3) it results that the quality function of

rules with low antecedent support is computed as if $\alpha - \sigma(X)$ transactions containing only X are added to the dataset. The resulting quality function value is lower than the actual confidence. Figure 2 illustrates how a rule for which the support of the antecedent is lower than the α threshold is transformed into a rule with a lower confidence.

The sensitivity of the proposed quality function is given by the following theorem:

THEOREM 1. *The sensitivity of the quality function q_α is α^{-1}.*

PROOF. Consider rule $r = X \to Y$ in dataset $\mathcal{D}$ with quality $q_{\alpha,\mathcal{D}} = \frac{\sigma(X \cup Y)}{\max\{\alpha, \sigma(X)\}}$. To simplify notation, we denote $\sigma(X \cup Y)$ by y and $\sigma(X)$ by x. Thus:

$$q_{\alpha,\mathcal{D}}(r) = \frac{y}{\max\{\alpha, x\}} \qquad (4)$$

For any sibling dataset $\mathcal{D}'$ we denote $\sigma(X \cup Y)$ by y' and $\sigma(X)$ by x', thus the quality function on $\mathcal{D}'$ is:

$$q_{\alpha,\mathcal{D}'}(r) = \frac{y'}{\max\{\alpha, x'\}} \qquad (5)$$

Given the sibling relationship between the datasets, there are four possible cases, as illustrated in Figure 3:

a) $\mathcal{D}' = \mathcal{D} \cup \{t\}$ and t contains both X and Y. In this case $x' = x + 1$ and $y' = y + 1$. Thus, for $x < \alpha$:

$$q_{\alpha,\mathcal{D}'}(r) = \frac{y+1}{\alpha} = q_{\alpha,\mathcal{D}}(r) + \frac{1}{\alpha} \qquad (6)$$

On the other hand, if $x \geq \alpha$:

$$q_{\alpha,\mathcal{D}'}(r) = \frac{y+1}{x+1} < q_{\alpha,\mathcal{D}}(r) + \frac{1}{x} \leq q_{\alpha,\mathcal{D}}(r) + \frac{1}{\alpha} \qquad (7)$$

b) $\mathcal{D}' = \mathcal{D} \cup \{t\}$ and t contains only X. In this case $y' = y$ and $x' = x + 1$. Thus, for $x < \alpha$:

$$q_{\alpha,\mathcal{D}'}(r) = \frac{y}{\alpha} = q_{\alpha,\mathcal{D}}(r) \qquad (8)$$

On the other hand, if $x \geq \alpha$:

$$\left| q_{\alpha,\mathcal{D}'}(r) - q_{\alpha,\mathcal{D}}(r) \right| = \left| y\left(\frac{1}{x+1} - \frac{1}{x} \right) \right| = \frac{y}{x(x+1)} \qquad (9)$$

But, we have $y \leq x$, so

$$\left| q_{\alpha,\mathcal{D}'}(r) - q_{\alpha,\mathcal{D}}(r) \right| \leq \frac{1}{x+1} \leq \frac{1}{\alpha+1} < \frac{1}{\alpha} \qquad (10)$$

c) $\mathcal{D}' = \mathcal{D} \setminus \{t\}$ and t contains both X and Y. In this case, $y' = y - 1$ and $x' = x - 1$. For $x \leq \alpha$:

$$q_{\alpha,\mathcal{D}'}(r) = \frac{y-1}{\alpha} = q_{\alpha,\mathcal{D}}(r) - \frac{1}{\alpha} \qquad (11)$$

And, if $x > \alpha$, since $0 \leq y \leq x$:

$$\left| q_{\alpha,\mathcal{D}}(r) - q_{\alpha,\mathcal{D}'}(r) \right| = \left| \frac{y}{x} - \frac{y-1}{x-1} \right| = \frac{x-y}{x(x-1)} \qquad (12)$$

Since $0 \leq y$, we have:

$$\left| q_{\alpha,\mathcal{D}}(r) - q_{\alpha,\mathcal{D}'}(r) \right| \leq \frac{1}{x-1} \leq \frac{1}{\alpha} \qquad (13)$$

d) $\mathcal{D}' = \mathcal{D} \setminus \{t\}$ and t contains only X. Then $y' = y$ and $x' = x - 1$. For $x \leq \alpha$ we have:

$$q_{\alpha,\mathcal{D}'}(r) = \frac{y}{\alpha} = q_{\alpha,\mathcal{D}}(r) \qquad (14)$$

And, if $x > \alpha$:

$$\left| q_{\alpha,\mathcal{D}}(r) - q_{\alpha,\mathcal{D}'}(r) \right| = \left| \frac{y}{x} - \frac{y}{x-1} \right| = \frac{y}{x(x-1)} \qquad (15)$$

Since in $\mathcal{D}'$ we have $y \leq x' = x - 1$ we obtain:

$$\left| q_{\alpha,\mathcal{D}}(r) - q_{\alpha,\mathcal{D}'}(r) \right| \leq \frac{1}{x} < \frac{1}{\alpha} \qquad (16)$$

Hence, in all cases the value $|q_{\alpha,\mathcal{D}}(r) - q_{\alpha,\mathcal{D}'}(r)|$ is bounded by α^{-1}, thus the sensitivity of q_α is α^{-1}. $\square$

Since the sensitivity of the quality function is $\Delta q_\alpha = \alpha^{-1}$ and the selection probability in the exponential mechanism is $\exp\left(\frac{\epsilon \times q_\alpha(r)}{2\Delta q_\alpha} \right)$, it results that a higher α value gives a greater weight to rules with higher confidence. That is, the distinction between the weights of any two rules is better if the ratio $\frac{q_\alpha}{\Delta q_\alpha}$ is higher.

In the next section, we focus on the rule sampling algorithm.

4. HCR SAMPLING ALGORITHM

The application of the exponential mechanism requires the computation of the quality function for each candidate rule. Given a set of n items, the total number of rules that can be generated is $3^n - 2^{n+1} + 1$. Extracting k rules from this set has computational complexity $O(k \times 3^n)$ (the quality function must be computed for each candidate in each of the k exponential mechanism execution rounds). This overhead is prohibitive even for moderate values of n. In this section, we investigate techniques that allow us to bring the computational complexity of private HCR to practical levels.

In addition to the number of distinct items n, the maximum length of a transaction, denoted by l_{max}, also has a significant impact on the size of the rule search space. We emphasize that, as opposed to existing techniques [23, 34], we do not restrict our solution to short length rules. However, we do take into account the fact that users may not be interested in rules that exceed a certain number of items. Therefore, we design our solution to take as input parameter from the user a maximum desired rule length l_{max}, and this bound allows us to prune the search space by only generating candidates up to this length. With this restriction, there are $\binom{n}{l_{max}}$ ways in which we can choose items to generate a rule. The search space is thus reduced from $O(3^n)$ rules to $O(\binom{n}{l_{max}} \times 3^{l_{max}}) \approx O(n^{l_{max}})$. However, this is still an excessive number of rules for most real-life datasets.

To further reduce the number of considered candidate rules, we prioritize rules according to the frequency of their composing items. The support of each itemset cannot exceed the support of any item it consists of. To that extent, we first determine privately, using the Laplace mechanism, the noisy supports for each item (i.e., singleton itemset) in the dataset, and sort the items in decreasing order of their noisy supports. Only a small fraction of the total privacy budget suffices for this operation, as we are not interested in the precise count values, but rather in their ordering, which tends to be relatively robust to noise addition, particularly for the higher-frequency items. Next, instead of generating all sets of l_{max} items, we only consider sets of l_{max} consecutive items in the ordering to generate rules. In addition, we account for the fact that the (small) counts of items at the end of the list are not accurate, due to the high noise-to-actual-value ratio, so we filter such items out. Specifically, we consider a threshold θ, which is a system parameter, and all items with noisy supports lower than θ are discarded. Finally, we slide a window of l_{max} items across this list and we generate all possible rules from that window. We emphasize that the values of threshold θ in our solution are very small compared to the dataset cardinality (e.g., in the experimental evaluation of Section 6 we show that 1% of the total number of transactions is a good setting for this parameter). The use of this parameter only eliminates few items. Therefore, our solution will still be able to find numerous low- and moderate-support rules, as opposed to competitor techniques that filter out a large proportion of items, and only keep very high-frequency ones (e.g., in excess of 50% of dataset cardinality).

Furthermore, in order to use the privacy budget judiciously, we need to ensure that we do not generate the same rule multiple times.

To achieve this, every time we slide the window of eligible items, we always generate rules that contain the newly included item. For instance, if the set of eligible items changes from $\{i_1, i_2, i_3, i_4\}$ to $\{i_2, i_3, i_4, i_5\}$, all the rules that are generated in the new step must contain item i_5. As a side effect, the complexity of the rule generation is also reduced. Apart from the first step when we need to generate $3^{l_{max}} - 2^{l_{max}+1} + 1$ possible rules, each subsequent step only needs to consider rules out of $2 \cdot 3^{l_{max}-1} - 2^{l_{max}}$ candidates. Since we need at most n steps (in the case when all items pass threshold θ), the computational complexity required to sample one rule is $O(n \times 3^{l_{max}}) \approx O(n)$ (assuming l_{max} is small).

The exponential mechanism of differential privacy is designed to produce a single output (in our case, a single association rule) per round. To extract k rules, the exponential mechanism needs to be independently executed k times, and the candidate rule populations, as well as associated quality function values must be generated in each round, for a resulting computational complexity of $O(kn)$. Moreover, at each round the algorithm needs to simultaneously keep in memory all weights of the candidate rules, which incurs a significant space complexity of $O(n \times l_{max})$. To address these performance problems, we employ a novel approach that combines the exponential mechanism with *reservoir sampling* [18]. We defer the proof of privacy for the resulting mechanism to Section 5.

The proposed differentially private reservoir sampling approach maintains a list of k candidate rules suitably constructed such that it always represents a valid sample of the rules generated until that moment. However, it only requires passing through the set of candidate rules a single time. Thus, we reduce the memory requirement to $O(k)$ and the time complexity to $O(n)$. We adapt the basic *Weighted Reservoir Sampling (WRS)* algorithm of [18] as follows: for each rule r we associate an exponentially distributed auxiliary variable v_r with the parameter of the distribution being the weight of the rule as given by the exponential mechanism, i.e., $\exp\left(\frac{\epsilon q}{2\Delta q}\right)$. That is, given a random variable U_r uniformly sampled from $[0, 1]$, we generate v_r as:

$$v_r = -\frac{\ln U_r}{\exp\left(\frac{\epsilon q}{2\Delta q}\right)} \qquad (17)$$

The first k rules which are generated are kept in the reservoir together with the associated v_r values, sorted in increasing order of v_r. Next, at each step when a new candidate rule is generated, its corresponding v_r value is computed. If v_r is smaller than the largest value currently contained in the reservoir, then the pair (r, v_r) is inserted into the reservoir. At any time during rule generation, and in particular at the the end of the process, the rules in the reservoir represent a valid sample of the entire rule population, and they are output as result by our algorithm.

The complete algorithm for HCR extraction is summarized in the pseudocode of Figure 4. The user provides as input the values for number of desired rules k, maximum rule length l_{max} and privacy budget ϵ. The algorithm first computes the budget split between the Laplace and exponential mechanisms (lines 1-2), according to the sequential composition property (Section 2.1). Similar to other work in the differential privacy domain that performs a pre-processing step computing low-budget estimations on counts [23], we choose ϵ_1 to be 10% of the total budget ϵ. Furthermore, the rule extraction loop (lines 10-16) samples k rules, so each rule must be sampled with a budget value set to $\epsilon_k = \frac{\epsilon_2}{k}$. Next, the algorithm computes the noisy supports $\sigma'(i)$ for items in the dataset ($i \in \mathbf{I}$) by adding Laplace noise with parameter $\frac{1}{\epsilon_1}$ to the

real supports $\sigma(i)$ (lines 5-7). The items are sorted in decreasing order of their noisy supports, and the list is truncated according to minimum support threshold θ (lines 8-9).

Subsequently, the algorithm constructs sliding windows of size l_{max} and generates all possible rules up to length l_{max} from the items in the sliding window. For each rule r we generate a new U_r value and the corresponding v_r, which is then compared to the maximum v_r found in the reservoir (lines 12-16). If v_r is smaller than the largest value in the reservoir, or if the reservoir contains fewer than k items, then the new rule is added to the reservoir. If the resulting reservoir has more than k items, the rule with the largest v_r is evicted. At the end of the algorithm, the set of all rules in the reservoir is returned as the result $\mathcal{R}_k$.

HCRMine

Input: Dataset $\mathcal{D}$, privacy budget ϵ, requested number of rules k, maximum length of rules l_{max}
Output: Set of k rules $\mathcal{R}_k$
Parameters: privacy budget ϵ_1, sanity bound α, minimum item support θ

1. $\epsilon_2 = \epsilon - \epsilon_1$;
2. $\epsilon_k = \epsilon_2 / k$;
3. $reservoir = \emptyset$;
4. $items = \emptyset$;
5.   **for** $i \in \mathbf{I}$ **do**
6. $\sigma'(i) = \sigma(i) + Laplace(\epsilon_1^{-1})$;
7. $items = items \cup \{(i, \sigma'(i))\}$;
8.   sort_decreasing($items, \sigma'$);
9.   truncate($items, \theta$);
10.   **for** sliding window w of length l_{max} of $items$ **do**
11.   **for** $r \in$ generate_rules(w) **do**
12. $U_r = $ Random();
13. $v_r = -\dfrac{\ln U_r}{\exp\left(\frac{\epsilon q_\alpha}{2\Delta q_\alpha}\right)}$;
14. $v_R = \max\{v_r | (r, v_r) \in reservoir\}$;
15.   **if** ($|reservoir| = k$ **and** $v_r < v_R$) **or** $|reservoir| < k$
16. $reservoir = reservoir \cup \{(r, v_r)\}$;
17. $\mathcal{R}_k = \{r | (r, v_r) \in reservoir\}$;
18.   return $\mathcal{R}_k$;

Figure 4: The pseudocode of the proposed approach

4.1 Rule Expansion Optimization

We introduce an optimization that improves the utility of the algorithm by generating more rules than the requested k. Specifically, the optimization uses properties of association rules to infer additional high-confidence rules starting from the set $\mathcal{R}_k$ of k rules returned by the algorithm. The problem formulation from Section 3.1 is slightly relaxed as follows:

PROBLEM 2. *Given a transaction dataset $\mathcal{D} = [t_1, t_2, \cdots, t_t]$ with t transactions containing items from $\mathbf{I} = \{i_1, i_2, \cdots, i_n\}$, a confidence threshold $c_0 \in [0, 1)$ and a value $k \in \mathbb{N}$ construct a set $\mathcal{R}'_k \subset \mathcal{R}_{\mathbf{I}}$ of association rules under differential privacy with budget ϵ, such that $|\mathcal{R}'_k| \geq k$ and for as many as possible $r \in \mathcal{R}'_k$ it holds that $c(r) \geq c_0$.*

Since we don't know the values of support and confidence for the rules that we have obtained so far, the only way in which we can add new rules with higher confidence is by doing lexical transformations on the rules in $\mathcal{R}'_k$. We are using the results of the following theorem.

THEOREM 2. *Given an association rule $X \to Y$ with $|Y| \geq 2$ for every item $i_y \in Y$ the rules $X \to Y \setminus \{i_y\}$ and $X \cup \{i_y\} \to Y \setminus \{i_y\}$ have at least the same confidence as the rule $X \to Y$.*

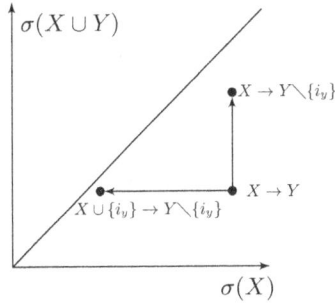

Figure 5: Lexical transformations of a rule $X \rightarrow Y$ which are guaranteed to have the same confidence or higher than the original rule. Item i_y can be any item from Y.

PROOF. Denote $Y \setminus \{i_y\}$ as Y_{i_y} and $X \cup \{i_y\}$ as X_{i_y}. So, the two new rules for i_y are $X \rightarrow Y_{i_y}$ and $X_{i_y} \rightarrow Y_{i_y}$. We know that $\sigma(X \cup Y_{i_y}) \geq \sigma(X \cup Y)$ and that $\sigma(X_{i_y}) \leq \sigma(X)$. Thus:

$$c(X \rightarrow Y_{i_y}) = \frac{\sigma(X \cup Y_{i_y})}{\sigma(X)} \geq \frac{\sigma(X \cup Y)}{\sigma(X)} \quad (18)$$

$$c(X_{i_y} \rightarrow Y_{i_y}) = \frac{\sigma(X \cup Y)}{\sigma(X_{i_y})} \geq \frac{\sigma(X \cup Y)}{\sigma(X)} \quad (19)$$

$$c(X \rightarrow Y) = \frac{\sigma(X \cup Y)}{\sigma(X)} \quad (20)$$

From the above relations we have that the confidence of the resulting rules is greater than the confidence of the original one. □

A graphical depiction of Theorem 2 is provided in Figure 5. While there are other possible lexical transformations of a rule, the two presented in Theorem 2 and Figure 5 are always guaranteed to increase the confidence of a rule.

5. PRIVACY ANALYSIS

In this section, we analyze the proposed method for private HCR mining that combines the exponential mechanism of differential privacy and reservoir sampling. Specifically, we show that: *(i)* the proposed method of sampling without replacement satisfies the requirements of differential privacy, and *(ii)* the proposed sampling method returns a valid sample.

THEOREM 3. *For any dataset $\mathcal{D}$, sampling without replacement item x and then item y using the exponential mechanism with the same privacy budget ϵ' and the same quality function satisfies differential privacy with parameter $2 \times \epsilon'$.*

PROOF. We first determine the probability to sample x followed by y from the dataset $\mathcal{D}$. Since sampling a certain item does not change the weights of any other item ($q_{\mathcal{D}} = q_{\mathcal{D} \setminus \{x\}}$) we have the following independence result:

$$p_{x,y,\mathcal{D}} = \Pr(y, x | \mathcal{D}) = \Pr(x | \mathcal{D}) \Pr(y | \mathcal{D} \setminus \{x\}) \quad (21)$$

But,

$$\Pr(x | \mathcal{D}) = \frac{\exp\left(\frac{\epsilon' q_{\mathcal{D}}(x)}{2\Delta q}\right)}{\sum_{t \in \mathcal{D}} \exp\left(\frac{\epsilon' q_{\mathcal{D}}(t)}{2\Delta q}\right)} \quad (22)$$

$$\Pr(y | \mathcal{D} \setminus \{x\}) = \frac{\exp\left(\frac{\epsilon' q_{\mathcal{D}}(y)}{2\Delta q}\right)}{\sum_{t \in \mathcal{D} \setminus \{x\}} \exp\left(\frac{\epsilon' q_{\mathcal{D}}(t)}{2\Delta q}\right)} \quad (23)$$

Thus,

$$p_{x,y,\mathcal{D}} = \frac{\exp\left(\frac{\epsilon'(q_{\mathcal{D}}(x) + q_{\mathcal{D}}(y))}{2\Delta q}\right)}{\sum_{t \in \mathcal{D}} \exp\left(\frac{\epsilon' q_{\mathcal{D}}(t)}{2\Delta q}\right) \sum_{t \in \mathcal{D} \setminus \{x\}} \exp\left(\frac{\epsilon' q_{\mathcal{D}}(t)}{2\Delta q}\right)} \quad (24)$$

Furthermore, for any sibling dataset $\mathcal{D}'$, the following holds:

$$
\begin{aligned}
\frac{p_{x,y,\mathcal{D}}}{p_{x,y,\mathcal{D}'}} &= \frac{\exp\left(\frac{\epsilon'(q_{\mathcal{D}}(x) + q_{\mathcal{D}}(y))}{2\Delta q}\right)}{\exp\left(\frac{\epsilon'(q_{\mathcal{D}'}(x) + q_{\mathcal{D}'}(y))}{2\Delta q}\right)} \times \\
&\quad \frac{\sum_{t \in \mathcal{D}'} \exp\left(\frac{\epsilon' q_{\mathcal{D}'}(t)}{2\Delta q}\right)}{\sum_{t \in \mathcal{D}} \exp\left(\frac{\epsilon' q_{\mathcal{D}}(t)}{2\Delta q}\right)} \times \\
&\quad \frac{\sum_{t \in \mathcal{D}' \setminus \{x\}} \exp\left(\frac{\epsilon' q_{\mathcal{D}'}(t)}{2\Delta q}\right)}{\sum_{t \in \mathcal{D} \setminus \{x\}} \exp\left(\frac{\epsilon' q_{\mathcal{D}}(t)}{2\Delta q}\right)}
\end{aligned}
\quad (25)
$$

Since q varies by at most Δq between sibling datasets, the first factor in the right-hand side of Eq. (25) is bounded as follows:

$$\exp\left(\frac{\epsilon'(q_{\mathcal{D}}(y) - q_{\mathcal{D}'}(y) + q_{\mathcal{D}}(x) - q_{\mathcal{D}'}(x))}{2\Delta q}\right) \leq \exp(\epsilon')$$

Similarly, for the other two factors we obtain:

$$\frac{\sum_{t \in \mathcal{D}'} \exp\left(\frac{\epsilon'(\Delta q + q_{\mathcal{D}})(t)}{2\Delta q}\right)}{\sum_{t \in \mathcal{D}} \exp\left(\frac{\epsilon' q_{\mathcal{D}}(t)}{2\Delta q}\right)} = \exp\left(\frac{\epsilon'}{2}\right) \quad (26)$$

$$\frac{\sum_{t \in \mathcal{D}' \setminus \{x\}} \exp\left(\frac{\epsilon'(\Delta q + q_{\mathcal{D}})(t)}{2\Delta q}\right)}{\sum_{t \in \mathcal{D} \setminus \{x\}} \exp\left(\frac{\epsilon' q_{\mathcal{D}}(t)}{2\Delta q}\right)} = \exp\left(\frac{\epsilon'}{2}\right) \quad (27)$$

Hence we obtain that $\frac{\Pr(y, x | \mathcal{D})}{\Pr(y, x | \mathcal{D}')} \leq \exp(2 \times \epsilon')$ which means that sampling without replacement using privacy budget ϵ' and not changing the values of the quality function between samples is differentially private with budget $2 \times \epsilon'$. □

To prove that the sample obtained by using reservoir sampling in conjunction with the exponential mechanims is valid, we adapt the original proof from Theorem 3.1 in [18], with the modification that our weights are given by the exponential mechanism. The re-stated theorem is as follows:

THEOREM 4. *Let $(r_1, r_2, \cdots r_k)$ denote the rules in the reservoir of the algorithm WRS after visiting all rules. Then*

$$\Pr(r_1, r_2, \cdots r_k) = \prod_{j=1}^{N} \frac{\exp\left(\frac{\epsilon' q(r_j)}{2\Delta q}\right)}{\sum_{r \notin \{r_1, r_2, \cdots r_j\}} \exp\left(\frac{\epsilon' q(r)}{2\Delta q}\right)} \quad (28)$$

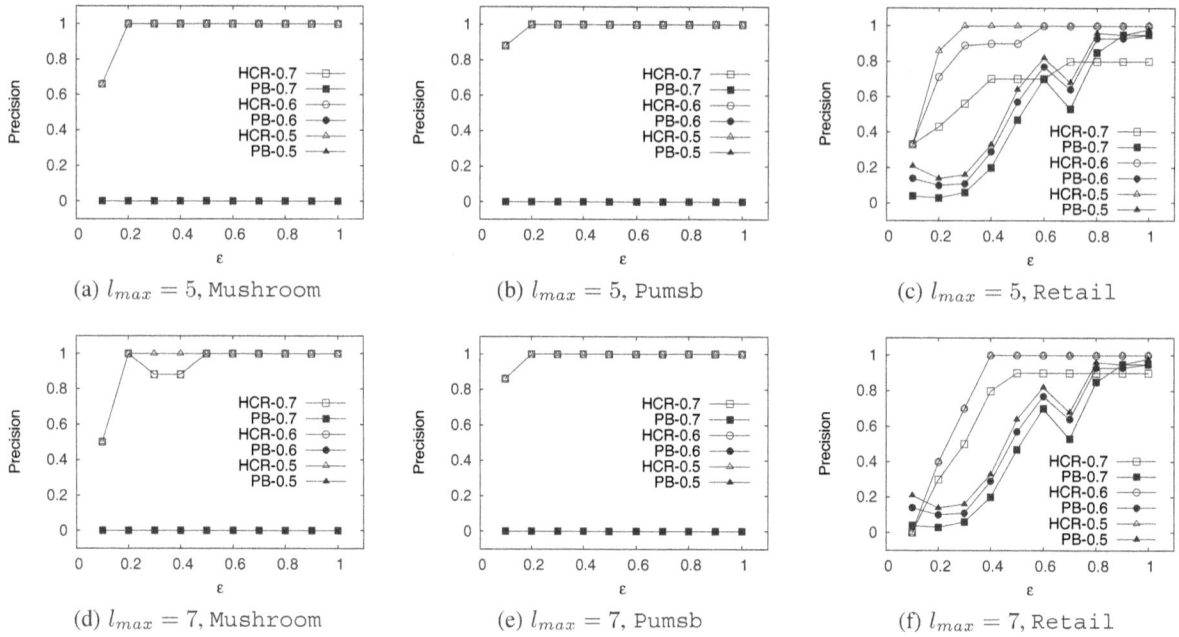

(a) $l_{max} = 5$, Mushroom   (b) $l_{max} = 5$, Pumsb   (c) $l_{max} = 5$, Retail

(d) $l_{max} = 7$, Mushroom   (e) $l_{max} = 7$, Pumsb   (f) $l_{max} = 7$, Retail

Figure 6: Comparison with *PrivBasis* [23]

Dataset	n	t	θ	θ_{PB}	k_{PB}
Mushroom	119	8124	81	4464	100
Pumsb	7116	49046	490	28613	200
Retail	16470	88162	881	1192	100

Table 1: Experimental dataset characteristics. Last two columns are parameters used by *PrivBasis* only

We provide only a sketch of the proof, which is similar to that of Theorem 3. In order to sample k rules using ϵ' privacy budget for each of them we need a total budget of $k \times \epsilon'$, which is expected since the reservoir sampling technique is used only to improve the complexity of the normal weighted sampling approach, but it still uses the same weights.

From (17), as well as taking into account the fact that the reservoir sampling technique uses only the relative ordering of v_r values, we replace these with v_r^* obtained by taking the logarithm of the expression in (17):

$$v_r^* = \ln\left(\ln\frac{1}{U_r}\right) - \frac{\epsilon' q}{2\Delta q} \tag{29}$$

This equation shows that the score of each rule in the reservoir is a linear combination of two terms: one is a random variable $(\ln(\ln U_r^{-1}))$ while the other is a linear term in the quality of the rule (for a fixed value of ϵ') or in ϵ' (for a fixed value of the rule's quality). This shows the importance of choosing a good $\frac{\epsilon' \times q}{\Delta q}$ value: the impact of randomness is reduced if this ratio is higher. While we have presented this analysis in the context of association rule mining, the result can be extrapolated to any approach which uses the exponential mechanism to sample multiple outcomes simultaneously.

6. EXPERIMENTAL EVALUATION

We evaluate experimentally the accuracy and performance of the proposed solution for differentially-private mining of high-confidence association rules (referred to in the remainder of the section as HCR). We implemented a C prototype of the proposed technique, and we ran our experiments on an Intel Core i7-3770 3.4 GHz CPU machine with 8 cores and 16 GB of RAM, running Linux OS. We first provide a description of the experimental settings used. Next, we evaluate the accuracy of HCR in comparison to *PrivBasis* [23]. Finally, we investigate the performance of HCR when varying several important system parameters. We consider three datasets with diverse characteristics (described in Table 1), frequently used in the data mining literature[3].

We vary the confidence threshold c_0 between 0.5 and 0.9, and the length of the mined rules l_{max} between 3 and 7. The privacy budget ϵ ranges between 0.1 and 1.0. For the proposed method, we set the minimum item support threshold parameter θ (Section 4) to 1% of the total number of transactions. Unless otherwise stated, the sanity bound of the quality function is set to $\alpha = 1000$. All reported measurements are obtained by averaging results over ten random seeds.

As discussed in Section 3.1, we measure the accuracy of private rule mining using precision, defined as the fraction of returned rules that actually satisfy the requested threshold c_0. Since we are interested in high-confidence rules with low and moderate support, we take into account only association rules for which the support is less than half of the dataset cardinality (i.e., occur in fewer than 50% of transactions).

First, we compare the proposed HCR method against *PrivBasis* [23], the state-of-the-art in differentially-private data mining. *PrivBasis* determines frequent itemsets and their supports, and based on these it is possible to generate association rules and compute their confidence. *PrivBasis* receives one system parameter k_{PB} that determines how many itemsets are mined. In our experiments, we use the same settings that the authors chose in [23], as illustrated in Table 1. The table also shows in column θ_{PB} the

---

[3]Available online at http://fimi.ua.ac.be/data/

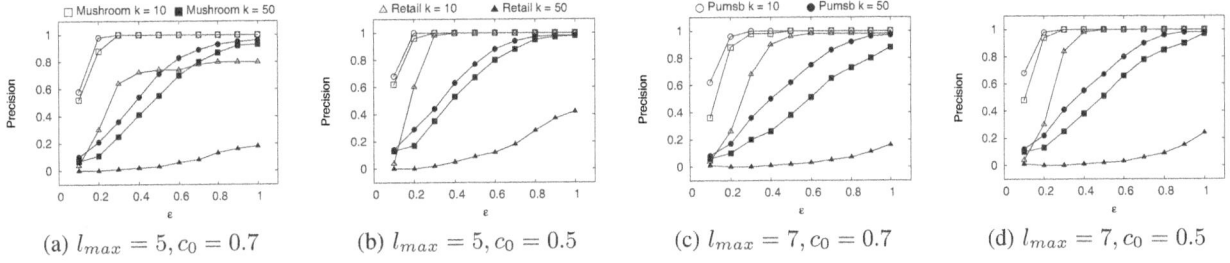

Figure 7: Effect of privacy budget ϵ for several settings of k, c_0 and l_{max}

(a) $l_{max} = 5, c_0 = 0.7$ (b) $l_{max} = 5, c_0 = 0.5$ (c) $l_{max} = 7, c_0 = 0.7$ (d) $l_{max} = 7, c_0 = 0.5$

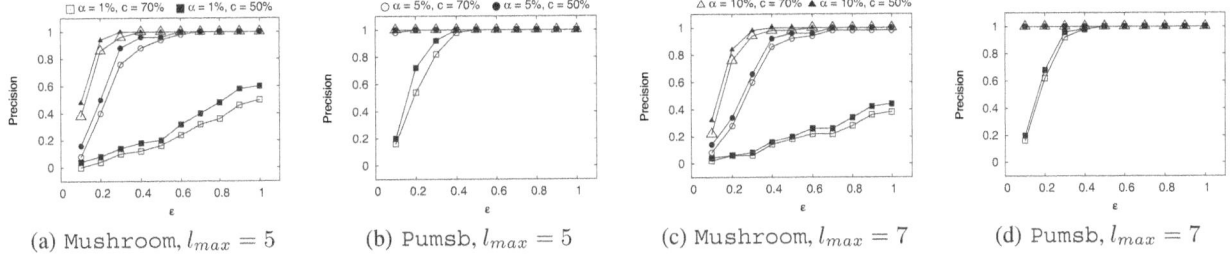

Figure 8: Effect of α, the quality function sanity bound, for several settings of c_0 and l_{max} (k=10)

(a) Mushroom, $l_{max} = 5$ (b) Pumsb, $l_{max} = 5$ (c) Mushroom, $l_{max} = 7$ (d) Pumsb, $l_{max} = 7$

minimum support of mined itemsets, i.e., the support of the k_{PB}^{th} most frequent itemset in each dataset.

Figure 6 summarizes the comparison results (for HCR, we set threshold $\alpha = 1000$ and $k = 10$). We consider three distinct minimum confidence threshold values $c_0 = 0.5$, 0.6 and 0.7 (shown as different lines in each plot). In the case of Mushroom and Pumsb datasets, *PrivBasis* (labeled PB in the graphs, and illustrated with full point shapes) is not able to find any rule with support less than 50%. This result captures the severe limitation of existing techniques for association rule mining, which only retain very-high support itemsets, and completely discard rules that are less frequent, even though many high-quality rules may have lower supports. In contrast, HCR is able to extract high-confidence rules with high accuracy. For privacy budgets in the upper half of the considered ϵ range, HCR obtains perfect accuracy, as all extracted rules exceed the required threshold c_0.

In the case of the sparser Retail dataset, *PrivBasis* is able to retrieve some rules, but the accuracy of HCR is consistently superior, except for a few isolated cases at very low and very high budgets, where the two methods obtain similar accuracy. Furthermore, HCR is able to judiciously use the available budget, as accuracy increases monotonically with ϵ. In contrast, the accuracy of *PrivBasis* oscillates with ϵ, and is subject to unpredictable influences by random factors in the dataset. Specifically, we noticed that the noisy confidence of the rules, computed as the ratio of the noisy supports of the complete rule and the antecedent, exhibits high variability with ϵ, which is the main cause for the non-monotonic behavior (division is not a stable operation in the presence of noisy counts). Due to its poor accuracy, we no longer consider *PrivBasis* in the rest of the experimental evaluation, and we focus on the behavior of HCR when varying its system parameters.

Next, we investigate the accuracy of HCR when varying privacy budget ϵ. We consider two distinct values of number of user-requested rules ($k = 10$ and $k = 50$) and two rule lengths, $l_{max} = 5$ and $l_{max} = 7$ (due to lack of space, we omit the $l_{max} = 3$ results for which we have observed similar trends as for the other lengths). We use two confidence threshold levels, $c_0 = 0.7$ and $c_0 = 0.5$. Figure 7 shows that, as expected, the preci-

sion is higher when the confidence threshold c_0 is lower. For higher c_0, there are fewer rules with actual confidence above the threshold, and due to noise, more lower-confidence rules are extracted by HCR. Furthermore, accuracy decreases when the number of requested rules k increases. This behavior is due to the way the exponential mechanism works. The budget for sampling rules (ϵ_2, as discussed in Section 4) is divided among all k extracted rules, as each invocation consumes ϵ_2/k budget. Therefore, the accuracy in determining the correct confidence for each individual rule decreases.

Among the three considered datasets, the accuracy for Pumsb and Mushroom is relatively high, whereas for the sparser Retail dataset lower values are obtained. Still, HCR obtains reasonable accuracy for smaller k values and shorter rule lengths (i.e., $l_{max} = 5$). For the other cases, the lower accuracy can be partly explained by the fact that we fixed α at 1000, regardless of the number of transactions in the dataset. All rules $X \rightarrow Y$ for which $\sigma(X) < \alpha$ are ranked poorly by the quality function q_α (as illustrated in Figure 2), so a better approach is to choose α differently for each dataset. We evaluate more closely the impact of α in the next experiment.

We evaluate the impact of parameter α used as a sanity bound in the quality function computation. We consider two settings of confidence threshold, $c_0 = 0.5$ and $c_0 = 0.7$, and two rule length values, $l_{max} = 5$ and $l_{max} = 7$. We set the number of requested rules to $k = 10$. Figure 8 presents the results for datasets Pumsb and Mushroom (we omit Retail due to space considerations). We set parameter α to 1%, 5% and 10% of the dataset cardinality. Each plot contains six lines, corresponding to combinations of the three α values times the two considered confidence threshold values.

As expected, precision is better when the confidence threshold is lower. However, we note that α also has a significant contribution on precision. The $\alpha = 1\%$ case obtains lower precision. In the case of the Mushroom dataset, the choice of α influences the entire privacy budget ϵ scale, and has a less significant impact for Pumsb, where precision quickly converges to 1 for $\epsilon > 0.3$. A clear increasing trend in precision can also be observed as α grows

Dataset	$l_{max} = 3$	$l_{max} = 5$	$l_{max} = 7$
Mushroom	0.03s	0.49s	5.48s
Pumsb	1.80s	27.54s	306.08s
Retail	0.03s	0.43s	4.58s

Table 2: Execution time of HCR (in seconds)

from 5% to 10%, although the gap is lower than the one from 1% to 5%. We conclude that a larger α value improves precision.

This is not surprising, as the net effect of a larger α is to prune away very low support rules, for which confidence is more difficult to compute. On the other hand, setting α too high will prevent low-support rules from being included in the result, and the higher the α value, the more our method behaves like *PrivBasis*. A value of $\alpha = 5\%$ seems to be a good choice in practice, as the precision loss is not high compared to the more restrictive 10% case, and the user of the system is able to retrieve rules with support in the range $5 - 10\%$. On the other hand, if the user already has a good indication that rules below a certain support threshold are not useful, then setting α to a higher value is indicated, to improve precision.

In our next experiment, we investigate how precision varies when the number of requested rules to be extracted (k) increases. We consider two settings of rule length, $l_{max} = 5$ and $l_{max} = 7$, and two confidence thresholds, $c_0 = 0.5$ and $c_0 = 0.7$. We set privacy budget $\epsilon = 0.5$. Recall from Section 4 that the privacy budget ϵ is shared among multiple invocations of the exponential mechanism, so as k increases we do expect precision to decrease. Figure 9 shows the obtained results. For the sparser Retail dataset, the precision drops significantly when k increases. It is well-understood in literature that highly-sparse data is more challenging to process with differential privacy. On the other hand, the precision for the other datasets degrades gracefully with k, and reasonable levels of precision may be obtained even for values of $k = 100$ and higher. The values of precision obtained for the longer $l_{max} = 7$ rules is lower, as the population of rules from which the exponential mechanism selects the output is larger (exponential in l_{max}).

Finally, we present results on the computational overhead of the proposed technique. Recall that, the computational complexity of HCR is influenced mainly by the number of total items in the dataset (n) and by the maximum length of extracted rules (l_{max}). Table 2 summarizes the results. Note that, in most cases, the algorithm finishes very quickly, with runtime of less than 30 seconds. The only exception is the denser Pumsb dataset, which also has high dimensionality. In this case, more candidate rules pass the support threshold, and for the larger $l_{max} = 7$ setting the execution time is higher. Nevertheless, even in this case the execution time is 5 minutes, which we believe is a reasonable time for a data mining task.

7. RELATED WORK

Privacy-preserving data publishing has been extensively studied in the literature in the context of relational data. The work in [2] employs random perturbation to prevent re-identification of records, by adding noise to the data. Later in [13] is is shown that an attacker could filter the random noise, and hence breach data privacy, unless the noise is correlated with the data. Furthermore, random perturbation may expose privacy of outliers when an attacker has access to external knowledge. Published data about individuals (*microdata*) may contain *quasi-identifier* attributes (QID), such as age, or zipcode, which may be joined with public databases to re-identify individual records.

Sweeney [30] introduced k-anonymity, a syntactic privacy-preserving paradigm which requires each record to be indistinguishable among at least $k - 1$ other records with respect to the set of QID attributes. Records with identical QID values form an *equivalence class*, or *anonymized group*. k-anonymity can be achieved through *generalization*, which maps detailed attribute values to value ranges, and *suppression*, which removes certain attribute values or records from the microdata. Several generalization techniques have been proposed, which attempt to minimize information loss, i.e., maximize utility of the data [4, 19, 20, 1, 33]. k-anonymity prevents re-identification of individual records, but it is vulnerable to *homogeneity* attacks, where many (or all) of the records in an anonymized group share the same sensitive attribute (SA) value. ℓ-diversity [26] addresses this vulnerability, and creates anonymized groups in which at least ℓ SA values are "well-represented". Generalization techniques have also been employed for transactional data [12, 24]. Another direction of research [3, 32] focuses on publishing *patterns*, and not data. The patterns (or rules) are mined directly from the original data, and the resulting set of rules is sanitized using generalization and suppression to prevent privacy breaches. However, syntactic methods (including generalization and suppression) are not able to protect against adversaries with background knowledge, and they only offer best-effort privacy, without any formal guarantees.

Differential privacy (DP) [9, 10] is a powerful semantic privacy model that transforms a dataset in a way that bounds the probability of an adversary of learning whether a particular individual is present in the dataset or not. DP has become the de-facto standard in privacy-preserving publishing and processing of sensitive data. Numerous works focus on differentially-private processing in various settings such as relational data [14, 21], location data [7, 5] or recommender systems [27]. DP has also been considered in the domain of data mining. For instance, the work in [11] shows how to construct a differentially private classifier. Closest to our work is the research in [23, 34], which focuses on mining frequent itemsets in a differential private way. Using the noisy itemset counts, one could in theory determine high-confidence rules, but as we show in Section 5, only rules with very high frequency are retained, whereas numerous high-confidence but only moderately-frequent rules are discarded. In contrast, our proposed technique is able to extract high-confidence rules that have moderate and low support.

8. CONCLUSION

In this paper, we proposed a novel technique for differentially-private mining of association rules with low and moderate supports. As opposed to existing methods that first mine very frequent itemsets using the Laplace mechanism, and then generate rules and compute their confidence, our technique directly samples high-confidence rules using the exponential mechanism. Doing so allows us to extract rules with a broad range of supports. To the best of our knowledge, this is the first differentially-private algorithm to directly extract high-confidence association rules. Experimental results show that the proposed technique clearly outperforms existing state-of-the-art in extracting quality rules with low and moderate supports.

In future work, we plan to extend our method to sample multiple rules in the same invocation round of the exponential mechanism. This can be achieved by grouping together multiple rules that are likely to have similar confidence, and associating quality functions to sets instead of individual rules. Such an approach will allow us to increase the number of extracted rules. In addition, we plan to explore alternative quality functions with lower sensitivity, and to devise more effective heuristics for rule pruning.

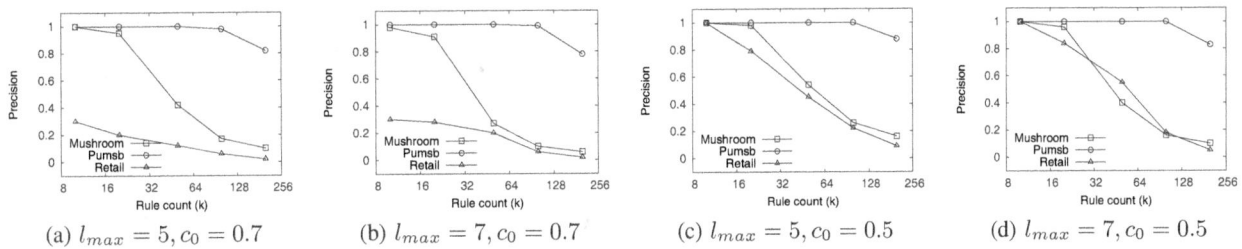

(a) $l_{max} = 5, c_0 = 0.7$ (b) $l_{max} = 7, c_0 = 0.7$ (c) $l_{max} = 5, c_0 = 0.5$ (d) $l_{max} = 7, c_0 = 0.5$

Figure 9: Effect of number of requested rules k for several settings of c_0 and l_{max}

Acknowledgments. This work has been supported by NSF award CNS-1111512.

9. REFERENCES

[1] G. Aggarwal, T. Feder, K. Kenthapadi, S. Khuller, R. Panigrahy, D. Thomas, and A. Zhu. Achieving Anonymity via Clustering. In *Proc. of ACM PODS*, pages 153–162, 2006.

[2] R. Agrawal and R. Srikant. Privacy preserving data mining. In *Proceedings of International Conference on Management of Data (ACM SIGMOD)*, 2000.

[3] M. Atzori, F. Bonchi, F. Giannotti, and D. Pedreschi. Anonymity preserving pattern discovery. *VLDB Journal*, 2008 (to appear).

[4] R. J. Bayardo and R. Agrawal. Data Privacy through Optimal k-Anonymization. In *Proceedings of International Conference on Data Engineering (ICDE)*, pages 217–228, 2005.

[5] R. Chen, B. C. Fung, B. C. Desai, and N. M. Sossou. Differentially private transit data publication: a case study on the montreal transportation system. In *Proceedings of the 18th ACM SIGKDD international conference on Knowledge discovery and data mining*, KDD '12, pages 213–221, 2012.

[6] D. W.-L. Cheung, J. Han, V. T. Y. Ng, A. W.-C. Fu, and Y. Fu. A fast distributed algorithm for mining association rules. In *PDIS*, pages 31–42, 1996.

[7] G. Cormode, C. Procopiuc, E. Shen, D. Srivastava, and T. Yu. Differentially private spatial decompositions. In *ICDE*, pages 20–31, 2012.

[8] W. Du, Y. S. Han, and S. Chen. Privacy-preserving multivariate statistical analysis: Linear regression and classification. In *2004 SIAM International Conference on Data Mining*, Lake Buena Vista, Florida, Apr. 22-24 2004.

[9] C. Dwork. Differential privacy. In *ICALP (2)*, pages 1–12. Springer, 2006.

[10] C. Dwork, F. McSherry, K. Nissim, and A. Smith. Calibrating noise to sensitivity in private data analysis. In *TCC*, pages 265–284, 2006.

[11] A. Friedman and A. Schuster. Data mining with differential privacy. In *Proceedings of the 16th ACM SIGKDD International Conference on Knowledge Discovery and Data Mining*, pages 493–502, Washington, DC, 2010.

[12] G. Ghinita, Y. Tao, and P. Kalnis. On the anonymization of sparse high-dimensional data. In *Proc. of ICDE*, pages 715–724, 2008.

[13] Z. Huang, W. Du, and B. Chen. Deriving private information from randomized data. In *Proceedings of International Conference on Management of Data (ACM SIGMOD)*, 2005.

[14] A. Inan, M. Kantarcioglu, G. Ghinita, and E. Bertino. Private record matching using differential privacy. In *EDBT '10*, pages 123–134.

[15] M. Kantarcioglu and J. Vaidya. Privacy preserving naive bayes classifier for horizontally partitioned data. In *the Workshop on Privacy Preserving Data Mining held in association with The Third IEEE International Conference on Data Mining*, Melbourne, FL, 2003.

[16] M. Kantarcıoğlu, J. Jin, and C. Clifton. When do data mining results violate privacy? In *Proc.of the ACM SIGKDD International Conference on Knowledge Discovery and Data Mining*, pages 599–604, Seattle, WA, Aug. 22-25 2004.

[17] D. E. Knuth. *The Art of Computer Programming, Volume II: Seminumerical Algorithms, 2nd Edition*. Addison-Wesley, 1981.

[18] M. Kolonko and D. Wäsch. Sequential reservoir sampling with a nonuniform distribution. *ACM Trans. Math. Softw.*, 32(2):257–273, June 2006.

[19] K. LeFevre, D. J. DeWitt, and R. Ramakrishnan. Incognito: Efficient Full-domain k-Anonymity. In *Proceedings of International Conference on Management of Data (ACM SIGMOD)*, pages 49–60, 2005.

[20] K. LeFevre, D. J. DeWitt, and R. Ramakrishnan. Mondrian Multidimensional k-Anonymity. In *Proceedings of International Conference on Data Engineering (ICDE)*, 2006.

[21] C. Li and G. Miklau. Optimal error of query sets under the differentially-private matrix mechanism. In *International Conference on Database Theory (ICDT)*, 2013.

[22] N. Li, T. Li, and S. Venkatasubramanian. t-closeness: Privacy beyond k-anonymity and l-diversity. In *ICDE '07*, pages 106–115, Istanbul, Turkey, 2007. IEEE.

[23] N. Li, W. Qardaji, D. Su, and J. Cao. Privbasis: Frequent itemset mining with differential privacy. *Proc. VLDB Endow.*, 5(11):1340–1351, July 2012.

[24] T. Li, N. Li, and J. Zhang. Modeling and Integrating Background Knowledge in Data Anonymization. In *Proc. of ICDE*, pages 6–17, 2009.

[25] J.-L. Lin and M. H. Dunham. Mining association rules: Anti-skew algorithms. In *ICDE*, pages 486–493, 1998.

[26] A. Machanavajjhala, J. Gehrke, D. Kifer, and M. Venkitasubramaniam. l-Diversity: Privacy Beyond k-Anonymity. In *Proceedings of International Conference on Data Engineering (ICDE)*, 2006.

[27] F. McSherry and I. Mironov. Differentially private recommender systems: Building privacy into the netflix prize contenders. In *Proceedings of the 15th ACM SIGKDD International Conference on Knowledge Discovery and Data Mining*, pages 627–636, Paris, France, 2009.

[28] F. McSherry and K. Talwar. Mechanism design via differential privacy. In *Proc. of Annual IEEE Symposium on Foundations of Computer Science (FOCS)*, pages 94–103, 2007.

[29] A. Savasere, E. Omiecinski, and S. B. Navathe. An efficient algorithm for mining association rules in large databases. In *VLDB*, pages 432–444, 1995.

[30] L. Sweeney. k-Anonymity: A Model for Protecting Privacy. *International Journal of Uncertainty, Fuzziness and Knowledge-Based Systems*, 10(5):557–570, 2002.

[31] J. Vaidya and C. Clifton. Privacy-preserving data mining: Why, how, and what for? *Security & Privacy Magazine*, 2(6):19–27, Nov.-Dec. 2004.

[32] V. Verykios, A. Elmagarmid, E. Bertino, Y. Saygin, and E. Dasseni. Association rule hiding. *IEEE Transactions on Knowledge and Data Engineering (TKDE)*, 16(4):434–447, 2004.

[33] J. Xu, W. Wang, J. Pei, X. Wang, B. Shi, and A. Fu. Utility-Based Anonymization Using Local Recoding. In *Proc. of SIGKDD*, pages 20–23, 2006.

[34] C. Zeng, J. F. Naughton, and J.-Y. Cai. On differentially private frequent itemset mining. *Proc. VLDB Endow.*, 6(1):25–36, Nov. 2012.

[35] N. Zhang, S. Wang, and W. Zhao. A new scheme on privacy-preserving association rule mining. In *The 8th European Conference on Principles and Practice of Knowledge Discovery in Databases (PKDD 2004)*, Pisa, Italy, Sept. 20-24 2004.

DetAnom: Detecting Anomalous Database Transactions by Insiders

Syed Rafiul Hussain
Dept. of Computer Science
Purdue University, USA
hussain1@purdue.edu

Asmaa Sallam
Dept. of Computer Science
Purdue University, USA
asallam@purdue.edu

Elisa Bertino
Dept. of Computer Science
and Cyber Center
Purdue University, USA
bertino@purdue.edu

ABSTRACT

Database Management Systems (DBMSs) provide access control mechanisms that allow database administrators (DBA) to grant application programs access privileges to databases. However, securing the database alone is not enough, as attackers aiming at stealing data can take advantage of vulnerabilities in the privileged applications and make applications to issue malicious database queries. Therefore, even though the access control mechanism can prevent application programs from accessing the data to which the programs are not authorized, it is unable to prevent misuse of the data to which application programs are authorized for access. Hence, we need a mechanism able to detect malicious behavior resulting from previously authorized applications. In this paper, we design and implement an anomaly detection mechanism, *DetAnom*, that creates a profile of the application program which can succinctly represent the application's normal behavior in terms of its interaction (i.e., submission of SQL queries) with the database. For each query, the profile keeps a signature and also the corresponding constraints that the application program must satisfy to submit that query. Later in the detection phase, whenever the application issues a query, the corresponding signature and constraints are checked against the current context of the application. If there is a mismatch, the query is marked as anomalous. The main advantage of our anomaly detection mechanism is that we need neither any previous knowledge of application vulnerabilities nor any example of possible attacks to build the application profiles. As a result, our *DetAnom* mechanism is able to protect the data from attacks tailored to database applications such as code modification attacks, SQL injections, and also from other data-centric attacks as well. We have implemented our mechanism with a software testing technique called concolic testing and the PostgreSQL DBMS. Experimental results show that our profiling technique is close to accurate, and requires acceptable amount of time, and that the detection mechanism incurs low run-time overhead.

Categories and Subject Descriptors

H.2.7 [**Database Management**]

General Terms

Security

Keywords

Database, Insider Attacks, Anomaly Detection, Application Profile, SQL Injection

1. INTRODUCTION

Data stored in databases is often critical to the organization's operations and sensitive, for example with respect to privacy. Therefore, securing data stored in a database is a critical security requirement. Data must be protected not only from external attackers, but also from users within the organizations [2]. A wide range of institutions from government agencies (e.g., military, judiciary etc.) to commercial enterprises are witnessing attacks by insiders at an alarming rate. The most important objective of these insiders is to either exfiltrate sensitive data (e.g., military plans, trade secrets, intellectual property, etc.) or maliciously modify the data for deception purposes or for attack preparation [1,6,11].

There are a number of facts that make the prevention of insider attacks more challenging compared with other conventional (external) attacks [3]. First, insiders are allowed to access machines and services inside the organization networks as they possess valid credentials. Second, the actions of insiders originate at a trusted domain within the network, and thus are not subjected to thorough security checks in the same way as external actions are. For instance, there is often no internal firewall within the organization network. Third, insiders are often highly trained computer experts, who have knowledge about the internal configuration of the network and the security and auditing control deployed. Therefore, they may be able to circumvent conventional security mechanisms.

Protecting data from insider threats requires combining different techniques. One important such technique is represented by the access control system that is implemented as part of the database management system (DBMS) code. An access control system allows one to specify which users/applications can access which data for which purpose. In addition to the access control system implemented as part of the DBMS, applications may also perform their own "application-level" access control in order to implement more complex access control policies. In such cases, accesses by users to the data stored in a database is mediated by the application programs. However, whereas the use of DBMS-level and application-level access control mechanisms provides a first layer of defense against insider threats, these mechanisms are unable to protect against malicious insiders that have access to the applications and can thus modify the code to change the queries issued to the database and also modify the logics of the application-level access control.

In order to address the above problem, one possible approach is to analyze the data access patterns of the application to create profiles on legitimate activities and then use at run-time these profiles to detect anomalous accesses by application programs.

The design of such an *anomaly detection* system is challenging, as the system should fulfill the following requirements:

• It should require minimal modifications to the code of the application program and the DBMS.

• It should not introduce significant delays that may negatively impact the performance.

• It should have the least possible number of false positives and false negatives.

In this paper, we propose *DetAnom*, an *anomaly detection* mechanism able to identify malicious database transactions that addresses above requirements. *DetAnom* consists of two phases: the *profile creation phase* and the *anomaly detection phase*. In the first phase, we create a profile of the application program that can succinctly represent the application's normal behavior in terms of its interaction (i.e., submission of SQL queries) with the database. For each query, we create a signature and also capture the corresponding preconditions that the application program must satisfy to submit the query. Note that an application program may execute different query sequences depending on different values of the input parameters. Hence, the profile of the application needs to consider all possible execution paths that lead to interactions with the database. Each query in the application belongs to one of these paths and has a set of preconditions (i.e., constraints) in order to be issued.

A major issue in our approach is that exploring all possible execution paths of an application program requires identifying all possible combinations of program inputs, which is sometimes not feasible. As a result, the unexplored paths introduce incompleteness in the application profile. The higher the number of paths explored, the more complete and accurate an application profile is. Hence, to make our profiling technique close to complete and accurate, we adopt concolic testing [19] [8], a widely used software testing methodology which ensures good coverage of the created profile. As the program may have different behaviors for different values of input parameters, our approach with concolic testing generates inputs automatically to explore all such program behaviors. Later in the *anomaly detection phase*, whenever the application issues a query, the corresponding signature and constraints are checked against the current context of the application. If there is a mismatch, the query is considered as anomalous. However, depending on the number of paths covered in concolic execution, the *anomaly detection phase* follows either the *'strict'* or the *'flexible'* policy. If the number of execution paths covered in the application profile is high, the *anomaly detection phase* verifies a query with more confidence and thus enforces the *'strict'* policy.

On the other hand, if the profile fails to cover a minimum number of execution paths, the *anomaly detection phase* is comparatively less confident and thus enforces the *'flexible'* policy. The *'strict'* policy raises an alert immediately upon detecting an anomalous query, whereas the *'flexible'* policy raises a flag for that query and observes any further query. The main advantage of our *anomaly detection* mechanism is that we need neither any previous knowledge of application vulnerabilities nor any example of possible attacks to build the application profiles.

The rest of the paper is organized as follows: Section 2 presents relevant preliminary concepts. Section 3 provides an overview of our system model. Section 4 and 5 describe the *profile creation phase* and the *anomaly detection phase*, respectively. Section 6 discusses implementation details. Section 7 presents an experimental evaluation of *DetAnom*. Section 8 surveys related work. Section 9 concludes the paper with a discussion on the future work.

2. PRELIMINARIES

In this section, we present some concepts that are used in this paper.

Software Testing is the process of examining the quality of a software product. It involves monitoring the actual program execution in the hope of observing unexpected behaviour (e.g., wrong output values, program crashes or early termination) which implies the existence of bugs. It can also give a perspective about the security and risks in the product or service under test. One of the main challenges that arises in software testing is the capability of testing all possible program inputs of an application to achieve high code coverage. *Concolic testing* is one of the widely used techniques in addressing this challenge.

Concolic Execution is a program analysis technique [8, 13, 19] that explores all possible execution paths of a program by acting according to the following steps. The program to be tested is first concretely executed with some initial random inputs. Then the concolic execution engine examines the branch conditions along the executed path's control-flow and uses a decision procedure to find an input that would reverse the branch conditions from true to false or vice-versa. This process is repeated to discover more inputs that trigger new control-flow paths, and thus more program states are tested. This technique is particularly useful for the automatic generation of high-coverage test inputs and for software vulnerability discovery.

3. SYSTEM MODEL

In this section, we introduce the *DetAnom* architecture and the adversary model that we consider.

3.1 DetAnom Architecture

The system architecture consists of several modules, supporting the two phases of *DetAnom*.

Profile creation phase: Figure 1 shows the modules supporting the *profile creation phase* and interactions between them. This phase starts with providing the application program as input to the *concolic execution (CE)* module which first instruments the application. Next, the *CE* module executes the instrumented application for a number of times and with different inputs, until all possible execution paths of the program are explored. Each time the application pro-

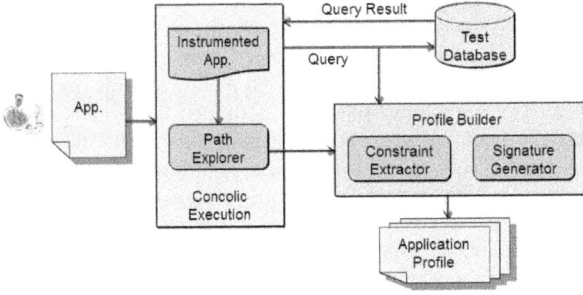

Figure 1: System architecture for profile creation

gram issues a query to the database, the *constraint extractor (CEx)* in the *profile builder (PB)* module extracts the constraints that lead the application program to follow the current path. These constraints compose a part of the *application profile*. On the other hand, each query submitted to the database is also forwarded to the *PB* module where the *signature generator (SG)* sub-module generates the signature of that query. Section 4 discusses details about the *CEx* and *SG* sub-modules. Finally, the *PB* module binds the query signature with its corresponding constraints and inserts this record into the *application profile*.

The database used in this phase is a *test database* that may be updated according to the requirement of concolic execution. This *test database* is necessary in the *profile creation phase* since the results returned by the database could be used in control-flow decisions later in the program.

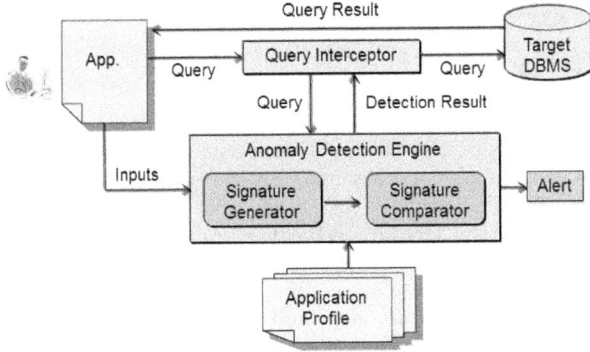

Figure 2: System architecture for anomaly detection

Anomaly detection phase: The main modules supporting the *anomaly detection phase* are: the *anomaly detection engine (ADE)*, the *query interceptor (QI)*, the *signature comparator (SC)*, and the *target database* as shown in Figure 2. The *target database* stores the data to be protected from insiders. The application interacts with this database through SQL queries. However, in this phase, any query issued by the application does not reach the *target database* directly; it is instead intercepted by the *QI* and forwarded to the *ADE* for anomaly detection. The *ADE* also includes the *SG* sub-module in order to generate the signature of the received query. Upon receiving the query, the *ADE* checks whether the current inputs of the program satisfy the constraints of some possible execution paths. If the constraints

are satisfied, the *SC* compares the signature associated with the satisfied constraint to that of the received query . If there is a match, the query is considered legitimate. This information is then sent to the *QI* to let it forward the legitimate query to the *target database* for execution. On the other hand, if the signatures do not match, the *ADE* module considers the query as anomalous and raises an alert.

3.2 Adversary Model

In our *DetAnom* system, we assume that every component involved in the *profile creation phase* is trusted. However, we assume that at run-time the application program can be tampered with and thus become untrusted. Therefore, we assume that while the program is executing, the program may issue a query that:

(a) has never encountered in the profile creation phase, i.e., the query does not belong to the application at all;

(b) belongs to the application but is not relevant to the current execution path;

(c) is relevant to the current execution path, but the program input variables do not satisfy that query's corresponding constraints.

4. PROFILE CREATION PHASE

In the *profile creation phase*, the application program interacts with the *test database* through SQL queries. We represent the queries internally in a specific format which we refer to as *signatures*. Queries' signatures and corresponding constraints are used to build the profile of the application. For each query, we record its signature and constraints, and refer to this pair as *query record (QR)*. All *QR*s of the program are organized in a hierarchical data structure which represents the control-flow of the application. We refer to this data structure as the *application profile*. In this section, we discuss the format of the query signatures and constraints, and the procedure for building the *application profile*.

4.1 Query Signature Representation

In our system, we consider standard SQL commands of types SELECT, INSERT, UPDATE, and DELETE. For instance, the format of a SELECT command is:

```
SELECT    [DISTINCT]    {TARGET-LIST}
FROM                    {RELATION-LIST}
WHERE                   {QUALIFICATION}
```

Our system internally represents an SQL query as a signature of the form (c, t, r, q, n). Here, c represents the type of the SQL command which takes one of the values: '1', '2', '3', and '4' in case of SELECT, INSERT, UPDATE, and DELETE commands, respectively. The second field, t, is a list that contains the identifiers (IDs) of the attributes projected in the query, i.e., the attributes that appear in the query result; this information is extracted from the TARGET-LIST of the query. Attributes are identified by two values: the ID of the table that the attribute belongs to and the ID of the attribute relative to that table. The third field, r, is a list that contains the IDs of the tables being accessed in the query, i.e., the tables that appear in the RELATION-LIST. The next field, q, is a list of IDs of attributes referenced in QUALIFICATION which corresponds to the WHERE clause of the query. And the last field, n, in the signature denotes the number

```
1  public static void salaryAdjustment(int profit, int
       investment){
2     Statement s;
3     ...
4     int employee_count = 0;
5     if(profit >= 0.5 * investment){
6        String query1 = "SELECT employee_id,
             work_experience FROM WorkInfo WHERE
             work_experience > 10";
7        resultSet1 = s.executeQuery(query1);
8        resultSet1.last();
9        if(resultSet1.getRow() > 100){
10          String query3 = "SELECT employee_id FROM
                WorkInfo WHERE work_experience > 10 AND
                performance = 'good'";
11          resultSet3 = s.executeQuery(query3);
12          ... // do other operations
13       } else{
14          String query2 = "UPDATE WorkInfo SET salary
                = salary * 1.2";
15          s.executeUpdate(query2);
16       }else{
17       String query4 = "SELECT p.employee_name FROM
             PersonalInfo p, WorkInfo w WHERE
             performance = 'poor' AND p.employee_id =
             w.employee_id";
18       resultSet2 = s.executeQuery(query4);
19       ... // do other operations
20    }
21  }
```

of predicates in the WHERE clause. Note that all attributes of the signature are extracted by parsing the query.

As an example, consider the relation schema in Table 1. ID's of tables and attributes are as shown in the table. Now, consider the query:

```
SELECT   employee_id, work_experience
FROM     WorkInfo
WHERE    work_experience > 10;
```

The signature of the above query is as follows: {1, {{200, 1}, {200, 2}}, {200}, {{200, 2}}, 1}

We explain this signature construction in order from left to right. The leftmost 1 represents the SELECT command. {200, 1}, and {200, 2} represent the IDs of attributes employee_id and work_experience, respectively. 200 represents the ID of the table WorkInfo. {200, 2} represents the attribute used in the WHERE clause, i.e, work_experience. The rightmost 1 corresponds to the number of predicates in WHERE clause.

Table 1: Relation schema

Table ID	Table name	Attribute ID	Attribute name	Type
100	PersonalInfo	1	employee_id	varchar(10)
		2	employee_name	varchar(50)
200	WorkInfo	1	employee_id	varchar(10)
		2	work_experience	number
		3	salary	number
		4	performance	varchar(20)

4.2 Constraint Extraction

This section describes how the constraints for executing a query are extracted during the *profile creation phase*. The

CE module takes the application program as input and instruments it to log each operation that may affect a symbolic variable value or a path condition. This module then executes the program concretely with some random input. In order to explore other paths, it examines the branch conditions (i.e., constraints) along the executed path, and uses a constraint solver to find inputs that would reverse the branch conditions. This concolic execution is repeated for a number of times until all the execution paths are explored. Note that the instrumented program may issue queries along some of these execution paths. The issued queries are forwarded to both the PB and the *test database*. Upon receiving a query, the CEx sub-module in the PB extracts the constraints that are prerequisite to execute that query.

We now explain the constraint extraction procedure by using as example the application program shown in Fig. 3. The salaryAdjustment program takes two inputs: profit, and investment. Depending on the values of inputs and results returned from the database, this application program issues different sets of queries. At first, assume that the CE module sets the values of profit, and investment to 60000 and 100000, respectively. When the program execution reaches the if statement at line 5, it encounters a branch condition that consists of these input variables. Assume that the CE module denotes the profit, and investment variables as x_1 and x_2, respectively. It then represents the constraint of the if branch as c_1, using x_1 and x_2, as shown in Table 2. As the initial inputs satisfy this constraint, the program enters into the if branch. It then issues $query_1$ at line 7 along its current execution path. Here, the constraint for $query_1$ is the same as the condition for the if branch, i.e, c_1. Upon receiving this query, the CEx sub-module extracts this constraint from the CE module and stores for use in profile creation.

4.3 Profile Creation

In this section, we show how the application profile is created using QRs, which are composed of query signatures and corresponding constraints. The definition of application profile is as follows:

Application Profile (AP): The profile of an application program P is a directed graph $T(V_P, E_P)$. Each node $v_i \in V_P$ is a QR of query q_i represented as $\langle sig(q_i), c_i \rangle$, where $sig(q_i)$ is the signature of q_i, and c_i is the set of constraints to execute q_i. An edge $e_{ij} \in E_P$ denotes that the query q_j is executed after query q_i and hence, node v_j is a child of node v_i.

To illustrate the profile creation procedure, we continue with the examples given in Section 4.1 and 4.2.

As $query_1$ is issued by the program, it is then passed to the PB where the SG sub-module generates the query signature as shown in Section 4.1. The CEx sub-module also extracts the constraint c_1 as described in Section 4.2. The PB module now generates the record of $query_1$ as $QR_1 = \langle sig(query_1), c_1 \rangle$ and inserts this record as the first child of the root of AP as shown in Fig. 4(a).

Afterwards, when the program reaches the if statement at line 9, the CE module identifies a branch condition that depends on the results returned by $query_1$. This is represented as a database constraint, c_2, as in Table 2. Now assume that the *test database* returns less than 100 rows of data to the application program for $query_1$. In this case, the program jumps to the else branch at line 13 and issues $query_2$. So,

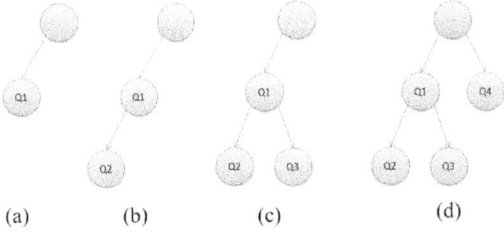

Figure 4: Steps of profile graph construction

Table 2: Constraints for queries

c_1	arithmetic: $1.0\ x_1 - 0.5\ x_2 >= 0.0$
c_2	database: $x_3 \leq 100.0$
c_3	database: $x_3 > 100.0$
c_4	arithmetic: $1.0\ x_1 - 0.5\ x_2 <= -1.0$

Table 3: Query signatures

Query	Signature
$query_1$	{1, {{200, 1}, {200, 2}}, {200}, {{200, 2}}, 1}
$query_2$	{2, {{200, 3}}, {200}, {∅}, 0}
$query_3$	{1, {{200, 1}}, {200}, {{200, 2}, {200, 4}}, 2}
$query_4$	{1, {{100, 2}}, {100, 200}, {{200, 4}, {100, 1}, {200, 1}}, 2}

Table 4: Query records

Query record	Contents
QR_1	$\langle sig(query_1), c_1 \rangle$
QR_2	$\langle sig(query_2), c_2 \rangle$
QR_3	$\langle sig(query_3), c_3 \rangle$
QR_4	$\langle sig(query_4), c_4 \rangle$

the precondition for $query_2$ to be executed is same as the condition of the **else** branch at line 13. This constraint, c_2, is extracted by the *CEx* as shown in Table 2, where x_3 denotes for `resultSet1.getRow()`. The *PB* module then creates the record of $query_2$ as $QR_2 = \langle sig(query_2), c_2 \rangle$ and inserts it in the *AP* as a child of QR_1 as shown in Fig. 4(b). Table 4 presents the signature of $query_2$, i.e., $sig(query_2)$.

Since for the current execution there is no further paths to explore after line 15, the *CE* module backtracks the execution to the **if** statement at line 9 and negates the branch condition to explore the **if** branch. To do so, the *CE* module inserts some random records into the database tables `PersonalInfo` and `WorkInfo` so that execution of $query_1$ returns more than 100 rows, and thus explores the **if** branch. Along this path when the program issues $query_3$, the *CEx* sub-module captures the corresponding constraint which is same as the condition of the **if** branch at line 9. This constraint is represented as c_3 (shown in Table 2). The *AP* is also updated as in Fig. 4(c) by inserting the query record $QR_3 = \langle sig(query_3), c_3 \rangle$ as another child of QR_1. Note that, insertion or deletion of records to the *test database* in the *profile creation phase* do not have any impact on the *target database* as these operations are executed only for extracting the database constraints properly. Finally, the *CE* module backtracks the execution of the program to the **if** statement at line 5, negates the branch condition, and uses a constraint solver to find values of `profit` and `investment` variables so that the program execution can explore the other branch, i.e., the **else** branch at line 16. Assume that it sets `profit` and `investment` variables to 49999 and 100000, respectively and enters the **else** branch at line 16. Executing along this path when the program issues $query_4$, the *CEx* extracts of the constraint c_4, as shown in Table 2. The *PB* inserts $QR_4 = \langle sig(query_4), c_4 \rangle$ to the *AP* as a child of the root as shown in Fig. 4(d). At this point, since the *CE* module has completed exploring all execution paths, the *profile creation phase* ends.

5. ANOMALY DETECTION PHASE

We now describe how application program profiles are used to distinguish between legitimate and anomalous database queries. The steps of the *anomaly detection* procedure are presented in Algorithm 1.

5.1 Detection of Anomalous Queries

In the *anomaly detection phase*, whenever the application program issues a query, the *QI* module intercepts the query and forwards it to the *ADE* module. The reason is that our system does not allow any query to reach the *target database* without verifying whether the query is anomalous or not.

When an application program starts executing in the *anomaly detection phase*, the *ADE* module sets the root node of the *AP* as the current parent node (v_p). Upon receiving the first query along an execution path of the program, the *ADE* considers all the children of v_p as *candidate nodes*. The *ADE* then takes the inputs from the executing application and for each *candidate node* it verifies whether the inputs satisfy the constraint in the *QR*. If the inputs satisfy constraint c_i, the program is expected to execute the query which is associated with the query record QR_i containing the satisfied c_i. As next step, the *SG* sub-module generates the signature of the received query and the *SC* sub-module compares it with the signature stored in QR_i, i.e., $sig(query_i)$. For a legitimate query, the signatures match. The verification outcome is then passed to the *QI* module which then sends the legitimate query to the *target database* for execution.

For subsequent queries issued by the program, the *ADE* module considers the *QR* of the most recently executed query as the current parent node, and verifies the signature and corresponding constraints in a similar way as described above.

Now consider the case of an anomalous query. In this case, the signature for that query generated by the *SG* sub-module will not match that in the *QR* for which the constraints are satisfied by the application program. As a result, the *SC* sub-module raises a flag and the *ADE* takes next steps based on either the *'strict'* or the *'flexible'* policy discussed in what follows.

5.1.1 Strict policy

In the *profile creation phase*, we use *concolic execution* to explore all possible paths of an application program. This technique statically estimates the number of possible branches in a program. Then while executing the program, it sets different values to the inputs and thus tries to explore new paths. However, it uses a bounded depth-first strategy, i.e., bounded DFS. With this searching strategy, there is a trade-off between the exploration of other execution paths and termination of the current path if its length is significantly large. If the length of an execution path exceeds the bound of the DFS, it stops that particular execution, and searches for new paths. In this case, the *concolic execution* leaves

Algorithm 1 Anomaly Detection

```
1:  Input: Application Profile (AP)
2:  v_p = root of AP
3:  while the program is executing do
4:      if a query q is issued then
5:          SG generates sig(q)
6:          for each child v_i of v_p do
7:              if c_i is satisfied then
8:                  SC compares sig(q) to sig(query_i)
9:                  if signatures match then
10:                     /* q is a legitimate query */
11:                     let the QI forward q to database
12:                     v_p = v_i
13:                 else
14:                     /* q is an anomalous query */
15:                     anomaly = 1
16:                     break
17:                 end if
18:             end if
19:         end for
20:         if anomaly == 1 || no c_i is satisfied then
21:             if policy is strict then
22:                 raise an ALERT
23:             else if policy is flexible then
24:                 if q is flagged more than k times then
25:                     raise an ALERT
26:                 else
27:                     raise a flag
28:                 end if
29:             end if
30:         end if
31:     end if
32: end while
```

some large execution paths unexplored that may contain queries. In the *strict* policy, we set the bound of the DFS high enough so that the *concolic execution* can explore almost all possible paths of the program and cover all the branches that are estimated statically. As a result, the profile of the application program gets close to be complete and the *ADE* module becomes strong enough to distinguish between legitimate and anomalous queries. So in this case, when the signature of an input query does not match, the *ADE* module identifies that query as anomalous with high confidence and raises an *alert* signal. This information is forwarded to the *QI* module.

5.1.2 Flexible policy

If the bound of the DFS for the *concolic execution* is not high enough, the *profile creation phase* may leave some large paths unexplored. For each query issued along an execution path that is within the DFS bound, if the *SC* does not find a match for its signature or the constraints are not satisfied, the *ADE* considers that query as anomalous. However, if the issued query is on an execution path that exceeds the DFS bound, the *SC* does not find a match for its signature. In this case, the *ADE* raises a flag for that query and asks the *QI* to drop it. If a particular query is flagged for more than k times (k is a threshold set in the *ADE* module), this module raises an *alert* signal, and requests the security officer (or some other trusted user) to check whether the query is actually anomalous or legitimate. If the query is assessed as anomalous, it is kept in the black-list of the *QI* so that future occurrences of such query are blocked automatically. If the query is assessed as legitimate, the *AP* is updated accordingly with its *QR*.

Also, consider the case in which the application program is compromised and its control-flow is hijacked. In this case, if some insider issues a query that belongs to the program but is not legal in the current execution path, the application inputs will fail to satisfy the constraints of any *candidate node*. In this case, the *ADE* will take an action according to the policy it adopts, as described above.

5.2 Case studies

In this section we present some case studies to illustrate how the *ADE* module works in the *anomaly detection phase*. We assume that the values of `profit` and `investment` variables are set to 60000 and 100000, respectively. We consider the following cases.

5.2.1 Execution of $query_1$ and $query_2$

According to the values of input variables, the application program is eligible to issue $query_1$. So in the *anomaly detection phase*, upon receiving the issued $query_1$, the *ADE* module takes the program inputs to check whether they satisfy the constraints of either QR_1 or QR_4. As c_1 is satisfied, the *SG* sub-module generates the signature of the input query and the *SC* sub-module compares it with the signature part of QR_1. The match is positive and hence $query_1$ is assessed as non-anomalous. Now assume that the number of records returned by $query_1$ is less than 100. In this case, the constraint c_2 is satisfied and the attempt to execute $query_2$ is considered non-anomalous because the signature of $query_2$ matches to that of the QR_2.

5.2.2 Execution of $query_1$ and $query_3$

In this case, $query_1$ is executed legitimately as described in the previous case. Afterwards, when the program issues $query_3$, the *SC* sub-module finds that the signatures of $query_3$ and that of the expected query do not match. As a result, the *ADE* module raises an alert indicating $query_3$ as anomalous.

5.2.3 Execution of a query that does not belong to the program

If a query is issued in the *anomaly detection phase* that is never encountered in the *profile creation phase*, the signature of that query does not match with any of the query records. In this case, the *ADE* module raises an *alert* or a *flag* based on the policy (*strict* or *flexible*) it adopts.

5.2.4 SQL injection attacks

Our approach is also able to detect SQL injection attacks. As these attacks typically modify the queries by adding new predicates, they can be easily detected by our anomaly detection mechanism because of its ability to profile the expected queries and compare them with the actual queries. We illustrate the detection of SQL injections with a sample application program. Such program has the function of displaying the medical records of an authenticated signed user. The user is authenticated by entering his `username` and `password`. The legitimate query execution would look like:

```
1  username = readInputUser();
2  password = readInputPassword();
3  SELECT * FROM MedicalRecords WHERE uname = ' + username
       + ' AND password = ' + password + ';
```

If the username is John and the password is Smith, then the query would be:

```
SELECT * FROM MedicalRecords WHERE uname = 'John'
AND password = 'Smith';
```

However, such query is vulnerable to SQL injection attacks by which the attacker can display the medical records of other users. This can be achieved if the attacker enters in the password input field the string password = ' OR uname = 'Carl'. If so, the following query would be issued which would display the medical records of the username Carl to the attacker.

```
SELECT * FROM MedicalRecords WHERE uname = 'John'
AND password = ' ' OR uname = 'Carl';
```

Such a vulnerability exists in any application that allows the user input to change the structure of an SQL query. Since SQL injection attacks are based on re-structuring the SQL query, our mechanism by comparing the query structure to the query signatures saved in AP is able to detect changes in the query. More specifically, as we count the number of predicates of the WHERE clause as part of the query signature, we are able to detect any additional predicates introduced by SQL injection. In the example above, the number of predicates is 2 before the injection, and it becomes 3 after the injection.

5.2.5 *Two-step SQL injection attacks*

These attacks are also referred to as second-order injection attacks and represent a complex form of data-centric attacks. The purpose of these attacks is to create an SQL injection attack that can be processed at a later time. This is achieved by injecting malicious input into the database that is legitimately saved into the database, but will result in an SQL injection attack at a later time when other types of queries perform actions on the maliciously inserted data. To clarify, consider an example of a web application that registers its users upon using their service. If a malicious user chooses (' OR '1' = '1') as his username, then adding this user to the database will execute the SQL query:

```
INSERT INTO users VALUES (' OR '1' = '1');
```

This is a legitimate query and will not result in an SQL injection attack, and thus the username ' OR '1' = '1' will be successfully created. However, if at a later time the malicious user or even the web administrator decides to delete this account, the executed SQL query is:

```
DELETE FROM users WHERE uname=' ' OR '1' = '1';
```

This is when the attack is effective as the query will result in deleting all the users in the database.

Our AD mechanism will be able to detect this type of attacks when the SQL injection is about to perform the intended attack action on the database. Consider the example above. Our AD mechanism will find a mismatch with the DELETE SQL query signature because of the change in the number of predicates in the WHERE clause. As a result, the ADE will assess the execution of such query as anomalous. Like the case of SQL injection attacks, additional predicates

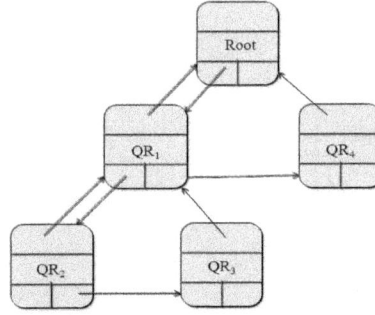

Figure 5: Profile graph

will result in a mismatch of the SQL injected queries when compared to the existing query signatures and therefore will result in the query being identified as anomalous.

6. IMPLEMENTATION

In this section, we discuss the implementation details of the following components: CEx, SG and AP. In our implementation, we consider J2EE based application programs through which an attacker may illegally access the *target database*. However, our proposed *anomaly detection* mechanism can be used for other kinds of application programs. For simplicity of implementation, we use PostgreSQL-9.1.8 [14] for both *test database* and *target database*. These databases are logically separate but contains identical relation schema.

Constraint Extractor: Our implementation of CEx is built on top of the JCute concolic testing framework [18]. This framework uses Soot [21] for instrumenting Java class files and lpsolve for solving linear programs. We instrument the executeQuery and executeUpdate statements of the application program using Soot to insert the instructions for the invocation of the CEx module. So, whenever a query is encountered, the CEx first captures the constraints of the current path from root to the intercepted query. Since CEx knows the constraints of the most recently executed query along this path, it extracts only the constraints that are extension of those of the most recent query and stores them in the AP along with the signature of the intercepted query.

Signature Generator: We use PostgreSQL-9.1.8 [14] to implement the SG module. PostgreSQL delivers all issued queries to the parser to generate a query parse tree using the method exec_simple_query(). In this method, our customized function for SG imports necessary query information (command, target list, relation list, and qualifiers) from the parse tree and creates the query signature.

Application Profile: The PB module creates *query records* by combining the query signatures generated from SG and the constraints extracted by CEx. These records are stored in a hierarchical data structure at PostgreSQL as shown in Fig. 5.

7. EXPERIMENTAL EVALUATION

We have evaluated the performance of our proposed *DetAnom* mechanism for both the 'strict' and 'flexible' policies. Our experiments have been performed on an Intel(R) Core(TM) i7-3540M CPU machine (number of core = 2) with a CPU speed of 3.00 GHz, running Ubuntu-11.10 operating system with 4GB of memory. Since the complete-

Table 5: Program constructs

Program ID (PID)	Lines of code	Number of nested if-else	Number of for loops	Maximum depth of a path	Number of branches	Total # of queries in a program	Average # of queries in each if-else branch	Average # of queries in each loop
1	794	30	-	30	32	200	7	-
2	586	20	-	20	22	200	10	-
3	322	10	-	10	12	200	20	-
4	826	30	5	∞	32	150	4	7

ness and accuracy of our *application profile* depend mostly on the performance of concolic testing [18, 19], we have implemented four different database applications with different program constructs to evaluate the performance of *DetAnom*. A detailed overview of these applications is shown in Table 5.

7.1 Evaluation Metrics

We analyze the performance of our proposed anomaly detection mechanism using the following metrics:

(a) *Profile creation time*: It is the time required to create the profile of an application program. We use the JCute [18] tool to measure the time elapsed for the concolic execution of the application program.

(b) *Branch coverage*: It is defined as the ratio of the number of branches covered in run-time in *profile creation phase* to the total number of branches in the program. If there are total n branches in a program and c branches are covered among them while creating the profile, the branch coverage is computed as:

$$Branch\ Coverage\ =\ \frac{c}{n} * 100\%$$

(c) *Run-time overhead:* It is defined as the ratio of additional time required by *DetAnom* to the time required by the program to execute without any anomaly detection mechanism. We denote the execution time of a database application without *DetAnom* as t_1 and with *DetAnom* as t_2. We then compute the run-time overhead as follows:

$$Run\text{-}time\ Overhead\ =\ \frac{t_2 - t_1}{t_1} * 100\%$$

(d) *False positive and false negative:* A *false positive* is a case in which a legitimate query is evaluated as anomalous by the detection engine, whereas a *false negative* means that an anomalous query is evaluated as legitimate.

Table 6: Different scenarios

Scenario ID	Program ID	Depth limit of bounded DFS
1	1	30
2	1	20
3	1	10
4	2	20
5	3	10
6	4	30
7	4	20
8	4	10

7.2 Results

In order to analyze our *DetAnom* system more rigorously, we have set different values for the depth of the bounded

Table 7: Profile creation time for different scenarios

Scenario ID	Profile creation time (seconds)
1	324.441
2	130.727
3	55.448
4	137.885
5	67.9425
6	1441.940
7	1148.475
8	755.192

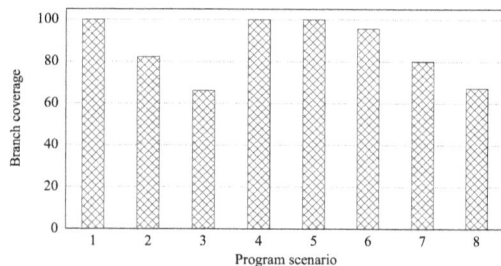

Figure 6: Branch coverage for different scenarios

DFS in concolic execution, which resulted in eight different scenarios shown in Table 6.

(a) *Profile creation time*: The amount of time required for creating the application profile for the eight different scenarios is reported in Table 7. The results show that setting the depth of the bounded DFS to a higher value takes a longer time to profile the application. The time elapsed for scenarios 6-8 is comparatively high because these scenarios include loops in the application program.

(b) *Branch coverage*: The branch coverage of the profiles for the eight different scenarios is shown in Fig. 6. Note that increasing the depth of the bounded DFS also increases the completeness and accuracy of the profile. For the scenarios where the depth is set equal to the maximum depth of the program, the branches are covered 100%. Also for a single application program, decreasing the depth of bounded DFS results in a low branch coverage.

(c) *Run-time overhead*: Fig. 7 reports the run-time overhead for the eight different scenarios. The run-time overheads for these scenarios do not differ to a large extent. The reason is that the *anomaly detection phase* takes almost the

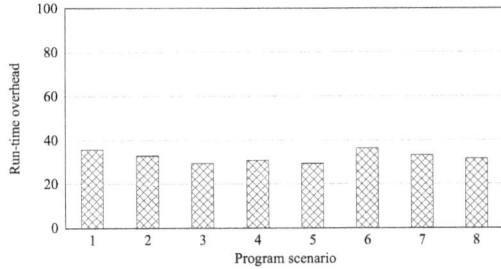

Figure 7: Run-time overhead for different scenarios

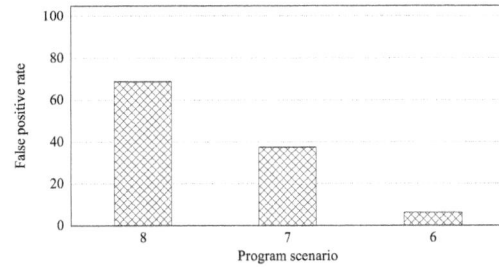

Figure 9: False positive rate for scenarios 6, 7, 8

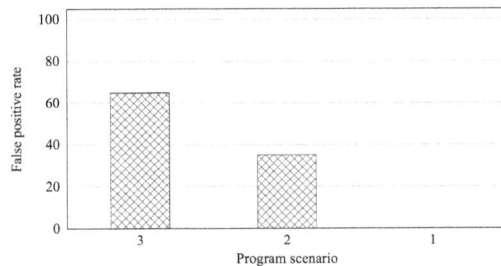

Figure 8: False positive rate for scenarios 1, 2, 3

same amount of the time in finding a match for each query issued.

(d) *False positive rate*: Fig. 8 shows the false positive rates for scenarios 1-3. In this experiment, false positive rates decrease with the increase of depth limits of bounded DFS set by the concolic execution in the *profile creation phase*. The higher the depth limit is set by the concolic execution, the more paths are covered by the application profile. Hence, scenario 1 covers all execution paths of the program and thus results in no false positives.

Fig. 9 also shows the false positive rates for scenarios 6-8. In this experiment, the termination condition of a `for` loop in the program is an input variable x, (e.g., `for (int i=0; i<x; i++) {...}`). One SQL query is issued from each iteration of this `for` loop. Hence, in the *profile creation phase* the `for` loop is iterated 30, 20, and 10 times in scenarios 6-8, respectively. So, in the *anomaly detection phase*, if the variable x is given the value 32, the number of false positives are 22, 12, and 2, respectively. Hence, it is evident that if the *profile creation phase* explores a large number of paths, the application profile becomes more complete and accurate.

Note that in our experiments we do not find any false negative as the *DetAnom* matches exact signature and constraints of a query.

8. RELATED WORK

Several approaches have been proposed to protect databases against malicious application programs. DIDAFIT [12] is an intrusion detection system that works at the applica-

tion level. Like our system, DIDAFIT works in two phases: training phase and detection phase. During the training phase, database logs are analyzed to generate fingerprints of the queries found in the log. Fingerprints are regular expressions of queries with constants in the where-clause replaced by place-holders that reflect the data types of the constants. During the detection phase, input queries are checked against such fingerprints. Queries that match some expression in the profiles are considered benign, and anomalous otherwise. DIDAFIT has however some major drawbacks. First, the system relies only on logs to create program profiles. There is therefore no guarantee that the log would contain all legitimate queries. To address this drawback, the authors propose a technique to generate new signatures from ones that are similar in all portions and have some predicates in common. While this solution works in some cases, the system would not be able to recognize queries that do not appear in the log. Another problem is that DIDAFIT does not take into account the control flow and data flow of the program, i.e., the algorithm neither checks the correct order of the queries, nor the constants in the predicates. The approaches proposed by Bertino et al. [4] and Valeur et al. [20] also analyze training logs for creating profiles of queries. Therefore they have the same drawbacks mentioned earlier. These approaches focus on the detection of web-based attacks like SQL Injection and Cross-Site Scripting (XSS) attacks and fail to detect other attacks performed through application programs, e.g., code modification attacks.

Our previous poster paper [17] outlines some preliminary ideas to protect against data exfiltration through malicious modification of the application program. However, the approach proposed in this paper reduces the performance overhead by allowing the *ADE* to simply traverse the *AP* instead of concretizing of the symbolic execution tree of the application program. Such concretization in the detection engine results in extra delay when verifying a query. In addition, our preliminary approach does not cover the combination of testing-based techniques with program analysis techniques nor cover implementation and assessment of the proposed approach. Also our current paper introduces the important notion of confidence for the profiles. According to the confidence obtained in the *profile creation phase*, our approach adopts either the '*strict*' or the '*flexible*' policy.

Programs profiling techniques have also been proposed for many other purposes, such as debugging and collecting usage statistics [16], monitoring system calls [10] [22] [9], and enhancing the performance of database applications. For example, the Pyxis system [5] uses static analysis of application code to partition the code into two pieces: one to be executed on the application server and the other on the database server, trying to reduce the control transfers and amount of exchanged data between the two components.

Dasgupta et al. [7] propose static analysis of database applications that use ADO.net APIs in order to extract features of SQL queries, query parameters, and usage of query results in order to detect SQL injection attacks and potential data integrity violations. Ramachandra and Sudarshan have developed DBridge [15], a tool that optimizes the performance of database applications by prefetching query results. Control-flow and data-flow analysis are used to find locations in the program where instrumented code can be added; at program runtime this code sends requests to the database to prepare results of queries predicted to be sent by the program at later points.

9. CONCLUSION AND FUTURE WORK

Though access control mechanisms deployed in DBMS are able to prevent application programs from accessing the data for which they are not authorized, they are unable to prevent data misuse caused by authorized application programs. In this paper, we have proposed an anomaly detection mechanism that is able to identify anomalous queries resulting from previously authorized applications. Our mechanism builds close to accurate profile of the application program and checks at run-time incoming queries against that profile. In addition to anomaly detection, our *DetAnom* mechanism is capable of detecting any injections or modifications to the SQL queries, e.g., SQL injection attacks. We have implemented *DetAnom* with JCute and PostgreSQL which results in low run-time overhead and high accuracy in detecting anomalous database accesses.

We are currently extending our work along several directions. Our current implementation of *DetAnom* exploits the constraints that JCute [18] supports, i.e., arithmetic, pointer and thread constraints. However, Emmi et al. [8] propose a concolic testing approach for database applications which considers the database constraints as discussed in Section 4.3. We are incorporating these database constraints to our current prototype which will enhance the accuracy and completeness of our *anomaly detection* mechanism. We plan to improve our signature signature generation scheme by incorporating information about program constants, variables, logical and relational operators used in the WHERE clause of a query as this information may enhance the accuracy of detection. We also plan to enhance the completeness and accuracy of our profile creation mechanism using both static and dynamic analysis of the program. In this approach, we will first analyze the program statically to find all the execution paths that contain SQL queries and then guide the concolic execution dynamically so that it does not leave any paths unexplored.

10. ACKNOWLEDGMENTS

The work reported in this paper has been funded in part under subcontract to Northrop Grumman Systems Corporation in support of a contract with Department of Homeland Security (DHS) Science and Technology Directorate, Homeland Security Advanced Research Projects Agency, Cyber Security Division under contract number HSHQDC-13-C-B0012. The views expressed in this work are those of the authors and do not necessarily reflect the official policy or position of the Department of Homeland Security or of Northrop Grumman Systems Corporation.

11. REFERENCES

[1] Cybersecurity watch survey: How bad is the insider threat? Technical report, Carnegie Mellon University, 2012. http://resources.sei.cmu.edu/asset_files/Presentation/2013_017_101_57766.pdf.

[2] E. Bertino. *Data Protection from Insider Threats.* Synthesis Lectures on Data Management. Morgan & Claypool Publishers, San Rafael, 2012.

[3] E. Bertino and G. Ghinita. Towards mechanisms for detection and prevention of data exfiltration by insiders: Keynote talk paper. In *Proceedings of the 6th ACM Symposium on Information, Computer and Communications Security*, ASIACCS '11, pages 10–19, New York, NY, USA, 2011. ACM.

[4] E. Bertino, A. Kamra, and J. P. Early. Profiling database application to detect sql injection attacks. In *IEEE International Performance, Computing, and Communications Conference, IPCCC 2007*, pages 449–458, April 2007.

[5] A. Cheung, S. Madden, O. Arden, and A. C. Myers. Automatic partitioning of database applications. *VLDB Endow.*, 5(11):1471–1482, July 2012.

[6] M. Collins, D. M. Cappelli, T. Caron, R. F. Trzeciak, and A. P. Moore. Spotlight on: Programmers as malicious insiders (updated and revised). Technical report, Carnegie Mellon University, 2013. http://resources.sei.cmu.edu/asset_files/WhitePaper/2013_019_001_85232.pdf.

[7] A. Dasgupta, V. Narasayya, and M. Syamala. A static analysis framework for database applications. In *Proceedings of the 2009 IEEE International Conference on Data Engineering*, ICDE '09, pages 1403–1414, Washington, DC, USA, 2009. IEEE Computer Society.

[8] M. Emmi, R. Majumdar, and K. Sen. Dynamic test input generation for database applications. In *Proceedings of the 2007 International Symposium on Software Testing and Analysis*, ISSTA '07, pages 151–162, New York, NY, USA, 2007. ACM.

[9] D. Gao, M. K. Reiter, and D. Song. Gray-box extraction of execution graphs for anomaly detection. In *Proceedings of the 11th ACM Conference on Computer and Communications Security*, CCS '04, pages 318–329, New York, NY, USA, 2004. ACM.

[10] J. T. Giffin, S. Jha, and B. P. Miller. Efficient context-sensitive intrusion detection. In *Proceedings of the 11th Annual Network and Distributed System Security Symposium NDSS*, 2004.

[11] C. Huth and R. Ruefle. Components and considerations in building an insider threat program. Technical report, Carnegie Mellon University, 2013. http://resources.sei.cmu.edu/asset_files/Webinar/2013_018_101_69083.pdf.

[12] S. Y. Lee, W. L. Low, and P. Y. Wong. Learning fingerprints for a database intrusion detection system.

In *Proceedings of the 7th European Symposium on Research in Computer Security*, ESORICS '02, pages 264–280, London, UK, UK, 2002. Springer-Verlag.

[13] R. Majumdar and K. Sen. Hybrid concolic testing. In *Proceedings of the 29th International Conference on Software Engineering, ICSE 2007*, pages 416–426, May 2007.

[14] PostgreSQL Global Development Group. *PostgreSQL-9.1.8*. http://www.postgresql.org/docs/9.1/static/release-9-1-8.html.

[15] K. Ramachandra and S. Sudarshan. Holistic optimization by prefetching query results. In *Proceedings of the 2012 ACM SIGMOD International Conference on Management of Data*, SIGMOD '12, pages 133–144, New York, NY, USA, 2012. ACM.

[16] T. Reps, T. Ball, M. Das, and J. Larus. The use of program profiling for software maintenance with applications to the year 2000 problem. In *Proceedings of the 6th European SOFTWARE ENGINEERING Conference Held Jointly with the 5th ACM SIGSOFT International Symposium on Foundations of Software Engineering*, ESEC '97/FSE-5, pages 432–449, New York, NY, USA, 1997. Springer-Verlag New York, Inc.

[17] A. Sallam and E. Bertino. Poster: Protecting against data exfiltration insider attacks through application programs. In *Proceedings of the 2014 ACM SIGSAC Conference on Computer and Communications Security*, CCS '14, pages 1493–1495, New York, NY, USA, 2014. ACM.

[18] K. Sen and G. Agha. Cute and jcute: Concolic unit testing and explicit path model-checking tools. In *Proceedings of the 18th International Conference on Computer Aided Verification*, CAV'06, pages 419–423, Berlin, Heidelberg, 2006. Springer-Verlag.

[19] K. Sen, D. Marinov, and G. Agha. Cute: A concolic unit testing engine for c. In *Proceedings of the 10th European Software Engineering Conference Held Jointly with 13th ACM SIGSOFT International Symposium on Foundations of Software Engineering*, ESEC/FSE-13, pages 263–272, New York, NY, USA, 2005. ACM.

[20] F. Valeur, D. Mutz, and G. Vigna. A learning-based approach to the detection of sql attacks. In *Proceedings of the Second International Conference on Detection of Intrusions and Malware, and Vulnerability Assessment*, DIMVA'05, pages 123–140, Berlin, Heidelberg, 2005. Springer-Verlag.

[21] R. Vallée-Rai, P. Co, E. Gagnon, L. Hendren, P. Lam, and V. Sundaresan. Soot - a java bytecode optimization framework. In *Proceedings of the 1999 Conference of the Centre for Advanced Studies on Collaborative Research*, CASCON '99, pages 13–. IBM Press, 1999.

[22] D. Wagner and D. Dean. Intrusion detection via static analysis. In *Proceedings of the IEEE Symposium on Security and Privacy, S&P 2001*, pages 156–168, 2001.

StaDynA: Addressing the Problem of Dynamic Code Updates in the Security Analysis of Android Applications

Yury Zhauniarovich
University of Trento
Trento, Italy
yury.zhauniarovich@unitn.it

Maqsood Ahmad
University of Trento
Trento, Italy
maqsood.ahmad@unitn.it

Olga Gadyatskaya
SnT, University of Luxembourg
Luxembourg
olga.gadyatskaya@uni.lu

Bruno Crispo
University of Trento, Italy
DistriNet, KU Leuven, Belgium
bruno.crispo@unitn.it

Fabio Massacci
University of Trento
Trento, Italy
fabio.massacci@unitn.it

Abstract

Static analysis of Android applications can be hindered by the presence of the popular dynamic code update techniques: dynamic class loading and reflection. Recent Android malware samples do actually use these mechanisms to conceal their malicious behavior from static analyzers. These techniques defuse even the most recent static analyzers (e.g., [12, 21, 31]) that usually operate under the "closed world" assumption (the targets of reflective calls can be resolved at analysis time; only classes reachable from the class path at analysis time are used at runtime). Our proposed solution allows existing static analyzers to remove this assumption. This is achieved by combining static and dynamic analysis of applications in order to reveal the hidden/updated behavior and extend static analysis results with this information. This paper presents design, implementation and preliminary evaluation results of our solution called STADYNA.

Categories and Subject Descriptors

D.4.6 [**Operating Systems**]: Security and Protection; D.2.5 [**Software Engineering**]: Testing and Debugging—*Code inspections and walk-throughs, Tracing*

Keywords

Android; Dynamic Code Updates; Security Analysis

1. INTRODUCTION

Mobile applications (apps for short) are complex programs that offer sophisticated user experiences by exploiting the whole spectrum of dynamic code update features provided by the Android platform.

Yet, these features (reflection and dynamic class loading) combined with the common practices adopted by mobile

app developers make the static analysis of mobile apps a challenging task. This is particularly daunting when static analysis is used in order to check the security of mobile applications (e.g., to detect the presence of malicious behavior). Indeed, Rastogi et al. [40] mention reflection among the techniques that make most of the current static analysis tools unable to detect malicious code. Additionally, static analysis is hindered by the code that evolves dynamically, because some parts of the code are impossible to discover or to analyze at installation time as they appear only at runtime. As a matter of fact, existing state of the art static analyzers for mobile applications (e.g., [12, 21, 31]) assume that the code base does not change dynamically and the targets of reflection calls can be discovered in advance. This is a clear simplification of what happens in the real world, where many apps rely on code base updated at runtime.

Wang et al. [43] demonstrate the difficulty to certify apps written by a malicious developer. They developed a proof of concept malicious iOS app that passed successfully the review process on Apple's App Store. The code submitted for review was benign, yet the app was able to update itself on the device in order to introduce malicious control flows and to perform illicit tasks (such as attacking other apps and exploiting kernel vulnerabilities). Similar proof of concept apps, which were able to bypass the Google Bouncer[1] check using dynamic code update features, were also developed for the Android platform [38].

At the same time, previous approaches that enhanced static analyzers of Java code in the presence of dynamic code update techniques (e.g., [17]) cannot be directly applied to Android due to the differences in the platforms (in Android, load-time instrumentation of classes is not available). Moreover, offline instrumentation also cannot solve the problem because this approach breaks the application signature, while some apps check it at runtime. If the signature does not correspond to some hardcoded value they may refuse to work. In case of malicious apps this check may be used to conceal illicit behaviour.

In this paper we present STADYNA, a system supporting security app analysis in the presence of dynamic code update features. Our main contributions can be summarized as follows:

---

[1] A system that checks applications uploaded by developers to Google Play for malicious functionality.

- We analyzed a large set of apps (downloaded from Google Play and third-party markets) and malware samples. Our findings show that extensive amount of Android apps relies on dynamic code update features.

- We designed and implemented STADYNA – a system that interleaves static and dynamic analysis in order to reveal the hidden/updated behavior. STADYNA downloads and makes available for analysis the code loaded dynamically, and is able to resolve the targets of reflective calls complementing app's method call graph with the obtained information. Thus, STADYNA can be used in conjunction with other static analyzers to make their analysis more precise.

- We release our tool as open-source[2] to drive the research in this direction.

- We evaluated STADYNA on a set of real applications. We report that STADYNA is useful in uncovering dangerous functionality not present (or not visible to static analyzers) in the initial distribution of the app.

The rest of the paper is organized as follows. §2 presents the results of our analysis of dynamic code update feature usage in Android apps. §3 provides a background on dynamic class loading and reflection in Android. §4 gives a high-level description of STADYNA, while §6 covers the implementation details. §5 presents our approach to build method call graphs and visualise them. §7 reports on the evaluation of STADYNA on real apps. §8 discusses the limitations of the current implementation, and envisages the future work. §9 overviews the related work, and §10 concludes.

2. ANALYSIS OF DYNAMIC CODE UPDATE FEATURES IN ANDROID APPS

To understand how significant is the use of reflection and dynamic class loading (DCL) in Android apps we performed a study of 13,863 packages from Google Play [10] (the official market maintained by Google), and 14,283 apps from several third-party markets gathered in July 2013, along with 1260 malware samples from [51]. Notice that for reflection cases we consider calls that influence the app method call graph (MCG), i.e., method invocation (invoke) and object creation (newInstance) functions, and do not study other reflection API capabilities like field modification (because they do not influence the MCG used for analysis in our system).

The aggregated results of the analysis with our modified version[3] of AndroGuard [1] are shown in Table 1. It is evident that dynamic code update features are widely used by application developers.

On Google Play we downloaded approximately 500 top free applications from each category. The analysis shows that on average 18.5% of dissected apps in Google Play contain DCL and 88% use reflection. On average, apps with DCL contain 1 DCL call and apps with reflection incorporate around 22 reflective calls. The categories *"BUSINESS"*, *"SHOPPING"* and *"TRAVEL_AND_LOCAL"* show minimal

Table 1: Usage of DCL and Reflection in Applications

Markets	Total Apps	DCL used by		Refl. used by	
		Apps	%	Apps	%
Google Play	13863	2573	18.5%	12233	88.2%
Androidbest	1655	35	2.1%	1088	65.7%
Androiddrawer	2677	379	14.1%	2596	96.9%
Androidlife	1677	117	6.9%	1368	81.5%
Anruan	4230	162	3.8%	2868	67.8%
Appsapk	2664	112	4.2%	1907	71.5%
F-droid	1380	11	0.07%	792	52.8%
Malware	1260	251	19.9%	1025	81.3%
Total	29406	3640	12.3%	23877	81.1%

DCL rates (at most 10% of apps use DCL). The most "dynamic" category is *"GAME"*: 38.3% of applications in this category use DCL[4].

We further downloaded apps from 6 third-party markets, namely, *androidbest* [4], *androiddrawer* [5], *androidlife* [6], *anruan* [7], *appsapk* [8] and *f-droid* [9]. The first 5 markets distribute only provided apk files, while the latter (*f-droid*) along with the final packages also provides links to the source code of the apps. The lowest fraction of applications with DCL calls were observed on the *f-droid* market that contains only open-source apps. In terms of individual usage, the average number of reflection calls is around 19 per app package across all third-party markets (with *f-droid* exhibiting again the lowest number of reflection calls at around 14).

Besides the analysis of benign applications, we studied malware samples provided in [51]. The average percentage of DCL usage across all malware samples is 19.9%, whereas 81% of all samples use reflection. However, this dataset is old, and DCL usage rates in more recent malware applications are expected to be significantly higher [38] because this functionality is used to conceal malicious payloads [26] from static and dynamic analyzers like Google Bouncer.

Listing 1 is a code snippet of the AnserverBot Trojan [50], which illustrates how reflection and DCL are used to thwart static analyzers from detection of malicious functionality. Line 16 shows an example of a dynamic class loading call in Android using the DexClassLoader class. The name of the file from which the code is loaded is computed at runtime in Line 8. Line 26 exhibits how to create an object of the loaded class using reflective call of the default constructor. Line 28 demonstrates a method invocation through reflection; the name of the invoked method is passed as a parameter and, thus, may not be available for static analysis.

3. REFLECTION AND DYNAMIC CLASS LOADING IN ANDROID

In order to understand the design of STADYNA, we first provide some background information on dynamic class loading and reflection implementation in Android. Notice that while in this paper we consider the Dalvik Virtual Machine (the Dalvik VM or DVM), the same functionality, i.e., DCL and reflection, is also present in the new Android runtime called ART that replaces DVM in the recent platform versions.

---

[2]https://github.com/zyrikby/StaDynA
[3]We found out that AndroGuard does not discover all possible cases of reflection and DCL.

[4]Mobile games can be very sophisticated and include realistic physics and a lot of graphics. Thus, developers often develop the original app as an installer that dynamically fetches additional code during the first run.

```
[com.sec.android.providers.drm.Doctype]
public static Object b(File pFile, String pStr1,
    String pStr2, Object[] pArrOfObj) {
  String s3;
  if (pFile == null) {
    String s1 = a.getFilesDir().getAbsolutePath();
    //get the name of the file to be loaded
    //9CkOrC32uI327WBD7n... -> /anserverb.db
    String s2 = Xmlns.d("9CkOrC32uI327WBD7n...");
    s3 = s1.concat(s2);
  }
  for (File locFile = new File(s3); ;locFile =
      pFile) {
    String s4 = locFile.getAbsolutePath();
    String s5 = a.getFilesDir().getAbsolutePath();
    ClassLoader locClassLoader = a.getClassLoader
      ().getParent();
    //get the class specified by "pStr1" from
      anserverb.db
    Class locCls = new DexClassLoader(s4, s5, null
      , locClassLoader).loadClass(pStr1);
    Class[] arrOfCls = new Class[5];
    arrOfCls[0] = Context.class;
    arrOfCls[1] = Intent.class;
    arrOfCls[2] = BroadcastReceiver.class;
    arrOfCls[3] = FileDescriptor.class;
    arrOfCls[4] = String.class;
    //get the method specified by "pStr2"
    Method locMtd = locCls.getMethod(pStr2,
      arrOfCls);
    //create new instance of the class
    Object locObj = locCls.newInstance();
    //invoke the method through reflection
    return locMtd.invoke(locObj, pArrOfObj);
  }
}
```

Listing 1: DCL and Reflection Usage in `AnserverBot`

3.1 Reflection

The ability of a program to manipulate as data something representing the state of the program during its own execution is called *reflection* [16]. Although Android is based on the Dalvik VM, the reflection API is almost the same as that of Java (with only several subtle differences). This API is used to access class information at runtime, create objects, invoke class methods, change the modifiers and the values of data field members [44]. More precisely, in Android the reflection API is used for the following purposes:

Hidden API method invocation. The developers of the Android OS may mark some methods as hidden (using `@hide` tag). In this case, the declaration and description of these methods does not appear in the SDK library and, thus, is not available for application developers. At the same time, app developers may use the reflection API to invoke these methods at runtime.

Access to the private API methods and fields. During compilation, the compiler ensures that the rules of access to fields and methods according to the specified modifiers hold. Yet, using the reflection API it is possible to manipulate with modifiers and, therefore, gain access to private members of a class at runtime.

Conversion from JSON and XML representation to Java objects. The reflection API is heavily used to generate automatically JSON and XML representation from Java objects and vice versa.

Backward compatibility. It is advised to use reflection to make an app backward compatible with the previous versions of the Android SDK. In this case, reflection is exploited

either to call the API methods, which have been marked as hidden in the previous versions of the Android SDK, or to detect if the required SDK classes and methods are present in the current framework version.

Plug-in and external library support. In order to extend the functionality of an application, the reflection API may be used to call plug-ins or external library methods provided at runtime using dynamic class loading functionality.

3.2 Dynamic Class Loading

The Dalvik VM allows a developer to load at runtime code obtained from alternative locations, such as the internal storage or over the network [19]. This functionality is usually used to:

Overcome the 64K method reference limit. Maximum number of method references in a dex file is 64K, but additional methods can be put in a separate dex file and loaded dynamically.

Extend app functionality at runtime. An app can provide stubs that process events using the pieces of code written by different developers. These pieces of code are called plug-ins, and DCL is widely used here to load the plug-in code into the memory.

Although Android allows developers to load and execute code dynamically, Google strongly recommends to avoid using this feature [3]. These recommendations are based on the fact that DVM does not provide a secure environment for the code supplied dynamically. Thus, this code has the same permissions as the app that loads this code. Moreover, DVM does not isolate code from the underlying operating systems capabilities and, thus, dynamically loaded code can operate with native libraries without any constraints [3]. These are crucial differences of the Android security architecture comparing with Java's one.

Class loaders are responsible for controlling the loading of classes into DVM. The process of loading classes in Android resembles the one implemented in Java [34,41]. As in JVM, Dalvik VM also has the *bootstrap* class loader responsible for loading core API classes. The *system* class loader is liable for loading application classes.

Similarly to Java, in Android class loaders form a tree. To organize this structure, each class loader holds a reference to its parent. The *bootstrap* class loader is the root of this tree; it has a `null` reference to its parent. An app may also define additional class loaders. In Android all particular class loaders are derived from `java.lang.ClassLoader` (possibly indirectly). Android provides several concrete implementations of this class, `PathClassLoader` and `DexClassLoader` being the most widely used ones.

4. AN OVERVIEW OF STADYNA

The architecture of STADYNA presented in Figure 1 comprises two logical components: a server and a client.

The static analysis of an application is performed on the server. In this respect, STADYNA allows an analyst to easily plug in and use any static analyzer in its architecture. The static analyzer on the server builds the initial *method call graph* (MCG) of the app, integrates the results of the dynamic analysis coming from the client, and stores the results of the scrutiny. The client part of STADYNA is a modified Android operating system, hosted either on a real device or an emulator. The client runs the application whenever dynamic analysis is required.

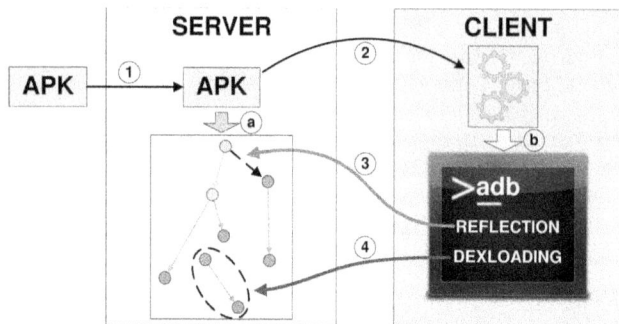

Figure 1: System Overview

In action, our system interleaves the execution of the static and dynamic analysis phases. However, to simplify the presentation, we describe them sequentially.

Preliminary analysis.

The server statically analyzes an app package and builds a MCG of that application (see Step *a* in Figure 1; solid arcs denote edges resolved statically). Dynamically loaded code cannot be analyzed during this phase and, thus, the corresponding nodes and edges are not present in the MCG. Further, the names of methods called through reflection may also not be inferred if they are represented as encrypted strings or generated dynamically. Still, a static analyzer can effectively detect the points in the MCG where the functionality of an application may be extended at runtime. Indeed, the usage of reflection and DCL requires to use specific API calls provided by the Android platform. The server detects these calls during the static analysis phase by searching for methods where DCL and reflection API calls are performed. We call these methods *methods of interest (MOI)*.

Dynamic execution.

If MOIs have been detected in the application, StaDynA installs the app on the client (Step *2*) and launches the dynamic analysis. The dynamic phase is exercised to complement the MCG of the app and to access the code loaded dynamically. The dynamic analysis is performed on a device (or an emulator) with a modified Android OS. The added modifications log all events when the app executes a call using reflection, or when additional code is loaded dynamically. Along with these events, the client also supplies some additional information, e.g., in case of a reflection call, the information about the called function and the stack trace (it contains the ordered list of method calls, starting from the most recent ones) is added. In case of DCL call, the path to the code file and the stack trace are supplied. The information collected by the client is passed back to the server side (Step *3*).

Analysis consolidation.

The server performs an analysis of the obtained information. In case a reflection call happens, the server complements the MCG of the app with a new edge (in Figure 1 it is represented by a dashed arc). This edge connects the node of the method that initiated the call through reflection (the node at the beginning) with the one corresponding to the called function (the node at the end).

When DCL is triggered the client infers which file was used to get the code. Using this evidence, the server downloads the file (Step *4*) containing the code, and performs the static analysis on it. The MCG of the app is then updated with the obtained information (see the part of the MCG in the dashed oval in Figure 1). Additionally, for each downloaded file the server analyzes whether it contains other MOIs. If it does, the list of the MOIs for the application is updated. This allows StaDynA to unroll nested MOIs. The stack trace data both for the reflection and DCL cases is used to detect which MOI initiated the call.

Marking suspicious behavior.

In Android, some API calls are guarded by permissions. Since APIs protected by the permissions could potentially harm the system or compromise user's data, the permissions must be requested in the `AndroidManifest.xml` file. However, there is no actual check which permissions are required to execute the written code and sometimes developers request more permissions than they actually use. In this case, those apps are called overprivileged. Many researchers, e.g., Bartel et al. [14], identified that malware, adware and spyware exploit additional permissions to get access to security sensitive resources at runtime.

Based on these considerations, we classify the following app behavior patterns as *suspicious*:

- An application dynamically loads the code that contains API functions protected with permissions. Indeed, malware may use this approach to evade detection by static analyzers, as the security-sensitive code is loaded dynamically.

- An application calls through reflection an API method protected with a *dangerous* permission[5]. This functionality can be used, for instance, to send malicious SMS, which cannot be detected by static analysis tools because the name of the SMS sending function is encrypted and decrypted only at runtime.

Detection of these suspicious patterns has been added to our tool. StaDynA raises a warning if such patterns occur during the analysis. Section 7 shows that indeed malware samples do expose such suspicious patterns.

5. METHOD CALL GRAPH

Method call graphs (or function call graphs) identify the caller-callee relationships for program methods. These structural representations of programs are widely used for different purposes. In the scope of Android, method call graphs are used, e.g., to detect malware [27, 29, 33], to identify potential privacy leaks in applications [23, 28, 49], to find vulnerabilities [42] and execution paths for automatic testing [48].

StaDynA extends the initial MCG generated with a traditional static analyzer with the information detected at runtime. Thus, if an application exposes dynamic behavior all mentioned approaches can benefit from the expanded MCG obtained with StaDynA.

---

[5]Google classifies as "dangerous" permissions with higher-risk level that guard access to private user data or device controls [2].

Example.

To visualize the capabilities of STADYNA and the process of method call graph expansion, we show the evolution on the example of a *demo_app*. Figure 2a shows the MCG of the app obtained with the AndroGuard static analyzer [1]. Figure 2b shows the one gained with STADYNA before dynamic execution phase, and Figure 2c presents it with dynamic execution phase. The *demo_app* dynamically loads some code from an external jar file at runtime and calls the loaded methods through reflection.

Figure 2a illustrates that AndroGuard identifies only the presence of ordinary methods and DCL calls (Ellipse 1) but no further analysis is done about those. Yet, Figure 2b shows that after preliminary analysis STADYNA selects 3 paths, which are surrounded by dashed ellipses. Ellipse 1 shows that a MOI (the dark grey node) invokes a constructor (the dark green node) through reflection. Similarly, Ellipse 2 displays a method invocation through reflection. Ellipse 3 depicts that a DCL call (the red node) is performed in a MOI (the dark grey node).

During the dynamic analysis STADYNA adds the edges that are outlined by Ellipses 4-7 (see Figure 2c). These ellipses show the cases when the MOIs are resolved and corresponding nodes and edges are added to the MCG. Ellipse 4 shows that as a result of a DCL call (the red node) a new code file has been loaded (the pink node). Ellipse 7 shows that a class constructor (the grey node) is called through reflection. Ellipse 5 shows a method invoked through reflection. This method contains an API call protected by the Android permission indicated by the blue node in Ellipse 6. There are also nodes and edges that appear as a result of the analysis of the code file (the pink node) loaded dynamically. These nodes and edges are connected with the rest of the graph through the reflection *new instance* call (see Ellipse 7).

Ellipses 2, 3, 8, 9 show other types of connections possible among nodes in a MCG obtained with our tool. Ellipse 2 shows the connection between the class and its constructor, Ellipse 3 shows an ordinary relation between two methods, Ellipse 9 connects the static initialization block and the class, and Ellipse 8 shows that the method is called from the static initialization block.

Each node type is assigned with a set of attributes, not shown in the figures. The analysis of values of these attributes can facilitate dissection of Android applications accompanied by the expanded method call graph. For instance, each method node is assigned with attributes, which correspond to a class name, a method name and a signature of this method. A permission node is assigned with a permission level along with the information about the API call that it protects.

6. IMPLEMENTATION

This section provides the implementation details of some key aspects of STADYNA. The workflow of our system operation is shown in Figure 3. App analysis starts at the server side. All occurrences of reflection and DCL methods are identified in the code of the application under analysis. In case neither of them is found, STADYNA builds a MCG of the app and exits. Otherwise, it starts the dynamic analysis on a device with the modified Android OS, which constitutes the client part of STADYNA.

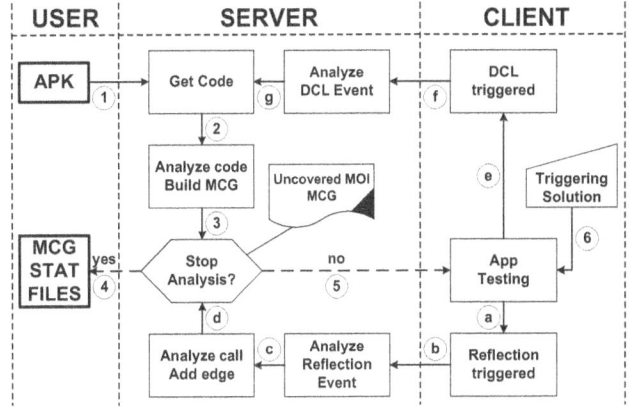

Figure 3: The STADYNA Workflow

6.1 The server

The server side of STADYNA is a Python program that interacts with a static analysis tool. Currently, STADYNA uses AndroGuard [1] as a static analyzer. AndroGuard represents compiled Android code as a set of Python objects that can be manipulated and analyzed. However, STADYNA can work with any static analysis tool that is able to analyze apk and dex files. To improve suspicious behavior detection we substituted the permission map embedded in AndroGuard (built for Android 2.2 in [25]) with the one generated by PScout [13] for Android 4.1.2.

Algorithm 1 App Analysis Main Function Algorithm

```
 1: function PERFORM_ANALYSIS(inputApkPath, resultsDirPath)
 2:     makeAnalysis(inputApkPath)
 3:     // Check if there are MOI
 4:     if !containsMethodsToAnalyze() then
 5:         performInfoSave(resultsDirPath)
 6:         return
 7:     end if
 8:     dev ← getDeviceForAnalysis()
 9:     package_name ← get_package_name(inputApkPath)
10:     dev.install_package(inputApkPath)
11:     uid ← dev.get_package_uid(package_name)
12:     messages ← dev.getLogcatMessages(uid)
13:     loop
14:         msg ← dequeue(messages)
15:         // analyzeStadynaMsg contains a switch statement
16:         // that selects a corresponding processing routine
17:         // shown in Algorithms 2 and 3 based on the msg type
18:         analyzeStadynaMsg(msg)
19:
20:         // Quit if a user finishes analysis
21:         if finishAnalysis then
22:             performInfoSave(resultsDirPath)
23:             return
24:         end if
25:     end loop
26: end function
```

The pseudo-code of the main server function is presented in Algorithm 1. The server starts the analysis of the provided app by extracting the classes.dex file (see Step *1*, *2* and *3* in Figure 3; Line 2 in Algorithm 1), and then dissects the extracted code. During this step STADYNA searches in the code all occurrences of reflection and DCL calls. The list of searched patterns for these API calls is presented in Table 2.

If MOIs are found, STADYNA selects a device (a real phone or an emulator) to perform the dynamic analysis on

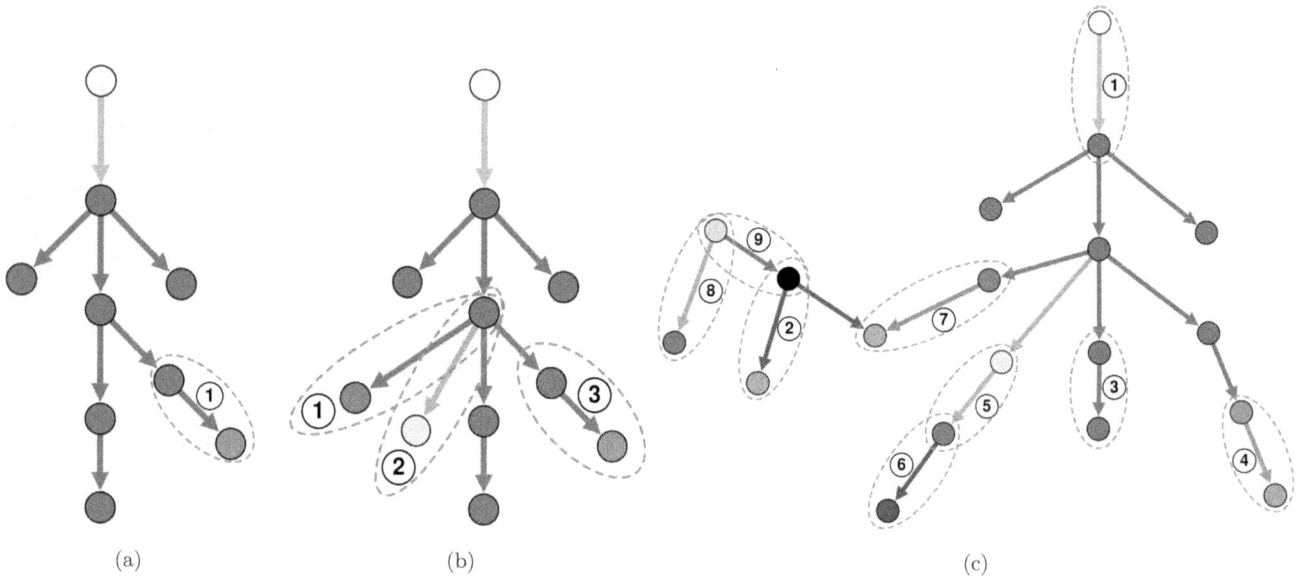

Figure 2: MCG of *demo_app* Obtained with a) AndroGuard b) STADYNA after Preliminary Analysis c) STADYNA after Dynamic Analysis Phase

Table 2: The List of Searched Patterns

Class	Method	Prot.
Dynamic class loading		
Ldalvik/system/PathClassLoader;	*< init >*	.
Ldalvik/system/DexClassLoader;	*< init >*	.
Ldalvik/system/DexFile;	*< init >*	.
Ldalvik/system/DexFile;	*loadDex*	.
Class instance creation through reflection		
Ljava/lang/Class;	*newInstance*	.
Ljava/lang/reflect/Constructor;	*newInstance*	.
Method invocation through reflection		
Ljava/lang/reflect/Method;	*invoke*	.

(Line 8) and installs the app under analysis (Line 10) onto the client (Step *5* in Fig. 3). After that the server obtains the UID of the installed package (Line 11) and starts a loop (Lines 13-25) that analyzes one by one messages (Line 12) obtained using the *logcat* utility from the *main* log file of the Android system. Basically, each obtained message is represented in the JSON format and contains values for the following fields: *UID* (required), *operation* (required), *stack* (required), *class* (optional), *method* (optional), *proto* (optional), *source* (optional), *output* (optional). The value of the `UID` field is used to select the messages produced by the analyzed app. If the user stops the analysis, STADYNA saves the results and finishes its execution.

The function `analyzeStadynaMsg` (Line 18) analyzes the selected STADYNA messages obtained from the client. It extracts the value of the `operation` field and based on this value selects the appropriate routine to analyze the message.

The routines for the reflection messages analysis are similar, so we consider them on the example when operation corresponds to *reflection invoke*. The algorithm for analysis of the *reflection invoke* messages is shown in Algo-

rithm 2[6]. Lines 2 - 4 extracts the method name along with its class name and the prototype, which has been called through reflection. Line 5 gets the stack from the message. Line 7 searches for the first *reflection invoke* occurrence in the stack. The next stack entry corresponds to the method that has performed the reflection call `invSrcFrStack` (Line 9). Then in the loop STADYNA compares this method with the list of MOIs extracted from the application executables (Lines 10 - 20). If the method is found STADYNA complements the MCG with the obtained information (Line 15), and deletes it from the list of uncovered invoke MOIs (Line 17). Otherwise, it adds this method to the list of vague methods (Line 21). This information is later analyzed to see why the method calling reflection was not found in the application executable during the static analysis phase.

The processing function for the DCL messages is slightly different (see Algorithm 3). From the message received from the client the server extracts the source path of the file containing the code loaded dynamically (Line 2). Using this information, STADYNA downloads the file locally (Line 4), and processes it (Line 5). This process includes computation of the file hash and copying the file into the results folder with a new filename, which includes the computed hash. The file hash allows us to check whether the file has been already loaded and avoid analysis of already checked code. Otherwise, the code analysis for MOIs is performed for the loaded code (Line 15). Function `getDLPathFrStack` (Line 6) searches for a pair of a DCL call and a MOI in the stack corresponding to the one extracted from the app executable. If this pair is found, then it is removed from the list of uncovered DCL calls (Line 11). Otherwise, STADYNA adds the information about the dynamic class loading call into the list of vague calls (Line 19).

---

[6]The algorithm for analysis of *reflection newInstance* messages is very similar so we do not show it.

42

Algorithm 2 Analysis of the Reflection Invoke Message

```
1:  function PROCESSREFLINVOKEMSG(message)
2:      cls ← message.get(JSON_CLASS)
3:      method ← message.get(JSON_METHOD)
4:      prototype ← message.get(JSON_PROTO)
5:      stack ← message.get(JSON_STACK)
6:      invDstFrCl ← (class, method, prototype)
7:      invPosInStack ← findFirstInvokePos(stack)
8:      thrMtd ← stack[invPosInStack]
9:      invSrcFrStack ← stack[invPosInStack + 1]
10:     for all invPathFrSrcs ∈ sources_invoke do
11:         invSrcFrSrcs ← invPathFrSrcs[0]
12:         if invSrcFrSrcs ≠ invSrcFrStack then
13:             continue
14:         end if
15:         addInvPathToMCG(invSrcFrSrcs, thrMtd, invDstFrCl)
16:         if invPathFrSrcs ∈ uncovered_invoke then
17:             uncovered_invoke.remove(invPathFrSrcs)
18:         end if
19:         return
20:     end for
21:     addVagueInvoke(thrMtd, invDstFrCl, stack)
22: end function
```

Algorithm 3 Analysis of the DCL Message

```
1:  function PROCESSDEXLOADMSG(message)
2:      source ← message.get(JSON_DEX_SOURCE)
3:      stack ← message.get(JSON_STACK)
4:      newFile ← dev.get_file(source)
5:      newFilePath ← processNewFile(newFile)
6:      dlPathFrStack = getDLPathFrStack(stack)
7:      if dlPathFrStack then
8:          srcFrStack ← dlPathFrStack[0]
9:          thrMtd ← dlPathFrStack[1]
10:         if dlPathFrStack ∈ uncovered_dexload then
11:             uncovered_dexload.remove(dlPathFrStack)
12:         end if
13:         addDLPathToMCG(srcFrStack, thrMtd, newFilePath)
14:         if !fileAnalyzed(newFilePath) then
15:             makeAnalysis(newFilePath)
16:         end if
17:         return
18:     end if
19:     addVagueDL(newFilePath, stack)
20: end function
```

Notice that the presented algorithms are simplified versions of the ones actually implemented in the server part. For instance, in a real application it is possible that the same MOI acts like a proxy used to call different targets (e.g., the same method could be used to load different code files). The real algorithms implemented in STADYNA are able to process these cases.

6.2 The client

The client side can run either on a real device or on an emulator. Using the emulator is more convenient because one can run the client and server on the same machine. The main drawback is that currently the Android emulator is quite slow. Moreover, mobile applications may suppress some functionality if they detect they are running in an emulated environment. With these limitations in mind, we implemented and tested our client on a real device. However, the code is not device-dependent so it can be easily ported to an emulator or another device.

To obtain the information required for analysis of reflection and DCL usage, we have modified the DVM and libcore components. To obtain the information related to DCL we added a hook to the method openDexFile of the DexFile class. This method is called when a new file with the code is opened. It gets three parameters as an input, where source-Name is of our interest. The added code forms a *JSON* message that contains the path to the file, from which the code is loaded (sourceName). Along with this information, the stack trace data and the *UID* of the process are also added into the message, which is then printed out to the *main* log file of Android.

To get the information about method invocation through reflection, a hook was placed into the invoke function of the Method class. Each Method object has declaringClass, name and parameterTypes member fields, which represent class name, method name and prototype of the invoked method respectively. This information along with the stack trace is put into the STADYNA message. Similarly, to log the information about new class creation through reflection, we put our hooks into the newInstance method of the Class and Constructor classes.

Each STADYNA message contains the stack trace information. Stack trace is a sequence of method calls performed in the current thread starting from the most recent ones. The information from a stack trace is usually used to find the origin of an exception in a program. In our case, the stack trace information is used to detect the MOI, which calls the reflection or DCL methods. In essence, a stack trace is an array of stack trace elements. Each stack trace element contains information about the class name, the method name and the line number of the method call in the source code. Unfortunately, using only this information it is not possible to uniquely identify the MOI, because we do not have access to the source code of the application. Moreover, due to function overloading it is possible to have several methods in a class with the same name. To overcome this limitation we modified the StackTraceElement class so that it can store the information about the method prototype. Method name and its prototype allow us to uniquely identify a method in a class.

A STADYNA message has a header and a body. To distinguish STADYNA messages from other log messages we add a special marker to the header. The second part of the message header is the part number. Currently, there is a limit on the length of the Android log entries specified by the constant LOGGER_ENTRY_MAX_PAYLOAD. To overcome this problem, we added the functionality to the client that allows it to split a message into several parts. The server takes care of assembling the original message.

7. EVALUATION

This section describes our application test suite and reports on the results of our experiments. In order to evaluate STADYNA we tested it on real applications, both benign and malicious. The server runs on a machine with 2.5 GHz Intel Core i5 processor and 4 GB DDR3 memory. The client is a Google Nexus S smartphone with the modified Android OS version 4.1.2_r2 connected to the server using a standard USB cable.

The evaluation test suite consists of a set of 5 benign and 5 malicious applications. The benign applications were selected based on their popularity and the presence of MOIs in the code. The malware samples were selected based on the study presented in Section 2 from the families exhibiting DCL as a part of malicious behavior. We also added two malware samples (FakeNotify.B and SMSSend) to our test suite based on the reports of antivirus companies [24,37].

Table 4: Evaluation: MCG Expansion

Apps	Nodes		Edges		Perm. Nodes	
	Init.	Final	Init.	Final	Init.	Final
Benign Applications						
FlappyBird	8592	8614	11014	11031	9	9
Norton AV	42886	55372	65960	85665	63	81
Avast AV	31317	32363	43554	44956	22	25
Viber	42536	46312	60078	65627	67	71
ImageView	5708	5713	6488	6496	7	7
Malicious Applications						
FakeNotify.B	148	171	137	191	1	2
AnserverBot	1006	1614	1138	2093	12	23
BaseBridge	1172	1780	1364	2333	14	25
DroidKungFu4	1550	21168	1779	23589	26	250
SMSSend	431	537	826	951	0	3

Table 5: Evaluation: Dangerous Permissions

App	Permissions	New
Benign Applications		
Norton AV	WRITE_SETTINGS	
	READ_PHONE_STATE	
	INTERNET	
	WRITE_SYNC_SETTINGS	X
	GET_TASKS	
Avast AV	INTERNET	
Viber	READ_PHONE_STATE	
	BLUETOOTH	
	INTERNET	
Malware		
FakeNotify.B	SEND_SMS	X
AnserverBot	INTERNET	
	READ_PHONE_STATE	
BaseBridge	INTERNET	
	READ_PHONE_STATE	
DroidKungFu4	CHANGE_NETWORK_STATE	X
	ACCESS_COARSE_LOCATION	
	BLUETOOTH	X
	INTERNET	
	BLUETOOTH_ADMIN	X
	WRITE_SETTINGS	X
	SET_TIME_ZONE	X
	WRITE_SYNC_SETTINGS	X
	READ_PHONE_STATE	
	CHANGE_WIFI_STATE	X
	MODIFY_AUDIO_SETTINGS	X
	MOUNT_UNMOUNT_FILESYSTEMS	X
SMSSend	READ_PHONE_STATE	X
	SEND_SMS	X

To evaluate STADYNA, the selected apps were manually inspected in order to trigger execution of MOIs. We also experimented with automatic triggering using the monkey tool [11]. This tool generates pseudo-random streams of user events and executes them on a device. Unfortunately, due to its random nature this tool was not useful for our experiments because STADYNA requires triggering of precise methods which contain reflection and DCL calls. To facilitate manual analysis, we extend our tool with the functionality that reports which MOIs have not been yet triggered. Observing this list an analyst may predict what actions will cause the execution of the uncovered MOIs. Here we report the results obtained using manual triggering.

Table 3 shows the numbers of detected MOIs for each operation ("Refl. Invoke", "Refl. NewInstance" and "DCL"). Each operation column has 3 subcolumns that present the number of MOIs in the initial application executable ("Init."), the number of detected MOIs after the analysis ("Final"), and the number of calls we managed to trigger during the analysis ("Triggered"). As STADYNA also analyzes the dynamically loaded code for MOIs, the numbers in the "Final" columns are usually higher than in the "Init." ones. The ratio between the numbers in the "Triggered" and "Final" columns can be considered as a coverage metric for STADYNA for every operation. Indeed, achieving 100% for this metric would mean that all MOIs were triggered at least once.

As the result of MOIs triggering, the MCG of the applications grows. Table 4 characterizes the effect of MCG expansion after STADYNA's analysis. MCG expansion is determined by two factors: a) STADYNA is able to analyze the code loaded dynamically and includes this information into the final MCG b) STADYNA can resolve the targets (unavailable in the initial graph) of reflective calls. The first subcolumn ("Init.") shows the number of nodes, edges and permission nodes in the initial MCG, while the second ("Final") presents the parameters of the MCGs obtained after analysis with STADYNA.

The column "Perm. Nodes" in Table 4 shows the number of detected API methods protected with dangerous permissions. Table 5 presents the analysis of the dangerous permission nodes discovered with the help of STADYNA. The column "Permissions" lists the names of the dangerous permissions required to run the code added by dynamic code updates features. A cross (**X**) in the column "New" shows the fact that the API calls protected with this permission were not discovered in the initial application executable. At the same time this permission is required to run the code

added by dynamic code updates features. These applications (with the cross in the column "New") will be considered as overprivileged by the tools [13, 14, 25], although in general, the apps do not belong to this category (because they use these permissions to run the dynamic code).

Results on benign apps.

ImageView does not contain the dynamic class loading functionality, thus its MCG was not expanded significantly by STADYNA. A popular game FlappyBird contains 1 DCL call, which was successfully uncovered during the analysis, and several instances of Reflection Invoke and Reflection NewInstance. However, the expansion of MCG produced by STADYNA was also relatively small (22 new nodes and 17 new edges). More complex applications like the mobile antiviruses Norton and Avast and the popular messenger Viber demonstrated significant expansion of their MCGs: more than 1000 of new nodes and edges were discovered by STADYNA for each app.

Norton AV, Avast AV and Viber also demonstrated suspicious behavior: they dynamically added code that invokes dangerous Android APIs protected by permissions. Notice that one of new API calls added by Norton AV (protected by the WRITE_SYNC_SETTINGS permission) was not even present in the original MCG. Thus, Norton AV would have been flagged as an overprivileged app (the one that requests more permissions than it actually uses in the code) by the tools [13, 14, 25].

Results on malware samples.

FakeNotify.B and SMSSend do not contain DCL calls, and new elements of their MCGs discovered by STADYNA appeared only as a result of reflection calls. Uncovered parts of MCGs of these apps are relatively small (while still revealing

Table 3: Evaluation: Number of MOIs for Each Operation

Apps	Refl. Invoke			Refl. NewInstance			DCL		
	Init.	Final	Triggered	Init.	Final	Triggered	Init.	Final	Triggered
Benign Applications									
FlappyBird	10	11	6	6	6	0	1	1	1
Norton AV	18	137	5	8	12	2	4	4	2
Avast AV	42	42	6	19	19	5	1	1	1
Viber	101	107	26	21	47	14	2	2	1
ImageView	6	6	5	2	2	2	0	0	0
Malicious Applications									
FakeNotify.B	68	68	68	9	9	9	0	0	0
AnserverBot	4	4	1	4	5	2	5	6	3
BaseBridge	5	5	1	2	3	2	2	3	3
DroidKungFu4	9	13	1	4	6	0	1	1	1
SMSSend	193	193	128	1	1	1	0	0	0

hidden suspicious functionality). More interesting results were demonstrated by STADYNA on AnserverBot, Basebridge4 and DroidKungFu43, where uncovered new parts of MCGs are comparable in size with the original statically produced graphs. In fact, the DroidKungFu43 code size exploded after dynamic class loading (an order of magnitude increase of the MCG size). This sample loaded the file settings.apk that contained approximately 13 times more nodes and edges than the original application.

The other two malware samples where DCL is present are from the AnserverBot and BaseBridge families. Both samples contain more than one instance of DCL. These samples both load two files with the names moduleconfig.jar and bootablemodule.jar. The former one contains no MOIs, whereas the latter contains *reflection invoke* and *DCL* calls. bootablemodule.jar then loads another file mainmodule.jar. This example shows how STADYNA unrolls nested calls.

In contrast to the benign apps, all evaluated malware samples exhibit suspicious functionality. This is an interesting result, as it shows that advanced malware indeed conceals its logic and reveals it only at runtime. E.g., SMSSend did not have any node labeled with a dangerous permission prior to the analysis. STADYNA has uncovered 4 such nodes (new nodes are protected with permissions READ_PHONE_STATE and SEND_SMS).

Our results show evidence that malware samples are more overprivileged (they contain more permission types required for the code loaded dynamically), so it is valid to identify the apps as suspicious if they are overprivileged. Yet, as benign apps can be overprivileged too, more research is required to understand if an application is benign or malicious, and STADYNA can be handy in exploration of this topic.

8. DISCUSSION

Our tool has space for future improvements. For STADYNA the coverage of MOIs (the ratio between the number of executed MOIs at least once and total number of discovered MOIs) is especially important. Currently, our system uses a manual approach to trigger MOI. Since we triggered the methods manually, STADYNA was not able to cover all MOIs in the apps because manual triggering is mostly GUI-based (it is challenging for a human analyst to produce a sufficient range of system events that might trigger all MOIs). As a way to improve STADYNA we plan to implement an automatic approach for triggering. As a first step in this direction we explored if the tools like *monkey* [11] can be handy. However, in our experiments we found out that pseudo-random events generated by the tool do not produce tolerable coverage values for MOIs. A possible approach to achieve satisfying values is to use systems like SmartDroid [48]. SmartDroid allows an expert to specify sensitive API methods required to be triggered. In case of STADYNA the sensitive API methods correspond to reflection and DCL calls. Other possible tools, which may be useful in developing fully automatic approach, are [15,39,45].

Another possible direction to reduce the amount of manual work is to resolve the targets of reflection calls statically at least those that are represented by constant strings [31]. The analysis performed in [25] has shown that it was possible to resolve automatically the targets of reflection calls in 59% of applications that used reflection. At the same time, the analysis was performed for the "closed world" scenario, which is not realistic, given that dynamic class loading is a popular technique for modern apps. Additionally, we can see that reflection is used more heavily today than in 2011 (88% of apps in our study versus 61% reported in [25]).

Usually, dynamic analysis allows an expert to explore only one execution path at a time. However, dynamic traces may differ depending on the context of the execution, e.g., some methods may contain calls invoked with parameters affecting the reflection call target. Therefore, another direction for improving STADYNA is to incorporate information obtained during different runs of analysis.

STADYNA has also other limitations. Its analysis is based on the UID of an application. However, it is possible in Android that several apps have the same UID. In this case, STADYNA will also collect the information produced by other apps with the same UID. At the same time, this information will not be used to complement MCG, but will be added to the category of vague calls that need to be later analyzed manually.

9. RELATED WORK

Being the most popular mobile OS, Android has won this position due to the openness of its ecosystem and the ease with which developers can publish apps on Google Play and third-party markets. Yet the openness comes at the price of large volumes of malware apps polluting the ecosystem. One approach to tackle security and privacy of mobile apps is to extend the security controls of the platform to detect misbehaving apps or to enforce the desired security policy [20,47]. Solutions following this approach, often require to modify the system image.

Another approach, more relevant to STADYNA, consists in the analysis of the mobile application code. Many static and dynamic analysis techniques have been proposed for Android. The ded system [23] re-targets Dalvik bytecode into Java class files that can be analyzed by the variety of tools developed for Java. In the original paper [23] the FortifySCA static analysis toolset was used for detecting vulnerabilities and dangerous functionality, like leaking the device IMEI. DroidAlarm [49] performs static detection of privilege-escalation vulnerabilities in apps by constructing paths in inter-procedural call graphs from a sensitive permission to a public interface accessible to other apps. STADYNA complements these static analysis techniques by completing inter-procedural call graphs.

Hu et al. proposed to explore functional call graphs (FCG) and rely on graph similarity metrics to detect malware based on known malware graph patterns [33]. Gascon et al. continue this research direction for Android with a technique to detect malware apps based on comparing FCGs that are mined with AndroGuard [27]. STADYNA can complement these techniques by providing more precise graphs required for analysis.

TaintDroid was among the first dynamic analysis tools for Android apps [22]; it allows to track propagation of information via the TaintDroid infrastructure-equipped smartphone software stack. Sources of sensitive information are typically the device sensors or private user information, and sinks are network interfaces; thus the main scope of TaintDroid is detection of privacy leaks. This approach is followed by Droid-Scope [45]. DroidScope allows to emulate app execution and trace the context at different levels of the Android software stack: at the native code level, at the Dalvik bytecode level, at the system API level, and at the combination of both native and Dalvik levels. While executing an app in Droid-Scope a security analyst can track events at different levels and instrument parameters of invoked methods to discover a malicious activity.

Dynamic analysis techniques are especially difficult to automate due to the need of emulating a comprehensive interactions of applications with the system and a user (UI interactions). Several approaches are proposed to automate the triggering of UI events, from random event generation [32] to more advanced approaches like AppsPlayground [39] and SmartDroid [48]. However, all of them still have many limitations on the type of events they can handle and the coverage.

Recently, Poeplau et al. [38] have identified the problem of dynamic code loading in Android apps. The authors selected possible vulnerable patterns of dynamic code loading and built a tool that can analyze Android apps for the found patterns. Moreover, they propose to use whitelists to prevent dynamic code loading that can potentially expose dangerous behavior. Whitelisting prevents unauthorized code from running. To get authorization the code must either signed [46] and its signature has to be included into a special list distributed by trusted authorities. However, as mentioned in the article [38], extraction of the dangerous behavior is a difficult problem by itself, especially when the protected API is called through reflection. In contrast, STA-DYNA aims not at preventing this loading (because a lot of legitimate apps use it and extra complications will not be welcomed by the developers) but at its analysis.

Reflection and Dynamic Class Loading in Java.

Gaps in the static analysis techniques in the presence of dynamic class loading, reflection and native code were previously studied for Java. For example, similarly to our approach, in [30] a pointer analysis (based on program call graphs) technique for the full Java language is extended by addressing dynamic class loading and reflection via an "online" analysis, when a call graph is built dynamically based on the program execution, and dynamic class loading, reflection and native code are treated in real time by modifying the pointer analysis constraints accordingly.

A run-time shape analysis for Java is investigated in [18]. Traditionally a shape analysis operates based on the call graph of a program, and it allows to conclude how the heap objects are linked to each other (e.g., if a variable can be accessed from several threads). Yet in Java the call graph produced from a program can be incomplete; and [18] suggests how to execute an incremental shape analysis when the call graph evolves dynamically. Our proposal does not involve a shape analysis, yet the ideas behind our proposal and [18] are similar.

Livshits, Whaley and Lam have studied the reflection analysis for Java [36]. They propose refinement for the static algorithms to infer more precise information on approximate targets of reflective calls, as well as to discover program points where user needs to provide a specification in order to resolve reflective targets.

Relevant to STADYNA is TamiFlex [17] that complements static analysis of Java programs in the presence of reflection and custom class loaders. Using the load-time Java instrumentation API TamiFlex modifies the original program to perform logging of class loading and reflection call events. This information is used to seed a tool that performs static analysis of the program having the information obtained during the dynamic analysis phase. This work differs from STADYNA in several aspects. First, TamiFlex uses a special Java API that is not available in Android. Second, although in Android it is possible to instrument an app before loading it on a device (offline instrumentation), some Android apps check the application signature in its code that is changed during the patching. Thus, for these applications the TamiFlex approach will not work in Android. Third, TamiFlex requires some debug information (the line number of the function call) to be present. In Android during the obfuscation phase this kind of information may be deleted from the final package. Therefore, the TamiFlex approach will not work, while STADYNA is able to process correctly this case due to the modifications we added to the Dalvik VM.

10. CONCLUSION

Today mobile applications make an extensive use of dynamic capabilities, namely reflection and dynamic class loading, available in the Android OS. Being adopted from Java, these techniques in Android incur an additional threat because the loaded code receives the same privileges as the loading one. Malicious apps can leverage these facilities to conceal their malicious behavior from analyzers.

In this paper we present STADYNA, a technique that interleaves static and dynamic analysis in order to scrutinize Android applications in the presence of reflection and dynamic class loading. Our approach makes it possible to expand the method call graph of an application by capturing additional modules loaded at runtime and additional paths of execution concealed by reflection calls. In order to produce the expanded call graph STADYNA does not require modification of the application itself.

The results produced by STADYNA can then be fed to the state of the art analyzers in order to improve their precision (for instance, a reachability analysis will be more precise over the expanded MCG than over the original one). Thus, STADYNA may help malware analysts by increasing their ability to detect suspicious samples.

11. ACKNOWLEDGEMENTS

This work has been partially supported by the EU project CAPITAL. We would like to thank Martina Lindorfer from the Andrubis project [35] for the provided dataset of malicious applications.

12. REFERENCES

[1] AndroGuard: Reverse engineering, malware and goodware analysis of Android applications. Available Online. https://code.google.com/p/androguard/.

[2] Android - App Manifest - Permission http://developer.android.com/guide/topics/manifest/permission-element.html.

[3] Android Security Tips. Available Online. http://developer.android.com/training/articles/security-tips.html.

[4] AndroidBest – Android market. http://androidbest.ru/.

[5] AndroidDrawer – Android market. http://www.androiddrawer.com/.

[6] AndroidLife – Android market. http://androidlife.ru/.

[7] Anruan – Android market. http://www.anruan.com/.

[8] AppsApk – Android market. http://www.appsapk.com/.

[9] F-Droid – Android market. https://f-droid.org/.

[10] Google Play – Android official market. https://play.google.com/store/apps.

[11] UI/Application Exerciser Monkey. Available Online. http://developer.android.com/tools/help/monkey.html.

[12] S. Arzt, S. Rasthofer, C. Fritz, E. Bodden, A. Bartel, J. Klein, Y. Le Traon, D. Octeau, and P. McDaniel. FlowDroid: Precise Context, Flow, Field, Object-sensitive and Lifecycle-aware Taint Analysis for Android Apps. In *Proceedings of the 35th ACM SIGPLAN Conference on Programming Language Design and Implementation*, pages 259–269, 2014.

[13] K. W. Y. Au, Y. F. Zhou, Z. Huang, and D. Lie. PScout: Analyzing the Android Permission Specification. In *Proceedings of the 2012 ACM Conference on Computer and Communications Security*, pages 217–228, 2012.

[14] A. Bartel, J. Klein, Y. Le Traon, and M. Monperrus. Automatically Securing Permission-based Software by Reducing the Attack Surface: An Application to Android. In *Proceedings of the 27th IEEE/ACM International Conference on Automated Software Engineering*, pages 274–277, 2012.

[15] R. Bhoraskar, S. Han, J. Jeon, T. Azim, S. Chen, J. Jung, S. Nath, R. Wang, and D. Wetherall.

Brahmastra: Driving Apps to Test the Security of Third-Party Components. In *23rd USENIX Security Symposium (USENIX Security 14)*, pages 1021–1036, August 2014.

[16] D. G. Bobrow, R. P. Gabriel, and J. L. White. Object-oriented programming. chapter CLOS in Context: The Shape of the Design Space, pages 29–61. MIT Press, 1993.

[17] E. Bodden, A. Sewe, J. Sinschek, H. Oueslati, and M. Mezini. Taming Reflection: Aiding Static Analysis in the Presence of Reflection and Custom Class Loaders. In *Proceedings of the 33rd International Conference on Software Engineering*, pages 241–250, 2011.

[18] J. Bogda and A. Singh. Can a Shape Analysis Work at Run-time? In *Proceedings of the 2001 Symposium on JavaTM Virtual Machine Research and Technology Symposium - Volume 1*, pages 2–2, 2001.

[19] F. Chung. Custom Class Loading in Dalvik. Available Online. http://android-developers.blogspot.it/2011/07/custom-class-loading-in-dalvik.html.

[20] M. Conti, B. Crispo, E. Fernandes, and Y. Zhauniarovich. CRêPE: A System for Enforcing Fine-Grained Context-Related Policies on Android. *IEEE Transactions on Information Forensics and Security*, 7(5):1426–1438, 2012.

[21] M. Egele, D. Brumley, Y. Fratantonio, and C. Kruegel. An Empirical Study of Cryptographic Misuse in Android Applications. In *Proceedings of the 2013 ACM SIGSAC Conference on Computer and Communications Security*, pages 73–84, 2013.

[22] W. Enck, P. Gilbert, B.-G. Chun, L. P. Cox, J. Jung, P. McDaniel, and A. N. Sheth. TaintDroid: An Information-flow Tracking System for Realtime Privacy Monitoring on Smartphones. In *Proceedings of the 9th USENIX Conference on Operating Systems Design and Implementation*, pages 1–6, 2010.

[23] W. Enck, D. Octeau, P. McDaniel, and S. Chaudhuri. A Study of Android Application Security. In *Proceedings of the 20th USENIX Conference on Security*, pages 21–21, 2011.

[24] F-Secure. Trojan:Android/FakeNotify Gets Updated. Available Online, Dec. 2011. http://www.f-secure.com/weblog/archives/00002291.html?tduid=f57e2769518f081721ffca586e797b2a.

[25] A. P. Felt, E. Chin, S. Hanna, D. Song, and D. Wagner. Android Permissions Demystified. In *Proceedings of the 18th ACM Conference on Computer and Communications Security*, pages 627–638, 2011.

[26] E. Fernandes, B. Crispo, and M. Conti. FM 99.9, Radio virus: Exploiting FM radio broadcasts for malware deployment. *Information Forensics and Security, IEEE Transactions on*, 8(6):1027–1037, 2013.

[27] H. Gascon, F. Yamaguchi, D. Arp, and K. Rieck. Structural Detection of Android Malware Using Embedded Call Graphs. In *Proceedings of the 2013 ACM Workshop on Artificial Intelligence and Security*, pages 45–54, 2013.

[28] C. Gibler, J. Crussell, J. Erickson, and H. Chen. AndroidLeaks: Automatically Detecting Potential Privacy Leaks in Android Applications on a Large Scale. In *Proceedings of the 5th International*

Conference on Trust and Trustworthy Computing, pages 291–307, 2012.

[29] M. Grace, Y. Zhou, Q. Zhang, S. Zou, and X. Jiang. RiskRanker: Scalable and Accurate Zero-day Android Malware Detection. In *Proceedings of the 10th International Conference on Mobile Systems, Applications, and Services,* pages 281–294, 2012.

[30] M. Hirzel, D. von Dinklage, A. Diwan, and M. Hind. Fast Online Pointer Analysis. *ACM Transactions on Programming Languages and Systems,* 29(2), 2007.

[31] J. Hoffmann, M. Ussath, T. Holz, and M. Spreitzenbarth. Slicing Droids: Program Slicing for Smali Code. In *Proceedings of the 28th Annual ACM Symposium on Applied Computing,* pages 1844–1851, 2013.

[32] C. Hu and I. Neamtiu. Automating GUI Testing for Android Applications. In *Proceedings of the 6th International Workshop on Automation of Software Test,* pages 77–83, 2011.

[33] X. Hu, T.-c. Chiueh, and K. G. Shin. Large-scale Malware Indexing Using Function-call Graphs. In *Proceedings of the 16th ACM Conference on Computer and Communications Security,* pages 611–620, 2009.

[34] S. Liang and G. Bracha. Dynamic Class Loading in the Java Virtual Machine. In *Proceedings of the 13th ACM SIGPLAN Conference on Object-oriented Programming, Systems, Languages, and Applications,* pages 36–44, 1998.

[35] M. Lindorfer, M. Neugschwandtner, L. Weichselbaum, Y. Fratantonio, V. van der Veen, and C. Platzer. Andrubis - 1,000,000 Apps Later: A View on Current Android Malware Behaviors. In *Proceedings of the the 3rd International Workshop on Building Analysis Datasets and Gathering Experience Returns for Security (BADGERS),* 2014.

[36] B. Livshits, J. Whaley, and M. S. Lam. Reflection Analysis for Java. In *Proceedings of the Third Asian Conference on Programming Languages and Systems,* pages 139–160, 2005.

[37] Pandalabs. New Malware Attack through Google Play. Available Online, Feb. 2014. `http://pandalabs.pandasecurity.com/new-malware-attack-through-google-play/`.

[38] S. Poeplau, Y. Fratantonio, A. Bianchi, C. Kruegel, and G. Vigna. Execute This! Analyzing Unsafe and Malicious Dynamic Code Loading in Android Applications. In *Proceedings of the 21st Annual Network & Distributed System Security Symposium,* 2014.

[39] V. Rastogi, Y. Chen, and W. Enck. AppsPlayground: Automatic Security Analysis of Smartphone Applications. In *Proceedings of the Third ACM Conference on Data and Application Security and Privacy,* pages 209–220, 2013.

[40] V. Rastogi, Y. Chen, and X. Jiang. DroidChameleon: Evaluating Android Anti-malware Against Transformation Attacks. In *Proceedings of the 8th ACM SIGSAC Symposium on Information, Computer and Communications Security,* pages 329–334, 2013.

[41] D. Sosnoski. Java programming dynamics, Part 1: Java classes and class loading. Available Online.

`http://www.ibm.com/developerworks/library/j-dyn0429/`.

[42] D. Sounthiraraj, J. Sahs, G. Greenwood, Z. Lin, and L. Khan. SMV-Hunter: Large Scale, Automated Detection of SSL/TLS Man-in-the-Middle Vulnerabilities in Android Apps. In *Proceedings of the 21st Annual Network and Distributed System Security Symposium,* San Diego, CA, February 2014.

[43] T. Wang, K. Lu, L. Lu, S. Chung, and W. Lee. Jekyll on iOS: When Benign Apps Become Evil. In *Proceedings of the 22nd USENIX Conference on Security,* pages 559–572, 2013.

[44] E. R. Wognsen and H. S. Karlsen. Static Analysis of Dalvik Bytecode and Reflection in Android. Master's thesis, Aalborg University, 2012.

[45] L. K. Yan and H. Yin. DroidScope: Seamlessly Reconstructing the OS and Dalvik Semantic Views for Dynamic Android Malware Analysis. In *Proceedings of the 21st USENIX Conference on Security Symposium,* pages 29–29, 2012.

[46] Y. Zhauniarovich, O. Gadyatskaya, and B. Crispo. DEMO: Enabling Trusted Stores for Android. In *Proceedings of the 2013 ACM SIGSAC Conference on Computer and Communications Security,* pages 1345–1348, 2013.

[47] Y. Zhauniarovich, G. Russello, M. Conti, B. Crispo, and E. Fernandes. MOSES: Supporting and Enforcing Security Profiles on Smartphones. *IEEE Transactions on Dependable and Secure Computing,* 11(3):211–223, May 2014.

[48] C. Zheng, S. Zhu, S. Dai, G. Gu, X. Gong, X. Han, and W. Zou. SmartDroid: An Automatic System for Revealing UI-based Trigger Conditions in Android Applications. In *Proceedings of the Second ACM Workshop on Security and Privacy in Smartphones and Mobile Devices,* pages 93–104, 2012.

[49] Y. Zhongyang, Z. Xin, B. Mao, and L. Xie. DroidAlarm: An All-sided Static Analysis Tool for Android Privilege-escalation Malware. In *Proceedings of the 8th ACM SIGSAC Symposium on Information, Computer and Communications Security,* pages 353–358, 2013.

[50] Y. Zhou and X. Jiang. An Analysis of the AnserverBot Trojan. Available Online, September 2011. `http://www.csc.ncsu.edu/faculty/jiang/pubs/AnserverBot_Analysis.pdf`.

[51] Y. Zhou and X. Jiang. Dissecting Android Malware: Characterization and Evolution. In *Proceedings of the 2012 IEEE Symposium on Security and Privacy,* pages 95–109, 2012.

Dimensions of Risk in Mobile Applications: A User Study

Zach Jorgensen
Department of Computer Science
North Carolina State University
Raleigh, NC
zjorgen@ncsu.edu

Jing Chen
Department of Psychological Sciences and CERIAS
Purdue University
West Lafayette, Indiana
chen548@psych.purdue.edu

Christopher S. Gates
Department of Computer Science and CERIAS
Purdue University
West Lafayette, Indiana
gates2@cs.purdue.edu

Ninghui Li
Department of Computer Science and CERIAS
Purdue University
West Lafayette, Indiana
ninghui@cs.purdue.edu

Robert W. Proctor
Department of Psychological Sciences and CERIAS
Purdue University
West Lafayette, Indiana
proctor@psych.purdue.edu

Ting Yu
Qatar Computing Research Institute
Doha, Qatar
tyu@qf.org.qa

ABSTRACT

Mobile platforms, such as Android, warn users about the permissions an app requests and trust that the user will make the correct decision about whether or not to install the app. Unfortunately many users either ignore the warning or fail to understand the permissions and the risks they imply. As a step toward developing an indicator of risk that decomposes risk into several categories, or dimensions, we conducted two studies designed to assess the dimensions of risk deemed most important by experts and novices. In Study 1, semi-structured interviews were conducted with 19 security experts, who also performed a card sorting task in which they categorized permissions. The experts identified three major risk dimensions in the interviews (personal information privacy, monetary risk, and device availability/stability), and a forth dimension (data integrity) in the card sorting task. In Study 2, 350 typical Android users, recruited via Amazon Mechanical Turk, filled out a questionnaire in which they (a) answered questions concerning their mobile device usage, (b) rated how often they considered each of several types of information when installing apps, (c) indicated what they considered to be the biggest risk associated with installing an app on their mobile device, and (d) rated their concerns with regard to specific risk types and about apps having access to specific types of information. In general, the typical users' concerns were similar to those of the security experts. The results of the studies suggest that risk information should be organized into several risk types that can be better understood by users and that a mid-level risk summary should incorporate the dimensions of personal information privacy, monetary risk, device availability/stability risk and data integrity risk.

Permission to make digital or hard copies of all or part of this work for personal or classroom use is granted without fee provided that copies are not made or distributed for profit or commercial advantage and that copies bear this notice and the full citation on the first page. Copyrights for components of this work owned by others than ACM must be honored. Abstracting with credit is permitted. To copy otherwise, or republish, to post on servers or to redistribute to lists, requires prior specific permission and/or a fee. Request permissions from permissions@acm.org.
CODASPY'15, March 2–4, 2015, San Antonio, Texas, USA.
Copyright © 2015 ACM 978-1-4503-3191-3/15/03 ...$15.00.
http://dx.doi.org/10.1145/2699026.2699108 .

Categories and Subject Descriptors

D4.6 [**Operating Systems**]: Security and Protection

General Terms

Human Factors, Security

Keywords

Android; smartphones; risk; mobile security

1. INTRODUCTION

In recent years, mobile devices such as smartphones and tablets have become pervasive. According to a 2013 survey by Pew Research, 91% of American adults own a cell phone, with 61% of those being smartphone owners [17]. Modern smartphones, which accompany a person at almost all times, are extremely capable mobile computers with a host of advanced sensors. By installing smartphone applications (apps), people can engage in activities that range from surfing the web and exchanging messages to shopping and banking online.

The convenience of smartphones is undeniable. But, along with that convenience come new risks in terms of security and privacy. Smartphones contain an unprecedented amount of personal and often sensitive data including contacts, call logs, browsing history, personal photos, financial information, and personal messages. Moreover, with advanced sensors such as Global Positioning Systems (GPSs), cameras, and microphones, smartphones are capable of fine-grained tracking and monitoring of a person's movements, communications, and surroundings. Thus, although smartphone apps can enable rich new functionality, they also pose risks to the personal privacy and security of smartphone users. Effective risk communication mechanisms are critical for helping users make safe and informed decisions regarding the apps that they install on their mobile devices.

In modern mobile platforms, such as Android, access to sensitive data and device resources is controlled through a permissions system. When a user installs an app on an Android device, for example, she is first shown a list of permissions used by the app, to which consent must be given before installation can proceed. The security and privacy provided by this mechanism therefore depends critically on the user's attention to, and accurate comprehension of, these permissions. The assumption that the user will attend to and comprehend permissions seems to be wishful thinking, though. Prior studies have shown that many users do not even look at the permissions when installing apps [2, 6], and those that do, often fail to understand many of them [6, 10].

A challenge to effectively communicating risk in mobile devices is that users differ in terms of their technical knowledge, the types of risks about which they care most, and how they respond to various risk signals. Moreover, risk is inherently a multi-dimensional concept [4, 15, 16]. Different apps may expose users to different types of risk, such as ones involving data privacy, monetary loss, device instability, and data integrity. Thus, any single approach to risk communication will be deficient for some users.

Motivated by these observations, we advocate a multi-dimensional, multi-granularity approach to risk communication. Within this approach the highest level is a summary risk index, which can be used to quickly and easily compare overall risks among multiple apps that provide similar functionality. Our research group has developed several risk scores suitable for this purpose in a recent series of papers [7, 8, 13, 14] and has provided evidence that provision of a summary risk index can increase the relative frequency with which users select the less risky option [1]. In addition to overall risk, many users will also want more detailed risk information for specific apps. Consequently, we envision an intermediate-level risk summary that aggregates risks along multiple dimensions (e.g., privacy and monetary) and integrates risk information extracted from multiple heterogeneous sources (e.g., permissions, reviews and ratings, and source code). An effective intermediate-level risk display will allow users to assess quickly the riskiness of an app according to the dimensions that are most important to them. From the intermediate-level display, users should be able to drill down to more detailed risk information for each dimension, if they desire to do so.

As a step toward developing new intermediate and high-granularity risk communication interfaces, we conducted user studies involving expert Android users and a broader user group recruited on Amazon's Mechanical Turk (MTurk) platform.[1] We chose to focus our attention on the Android platform because of its openness, as well as its dominance in the global smartphone market, with almost 85% of the market share as of the second quarter of 2014[2]. Our studies were aimed at answering the following questions:

1. What do expert Android users regard as the main dimensions of risk associated with installing mobile apps, and which permissions do they identify as contributing to the risks?

2. What key sources of risk information other than permissions do expert users consider when deciding whether to install a mobile app?

3. Which risk dimensions do typical Android users care about the most when making installation decisions?

4. How do users of different technical backgrounds and levels of Android experience compare in terms of the risks they care most about and the signals they use to assess risk in mobile apps?

The first study (Section 3) involved expert Android users— these were computer science graduate students with at least a year of experience with Android and knowledge of mobile and/or computer security fundamentals. We used two qualitative approaches to identify the primary risk dimensions and risk signals, drawing on the knowledge and perspectives of the expert users. Specifically, we conducted semi-structured interviews, in which participants answered questions about the types of risks posed by third-party apps and the relative importance of each of the risk types. We also solicited information about the specific risk signals the experts use to assess the risks of the apps they install, and how they use those risk signals. Following the interviews, we conducted a card sorting task in which the expert users were asked to sort a list of Android app permissions into groups based on the associated risk(s).

Whereas Study 1 was aimed at using the collective knowledge and experience of a group of expert users to identify the main risk dimensions and risk signals, Study 2 (Section 4) was designed to identify (1) which of those risk dimensions are most important to typical users, and (2) which of the identified risk signals they rely on most when installing apps. The study, conducted online through the MTurk platform, surveyed typical Android users about the types of risks with which they are most concerned and the types of risk signals they use when installing apps. The survey questions and answer choices were derived from the responses received during the first study.

Our main findings show that risk in mobile devices can be decomposed into a small set of risk dimensions, with the main ones being personal information privacy, monetary risk, device availability/stability risk, and data integrity risk. The identified risk dimensions and the insights regarding their relative importance to users should provide valuable guidance regarding which dimensions of risk to emphasize in future intermediate-level risk displays, enabling users to assess apps easily in terms of the risk dimensions that matter most to them.

2. RELATED WORK

Several recent studies (e.g., [6, 10]) have demonstrated that Android's current risk communication interface, which displays a list of permissions requested by an app before installation, is ineffective. For example, in a laboratory study conducted by Felt et al.[6], only "17% of participants paid attention to permissions during a given installation" (p. 2) and less than a quarter of participants demonstrated a competent understanding of the risks associated with specific permissions. Similarly, through semi-structured interviews with 20 participants, Kelley et al. [10] concluded that most users do not understand permissions and tend to ignore them in favor of more easily understood indicators, such as ratings, reviews, and word of mouth.

Researchers have attempted to address Android's limitations regarding risk communication. Chin et al. [2] noted that users appear disinterested in existing indicators and suggested the need for new, more usable security indicators in app marketplaces. Felt et al. [5] surveyed 3,115 users

---

[1]We received Institutional Review Board (IRB) approval from our institutions prior to conducting both studies.
[2]IDC Worldwide Mobile Phone Tracker, August 14, 2014: http://www.idc.com/getdoc.jsp?containerId=prUS25037214

on Amazon's MTurk platform about their level of concern for 99 specific risks associated with a selection of 54 app permissions. From the responses, they generated a ranking of the risks by level of user concern. They also concluded that "warnings in current smartphone platforms do not correspond to users' concerns" and recommended that "future permission systems should consider user concerns when deciding which privileges are protected with warnings" (p. 33). Our work in the present paper differs from [5] in that we are interested in identifying and gauging concern for a broad set of *risk dimensions* to emphasize in an intermediate-level risk display, rather than ranking specific risks associated with permissions.

Several recent works [3, 9, 11, 12] have focused specifically on the privacy risks posed by mobile apps. Kelley et al. [11] found that displaying high-level "privacy facts" enumerating the types of information accessible by an app can affect selection decisions among similar apps. Lin et al. [12] used crowd-sourcing to capture user expectations regarding an app's functionality and proposed a privacy summary interface that highlights permissions that go against those expectations. Choe et al. [3] investigated various visual displays for communicating privacy risks and aiding users in avoiding privacy-invasive apps. In particular, they studied the impact of framing effects (e.g., displaying how privacy-preserving vs. privacy-invasive an app is) on users' perceptions of an app's trustworthiness. Harbach et al. [9] proposed making the privacy risks associated with certain permissions more concrete through the use of "personal examples". For instance, if an app requested access to the *read contacts* permission, the permissions dialog would display three randomly selected contacts from the user's actual address book. Users were found to make more privacy-conscious installation decisions with the proposed interfaces. Although privacy is a critical dimension of risk, it is but one of the dimensions about which users care. Consequently, in the present research we also investigate users' concerns for other risk dimensions, such as data integrity, monetary risk, and threats to device stability and availability.

In a recent series of papers [7, 8, 13, 14], our research group has developed and evaluated several high-level risk signals generated from permission requests. Sarma et al. [14] proposed to identify risky apps as those that request permissions that are rarely requested by apps in the same category. Rather than a binary risk signal, Peng et al. [13] proposed risk scoring functions based on probabilistic generative models, which can be used to easily assess the risk of apps relative to one another. Gates et al. [7, 8] evaluated the effectiveness and usability of high-level risk summary indicators.

Such high-level risk indicators only tell part of the story, however. Because risk is a multi-dimensional concept [15, 16], multi-dimensional risk information also needs to be displayed for users that want a more detailed view of the risks posed by an app. Thus, the main focus of the present work was (1) to identify the most meaningful dimensions of risk and understand users' perceptions of those risks, and (2) to better understand other sources of risk information (in addition to permissions) and how such information is used by experts and average Android users to assess apps. The findings of our studies will inform the design of effective intermediate-level and high-granularity risk interfaces in the future.

3. STUDY 1: EXPERT USERS

The initial investigation that we report in detail is a laboratory study involving 19 expert Android users, which had two primary goals: (a) to determine the main dimensions of risk associated with installing Android apps, and (b) to identify the various signals considered by expert users to assess the risk of the apps they install. We used two qualitative methods to draw on the collective knowledge and perceptions of the expert users to identify the primary risk dimensions and risk signals. Specifically, semi-structured interviews were conducted, in which participants answered questions about the types of risks posed by third-party apps and the relative importance of each of the risk types. The interviewers also solicited information about the specific risk signals they use to assess the risks of the apps they install, and how they use those risk signals. Following the interviews, the expert users performed a card sorting task in which they placed individual Android app permissions into groups based on the associated risk(s).

3.1 Methodology

3.1.1 Participants

A total of 19 participants were recruited through posted fliers in the computer science building at one of our institutions and through direct emails to graduate students in security-related research areas at both institutions. The participants had experience with Android mobile devices and knowledge of computer/mobile security. Participants received a $20 Amazon.com gift card for completing the study.

The headline for the flier read "Volunteers Needed for Smartphone Security Research." The flier listed the following eligibility requirements:

We are recruiting security-minded individuals (knowledge of computer/smartphone security fundamentals) who have experience with Android smartphones. Participants must be at least 18 years old.

The task was described as follows:

Participants will be interviewed in a one-on-one setting with the researcher to share their thoughts and perceptions of the risks associated with installing/using smartphone apps. Participants will then be asked to sort a list of Android security permissions by risk type.

Although we asked questions about the subjects' security backgrounds during the interviews, we did not formally verify their reported qualifications.

3.1.2 Procedure

Participants met one-on-one with a researcher in an on-campus location. The study involved two parts: a semi-structured interview and a card sorting task.

Interview. The purpose of the interview was to understand how expert users perceive risks associated with installing and using mobile apps and the process by which they evaluate the apps they install on their personal devices. The interviews were audio recorded (with permission from the participants) for later transcription.

We began the interviews by asking questions about the participants' experience with Android devices and general usage patterns, such as types of device(s) used, number of apps installed, and installation frequency. We also queried participants about their background in information security.

Next, we asked participants to explain their personal process for vetting apps prior to installation, including a discussion of the different types of risk signals they use and why. We also asked participants to rank the risk signals based on their importance to the decision-making process.

We then asked participants to describe the different types of risks they perceive to be associated with installing mobile apps. After participants had finished describing all of the risks of which they could think, they were instructed to provide a ranking of the risks in terms of perceived severity. A general risk that was mentioned by every participant was personal information privacy. Whenever this risk was mentioned, we asked the participant to elaborate by listing the various types of personal information that he or she perceived to be at risk on mobile devices and to rank them by the level of importance placed on the privacy of each item.

The researcher asked clarifying and follow-up questions throughout the interviews in an attempt to resolve ambiguity and to get the participants to elaborate on interesting statements. The interviews lasted an average of 35 minutes.

Card Sorting. Following the interview, the participants performed an electronic card sorting task in which they sorted a list of Android permissions into groups based on the perceived risk type(s) associated with the permissions. This was an *open card sorting* task, meaning that participants were *not* provided specific categories, but rather had to form and name their own groupings of permissions. Participants were given the following instructions: (1) sort the permissions into groups based on the type of risk that you feel is associated with each permission (a single permission may be assigned to more than one group); and (2) give each group of permissions a name describing the risk type. Participants were given an opportunity to ask the researcher any clarifying questions about the instructions.

The task was conducted on a laptop using a web-based card sorting software package[3]. After reading the instructions explaining the task and how the software interface worked, the participants were shown a screen listing 74 permissions defined by the Android operating system. Although the Android operating system defines over 200 different permissions (as of August, 2013), we only included the 74 permissions that were usable by third-party apps[4]. The omitted permissions are only usable by system apps, or by apps that are cryptographically signed by Google or the device manufacturer; such apps are typically pre-installed on Android devices, rather than downloaded directly by users. Participants were also provided with a physical printout of the list of permissions, including a brief one-sentence description of each permission. The list and descriptions were obtained from developer.android.com[5]. After completing the sorting task, participants were asked to verbally explain their chosen groupings to the researcher.

3.2 Results

3.2.1 Demographics

Among the 19 participants, four were female and the rest were male. Fifteen of the participants were in the age range

23–30 years; two participants were of the age 18–22 years and two participants were in the range 31–35. The participants reported having an average of 2.5 years of experience with Android, with all participants having at least one year of experience. They all were computer science graduate students and reported varied computer security backgrounds. Eight participants were directly involved in smartphone/Android security research, whereas the others were involved in other security-related research areas or had taken or served as a teaching assistant for security courses in the past.

3.2.2 Interview Data

The audio recordings of the interviews were transcribed by paid graduate assistants and the researchers. When the transcriber could not understand a particular word or statement, question marks were entered into the transcripts. The interviewers checked each unclear statement and entered the correct words except in a few cases where they could not be discerned.

Risk Signals. We coded responses to the question, "What signals do you use to vet apps before you install them?" into 11 distinct risk signals. In descending order, by the number of responses, the risk signals are: user reviews, permissions, number of downloads, developer reputation, reviews/ratings summary[6], app description, screenshots, word-of-mouth, information from Google search, app maturity[7], and whether an app is open source. All but the last two signals were mentioned by at least two participants. Additionally, although it is not an install-time risk signal, six participants mentioned that they observe the "post-install behavior" of apps and immediately uninstall them if they notice signs of suspicious behavior. Table 1 summarizes the data.

Table 1: Summary of responses to the question "What signals do you use to vet apps before you install them, and how would you rank them in terms of importance?" The second column shows the number of participants that mentioned a risk signal, and the third column shows the number of participants that ranked the signal as most important.

Risk Signal	Mentioned by	Ranked 1st
User reviews	16	6
Permissions	13	6
No. of downloads	13	5
Developer reputation	11	5
Review/rating summary	11	5
App description	8	4
Post-install behavior	6	1
Screenshots	3	2
Word of mouth	3	1
Google search	3	0
App maturity	1	0
Is open source?	1	0

Participants were asked to rank any risk signals that they mentioned in terms of their relative importance to the decision making process[8]. Permissions and user reviews were ranked as the most important by the greatest number of participants, six. Moreover, of the 12 participants who men-

---

[3]http://www.ConceptCodify.com

[4]We used the permissions with a protection level of "normal" or "dangerous".

[5]http://developer.android.com/reference/android/Manifest.permission.html

[6]Includes the total number of reviews as well as a histogram of ratings for the app.

[7]May include things like the release date, version number or other information that would indicate how mature the app is.

[8]The rankings given during the interviews were relative in nature and many participants ranked multiple signals on the same level; this resulted in more than one signal being ranked as most important in some cases.

tioned using both signals, half ranked reviews as more important than permissions, whereas the other half ranked permissions as more important than reviews. Three signals were each ranked as most important by five participants: developer reputation, number of downloads, and reviews/ratings summary. Based on the relative ranking information, developer reputation appeared to be more important than the other two, which were generally regarded with the same level of importance. Four participants ranked app description as most important; however, most participants reported using the app description as auxiliary information to determine whether permissions were appropriate or for interpreting user reviews, rather than as a risk signal itself. The remaining risk signals were mentioned by three or fewer users and were ranked as most important by two or fewer users.

Regarding permissions, seven participants explicitly stated that the primary way in which they use the permissions is to look for inconsistencies with the stated or understood function of the app, the presence of which raises their perceived risk for the app (e.g., a game that requests permission to read SMS messages). Only three participants explicitly stated that they look for specific permissions that they consider to be especially risky and are extra cautious of any apps requesting one or more of those permissions. Some examples of risky permissions given include: access to contacts, send SMS, camera, audio recording, access to external/internal storage, location access, and call phone. Two participants explicitly mentioned that they appreciate when developers provide a reason for requesting certain permissions in the app description; such explanations will sometimes satisfy concerns about apparently inconsistent permission requests. One participant explained that he did not consider the permissions to be an informative risk signal because it was not possible to determine how an app was actually using a given permission or whether the permission was actually needed or not.

Participants reported using several different strategies for reading user reviews. Three participants explicitly stated that they focus primarily on the top few reviews. Another stated that he focuses on the most recent reviews. Two participants explicitly stated that they focus on the reviews corresponding to high ratings (four or five stars) and reviews corresponding to one-star ratings, as they feel that these contain the most useful information. As far as what participants look for when reading reviews, some participants indicated that they just check the general sentiment of the reviews, whereas others look for mentions of specific bugs, high data or battery usage, or threats to device availability or integrity. One participant mentioned using review content primarily to determine the maturity and stability of an app, rather than as a security related signal.

Regarding developer reputation, three participants explicitly stated that if an app is from a trusted developer, they will typically install the app without further scrutiny or will overlook otherwise suspicious permission requests. Despite stating that the number of downloads and ratings can be useful risk signals, several participants acknowledged that they can be misleading due to easy manipulation.

Risk Dimensions. We coded responses to the question "What do you think are the risks associated with installing applications?" into 13 response categories, nine of which described specific types of risks. The risk types (see Table 2), presented in order of the number of participants mentioning

each, are: personal information privacy, device stability and availability, location privacy, monetary or financial, spam and phishing, eavesdropping and surveillance, data integrity, behavioral profiling, and social embarrassment (e.g., an app publishes private messages or pictures). Aside from social embarrassment, all of the risk types were mentioned by at least two participants. Merging location privacy and social embarrassment into personal information privacy, and behavioral profiling into eavesdropping/surveillance, leaves six distinct risk dimensions. The four response categories considered not to describe risk types (bottom of Table 2) are best classified as describing types of attacks; these attacks are: privilege escalation, malware, attacks involving physical access to a device (e.g., theft of the device or reading sensitive data from RAM, such as credentials), and attacks targeting vulnerabilities in older, unpatched versions of Android.

Table 2: Summary of responses to the question "What do you think are the risks associated with installing applications?"

Category	Mentioned by	Ranked 1st
Personal Info. Privacy	19	14
Monetary	10	5
Device Instability	10	3
Location Privacy	7	2
Spam/Phishing	4	2
Eavesdropping	3	0
Data Integrity	2	0
Behavioral Profiling	2	0
Social Embarrassment	1	0
Privilege Escallation	7	5
Malware	3	1
Physical Access	2	2
Unpatched Vulnerabilities	1	1

The top three risk dimensions, in terms of the number of users who ranked[9] them as most important, were: personal information privacy, monetary risk, and device stability/availability risks. Each of these risk types was mentioned by over half of the participants. Regarding the three remaining risk types, spam/phishing was mentioned by four participants, two of whom ranked it as the most important risk; eavesdropping/surveillance and data integrity were mentioned by three and two participants, respectively, and there was no clear ranking of those risks.

Information privacy was the dominant concern for the participants; it was mentioned by every participant, with 74% of them ranking it as the most important risk type. When participants mentioned this risk type during the interviews, they were asked to list specific types of personal information that they believed to be at risk on mobile devices. Participants listed a total of 14 distinct types of personal information. In descending order of the number participants who mentioned concern for that type of information, they are: address book (i.e., contacts), location, photos/videos, files, messages (email, chat, SMS), financial information (e.g., banking credentials, credit card info.), personally identifying information (e.g., SSN, phone number, date of birth), login credentials, call logs, notes, todo lists, device ID/IMEI, browser history, and calendar (see Table 3 in Appendix A). In addition to being mentioned by the most participants (15

---

[9]The rankings were relative in nature and many participants ranked multiple risk types on the same level.

out of 19), "address book" was ranked as the most important type of information by the most participants, seven. The main reason for participants' concerns about the address book was the potential for the information to be misused for spamming or phishing. One participant indicated that the address book was not a big concern for him because his personal contacts are already easily obtainable from various social networking platforms like Facebook and Twitter. Location data were ranked next highest (ranked most important by five participants), followed by photos/videos, files, financial information, personally identifying information, and login credentials, each of which was ranked most important by three participants. The remaining information types were ranked most important by two or fewer participants. Somewhat surprisingly, only one participant ranked private messages (SMS, email, chat) as most important.

Monetary risk was mentioned by 10 participants, five of whom ranked it as the most important risk type. Participants mentioned the threat of apps that send text messages to premium numbers or make premium calls, apps with excessive data usage resulting in overage fees, and apps that steal financial information or make unauthorized accesses to financial accounts.

Ten participants mentioned device availability/stability risks, three of whom ranked it as most important. Participants mentioned things like battery drain and prevention of outgoing calls. Although we merged location privacy into the personal information privacy dimension above, it is worth mentioning that seven participants made a specific distinction between the two risks, five of whom ranked location privacy as less important than personal information privacy in general (the other two ranked them the same).

3.2.3 Card Sorting Data

On average, participants created 6.5 risk categories (standard deviation = 2.5; max 12, min 3). To get an aggregate picture of how the expert users categorized the permissions, we performed hierarchical clustering on the card sorting data. The input to the clustering algorithm was a 74×74 matrix containing a *dis-similarity score* for every pair of permissions. The dissimilarity between a pair of permissions i, j was computed as $1 - \frac{A}{\max(I,J)}$, where A is the number of times the two permissions were sorted into the same group by participants, and I and J are the counts of the number of groups into which i and j were sorted, respectively[10]. The dissimilarity scores fall into the range [0,1], where 0 means that i, j were sorted into the same group(s) by all participants, and a score of 1 means that no participants placed the two permissions into the same group.

The dissimilarity matrix was used as input to an agglomerative, hierarchical clustering algorithm using the *average* linkage method, which is the standard choice in the literature [18]. The output of the clustering procedure takes the form of a dendrogram, which is pictured in Fig. 1, with the clusters outlined. The summary labels for the clusters were derived from the group names generated by users during the sorting task. We coded each of the user-supplied group labels into one of 16 different summary labels based on the risk concept that it seemed to describe. We then labeled each cluster in the dendrogram with the summary label most frequently associated with the permissions in the

---

[10]Recall that a permission could be sorted into more than one group by the same participant.

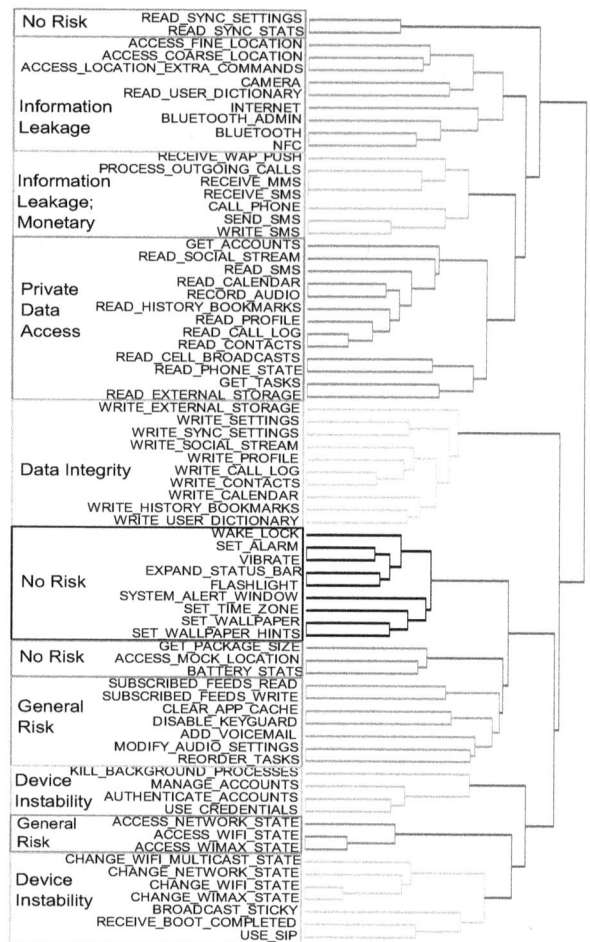

Figure 1: Dendrogram constructed from card sorting data.

given cluster. Eleven main clusters of permissions can be distinguished from the dendrogram, representing four distinct dimensions of risk: information leakage, private data access, data integrity, and device instability. The two clusters labeled as "general risk" appear to contain permissions that many participants felt were risky but were unsure about which specific risks to associate them with. The three "no risk" clusters contain permissions that were generally regarded as posing little risk. We note that the second most common label for the permissions in the main "no risk" cluster (the one containing wake_lock, set_alarm, etc.) was "annoyances", indicating that these permissions could enable actions that, while not necessarily risky, are nevertheless annoying to users (such as changing the wallpaper or setting random alarms).

The two "information leakage" clusters contain permissions that could enable an app to send data off of a device (e.g., via the Internet, SMS, bluetooth or near field communication) as well as various permissions that could be used to collect sensitive information that is of a dynamic nature (e.g., SMS/MMS messages, location, images from the camera). Within the second information leakage cluster, the 'call_phone', 'send_sms' and 'write_sms' permissions form a sub-cluster in which the most frequent label was "monetary", indicating that misuse of these permissions could cost the user money. The "private data access" cluster includes permissions that could be used to gather potentially sensitive data that is stored on the device, such as calendar information, contacts and call logs, browser history, and data on external storage (i.e., SD card). The permissions in the "data integrity" cluster allow apps to modify or delete data from a user's device (such as contacts, appointments or bookmarks) or from external storage. The two "device instability" clusters contain permissions with which an app could impact the stability or availability of the device (e.g., terminating background processes of other apps, introducing memory leaks, or affecting network connectivity).

3.3 Summary

The security experts indicated that they attend primarily to user reviews, permissions, and number of downloads when choosing whether to install apps. For the most part, they specified that they use the permissions to locate inconsistencies with the supposed functionality of the app. When queried about risk types, there was considerable agreement among the experts, with the categories of personal information privacy, monetary risk, and risks to device availability or stability mentioned most often. Three other risk categories that were also mentioned were spam/phishing, eavesdropping or surveillance and risks to data integrity. The card sorting data revealed 11 main clusters of permissions representing five distinct categories of risk: information leakage, private data access, data integrity, device instability and general risk. Although data integrity was only mentioned by two participants during the interviews, it emerged as a primary risk dimension from the card sorting data. The main points from this study are that security experts weight the user reviews, permissions, and number of downloads as important in their decisions and decompose risk into a few distinct categories. Thus, it would seem to be valuable to display mid-level risk information for which overall risk is decomposed into a few basic categories.

4. STUDY 2: TYPICAL USERS

Whereas the previous study was aimed at using the collective knowledge and perceptions of expert users to identify the main risk dimensions and risk signals, Study 2 was designed to identify (1) which of those risk dimensions are most important to typical users, and (2) which of the identified risk signals typical users rely on most when installing apps. The study was conducted online through the MTurk platform. We surveyed a broad group of Android users about the types of risks they are most concerned about and the types of signals they use when deciding whether to install new apps on their mobile device(s). The survey questions and answer choices were derived from the responses received during Study 1.

4.1 Methodology

4.1.1 Participants

A total of 400 users were recruited through Amazon's MTurk platform. Participants were required to be at least 18 years of age and reside in the United States.

The study was listed under the title "Android Installation Survey" and described as follows:

We are conducting research to study users' behavior while choosing apps for smartphones or other mobile devices. You will be presented with a survey that asks questions concerning demographic information, experience with mobile devices, how you choose apps to install, and the types of risk you think about when using your device(s).

4.1.2 Procedure

The survey questions were similar to those asked during the interviews with the expert users, except that they were mostly multiple choice. The multiple choice answers were derived from analysis of the interview transcripts. Participants were required to complete the questions on each page before continuing to the next page and were restricted from returning to a previous page after advancing. The survey questions included the following.

- Basic demographic information, such as age, gender, and level of education.
- Questions relating to mobile device usage: device(s) used, device used most often, frequency of use, sources of downloaded apps (e.g., Google Play, Amazon, third-part sites), and app installation frequency.
- A list of 14 different types of information available for apps in the Google Play Store (as of August, 2013): Participants rated each item on a five-level scale from "never" to "always", according to how often they considered that item when installing apps. We included labeled screenshots of the Google Play interface for reference (see Fig. 2).
- A free response question: "In a few words, what do you personally feel is the biggest risk associated with installing an app on your mobile device(s)?"
- Seven specific risk types: Participants rated their level of concern for each risk, on a five-point scale ranging from "not at all" to "extremely". The risk types included the following: personal data integrity, monetary or financial risks, physical damage to device, device instability, eavesdropping or spying, personal privacy, and spam. The order of the list was randomized for each participant. A text box was also provided for participants to list any additional risks that came to mind.
- 13 different types of personal information commonly found on mobile devices: Participants rated their concern for apps having access to that information, on the same five-point scale as in the previous question. A text box was included for participants to list any additional types of information that came to mind. The order of the list was randomized for each participant.
- Level of computer security expertise: Participants chose one from computer novice, regular user, highly skilled (programmer, sys admin, etc.), security expert (work in security related field), or I don't know.

Participants were paid $0.75 for completing the survey, which took approximately eight minutes. Although 400 users completed the survey, 49 of them indicated that they did not own an Android device, and one indicated that s/he was under the age of 18. Therefore, our analysis included only the responses from the other 350 users.

4.2 Results

4.2.1 Demographics

Of the 350 Android users that responded to the survey, 65% were male and the rest female. The breakdown of ages in years was as follows: 18–24 (34%), 25–34 (47%), 35–44

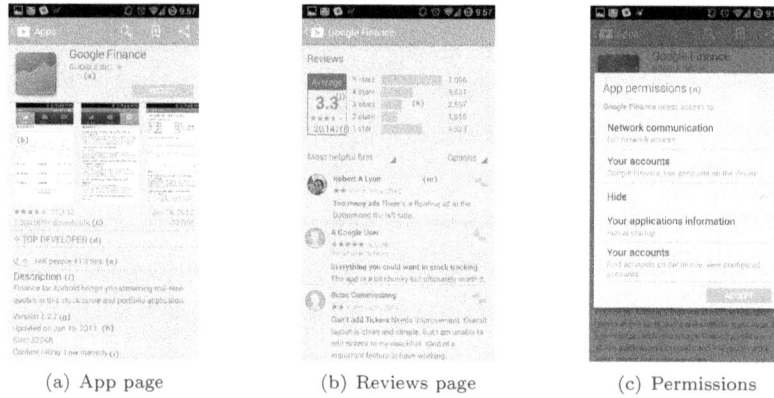

| (a) App page | (b) Reviews page | (c) Permissions |

Figure 2: Google Play Store interface (as of August, 2013). The survey participants were asked to indicate how often they considered each of the labeled interface elements when installing new apps.

(11%), 45–54 (4%), and 55-64 (3%). In terms of education level (highest achieved), 34% of participants had a bachelor's degree, while another 34% had completed some college credit (no degree). The breakdown for the other participants was as follows: high school graduate or below (11%), trade/technical/vocational training (2%), associate degree (11%), master's degree (6%), professional or doctorate degree (2%). In terms of reported computer security expertise, the majority of the participants (2%) identified themselves as "computer novice", 70% as "regular user", 28% as "highly skilled", and 1% as "security expert".

Among these Android users, 92% of them reported using Android smart phones, and 43% reported using Android tablets (35% used both). When asked which mobile device they used most often, 78% chose Android smart phone, 9% chose Android tablet, and the remainder chose other devices such as iPhone as their primary device. These participants reported using their Android devices often: 93% of them reported using their Android device(s) daily, 4% 2–3 times a week, 1% once a week, and 1% 2–3 times a month.

Regarding app installation activities, 95% of the participants indicated that they installed new apps from the Google Play Store, the interface on which the current study is based; some of them also went to the Amazon Appstore (30%), Samsung Apps (9%), and third-party websites (17%). For app installation frequency, 2% of the participants reported installing new apps on a daily basis, 15% 2–3 times a week, 25% once a week, 29% 2–3 times a month, 15% once a month, 13% less than once a month, and 1% reported that they had never installed any new apps on their primary mobile devices.

4.2.2 Survey Data

Risk Signals. Participants were shown a list of information elements displayed for an app in the Google Play Store (as shown in Fig. 2), and were asked how often they consider these components when deciding whether to install an app on a five-point scale (never, rarely, sometimes, often, and always). To analyze the responses, we assigned scores from 0 to 4 to the five frequency levels, and computed a mean score for each element weighted by the number of participants who selected a certain level of frequency. In order of their weighted means, they are: Description, Average rating, Content of reviews, Number of ratings, Screenshots, Ratings distribution, App permissions, Number of downloads, Content Rating, "Top Developer" designation, Number of

+1's[11], Updated On date[12], Developer's name, and Version number (see Table 4 in Appendix A). Chi-squared analysis was conducted to compare the difference among participants' responses for the elements, by transforming the five-point scale into a binary one. The transformation was done through combining "never consider" and "rarely consider" into a "negative" category and combining "often consider" and "always consider" into a "positive" category. The chi-squared results showed that, using a $p = .05$ criterion, participants' responses on the information elements can be divided into five groups. The elements within each group did not differ significantly from each other, but had significantly different responses from elements in the other groups. The five groups were: (1) Description and Average rating; (2) Content of reviews, Number of ratings, and Screenshots; (3) Ratings distribution, App permissions, and Number of downloads; (4) Top Developer designation, Number of +1's, and Updated On date; and (5) Developer's name and Version number.

Free-response Question. Participants were asked to describe, in a few words, what they personally think is the biggest risk associated with installing an app on their mobile device(s). We asked this question to get an idea of the participants' most significant concerns before asking them about specific risk types in the following question. They were not able to proceed to the next question until answering this free response question. We grouped all of the responses that appeared to be describing the same type of risk and then gave each group a representative label. The coding process was performed by two of the authors; responses that were too general or ambiguous, or for which an agreement could not be reached by the two authors, were discarded. Some responses described more than one type of risk, and were therefore assigned to multiple response groups. In total, 43 of the responses were discarded, leaving 307 responses. In order of frequency, the nine resulting response categories were: information privacy (154), malware (58), device instability (45), over-privileging (23), functionality (20), spam (12), unknown/untrusted developer (10), monetary (10) and insecure behavior (5); only seven participants explicitly stated that they had no concerns. Table

---

[11] +1's are used by users of the Google Plus social networking service to indicate that they "like" an app.

[12] This is the date on which the app developer last updated the app in the Google Play Store.

5 (deferred to Appendix A) summarizes the categories and describes typical responses in each category.

Risk Dimensions. Participants were presented with a list of the six main risk dimensions identified in Study 1 (Sec. 3), along with one additional risk type (physical damage to device). Next to the name of each risk dimension we included a short description including brief examples of risks in that dimension. Participants were asked to rate their level of concern for each risk dimension, with respect to installing apps on their mobile device(s), on a five-point scale (not at all, slightly, somewhat, moderately, and extremely), and weighted means were computed similarly as in the previous question. The types of risks ranked in terms of their weighted means are: personal privacy, personal data integrity, eavesdropping or spying, device instability, spam, monetary or financial risks, and physical damage to device (see Table 6 in Appendix A). Chi-squared analyses were also conducted on the binary data transformed from the five-point scale to compare the difference between the risk types of different ranks. Again, most of the analyses showed significant differences ($ps < .05$) among the risk types with different rankings, except those between personal data integrity and eavesdropping/spying, eavesdropping/spying and device instability, device instability and spam, and spam and monetary/financial risks.

Only 18 participants entered a response in the space for "other risks"; however, we found that all of the responses either described risks that could be categorized into one of the provided risk types or did not describe a specific risk (e.g., "viruses" and "addictive"). Although this seems to indicate that the risk types identified by the expert users and used in this study are appropriately comprehensive, there may be better names or descriptions that could be used to convey the scope of the risk types. In particular, a third of the responses described things that we consider to fall under the "device instability" risk type, which may indicate the need for a better descriptor for that risk type.

We conducted a correlational analysis to determine whether there were any significant correlations between the types of risks users are most concerned about and the specific risk signals they use when installing apps. Most of the correlations that were significant had small correlation coefficients. The most significant correlations involved the element "App permissions": the more often participants considered app permissions when installing an app, the more concerned they were about personal privacy (Spearman correlation coefficient $\rho = 0.361$, $p < .001$), personal data integrity ($\rho = 0.386$, $p < .001$), and eavesdropping or spying ($\rho = 0.293$, $p < .001$).

Personal Information Privacy. As noted above, the surveyed users were most concerned about personal information leakage. We queried participants about their concern for apps having access to each of 13 types of personal information. The same five-point scale was used and analyzed in the same way as in the previous question. The types of information, ranked in terms of the weighted means were: Personally identifying information, Passwords and login credentials, Financial information, Texts/emails/chat messages, Personal photos/videos, Exact location (i.e., GPS), Contacts, Files, Call logs, General location, Web browsing history, Calendar, and Notes or todo lists (see Table 7 in Appendix A). Similarly, chi-squared analyses showed that, using a $p = .05$ criterion, these different types of personal information can

be put into four groups that differ in terms of how concerned the participants were about them: (1) personally identifying information, passwords and login credentials, and financial information; (2) texts/emails/chat messages, personal photos or videos, exact location, contacts, and files; (3) call logs, general location, and web browsing history; (4) calendar and notes or todo lists.

Only five participants entered a response in the space provided for "other types of personal information"; however, all of the responses described one of the listed information types (e.g. "my bank information or my credit card") or did not refer to a specific information type (e.g., "anything that has to do with my personal information").

Group Differences. We compared the participants' responses across reported expertise, by treating the computer novices and regular users as *unskilled* users, and treating highly skilled and security experts as *skilled* users. For the question asking how often users consider the various information elements, Mann-Whitney U tests showed that the skilled users consider the developer's name, screenshots, number of downloads, and app permissions more often and content rating less often than do the unskilled users ($ps < .05$). No significant difference was observed for the other elements ($p > .05$). Regarding concern for different risk types, no difference was found between the two groups ($ps > .05$). For the question regarding concern for different types of personal information, the only significant difference between the two groups of users was with respect to the call logs, where the skilled users showed greater concern ($p < .05$).

A similar analysis was also conducted to compare male and female participants. We found that the male users considered the "Top Developer" designation more often and content rating less often than did the female users ($ps < .05$). Males were also less concerned about physical damage to their devices than were females ($p < .05$). Finally, males were less concerned about their general location being accessed by an app than were females ($p < .05$).

4.3 Summary

Users showed the most concern for information privacy risks, followed by data integrity, eavesdropping/spying, device instability, spam, monetary risks and finally, physical device damage. In contrast to the expert users from Study 1, the surveyed users showed greater concern for data integrity risks, but less concern for monetary risks. Although data integrity was not mentioned by any of the participants in the free-response question, participants ranked it as one of the top risks when queried about it directly. Also in contrast to the expert users from Study 1, the users surveyed in Study 2 ranked permissions relatively lower and descriptions and screenshots relatively higher among the sources of risk information that they consider when installing apps. Participants who reported considering app permissions more often expressed more concern about personal privacy, data integrity, and eavesdropping/spying than participants who considered permissions less often.

5. DISCUSSION

5.1 Limitations

Both studies involved participants' subjective reports of their concerns and thoughts regarding risks associated with

Android apps. These self-reported answers may not be exactly the same as the participants' actual app selection behavior. Measuring users' actual app selection and distilling users' preferences from that is beyond the scope of this paper. In Study 2, we tried to minimize possible inconsistencies by showing participants the Google Play interface (Fig. 2) as a prompt to retrieve the actions they have taken when using it.

The interviews in Study 1 were semi-structured and were conducted by two different researchers in two of our institutions. Although both interviewers used the same script, there may have been differences in their interviewing styles that could have led to under-reporting or over-reporting in some cases. We attempted to minimize differences by having the second interviewer listen to interview recordings of the first interviewer. We note that 16 of the 19 interviews were conducted by a single interviewer and so we would expect any effects on the conclusions to be small.

5.2 Dimensions of Risk

Through semi-structured interviews and a card sorting task with a group of security experts, we found that risk in mobile apps can be decomposed into a small set of distinct risk dimensions, with the main dimensions being personal information privacy, monetary/financial risk, and risks to the stability or availability of one's device. Additional risk dimensions identified were spam/phishing, eavesdropping or surveillance and data integrity. The card sorting task yielded several useful clusters of permissions associated with the main risk dimensions as well as highlighting data integrity. An online survey of 350 typical Android users confirmed the comprehensiveness of the identified risk dimensions and revealed valuable insights into which dimensions average users are most concerned about.

The predominant concern, for users across both studies, was personal information privacy, suggesting that recent work on developing interfaces for communicating privacy risks (e.g., [3, 9, 10, 12]) is a step in the right direction. We found that concern for different types of personal information was similar across the two studies. A notable exception was contacts (i.e., address book), which was ranked first by the expert users but seventh by the users in Study 2. The expert users expressed concern about contacts being used for spam/phishing purposes. It is possible that average users are less aware of the risks associated with the leakage of contacts. Another possible explanation is that, with the pervasiveness of social networking sites like Facebook and Twitter, users have become more accustomed to sharing their contacts with third-party services.

We found no significant differences in concern for specific risk types among users of different reported expertise in Study 2. However, we did observe some differences in concern across the two studies, particularly with regard to monetary/financial risk and data integrity. Specifically, the experts in Study 1 regarded monetary risk as one of the top-ranked risks, whereas the users surveyed in Study 2 ranked their concern for that dimension near the bottom. It is possible that typical users are less aware of the monetary risks posed by apps (e.g., calling or texting premium-rate numbers). However, Felt et al. [6] found that a ranking of 99 different risks by typical mobile device users included three risks related to monetary loss ranked among the top five. A possible explanation for the low ranking of monetary risk in

our Study 2 is that most users have not personally experienced any monetary loss from installing apps and thus are not very concerned. Security experts on the other hand are accustomed to thinking in worst-case terms and are more aware of the potential risks.

Although data integrity was only mentioned by two of the expert users interviewed in Study 1, it was identified in the ratings of each risk type as a top concern for the users in Study 2. However, we also note that data integrity was not mentioned by users in their answers to the free-response question in Study 2. It is possible that many of the expert users did not think of this risk during the interviews but might have indicated concern had they been directly queried about it, as the users in Study 2 were. It may also be that expert users are more likely to make regular backups of their data than average users and are therefore less concerned about data integrity. Regardless, the infrequent mention of data integrity in both the free-response question and the expert interviews suggests that it is not on the forefront of most users' minds, regardless of their level of concern for it.

Implications for Risk Communication. Prior work on risk communication in mobile devices has focused on high-level risk indicators(e.g., [13, 14]) and on developing new interfaces for communicating risk information about a single type of risk, particularly privacy (e.g., [3, 9, 10, 12]). However, our findings show that risk, in the context of mobile apps, is multi-dimensional. Thus, to make informed decisions about which apps to install, users need to be able to assess quickly and easily the risk posed by an app along the dimensions that matter the most to them. The identified risk dimensions and the evidence regarding their relative importance to users should provide valuable guidance regarding which dimensions of risk to emphasize in an intermediate-level risk display. The permissions clusters identified from the card sorting results should be useful in developing risk indices for each dimension, or identifying which permissions to highlight in high-granularity displays for individual risk dimensions. Similarly, our findings regarding concern for the various types of personal information should be helpful in guiding the design of high-granularity interfaces for the information privacy dimension.

5.3 Sources of Risk Information

Our semi-structured interviews with expert users revealed 11 possible sources of risk information, with permissions and user reviews ranked as the most important. Other signals identified as useful were developer reputation, number of downloads, and reviews/ratings summary. Despite the importance of permissions in determining risk, the typical users surveyed in Study 2 ranked permissions relatively low in terms of information they consider when installing apps, instead focusing more often on the app description, user ratings, and reviews. This finding is consistent with that of prior studies reporting that users often ignore permissions (e.g., [2, 6]). Comparing the users of different self-reported expertise in Study 2, we also found that highly skilled and expert users were more likely to consider permissions, developer reputation, screenshots, and number of downloads than were novice and regular users.

Implications for Risk Communication. Although permissions are an important source of risk information and have been the primary focus of prior work (e.g., [11, 12, 14]), our findings highlight that useful risk information can also be found in other sources, such as user reviews, number of downloads, and developer reputation. The findings also confirm that average users and expert users tend to rely on different sources of risk information when making installation decisions. Our work points to the need to develop techniques to extract and present risk information from other important signals that are often under-utilized by typical users, so as to ensure that users are making informed installation decisions.

6. CONCLUSION

We conducted two user studies designed to identify the main dimensions of risk associated with mobile apps, as perceived by both experts and typical Android users. We found that risk in mobile apps can be decomposed into a small set of distinct risk dimensions including personal information privacy, monetary risk, device availability/stability risk and data integrity risk. Guided by these findings, our future work will focus on developing and evaluating new intermediate and high-granularity risk communication interfaces to enable users to quickly and accurately assess an app's risk in terms of the dimensions that matter most to them.

Acknowledgment

The authors are grateful to the anonymous reviewers for their helpful feedback. This work is supported in part by the National Science Foundation under the awards CNS-1314688 and CNS-1314229.

7. REFERENCES

[1] J. Chen, C. S. Gates, R. W. Proctor, and N. Li. Framing of summary risk/safety information and app selection. In *HFES*, pages 1461–1465. HFES, 2014.

[2] E. Chin, A. P. Felt, V. Sekar, and D. Wagner. Measuring user confidence in smartphone security and privacy. In *SOUPS*. ACM, 2012.

[3] E. K. Choe, J. Jung, B. Lee, and K. Fisher. Nudging people away from privacy-invasive mobile apps through visual framing. In *INTERACT: IFIP TC13*, pages 74–91. Springer, 2013.

[4] A. H. Crespo, I. R. del Bosque, and M. G. de los Salmones Sanchez. The influence of perceived risk on internet shopping behavior: a multidimensional perspective. *J. Risk Res.*, 12(2):259–277, 2009.

[5] A. P. Felt, S. Egelman, and D. Wagner. I've got 99 problems, but vibration ain't one: a survey of smartphone users' concerns. In *SPSM*, pages 33–44. ACM, 2012.

[6] A. P. Felt, E. Ha, S. Egelman, A. Haney, E. Chin, and D. Wagner. Android permissions: User attention, comprehension, and behavior. In *SOUPS*. ACM, 2012.

[7] C. Gates, J. Chen, N. Li, and R. Proctor. Effective risk communication for Android apps. *IEEE TDSC*, 11(3):252–265, 2014.

[8] C. S. Gates, N. Li, H. Peng, B. P. Sarma, Y. Qi, R. Potharaju, C. Nita-Rotaru, and I. Molloy. Generating summary risk scores for mobile applications. *IEEE TDSC*, 11(3):238–251, 2014.

[9] M. Harbach, M. Hettig, S. Weber, and M. Smith. Using personal examples to improve risk communication for security & privacy decisions. In *CHI*, pages 2647–2656. ACM, 2014.

[10] P. G. Kelley, S. Consolvo, L. F. Cranor, J. Jung, N. Sadeh, and D. Wetherall. A conundrum of permissions: installing applications on an android smartphone. In *FC*, pages 68–79. Springer, 2012.

[11] P. G. Kelley, L. F. Cranor, and N. Sadeh. Privacy as part of the app decision-making process. In *CHI*, pages 3393–3402. ACM, 2013.

[12] J. Lin, S. Amini, J. I. Hong, N. Sadeh, J. Lindqvist, and J. Zhang. Expectation and purpose: understanding users' mental models of mobile app privacy through crowdsourcing. In *Ubicomp*, pages 501–510. ACM, 2012.

[13] H. Peng, C. Gates, B. Sarma, N. Li, Y. Qi, R. Potharaju, C. Nita-Rotaru, and I. Molloy. Using probabilistic generative models for ranking risks of android apps. In *CCS*, pages 241–252. ACM, 2012.

[14] B. P. Sarma, N. Li, C. Gates, R. Potharaju, C. Nita-Rotaru, and I. Molloy. Android permissions: a perspective combining risks and benefits. In *SACMAT*, pages 13–22. ACM, 2012.

[15] L. Sjöberg. Factors in risk perception. *Risk Anal.*, 20(1):1–12, 2000.

[16] P. Slovic. Perception of risk. *Science*, 236 (4799):280–285, 1987.

[17] A. Smith. Smartphone ownership–2013 update. *Pew Research Center: Washington DC*, 2013.

[18] R. Xu and D. C. Wunsch. Clustering algorithms in biomedical research: a review. *IEEE R-BME*, 3:120–154, 2010.

APPENDIX

A. SUPPLEMENTAL DATA

Table 3: (Study 1) Summary of responses to the question "What specific types of personal information do you believe are at risk on mobile devices, and how would you rank those in terms of your level of concern?"

Information Type	Mentioned by	Ranked 1st
Address book (contacts)	15	7
Location	14	5
Photos/videos	11	3
Files	9	3
SMS/Email/Chat messages	9	1
Financial info.	6	3
Personally identifying info.	5	3
Login credentials	5	3
Call logs	4	1
Notes	2	2
Todo lists	2	1
Device ID/IMEI	2	0
Browser History	1	1
Calendar	1	1

Table 4: (Study 2) Frequencies of ratings for each app element in response to the question, "How often do you consider that type of information when deciding whether to install an app on your device(s)?" The information elements were ranked (leftmost column) by the mean scores (rightmost column), which were computed as an average of the scores weighted by the response frequency.

Rank	Element	Never (0)	Rarely (1)	Sometimes (2)	Often (3)	Always (4)	Mean Score
1	Description	1	3	37	133	176	3.37
2	Average rating	5	6	27	133	179	3.36
3	Content of reviews	7	16	53	149	125	3.05
4	Number of ratings	10	18	76	147	99	2.88
5	Screenshots	3	27	94	158	68	2.75
6	Ratings distribution	29	32	73	128	88	2.61
7	App permissions	22	41	91	101	95	2.59
8	Number of downloads	12	37	99	143	59	2.57
9	Content Rating	58	38	44	103	107	2.47
10	"Top Developer" designation	58	90	88	81	33	1.83
11	Number of +1's	83	75	79	85	28	1.71
12	Updated On date	62	93	109	60	26	1.70
13	Developer's name	82	131	77	46	14	1.37
14	Version number	91	133	72	40	14	1.29

Table 5: (Study 2) Risk categories derived from the free-response question: "In a few words, what do you personally feel is the biggest risk associated with installing an app on your mobile device(s)?" The frequencies of responses in each category and descriptions of their contents are also provided.

Response Category	# of Responses	Description of Typical Responses
Information Privacy	154	leakage or theft of sensitive information; identity theft; unauthorized data collection; behavioral profiling or tracking for ad purposes
Malware	58	viruses, trojans, spyware, etc.
Device Instability	45	excessive battery or storage space usage; apps that cause device to become sluggish, freeze or restart unexpectedly; apps that interfere with other apps; apps that are difficult to uninstall; apps that cause physical damage to device
Over-privileging	23	apps that request more permissions than legitimately needed, or misuse granted permissions for purposes other than those implied by the app's understood functionality
Functionality	20	apps that function poorly or not at all; apps that do not work as expected or implied by description
Spam	12	SMS (i.e., text) or email marketing; obtrusive notifications or ads
Unknown/Untrusted Developer	10	granting permissions to an unknown or untrusted developer
Monetary	10	unauthorized access to financial information or accounts; accidental purchases; app not being worth the price paid
Insecure Behavior	5	apps that expose device to vulnerabilities due to negligence (e.g., transferring sensitive data over an insecure connection)
None	7	not concerned; no perceived risks

Table 6: (Study 2) Frequencies of ratings for each risk type in response to the question, "Please indicate how concerned you are about that type of risk when installing apps on your mobile device(s)." The risk types were ranked by the mean scores, which were computed as an average of the scores weighted by the response frequency.

Rank	Risk Type	Not at all (0)	Slightly (1)	Somewhat (2)	Moderately (3)	Extremely (4)	Mean Score
1	Personal privacy	6	14	44	111	175	3.24
2	Personal data integrity	12	25	47	116	150	3.05
3	Eavesdropping or Spying	19	23	61	93	154	2.97
4	Device instability	8	43	96	121	82	2.65
5	Spam	17	44	90	109	90	2.60
6	Monetary or financial risks	27	59	66	83	115	2.57
7	Physical damage to device	113	68	38	60	71	1.74

Table 7: (Study 2) Frequencies of ratings in response to the question, "Thinking about your personal privacy, how concerned are you about apps having access to each of the following types of information?" The information types were ranked by the mean scores, which were computed as an average of the scores weighted by the response frequency.

Rank	Information Type	Not at all (0)	Slightly (1)	Somewhat (2)	Moderately (3)	Extremely (4)	Mean Score
1	Personally identifying information	7	22	34	66	221	3.35
2	Passwords and login credentials	11	18	33	70	218	3.33
3	Financial information	14	15	35	81	205	3.28
4	Texts/emails/chat messages	16	40	57	112	125	2.83
5	Personal photos or videos	19	43	56	114	118	2.77
6	Exact location	19	43	80	82	126	2.72
7	Contacts	19	38	72	120	101	2.70
8	Files	17	47	69	115	102	2.68
9	Call logs	38	56	73	104	79	2.37
10	General location	29	68	79	101	73	2.35
11	Web browsing history	43	54	90	89	74	2.28
12	Calendar	113	81	68	52	36	1.48
13	Notes or todo lists	122	77	64	55	32	1.42

SemaDroid: A Privacy-Aware Sensor Management Framework for Smartphones

Zhi Xu
Pennsylvania State University
University Park, PA, USA
zhi.xu.cs@gmail.com

Sencun Zhu
Pennsylvania State University
University Park, PA, USA
szhu@cse.psu.edu

ABSTRACT

While mobile sensing applications are booming, the sensor management mechanisms in current smartphone operating systems are left behind – they are incomprehensive and coarse-grained, exposing a huge attack surface for malicious or aggressive third party apps to steal user's private information through mobile sensors.

In this paper, we propose a privacy-aware sensor management framework, called *SemaDroid*, which extends the existing sensor management framework on Android to provide comprehensive and fine-grained access control over onboard sensors. SemaDroid allows the user to monitor the sensor usage of installed apps, and to control the disclosure of sensing information while not affecting the app's usability. Furthermore, SemaDroid supports context-aware and quality-of-sensing based access control policies. The enforcement and update of the policies are in real-time. Detailed design and implementation of SemaDroid on Android are presented to show that SemaDroid works compatible with the existing Android security framework. Demonstrations are also given to show the capability of SemaDroid on sensor management and on defeating emerging sensor-based attacks. Finally, we show the high efficiency and security of SemaDroid.

Categories and Subject Descriptors

C.2.m [**Computer-Communication Networks**]: Miscellaneous;
C.2.0 [**General**]: Security and protection

Keywords

Sensor management, phone sensing, smartphone, Android, privacy-aware

1. INTRODUCTION

Nowadays, high-resolution sensors have been widely applied in mobile applications to support innovative mobile user interfaces [15] [5], user authentication [4] [1], context-aware applications [44] [3], well-being monitoring [30] [2], wearable devices (e.g., GoogleGlass), and collaborative data collection applications [17, 7]. In all these apps, various types of sensors are either shipped within the smartphone or equipped on wearable devices. The data collected from those sensors are gathered by the smartphone OS and then dispatched to different mobile apps.

As more and more high-precision sensors are introduced, greater concerns are raised that the collected sensing data may be abused by installed third party apps to infer sensitive information that users do not want to share. Recently, many sensor-based mobile context inference techniques [34, 33] and user activity recognition techniques [32, 33] have been developed for good purposes. However, such techniques can be equally abused to infer user's sensitive information. Recent studies on offensive technologies have also shown prototypes of innovative sensor-based attacks on smartphones, including location tracking attacks (with GPS [29, 19] and accelerometer [22]), stealthy video capturing attack (with camera [45]), audio-based logging attack (with microphone [42]), vibration-based logging attack on keystrokes of nearby keyboards (with accelerometer [35]), vibration-based logging attack on user touchscreen inputs (with motion sensors [46, 11, 40]).

These merging sensor-based attacks expose the flaws and ineffectiveness of existing permission-based sensor management systems, which were designed to protect traditional types of sensitive information, such as contact lists and confidential files. Differently, the sensitivity of sensor data depends on the context in which the data was collected and the quality of data (e.g., precision). Existing permission-based access control can only help decide if an app is allowed to access particular sensors. Once permissions are granted, the user has no knowledge or control over the actual sensor usage. For example, the trojan app Soundcomber [42] first tricks the user to grant the permission for audio recording and then stealthily abuses the privilege to record the voice of a user during phone calls. Thus, simply introducing more permissions for onboard sensors will not help protect users from sensor-based attacks.

In this paper, we propose a privacy-aware sensor management framework, named *SemaDroid*. Extending the existing sensor management framework on Android, SemaDroid is a general framework for managing a comprehensive list of on-board sensors to enable flexible and effective sensor data access control. It covers not only the permission-associated sensors, e.g., GPS and camera, but also sensors overlooked by the existing sensor management system, e.g., accelerometer, orientation, and proximity sensors.

Specifically, we consider the onboard sensors as *Service Providers*, the installed sensing apps as *Service Consumers*, and then introduces the notion of *Quality-of-Sensing (QoSn)* to measure the quality of sensor data supplied by sensors to sensing apps. Based on this provider-consumer relation, SemaDroid allows the user to monitor the sensor usage of an installed third party app from the perspectives of (1) the context under which the sensor data is collected and (2) the QoSn of data that is collected from the onboard sensors. Then, SemaDroid allows the user to manage the sensor usage by specifying context-aware and QoSn-based sensor usage policies and enforcing the policies in real time. Our sensor data management model supports not only local third-party apps, but also general-purpose participatory sensing applications (e.g., citizen science and journalism, building noise/pollution/WiFi maps) where participating phones contribute their own sensing data to a remote data collector. Instead of installing one third-party app for each type of participatory sensing, which might be privacy-invasive itself, our model results in a new paradigm for participating sensing by downloading and enforcing third-party sensing policies that must conform to user's local sensing policy.

To balance the privacy and desired functionalities, SemaDroid provides a *Privacy Bargain* feature, which allows the user to interactively refine the SemaDroid sensor usage policies. This is based on the observation that the content of sensor data collected may always contain more or less information about the user, and the user may be willing to bargain the QoSn of a sensor in exchange for relative rewards of desired functionalities. Moreover, SemaDroid provides QoSn adjustment services that generates continuous adjusted sensor data for different types of sensors. The generated data can simulate the real sensor readings with little private information, or are purely random data. Such services allow the user to feed the sensing app with quality-adjusted data in order to keep the app running while not sacrificing (much) user privacy.

We present the design of SemaDroid on Android version 4.0.3. Framework design and implementation details are presented to show that SemaDroid works compatible with the existing permission based access control system on Android from 4.0 to 4.4.

2. SENSING ON SMARTPHONES

Phone sensing applications rely on apps installed on smartphones to receive sensor data from OS [31]. Those collected data may be consumed locally or forwarded to a more powerful remote server [17]. In this paper, our study focuses on the management of sensor data collection performed by installed third party apps.

2.1 Sensors on Smartphones

According to the associated security permissions, we classify sensors on Android into two groups, unrestricted sensors and restricted sensors. Accessing unrestricted sensors requires no security permission. These types of sensors are all governed by the *SensorManager* system service on Android. Accessing restricted sensors requires the app to declare corresponding security permissions (e.g., *CAMERA*) in its Manifest file. Each type of restricted sensor has its specific sensor management service, e.g., the *LocationManagerService* for GPS. Specifically,[1]

- Unrestricted sensors include accelerometer, ambient temperature sensor, gravity sensor, gyroscope sensor, light sensor, magnetic field sensor, orientation sensor, atmosphere pressure sensor, proximity sensor, etc.
- Restricted sensors include GPS, camera, and microphone.

To investigate the popularity of sensor usage, we downloaded more than 12, 000 top ranked free apps from 7 popular categories

---

[1]Communication sensors are not considered in this paper, such as cellular network, wifi, bluetooth, and NFC. Also, touchscreen is not included because, on Android, only the app running in foreground and displayed on the touchscreen is allowed to receive touch event information from the touchscreen. Furthermore, featured sensors, such as the fingerprint reader [36], are not considered as they have only been equipped on selected smartphone models and are not supported by standard Android SDK.

Table 1: **Percentage of apps using different sensors**

Category	Unrestricted sensors	GPS	Camera	Microphone
Game	53.57%	57.92%	20.81%	2.52%
Business	15.77%	54.73%	12.24%	2.98%
Book & Reference	7.91%	47.84%	2.38%	0.15%
Comics	25.85%	33.47%	12.24%	2.98%
Communication	15.62%	38.51%	9.76%	6.43%
Education	16.67%	42.01%	6.96%	6.39%
Entertainment	14.24%	40.13%	5.61%	3.41%
Average	22.65%	47.89%	11.39%	2.52%

in the Google Play App store. Static analysis is then performed with the help of reverse engineer tool [9] to analyze the sensor usage of individual apk. The number of apps downloaded from each category is slightly different. For example, the comics category in Google lists much fewer apps than the game category. As listed in Table 1, Game is the category that accesses sensors the most, and GPS is the most popular sensor type. Overall, from the dataset we collected, we observed that accessing sensors (e.g., GPS and unrestricted sensors) is a common behavior of third party apps.

2.2 Workflow of Sensor Data Collection

We use an example of accessing the accelerometer sensor to briefly illustrate the procedure of sensor data collection on Android. To request sensor data from accelerometer, an installed sensing app first sends a registration request to the *SensorManager* system service. In the request, the sensing app specifies the desired sensor type (e.g., accelerometer), the (recommended) data sampling rate, and the *SensorEventListener* that is implemented within the sensing app. Upon receiving the request, the *SensorManager* creates a *ListenerDelegate* thread for this sensing app, passes the parameters to the thread, and then maps the thread to a *SensorThread*, which receives sensor events from the accelerometer driver. For accelerometer, a sensor event includes a vector of sampled *values[]* and a timestamp of sampling. The sensor event will be passed backwards to the designated *SensorEventListener* in the sensing app. The procedures of sensor data collection on other sensors are similar to that of accessing the accelerometer. Furthermore, accessing restricted sensors requires certain security permissions.

2.3 Existing Sensor Management on Android

The existing sensor management system on Android relies on a general permission-based access control system. During the installation of a sensing app, the smartphone user will be notified of security permissions claimed by this app. The installation will be pursued only if the user agrees to grant all the claimed security permissions. If an app attempts to access a sensor whose security permission is not stated in the Manifest file, the access will be denied by Android OS and a security exception will be thrown. Clearly, the existing permission-based access control system is not suitable for sensor management as it only provides management on the access privileges without any management on the sensor usage. Because Android supports multitasking, installed apps running in the background can stealthily collect sensor data from desired sensors, as long as the sensors are unrestricted or the corresponding security permissions have been granted.

2.4 Security Model

2.4.1 Attack Model

The attackers in our work are installed third party apps which attempt to collect sensor data when a user is not willing to share it. Such apps include (1) malware (e.g., Trojan apps proposed in [46,

42]) that attempt to infer sensitive user information from collected sensor data; and (2) adware that attempt to improve their functionalities, e.g., collecting location information for ads targeting and news delivery [16]. As the third party apps have already been installed on the smartphone, we assume that they have gained permissions to access the sensors they request. Also, we assume that all apps access the sensors via APIs specified in the standard Android sdk (Android 4.0.3 SDK [20]). Web applications running in mobile browsers may also be able to access onboard sensors (e.g., GPS) via APIs provided by mobile browsers. In this case, these web applications will be treated the same as the web browser.

2.4.2 Trust Model

We assume that the Android OS is not compromised. SemaDroid is implemented within the Application Framework layout of Android OS. Hence, the security of SemaDroid is protected by the Android OS. SemaDroid only communicates with components within the Android OS and none of its APIs is exposed to third party apps. Third party apps have neither the knowledge about the existence of SemaDroid, nor the access to the APIs of SemaDroid.

3. SEMADROID DESIGN

In this section, we present the design of *SemaDroid*, which allows the user to track the sensor usage of installed apps and then control the sensor usage by enforcing user customized policies.

3.1 SemaDroid Framework Design

In Figure 1, we present an overview of sensor usage management in SemaDroid. Basically, SemaDroid consists of four components and a set of hooks (named *SemaHook*) embedded within the existing modules of Android.

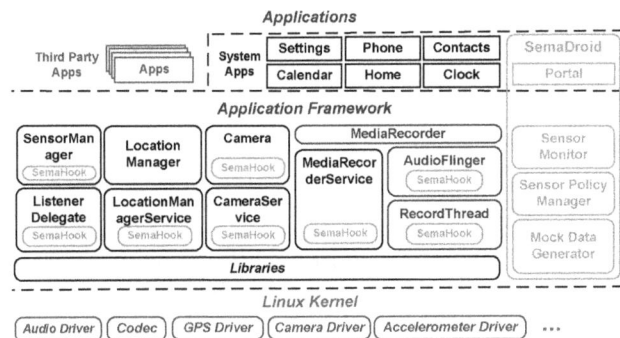

Figure 1: The design of SemaDroid framework on Android

Portal App is a SemaDroid app located within the $/system/app$ folder, like the default *Contact* and *Settings* apps of Android. It is implemented as a user interface app that allows the user to interact with the SemaDroid framework. Through the Portal app, the user can view the sensor usage of all installed third party apps, create sensor usage policies, and enforce the policies in real-time.
SensorMonitor is implemented as a system service with APIs accessible only inside the Android OS or by the Portal app. Sensor Monitor provides two services. First, Sensor Monitor keeps tracking the sensor usage of every installed app so that the Portal app can retrieve the sensor usage information and show it to the user for review. Second, SensorMonitor is the interface for SemaHook to query for sensor usage policies. When receiving a policy query from a SemaHook, SensorMonitor will fetch the corresponding sensor usage policy from the *SensorPolicyManager* service, extract the enforcement rules from policies, and then return the rules to the requester SemaHook for enforcement.

SensorPolicyManager is implemented as a system service with APIs accessible only by SensorMonitor and Portal. It maintains all sensor usage policies and answers policy queries from SensorMonitor. Besides, together with the Portal, Sensor Policy Manager allows the user to create and customize the sensor usage policies.
MockSensorDataGenerator is a featured service provided by SemaDroid. Briefly, it maintains a set of threads that generate mock sensor data for different sensor types. SemaDroid allows the user to replace the real sensor data with mock data so as to keep the app running while not sacrificing his privacy.
SemaHooks are codes we place within the existing Android components. The major functions of SemaHooks include intercepting sensor access requests from apps, communicating with SensorMonitor service, and enforcing sensor usage policies during the sensor data collection.

3.2 SemaDroid Workflow

We briefly explain how SemaDroid works from two aspects.

3.2.1 Allowing Sensor Usage Management

The smartphone user interacts with SemaDroid through the *Portal* app, which provides a sensor usage review function and a policy management function. With the sensor usage review function, the user can review a sensor usage report for an individual app. Figure 2 shows a simple user interface for reviewing low-level sensor usage (More user friendly UI can also be designed to aggregate low-level usage information for more in-depth usage anomaly analysis.) A sensor usage report consists of sensor usage records on all accessed sensors. Each usage record is described by the starting time, usage duration, and a set of phone state descriptions within this duration. The phone state descriptions are used to indicate the context of sensor data usage. The Portal app shows the existing SemaDroid policies associated with each installed app. It allows the user to create new sensor usage policies and customize the existing sensor usage policies.

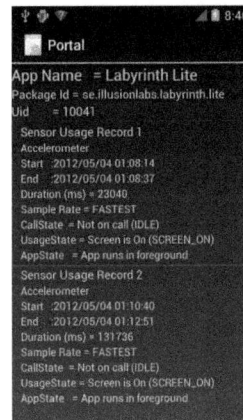

Figure 2: A demonstration of sensor usage report

3.2.2 Enforcing Sensor Usage Policies

In SemaDroid, the policy enforcement workflow starts from the embedded SemaHook when a sensor access request is intercepted. Here, we briefly explain the common steps in policy enforcement. Enforcement details will be presented in Section 6.
Step 1 Interception: When a sensor access request is intercepted, SemaHook will send the requested sensor type with the requester app's *uid* to the *SensorMonitor* service, asking for rules to enforce.

Step 2 Policy Retrieval: With the sensor type and *uid*, *SensorMonitor* retrieves a set of stored sensor usage policies (if existing) from the *SensorPolicyManager*. Each policy contains a description of its enforcement context, detailing the context under which this policy can be applied (as in Figure 3). *SensorMonitor* will filter the retrieved policies with the current context, such as current time and phone states. With the policies applicable in the current context, *SensorMonitor* retrieves the enforcement rules of the requested sensor type and returns them to SemaHook for enforcement.

Step 3 Rule Enforcement: Those received enforcement rules contain the guidance about how this sensor data collection should be performed. SemaHook will then enforce the received enforcement rules during sensor data collection.

4. SENSOR USAGE POLICY DESIGN AND ENFORCEMENT

SemaDroid allows the user to control sensing apps by placing fine-grained policies on their sensor usages instead of simply following the privileges of sensor access. A sensor usage policy describes in what context sensor data collection can be performed and the best quality of sensor data that is allowed to collect. For example, an informal example sensor usage policy may state *"app A is allowed to collect sensor data from accelerometer, between 1:00 am and 8:00 am, with sample rate no greater than 20 Hz"*.

In SemaDroid, a sensor usage policy consists of three sections: *Policy Property*, *Enforcement Context*, and *Quality-of-Sensing(QoSn) based Enforcement Rules*. A policy file is organized in standard XML format as shown in Figure 3.

```
<!-- Enforcement Rules -->
<rule sensortype="Accelerometer" originalmanager="SensorManager" sensorid="1">
 <!-- lower the sampling rate -->
 <action type="Rate" method="Times">
  <parameter>0.5</parameter>
 </action>
</rule>
<rule sensortype="Magnetic Field" originalmanager="SensorManager" sensorid="2">
 <!-- lower the precision of sensor readings -->
 <action type="Manipulate" method="Round">
  <parameter>values</parameter><parameter>1</parameter><parameter>0.1</parameter>
 </action>
</rule>
```

Figure 3: An example of SemaDroid policy

4.1 Policy Property

The Policy Property section includes the information about the app under management and the policy modification information.

app-info Section: A sensor usage policy supports one or multiple apps. Each app is identified by its package identification. When the *SensorPolicyManager* service loads the policy, it will contact the *PackageManager* and get the corresponding *uid*. Policy enforcement is based on *uid* instead of package name. Multiple apps with the same uid can share policies with one another.

SemaDroid also supports two special app package names. One is *"***.***.app"*, called *all-app*, which represents all third party apps. The other is *"***.***.root"*, called *all-root*, which represents all *uids* including system apps.

policy-info Section: The *policy-info* section keeps the version information of the policy. User can create a policy through the SemaDroid Portal system app, or load a policy file from the sd card.

4.2 Policy Enforcement Context

The *Enforcement Context* section specifies the context restrictions for policy enforcement. The policy can be applied if and only if all restrictions described in the *Context* sections are satisfied. Currently, SemaDroid supports the following restrictions:

Temporal Duration restriction describes the effective date and expiration date (*startdate* and *enddate*), repeating starting time and end time in a day (*repeatstarttime* and *repeatendtime*), etc.

Phone State restriction is tagged by *"phonestate"*. SemaDroid supports the set of telephone states maintained by *TelephonyManager* [20]. For example, *CALL_STATE_IDLE* indicates that the user is not making phone calls. SemaDroid determines the current telephone state by querying the *Context.TELEPHONY_SERVICE*.

Usage State restriction is determined by monitoring the Intent broadcasted by Android. Currently, we heuristically select several typical states according to the attacks we attempt to defeat. One example is the *SCREEN_ON* state, which states that the screen is turned on.

App State restriction describes the running status of sensing apps. SemaDroid determines the running status of an app, either foreground or background, by contacting the *ActivityManager* for the *RunningAppProcessInfo* of app.

These stated restrictions help make context-aware sensor usage policies. For example, enforcing policy on microphone when the user is on the call can easily defeat the attacks that stealthily record audio during phone calls, and enforcing policy on motion sensors when the screen is turned on can defeat the attacks that infer user inputs via tapping touchscreen.

Location-based restrictions are not currently supported because checking the current location upon every policy query will introduce significant delay. While keeping tracking the location information may lower the delay, it is costly in battery consumption.

4.3 Quality-of-Sensing based Enforcement Rules

The QoSn-based *Enforcement Rules* allow the user to manage the sensor usage of a sensing app by controlling the quality of sensor data supplied to this app. When no enforcement rule is applied, the sensing app will always get the sensor data with finest QoSn (a.k.a., *Original QoSn*), which is determined by hardware specification, the sensor driver, and the version of Android OS.

By enforcing the rules, SemaDroid allows the user to lower the QoSn by adjusting sensing parameters, manipulating sensor data, and even supplying mock data. For example, in Figure 3, the enforcement rule on accelerometer states that, the actual sampling rate of accelerometer will be 0.5 times of the original sampling rate specified by the sensing app. The enforcement rule on magnetic field sensor states that the first reading in the *value[]* of collected *SensorEvent* will be round to a multiple of 0.1. The round-off errors from the raw reading are intentionally introduced to lower the QoSn of sensing service provided by the onboard magnetic field sensor.

4.4 Policy Enforcement

Sensor usage policies are enforced by SemaHooks through either the sensing parameters or the collected sensor data.

Through Parameters: Android allows the sensing app to guide the sensor data collection by specifying sensing parameters, such as the sampling rate for accelerometer and the image size for camera. These specified parameters will be intercepted by *SemaHook* with the sensing request. SemaDroid allows the user to specify enforcement rules to manipulate the values of original parameters, such as the sampling rate in Figure 3. Adjusting sensing parameters is the simplest approach to control the QoSn.

Through Collected Sensor Data: when the sensor data collected by the Sensor Driver arrives at the *Application Framework* layer, the *SemaHook* will intercept the sensor data and enforce sensor usage policies before forwarding it to the sensing app. For example, in Figure 3, the enforcement rules on magnetic field sensor is enforced on collected sensor data.

5. PRIVACY BARGAIN

User privacy has been defined in different research fields. In the context of mobile sensing, sensors act as service providers supplying user's personal (context) information to sensing apps. Thus, we adopt the definition of user privacy that is widely accepted in personal information privacy study: *user privacy is the ability of an individual to control the access others have to his/her personal information* [14]. The control of user's privacy refers to the ability to decide the amount and depth of information collected through the sensor data collection procedure.

In this section, we show how *SemaDroid* can allow the user to bargain over their personal information in exchange of desired functions of sensing apps.

5.1 Definition of Privacy Bargain

Privacy Bargain is a concept where the users are willing to trade off privacy for desired functions or to bargain the release of personal information in exchange of relatively small rewards [6, 12, 23]. Privacy bargain has been widely studied in the individual decision process with respect to user information privacy [6] and user online information privacy [12, 23].

During sensor data collection, the readings collected from onboard sensors contain user's personal information as these readings are measured by examining the surrounding context of smartphones. For example, readings collected from motion sensors are widely used to infer the type of user activities [32, 33]. Thus, in our case, privacy bargain stands for the case when the user releases sensing information to sensing apps in return for desired functions of sensing apps.

5.2 Bargain Procedure using SemaDroid

SemaDroid provides the privacy bargain capacity by allowing the user to review the sensor usage report of a sensing app via the Portal app, and then adjust the QoSn of sensing data by changing the policies. For example, at the higher sampling rate or the higher precision the readings are generated, the better QoSn the sensor can provide, thus more private information the sensing data may carry. Admittedly, lowering the QoSn (e.g., providing vague or mock sensor data) may affect some functionalities of sensing apps. However, from the perspective of users, if the functionalities are not desired, such as ads, feeding vague or mock sensing data would not be a problem as long as their desired functionalities, e.g., game control, are not affected.

5.3 QoSn Adjustment using SemaDroid

To adjust the QoSn, SemaDroid supports three types of enforcement rules: *Data Adjustment Rules*, *Data Manipulation Rules*, and *Mock Data Rules*. The differences lie on the operations supported on the collected sensor data.

5.3.1 Data Adjustment Rules

Data Adjustment Rules do not alter the content of collected sensor data directly. Instead, they are rules for adjusting the sampling rate, or dropping selected sensor readings according to certain criteria. *Data Adjustment Rules* can be applied when the user is conservative in providing sensing data, but the correctness of reported sensor events is critical to the desired functionalities of the sensing app. The user would lower the QoSn but still provide accurate sensor data. For example, the user may adjust the sampling rate of GPS to a monitoring app to avoid precise location tracking.

5.3.2 Data Manipulation Rules

Data Manipulation Rules allow the user to manipulate the content of collected sensor data or adding noise. Typical *Data Manipulation Rules* include rounding the values in the sensor data to approximate values, replacing particular sensor readings by mock readings, manipulating the content of sensor events (e.g., adding watermarks to images taken by the camera), and adding noise such as mock readings. The mock readings are either generated randomly according to the specification of rules, or loaded from sensor events recorded previously in a trace file.

Data Manipulation Rules are suitable in cases when the user is suspicious of sensor data abuse in certain sensing apps. For example, to avoid inferring sensitive tap events on the touchscreen from collected motion sensor readings in the TapLogger attack [46], the user may intentionally add noise to the reported readings.

5.3.3 Mock Data Rules

Mock Data Rules allow the user to completely replace the collected sensor data by mock data. This option enables the user to prohibit particular apps from getting any real context information, while keeping the app running. For example, many apps require sensor data from GPS for the ads libraries [16, 25]. If the user is not interested in the content of advertisement, SemaDroid allows the user to provide mock GPS information to the app.

5.3.4 Rules Refinement

The *Privacy Bargain* function allows the user to refine their specified enforcement rules. Briefly, the user may keep reducing the QoSn starting from the *Data Adjustment Rules* until the *Mock Data Rules*. If feeding the sensing apps with the current enforcement rules causes little or even no side effect to the desired functionalities, the user can safely enjoy the desired functionalities without sacrificing his/her privacy.

6. IMPLEMENTATION OF SEMADROID

An overview of SemaDroid implementation was presented in Figure 1. In this section, we present some implementation details on Android (version 4.0.3). Due to space limit, we take the set of sensors managed by *SensorManager* and GPS as two examples to explain the detailed policy enforcement procedure with SemaDroid. For SemaDroid implementations with camera and microphone, we briefly explain the differences in their implementations and enforcement procedures. A summary of all currently supported enforcement rules are listed in Table 2 for reference. Besides, as to SemaDroid itself, we focus on the *Mock Data Generator* service whose details have not been discussed.

6.1 Unrestricted Sensors

In Android, *SensorManager* is a system service that allows sensing apps to access all unrestricted sensors, including accelerometer, ambient temperature sensor, gravity sensor, gyroscope, ambient light sensor, magnetic field sensor, orientation sensor, atmosphere pressure sensor, proximity sensor, relative humidity sensor, and temperature sensor [20]. All sensors governed by *SensorManager* require no security permission to access and can be accessed by apps running in the background. Figure 4 shows how SemaDroid enforces sensor usage policies on these unrestricted sensors.

6.1.1 Normal Sensor Data Collection

To access an unrestricted sensor, a sensing app will first prepare a class *SensorEventListener* for the coming sensor events[2],

---

[2] The sensing app may also specify a *Handler* for sensor events

Table 2: Enforcement rules supported by SemaDroid on different sensors(variables in () are parameters)

Sensor Types	Enforcement Targets	*Type* in Rules	*Method* in Rules
Unrestricted Sensors (accelerometer, orientation sensor, etc.)	On Parameters (Delay)	Rate	Set, Times, AllowedRange;
	On Collected Sensor Data (a *SensorEvent* consists of accuracy, timestamp, values[])	AdjustSampleRate	Times;
		AdjustTimeInterval	Set, Times;
		Manipulate	FilterWithFixed,FilterWithRandom, Times, Set, Round;
		Mock	Random, TraceFile;
GPS	On Parameters (minTime, minDistance, criteria, etc.)	minTime, minDistance, criteria, etc.	Set, AllowedRange;
	On Collected Sensor Data (A *Location* consists of latitude, longitude, etc.)	AdjustSampleRate	Times;
		AdjustTimeInterval	Set, Times;
		Manipulate	FilterWithFixed,FilterWithRandom, Set, Round;
		Mock	Random, TraceFile;
Camera (picture)	On Parameters (output file, picture size, flash mode, etc.)	output file, picture size, flash mode, etc.	Set, AllowedRange;
	On Collected Sensor Data (A picture is represented by a byte[])	Manipulate	WaterMark, FilterWithFixed,FilterWithRandom, Set;
		Mock	Random, TraceFile;
Microphone (Audio Recording)	On Parameters (output file, output format, audio encorder, etc.)	output file, output format, audio encorder, etc.	Set;
	On Collected Sensor Data (A frame is represented by a Buffer object)	Manipulate	FilterWithFixed,FilterWithRandom, Set;
		Mock	Random, TraceFile;
Microphone and Camera (Video Recording)	On Parameters (output file, video size, video frame rate, etc.)	output file, video size, video frame rate, etc.	Set;
	On Collected Sensor Data (On the output file directly)	Manipulate	Cut
		Mock	Empty, TraceFile;

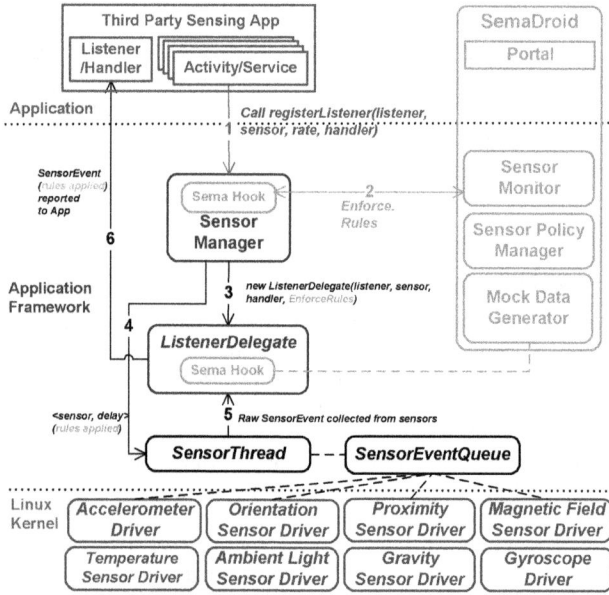

Figure 4: Enforcing sensor usage policies on sensors managed by *SensorManager* with SemaDroid

and then register the listener to the *SensorManager* by calling the function *registerListener()*. Within *SensorManager*, a *ListenerDelegate* thread will be created and associated to the *SensorThread* that keeps monitoring the *SensorEventQueue* by calling *sensors_data_poll*. When a sensor event is polled from the SensorEventQueue, the *SensorThread* will report the sensor event to all *ListenerDelegate* threads that care about it. A *ListenerDelegate* then forwards the received sensor event to *SensorEventListener* within the sensing app.

During the collection, the sensing app is only allowed to send a sampling rate option with the registration request. This option is one of the following: (*SENSOR_DELAY*)_*FASTEST*, _*GAME*, _*UI*, and _*NORMAL* (from the fastest to the slowest). Within *SensorManager*, the sampling rate option is converted into different delays between two sampling actions, e.g., *SENSOR_DELAY_NORMAL*

is converted into 200000ns.[3] A sensor event collected from sensor driver is a vector of values $< accuracy, sensor\_type, timestamp, values[] >$.

6.1.2 Policy Enforcement with SemaDroid

SemaDroid intercepts the sensor request by the *SemaHook* placed in *SensorManager*. When a sensor request is intercepted, the *SemaHook* will send the requested sensor type and the *uid* of requester app to the *SensorMonitor* service, which retrieves sensor usage policies from *SensorPolicyManager* and returns the enforcement rules applicable in the current context to the *SemaHook*. The enforcement rules can be applied either by the SemaHook in *SensorManager* on sampling delay, or by the SemaHook in *ListenerDelegate* on collected raw sensor events. We list the supported enforcement rules in Table 2.

6.2 GPS and Network Location Providers

Figure 5(a) shows the implementation of SemaDroid with GPS.

6.2.1 Normal Sensor Data Collection

In Android, the source of location information is called *Location Provider*. SemaDroid supports all types of location providers, including *GPS* that determines locations using satellites, *Network* that determines locations using cell towers and WiFi access points, and *Passive* that passively monitors location updates reported by other providers. Here we take GPS as the default location provider in our discussion.

Specifically, Android allows installed third party apps to access the location information by two approaches through the *LocationManager* system service. One approach is to register an update listener, such as *LocationListener* or *BroadcastReciver* (updates sent out as *Intents*), which obtains periodic updates of smartphone's geographical locations from the location provider. The sensing app

---

[3]Note that, this (recommended) delay will be sent to the sensor driver; but, the actual sampling rate is ultimately determined by the sensor driver. Thus, the real sampling delay on the device might not be the recommended value.

can specify a set of parameters (e.g., a criteria) with the registration request to guide the sampling of location updates. The other approach is to get the last known location record stored by the *LocationManagerService*.

As shown in Figure 5(a), the request for location information is actually fulfilled by the *LocationManagerService*. Unlike the unrestricted sensors, GPS in Android is associated with security permissions, e.g., *ACCESS_FINE_LOCATION*. Thus, a permission check will be performed before starting sampling. A location update collected is a *Location* object, containing location information including latitude, longitude, timestamp, altitude, etc. When an update is received by the *LocationManagerService*, it will be forwarded to the listener of the sensing app and be used to renew the last known location record.

6.2.2 Policy Enforcement with SemaDroid

Similar to that with *SensorManager*, SemaDroid places one SemaHook right after the permission check to intercept the location request from sensing apps, and get the enforcement rules from the *SensorMonitor*. According to the content, the received rules will be either enforced locally on the parameters with the request, or be enforced by the other two SemaHooks on the collected location updates (i.e., the sensor data).

Several system services also provide a location tagging option. For example, when taking images from the camera, the app is allowed to add geographic location tags into the image taken. In this case, the location request will not go through the *LocationManager*, but be handled by *LocationManagerService*. In either case, the location tagging service is under the management of SemaDroid policies.

6.3 Camera

Camera in Android provides two functions, taking pictures and recording video clips. Both functions allow the sensing app to specify an output file location for the sensor data collected from camera (i.e., pictures and video clips). Android also supports a preview function that allows the app running on the screen to display a preview window of camera. However, this sensing app does not have access to the data in the preview window as the display and the data received in the preview window is controlled by Android OS. Thus, SemaDroid focuses on the case when the collected sensor data is saved into designated files.

Android supports two approaches to take pictures by an app. One approach is by directly calling the function Camera.takePicture(). A *PictureCallback* function has to be specified in the sensing app to handle the collected picture. The other approach is by using other camera services (e.g., that of the Camera system app of Android) to take pictures. In this case, the sensing app has to specify the *onActivityResult* function for pictures returned through *Intents*. For both approaches, the picture taking request will be handled by *CameraService*, which assigns a *Client* to perform the sensor data collection and return the collected pictures to the app.

SemaDroid places a SemaHook right after the permission check (i.e. *CAMERA* permission) in the *CameraService* so as to intercept the request and enforce the sensor usage policies on the parameters specified by the sensing app. When the Client receives the picture (an array of data), the SemaHook in the Client will enforce the policies on the collected image, if a policy exists.

6.4 Microphone

Android allows the sensing app to record audio data from microphone to a designated output file. To the sensing app, the microphone is accessed by creating a *MediaRecorder* object and specifying the parameters for it. Inside Android, the sensing request will be handled by *AudioFlinger* service, which creates a *RecordThread* for sensor data collection. Specifically, the audio data is sampled frame by frame and each frame consists of an array of values.

SemaDroid places a SemaHook right after the *AUDIO* permission check in the *AudioFlinger* for policies enforced through parameters. When the *RecordThread* is assigned to this sensing request, the enforcement rules on collected sensor data will be passed to the SemaHook in the *RecordThread*.

6.5 Media Recorder

Similar to picture taking, the sensing app records video clips either through the *MediaRecorder* or the Intent (i.e., requesting the video recording service provided by other apps). Inside Android, the recording request is handled by the *MediaRecorderClient*.

Thus, SemaDroid places a SemaHook right after the permission check in the *MediaRecorderClient* for policies enforced on parameters. Different from picture taking, *MediaRecorderClient* relies on the underlying libraries to perform the recording task. Briefly, within the libraries, a buffer will be created for the frames captured from camera. Data in the buffer will be streamed to the designated output file directly. Thus, for enforcement rules on collected sensor data, the SemaHook in the *MediaRecorderClient* will enforce the rules on the output file, not on the stream video data.

6.6 Mock Data Generator Service

The *Mock Data Generator* service maintains a set of worker threads that generate mock data values according to the specified sensor types and enforcement rules. For every mock data request from SemaHook, the *Mock Data Generator* service assigns a separate worker thread. This thread ends when notified by the requester SemaHook. For example, when the sensing app unregisters a listener for the GPS, its serving worker thread will be ended.

To lower the workload of a worker thread and improve the scalability, the worker thread only generates a sequence of values used for policy enforcement instead of (complete) sensor events. For example, if the enforcement rule is to generate mock longitude and latitude for GPS, the worker thread will generate a vector of only two values for a sensor event from GPS, instead of making an Android *Location* object. During enforcement, the SemaHook receiving this vector of values will then replace the longitude and latitude values of the genuine *Location* object received from GPS with the mock values. To the sensing app, the received location information will be mostly real except the longitude and latitude values.

We note that for testing purpose, Android provides a *Mock_Location* provider function that allows the app to create a mock location provider with one fixed mock location, and read this fixed mock location from it. However, this mock location provider does not generate continuous location updates. Moreover, for the app under test, it requires a security permission *ACCESS_MOCK_LOCATION* to create such a mock location provider. It also needs the cooperation from the user by turning on the mock location option in the settings.

7. APPLICATIONS AND DEMONSTRATION

7.1 Preventing Sensitive Sensor Data Leakage

The Portal app allows the smartphone user to review the sensor usage reports of all installed apps. When suspicious sensor usages are detected, the user can create fine-grained sensor usage policies to place restrictions to such apps. Here, we select two sensor-based trojan attacks *Soundcomber* [42] and *TapLogger* [46] as examples to demonstrate the effectiveness of SemaDroid.

7.1.1 Sensor Usage Review

Briefly, *Soundcomber* is a trojan app that stealthily records the voice of user during phone calls, and then extracts sensitive information (e.g., credit card number) from the logged audio records. With SemaDroid, all the accesses to the microphone sensor by *Soundcomber* will be logged. By reviewing the sensor usage reports, the user can see that *Soundcomber* always accesses microphone during phone calls (i.e., "*phonestate = OnCall*").

TapLogger is a trojan app that stealthily monitors the motion changes of smartphones so as to infer the password of screen lock and the numbers entered during a phone call (e.g., credit card). With SemaDroid, all the accesses to accelerometer and orientation sensors by *TapLogger* will be logged. By reviewing the sensor usage reports, the user may see that the *TapLogger* always accesses these two sensors in the background (i.e., "*appstate = Background*"), when the screen is on (i.e., "*usagestate = ScreenOn*"). If the attacks are performed during phone calls, the "*phonestate*" will also be *OnCall*.

7.1.2 Privacy Policy Design

With the suspicious access behavior detected, the user may decide to uninstall the corresponding sensing apps. However, suppose the suspicious accesses only happen occasionally or the user is not certain about the suspicion. The user may still want to keep the suspicious app for certain desired functionalities. In this case, SemaDroid allows the user to create sensor usage policies to place restrictions on those suspicious apps.

Informally, we describe the corresponding policies as follows:
(1) To defeat *Soundcomber*, the user may create a policy stating that *if the Soundcomber app tries to access from microphone when the phone state is OnCall and the app is running in the background, feed the Soundcomber app with mock audio data.*
(2) To defeat *TapLogger*, the user may create a policy stating that *if the TapLogger app tries to access the accelerometer and orientation sensor when the app is running in the background, lower its sampling rate to 1/10 of its original sampling rate.*

Note that even when no suspicious sensor usage is detected, the user may still specify preventative policies to prevent possible attacks, e.g., *"Apps attempting to access microphone (or camera, GPS) will be supplied with mock sensor data."*.

7.2 Managing Sensor Usages

We present two demonstrations to show the effectiveness of SemaDroid in managing accesses to sensors. In Figure 5(b), we present a demonstration of supplying a location tracking app (*My Tracks by Google*) with mock location information. Briefly, in this experiment, we first use another app to record the location changes when a user is excising in a park. Then, when sitting indoor, we launch the *My Tracks* app and supply it with mock sensor data from GPS. This enforcement is performed with SemaDroid specifying supplying mock data from the trace file in the sensor usage policy on *My Tracks*. As shown in the Figure 5(b), the *My Tracks* app "thinks" the smartphone (and the user) is moving in a park.

In Figure 5(c), we present a demonstration of manipulating the sensor data collected from microphone. The app in the experiment is *TapeMachine Lite Recorder*, a popular audio recording app on Google's app market. In the experiment, we create a sensor usage policy for this app that manipulates the collected audio sensor data by setting their values to 0. For comparison, we run both the same *TapeMachine Lite Recorder* app on two Android phones that are placed close to a speaker. In Figure 5(c), we can observe that the left phone without SemaDroid can record the music played but the right phone with SemaDroid cannot. This is because SemaDroid blocks the audio input collected from microphone.

8. DISCUSSIONS AND FUTURE WORK

8.1 Applicability to iOS and BlackBerry

Besides Android, other platforms like iOS and BlackBerry have also overlooked the sensor management issue. For example, accessing accelerometer and orientation sensors on both iOS and BlackBerry require no security permission. Also, existing sensor management systems on both iOS and BlackBerry rely on permission-based access control systems, not on sensor usage. Although iOS does not support multitasking thus preventing any stealthy sensor data collection by apps running in the background. Yet, it is still necessary to build a comprehensive sensor management framework like SemaDroid so as to protect the user's private information, such as location information, from the perspective of sensor usage. Further, the design of SemaDroid should apply to iOS and BlackBerry, especially the sensor usage policy design. The actual implementations on iOS and BlackBerry will vary.

8.2 Coverage of SemaDroid

8.2.1 Sensor Coverage

For unrestricted sensors managed by SensorManager, all accesses must be through the SensorManager. Thus, by placing *SemaHook* within the *SensorManager*, SemaDroid is able to govern *all* accesses to sensors managed by SensorManager. For other sensors, such as GPS, camera, and microphone, accessing these sensors require permission checks. To guarantee the interception of sensor accesses, we place a SemaHook right after every occurrence of the corresponding permission check. For example, accessing camera requires permission *android.permission.CAMERA*. By examining the source code of Android, the permission check with *android.permission.CAMERA* only occurs twice. One is in the *CameraService* for image capturing, and the other is in the *MediaRecorderClient* for video recording. As such, SemaDroid places SemaHooks in both occurrences to guarantee the coverage of policy checking.

8.2.2 App Coverage

SemaDroid can specify policies for multiple apps or even all apps (with *all-app* package name), as discussed in Section 4. For suspicious apps, SemaDroid supports the privacy bargain and applies fine-grained sensor usage policies even with mock sensor data.

8.3 Malware Detection and Classification

As mentioned in Section 7.1, SemaDroid provides detailed sensor usage reports of installed apps and allows the user to discover the abnormal sensor usages from the report. Admittedly, our current abnormal detection approach is still based on heuristics and experience. But, we see the potential of developing new approaches for overprivilege detection [18] and malware classification.

8.4 Policy Design and Revocation

SemaDroid supports generic policies that are not specifically for known attacks. For example, the user can specify a policy that mutes the microphone for all apps (or selected apps) when entering a sensitive context. So, it is not necessary for the user to detect malicious apps first and then apply precise SemaDroid policies for them. By specifying generic policies, the user can place restrictions according to their demands. On the other hand, a policy targeting at one app will not affect other apps that uses the same types of sensors. SemaDroid is able to identify the originating app of sensor

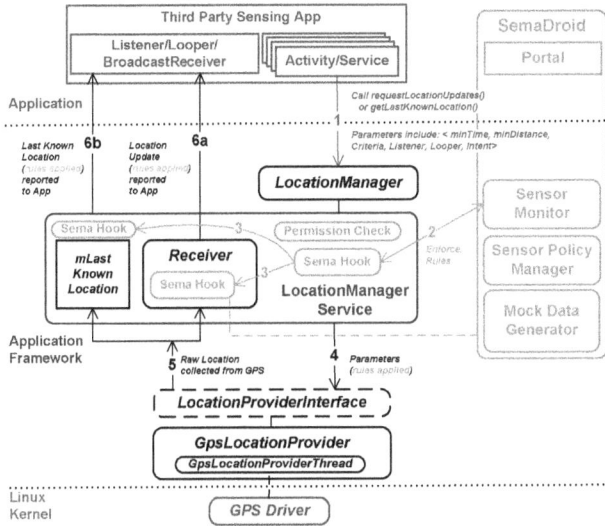

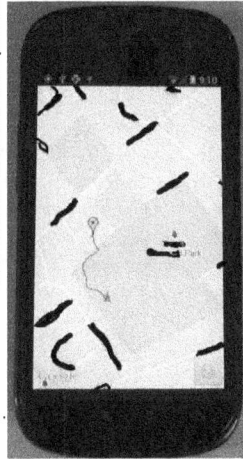

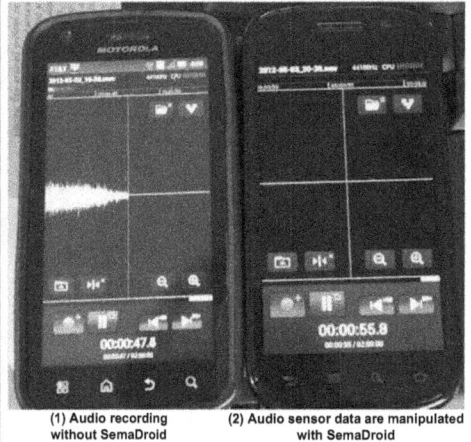

(a) Enforcing SemaDroid Policies on GPS managed by Location-Manager on Android

(b) Supplying running apps with mock GPS location information

(c) Supplying apps with mock audio data data

Figure 5: Implementation of SemaDroid on Android

data request, and enforces different policies on different apps when requesting the same sensors.

For greater usability of SemaDroid, one of our future work is to generate sensor usage policies automatically. The research challenge here is to learn automatically whether each sensor data access is necessary for the main functionality of the sensing app. While it might be possible for doing so through static code analysis, a more practical solution seems to be learning from app descriptions. In WHYPER [41], the authors have successfully applied natural language processing (NLP) techniques over app descriptions to infer why each type of permission is needed for the functionality of the app. For our future work, we may extend their techniques for our purpose here.

The policy revocation of SemaDroid depends on the type of policy. If the enforcement of policy is on the parameter of sensing task, then the revocation or update of policy will require restarting the sensing app. However, if the policy is enforced on the collected sensor data, it is possible to adjust the policy and enforce it in real-time. For example, adjusting the quality of audio recording (e.g. sampling rate) will require restarting the app. However, if an app is already recording audio and it is possible for SemaDroid to mute the app by manipulating the audio data collected for it.

All policies enforced by SemaDroid are stored in system space. Loading policies from SD card is only a feature that allows the user to manually load a policy file from SD card and display the policy on the SemaDroid Portal app. If the user likes the policy, he can save the content of the policy (not copy the policy file from SD card directly) into the system space. Therefore, malware cannot tamper the user defined policies stored in system space by manipulating the policy files stored on SD card.

8.5 Overhead Analysis

SemaDroid is compatible with the existing permission system with little overhead on Android. Firstly, the three system services of SemaDroid are simple and single functioned. The MockData-Generator service maintains a set of worker threads, which are lightweight and can be reused. Secondly, only the policy files will be loaded into memory. The mock data stored in trace files is loaded only when needed and cleaned when the worker thread

ends. Thirdly, the delay caused by policy enforcement is usually neglectable with the SemaHook because most rules supported are simple operations.

8.6 New Paradigm for Participatory Sensing

SemaDroid supports loading sensor usage policies (i.e., in XML form) from SD card. The sensing application developers and vendors are encouraged to publish recommended sensor usage policies for their apps, describing in what contexts their apps will perform the sensing tasks and how the sensor data collection will be performed. The recommended policies can help app vendors to promote their sensing apps by mitigating the user's concern of leaking private information by installing third-party apps. This is because with SemaDroid, one would only require downloading third-party sensing policies instead of installing individual third-party sensing apps that might be privacy invasive. On the user side, enforcing the recommended policies with SemaDroid guarantees that the sensing app will collect sensing data as claimed in its recommended policies. Of course, the user can make adjustments on the recommended policy via the SemaDroid Portal for customization. As such, with SemaDroid, many kinds of participatory sensing can be easily supported without installing separate apps.

8.7 Limitations of SemaDroid on Android

To bypass SemaDroid, an approach would be receiving sensor data from other installed helper apps (with different uids) through side channels. In this case, the helper app may cause suspicion and may be blocked by sensor usage policies for the helper app. Furthermore, SemaDroid allows the user to prohibit all sensing tasks (including those performed by root privileges)[4]. However, some system features may be affected in this case, such as the automatic screen rotation feature.

---

[4]within the existing android permission system, the access control on sensors (if exist) is based on the uid of requester thread. If a requester thread has root privilege, the access to sensor will always be allowed without checking. SemaDroid identifies the originating app by the uid of requester thread. Thus, it is feasible for the user to create a policy that supplying even system apps/thread with manipulated sensor data.

9. RELATED WORKS

Compared to the existing literature, SemaDroid distinguishes itself from them by focusing on managing the sensor data collected from onboard sensors. As mentioned in previous sections, sensors are different from traditional sensitive resources such as SMS and contact lists. Firstly, sensors provide continuous sensor data to the installed sensing app. Thus, SemaDroid considers a sensor as a service provider rather than a stored data file. Secondly, the traditional context-aware access control policies may look fine-grained for traditional data files, but is not fine-grained enough for sensor data, especially because sensor data collection is context aware. Thus, we introduce sensor management policies not only on the permission to access a sensor but also on the quality of sensor data an app can get. Thirdly, existing mock data techniques do not suit sensor data. For example, Android provides a *Mock_Location* provider function for testing purpose. It allows the app to create a mock location provider with a fixed location. However, as the mock location is fixed, apps relying on location updates will crash. The proposed *Mock Data Generator* service in SemaDroid that is able to provide continuous mock sensor data.

9.1 Access Control on Smartphones

Some literature work have been proposed to provide access control on smartphones. Few literatures mentioned sensor management because they did not realize the differences between sensors and other types of resources (like contact list).

[8] proposes a system, named MockDroid, that feeds third party applications with fixed fake values for location, phone identifiers, Internet connection status, intent broadcasts, SMS/MMS, calendar, and contacts. [47] proposes a system, named TISSA, that implements a privacy mode on Android. In the privacy mode, the user is allowed to specify the contents of location, phone identity, contacts, and call log for each third party application. However, sensors with continuous sensor data feeding are not mentioned. Moreover, SemaDroid offers other important features such as privacy bargin and QoSn, which are important for mobile sensing applications.

[26] proposes a system, named AppFence, that allows users to withhold data from imperious applications by substituting real data with innocuous shadow data. Specifically, AppFence shadows browser metadata, SMS/MMS messages, subscribed feeds, contacts, accounts, and calendar entries by returning a set of predefined fake data. However, sensor data is not mentioned in AppFence. As explained, sensor data is different from the ordinary sensitive resources. AppFence cannot be applied in sensor management.

Both Saint [39] and Apex [38] study extending the existing Android permission system in order to support additional run-time permissions. However, firstly, sensors not covered by the existing Android permission system are not covered by Saint and Apex. Secondly, both works study the problem of granting the permissions basing on context. Differently, SemaDroid focuses on how to manage the sensor data (so as to protect user privacy) even if the access to the sensor is allowed.

9.2 Sensor Management on Smartphones

[37] introduces a privacy architecture, called Personal Data Vaults (PDVs), that provides the user the access control over the sensor data shared with content-service providers. Different from our approach, PDV provides the privacy control on a server called PDVs. Sensing data are collected and uploaded to the PDVs server first, and the user then decides data sharing in PDVs. SemaDroid provides solutions on the smartphone directly.

[24] focuses on the data usage side and presents a general-purpose policy language for usage control, called Obligation Spec-ification Language (OSL), which may help one define the usage policy in the framework. Differently, we protect the user at the data collection side.

[21] proposes a personalized ad delivery system in which users can decide how much information about their private context they are willing to share with the ad-server. This work is for individual sensing apps. That is, the app of this system is equipped with sensing management mechanism. We are proposing a framework for managing all apps and no sensor management mechanism is prerequisite.

[13] discusses how to balance the issues of energy consumption, latency and accuracy for mobile sensing. The mentioned factors affecting mobile sensing are useful to describe our Quality-of-Sensing measures. Also, this paper discusses the enforcement of QoS measures.

TrustDroid [10] introduces a domain isolation approach that groups the apps and stored data by different trust levels. However, Tust-Droid focuses on preventing the untrusted apps from accessing trusted data, e.g. SMS and Calendar. No sensor is mentioned in this work.

Recently, the increasing popularity of wearable devices such as GoogleGlass has also raised great user privacy concerns as they may record others without consent. [43, 28] both proposed access control schemes which first infer the current context of sensing based on collected sensor data, and then apply context-aware policies to mediate access of apps to sensors.

[27] proposed DARKLY, an architecture which supplies perceptual applications of different trust levels with different sensing data. The system is implemented with the OpenCV library to support computer-vision tasks.

10. CONCLUSION

While phone sensing applications are booming, the privacy concern arises about leaking user private information through sensor data collected by installed third party apps. In this paper, we propose SemaDroid, a privacy-aware sensor management framework for Android. SemaDroid provides a fine-grained and context-aware sensor management that allows the user to specify sensor usage policies by balancing the privacy and desired functions of apps with the privacy bargain function. Detailed design, implementation, and demonstrations are presented to show the capacity of SemaDroid in defeating sensor-based attacks on smartphones.

11. ACKNOWLEDGMENTS

We thank the reviewers for the valuable comments. This work was supported in part by NSF grant CCF-1320605. The views and conclusions contained in this document are those of the author(s) and should not be interpreted as representing the official policies, either expressed or implied, of NSF or the U.S. Government.

12. REFERENCES

[1] Apple pay.
    https://www.apple.com/iphone-6/apple-pay/.
[2] Apple watch. http://www.apple.com/watch/.
[3] Awareness! the headphone app. http://www.essency.co.uk/awareness-the-headphone-app/.
[4] Samsung fingerprint sdk.
    http://developer.samsung.com/develop.
[5] Samsung gear vr. http://www.samsung.com/global/microsite/gearvr/gearvr_features.html.
[6] A. Acquisti and J. Grossklags. Privacy attitudes and privacy behavior: Losses, gains, and hyperbolic discounting. *Jean Camp and Stephen Lewis (Eds.) "The Economics of Information Security"*, pages 165–178, 2004.

[7] X. Bao and R. Roy Choudhury. Movi: mobile phone based video highlights via collaborative sensing. In *Proc. of the 8th international conference on Mobile systems, applications, and services*, MobiSys '10, pages 357–370, New York, NY, USA, 2010. ACM.

[8] A. Beresford, A. Rice, N. Skehin, and R. Sohan. Mockdroid: Trading privacy for application functionality on smartphones. In *Proc. of the 12th Workshop on Mobile Computing Systems and Applications (HotMobile)*, 2011.

[9] Brut.alll. Android-apktool: A tool for reverse engineering android apk files. `https://code.google.com/p/android-apktool/`.

[10] S. Bugiel, L. Davi, A. Dmitrienko, S. Heuser, A.-R. Sadeghi, and B. Shastry. Practical and lightweight domain isolation on android. In *Proc. of the 1st ACM workshop on Security and privacy in smartphones and mobile devices*, SPSM '11, pages 51–62, New York, NY, USA, 2011. ACM.

[11] L. Cai and H. Chen. Touchlogger: Inferring keystrokes on touch screen from smartphone motion. In *Proc. of HotSec'11*, 2011.

[12] R. K. Chellappa and R. Sin. Personalization versus privacy: An empirical examination of the online consumerŠs dilemma. In 2002 Informs Meeting, 2002.

[13] D. Chu, N. D. Lane, T. T.-T. Lai, C. Pang, X. Meng, Q. Guo, F. Li, and F. Zhao. Balancing energy, latency and accuracy for mobile sensor data classification. In *Proc. of the 9th ACM Conference on Embedded Networked Sensor Systems*, SenSys '11, pages 54–67, New York, NY, USA, 2011. ACM.

[14] M. J. Culnan. "how did they get my name?": An exploratory investigation of consumer attitudes toward secondary information use. *MIS Quarterly*, 17(3):pp. 341–363, 1993.

[15] Electronic Arts. Need for speed shift on iphone. `http://itunes.apple.com/us/app/need-for-speed-shift/id337641298?mt=8`.

[16] W. Enck, D. Octeau, P. McDaniel, and S. Chaudhuri. A study of android application security. In *Proc. of Usenix Security'11*, 2011.

[17] M. Faulkner, M. Olson, R. Chandy, J. Krause, K. M. Chandy, and A. Krause. The next big one: Detecting earthquakes and other rare events from community-based sensors. In *Proc. ACM/IEEE International Conference on Information Processing in Sensor Networks (IPSN)*, 2011.

[18] A. P. Felt, E. Chin, S. Hanna, D. Song, and D. Wagner. Android permissions demystified. In *Proc. of the 18th ACM conference on Computer and communications security*, CCS '11, pages 627–638, New York, NY, USA, 2011. ACM.

[19] P. Golle and K. Partridge. On the anonymity of home/work location pairs. In *Proc. of the 7th International Conference on Pervasive Computing*, Pervasive '09, pages 390–397, Berlin, Heidelberg, 2009. Springer-Verlag.

[20] Google. Android 4.0.3 platform. `http://developer.android.com/sdk/android-4.0.3.html`.

[21] M. Glotz and S. Nath. Privacy-aware personalization for mobile advertising. Technical report, MSR, 2011.

[22] J. Han, E. Owusu, T.-L. Nguyen, A. Perrig, and J. Zhang. ACComplice: Location Inference using Accelerometers on Smartphones. In *Proc. of COMSNETS'12*, 2012.

[23] I.-H. Hann, K. L. Hui, S.-Y. T. Lee, and I. P. L. Png. Online information privacy: Measuring the cost-benefit trade-off. In F. Miralles and J. Valor, editors, *ICIS*, page 1. Association for Information Systems, 2002.

[24] M. Hilty, A. Pretschner, D. Basin, C. Schaefer, and T. Walter. A policy language for distributed usage control. In *Proc. of ESORICS'07*, 2007.

[25] P. Hornyack, S. Han, J. Jung, S. Schechter, and D. Wetherall. These aren't the droids you're looking for: retrofitting android to protect data from imperious applications. In *Proc. of the 18th ACM conference on Computer and communications security*, CCS '11, pages 639–652, New York, NY, USA, 2011. ACM.

[26] P. Hornyack, S. Han, J. Jung, S. Schechter, and D. Wetherall. Şthese arenŠt the droids youŠre looking forŤ: Retrofitting android to protect data from imperious applications. In *Proc. of the 18th ACM Conference on Computer and Communications Security (ACM CCS)*, 2011.

[27] S. Jana, A. Narayanan, and V. Shmatikov. A scanner darkly: Protecting user privacy from perceptual applications. In *Proc. of the 2013 IEEE Symposium on Security and Privacy*, SP '13, pages 349–363, Washington, DC, USA, 2013. IEEE Computer Society.

[28] J. Jung and M. Philipose. Courteous glass. In *Proc. of the 2014 ACM International Joint Conference on Pervasive and Ubiquitous Computing: Adjunct Publication*, UbiComp '14 Adjunct, pages 1307–1312, New York, NY, USA, 2014. ACM.

[29] J. Krumm. Inference attacks on location tracks. In *Proc. of the 5th international conference on Pervasive computing*, PERVASIVE'07, pages 127–143, Berlin, Heidelberg, 2007. Springer-Verlag.

[30] N. D. Lane, T. Choudhury, A. Campbell, M. Mohammod, M. Lin, X. Yang, A. Doryab, H. Lu, S. Ali, and E. Berke. Bewell: A smartphone application to monitor, model and promote wellbeing. In *Proc. of 5th International ICST Conference on Pervasive Computing Technologies for Healthcare*, 2011.

[31] N. D. Lane, E. Miluzzo, H. Lu, D. Peebles, T. Choudhury, and A. T. Campbell. A survey of mobile phone sensing. *Comm. Mag.*, 48(9):140–150, Sept. 2010.

[32] N. D. Lane, Y. Xu, H. Lu, S. Hu, T. Choudhury, A. T. Campbell, and F. Zhao. Enabling large-scale human activity inference on smartphones using community similarity networks (csn). *Pattern Recognition*, pages 355–364, 2011.

[33] H. Lu, A. B. Brush, B. Priyantha, A. Karlson, and J. Liu. Speakersense: Energy efficient unobtrusive speaker identification on mobile phones. In *Proc. of the 9th International Conference on Pervasive Computing (Pervasive'11)*, 2011.

[34] H. Lu, W. Pan, N. D. Lane, T. Choudhury, and A. T. Campbell. Soundsense: Scalable sound sensing for people-centric sensing applications on mobile phones. In *Proc. ofâ7th ACM Conference on Mobile Systems, Applications, and Services (MobiSys '09)*, 2009.

[35] P. Marquardt, A. Verma, H. Carter, and P. Traynor. (sp)iphone: decoding vibrations from nearby keyboards using mobile phone accelerometers. In *Proc. of the 18th ACM conference on Computer and communications security*, CCS '11, pages 551–562. ACM, 2011.

[36] Motorola. Writing fingerprint-enabled apps. `http://developer.motorola.com/docs/writing-fingerprint-enabled-apps/`.

[37] M. Mun, S. Hao, N. Mishra, K. Shilton, J. Burke, D. Estrin, M. Hansen, and R. Govindan. Personal data vaults: A locus of control for personal data streams. In *Proc. of ACM CoNEXT 2010*, 2010.

[38] M. Nauman, S. Khan, and X. Zhang. Apex: extending android permission model and enforcement with user-defined runtime constraints. In *Proc. of ASIACCS '10 Proc. of the 5th ACM Symposium on Information, Computer and Communications Securit*, 2010.

[39] M. Ongtang, S. McLaughlin, W. Enck, and P. McDaniel. Semantically rich application-centric security in android. In *Proc. Annual Computer Security Applications Conf. ACSAC '09*, pages 340–349, 2009.

[40] E. Owusu, J. Han, S. Das, A. Perrig, and J. Zhang. ACCessory: Keystroke Inference using Accelerometers on Smartphones. In *Proc. of Workshop on Mobile Computing Systems and Applications (HotMobile)*, 2012.

[41] R. Pandita, X. Xiao, W. Yang, W. Enck, and T. Xie. Whyper: Towards automating risk assessment of mobile applications. In *Proc. of the 22Nd USENIX Conference on Security*. USENIX Association, 2013.

[42] R. Schlegel, K. Zhang, X. Zhou, M. Intwala, A. Kapadia, and X. Wang. Soundcomber: A stealthy and context-aware sound trojan for smartphones. In *Proc. of the 18th Annual Network and Distributed System Security Symposium (NDSS)*, 2011.

[43] R. Templeman, A. Kapadia, R. Hoyle, and D. Crandall. Reactive security: Responding to visual stimuli from wearable cameras. In *Proc. of the 2014 ACM International Joint Conference on Pervasive and Ubiquitous Computing: Adjunct Publication*, UbiComp '14 Adjunct, pages 1297–1306, New York, NY, USA, 2014. ACM.

[44] B. van Wissen, N. Palmer, R. Kemp, T. Kielmann, and H. Bal. Contextdroid: an expression-based context framework for androidă. In *Proc. of PhoneSense'11*, 2011.

71

[45] N. Xu, F. Zhang, Y. Luo, W. Jia, D. Xuan, and J. Teng. Stealthy video capturer: a new video-based spyware in 3g smartphones. In *Proc. of the second ACM conference on Wireless network security*, 2009.

[46] Z. Xu, K. Bai, and S. Zhu. Taplogger: inferring user inputs on smartphone touchscreens using on-board motion sensors. In *Proc. of the fifth ACM conference on Security and Privacy in Wireless and Mobile Networks*, WISEC '12, pages 113–124, New York, NY, USA, 2012. ACM.

[47] Y. Zhou, X. Zhang, X. Jiang, and V. Freeh. Taming information-stealing smartphone applications (on android). In *Proc. of the International Conference on Trust and Trustworthy Computing (TRUST)*, 2011.

APPENDIX

A. ADDITIONAL DEMONSTRATIONS

In Figure 6(a), we present a demonstration of adding noise to sensor data collected from accelerometer (managed by *SensorManager*). The screenshot was taken by app *Accelerometer Values*. In Figure 6(b) we present a picture taken by the camera with content manipulated by SemaDroid according to the sensor usage policy.

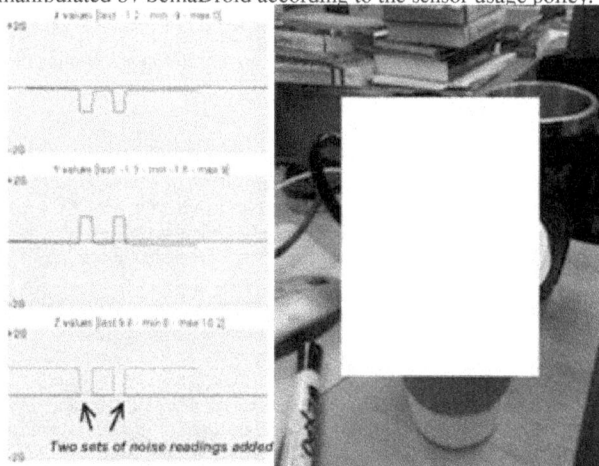

(a) Demonstration of adding noise to sensor data collected from accelerometer

(b) Demonstration of sensor data manipulation on pictures collected from camera

Figure 6: Demonstrations of enforcing sensor usage policies with SemaDroid

B. ADDITIONAL DETAILS OF IMPLEMENTATION

In Figure 7, 8, 9, we present the implementation of SemaDroid with policy enforcement on camera and microphone.

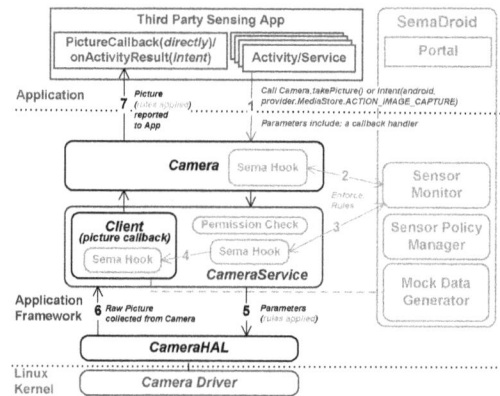

Figure 7: Enforcing SemaDroid policies on Camera when taking pictures

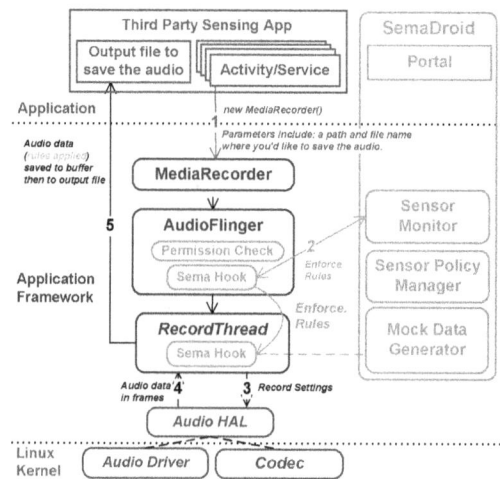

Figure 8: Enforcing SemaDroid Policies on microphone

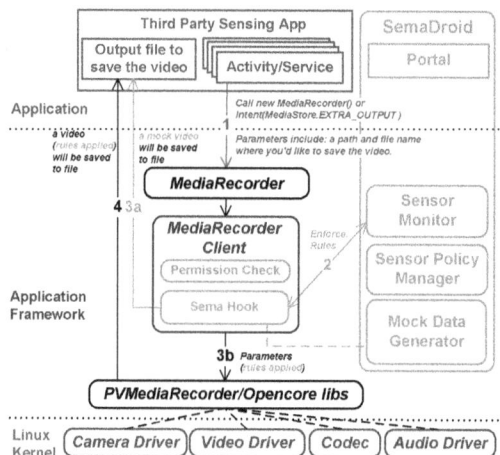

Figure 9: Enforcing SemaDroid Policies on camera and microphone when recording video clips

Collecting, Analyzing and Responding to Enterprise Scale DNS Events

William Horne
Hewlett-Packard Laboratories
5 Vaughn Drive, Suite 301
Princeton, NJ 08540
william.horne@hp.com

ABSTRACT

DNS is an important data source for security for many reasons. If the DNS infrastructure can be brought down, many networking tasks would be impossible to complete. If the integrity of the mapping between domain names and IP addresses is compromised, attackers can redirect users undetectably to IP addresses of their choosing. And malware of many types must in one way or another use the DNS infrastructure as part of their operations. For example, botnets often use fast flux techniques and domain name generation algorithms to rendezvous with command and control servers.

Collecting DNS is a significant challenge. In HP, our core internal DNS clusters process approximately 16 billion DNS packets every day. Ideally, we would like to turn each and every one of those packets into an event for our security information and event management (SIEM) system. However, we would have to grow our SIEM, which is one of the largest deployments in the world, by a factor of six to collect this data. Moreover, traditional logging has a substantial performance impact on the DNS infrastructure, and therefore from an operational perspective enabling logging is also impractical. Finally, DNS servers generally do not log the information necessary to detect many security problems.

To deal with these problems we collect and filter this traffic using hardware network packet sniffers, which have no impact on the performance of the DNS servers and allows us to collect all of the information we need for security purposes. We model known good traffic, and discard it, keeping only anomalous data.

We developed a custom analytics engine, which analyzes this data looking for evidence of botnet infections, blacklist hits, cloud platform abuse, beaconing, data exfiltration, and cache poisoning attempts. The results of these analyses is turned into a set of alerts which are sent to our Security Operations Center (SOC). We've also developed a user interface including various visualizations to help analysts explore the data.

The system has been up and running in HP since June 2014. The SOC processes on average about 20 of our alerts per day, with very low false positive rates. We've worked closely with the SOC to make sure the tool is fully integrated into the workflows that the SOC analysts use and meets the needs of the analysts.

In this talk, I will describe our experiences developing this tool and the lessons we learned in the process.

Categories and Subject Descriptors

K.6.5 [**Management of Computing and Information Systems**]: Security and Protection – *invasive software, unauthorized access.*
C.2.3 [**Computer-Communication Networks**]: Network Operations – n*etwork monitoring.*

General Terms

Security.

Keywords

Domain Name System, Security Information and Event Management, Security Operations

Bio

Bill Horne has served as a Research Manager in the Security and Cloud Lab of HP Laboratories in Princeton, NJ since August 2002. He directs research on systems and network security, cryptography, privacy and risk management, and is responsible for transferring security technology developed in HP Labs to customers and business units.

He is a Principal Investigator for a DHS Science and Technology funded project Improving CSIRT Skills, Dynamics, and Effectiveness. He is currently an associate editor for IEEE Security and Privacy Magazine.

Prior to joining HP, he held industrial research positions at InterTrust Technologies and NEC Research Institute. He has an MSEE and PhD in Electrical Engineering from the University of New Mexico, and a BS in Electrical Engineering from the University of Delaware.

CODASPY'15, March 2–4, 2015, San Antonio, Texas, USA.
ACM 978-1-4503-3191-3/15/03.
http://dx.doi.org/10.1145/2699026.2699027

CoinParty: Secure Multi-Party Mixing of Bitcoins

Jan Henrik Ziegeldorf, Fred Grossmann, Martin Henze, Nicolas Inden, Klaus Wehrle
Communication and Distributed Systems (COMSYS), RWTH Aachen University, Germany
lastname@comsys.rwth-aachen.de

ABSTRACT

Bitcoin is a digital currency that uses anonymous cryptographic identities to achieve financial privacy. However, Bitcoin's promise of anonymity is broken as recent work shows how Bitcoin's blockchain exposes users to reidentification and linking attacks. In consequence, different *mixing services* have emerged which promise to randomly mix a user's Bitcoins with other users' coins to provide anonymity based on the unlinkability of the mixing. However, proposed approaches suffer either from weak security guarantees and single points of failure, or small anonymity sets and missing deniability. In this paper, we propose *CoinParty* a novel, decentralized mixing service for Bitcoin based on a combination of decryption mixnets with threshold signatures. *CoinParty* is secure against malicious adversaries and the evaluation of our prototype shows that it scales easily to a large number of participants in real-world network settings. By the application of threshold signatures to Bitcoin mixing, *CoinParty* achieves anonymity by orders of magnitude higher than related work as we quantify by analyzing transactions in the actual Bitcoin blockchain and is first among related approaches to provide plausible deniability.

Categories and Subject Descriptors

K.4.4 [**Electronic Commerce**]: Cybercash, digital cash

Keywords

Bitcoin; Anonymity; Secure Multi-Party Computation

1. INTRODUCTION

Bitcoin was proposed in 2008 by Nakamoto [24] as a decentralized digital currency. The market cap of circulating Bitcoins amounts to nearly $5 Billion [4] as of December 2014 which shows the wide adoption of Bitcoin. Instead of using central entities, i.e., banks, to establish trust in the currency, Bitcoin stores all transactions in a distributed public ledger, the *blockchain*, to prevent double spending and keep track of the balances. Bitcoins are stored at and transferred between addresses, cryptographic identities corresponding to

Elliptic Curve Digital Signature Algorithm (ECDSA) public keys. Addresses and thus transactions are anonymous as long as addresses cannot be linked to their owners. It is especially this promise of financial privacy that has drawn great interest towards the Bitcoin currency.

However, this promise is broken, as recent works [2, 22, 25, 26] show how a user's transactions and addresses can often be linked back together by analyzing the transaction graph in the publicly available blockchain. Though, any user, Alice, can generate fresh unlinkable addresses, transferring funds to them would again link the address back to her. Basically, what Alice needs is a way to send funds to her new address in an unlinkable manner. As of today, `bitcoin.it` lists no less than thirteen commercial mixing services [6] that promise to provide exactly this: If Alice sends her funds to the mixing service, the mix will, for a small fee, pay her back with the funds of some random other user after a certain waiting period. To any outsider observing the blockchain the resulting mixing transactions are indistinguishable from other contemptuous transactions in the blockchain. This property is desirable since it provides for large anonymity sets and allows users to plausibly deny their participation in the mixing operation.

This first generation of mixes, however, suffers from two severe drawbacks which are well-known to the Bitcoin community: First, users need to blindly trust the operators not to steal their funds. Second, the mixing service knows how funds were mixed and may be forced or otherwisely incentivized to reveal this knowledge. This has led to new decentralized approaches that promise better security and stronger anonymity [20, 28, 31]. However, most of these approaches require that all mixing transactions are issued in one single *atomic* transaction with multiple inputs and outputs. This serves to prevent malicious peers from aborting the protocol after they have received their funds thereby leaving another peer unpaid. However, the characteristic form of such *group transactions* renders them easily identifiable in the blockchain. This introduces two severe limitations when they are used in mixing services: First, the resulting anonymity set of the mixing is limited to the number of users participating in a particular mixing operation. Second, since such bundled mixing transactions are clearly identifiable in the blockchain, users have no means of plausibly denying that they participated in the mixing.

Our contribution. In this paper, we propose *CoinParty*, an efficient decentralized Bitcoin mixing service with stronger anonymity guarantees, plausible deniability, and lower costs. *CoinParty* takes a two stage approach. Our core idea is to introduce a set of *mixing peers* that in a decentralized yet secure fashion carry out the mixing in multiple one-to-one Bitcoin transactions thereby replacing the disadvantageous group transactions used in the related work. The key challenge is to ensure that all mixing transactions succeed even when mixing peers fail or behave maliciously. We show how to achieve this by employing a threshold variant of the ECDSA scheme realized using general Secure Multi-Party Computation (SMC) protocols. This scheme allows to distributedly create Bitcoin addresses from which funds can only be redeemed in a *threshold transaction*, i.e., only when a majority of the controlling peers agrees to do so. *CoinParty* can thus realize the advantages of *both* the early centralized approaches and of the later decentralized approaches, achieving notable improvements compared to the related work:

Improved anonymity: To outsiders and the fellow mixing participants observing the blockchain, *CoinParty*'s threshold transactions are indistinguishable from other non-threshold transactions. Thus, *CoinParty*'s mixing transactions are anonymous among *all contemptuous* transactions with the same value. We conduct a quantitative analysis on the blockchain to show that this increases anonymity by orders of magnitude.

Plausible deniability: In [9] the authors briefly mention *deniability* as one desirable property for mixings. *CoinParty* is first among related approaches for mixing Bitcoins to provide its users with plausible deniability.

No fees: *CoinParty* issues multiple small transactions that do not require transaction fees. Since *CoinParty* is run in absence of any trusted third party, i.e., a service provider, no mixing fees are charged either. Related approaches require at least transaction or mixing fees.

Applicability: *CoinParty* is fully compatible with the existing Bitcoin network. We evaluate a proof-of-concept implementation in a real-world network setting to show that *CoinParty* incurs only small overheads even when scaling to large numbers of participants.

The remainder of the paper is structured as follows: We present background information on the Bitcoin digital currency and SMC in Section 2. Section 3 formalizes the problem and requirements of Bitcoin mixing. Section 4 describes the protocol and system design of *CoinParty*. Section 5 provides a comprehensive analysis, evaluation, and discussion of the mixing correctness, performance, anonymity, and further system requirements. Finally, Section 6 compares *CoinParty* to related work and Section 7 concludes this paper.

2. BACKGROUND

We briefly cover the relevant background on Bitcoin and SMC as the underlying foundation of our approach.

2.1 Bitcoin

Bitcoin is best understood as a decentralized P2P network that keeps track of all money transfers between its users. Transfers are recorded in a public ledger, the blockchain, which is constantly validated by the Bitcoin participants through a proof-of-work. Double spending of Bitcoins is thereby ruled out as long as the majority of computation power is contributed by honest, non-colluding participants.

Addresses. Bitcoin users can have a virtually unlimited amount of cryptographic identities, called addresses. Addresses are used to store and receive Bitcoins. An address is basically the hash of an ECDSA public key and a user in possession of the corresponding private key is said to *own* the address. Addresses serve as pseudonyms and frequently using fresh ones is the basis for anonymity in Bitcoin.

Transactions. A transfer of Bitcoins between addresses is called a transaction. To issue a transaction, a user specifies one or more *input addresses* $I_1, ... I_n$ from where the transaction amount is collected. The transaction amount can be distributed arbitrarily to one or more *output addresses*, $O_1, ..., O_m$. We formally write $\{I_1, ..., I_n\} \overset{\nu_1,...,\nu_m}{\to} \{O_1, ..., O_m\}$, for a transaction of ν_i Bitcoins to O_i, respectively, or simply $I \overset{\nu}{\to} O$ when only one particular input and output address is relevant in the transaction. The user signs the transaction with the private key corresponding to the input address to proof that she indeed owns the respective address. The complete transaction is then broadcasted into the Bitcoin network where it is grouped and validated together with other transactions in *blocks*. The transaction is usually considered valid by the other Bitcoin participants after six further blocks have been processed. Blocks are linearly chained in the blockchain which represents the complete *accepted* history of Bitcoin transactions and has been the primary target for deanonymization attacks.

Transaction fees. The difference between the sum of a transaction's input and output values can be collected as a transaction fee. Transaction fees motivate *Bitcoin miners*, i.e., users who invest computing power to find new blocks, to include the transaction in the blockchain. Fees are not mandatory and many transactions are indeed processed with no fee at all, e.g., those not exceeding a size of 1 KB [7].

2.2 Secure Multi-Party Computation

SMC considers the basic problem of how a group of peers can compute some known functionality $\mathcal{F}(x_1, .., x_n)$ in absence of a trusted third party without anyone learning the private inputs $x_1, ..., x_n$. Among the different proposed solutions, constructions based on linear secret sharing are widely used and we quickly cover the basics here. At the beginning, each input party creates $[x] := (f_x(1), ..., f_x(i), ..., f_x(m))$, a sharing of her private input x where $f_x \in \mathbb{Z}_p[X]$ is a random t-degree polynomial with $f_x(0) = x$. $[x]$ is called a t-out-of-n secret sharing of x, where $[x]_i$ is called the i-th share of x. Any subset of t or less shares does not reveal anything about the secret, while any $t + 1$ or more shares are sufficient to reconstruct x using Lagrange interpolation. t is thus often called the reconstruction threshold:

$$x = f_x(0) = \sum_{i=i_1}^{i_{t+1}} [x]_i \cdot \underbrace{\prod_{j=0 \atop j \neq i}^{j} \frac{j}{i - j}}_{=: \lambda_i} \qquad (1)$$

To realize the desired functionality $\mathcal{F}$ securely, it is first expressed as an arithmetic circuit which is subsequently evaluated by a set of *privacy peers*. The input peers share their secrets to the m privacy peers, i.e., privacy peer P_i receives $[x]_i$, and the privacy peers then compute the required additions and multiplications on these shares, i.e., without learning the secret inputs. In *linear* secret sharing schemes, addition and thus also scalar multiplication can be computed locally, i.e., $[x] + [y] = [x + y]$ and thus $[x] \cdot s = [x \cdot s]$. Multiplication of two secret-shared values $[x]$ and $[y]$ can be implemented in a simple protocol which requires one round of communication between the privacy peers. Based on addition and multiplication, theoretically any functionality can be implemented, while practically processing and communication overheads limit what is feasible.

Adversary models. Security of SMC protocols is usually analyzed in either the *semi-honest* adversary or the *malicious* adversary model [18]. Semi-honest adversaries, also referred to as passive adversaries, are assumed to follow the protocol correctly, but may analyze the protocol transcript to gain additional information about the participants' private inputs, e.g., to break anonymity. In the *semi-honest* model, we typically set the reconstruction threshold to $t = \lfloor (m - 1)/2 \rfloor$ which achieves security against an adversary that corrupts any minority of the m privacy peers. Contrarily, a *malicious* adversary is not bound by the protocol specifications and may actively try to cheat. Because of the involved monetary values, we argue that it is mandatory to provide security against malicious adversaries in the context of our work. Notably, all of the SMC primitives we use in this work are based on Damgård et al.'s protocol for general Secure Multi-Party Computation [14]. Damgård's construction builds on linear secret sharing and is secure against a malicious adversary that corrupts less than $m/3$ of the m privacy peers, i.e., the reconstruction threshold is $t = \lfloor (m - 1)/3 \rfloor$. An efficient implementation of [14] exists in the VIFF framework [30] on which we base our protocol implementation.

3. PROBLEM STATEMENT

Motivated by recent work on de-anonymization of Bitcoin transactions [2, 22, 25, 26], we consider the problem of how a user can mix Bitcoins with other users to preserve her financial privacy. Formally, n input peers which each have a certain amount of ν Bitcoins available at input addresses $I_1, ..., I_n$ want to mix that amount to a set of output addresses $O_1, ..., O_n$ such that (1) each input peer receives back ν Bitcoins on her output address, and (2) input and output addresses are unlinkable, i.e., only input peer i knows that I_i and O_i belong together. Essentially, this means that each input peer i issues the transaction $I_i \xrightarrow{\nu} O_{\pi(i)}$ where π is a random and *secret* permutation over $\{1, ..., n\}$. Such a mixing service needs to fulfil the following requirements:

Mixing correctness: Bitcoins must not be lost, stolen, or double-spent by any inside or outside party even in the presence of a malicious adversary. Honest input peers should receive their funds in a timely manner.

Anonymity: The mixing must be anonymous, i.e., a malicious adversary must not be able to create a link between input address I_i and output address O_i for any input peer i.

Deniability: Input peers should be able to plausibly deny having participated in a mixing operation.

Performance: The protocol should scale to large numbers of input peers without imposing prohibitive overheads upon the mixes or the Bitcoin network.

Compatibility: The mixing protocol must be fully compatible with the current Bitcoin network and produce legitimate Bitcoin transactions.

Cost-efficiency: The protocol must be cost-efficient in terms of involved transaction and mixing fees.

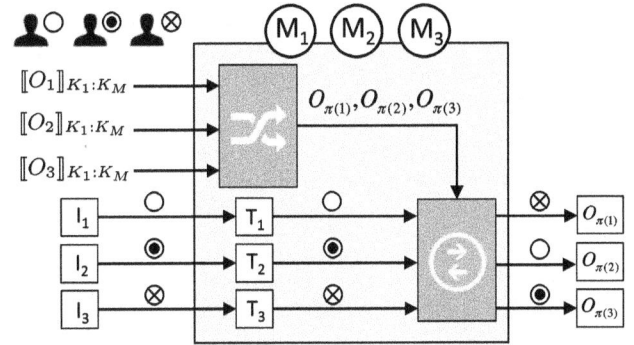

Figure 1: Overview of *CoinParty* with three participants. The shuffling and transaction (grey) are executed collaboratively by the mixing peers M_1, M_2 and M_3.

Clearly, the first generation of centralized mixes [5,6,8,11] does not provide correctness in the presence of a malicious mix that steals funds. Furthermore, anonymity is provided not even against weaker passive adversaries because the mixing service knows the permutation applied to the output addresses. The improvements proposed in [9, 20] protect against theft from malicious adversaries, but users still need to entrust the mix with their anonymity. Recent works on decentralized mixes provide anonymity also in the presence of a malicious adversary corrupting the mixing service itself. However, they are either inefficient [21, 23, 31], uneconomical [21], achieve only suboptimal anonymity and deniability [20, 28], are incompatible with the current Bitcoin network without substantial modifications [3, 23], or have not evolved beyond discussions on forums and blogs [16,21,27,31]. Thus, secure and anonymous mixing of Bitcoins is an open problem. In the following, we propose *CoinParty* which combines the advantages of centralized and decentralized approaches to Bitcoin mixing and fulfils the stated requirements.

4. PROTOCOL DESIGN

CoinParty takes a decentralized approach at Bitcoin mixing by introducing a set of mixing peers which emulate a Trusted Third Party through SMC to realize a secure and anonymous mixing of Bitcoins between the participating users. Note that in the context of this work, we refer to the privacy peers executing the SMC protocol as *mixing peers*. Figure 1 gives an overview of one exemplary protocol run of the *CoinParty* system with three participants. *CoinParty* runs in three phases, (1) commitment (Section 4.1), (2) shuffling (Section 4.2), and (3) transaction (Section 4.3). A fourth error and reversion protocol phase (Section 4.4) is invoked when an error or malicious behaviour is detected in the three previous phases. We describe each of these phases in detail now, while deferring discussions of security and anonymity to Sections 5.1 and 5.2.

4.1 Commitment

The goal of the commitment phase is to make the input peers commit the required funds for mixing to a temporary escrow address T_i. Of course, the escrowed funds must be protected against theft by malicious mixing peers. To achieve this, T_i is generated from a fresh *threshold* ECDSA key pair so that T_i is under joint control by the mixing peers and a majority of mixing peers must collaborate to create a valid signature in order to transfer funds. Inspired by the scheme of Ibrahim et al. for threshold signatures [17], we show how to generate escrow addresses T_i and the corresponding key pair in a distributed fashion so that no central trusted entity is required:

(C1) Using Pseudo-Random Secret Sharing (PRSS) [13], each mixing peer M_j obtains a share $[d_i]_j$ of an unknown random value d_i that represents the private key.

(C2) Each M_j computes locally her share of the public key Q_i: $[Q_i]_j = [d_i]_j \cdot G$, with G the generator of the elliptic curve (i.e., secp256k1 in the case of Bitcoin).

(C3) Each mixing peer M_j broadcasts her share $[Q_i]_j$ to the other mixing peers.

(C4) Each M_j receives the shares of the other peers and reconstructs the public key $Q_i = \sum_{j=1}^{m} \lambda_j [Q_i]_j = \sum_{j=1}^{m} \lambda_j [d_i]_j G = d_i G$, with λ_j the Lagrange basis polynomial at point $x = 0$.

(C5) Each M_j creates the address T_i from Q_i according to the technical specifications of the Bitcoin protocol.

Mixing peers precompute a set of escrow addresses in advance and announce a different escrow address T_i to each input peer i on demand. If an input peer receives two different escrow addresses $T_i \neq T_i'$, e.g., from a malicious mixing peer that tries to divert funds to her own address, the input peer aborts the protocol immediately and notifies the other mixes of the equivocation. Otherwise, the input peer transfers the required funds ν from her input address I_i to the escrow address T_i, i.e., issues transaction $I_i \xrightarrow{\nu} T_i$. The mixing peers wait the recommended six blocks until the commitment is considered accepted by the Bitcoin network.

4.2 Address Shuffling

The goal of the shuffling phase is to permute the set of output addresses given by the input peers under a secret permutation π, such that nobody, not even the mixing peers, can link input addresses $I_1, ..., I_n$ to the corresponding output addresses $O_1, ..., O_n$. *Verifiable shuffling* is a well-known problem, e.g., in anonymous communications, and can be solved using decryption mixnets as proposed in [10,12] and applied to Bitcoin mixing in [28]. While our use of decryption mixnets for address shuffling is inspired by [10,12,28], we use a different approach to verify the integrity of the shuffling which allows for deniability and improves performance. We first outline our shuffling protocol and then discuss our modifications.

(S1) Each input peer i encrypts and broadcasts her output address O_i using the public keys $K_1, ..., K_m$ of the mixing peers in a layered encryption $[\![O_i]\!]_{K_1:K_m} := E_{K_1}(E_{K_2}(...E_{K_m}(O_i)))$. Also, each input peer i secret-shares the hash $H(O_i)$, i.e., sends $[H(O_i)]_j$ to $M_{j=1..m}$.

(S2) The mixing peers now enter m rounds of decryption and shuffling. M_j removes the outermost decryption E_{K_j}, then applies a private permutation π_j and sends $S^j = [\![O_{\pi_j \circ ... \circ \pi_1(1)}]\!]_{K_{j+1}:K_m}, ..., [\![O_{\pi_j \circ ... \circ \pi_1(n)}]\!]_{K_{j+1}:K_m}$ to the next mixing peer M_{j+1}.

(S3) M_m removes the last layer of encryption E_m. M_m then sorts the output addresses lexicographically (permutation π_m) and broadcasts the resulting S^m.

(S4) Each M_j computes a share of a checksum $[C]_j := [\sum_{i=1}^{n} H(O_i)]_j = \sum_{i=1}^{n} [H(O_i)]$, broadcasts $[C]_j$ to the other mixes, waits for the other peers' shares and then reconstructs C.

(S5) Each M_j validates that (1) S^m is lexicographically ordered and (2) the correctness of the checksum $C = \sum_{i=1}^{n} H(O_{\pi_m \circ ... \circ \pi_1(i)})$ by hashing the addresses in S^m. Otherwise, M_j enters the error and reversion phase.

(S6) On success, each M_j seeds a pseudo-random number generator (PRNG) with the checksum C to obtain a common final permutation π_{m+1} that is applied to S^m to get $S^{m+1} = O_{\pi(1)}, ..., O_{\pi(n)}$ with $\pi := \pi_{m+1} \circ \pi_m \circ ... \circ \pi_1$.

Though our shuffling protocol is inspired by the related work [10,12,28], we introduce two core modifications. First, we use secret sharing to validate the correctness of the shuffling in Steps (S4) and (S5). This obsoletes involving input peers in the verification of the shuffling which strengthens anonymity guarantees and allows for deniability as analyzed in Sections 5.2 and 5.3. Second, in [28] the last mixing peer controls the outcome of the shuffling which is undesirable as we explain in Appendix A. In [10,12] this is prevented at the costs of a second encryption layer. Our Steps (S3) and (S5) prevent M_m from controlling the shuffling while Step (S6) ensures that the final shuffling is indeed random. We thus fix this vulnerability of the shuffling protocol in [28] while maintaining its superior performance compared to [10,12].

4.3 Transaction

In the transaction phase, the mixing peers create transactions $T_i \xrightarrow{\nu} O_{\pi(i)}$ which requires them to compute one ECDSA signature per transaction. Since the private key d_i corresponding to an escrow address T_i is *shared* across the mixing peers, the standard ECDSA algorithm cannot be used. Instead, the mixing peers need to collaboratively sign the transaction to spend any of the funds located at T_i. We employ a threshold variant of the ECDSA algorithm according to Ibrahim et al. [17], which we use to create and sign a Bitcoin transaction as follows:

(T1) The mixing peers use PRSS [13] to obtain shares $[k]_i$ of an unknown random value k. They use the reciprocal protocol from [17] to obtain $[k^{-1}]_i$.

(T2) Each mixing peer M_j creates $e = \text{SHA-1}(T_i \xrightarrow{\nu} O_{\pi(i)})$ according to the Bitcoin protocol specifications.

(T3) Using the generator of the curve G, each M_j computes $[kG]_j = [k]_j G$ and broadcasts her share $[kG]_j$. M_j receives the other peers' shares and reconstructs kG.

(T4) With $(x, y) := kG$ and $R := x \bmod n$, the mixing peers compute $[S] = [k^{-1}] * (e + [d] \cdot R)$ and reconstruct S.

(T5) The mixing peers output the ECDSA signature (R, S) and with it build and broadcast $T_i \xrightarrow{\nu} O_{\pi(i)}$.

We introduce the following modifications to improve the performance and robustness compared to [17]: The mixing peers precompute the first part of the signature R, e.g., along with the precomputation of the escrow addresses T_i. This only requires mixing peers to precompute $[k]$, its reciprocal

$[k^{-1}]$ (T1) and then kG (T3). We further split the computation of the second signature part S (T4) into two parts, i.e., $[S] = [k^{-1}] * e + [k^{-1}] * [d] \cdot R$. Then, also the critical multiplication on shares $[k^{-1}] * [d] \cdot R$ can be precomputed. To create the actual signature, the mixing peers now only need to compute locally the hash e (T2), the scaler multiplication $[k^{-1}] \cdot e$ (T4) and then reconstruct $[S]$. Thus, signature generation becomes much faster and more robust against halting or failing peers.

4.4 Error and Reversion

When an error is detected during the commitment or shuffling phase, the mixing peers transfer all funds from the escrow addresses T_i back to the input addresses I_i. The necessary steps are the same as in the transaction phase. As we analyze in Section 5.1, these transaction are guaranteed to succeed even in the presence of malicious adversaries such that no funds can be stolen, diverted, or lost.

Detecting a malicious mix that announces a different $T_i' \neq T_i$ to input peer i in the commitment phase is straightforward. It is slightly more difficult to hold mixing peers accountable for malicious behaviour during the shuffling phase. However, as this has been previously explained in [12, 28], we restrict ourselves to briefly sketch the basic idea. Other than for mixnets used for anonymous communications [12], the shuffled messages, i.e., the output addresses, need not be kept secret in case of an error. If the mixing fails, input peers simply dispose of the potential contaminated, yet unused output addresses O_i. They can then reveal the randomness used to produce the layered encryptions $[\![O_i]\!]_{K_1:K_m}$ which allows honest mixing peers to trace the malicious mix by successively reconstructing the intermediate shufflings S^j. Because mixing peers need to sign all their messages, they can then be held accountable for their wrong doing. Note that as a consequence input peers need to generate fresh output addresses for the next mixing, which is accpeted good practice even for correct protocol runs.

5. DISCUSSION OF SYSTEM PROPERTIES

In this section, we show that *CoinParty* fulfils the requirements presented in Section 3. We explain why *CoinParty* achieves a random and correct mixing even in the presence of malicious adversaries in Section 5.1. In Section 5.2 we quantitatively evaluate the achieved anonymity. This is also the basis for our discussion of deniability in Section 5.3. We present a comprehensive performance evaluation of *CoinParty* in Section 5.4. Finally, Sections 5.5 and 5.6 briefly discuss compatibility and cost-efficiency of *CoinParty*.

5.1 Mixing correctness

To prove the correctness of our protocol in the presence of malicious adversaries, we now show that each protocol phase, i.e., commitment, shuffling, and transaction, is either completed correctly or an error is detected and funds are restored to the input addresses of the participants.

5.1.1 Commitment phase

Malicious Input Peers. In the commitment phase, input peers transfer the required mixing amount to the escrow addresses T_i. The correctness of the commitment phase only depends on the correctness of the transactions $I_i \xrightarrow{v} O_i$, which is ensured by the Bitcoin network itself and independent of our system. Further, we note that input peers cannot

stall this protocol phase, since refusal to commit funds just means that the mixing starts without the particular input peer. An input peer could DoS our system by repeatedly requesting escrow addresses, however this can be thwarted using standard puzzle mechanisms. Thus, the commitment phase is secure against any number of malicious input peers.

Malicious Mixing Peers. A malicious adversary that controls a fraction of the mixing peers can try to corrupt the ECDSA key generation and with it the generation of escrow addresses T_i. However, to implement the key generation we use the general SMC protocol from [14], which is secure against a malicious adversary that corrupts less than $m/3$ of the mixing peers. In other words, the protocol in Section 4.1 will generate a valid address T_i with the honest mixing peers holding consistent shares of the corresponding private key d_i, even if one third of the mixing peers are compromised and behave arbitrarily, e.g., submit wrong inputs. Thus, the commitment phase is secure against an $m/3$ malicious adversary.

5.1.2 Shuffling phase

We show that the shuffling finishes and that its integrity holds even in the presence of a malicious adversary. Unlinkability and randomness of the shuffling are proved in Section 5.2. We define *integrity* analogous to [10]: Either exactly the given output addresses are contained in the final shuffling, or the honest mixing peers are informed that some input peer's output address has been substituted. Note that though our shuffling phase is inspired by [10, 12, 28], our method of verifying the integrity of the shuffling is different and thus requires a dedicated proof of correctness.

Malicious Input Peers. Input peers only broadcast a layered encryption of their output address and secret-share its hash value. Other than related work based on decryption mixnets [10, 12, 28], the input peers are not involved in the verification of the shuffling. Malicious input peers have no incentive in announcing a wrong or broken address, since this would only result in the loss of their own funds. However, malicious input peers can share out a wrong hash value in order to mount a DoS attack against the verification step. In this case, the protocol proceeds by transferring back the funds to the input addresses, which is the same as one run of the transaction phase and thus not further analyzed here. While such malicious behaviour of input peers can be traced back to the peer, e.g., by reconstructing the hashes from the sharings $[\![H(O_i)]\!]$ on error, it cannot be prevented. We note that related work [10, 12, 28] is also vulnerable to such DoS attacks by single malicious input peers. However, unlike related work which involves the input peers in the verification of the shuffling, our approach is robust against halting input peers or random failures.

Malicious Mixing Peers. Any malicious mixing peer M_j can substitute the outputs in the shuffling with her own output addresses by encrypting them with the known public keys of the remaining mixes and announcing $S'^j = [\![O_1']\!]_{K_{j+1}:K_m}, ..., [\![O_m']\!]_{K_{j+1}:K_m}$. However, this will be detected in (S5) unless the attacker finds $O_1', ..., O_m'$ with $C = \sum_{i=1}^{m} H(O_i) = \sum_{i=1}^{m} H(O_i')$. For all but the last mixing peer, this is clearly infeasible since M_j, $j < m$, needs to announce the shuffling S^j before even learning C in (S4).

The last mixing peer M_m, however, removes the last layer of encryptions and learns the output addresses in clear. M_m can thus derive the checksum C *before* announcing the shuffling S^m. To steal the mixed funds, M_m must thus find suitable output addresses $O'_1, ..., O'_n$ that sum up to the same checksum C. Since the attacker can generate an arbitrary amount of addresses, this corresponds to solving a high density *Random Modular Subset Sum* (RMSS) problem, which is likely to have a solution. However, we show in Appendix B that large problem instances as involved in *CoinParty* are not practically solvable in reasonable time and thus the attack is thwarted by limiting the time for Step (S3). We can also prevent the attack on the protocol level by introducing random nonces into the hashes, i.e., the input peers share $[H(O_i|n_i)]$ in (S1). Since the nonces n_i link in- and output addresses, the nonces need to be encrypted as well. By shuffling and decrypting them only *after* mixing peer M_m has committed to the final shuffling S^m in (S3), M_m cannot predict the checksum C and mount the RMSS attack anymore. Note that this comes at the cost of a complete shuffling.

The chances of the attacker to recover C do not increase, even if he can compromise up to $n-1$ of the input peers and up to t mixing peers, where $t+1$ is the reconstruction threshold of the secret sharing scheme. Aside from substituting addresses, a malicious attacker can announce an incorrect share of C in Step (S4) to let the verification fail. As in the commitment phase, we can tolerate up to $t < m/3$ inconsistent shares of malicious mixing peers and still correctly reconstruct C. We conclude that the shuffling phase is secure against an $m/3$ malicious adversary.

5.1.3 Transaction phase

The transaction phase does not involve input peers and thus we focus on malicious mixing peers. Steps (T1), (T3), (T4), and (T5) of the transaction phase involve only addition, multiplication, and reconstruction of shares. Thus, as with the commitment phase, the security of theses steps against a $m/3$ malicious adversary follows directly from the security guarantees of Damgård's general SMC protocol [14]. Computing a wrong hash $m' \neq m$ in Step (T2) and using it to construct S in Step (T4) results in inconsistent shares of S. As long as no more than $m/3$ shares are inconsistent, the inconsistent shares can be filtered out using techniques from error detection codes. Since, our modifications shift all critical operations to the precomputation phase, the transaction phase succeeds even if up to $2m/3$ mixing peers fail or halt the protocol, i.e., without announcing inconsistent shares, because reconstruction requires only $t+1 = \lfloor (m-1)/3 \rfloor + 1$ consistent shares. Finally, a malicious peer could announce an incorrect signature and thus an invalid transaction in Step (T5), which will then be rejected by the Bitcoin network. However, since the protocol finishes correctly under the mentioned assumptions, the remaining honest mixing peers will announce the correct transaction to the Bitcoin network.

5.2 Anonymity

We first argue why *CoinParty* performs a random and unlinkable shuffling and then analyse in detail which level of anonymity is guaranteed by this shuffling.

5.2.1 Unlinkability and randomness

We note that unlinkability and randomness depend only on the shuffling phase (Section 4.2). If there is an error in this phase, the protocol enters the error and reversion phase (Section 4.4) and funds are restored to the inputs while the output addresses are considered burnt and are discarded. Thus, errors during the shuffling phase have no impact on unlinkability and we only need to consider correct runs of this phase in our anonymity analysis.

The proof for unlinkability is then basically the same as for Brickell and Shmatikov [10] and we only sketch it here. The argument for unlinkability of in- and output addresses is that by using an encryption scheme E which is IND-CCA2 and length regular, the ciphertexts $[\![O_{i=1...m}]\!]_{K_j:K_m}$ are *indistinguishable*. Concretely, the attacker, given the public key K_j of mix M_j, cannot decide which ciphertext $[\![O_{i'=1...m}]\!]_{K_j:K_m}$ corresponds to the encryption of $[\![O_{i=1...m}]\!]_{K_{j+1}:K_m}$. Thus, the attacker cannot link ciphertexts in S^j and S^{j+1}, i.e., he cannot observe the permutation π_j applied by M_j. Furthermore, the decryption mixnet ensures participation of all mixing peers in the shuffling, i.e., in particular that M_j cannot be skipped. Hence, a single honest mixing peer can ensure the unlinkability of the shuffling.

We now show that the shuffling is random. The permutations $\pi_{j<m}$ only ensure that the last mix M_m decrypts the output addresses under an unknown shuffling, but do not contribute towards the randomness of the shuffling since the permutation π_m applied by M_m is a lexicographic ordering and thus fixed. The lexicographical ordering is verifiable by all other peers, thus preventing any attempt of M_m to undermine the randomness of the shuffling (cf. Appendix A). The source of randomness is the final permutation π which is obtained from a PRNG seeded with the checksum C, i.e., the sum over the hashes of all output addresses. Thus, if at least one honest input peer chooses a random output address, C is random within the range of the hash function and hence π is a also random. We conclude that *CoinParty* performs a random and unlinkable shuffling as long as at least one input and one mixing peer honestly follow the protocol.

5.2.2 Anonymity Level

Based on observations of the blockchain an attacker can try to guess the mapping between a mixing participant's input and output address. The set of addresses among which the attacker has to guess is the *anonymity set* and its size the achieved *anonymity level*. A larger anonymity set leads to a smaller probability of a correct guess and hence more anonymity. In the following, we analyze an input peer's anonymity against (i) outside attackers who only observe the blockchain, (ii) other input peers, and (iii) the mixing peers.

Outsiders. Our threshold transactions are indistinguishable from standard Bitcoin transactions. Thus, *CoinParty*'s mixing transactions can only be identified as such by (i) their correlation in time and (ii) the reoccurring output value of ν Bitcoins, i.e., the mixing amount. Generally, *CoinParty* produces mixing transaction chains of length two: First, input peer i commits at least ν funds to the escrow address T_i during $[t_0, t_1]$ in one transaction $I_i \xrightarrow{\nu} T_i$. In the transaction phase $[t_1, t_2]$, ν Bitcoins from T_i are mixed to another participant's output address $O_{\pi(i)}$ in a second transaction $T_i \xrightarrow{\nu} O_{\pi(i)}$. Note that the mixing amount ν is known to the input peers and we thus assume it is also known to the attacker. The question is whether this transaction pattern is unique enough to distinguish mixing from non-mixing transactions in the blockchain.

To establish a *lower bound* for the anonymity level, we first assume that an attacker is able to distinguish the n

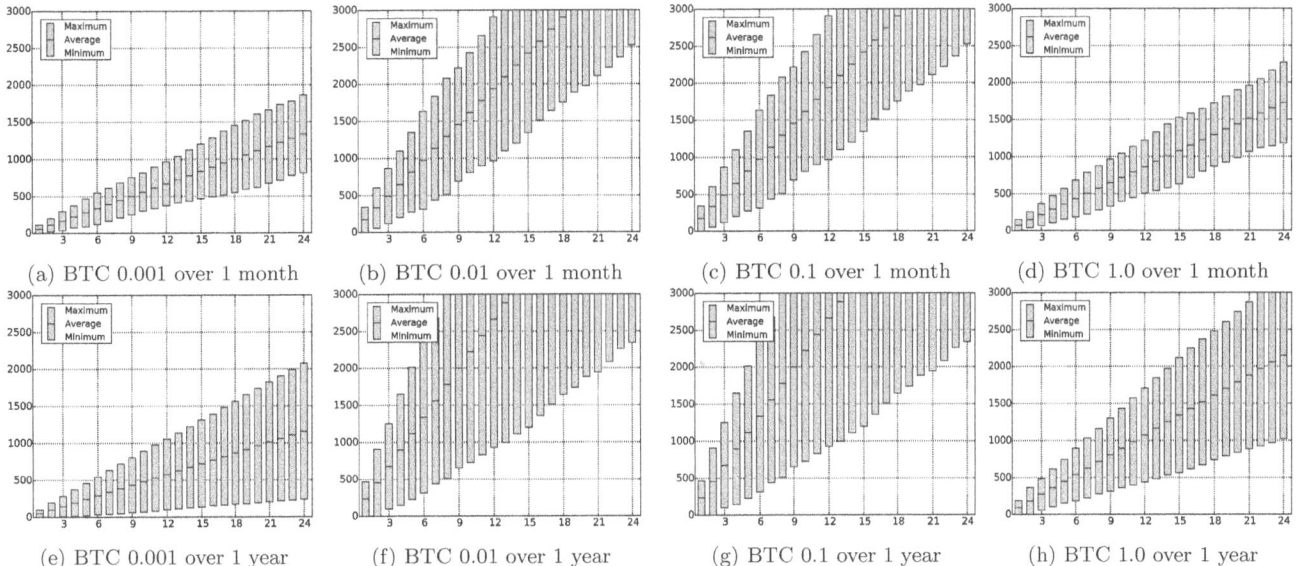

Figure 2: Size of the anonymity set (minimum, average, and maximum) for different mixing windows $w = 1, ..., 24$ hours and mixing values $\nu = 0.001, 0.01, 0.1, 1.0$ BTC in June 2014 (top (a)-(d)) and from June 2013 to July 2014 (bottom (e)-(h)).

mixing transaction chains produced by *CoinParty* from all other transactions in the blockchain during the time frame $[t_0, t_2]$ for commitment and transaction. The attacker however cannot distinguish between the n transactions belonging to the same mixing operations. Thus, the anonymity level against outsiders is at least n, or even $k \cdot n$ if there are k contemptuous mixing operations with n participants each.

We now show that our approach of mixing in multiple one-to-one transactions instead of using one single group transaction significantly increases the anonymity set to sizes similar to those realized by the early centralized mixing services. We note that input peers can vary the transaction amount in the commitment phase by transferring arbitrary amounts $\nu' \geq \nu$ to T_i (they just receive the leftovers $\nu' - \nu$ after the mixing on a fresh change address). The commitment $I_i \rightarrow T_i$ thereby becomes indistinguishable from all other transactions in $[t_0, t_1]$ with an amount $\geq \nu$. However, we cannot hide the tell-tale ν transaction $T_i \xrightarrow{\nu} O_{\pi(i)}$ during the transaction phase $[t_1, t_2]$ with the same trick, since our current design of the shuffling phase limits us to mix the same amount ν between all mixing participants. The size of the anonymity set for the transactions $T_i \xrightarrow{\nu} O_{\pi(i)}$ is thus the number of other transactions with an output value of ν BTC in the time frame $[t_1, t_2]$. We have analyzed the transactions in the blockchain between June 2013 and July 2014 (long term) and in June 2014 (short term) in order to determine how to sensibly choose ν to provide a high anonymity level. We choose a long and short observation period to show that results are consistent for the past and present and are thus also good indication for the future. Although some differences can be observed, $1, 0.1, 0.01$, and 0.0001 BTC are notably popular output values in both time spans. E.g., there are $120\,318$ transactions for 0.01 BTC in June 2014. These values are promising choices for ν.

Even when using these popular values, releasing all mixing transactions at the same time would render them easily distinguishable from non-mixing transactions by their strong correlation in time. Thus, the length of the transaction phase $[t_1, t_2]$ over which transactions are released to the Bit-

coin network, referred to as *mixing window*, has to be chosen reasonably in order to hide *CoinParty*'s mixing transactions among normal Bitcoin transactions. We again analyzed the blockchain to quantify how much different mixing windows increase the anonymity level. Figure 2 plots the minimum, average, and maximum anonymity level for mixing windows of 1 up to 24 hours for the four popular transaction values $1, 0.1, 0.01$, and 0.001 BTC. We moved a sliding window of the respective size, i.e. 1 to 24 hours, over the blockchain and calculated minimum, maximum, and average over all window positions. We observe that increasing the mixing window greatly increases the achieved minimum, average, and maximum anonymity levels. Already a mixing window of 3 hours provides for nearly all cases (except (e)) a minimum additional anonymity level > 0 and an average additional anonymity level of 100 to 500. Results for the long (past) and short (present) observation period are consistent and thus provide a good indication for choosing mixing windows also in future. It is important to note that these anonymity levels, denoted by N, are *in addition* to the anonymity level of the mixing operation itself, i.e., the lower bound established above. Thus, even in case (e) with a mixing window of 3 hours where non-mixing transactions do not necessarily offer additional anonymity, i.e., $N = 0$, the anonymity level is still at least $k \cdot n$, if k parallel mixings each with n participants take place within this mixing window.

Input peers. If all input peers are honest, anonymity of one input peer against the others is practically the same as for protocol outsiders, since input peers do not know which other input peers participate in the shuffling. We achieve this by introducing dedicated mixing peers and modifying the verification of the shuffling to not require involvement of any input peer (Section 4.2), unlike related work [28].

The case is different, when an attacker compromises c of the n input peers. He can then distinguish a mixing transaction from the other non-mixing transactions in the blockchain, if one of the compromised input addresses is mapped to an honest input peer's output address or vice versa. This allows the adversary to tie one transaction with probability

$p = 1 - (1 - c/n)^2$ to the mixing. A plot of p versus c/n is included in Appendix C, e.g., showing that the attacker needs to compromise only $c/n = 50\%$ of the input peers to identify 75% of the mixing's transactions. We now assume the attacker has thereby tied input address I_i to the mixing and now tries to link it to the corresponding output address O_i. It can be showed using basic probability theory that in our approach the attacker then has a success probability of $p' = p/(n-c) + (1-p)/(n-c+N')$ where $N' := N/(1-p)$ to guess the corresponding output address. In related work this probability is $1/(n-c)$. Our scheme thus provides equal anonymity for $N' = 0$ and is better for $N' > 0$. To give an example, for $n = 100$ participants of which $c/n = 10\%$ are compromised, the attacker guesses correctly with $p = 0.011$ for the related work and only $p = 0.003$ for our scheme with $N = 500$ (e.g., for a mixing amount of 0.01 or 0.1 BTC and a mixing window of at least 3 hours according to Figure 2).

Such sybil attacks seem endemic to Bitcoin mixes where participation is free or very cheap (cf. Section 5.6): The adversary can use the mixing service to generate untraceable Bitcoin addresses which can then be used as input addresses to attack anonymity in another mixing. An obvious solution is to make such attacks expensive by charging mixing fees, resulting in a trade-off with our *cost efficiency* requirement.

Mixing peers. The *mixing peers* inevitably learn which input and output addresses are involved in the mixing operation, as they have to sign the corresponding transactions and release them to the Bitcoin network. However, since mixing peers do not learn which output belongs to which input address as proved in Section 5.2.1, the anonymity level against mixing peers is equal to the number of participants in the mixing n which is as good as the related work [28, 31] and significantly better than [9, 20].

We conclude our analysis with the remark that our results are consistent with the results from the field of anonymous communications: Mixing inputs and outputs must occur over a sufficiently long time span, the longer the time span the higher the achieved level of anonymity. Here, our results provide concrete indication that time windows around 3 hours are reasonable and practical for Bitcoin mixing services. More importantly, the results show that *CoinParty* can provide levels of anonymity that are orders of magnitude higher than those achieved by related work [20, 28, 31], even when a fraction of the input peers is compromised.

5.3 Deniability

A user can simply deny having participated in a mixing if she can plausibly deny owning a Bitcoin address. However, the recent works on identifying ownership of addresses and even real identities of Bitcoins users render this option questionable. Indeed, these results are the main motivation for the development of mixing services. Thus, instead we need to analyze whether a user can plausibly deny that one of her addresses was part of a mixing operation.

Outsiders. Deniability against outsiders is achieved by the indistinguishability of mixing and normal transactions. We argue that if there are at any point many more non-mixing than mixing transactions in the Bitcoin network, a user can plausibly deny having participated in a mixing. Our analysis of the blockchain in the previous section shows that there are indeed many non-mixing transactions of the same form as those issued by *CoinParty*, if a mixing window of sufficient size and popular mixing values are used.

Input peers. In our anonymity analysis, we have showed that an adversary that corrupts c input peers can tie a fraction of $p = 1 - (1 - c/n)^2$ of the transactions to the mixing. Thus, an honest input peer is not bound to the mixing with probability $1 - p = (1 - c/n)^2$ and can deny her participation. Again, we refer to Appendix C for a plot of c/n versus p. Note that due to our modifications to the shuffling protocol (cf. Section 4.2, Appendix A) it is ensured that the shuffling is random. Thus a targeted attack on a specific input peer only succeeds with probability p.

Mixing peers. Deniability against mixing peers is not achieved because they learn which in- and output addresses participated in the mixing during the shuffling phase. Achieving deniability against the mixes would require blindly signing transactions. The cryptographic primitives for blind signatures exist but we consider this future work.

5.4 Performance Evaluation

In this section, we analyze whether *CoinParty* fulfils the *performance* requirement as presented in Section 3. To this end, we present a quantitative evaluation of our prototype in a real world network setting. A qualitative analysis is presented in Appendix D due to space constraints. Input peers in the *CoinParty* protocol only need to compute a small constant amount of ECDSA signatures and encryptions of their output addresses during the commitment phase. We include a brief evaluation of their overhead in Appendix E and concentrate our analysis here on the mixing peers which shoulder most of the overhead. We also consider only successful protocol runs, as the performance of the error and reversion phase (excluding mechanisms for tracing malicious peers) is the same as for a successful transaction phase run.

Quantitative Analysis. We have implemented a prototype of *CoinParty* in Python 2.7 based on the *VIFF* SMC framework [30] which provides primitives secure against malicious adversaries. We use the *Elliptic Curve Integrated Encryption Scheme* (ECIES) over the `secp256k1` curve as encryption scheme E in the shuffling phase. ECDSA is used for signatures on protocol messages in the shuffling phase. VIFF uses the asynchronous communication framework *Twisted* to handle communication between peers while communication in the shuffling phases is implemented using separate TCP sockets between each pair of mixing peers. Functionality related to the Bitcoin protocol, e.g., generating addresses and transactions, has been implemented using *bitcointools* [1]. All functionality related to elliptic curves cryptography is based on *pyelliptic* [15].

We have carried out an extensive evaluation on Microsoft's Azure Cloud, varying the number of mixing and input peers. Each mixing peer runs in a small (A1) instance with one virtual core and 1.75 GB RAM running Ubuntu 12.04 LTS. In all evaluation settings, virtual machines are distributed over different geographical locations in Western and Northern Europe as well as Western and Eastern US. The pairwise round trip times (RTTs) between mixing peers are 50 - 100 ms for Europe ↔ Europe and US ↔ US as well as 150 - 200 ms for Europe ↔ US. Bandwidth measurements range from 5 to 15 MBit/s. Each evaluation setting is aggregated over 10 runs. We repeated all experiments on a single machine (32 cores, 32 GB RAM, Ubuntu 12.04 LTS), running each mixing peer as a separate process on one of the cores and all communication between peers over the local loopback interface. The experiments in the local setting serve

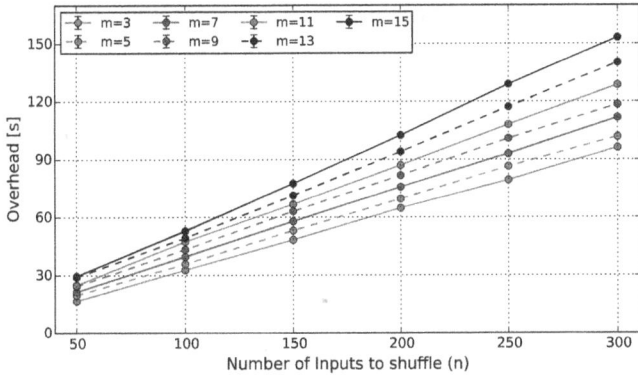

(a) Performance in the cloud network setting.

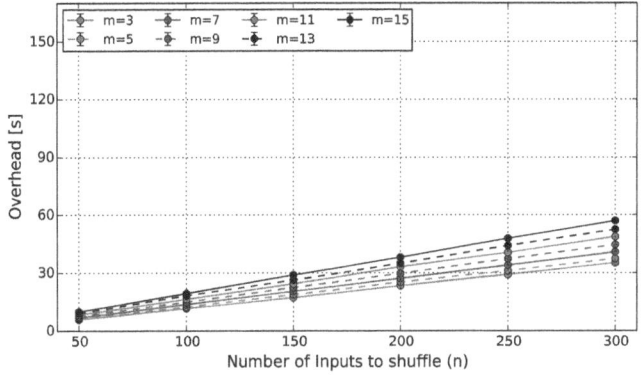

(b) Performance in the local network setting.

Figure 3: Performance in the cloud (left) and local network setting (right) for 50 to 300 input and 3 to 15 mixing peers.

to distinguish time spent for processing from time spent for communication which is difficult to measure separately due to the asynchronous communication model in VIFF.

Figure 3 shows the time for the complete protocol, i.e., including precomputations, for both the cloud (a) and the local network setting (b). We show the performance for $m = 3, 5, 7, 9, 11, 13, 15$ mixing peers, respectively, running a mixing over $n = 50, 100, 150, 200, 250, 300$ inputs including the standard deviation which was clearly below 1 s for all experiments. The results show that the runtime scales approx. linearly with the number of inputs to mix. Furthermore, the runtime is higher and grows stronger in n if a larger number of mixing peers m is chosen due to the increased number of communication rounds. The comparison with the local setting clearly shows that at least half of the overhead is due to communication. In all settings, *CoinParty* finishes in less than three minutes which clearly shows that *CoinParty* is feasible in real world settings. The online runtime of *CoinParty* is even faster because approx. 70 % of the runtime in both settings are spent on precomputations. In all settings, the communication overhead ranges from a few hundreds of KBs to a few MBs per mixing peer. Hence, we conclude that *CoinParty* fulfils the stated performance goals.

5.5 Compatibility

CoinParty deviates from standard Bitcoin clients in two ways: First, *CoinParty* implements a distributed generation of Bitcoin addresses with shared private keys while in standard Bitcoin clients addresses are generated locally and the client owns the complete private key. Apart from the correct format, generating a valid Bitcoin address thus boils down to generating a correct ECDSA key pair. We have reconstructed the private keys and tested that the generated private and public keys form correct ECDSA key pairs. Second, *CoinParty* replaces the standard ECDSA signature with a threshold ECDSA signature computed collaboratively by the mixing peers. In order to form correct Bitcoin transactions, the generated signatures need to be verifiable using the public key corresponding to the escrow addresses T_i which we have successfully tested. Thus, transactions created by *CoinParty* are fully compatible with the Bitcoin protocol.

5.6 Cost efficiency

A Bitcoin mixing service can principally involve two kinds of fees, (i) transaction fees which are paid for including the

issued mixing transactions in the blockchain and (2) mixing fees demanded by the mixing services themselves.

Transaction fees. Unlike other decentralized Bitcoin mixing protocols, *CoinParty* does not bundle mixing transactions into one joint transaction with many inputs and outputs. Instead, *CoinParty* issues one transaction with one input and a few outputs per mixing input, i.e., n separate transactions. As of today, Bitcoin transactions smaller than 1 KB can be safely sent without fees [7]. Transactions in *CoinParty* do not exceed this size and would not require any transaction fees at all. If desired, transaction fees τ can be paid nevertheless. Input peers then commit at least $\nu + \tau$ funds to T_i but only ν funds are transferred in the mixing transaction $T_i \xrightarrow{\nu} O_{\pi(i)}$.

Mixing fees. Anyone can set up a *CoinParty* mixing peer and collaborate with others to provide mixing services. Even the input peers themselves can function as mixing peers. Thus, *CoinParty* does not require any third party services that could charge mixing fees. On the other side, as we note in Section 5.2, it might be reasonable to charge fees to make sybil attacks expensive money-wise. Mixing fees must be handled with care so that they do not identify mixing transactions which would decrease anonymity and chances of deniability. This effect and possible solutions have been discussed in detail in [9].

6. RELATED WORK

In the following we analyze previously proposed approaches to secure and anonymous Bitcoin mixing and highlight the differences to *CoinParty*, as summarized in Table 1.

1st *Generation Bitcoin mixes* [5,6,8] operate centrally and do not provide any guarantees that Bitcoins are actually mixed or even returned. Furthermore, a centralized mix can link input to output addresses and could be forced to reveal this information, e.g., by subpoena. Most of the 1st *Generation mixes* also demand significant mixing fees. However, mixing transactions cannot be distinguished from nonmixing transactions, if the mixing service provides fresh addresses for each input. Thus, deniability is provided against outsiders but not against the mix itself. Also, sybil attacks can be mounted by malicious participants to decrease anonymity as shown in Section 5.2.

Mixcoin [9] still depends on a centralized mixing service but introduces a mechanism to hold a mix accountable if funds are not returned. However, anonymity against the

Approach	Security	Anonymity Level			Deniability	Mixing Delay	Fees	Comp.
1st Generation [5,8]	None	0	$>> n$	$>> n$	Yes	1 window	Mix fees	Yes
Mixcoin [9]	Accountability	0	$>> n$	$>> n$	Yes	1 TX + 1 window	Mix fees	Yes
CoinJoin [20]	Group TX	0	$n - c$	n	No	1 TX	TX fees	Yes
CoinShuffle [28]	Group TX	n	$n - c$	n	No	1 TX	TX fees	Yes
SMC [27,31]	Group TX	n	$n - c$	n	No	1 TX	TX fees	Yes
ZeroCash [3,23]	ZKPs	∞	∞	∞	Yes	-	-	No
CoinParty	2/3 honest	n	$> n - c$	$n + N$	$(1 - c/n)^2$	2 TX + 1 window	None	Yes

Table 1: Comparison of our *CoinParty* system to the related works by the most important design requirements. The denoted anonymity level denotes the anonymity an input achieves against (1) the mixing peers (2) c of n malicious input peers, and (3) outsiders, where N depends on the mixing windows as analyzed in Section 5.2.

mix is not provided and the authors propose as a fix to chain multiple mixes. While this potentially achieves anonymity levels similar to *CoinParty*, chaining mixes incurs significant mixing fees and increases the risk of theft as well as the mixing delay. Transactions issued by Mixcoin are indistinguishable from those created by 1st generation Bitcoin mixes and thus Mixcoin provides the same means for deniability.

CoinJoin [20] was first to achieve security against stealing mixes by using group transactions. Still, CoinJoin depends on a central service to shuffle the output addresses and thus provides no anonymity against insiders. Furthermore, the use of group transactions limits the anonymity level to the number of participants n, prevents plausible deniability and requires transaction fees for larger mixing groups.

CoinShuffle [28], like CoinJoin, uses group transactions to ensure correctness and thus shares the corresponding disadvantages, i.e., limited anonymity levels, no deniability, and potential transaction fees. CoinShuffle improves over CoinJoin by using decryption mixnets for address shuffling which achieves anonymity against insiders. However, in CoinShuffle the last peer is in the unique position to determine the outcome of the shuffling and might exploit this to select preferred input addresses to her own outputs addresses. Our proposed shuffling protocol fixes this issue.

The applicability of SMC to Bitcoin mixing was first recognized by member *hashcoin* of the *bitcointalk* forum [16] who brought up the crude idea to use SMC for shuffling output addresses. Later, Rosenfeld [27] and Yang [31] elaborated on this idea in blog posts. However, the presented schemes do not scale with the number of inputs and have not been thoroughly specified. Furthermore, all of the proposed schemes rely on group transactions with the mentioned disadvantages w.r.t. anonymity, deniability, and costs.

Finally, *ZeroCoin* [23] and later *ZeroCash* [3] have been proposed which basically replace Bitcoin's public transaction history by Zero-Knowledge Proofs (ZKPs) to ensure validity of transactions. A payment in *ZeroCash* is fully unlinkable since it reveals neither the origin or destination nor the amount of the transaction. However, those approaches are extensions to Bitcoin that cannot be deployed without significant modifications to the Bitcoin system.

Compared to related work, *CoinParty* introduces several improvements. First and most important, *CoinParty* leverages threshold ECDSA signatures for Bitcoin mixing, instead of depending on group transactions. This allows the mixing to take place in one-to-one transactions which increases the achievable anonymity level by orders of magnitude as analyzed in Section 5.2 and additionally provides plausible deniability against outsiders (Section 5.3). Second, due to the improved shuffling verification scheme the

increased anonymity level and deniability are, with some restrictions, also guaranteed against malicious input peers, other than in *CoinShuffle* where input peers actively participate in the protocol. Finally, using several small transactions as opposed to one large group transaction requires no transaction fees at all. The mixing delay is slightly larger than for *CoinJoin, CoinShuffle*, and the approaches by Yang and Rosenfeld which require only one transaction. Especially, waiting the desired mixing window $[t_1, t_2]$, as analyzed in Section 5.2, increases the mixing delay. However, we believe this can and must be tolerated if strong anonymity is desired. Compared to *MixCoin* which provides a similar anonymity level when chaining multiple mixes, *CoinParty*'s mixing is by orders of magnitude faster and fully secure.

7. CONCLUSION

Different works successfully attacked anonymity of Bitcoin addresses by analyzing transactions in the blockchain [2, 22, 25, 26, 29]. Those works make evident the necessity of mixing services and several such systems have been recently proposed [9, 20, 28]. However, a detailed analysis reveals disadvantages with each of those systems (Sections 3 and 6).

In this paper, we have thus presented *CoinParty*, a novel mixing service for Bitcoins that improves significantly over the related work by combining the advantages of centralized and decentralized mixes in a single system. *CoinParty* achieves this by employing two existing building blocks, i.e., threshold ECDSA [17] and decryption mixnets [12, 28]. We introduce several modifications that improve on robustness, anonymity, and deniability that are relevant also beyond the scope of our work. Importantly, we show by analyzing the actual Bitcoin blockchain how our single transaction pattern provides anonymity by orders of magnitude higher than what is achieved by the group transaction pattern that the majority of related work depends on. An extensive evaluation of our implemented prototype demonstrates that *CoinParty* scales better than related work, e.g., [28], due to the possible separation of input and mixing peers. The threshold ECDSA scheme implemented as part of the prototype is efficient and secure against malicious adversaries and can be used beyond our work, e.g., for securing Bitcoin wallets. Finally, although we focused on Bitcoin, our work is directly compatible with other crypto-currencies which use the same ECDSA primitive, e.g., Litecoin and Mastercoin.

Acknowledgments

This work has been co-funded by the Excellence Initiative of the German federal and state governments and the German Research Foundation (DFG) CRC 1053 "MAKI".

8. REFERENCES

[1] G. Andresen. bitcointools, 2014.
https://github.com/gavinandresen/bitcointools.

[2] E. Androulaki et al. Evaluating User Privacy in Bitcoin. In *FC*. Springer, 2013.

[3] E. Ben-Sasson et al. Zerocash: Decentralized Anonymous Payments from Bitcoin. In *Security & Privacy*. IEEE, 2014.

[4] Bitcoin Charts, 2014.
http://bitcoincharts.com/bitcoin/.

[5] Bitcoin Fog, 2014. http://www.bitcoinfog.com/.

[6] Bitcoin Wiki. Mixing Services, 2014.
http://en.bitcoin.it/wiki/Category:Mixing_Services.

[7] Bitcoin Wiki. Transaction fees, 2014.
https://en.bitcoin.it/wiki/Transaction_fees.

[8] BitLaundry, 2014. http://bitlaundry.appspot.com/.

[9] J. Bonneau et al. Mixcoin: Anonymity for Bitcoin with accountable mixes. In *FC*, 2014.

[10] J. Brickell and V. Shmatikov. Efficient Anonymity-Preserving Data Collection. In *SIGKDD*. ACM, 2006.

[11] CoinSplitter, 2014. http://coinsplitter.org/.

[12] H. Corrigan-Gibbs and B. Ford. Dissent: Accountable Anonymous Group Messaging. In *CCS*. ACM, 2010.

[13] R. Cramer, I. Damgård, and Y. Ishai. Share Conversion, Pseudorandom Secret-Sharing and Applications to Secure Computation. In *Theory of Cryptography*. Springer, 2005.

[14] I. Damgård et al. Asynchronous Multiparty Computation: Theory and Implementation. In *PKC*. Springer, 2009.

[15] Y. Guibet. pyelliptic, 2014.
https://pypi.python.org/pypi/pyelliptic.

[16] hashcoin. Blind Bitcoin Transfers. Forum Post, 2011.
https://bitcointalk.org/index.php?topic=12751.
msg315793#msg315793.

[17] M. Ibrahim et al. A robust threshold elliptic curve digital signature providing a new verifiable secret sharing scheme. In *Circuits and Systems*. IEEE, 2003.

[18] Y. Lindell and B. Pinkas. Secure Multiparty Computation for Privacy-Preserving Data Mining. *Journal of Privacy and Confidentiality*, 1(1), 2009.

[19] V. Lyubashevsky. The Parity Problem in the Presence of Noise, Decoding Random Linear Codes, and the Subset Sum Problem. In *RANDOM*. Springer, 2005.

[20] G. Maxwell. CoinJoin. Forum post, 2013.
https://bitcointalk.org/index.php?topic=279249.

[21] G. Maxwell. CoinSwap. Forum post, 2013.
https://bitcointalk.org/index.php?topic=321228.

[22] S. Meiklejohn et al. A Fistful of Bitcoins: Characterizing Payments Among Men with No Names. In *IMC*. ACM, 2013.

[23] I. Miers et al. Zerocoin: Anonymous Distributed E-Cash from Bitcoin. In *Security & Privacy*. IEEE, 2013.

[24] S. Nakamoto. Bitcoin: A Peer-to-Peer Electronic Cash System. bitcoin.org, 2008.

[25] F. Reid and M. Harrigan. An Analysis of Anonymity in the Bitcoin System. In *PASSAT*, 2011.

[26] D. Ron and A. Shamir. Quantitative Analysis of the Full Bitcoin Transaction Graph. In *FC*. Springer, 2013.

[27] M. Rosenfeld. Using mixing transactions to improve anonymity. Forum post, 2012.
https://bitcointalk.org/index.php?topic=54266.

[28] T. Ruffing, P. Moreno-Sanchez, and A. Kate. CoinShuffle: Practical Decentralized Coin Mixing for Bitcoin. In *HotPETS*, 2014.

[29] M. Spagnuolo, F. Maggi, and S. Zanero. BitIodine: Extracting Intelligence from the Bitcoin Network. *FC*, 2014.

[30] VIFF Development Team. VIFF, the Virtual Ideal Functionality Framework, 2010. http://viff.dk/.

[31] E. Z. Yang. Secure multiparty Bitcoin anonymization. Blog post, 2012. http://blog.ezyang.com/2012/07/secure-multiparty-bitcoin-anonymization/.

APPENDIX
A. RANDOMNESS OF SHUFFLING

The randomness of the performed shuffling (Section 4.2) is an important property. If an attacker can control the outcome of the shuffling, he can (i) select which output address receives funds from which input address and (ii) break deniability for specific users in a targeted fashion (Section 5.3). As we show, the closely related CoinShuffle [28] does not achieve a random shuffling. After the first $m-1$ shuffling steps in CoinShuffle, the mixing peer M_m receives from M_{m-1} the shuffling S^{m-1}, with only one layer of encryption left, i.e., E_{K_m}. Note that a malicious M_m can first lift E_{K_m} and then, with knowledge of the output addresses, apply a final permutation π_m. By choosing π_m accordingly, M_m can thus completely determine the outcome of the shuffling. This cannot even be detected by the other mixing peers.

CoinParty fixes this issue by requiring M_m to apply a publicly verifiable permutation, i.e., a lexicographic sorting. The randomness of the final shuffling π then depends only on the sum of the hashed output addresses, i.e., $C = \sum_{i=1}^{n} H(O_i)$. To control π, an attacker needs to choose *all* output addresses $O_1, ..., O_m$ which is clearly neither a realistic nor rational attack scenario (as this would also mean that the attacker controls *all* input addresses).

B. OUTPUT ADDRESSES SUBSTITUTION

We show how a malicious adversary can steal funds during the shuffling phase (Section 4.2), if he can solve an instance of the *Random Modular Subset Sum* problem. The last mixing peer M_m can substitute the original output addresses $O_1, ..., O_n$ with his own $O'_1, ..., O'_n$ without being detected iff $C = \sum_{i=1}^{n} H(O_i) = \sum_{i=1}^{n} H(O'_i)$. Finding such a sequence $O'_1, ..., O'_n$ requires solving a *Random Modular Subset Sum* (RMSS) problem, with modulus $M = 2^{len(H)}$, random elements $\{a_1, ..., a_N\} \in_U [0, M)$ and target sum C. $\delta = N/log(M)$ is called the density of the problem and high density RMSS instances are very likely to have a solution. The attacker can generate such a high density instance of the problem by pre-generating a large number of addresses O'_i and corresponding hashes $a_i = H(O'_i) \in [0, M)$. The best known algorithm for solving such instances has runtime $M^{O(1/log(N))}$ [19]. Clearly, the runtime decreases if N grows, i.e., if we generate a larger pool of hashes to select the n addresses O'_i from. Contrarily, as M, the length of the hash function, grows, the runtime increases.

We make a practical estimate, which sizes of the RMSS problem are solvable in reasonable time. As a concrete example, we assume our checksum C is computed from 512-bit hashes, i.e. $M = 2^{256}$. Then, generating 10^{12} hashes amounts to roughly 58 TB of storage and we assume it is not feasible to generate more than $N \leq 10^{12}$ such hashes. Thus, setting $N = 10^{12}$ gives a lower bound on the runtime. Assuming there is a solution at all, it can then be found in $(2^{512})^{1/log(10^{12})} = 2^{512/12} = 2^{52}$ operations, which is already quite challenging to solve practically. Using 1536-bit hashes, i.e. $M = 2^{1536}$, we get a runtime of 2^{128} operations which is comparable to the complexity of breaking keys for long term security for AES. Note that using 1536-bit or even longer hashes for the checksum computation does not significantly increase the overhead of the protocol. Thus we conclude that the RMSS attack can be thwarted by putting a time-bound on the Step (5) of the shuffling phase 4.2.

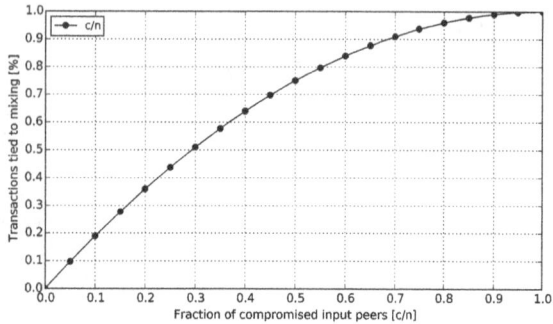

Figure 4: Fraction of identified mixing transactions vs fraction of compromised input peers.

C. SYBIL ATTACKS

An attacker that controls c of the n input peers can tie a fraction $1 - (1 - c/n)^2$ of the n mixing transactions to the mixing. Figure 4 plots the fraction of identified transactions versus the fraction c/n of compromised input peers. The plot, e.g., shows that an attacker can already tie 75 % of the transactions to the mixing, if he can compromise 50 % of the participants. Because *CoinParty* ensures randomness of the shuffling (Appendix A), the attacker cannot choose which transactions to tie to the mixing.

D. QUALITATIVE OVERHEAD PER MIXING PEER

In addition to our quantitative performance evaluation (cf. Section 5.4), Table 2 qualitatively summarizes the overhead of *CoinParty* for the three protocol phases, i.e., commitment, shuffling, and transaction. Communication rounds contain only the sequential synchronization points between mixing peers, i.e., message exchanges that cannot be batched and processed in parallel. We divide our discussion into precomputation efforts and online overhead. Notably, precomputations allow us to speed up the mixing process by utilizing otherwise idle resources before the actual mixing.

Precomputing the escrow addresses T_i requires n pseudorandom secret sharings (*PRSS*) in order to draw the shares $[d_i]$ of the secret key d_i. Then, n scalar-point multiplications over the elliptic curve (*EC-Mul*) are required to obtain $[Q_i] = [d_i G]$. Finally, we obtain the public key Q_i corresponding to T_i in n reconstructions (*S-Open*) in one round. For the shuffling phase, it is not possible to benefit from precomputations. For the transaction phase, we precompute for each T_i, $[k_i]$, $[k_i^{-1}]$, $[k_i^{-1}] * [d_i] \cdot R$ and kG as explained in Section 4.3. This first requires n PRSS for drawing the $[k_i]$. Computing the inverses $[k_i^{-1}], i = 1...n$, costs n PRSS, n multiplications on shares (*S-Mul*) batched into one round, and n *S-Open* batched into one round. Deriving $[k_i^{-1}] * [d_i] \cdot R, i = 1...n$, requires n *S-Mul* in one round and n *EC-Mul*. Finally, precomputing $k_i G, i = 1..n$, can be done in another n *EC-Mul* and n *S-Open* in one round.

Because of the extensive precomputations, the online phase of *CoinParty* is considerably cheaper. The commitment incurs no significant overhead, because the mixing peers only need to check that all input peers transferred their funds to the respective addresses T_i. In the shuffling phase, the processing overhead per mixing peer consists of one signature verification (*Ver*) for the received shuffling, n decryption operations (*Dec*) as well as one signature operation (*Sig*) to

Phase	Processing per Mixing Peer	Rounds
Precomputation		
Commit	n PRSS + n EC-Mul + n S-Open	1
Shuffle	-	-
Transaction	$2n$ PRSS + $2n$ S-Mul $+ n$ EC-Mul + $2n$ S-Open	4
Online		
Commit	-	-
Shuffle	1 S-Open + n Dec + 1 Sig + 1 Ver	$m + 1$
Transaction	n S-Open	1

Table 2: Qualitative overhead per mixing peer.

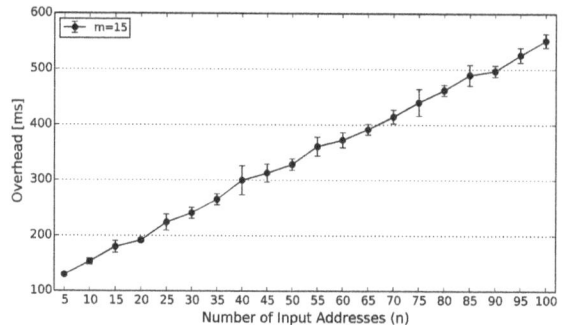

Figure 5: Overhead on one input peer in *CoinParty*.

create the next shuffling and finally one share reconstruction for the checksum C. However, the predominant overhead results from the necessary communication, because the shuffling requires m consecutive rounds of decryption and permutation plus one subsequent round for reconstructing C. Finally, the online overhead of the transaction phase is comparably small with just n reconstructions batched into one round to obtain the signature part S from the shares $e[k^{-1}] + [k^{-1}] * [d] \cdot R$.

E. OVERHEAD PER INPUT PEER

Additionally to our performance evaluation of the mixing peers (Section 5.4), we also consider the performance impact on the input peers in this section. The overhead for one input peer i to participate in one mixing operation consists of three steps. First, input peer i must compute the layered encryption of her output address $[\![O_i]\!]_{K_1:K_m}$. This requires m ECIES encryptions, one for each of the m mixing peers. Second, the input peer must compute and share the hash of her output address to all mixing peers, i.e., distribute the sharing $[H(O_i)]$. Third, the input peer must transfer ν Bitcoins to T_i. Peer i can collect the required funds from multiple input addresses, i.e., creating a transaction $\{I_i^1, ..., I_i^n\} \xrightarrow{\nu} T_i$. For each input address I_i^j, input peer i needs to compute one ECDSA signature. Figure 5 shows the resulting processing overhead for a variable number of $n = 5$ to 100 input addresses and $m = 15$ mixing peers. This does not include the communication overhead for distributing $[\![O_i]\!]_{K_1:K_m}$ and $[H(O_i)]$ to the mixing peers, since this can take place any time during the commitment phase $[t_0, t_1]$. The plain processing overhead is considerably small even when collecting funds from $n = 100$ input addresses. Communication will add another $50 - 200$ ms, depending on the latency between the input peer and the mixing peers. With a total overhead well below 1 second, the overhead per input peer is small enough to not influence the applicability of *CoinParty*.

The BORG: Nanoprobing Binaries for Buffer Overreads

Matthias Neugschwandtner
Vienna University of Technology
SBA Research

Istvan Haller
VU University Amsterdam

Paolo Milani Comparetti
Lastline Inc.

Herbert Bos
VU University Amsterdam

ABSTRACT

Automated program testing tools typically try to explore, and cover, as much of a tested program as possible, while attempting to trigger and detect bugs. An alternative and complementary approach can be to first select a specific part of a program that may be subject to a specific class of bug, and then narrowly focus exploration towards program paths that could trigger such a bug.

In this work, we introduce the BORG (Buffer Over-Read Guard), a testing tool that uses static and dynamic program analysis, taint propagation and symbolic execution to detect buffer overread bugs in real-world programs. BORG works by first selecting buffer accesses that could lead to an overread and then guiding symbolic execution towards those accesses along program paths that could actually lead to an overread. BORG operates on binaries and does not require source code. To demonstrate BORG's effectiveness, we use it to detect overreads in six complex server applications and libraries, including lighttpd, FFmpeg and ClamAV.

1. INTRODUCTION

Buffer overreads are an increasing security concern in modern computer systems. Virtually all of today's major operating systems employ advanced protection mechanisms like Address Space Layout Randomization (ASLR) and Data Execution Prevention (DEP) to prevent attackers from diverting the control flow of a program to executable code. Because code addresses are no longer easily guessable, attackers rely on memory disclosures such as buffer overreads to find them. Typically, even a single disclosure suffices to bypass even these powerful defenses [36, 37]. Besides addresses, buffer overreads may leak sensitive user information and lead to crashes. A very recent example is the Heartbleed bug in OpenSSL [14] that allows exfiltration of cleartext data.

Even so, the problem of overreads in binaries has received little attention by the research community. The problem is that finding buffer overread vulnerabilities is hard enough if the program's source code is available, but without the source or debug symbols, it is almost impossible. Unfortunately, most commercial software consists of optimized, stripped binaries. Analysis of binary programs is desirable for developers that rely on compiled third-party COTS libraries or programs as well as security analysts auditing binary programs.

In this work, we introduce the BORG (Buffer Over-Read Guard), a tool for finding buffer overread bugs with guided symbolic execution. BORG is based on S2E [12] and works on binaries, with no source code required. At the core of our system are novel techniques for guiding the execution to a potentially vulnerable access while at the same time trying to trigger an overread on this access. To the best of our knowledge, BORG is the first automated bug finding tool targeted at finding buffer overread bugs, so we believe it can be useful in practice to harden programs against memory disclosure vulnerabilities.

The BORG's guided symbolic execution. Symbolic execution is a powerful technique for finding bugs in software. By executing a program under symbolic inputs and forking execution to explore many different program paths, symbolic execution can automatically find bugs, as well as provide concrete input values that trigger them. The fundamental limitation of this approach, of course, is that it is infeasible to explore all possible program paths. Symbolic execution suffers from "path explosion", because the number of program paths to explore grows exponentially with the number of branch points encountered. This problem is compounded by the computational cost of symbolic execution: At each branch point, a symbolic executor will invoke a costly constraint solving step to decide which branches can be reached. This difficult problem gets even harder when source code is not available and the solver must reason on binary code. Furthermore, keeping track of program state for all of the as yet unexplored paths puts pressure on memory, further impacting performance.

Whenever symbolic execution reaches a branch point, we must decide which branch to execute first. The strategy used to select paths to execute is essential to the effectiveness of symbolic execution. For testing code and finding bugs, the goal of the path selection strategy is typically to improve the overall code coverage of symbolic testing. To this end, for instance, KLEE [8] alternates between a code-coverage based path selection heuristic and random selection.

Instead of trying to cover as much code as possible, a different approach is to guide execution towards "interesting" parts of the program under test. This is the approach we follow in this work. The general idea is to first select specific parts of the tested program that are more likely to be subject to specific bug classes, in our cases overreads, and to then use a path selection strategy that guides execution towards these interesting parts while trying to violate an integrity assumption.

BORG uses such guided symbolic execution to steer the program exploration toward code that may allow for overreads. Beyond the concrete implementation for overread detection, however, we will argue that the proposed approach is general and can be applied to several classes of bugs, so long as we are able to:

1. Select potential targets in the tested program that are more likely to be vulnerable to bugs of a certain class.
2. Guide execution towards those targets.
3. Detect the occurrence of a bug as the violation of an integrity constraint.

The techniques we introduce for item 2 (guidance) are quite general. Furthermore, there are well-understood ways to express many classes of bugs as the violation of an integrity constraint (item 3). Therefore, the applicability of the techniques proposed in this paper to different classes of bugs is restricted chiefly by item 1: That is, by our ability to select targets that have a high enough likelihood of being subject to such bugs.

Contributions. To summarize, the contributions of this work are the following:

- We develop novel techniques for guiding symbolic testing of a program towards a potentially vulnerable target while trying to break an integrity constraint.
- We build a system called BORG that combines these techniques with a selection heuristic and a detection mechanism for potential buffer overreads to automatically discover such vulnerabilities.
- All of the techniques we introduce work on binary code and do not require source code.
- We apply BORG to six complex, real-world programs including lighttpd, FFmpeg, and ClamAV, and show that our system is able to automatically trigger buffer overreads in these programs.

2. OVERVIEW

Figure 1 shows a high-level overview of BORG. Given a binary

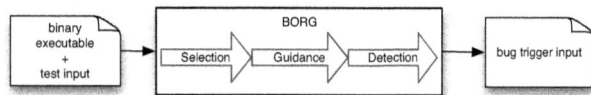

Figure 1: High-level overview of BORG

program and test data as an input, BORG will set out to find an execution path that violates a security assumption and output the corresponding malformed input. The core of our tool is an online symbolic execution engine that runs the program and generates new states on every conditional control-flow branch that depends on the program's input. Three main components that build around and on top of this core principle are essential to BORG's functionality:

Selection. Given a specific integrity assumption, the goal of this first step is to identify potentially vulnerable spots, i.e. security critical code regions that are likely to violate the integrity assumption.

Guidance. The purpose of the guidance mechanism is to select the most promising states produced by the symbolic execution engine for exploration. Promising states are more likely to lead to a violation of the integrity assumption. Therefore the states are ranked based on their likelihood to (1) actually hit the potentially vulnerable spot and (2) allow actually triggering the bug based on the state's path constraints. To this end the guidance regularly assesses the states' properties and picks the state that is ranked highest.

Detection. While the guidance attempts to trigger a bug, the detection mechanism has to check whether the integrity assumption is violated. In case of a violation BORG will terminate the current state and output a test case for this execution path.

While the principles outlined so far are fairly general, our implementation of BORG focuses on detecting overread bugs. We will discuss additional classes of bugs to which our approach could be applicable in Section 8.

2.1 Testing Process

Figure 2 shows an overview of the steps and components involved in BORG's testing process. As input, BORG will accept a binary executable along with test inputs. To obtain inputs for the tested programs, we can use inputs in the program's test suite, if available. If the program itself does not have a test suite, provided that we know at least which kind of protocol or data format the program will handle, we can use test cases from existing test suites for the corresponding protocol or data format. Concrete examples from our evaluation are the HTTP protocol and the JPG file format. If on the other hand the expected input format is unknown, we can start from any real-world input data.

Preliminary Analysis. The preliminary analysis stage combines static and dynamic analysis to gather information about the tested program. First, we perform an instrumented, concrete execution of the tested program for each available test input. During this execution, we use dynamic taint analysis to propagate taint from the test input. We thus generate detailed execution traces that include taint information for instruction operands.

The first goal of the preliminary analysis phase is to generate an accurate model of the program's intra- and inter-procedural Control Flow Graph (CFG). For this, we refine a CFG obtained from static analysis with knowledge from the dynamically generated execution traces. The dynamic execution provides information that is not easily available from static analysis, such as possible targets of indirect control flow transfers.

We further use the execution traces to collect buffer access profiles that will later be used to detect out-of-bounds buffer accesses. Specifically, we record which buffers in the program's memory are accessed by which of the program's instructions.

Target Selection. After the preliminary analysis has been completed, the next step is to select targets for testing. That is, we aim to select specific instructions in the program under test that are more likely to trigger a bug, so we can guide our testing towards those instructions. For the detection of buffer overread bugs, BORG selects all memory reads from a tainted address: That is, from an address that is derived from the program's input. We also target sensitive functions such as memcpy and strcpy if their parameters are tainted. It is easy to see that whenever a buffer access's address depends on data that can be influenced by an attacker, there is a possibility that the access will go out of bounds if we can find a program path along which the address is not calculated or sanitized correctly. For this reason, these accesses are good candidates for targeted testing. As we will show, this selection strategy is already effective for finding non-trivial bugs in real programs. On the other hand, we must point out that it is not on its own sufficient to target all accesses that can lead to overreads, because overreads can also happen with no direct data flow from user inputs to addresses. Additional selection strategies for potential overreads could be employed alongside this one to obtain additional targets and find more bugs: one approach is to rank accesses in loops based on some measure of the complexity of the code that computes the accessed address [23].

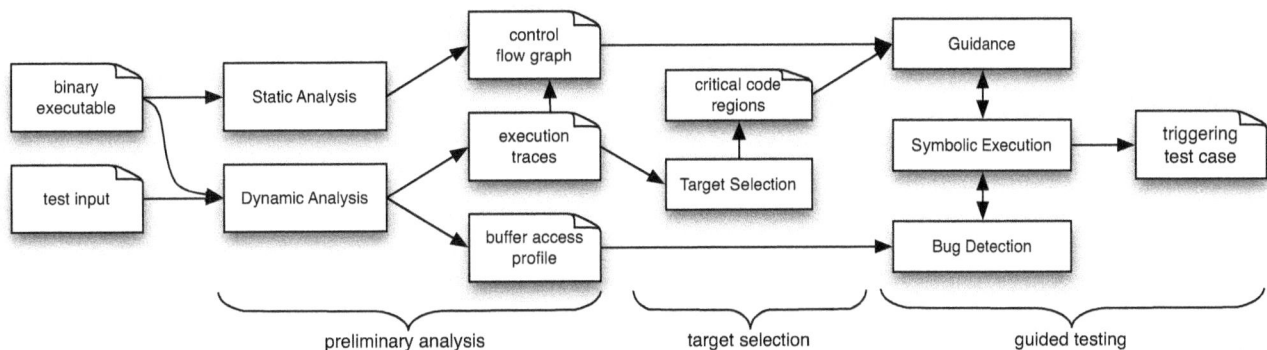

Figure 2: Overview of the testing process executed by BORG. The preliminary analysis applies both static and dynamic analysis to the binary program under test to produce information that is required for the components of the main testing phase. After the critical code regions have been identified based on the dynamic execution traces, guidance can use those in combination with control flow data to home in on the targets. At the same time, the detection component uses the buffer access profiles to detect overreads.

Guided Testing. Once the targets have been identified, we can begin to test the program using guided symbolic execution. We perform the guided testing step separately for each identified target. We consider as symbolic the entire program input (such as a video file for *FFmpeg*, or the input from a network socket for the *lighttpd* web server). Since we use an online symbolic executor, states that capture the complete current state of the program executed are forked whenever the execution encounters a branch point where the branch condition is based on symbolic input.

Two components constantly interact with the symbolic executor: guidance and detection. The guidance regularly assesses a number of characteristics of each state to establish a ranking that corresponds to the likelihood of triggering a bug. The symbolic executor will always execute the state with the highest rank. Intuitively, the ranking is designed to prefer states that are near to the target in the program's control flow graph and have path constraints compatible with the violation of the integrity assumption. Furthermore, the ranking uses additional heuristics aimed at privileging execution paths that are more likely to lead to an overread. Section 3 explains the guidance mechanisms in detail.

To find a bug, in addition to triggering its occurrence, we also need to detect that it was indeed triggered. Detecting a bug is not as straightforward as executing the faulty code since silent failures are typical for buffer overreads. To detect buffer overreads we have developed a technique that is effective for memory accesses that use either concrete or symbolic addresses. In some cases, detecting an overread may be trivial. As an example, if the address of a memory access can be made to point outside the program's allocated memory pages, it is obvious that an overread is possible. To detect a wider class of overreads, however, we need more fine-grained detection methods that are aware of buffer boundaries within the program's memory space. We will discuss in Section 4 how we obtain this information about a binary. To detect overreads, we make use of the buffer access profiles collected during the preliminary analysis. This profile associates each program state with the buffers accessed in that state during any of the the test runs in the preliminary analysis phase. Here, a program state is a combination of an instruction with the current call stack. During symbolic execution we again check, for each memory access, whether a buffer is being accessed. We then compare this information with the profile for the current program state. Based on this comparison we distinguish three conditions:

Valid access. If the access hits a buffer that has been recorded before in the current state's profile, the access is clearly valid.

Buffer accesses in code that have not been covered by the preliminary analysis (for which we have no profile) are also regarded as valid.

Suspicious access. In cases where the access is within a buffer that is not contained in the profile for the current program state, we report a suspicious access. While in the case of library functions that operate on buffers, such as memcpy, this might be a legitimate behavior, it could also be an overread from a neighboring buffer.

Out of bounds access. If the program accesses memory at a region outside any known buffer allocation sites, but the profile lists buffers for this program state, an out of bounds access is highly probable. When the referenced memory address is a symbolic expression, even stronger conclusions can sometimes be drawn: if the expression can evaluate to both an address within a buffer as well as outside it, an out of bounds access is possible.

3. GUIDANCE

Instead of trying to cover all the code of the program under test, we direct our efforts toward a specific, potentially vulnerable point in the program. For this, precise guidance of the symbolic execution is crucial: We need to avoid getting lost in uncontrolled state-space explosion. Instead, we want to quickly and comprehensively explore the execution paths that are most relevant to the vulnerability we are trying to trigger. This guidance takes several forms. First of all, we can use the control flow information collected in the preliminary analysis phase as a "map" that helps us to quickly lead execution towards the potentially vulnerable spot. Furthermore, we can take into account the path constraints associated with each state in the symbolic execution. Specifically, we are interested in any constraints on the bytes of input on which the address of the memory accesses we are testing may depend. As we will see, these constraints can help us reach the target program point along paths that are interesting because they differ in the way they calculate the address for the targeted memory access.

BORG starts by using concolic execution (Section 3.1). This provides us with an initial, successful execution of the program based on real world input data. From then on, several assessment functions evaluate each state based on criteria that are relevant for triggering the target vulnerability. Depending on the importance of each criterion, the combination of the assessment functions establishes a ranking of all the states. This ranking is computed periodically, and the top ranked state is then selected for execution.

In detail, the assessment involves the following steps:

1. Evaluate whether the target instruction is reachable from each state.
2. Based on the path constraints, evaluate whether an out-of-bounds access is possible from each state.
3. Rank states based on their proximity to the vulnerable spot.
4. At a branch point, evaluate whether a newly forked state would either exit or stay in a loop.
5. Among freshly forked states, prefer those whose path constraint affects parts of the input that are involved in the targeted buffer access.

Both reachability of the target instruction (1) and the satisfiability of the out-of-bounds constraint (2) are strong selectors: we are not going to explore states in which either the targeted access is unreachable, or the path constraints rule out a violation of the integrity assumption. Therefore, such states are simply discarded. All states that pass these filters are evaluated for further exploration. The following assessment criteria do not rule out states in general. Instead, they express a preference in which states will be explored first. The proximity metric (3) measures an approximation of the minimum number of instructions needed to reach the target instruction from each state. We discuss this metric in Section 3.2. To try to trigger an overread, we prefer states that stay inside a loop to states that exit the loop prematurely (4). Our handling of loops is discussed in Section 3.3. Finally, we try to explore states with a variety of path constraints involving the inputs that affect the targeted buffer access (5). Our use of path constraints for selecting states is discussed in Section 3.4.

3.1 Concolic Testing

Concolic testing [32] complements symbolic execution by backing the symbolic input data with a concrete value assignment. This concrete input data can be used to make a branch decision: the symbolic executor will, by default, follow the branch for which the path constraints evaluate to true based on the concrete assignment.

With BORG, we use concolic execution to get an initial, successful execution path through the program that allows to explore states deep in the program's logic. As input we use the real-world data from the preliminary testing phase that revealed the vulnerable spot.

Every path that is generated during symbolic execution requires a concrete assignment that match the constraint set of the path. While a new concrete assignment can be generated by the constraint solver, this will likely overwrite values from the original input. With BORG we strive to preserve as much concrete information from the original input as possible as it contains realistic data that allowed us to reach deep states. Therefore, whenever we pick a branch that leaves the initial execution path, we examine the path constraint generated by that branch and determine the exact parts of the input that caused this path constraint. We then replace only these parts of the original assignment with new values obtained by querying the constraint solver.

An important side-effect of always having a valid, concrete assignment of the input available for every state is that it will speed up symbolic execution significantly. During symbolic execution, the engine often needs a concrete sample value for a given symbolic expression, for example S2E uses this for its internal memory management. In such a case, the engine would normally issue a costly query to the constraint solver for a value. This is of special significance with memory operations: with plain symbolic execution, the constraint solver needs to be queried for a valid value whenever a memory operation depends on symbolic input and the address expression needs to be evaluated against the path constraints. If such

a memory operation is executed within a loop, this can cause a significant slowdown. Provided that we always have a valid, concrete assignment at hand, however, the address expression can be evaluated in a straightforward manner.

3.2 Proximity Rating

To exercise the vulnerable spot as often as possible in different execution paths, we pick states that are in close proximity to the target instruction. The rationale behind this approach is that the closer we are to the target, the fewer branch instructions will be in our way that can lead us astray.

To estimate proximity, we require a distance metric between a program's current execution state and a target instruction. The general requirement for the metric is an ideal tradeoff between *fast* and *precise* computation that can be performed at every execution state change of the program. We define an execution state as the combination of the current basic block executed and the associated callstack. As a distance metric, BORG uses the minimum number of instructions that have to be executed to reach the target instruction from the current execution state.

To accurately compute this distance, we require precise information about the control flow of the program. For this, we rely on the control flow graph that was extracted during the preliminary analysis phase. However, standard graph search algorithms cannot be directly applied to searching within a control flow graph, as they do not take the call-return semantics into account: return edges must always match their preceding call edges. The main idea of our solution is to pre-calculate distance information for all execution states that can reach the target instruction by performing a backward search from the target instruction. Since it is not feasible to compute reachability and exact distance to the target for all possible program states in advance, we split the problem into two steps:

1. Static, offline calculation before guided testing. Function `calcdist` of Algorithm 1 calculates distance information based on the control flow graph.
2. Lightweight on-the-spot calculation during guided testing to calculate the actual distance to the target for a given program state based on the distance information.

Generating Distance Information.

To address the fact that storing one distance per execution state does not scale to large programs and that programs often call a function more than once, we devised an efficient way of storing distance information. We split the information into *absolute* and *relative* distance information. Relative distances are measured intraprocedurally, for a given basic block they are defined as the minimum distance until the function returns. Absolute distances are measured inter-procedurally, for a given basic block they are defined as the minimum distance until the target instruction is reached. To generate these different kinds of distance information, the algorithm operates in two modes: If the `rel` parameter is set, intraprocedural distances are calculated, otherwise interprocedural distances are calculated.

The `calcdist` function follows a typical worklist approach that will start from the target instruction and traverse the CFG backwards. As input it requires the predecessors (`pred`) for each basic block and knowledge about whether a basic block is a callsite (`cs`) or ends a function (`ret`). In addition, it requires a mapping between function exit blocks and their corresponding function heads (`fh`) as well as return sites and their call site (`call`). All this information is retrieved from the interprocedural CFG.

The operation of the function is based on the well-known Dijkstra algorithm [16], with basic blocks as nodes, predecessors being their neighbors and distance information initialized to infinity except for the target. As long as the function $F(c)$ of the current basic block c is equal to that of a predecessor p, i.e. $F(p) == F(c)$, the algorithm proceeds like ordinary Dijkstra. However, predecessors breaching a function boundary need special treatment:

Function return. If p is a return from $F(p)$ to $F(c)$ (line 13), we recursively invoke calcdist for $F(p)$. To calculate the minimum distance of executing $F(p)$, we need distances relative to p and thus run calcdist in intraprocedural mode with p as the target. Once $F(p)$ is explored and calcdist returns, we continue with the callsite of $F(p)$ in $F(c)$, i.e. the intraprocedural predecessor of c (line 16). To calculate the distance of the callsite, we sum up the distance of the current block dist[c], the distance of the function head of $F(p)$, rel_dist[fh(p)] and the size of the basic block that contains the callsite size[call[c]] (line 15). The remaining procedure is the same as with an ordinary predecessor: If the resulting distance is lower than a previously stored distance, we update its distance and add it to the worklist.

Function call. If p is a call from $F(p)$ to $F(c)$, processing depends on the mode the algorithm is operating in. In intraprocedural mode, we are restricted to the scope of $F(c)$ and thus skip p (line 12). In interprocedural mode, we treat p like a normal predecessor as we are calculating absolute distances.

Putting it together, calcdist is invoked in interprocedural mode with the given target. Whenever it hits a predecessor that is returning from a function, it switches to intraprocedural mode to calculate relative distances within that function.

Since we only store the information per basic block and not per state, memory consumption scales linearly to the size of the program. Apart from that, we do not explore functions multiple times once they have been covered completely.

Calculating Actual Distances.

During guided testing, we use the distance information to calculate the actual distance for a given execution state. The execution state is given by a stack of return addresses with the address of the current basic block on top. The optimum distance to the target is then calculated by summing up the distance information of the basic blocks on the callstack. Beginning with the item on top of the stack, we stop at the first item for which absolute distance information is available. If an item's distance information is unknown (i.e. the target is unreachable), we set it to infinity. This on-the-spot calculation's runtime is linear in the number of items on the callstack and can thus be performed very fast.

It is possible that during the guided testing phase, execution reaches a basic block that is not part of the CFG constructed in the preliminary analysis phase because of incomplete indirect call target information. Such basic blocks need special treatment, because we do not have distance information on them. For states that have reached new code, we retain the state's last distance assessment and dynamically enhance the CFG with the new information. As soon as we are back on a known basic block, we pause the guided testing and re-run Algorithm 1 on the expanded CFG.

3.3 Loop Handling

Branch points within loops can lead to a massive state explosion in symbolic execution. Thus a common guiding approach for symbolic execution is to perform one loop iteration and exit as soon as possible. While this is a reasonable strategy if just aiming for code coverage, it is less suited for our class of bugs. Programs typically use loops to parse and validate their inputs. Among the case stud-

---

Algorithm 1 Offline distance information generation.

Require: pred[bb] $\forall$ bb $\in$ basic_blocks
Require: ret[bb] := true iff bb ends with return
Require: cs[bb] := true iff bb is a callsite
Require: call[bb] callsite for a given return site
Require: fh[bb] function head for a given function exit

```
 1: function calcdist(target:address,rel:bool)
 2:     worklist ← {target}
 3:     if rel then
 4:         dist ← rel_dist
 5:     else
 6:         dist ← abs_dist
 7:     dist[target] ← 0
 8:     for c ∈ worklist do
 9:         worklist ← worklist \ {c}
10:         for p ∈ pred[c] do
11:             if cs[p] ∧ rel then
12:                 continue
13:             if ret[p] then
14:                 calcdist(p, true)
15:                 d ← dist[c] + size[call[c]] + rel_dist[fh[p]]

16:                 p ← call[c]
17:             else
18:                 d ← dist[c] + size[pred]
19:             if d < dist[p] then
20:                 dist[p] = d
21:                 worklist ← worklist ∪ {p}
```

---

ies in this work for instance, lighttpd and SSSD use loops for input validation, while libexif iterates over the input to return the index of a specific marker. In all cases triggering the bug depends on a successful, exhaustive completion of the loop.

Figure 3 shows the control flow of such an input processing loop that iterates over every character of the input string. Branch points B1-B3 will exit the loop prematurely on a special control character, while branch point B4 will iterate through the loop until it encounters a terminator. Given a target some place after the loop exit, proximity guidance will always pick one of the break edges as their distance to the target is smaller than completing the iteration or even taking the back edge. This way we would, per input character, explore three unsuccessful states before going for another iteration.

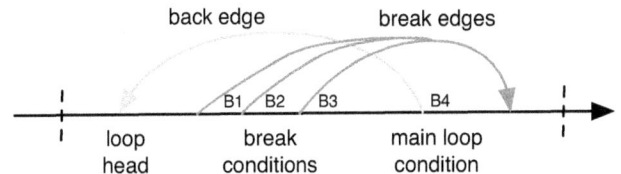

Figure 3: A typical input processing loop. States forked at branch points B1-B3 will be preferred by the proximity rating over taking the back edge.

Our solution to this issue is to prefer branch targets that stay within the loop. To pick branch targets that stay within the loop, we perform an intra-procedural loop detection for every branch point: We apply the Kosaraju-Sharir [34] algorithm on the intra-procedural control flow graph to identify strongly connected components. If the branch point is actually within such a component (i.e. loop), we examine its branch targets. Only if one of them points outside and one inside the loop, we mark the outside target as a loop exit.

3.4 Security Constraints

The goal of BORG is to find an execution path that performs an out-of-bounds access, thus violating an integrity assumption. Since we are targeting tainted accesses, the memory address accessed is a symbolic expression that has a relationship with some parts of the input. A typical scenario would be a pointer dereference where the program calculates the final memory address m by adding a symbolic offset to a concrete base address. Combining this information with the supposed target of the access, we can create security constraints that specify an out-of-bounds condition. In the case of a buffer that ranges from a start address s to an end address e, the security constraint SC would read $s \leqslant m \wedge m < e$. By querying the solver with the combination of the normal path constraints and this security constraint, we can filter any state as soon as $\neg SAT(PC \wedge \neg SC)$.

We can also leverage another feature of security constraints for guidance. During symbolic execution we do not just see the final address m in case of a symbolic memory access, but the whole expression that represents all the calculation steps that involved symbolic input. Knowing which input bytes are involved in a security constraint allows us to prefer states that have been forked at branch points whose path constraints affected those very input bytes. This way we can explore the possible values of m more efficiently.

4. OVERREAD DETECTION

In contrast to overread detection that works at the source-code level like AddressSanitizer [33], BORG has to overcome the loss of high-level semantics at the binary level: Instead of an access expression like buf[i], which readily provides the target buffer as well as the index of the read, BORG just sees a read access to a memory location.

Therefore, BORG first needs to associate memory accesses with buffers. On each memory access, it checks whether the accessed address falls inside the range of a buffer. To do so, it needs to identify the exact locations of buffers in memory beforehand. From a program's point of view, buffers can be located on the stack, on the heap or, in the case of global variables, in the bss or data segments.

While buffers on the heap, or global buffers in bss, or in the data segment are easy to track as they stay at the same memory location once they are allocated, stack-based buffers require more effort. Both their addressing as well as their scope depends on the current stack frame. They need to be validated and invalidated upon entering and exiting the function in which they have been declared. To calculate the actual memory location we need an offset of the stack buffer that is either relative to the base frame pointer or the stack pointer on function entry. While we resort to DWARF information for this special task only, the information can also be obtained for stripped binaries by statically identifying large variables located on the stack as suggested in [17] or by more sophisticated methods that evaluate dynamic access patterns [35]. For heap-based buffers we intercept all common allocation routines, such as malloc and free. Again, we focus on general purpose allocation routines like malloc() and mmap() in our implementation. In case of custom memory allocators, we can use tools like MemBrush [11] to extract these routines first.

To be able to check accesses, we need a way to refer to buffers across multiple executions of the program under test. Global buffers can simply be identified by their absolute address. For stack buffers, we record the allocation site (i.e. the function) as well as the offset from either the stack pointer or the base frame pointer. Finally, for heap buffers, we hash the program state (callstack + program counter) of the allocation site (i.e., where malloc was called).

Library functions that have well-known semantics and operate on buffers allow us to use performance optimizations. For example, memcpy contains a loop that copies four-byte chunks from source to destination. If an address provided to memcpy is symbolic, our system needs to perform a costly query to the constraint solver at each iteration. However, knowing the semantics of memcpy, we only need to intercept the function call and issue a single query to check whether the supplied parameters would allow an out-of-bounds access.

5. IMPLEMENTATION

The implementation of BORG's core, the guided testing, is based on S2E, a full-system selective symbolic execution engine [12]. S2E itself uses the Qemu emulator [3] and modifies its dynamic translation engine TCG to translate the binary guest code to LLVM instead of native host code. The generated LLVM code can then be run in the KLEE [8] symbolic virtual machine. KLEE uses STP [18] as its constraint solver. Figure 4 shows how BORG is based on S2E. The S2E base layer links KLEE and Qemu and expands KLEE's state concept to the operating system level. S2E also provides a plugin API that is used by BORG's main components.

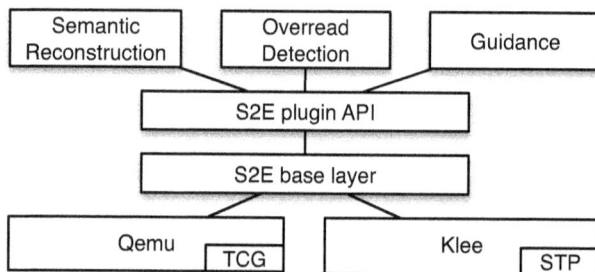

Figure 4: The BORG testing system. We implemented three extensions on top of the plugin API provided by S2E: Semantic view reconstruction restores OS concepts such as processes, overread detection monitors the process under test for buffer overreads and guidance tells S2E which states to execute.

The advantages of bringing symbolic execution to the operating system level are evident: binary applications can be symbolically executed in their native, real environment, even if they depend on libraries and devices. On the other hand, this high degree of symbolic execution support and integration at a comparably low level comes at a price. For instance, when symbolic input arrives via a network socket, it has to pass through all of the network stack in the kernel, adding significant overhead in symbolic execution. Similarly, even though S2E employs a copy-on-write memory concept, it still has to keep track of the whole OS state on a fork. Performance aside, a problem with operating at the level below the operating system itself is the lack of semantic information at the system level–an issue that we discuss in more detail presently.

Semantic view reconstruction. To improve execution performance of unrelated code, S2E needs to know when the program under test is executed and where it resides in memory. We implemented a plugin for S2E to reconstruct this information for Linux. Whenever the kernel starts a thread, the plugin extracts the memory layout and the name of the new task from the guest's memory. It then associates this information with the task's page table base address, which is unique per process and thus well-suited as a process identifier. We further track whether the program under test has terminated and we can thus kill the corresponding state. For the special case that the program is terminated by a signal, we additionally intercept signals to be able to report e.g. segmentation violations.

Tracking the program state. In BORG, all buffer accesses are associated with a program state. As already mentioned in Section 2.1, we define the program state as a combination of the address of the current instruction and the associated callstack. To remove all possible ambiguity, the callstack is represented by the return addresses, as they identify not only the function invoked, but also the callsite.

While determining the current instruction pointer is straightforward, the callstack needs more effort. In a nutshell, we keep track of all function invocations and returns throughout the program execution on a per-state basis. Since programs are not bound to follow the call-return semantics at the assembly level, we maintain the callstack on a best-effort basis.

The reasons for not adhering to the normal call-return convention vary. The best known example is position independent code. Such code may need to determine its current address; A popular way to do so is by means of a call instruction, as it pushes the address of the next instruction onto the stack. Besides, calls without returns also occur in exception handlers and event-based programming. To account for these cases, our callstack handling keeps track of the expected return addresses. Upon executing a return instruction, we distinguish two cases: If a return target is not contained in the callstack, the callstack is left untouched. Otherwise, we pop all items from the callstack until we reach the matching return address.

Preliminary analysis. For the static phase of the preliminary analysis, we leverage the IDA Pro disassembler. Our CFG generation script starts with the main function and descends into every called function, splitting the code on control transfer boundaries into basic blocks. To compensate for the shortcomings of this static approach, we additionally explore all functions we encounter during dynamic analysis and also extract the targets of indirect jumps.

For the dynamic phase we first run the program under test in a modified version of the lightweight taint tracker Minemu [4]. This will output all memory accesses encountered that depend on tainted input data. To produce the buffer profiles, we additionally run the tested program in S2E with symbolic execution completely disabled and only the semantic reconstruction and overread detection plugins enabled.

6. EVALUATION

To evaluate the effectiveness of BORG, we selected a number of recent out-of-bound vulnerabilities in real-world server applications and commonly used libraries. We selected the programs by querying the NVD database of NIST [28] for the most recent and critical buffer overread vulnerabilities in open source programs that S2E was able to execute. We used open source programs and known bugs so we could verify the results accurately.

Table 1 lists characteristics of the programs under test as well as results from being analyzed by BORG. The *basic block count* is an indicator of both size and complexity of the program. It shows that BORG also works on large applications such as ClamAV with over 38,000 basic blocks. The *candidate* column lists how many critical accesses were identified by BORG's target selection. For libexif our target selection could not come up with candidates, so we chose to use the selection strategy of Dowser [23] for this case. The size of the *symbolic input* supplied to each program under test varied significantly, based on the kind of input processed by the program: While the communication protocol of SSSD uses only a small 42 byte message, the test input to libmagic, an MS Office document, was more than 170 times as large. The sum of the *preliminary analysis* and *guided testing* column states how long it took BORG to trigger a vulnerability. Finally the *state space* is the number of states generated during symbolic execution and the *states explored* the part of

the state space that was explored by guided testing.

In the following we will provide insight on the programs and on how BORG dealt with their vulnerabilities.

Lighttpd. Lighttpd is a lightweight, yet standards-compliant web server that is used, amongst others, by YouTube. Using the supplied test cases for authentication, BORG found two tainted memory accesses during preliminary analysis. One of them corresponds to a buffer overread vulnerability specified by CVE-2011-4362. It is located in a function that handles base64 decoding of the username supplied in an HTTP request with basic authentication, where part of the input is used as an offset into a conversion table:

```
 1 static unsigned char * base64_decode(buffer *out,
      const char *in) {
 2   unsigned char *result = (unsigned char *)out->ptr;
 3   int ch = in[0];
 4   for (size_t i = 0; i < strlen(in); i++) {
 5     ch = in[i];
 6     if (ch == '\0' || ch == base64_pad) break;
 7     ch = base64_reverse_table[ch];
 8     if (ch < 0) continue;
 9     switch(i % 4) {
10       case 0:
11         result[j] = ch << 2;
12         break;
13                              ⋮
14     }
15   }
16   return result;
17 }
18 int http_auth_basic_check(..., const char *realm_str)
        {
19   buffer *username, *password;
20                              ⋮
21   username = buffer_init();
22   if (!base64_decode(username, realm_str)) return 0;
23                              ⋮
24 }
```

The realm_str pointer (line 18, 22) directly references input data. The base64_decode function will iterate over each byte of the input (line 4) unless it encounters a termination character. It decodes each character by means of the base64_reverse_table (line 7) and writes the result to the output pointer. The problem is the missing bounds check for ch when using it as an offset into the array in line 7. Since the array has 256 entries one might first not think that an overread is possible, as this perfectly matches the maximum value of an unsigned character. However, before being used as an index, the character is first casted to a signed integer (line 3). Therefore all values above 0x7f will turn into negative offsets into the table.

Still, the generated out-of-bounds constraint does not evaluate to true in the initial state, as the path constraints do not allow for it. After guidance dismissed all irrelevant states using the security constraints, the closest valid states based on the proximity ranking pointed to a validation loop that happens at a very early stage in the program. As it turns out, each character of the request header (line 2) is first checked for validity:

```
1 for (; i < con->parse_request->used && !done; i++) {
2   char *cur = con->parse_request->ptr + i;
3                              ⋮
4   if (*cur >= 0 && *cur < 32 && *cur != '\t') break;
```

At this point we fork a state for every header character. The compiled assembly version of this if-clause will only pass if *cur is negative, bigger than 0x1f or if it is not equal to 0x9. Our test input passes this if-clause, because all characters' values exceed 0x1f. The path constraints generated corresponding to this input are the

Program	Basic Blocks	Candidates	Symbolic Input	Preliminary Analysis		Guided Testing	State Space	States Explored
				static	dynamic			
Lighttpd	7,139	2	63 byte	3s	1m 52s	3m 36s	369	10
FFmpeg	4,654	4	5,120 byte	2s	10m 42s	3m 54s	10	1
libmagic	512	14	7,168 byte	<1s	19s	3h 46m 37s	762	1
libexif	2,506	(87)	678 byte	<1s	10s	1m 45s	1,804	503
SSSD	9,938	4	42 byte	6s	2m 40s	2m 56s	116	7
ClamAV	38,037	12	3,505 byte	51s	5m 26s	12h 40m 09s	3,792	1

Table 1: Programs analyzed using BORG. For libexif, we used Dowser's selection strategy.

reason why an invalid offset was not possible for the initial path: they effectively limit the possible range for values to 0x1f-0x7f. By taking a different branch that allows for a different set of input characters, BORG can trigger the vulnerability. In this case loop handling prefers states that do not lead to the break condition.

Given the depth of the bug and the fact that BORG forks hundreds of states until it triggers the vulnerability, an uninformed exploration strategy is highly likely to fail – each path that does not hit or trigger the bug will fork off a large number of new states during exploration.

SSSD. The System Security Services Daemon (SSSD) is installed per default on Fedora-related Linux distributions. It provides remote access to various identity and authentication resources through a common framework. We tested the SSH-module, which is susceptible to a buffer overread specified in CVE-2013-0220. As the supplied test suite is only targeted at testing the internal database, we intercepted network traffic from the supplied client. Based on this test input, BORG identified four target candidates, all of them located in a function that parses the incoming request.

```
1  static errno_t ssh_cmd_parse_request(struct
       ssh_cmd_ctx *cmd_ctx) {
2      struct cli_ctx *cctx = cmd_ctx->cctx;
3      uint8_t *body;
4      size_t body_len;
5      size_t c = 0;
6      uint32_t flags, name_len, alias_len;
7      char *name;
8
9      sss_packet_get_body(cctx->creq->in, &body,
           &body_len);
10     memcpy_c(&flags, body+c, body_len, &c);
11     memcpy_c(&name_len, body+c, body_len, &c);
12     if (flags > 1) {return EINVAL;}
13     if (name_len == 0) {return EINVAL;}
14     name = (char *)(body+c);
15     if (!sss_utf8_check(name, name_len-1) ||
           name[name_len-1] != 0) {
16         return EINVAL;
17     }
18     c += name_len;
19            ⋮
20     if (flags & 1) {
21         memcpy_c(&alias_len, body+c, body_len, &c);
22            ⋮
```

The body pointer used in this function references part of the data received from the network. The memcpy_c function is a wrapper around the ordinary memcpy that will add the length parameter to its last parameter. The problem is the name_len variable that is parsed from the input data in line 11 and, without any further validation, used as an offset in lines 15, 18 and 21. However, the out-of-bounds constraint does not evaluate to true on the initial path, because the sss_utf8_check function in line 15 generates path constraints that limit name_len to the actual length of the corresponding part of the input. Proximity rating and security constraints take us

back to the states that have been forked last in the validation loop in sss_utf8_check. Loop handling dismisses numerous states that would exit the loop prematurely. One of the high-ranked states triggers a different behavior of sss_utf8_check: if the length parameter is negative, it assumes a zero terminated string and returns true if the characters up to the termination character are in conformance to UTF8. Since this is the case, name_len is now negative and all subsequent accesses that use it as part of their offset potentially overread. This case shows that BORG is also effective using observed real-world input data when no test cases are available.

FFmpeg. FFmpeg is a collection of libraries that provide functionality to record, convert and stream audio and video of various formats. Since it is not a standalone program, we implemented a very basic test program that will open, identify and read a file. As concrete test input we used a typical stream in the DV format, truncated to a limited number of frames. Among the four candidates given by BORG's target selection was the overread vulnerability specified by CVE-2011-3936.

```
1  static const uint8_t *dv_extract_pack(uint8_t *frame,
       enum dv_pack_type t) {
2      int offs;
3      switch (t) {
4      case dv_audio_source:
5          offs = (80*6 + 80*16*3 + 3);
6          break;
7              ⋮
8      }
9      return frame[offs] == t ? &frame[offs] : NULL;
10 }
11 static int dv_extract_audio(uint8_t *frame, ...) {
12             ⋮
13     as_pack = dv_extract_pack(frame, dv_audio_source);
14     if (!as_pack) return 0;
15     freq = (as_pack[4] >> 3) & 0x07;
16     size = (sys->audio_min_samples[freq] + smpls) * 4;
17 }
```

In this case, part of the input is modified by a number of logic operations before it is used as an array offset: The frame pointer passed to dv_extract_audio is a direct reference to the supplied input. Since our input has the dv_audio_source type set at the offset required by dv_extract_pack, symbolic execution follows the else branch of the conditional and continues. Now freq is calculated by masking a value of as_pack (that refers directly to the input) with 0x7. In line 16, freq is used as an offset into the audio_min_samples array that only contains three entries, although the bitmask allows values up to seven. Since no (path) constraints apply to the value in as_pack[4], the out-of-bounds constraint we generate is already satisfiable and BORG reports the possible overread and outputs a test case without exploring additional states.

Libmagic. Libmagic is the library behind the popular "file" command line tool that will try to determine the type of a given file based on its content. It is also used by larger programs such as the Apache web server. While most file types are covered by magic bytes contained in the magic database, libmagic performs further processing for a limited number of file types, such as CDF, Microsoft Office's composite document format. Since libmagic does not come with a testfile for the CDF format, we used Microsoft Office to produce an empty CDF document. BORG's target selection identified 14 candidates, one of them being an overread specified by CVE-2012-1571. In this case, the overread is caused by lacking validation of the source pointer on a call to memcpy. Again, BORG is able to query the constraint solver for a test case that triggers the vulnerability in the first state, since the path constraints allow for it.

The comparably long time it took until the vulnerability was triggered is caused by the combination of a rather large symbolic input size and the large number of constraints generated. This causes queries to the constraint solver to take up to 90s each.

Libexif. Libexif reads and writes EXIF metadata information from and to JPG image files. It is a popular library used by various image processing applications such as ImageMagick. Being a library, we tested its main functionality that extracts EXIF data from a memory region. As input we used a sample JPG image shipped with the libexif library.

In this case, BORG's target selection could not come up with candidates because none of the buffer accesses used tainted input for the address calculation. Having the source code available, we chose to try Dowser's selection heuristic in this case. While being based on taint tracking as well, it employs special methods to handle implicit flows. Indeed, it provided us with an access affected by CVE-2012-2836 that is ranked at place 13 out of 87 loops. In the following BORG's guided testing managed to trigger the vulnerability, showing the effectiveness of the proximity rating.

Compared to the other examples, the bug in libexif is located at a rather shallow position in the program's logic. Still, when we turned off our guiding enhancements and ran libexif with concolic execution and a standard depth-first exploration guidance, the bug was not triggered within 29 hours.

ClamAV. ClamAV is a widely used anti-virus engine that offers its capabilities in a library. When used on a password-protected PDF file, target selection identified 12 security critical accesses. This is in accordance with CVE-2013-2021, which indicates an overread vulnerability with encrypted PDF files: The user password checking function in ClamAV's PDF scanner passes user input directly to memcpy as a length parameter. Since the out-of-bound constraints already hold in the first state, BORG was able to generate a test case for the overread right away. As ClamAV is by far the biggest program we applied BORG on, its size is being reflected by the long time it took to trigger the bug compared to the other programs.

7. RELATED WORK

The use of symbolic execution to find bugs in programs has been subject to a substantial body of recent research, including CUTE [32], DART [19], EXE [9], KLEE [8], SAGE [20]. Other than SAGE, these approaches require source code. Unlike BORG, their goal is to achieve high code coverage of the tested program and find bugs throughout the program.

SE targeted at specific bugs. A number of papers investigate how symbolic execution can be applied in a more targeted fashion to attempt to detect specific bugs.

In [23] we present Dowser, a guided symbolic execution strategy geared towards buffer overflow bugs. It uses static analysis to identify possible locations for buffer overflow bugs within loops and ranks them based on a metric that evaluates the complexity of the access. Dowser's static analysis techniques heavily rely on the expressiveness of source code, porting them to support binaries rep-

resents a challenge in itself that we leave to future work. While Dowser's heuristics for target selection can enhance BORG's efficiency, it is not sufficient by itself, as it only focuses on accesses within loops. It thus fails in all our evaluation examples except for the libexif case.

Cui et al. [15] aim to discover bugs in the enforcement of higher level policies, such as heap or file descriptor misuse. They use path slicing to statically infer execution paths that are not relevant for the given testing run. While the paper demonstrates the effectiveness on coarse-grained bugs, program slicing is less suitable for dealing with fine-grained bugs like memory errors: In a typical application that first parses the input before the program logic takes effect, the parser will be data-dependent on the whole input, thus leaving nothing for path slicing to prune. The same applies to DiSE [29] and its simplification based on "unaffected" nodes. Program slicing is also significantly more difficult to perform on stripped binaries where pointer aliasing is an unsolvable problem.

In Zesti [27] the authors use symbolic execution to improve testing of sensitive instructions. They limit their exploration to paths that do not exceed a certain fork depth, measured backwards from a targeted sensitive instruction. In order to scale, they use a fork depth of ten forks. Thus their approach would fail with programs such as lighttpd where the path constraint that allows for a bug to occur is in a validation loop "far" (in terms of fork depth) from the actual bug.

Babić et al. [2] describe a guided analysis method similar to BORG that, in contrast to the aforementioned systems, also works on binaries. The authors use a data-flow graph to identify possible vulnerabilities first, and a shortest-path distance heuristic based on a control flow graph as a second step to guide symbolic execution to the vulnerabilities. In contrast to this work, BORG's selection strategy also uses dynamic analysis to both resolve indirect call targets and dynamically allocated memory. BORG additionally uses security constraints for guidance and employs a more fine grained distance metric that uses the current basic block and the runtime call stack, while this system only uses the current basic block. Finally, unlike BORG, this work has not been tested on real-world programs, but only historic and simplified vulnerabilities.

SE aimed at known vulnerabilities. Symbolic execution has also been leveraged to replay or extend existing vulnerabilities. Such approaches typically involve strong guidance strategies, but are based on stronger assumptions regarding existing information about faulty application behavior. ESD by Zamfir et al. [39] applies a distance based guidance strategy aiming to replicate inputs responsible for crashes based on existing core dumps. Even though their distance heuristic is rather coarse, their method proves that distance based guidance is a strong tool for eliminating the potential exponential explosion of symbolic execution. On a similar note, some researchers aim to increase the threat level of existing bugs using guided symbolic execution. Avgerinos et. al. [1] and Cha et al. [10] developed techniques for guided symbolic execution with the purpose of exploit generation. They assume knowledge about existing bugs that are considered benign from a security perspective and transform them into full blown security exploits.

Approaches to guidance. The general idea of using the program's structure in form of a CFG for guiding symbolic execution was introduced by [7]. Ma et al. [26] show that distance calculation is generally suited to navigate symbolic execution towards specific target instructions, but might lead to inferior results when a longer path is required. While they propose a form of backward symbolic execution that is not feasible with an online symbolic executor, BORG addresses these problems by its additional guiding techniques. Both Rungta and Cho [13, 30] leverage program models for guidance.

While models are suited to guide symbolic execution to specific high-level states, they are only a coarse approximation of the real program that is possibly incomplete and might thus miss specific bugs. Fitnex [38] selects those paths that are more likely to satisfy a certain target predicate. BORG does not use fitness guidance because a measure of how well an access is within bounds does not relate to how likely the access might go out-of-bounds. In contrast, BORG's boolean security constraints prune states that are in bound and put much less strain on the constraint solver.

Improving symbolic execution. A significant body of research focusing on improving symbolic execution in general. Approaches include parallelization [5], swapping states to disk [10], efficient handling of array accesses in loops [31], summarizing loops [21] and state merging [6, 25]. By extending the underlying symbolic execution engine with the techniques presented above, the overall performance of BORG would improve, enabling even larger applications to be tested. The benefit of guidance would still be relevant since it is offers a relative improvement to the underlying symbolic execution engine.

8. EXTENDING BORG

Our overall approach and the guidance techniques discussed in Section 3 have applications beyond the ones we address in this work, which only targets a specific class of bugs (buffer overreads), and the subset of bugs in this class that can be targeted by the selection strategy we propose.

To be able to effectively apply our guided symbolic execution approach to a class of bugs, we need to have at least one target selection strategy that is able to identify a limited number of program instructions that could potentially trigger a bug of that class. Note that, to be useful, a target selection strategy does not need to be able to target all possible bugs within a class: It is enough that it can target some bugs that would be hard to find with unguided testing. A comprehensive, practical approach to automated bug detection could then be to execute both unguided testing runs that aim to maximize code coverage, and guided testing runs led by a number of selection strategies for different types of bugs. In the following, we will discuss a few possible selection strategies for different classes of bugs.

Buffer Boundary Violations. All of the techniques that BORG applies to buffer overreads can trivially be adapted to similarly detect buffer overflows. As discussed, our target selection strategy for this application targets memory accesses that use tainted memory address. To detect additional overread and overwrite bugs, we could introduce additional selection strategies, such as the one proposed in Dowser [22, 23].

Format String Vulnerabilities. Comparable to buffer boundary violations, format string vulnerabilities can also be exploited to write to or read from a program's memory in unexpected and potentially harmful ways. These vulnerabilities occur when attackers are able to control the format string provided as input to functions in the *printf* family and to introduce unexpected modifiers, such as %x or %n. Format string modifiers can cause the function to read data from and write data to arbitrary memory regions.

For this class of bug, an effective selection strategy is to target all invocations of functions in the *printf* family where the format string is derived from user input. Often logging functions turn out to be such candidates. During exploration, guidance can automatically assess whether the path constraints allow for certain modifiers to end up in format strings at all. Finally, whenever a candidate function is executed, the detection component can check whether it will actually access memory regions it is not supposed to.

Control Flow Integrity. If an offset into a jump table is calculated based on program input, malformed input that is not sufficiently validated may cause a violation of control flow integrity: The program could either pick a target in the table it is not supposed to jump to at this moment, or, if the final address is not bounds-checked against the size of the table, it could jump to an arbitrary memory location.

One selection strategy for this class of bugs can be to target all indirect control flow transfer instructions whose target depends on user input. During symbolic execution, guidance prefers states whose path constraints are relaxed enough to allow for a wide range of possible offsets. In the preliminary analysis phase we construct a profile of valid jump targets for every control flow transfer. Whenever a control flow transfer happens, the detection component can then check whether we can pick a target outside the ones recorded.

9. LIMITATIONS AND FUTURE WORK

BORG's effectiveness or applicability is limited by the target selection method. While the evaluation shows that the current selection method allows it to find deep bugs in complex, real-world programs, there is certainly room for improvement. One issue is that BORG's current selection strategy does not track implicit flows, which prevented it from finding candidates in the libexif case, as well as CVE-2012-1798 of libmagick and CVE-2012-3425 of libpng. We plan to look into possible solutions that have been proposed for this issue [24]. Another issue is BORG's dependence on concrete input: it cannot find bugs in code that is not covered by any test input. This limitation can be alleviated by introducing additional selection strategies that are based purely on static analysis.

Our overall approach and the guidance techniques discussed in Section 3 have applications beyond the ones we address in this work. In future work, we plan to develop a number of additional selection strategies as outlined in Section 8.

Finally, our implementation of symbolic execution, which is based on S2E, is rather slow and uses a large amount of memory per state. This prevented us from evaluating BORG on CVE-2012-2141 of net-snmp. A more efficient implementation of the core engine could allow BORG to find more bugs faster.

10. CONCLUSION

In this paper we presented BORG, a tool for finding out-of-bounds buffer accesses in binaries. Unlike many testing techniques, BORG does not aim to cover as much code as possible in the tested program. Instead, it selects specific points in the program that may be vulnerable, and then proceeds to thoroughly test them by exploring program paths that lead to those points, while trying to trigger and detect a bug. For this, we introduce techniques to guide symbolic execution and make it focus on execution paths that are most relevant to the selected targets and the bugs that may lurk there. As a result, BORG can output concrete program inputs that trigger a buggy behavior. Our novel guidance approach allows BORG to reach and trigger bugs deep in the logic of the programs under test as we show in case studies on six real-world applications.

While BORG focuses on detecting overread bugs, the guidance techniques we introduce could be used to target different classes of bugs, such as buffer overflows, format strings vulnerabilities and control flow integrity violations.

Acknowledgments

The research leading to these results has received funding from the European Union Seventh Framework Programme under grant agreement 257007 (SysSec), the European Research Council through project ERC-2010-StG 259108 (ROSETTA), the MSR Ph.D. Scholarship 2011-049 and the FFG – Austrian Research Promotion under grant COMET K1.

11. REFERENCES

[1] T. Avgerinos, S. K. Cha, B. L. T. Hao, and D. Brumley. AEG: Automatic Exploit Generation. In *Proceedings of the Network and Distributed System Security Symposium (NDSS)*, 2011.

[2] D. Babić, L. Martignoni, S. McCamant, and D. Song. Statically-directed dynamic automated test generation. In *Proceedings of the Symposium on Software Testing and Analysis (ISTA)*, 2011.

[3] F. Bellard. Qemu, a fast and portable dynamic translator. In *Proceedings of the USENIX Annual Technical Conference (USENIX ATC)*, 2005.

[4] E. Bosman, A. Slowinska, and H. Bos. Minemu: The World's Fastest Taint Tracker. In *Proceedings of the Symposium on Research in Attacks, Intrusions and Defenses (RAID)*, 2011.

[5] S. Bucur, V. Ureche, C. Zamfir, and G. Candea. Parallel symbolic execution for automated real-world software testing. In *Proceedings of the European conference on Computer systems (EuroSys)*, 2011.

[6] S. Bugrara and D. Engler. Redundant State Detection for Dynamic Symbolic Execution. In *Proceedings of the USENIX Annual Technical Conference (USENIX ATC)*, 2013.

[7] J. Burnim and K. Sen. Heuristics for scalable dynamic test generation. In *Proceedings of the IEEE/ACM Conference on Automated Software Engineering (ASE)*, 2008.

[8] C. Cadar, D. Dunbar, and D. Engler. Klee: unassisted and automatic generation of high-coverage tests for complex systems programs. In *Proceedings of the USENIX Conference on Operating Systems Design and Implementation (OSDI)*, 2008.

[9] C. Cadar, V. Ganesh, P. M. Pawlowski, D. L. Dill, and D. R. Engler. Exe: Automatically generating inputs of death. In *Proceedings of the ACM Conference on Computer and Communications Security (CCS)*, 2006.

[10] S. K. Cha, T. Avgerinos, A. Rebert, and D. Brumley. Unleashing mayhem on binary code. In *Proceedings of the IEEE Symposium on Security and Privacy (S&P)*, Washington, DC, USA, 2012.

[11] X. Chen, A. Slowinska, and H. Bos. Who allocated my memory? Detecting custom memory allocators in C binaries. In *Proceedings of the Working Conference on Reverse Engineering (WCRE)*, Koblenz, Germany, 2013.

[12] V. Chipounov, V. Kuznetsov, and G. Candea. S2e: a platform for in-vivo multi-path analysis of software systems. In *Proceedings of the Conference on Architectural Support for Programming Languages and Operating Systems (ASPLOS)*, 2011.

[13] C. Y. Cho, D. Babić, P. Poosankam, K. Z. Chen, E. X. Wu, and D. Song. MACE: Model-inference-Assisted Concolic Exploration for Protocol and Vulnerability Discovery. In *Proceedings of the USENIX Security Symposium (USENIX SEC)*, 2011.

[14] Codenomicon. The Heartbleed Bug. heartbleed.com.

[15] H. Cui, G. Hu, J. Wu, and J. Yang. Verifying systems rules using rule-directed symbolic execution. In *Proceedings of the Conference on Architectural Support for Programming Languages and Operating Systems (ASPLOS)*, 2013.

[16] E. W. Dijkstra. A note on two problems in connexion with graphs. *Numerische Mathematik*, 1959.

[17] C. Eagle. *The IDA Pro Book*. William Polloc, 2011.

[18] V. Ganesh and D. L. Dill. A decision procedure for bit-vectors and arrays. In *Proceedings of the Conference on Computer Aided Verification (CAV)*, 2007.

[19] P. Godefroid, N. Klarlund, and K. Sen. Dart: Directed automated random testing. In *Proceedings of the ACM Conference on Programming Language Design and Implementation (PLDI)*, 2005.

[20] P. Godefroid, M. Levin, and D. Molnar. Automated whitebox fuzz testing. In *Proceedings of the Network and Distributed System Security Conference (NDSS)*, 2008.

[21] P. Godefroid and D. Luchaup. Automatic partial loop summarization in dynamic test generation. In *Proceedings of the Symposium on Software Testing and Analysis (ISTA)*, 2011.

[22] I. Haller, A. Slowinska, and H. Bos. Dowser: a guided fuzzer to find buffer overflow vulnerabilities. In *Proceedings of the European Workshop on System Security (Eurosec)*, 2013.

[23] I. Haller, A. Slowinska, M. Neugschwandtner, and H. Bos. Dowsing for overflows: A guided fuzzer to find buffer boundary violations. In *Proceedings of the USENIX Security Symposium (USENIX SEC)*, 2013.

[24] M. G. Kang, S. McCamant, P. Poosankam, and D. Song. DTA++: Dynamic Taint Analysis with Targeted Control-Flow Propagation. In *Proceedings of the Network and Distributed System Security Symposium (NDSS)*, 2011.

[25] V. Kuznetsov, J. Kinder, S. Bucur, and G. Candea. Efficient state merging in symbolic execution. In *Proceedings of the ACM Conference on Programming Language Design and Implementation (PLDI)*, 2012.

[26] K.-K. Ma, K. Y. Phang, J. S. Foster, and M. Hicks. Directed symbolic execution. In *Proceedings of the Conference on Static Analysis*, 2011.

[27] P. D. Marinescu and C. Cadar. make test-zesti: a symbolic execution solution for improving regression testing. In *Proceedings of the International Conference on Software Engineering (ICSE)*, 2012.

[28] NIST. National Vulnerability Database. web.nvd.nist.gov.

[29] S. Person, G. Yang, N. Rungta, and S. Khurshid. Directed Incremental Symbolic Execution. In *Proceedings of the ACM Conference on Programming Language Design and Implementation (PLDI)*, 2011.

[30] N. Rungta, E. Mercer, and W. Visser. Efficient testing of concurrent programs with abstraction-guided symbolic execution. In *Model Checking Software*, LNCS. 2009.

[31] P. Saxena, P. Poosankam, S. McCamant, and D. Song. Loop-extended symbolic execution on binary programs. In *Proceedings of the Symposium on Software Testing and Analysis (ISTA)*, 2009.

[32] K. Sen, D. Marinov, and G. Agha. CUTE: a concolic unit testing engine for C. In *Proceedings of the European Software Engineering Conference*, 2005.

[33] K. Serebryany, D. Bruening, A. Potapenko, and D. Vyukov. Addresssanitizer: A fast address sanity checker. In *Proceedings of the USENIX Annual Technical Conference (USENIX ATC)*, 2012.

[34] M. Sharir. A strong connectivity algorithm and its applications to data flow analysis. In *Computers and Mathematics with Applications*, 1981.

[35] A. Slowinska, T. Stancescu, and H. Bos. Howard: a dynamic excavator for reverse engineering data structures. In *Proceedings of the Network and Distributed System Security Symposium (NDSS)*, 2011.

[36] K. Z. Snow, F. Monrose, L. Davi, A. Dmitrienko, C. Liebchen, and A.-R. Sadeghi. Just-in-time code reuse: On the effectiveness of fine-grained address space layout randomization. In *Proceedings of the IEEE Symposium on Security and Privacy (S&P)*, 2013.

[37] A. Sotirov and M. Dowd. Bypassing Browser Memory Protections: Setting back browser security by 10 years. In *Blackhat*, 2008.

[38] T. Xie, N. Tillmann, P. de Halleux, and W. Schulte. Fitness-guided path exploration in dynamic symbolic execution. In *Proceedings of the Conference on Dependable Systems and Networks (DSN)*, 2009.

[39] C. Zamfir and G. Candea. Execution synthesis: a technique for automated software debugging. In *Proceedings of the European conference on Computer systems (EuroSys)*, 2010.

How Your Phone Camera Can Be Used to Stealthily Spy on You: Transplantation Attacks against Android Camera Service

Zhongwen Zhang [1] [3], Peng Liu [2], Ji Xiang [1], Jiwu Jing [1], Lingguang Lei [1]

[1]Institute of Information Engineering, CAS, Beijing, China
[2]Pennsylvania State University, University Park, PA, US
[3]University of Chinese Academy of Sciences, Beijing, China

[1]zwzhang@lois.cn [2]pliu@ist.psu.edu [1](jixiang, jing, lglei)@lois.cn

ABSTRACT

Based on the observations that spy-on-user attacks by calling Android APIs will be detected out by Android API auditing, we studied the possibility of a "transplantation attack", through which a malicious app can take privacy-harming pictures to spy on users without the Android API auditing being aware of it. Usually, to take a picture, apps need to call APIs of Android Camera Service which runs in *mediaserver* process. Transplantation attack is to transplant the picture taking code from *mediaserver* process to a malicious app process, and the malicious app can call this code to take a picture in its own address space without any IPC. As a result, the API auditing can be evaded. Our experiments confirm that transplantation attack indeed exists. Also, the transplantation attack makes the spy-on-user attack much more stealthy. The evaluation result shows that nearly a half of 69 smartphones (manufactured by 8 vendors) tested let the transplantation attack discovered by us succeed. Moreover, the attack can evade 7 Antivirus detectors, and Android Device Administration which is a set of APIs that can be used to carry out mobile device management in enterprise environments. The transplantation attack inspires us to uncover a subtle design/implementation deficiency of the Android security.

Categories and Subject Descriptors

D.4.6 [**Operating Systems**]: Security and Protection; K.4 [**Computers and Society**]: Privacy

Keywords

Android, Spy on Users, Transportation Attack, Android Camera Service

1. INTRODUCTION

In May, 2014, a news feature story from the USAToday Newspaper reported that users' phone camera can be used to spy on them [11]. "One segment was particularly troubling. In it, Snowden described how a hacker could potentially hijack the camera in William's pre-paid smartphone and use it to capture photos, video, and audio without his knowledge." With this news, that the camera can be used to spy on users becomes well known.

Regarding how the Camera device in a smartphone can be hijacked, a typical way is as follows.

Motivation example. To achieve stealthiness, the attacker can use a QR-code scanner app to spy on users. QR-code scanner can be used in many places, such as comparing price when shopping, downloading a coupon or an app, getting other users' business card. Because the Camera device is used when scanning, the scanner app should have the CAMERA permission. To misuse this app to spy on users, the attacker can maliciously repackage this app to take pictures. According to [36], 86% malware are repackaged version of legitimate apps.

Motivation. This work is motivated by a key observation in launching spy-on-user attacks, which is that getting the CAMERA permission does not address all the concerns of the attacker. Even with the CAMERA permission, the attack is still concern with what the defences can do. Because the repackaged scanner app has to use Android APIs to take a picture, the Framework code of Android, e.g., PackageManager Service, Camera Service, can be extended to do at least 2 things. First, it can do API auditing. API auditing will give users substantial awareness and alerting. For example, one day, users only use the QR-code scanner during 5pm to 6 pm to compare price when shopping, but the audit record shows the camera usage APIs are called every 30 minutes all day. That is a big alerting, and users will gain full awareness of being spied by attackers. Second, a simple image processor can be added (to Camera Service) to verify whether the picture just token is QR-code. If not, the Framework code (Camera Service) can reject returning the picture back. This will fail the attack.

To avoid the second defence, the attacker could use a standard picture-taking app instead of QR-code scanner app to add spy-on-user code. However, even if using a standard picture-taking app cannot confront the first defence.

Our goal is to enable the spy-on-user attack to achieve superb stealthiness. By superb stealthiness, we mean that neither the first nor the second defence way will deter the spy-on-user attack. Through the proposed *transplantation attack*, the attacker can spy on users without calling any Android API.

On Android phones, to capture a picture, attackers could call picture taking APIs provided by Android SDK. However, from the attackers' point of view, this kind of spy-on-user attack is not stealthy. It cannot evade the Android API auditing detection, which records when and which API is called.

Android API auditing is important to both enterprise environments and individual users. In enterprise environments, employees can fulfill their job responsibilities on their Android phones anywhere. Even with permission controls, abuse (by attackers) or misuse (by employees) of apps can still bring security risk to companies. Therefore, as important as Windows/Linux audit in PC world, it is critical to deploy API auditing on employee phones. No matter it is a COPE (Corporate Owned, Personally Enable) phone or a BYOD (Bring You Own Device) phone, the company must deploy Android API auditing before the phone can be used to do any business.

Besides enterprise environments, individual users face security risk as well. The news feature story indicates that users' smartphone camera could be turned on without their knowledge. Such spy-on-user news will make individual smartphone users increasingly concerned about their privacy. Therefore, more and more individual users should do API auditing on their phones.

Android API auditing helps defend the spy-on-user attack in at least three ways. First, it offers awareness to users. Company administrators and individual users can look into the audit files to check if there are camera-access APIs been called. Second, it can do intrusion detection. The API auditing can automatically do intrusion detection according to some (user-provided) detection rules. Third, based on the intrusion detection results, company administrators and individual users can uninstall the malicious apps.

Moreover, either employee phones or individual phones may contain Antivirus (AVs). One of the functionalities of AVs is antispyware, which is used to protect the user's phone from being turned into a voice or video recorder or to see what the phone's camera sees by malicious code. Regularly calling the picture taking APIs will face the threat of being detected by AVs.

In enterprise environments, besides API auditing and AVs, the MDM (Mobile Device Management) is another safety measure, which can control the usage of picture taking APIs. MDM apps can enable or disable Camera Service. Once the Camera Service is disabled, the picture taking APIs cannot work. As a result, the spy-on-user goal cannot be achieved, either.

Problem Statement. Security measures like API auditing, AVs, MDM hinder the existing spy-on-user attacks which relying on picture taking APIs. Motivated by this key observation, in this paper, we focus on a new spy-on-user attack, i.e. how to take pictures without calling any picture taking APIs.

Besides API auditing, log auditing is another way to detect abnormal behavior. However, on Android system, picture taking logs are only generated after picture taking APIs

are called. As no picture taking APIs will be called in the new attack, picture taking logs will not be generated. Therefore, this new attack can also evade log auditing.

We have the following insights about this attack. (1) When an app takes a picture, the app will send a request to the *mediaserver* process, in which the Camera Service runs, via Binder IPC (Inter-process Communication). Then, the *mediaserver* process sends a request to the *systemserver* process, in which API auditing can be done. (2) The picture taking code of Camera Service run in the *mediaserver* process, and they exist in the form of *.so* libraries. (3) The camera driver could be directly accessed by the *.so* libraries without the app having any Binder IPC.

Base on the above insights, we could transplant the needed *.so* libraries from *mediaserver* process to a malicious app process, and let the malicious app access camera drivers to take pictures, directly. We denote this attack as **transplantation attack**. To make this happen, the malicious app should be able to access camera drivers. If a camera driver is globally accessible (i.e. has a Linux permission of 666 or 777), the malicious app can directly access it. Otherwise, the malicious app should become a member of *camera* group, which can be achieved by applying CAMERA permission [1]. In this case, the transplantation attack needs CAMERA permission as well. Our survey reveals that among the top 758 apps gotten from Google Play, 24.27% of them request the CAMERA permission. These apps provide a lot of chances to make transplantation attack become a real-world threat (e.g., by repackaging).

Going through a series of failures, we have finally constructed a novel spy-on-user attack. Accordingly, this spy-on-user attack has the following characteristics: 1) A malicious app can take a (potentially privacy-harming) picture at anytime without calling any picture taking APIs. 2) No Binder IPC is involved when the malicious app is taking pictures. 3) The transplantation attack can evade the Android API auditing. 4) The transplantation attack, when being applied to the Camera Service, results in stealthiest and *unnoticed* picture taking. That is, privacy-harming pictures can be taken by the malware without the Android API auditing being aware of it.

Research Contributions. The main contributions of this paper are listed as follows.

- To the best of our knowledge, this work is the first one on the transplantation attack. We have searched the CVE (Common Vulnerabilities and Exposures) list [2]. Among the 448 CVE entries that match the keyword *Android*, we found there was no such kind of attack happened before.

- We have conducted a set of real world experiments on 69 phones. 46.38% of the smartphones (manufactured by 8 vendors) tested by us let the transplantation attack succeed. We have also evaluated the *evasiveness* of the transplantation attack against 7 Antivirus detectors, and Android Device Administration (mainly used to do MDM). The evaluation results show that the transplantation attack can evade all of these defenses.

---

[1] That is because, Android will automatically put an app with CAMERA permission to *camera* group, which will be discussed in Section 4.1

- Transplantation attack indicates a design deficiency of the Android security. Android will automatically put an app with CAMERA permission into *camera* group, which is the primary reason that transplantation attack happens. However, our experiment shows that doing this is not necessary. Therefore, we believe putting an app into *camera* group is a design deficiency.

The remaining part of this paper is organized as follows. Section 2 gives attack overview. Section 3 describes the workflow of the Camera Service. Section 4 shows construction of transplantation attack. Section 5 shows the evaluation result. Section 6 shows the discussion. Section 7 shows related works. Section 8 shows our conclusion.

2. ATTACK OVERVIEW

In real world, camera drivers on most phones cannot be globally accessed, instead, they are assigned with a Linux permission of 660. Therefore, in most cases, the transplantation attack needs to apply CAMERA permission (to be put in the *camera* group).

To initiate transplantation attack, attackers can simply write an app with CAMERA permission. However, attacking through this app has limited coverage if this app is not downloaded by many phones. To maximize the coverage, re-packaging a wildly downloaded app is an effective way. According to [34], 5% to 13% apps in the third party markets are repackaged. According to [36], 86% malware are repackaged versions of legitimate apps. Therefore, it is quite likely that innocent users will download a repackaged app.

Our survey reveals that among the top 758 apps gotten from Google Play, 24.27% of them request the CAMERA permission. Stowaway [13] reveals that among the 940 apps getting from Google Play, 6% of them require the CAMERA permission but not use it. We also collect 19 phones from our labmates, an average of 35.3% apps on each phone have the CAMERA permission. These apps either in the wild or is widely distributed on users' phones give attackers a lot of opportunities to exploit these apps to spy on users.

We assume attackers would repackage an app that already has CAMERA permission. Therefore, our attack goal has nothing to do with obtaining the CAMERA permission. The malicious repackaging can work as flows.

First, the repackaging does not need to modify **any** existing functionalities, including functionalities using the Camera Service to take pictures, or to scan QR-codes. Second, attackers only need to add the malicious code to spy on users. In Section 4, we will tell how to construct the malicious code. Third, after repackaging is done, attackers should resign the app using *jarsigner*. At last, attackers can submit the repackaged app(s) to, e.g., third party markets to distribute it. Of course, the repackaged app can be submitted to any markets. Even the official Android Market has 1% of repackaged apps [33].

When repackaged apps are running, users' experience is exactly the same as before. User-initiated camera usage will be audited by the API auditing and appears in the audit. However, the attack goal is that the spy-on-user part of accessing the camera hardware will not appear in the audit, which is a stealthy way. Exploiting this stealthy way of accessing the camera hardware, attackers can spy on users without being detected.

3. WORKING MECHANISM OF CAMERA SERVICE

Camera Service provides the functions of using the camera device to, e.g., take a picture, record a video, etc. The workflow of Camera Service is quite different between 2.x and 4.x. In this section, we will analyze the working mechanism of the Camera Service based on Android 4.x, which according to Google's survey [16] becomes the main stream Android version nowadays.

3.1 Camera Service Workflow

Android system is running on top of a Linux kernel. The Android system is essentially a set of processes (address spaces), including daemon processes, the *mediaserver* process, the *systemserver* process, the *servicemanager* process, and the Android application processes.

3.1.1 Overview.

Camera Service belongs to *mediaserver* process, which is a native process. The Camera Service's workflow is shown in Figure 1. The workflow is illustrated using a client process and the *mediaserver* process.

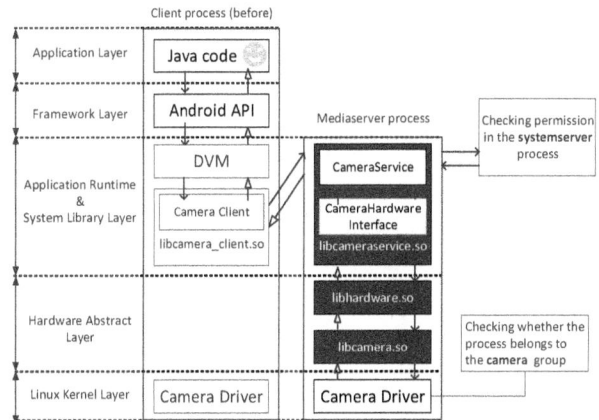

Figure 1: The workflow of the Camera Service

The client represents any app using the Camera Service. The client process has a standard 5-layer structure, which includes Application layer, Framework layer, Android Application Runtime layer (Runtime layer), Hardware Abstract Layer (HAL), and Linux Kernel layer. The Application layer and the Framework layer are written by Java code. The Runtime layer contains a Dalvik Virtual Machine (DVM) to execute Java code. This layer also includes certain native libraries to take care of the IPC needs, e.g. *libcamera_client.so*. In the HAL layer, since the client process does not need to directly interact with Camera device, this layer does not contain any code talking with camera driver. Regarding the Linux kernel layer, since the memory pages containing the kernel code are shared by every process, the client address space also contains the camera driver code.

The *mediaserver* process is a native process. Native processes do not contain Java code, therefore the *mediaserver* process does not need the DVM. The *mediaserver* process only has 3 layers (see Figure 1). The top layer only contains system libraries written in native code (*.so* libraries), therefore, we call this layer as System Library layer. The

System Library layer *.so* libraries are used to handle the request coming from a client, forward the request to the HAL layer, get the response from the HAL layer, and forward the response to the client. The HAL layer also contains *.so* libraries. Different from the System Library layer, libraries in this layer are used to talk with the camera driver. The HAL layer is doing most of the work assigned to the *mediaserver* process. The *mediaserver* process's Linux kernel layer also contains the camera diver.

3.1.2 Request Sending Workflow.

To communicate with the Camera Service, the client should firstly query the *servicemanager* process for the Camera Service's reference through binder IPC. The *servicemanager* is a native process managing a list of registered system services and their references. Querying *servicemanager* for the Camera Service's reference is a quite common IPC transaction, therefore it is not shown in the figure.

After the reference of the Camera Service is obtained, the general workflow of the Camera Service can be described as follows. If the client wants to, for example, take a picture, it should get connected with the Camera Service first. After the connection is established, the client could use all functions provided by the Camera Service. To get connected, the client first calls an Android API from its Java code. The Android API, through a system library (*libcamera_client.so*), sends the *CONNECT* binder request to the *mediaserver* process.

When the binder request is received by *mediaserver* process, the *CameraService* part (see Figure 1) of the System Library layer will parse the request type from binder data structure. If the request type is *CONNECT*, the *CameraService* part will let the *systemserver* process check the client's permission first. This step can be used to do API auditing, which will be discussed in Section 3.2. Only after the client passes permission check, the *CameraService* part will call the *CameraHardwareInterface* part of the System Library layer to initialize the camera device. The functions in the *CameraHardwareInterface* part will call the functions in the HAL layer to interact with the camera driver in the Linux kernel.

3.1.3 Image Data Transfer Workflow.

After a picture is taken, the picture (a frame of image data) will be transferred back (see the –▷ flow in Figure 1).

In the HAL layer, there is a *notification* thread that keeps listening on the camera driver and waits for camera events, such as Camera has focused, or focus has moved. When the camera device finishes taking a picture, the camera driver will send an event to the *notification* thread. After the *notification* thread receives the event, it will transfer the image data back to the System Library layer of the *mediaserver* process from the bottom up by calling the callback functions. The image data has already been compressed (by the camera driver) to a certain picture format (e.g. *jpeg*); the *CameraService* part could directly forward the image data to the client process via Binder IPC.

In the client process, after the image data is received by the *CameraClient* in the Runtime layer, it will be forwarded to the Framework layer. Then, the Framework layer posts the image data to the screen and the user will see. The image data could be saved as a picture file in the Application layer, which could be done by developers.

3.2 Android API auditing

Android provides various APIs to access phone hardware (e.g., camera), Wifi and networks, user data, and phone settings. Some of those APIs are protected by permissions. These APIs are implemented either in framework code or in system libraries. When a protected API is called, the implementation code of the API will send a request to the *systemserver* process to check the caller's permission.

The request is sent to the *PackageManager* thread of the *systemserver* process via Binder IPC, particularly. This thread can know when and which API is called, and can get the caller's UID (user ID) and PID (process ID). Therefore, through this thread, Android API auditing can be easily done. Through the audit record, intrusion detection can be done as well.

In Camera Service, when a picture-taking request is received, the *mediaserver* process will send a request to the *PackageManager* thread to check the caller's permission. In the meanwhile, the picture taking API can be audited.

4. CONSTRUCTION OF THE TRANSPLANTATION ATTACK

In this work, our goal is to take a picture without being audited by the API auditing, which should not have IPC with the *mediaserver* process. We assume an attacker would use a repackaged app with CAMERA permission to start transplantation attack. The repackaging should add the malicious code described in this Section.

4.1 First Idea

The first idea of transplantation is to transplant the code both in the System Library layer and the HAL layer from the *mediaserver*'s address space to the malicious app's address space directly. The code in the two layers exist in the form of *.so* libraries. It should be noticed that the camera-related *.so* libraries in the *mediaserver* process do not exist in any normal Android app's address space in the real world.

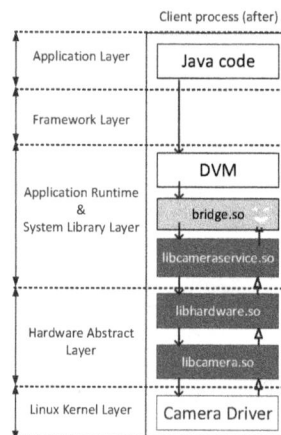

Figure 2: The address space of the malicious app

If the *.so* libraries in the *mediaserver* process can be successfully loaded into the malicious app's address space, the result will look like the one shown in Figure 2 without the *bridge.so* part. The Java code in the Application layer could get through the Framework layer and access the transplanted *.so* libraries in the Runtime layer. Then functions in the Runtime layer call the functions in the HAL layer to talk

102

with the camera driver in the Linux kernel layer. The execution flow of taking a picture goes from top to bottom within the malicious app's address space. The image data is transferred back from the bottom up inside the app's address space as well.

To make the above workflow work, three steps are needed. The first step is to get the capability of accessing the camera driver in the Linux kernel layer. Camera is a device file, who is assigned to the *camera* group. To get the access capability, the malicious app could become a member of *camera* group. In Android system, apps granted the CAMERA permission will be automatically put into the *camera* group [2]. Therefore, attackers should choose an app with CAMERA permission to repackage, then the repackaged malicious app will be put into *camera* group and can access camera drivers. On the condition that vendors have mistakenly configured the file access permission of camera driver as *rw-rw-rw-* (666) [35], camera driver can be globally accessed. In this case, the malicious app does not need to become a member of *camera* group. That is to say, the malicious app does not need to apply the CAMERA permission. We will discuss this case in the related work section.

The second step is to load the *.so* libraries into the malicious app's address space. There are two ways to load the system *.so* libraries into a process's address space in Android. The first one is loading all the required *.so* libraries when the process is created. This way needs the header files of the *.so* libraries. The other one is loading the required *.so* libraries when they are accessed. Using this way should call the *dlopen* and *dlsym* function, which are special functions provided by Android NDK. We have verified that both of the two ways are workable in loading *.so* libraries.

The third step is to enable the Java code in the Application layer to call the transplanted *.so* libraries in the Runtime and HAL layer. We know that Android provides Java Native Interface (JNI) for Java code to **inter-operate** with native code through DVM. Taking advantage of JNI programming, we can use native code as a bridge to connect the Java code and the transplanted *.so* libraries. The native code will be compiled to a *.so* file, and we name the *.so* file as *bridge.so*, which is shown in Figure 2.

The first and second step are easy to achieve, however, the third step is complicated. We meet several challenges in constructing the *bridge.so*: choosing a reasonable start point, setting up the execution context, and obtaining image data and save it as a picture file, which will be talked in the following sections.

4.2 Choose the Start Point of Transplantation

In step three, when we construct the transplantation attack and when we write the native code, a primary thing is to determine the start point of transplantation, i.e., which function of the transplanted *.so* library to be first called.

In the Runtime layer, the *.so* library we transplanted from the *mediaserver* process is the *libcameraservice.so*. We observed that after API auditing is finished, the first function of the *libcameraservice.so* library executed is the *connect* function. So, we try to start transplantation at this function. Before calling this function, the *bridge.so* also need to

first call several *constructor code* to generate some variables needed by the *connect* function.

Till now, the native code contains the *constructor code* and the *connect* function. Then, we try to compile the native code. Unfortunately, the compilation fails. That is because some parameters, global variables, as well as *constructor code* used in the *connect* function are implemented as **private** in Object Oriented Programming. They cannot be used outside their definition class. Therefore, starting at the *connect* function does not work, and we should look for another start point.

If we move the start point upstream of the workflow, the malicious app will cannot evade API auditing, which fails our goal. In addition, we noticed that functions really working are at the downstream of the workflow and these functions are not private. Therefore, moving the start point downstream of the workflow is an option.

We find that, logically, the *libcameraservice.so* library can be broken into two parts: the *CameraService* part and the *CameraHardwareInterface* part. The primary duty of the *CameraService* part is handling Binder request; and it is the *CameraHardwareInterface* part really processing the request by calling functions in the HAL layer. The spy-on-user goal is to take pictures without using any IPC, so, we just need to jump over the *CameraService* part and start at the *CameraHardwareInterface* part, instead.

Although starting at the HAL layer also can call the camera accessing functions, it will encounter more incompatibility problems than starting at the *CameraHardwareInterface* part. That is because, the HAL layer is more closely linked with the driver than the *CameraHardwareInterface* part. According to [35], making hardware work is the primary reason for vendors to customize Android system. Therefore, the closer to the driver, the possible the code will be modified. Another reason to start at the *CameraHardwareInterface* part is that the number of functions in this part is much less than that of the HAL layer.

Starting at the *CameraHardwareInterface* part does not change the address space shown in Figure 2. We still need to transplant the *libcameraservice.so* into the malicious app's Runtime layer. The difference is that the *CameraService* part is no longer executed in the malicious app's address space.

4.3 Set up the Execution Context of Picture Taking

Without proper execution context, the function of taking a picture cannot be executed. *CameraService* part plays a significant role in setting up the execution context needed by the functions in the *CameraHardwareInterface* part. That the *CameraService* part will not be executed will lead to missing of execution context. As a consequence, functions in the *CameraHardwareInterface* part cannot be executed.

To take a picture, the *bridge.so* at least needs to call the *initialize* function (to initialize camera driver) and the *takePicture* function (to take a picture). The execution context needed by the *initialize* function is a data structure *hw_module_t*, which contains a set of camera metadata and a set of function pointers pointing to the functions in the HAL layer. To get this data structure, we need to call the *hw_get_module* function of the *libhardware.so*. After successfully obtain the data structure, the *bridge.so* can call *initialize* function to initialize camera driver.

---

[2] Android has bound several permissions to some group IDs in a metadata file named *platform.xml*. In the file, CAMERA permission has been bound to camera group

Although the camera device is initialized, the execution context needed by the *takePicture* function is still missing. We notice that before taking a picture, it should start a preview first. The execution context of preview should be gotten from a data structure transferred by binder. Since there is no IPC in the malicious app's workflow, there is no binder data to use.

The execution context needed by preview is a native window variable, which is created by using a Java parameter obtained from a binder data structure. The Java parameter (*Surface* object) is created in the Application layer of the workflow shown in Figure 1. Noticing this, we could create the Java parameter using Java code and let the native code get the Java parameter by programming with JNI.

After the native window variable is created, we first start a preview, and try to take a picture two seconds later. As expected, the preview is successfully shown on the screen. And, two seconds later, the preview window is successfully frozen, which means the *takePicture* function is successfully executed.

4.4 Store Image Data as Picture File

Although picture/image data can be shown on the screen, it does not mean the picture files have been generated. We need to get the picture/image data and store the data as a picture file.

As we mentioned in Section 3.1.3, the image data is transferred through callback functions. The *CameraHardwareInterface* part also provides the *setCallbacks* function to set up callback functions. There are three callback functions: *notifyCallback*, *dataCallback*, and *dataCallbackTimestamp*. Their usage can be inferred from the function's name. The *notifyCallback* function tells user such things as the Camera has focused or the focus has moved. In this attack, we do not want the user to receive those notifications. Instead, we want to stealthily take a picture and send the picture to someone else. Therefore, we focus on getting the image data, which needs to implement the *dataCallback* function.

After the *dataCallback* function being added to the *bridge.so*, we rerun the malicious app. Out of our expectation, the *dataCallback* function is not called. As a result, the picture cannot be obtained.

The possible reasons are analyzed as below. First, Android may restrict that the image data only can be transferred to the *mediaserver* process only. However, since we already succeed in previewing the image data on the screen, the malicious app **can** receive the image data coming from camera driver. Therefore, this reason is not valid.

Second, the image data may exist in the kernel space since the camera driver runs in the Linux kernel, and native code running in the user space cannot get the data. However, all transplanted code is also executed in the user space of the *mediaserver* process. Since the image data can be gotten in the *mediaserver*'s user space, it also should be gotten from malicious app's process. This reason is not valid, either.

Third, there may be other missing steps in our transplantation. In the *mediaserver* process, the callback functions are set in the *CameraService* part, whose code is 3.67 times as much as the code of the *CameraHardwareInterface* part[3]. The *CameraService* part is not executed in the malicious app's address space, which may lead to other execution context not being set up or some functions not being executed.

---

[3]The comparison is between the .*cpp* files on Android 4.1.2 version.

To see if this reason is valid, we do a dynamical analysis. We take advantage of the *log* mechanism provided by Android to print the names of the functions executed in a picture taking workflow. To see if there are missing steps, we compare the functions executed in the *mediaserver* process and the malicious app process by analyzing the logs. The result shows that several functions in the HAL layer are not called in the malicious app's address space. For example, functions used to detect users' face, to play shutter sound, and to enable/disable an event message type to get/drop a notification are not called.

We care about the functions about notification, whose names are *enableMsgType* and *disableMsgType*. They are used in pairs. There are several message types enabled in the *mediaserver* process when taking a picture. What really matters is the event message type *CAMERA_MSG_COMPRESSED_IMAGE*. Enabling this message type will make the *dataCallback* function be called. Motivated by this special trigger condition, we let the native code call the *enableMsgType* and *disableMsgType* functions provided by the *CameraHardwareInterface* part. In addition, we let the native code call the *stopPreview* function to stop the preview and the *release* function to close the camera device. These steps make the malicious code clean and tidy.

After all the above functions are added into the malicious app's native code, we rerun the app. The good news is the *dataCallback* function is called, however, the image data remains not received. To diagnose, we do a static analysis, and we find the image data is transferred back by the *notification* thread (see Section 3.1). The *notification* thread needs to wait for image data coming from the camera driver, which is time consuming. To the contrary, the native code is executed in another thread, which takes much less time. The two threads are not synchronized. Therefore, before the image data is transferred back, the *CAMERA_MSG_COMPRESSED_IMAGE* message type may be disabled or the camera may be closed.

Based on this observation, we add synchronization for the two threads. This time, we successfully get the image data transferred by the *dataCallback* function in the native code. Moreover, the image data is successfully stored to a picture file in the *dataCallback* function.

4.5 How to Hide

To make the spy-on-user attack be stealthily carried out, we assume the attacker would need the following requirements when executing the malicious code of picture taking.

Hiding the user interface. As an app, the attacker's Java code should be implemented in the form of Android components. Among the four kinds of components (*Activity*, *Service*, *Content Provider*, and *Broadcast Receiver*), we prefer the *Service* component to hold the malicious Java code of creating the Java parameter needed in preview and calling the malicious native code. It is because this component does not contain a user interface and runs in the background. When the *Service* component is running, users will not feel any abnormal things on the screen.

Hiding the preview window. At the meanwhile of hiding user interface, we need a window view (*window* variable) to preview when taking a picture. A view occupies a rectangular area on the screen, which could be seen by the user. We have two ways to hide the preview window. The first one is minimizing the window view's size to such as 1 pixel

× 1 pixel, so that it cannot be seen by humans' eyes. What worth mentioning is that the size of the preview window does not affect the size of the picture. The other way to hide the preview window is not transferring the image data to the window view when previewing. As there is no image data received, the window view cannot be seen on the screen. However, the view still stays on the screen. If coincidentally the malicious app is taking a picture and users touch the window view area, e.g., to launch a new app, there will be no response happens, which will make users suspicious. Therefore, we prefer the first way to hide the preview window.

Hiding the flashlight and shutter sound. The flashlight and shutter sound can be controlled by the *bridge.so*. To minimize the picture taking signs, we prefer not to use them. At daytime, the nature light is enough for taking a picture. While at night, the evening light is not suitable for photographs without flashlight. Therefore, the attack should choose not to take pictures after 8pm. Without flashlight and sound, the user can hardly feel the signs of picture taking. It may be considered that a camera indicator light may be shown when taking pictures. However, all the experiment phones used by our labmates (see Table 3) do not show it. Further, provided the camera indicator light is shown, the nature light will make it hardly be noticed.

Stealthily sending the picture out. There are several ways that can be used to send pictures out, such as MMS (multimedia message), Bluetooth, 3G, and Wifi. To achieve the stealth goal, we should not cost the user's money, leave any audit records, or light on any icon on the desktop. Users care about the MMS they send, as these will cost their money, so we should not use them to send pictures. Sending data out through the Bluetooth has the shortcomings that it will leave an audit record and does not fit for long distance transfer, so we do not use it, either. Since 3G and Wifi do not suffer the two shortcomings as Bluetooth, we prefer to use them to send pictures out. To avoid lighting on their icon on the screen, we let the malicious app send pictures out **after** the 3G/Wifi is turned on by the user. Nowadays, 3G traffic is quite cheap and has no toplimit; it is not a big concern of users any more.

Do not drain the battery too quickly. If the malicious app takes pictures too frequently, the battery may be drained too quickly, which will make the user suspicious. To determine the frequency of picture taking, we measured the power consumption of taking ten pictures, playing *Angry bird* and *Sudoku* for ten minutes respectively on the same phone using *PowerTutor*. The result shows that the power consumed by playing 10 minutes of *Angry bird* can support taking 41.7 pictures, while playing 10 minutes of *Sudoku* can support taking 30.2 pictures. So, taking 36 pictures every day will not be perceived by the user. Further, we do not take pictures at night because the flashlight cannot be used, this will also save energy. To make the balance between the battery consumption and the frequency of picture taking, the attacker could set the malicious app to take a picture every 20 minutes during 8am to 8pm (36 pictures in total).

4.6 Other Things That Attackers Should Do

In the real world, the first step to launch the transplantation attack is to choose an app with CAMERA permission to repackage. For example, scan-QR-code apps need CAMERA permission to open camera and scan QR code, attackers can choose this kind of apps to repackage. A great number of scan-QR-code apps can be found on Google Play, Amazon, or other markets. Attackers can easily choose a widely downloaded one on Google Play to repackage, and then attackers could submit the repackaged app to third party markets to distribute. Also, the target app can be chosen on third party markets and submit to Google Play.

Assuming that the malicious repackaged app has been successfully installed into the user's phone, the next step is letting the app obtain the CPU cycles to run itself. Attackers would like that the malicious app is able to get the CPU cycles every 20 minutes. A possible way is letting the malicious app be started immediately after the phone has been booted up. To do this, the malicious app should receive a BOOT_COMPLETED broadcast, which is sent by the Android system when the system has been boot up. The stealthy picture taking functionality can be implemented as a service, which can be denoted as picture taking service. In the broadcast receiver, the attacker put a piece of code that denoted as *timer* and let the *timer* to start the picture taking service every 20 minutes.

Some Antivirus allow users to block apps from receiving the BOOT_COMPLETED broadcast. In this case, the stealthy picture taking can be trigged by motion sensors, such as accelerometer sensor, orientation sensor. There are plenty of open sources towards how to use motion sensors to infer position of smartphones publicly available on many websites. Therefore, attackers can easily get those code and add them into the repackaged app to make the stealthy picture taking triggered by motion sensors. Using motion sensors does not need any permission.

To send pictures out, the malicious app needs to apply the INTERNET permission. According to [19], there are 88% apps with the INTERNET permission. Most of apps use INTERNET permission to fulfill the advertisement needs. It is not a strange thing that a scan-QR-code app to apply this permission, e.g, to show advertisements.

Front and Rear Camera Nowadays, most smartphones shipped with front and rear Cameras. Sometimes, attackers want to see users' expression, and sometimes, attackers want to see the environment where users stay in. This can be archived by specifying the camera ID of front Camera or rear Camera in the *bridge.so*. Usually, the ID of front Camera is 0, and the other one is 1, which is true on the successful ones of 69 phones (See Section 5). Still, there exists a possibility that vendors may change their Camera IDs. In this case, analyzing the phone logs or brute force may be help to find the IDs.

5. EVALUATION

We evaluate the transplantation attack in the aspects of success rate on real phones, detection rate of Antivirus (AVs), and the Android Device Administration, respectively.

5.1 Success Rate

To know the effectiveness of the transplantation attack, we run the malicious app on different phones shipped with different Android versions in the real world. We choose 8 different vendors, 69 different phones, and 7 different Android versions. The result is shown in Table 1 and Table 2.

Among the tested phones, 14 of them are collected from our labmates, 62 of them are achieved from *Baidu* app test platform [1]. 7 of 62 phones have the same model and the same Android version with some of the 14 ones. So, the total number of **different** phones is 69. On the *Baidu* app test platform, all phones used to test apps are real phones not emulators.

On our labmates' phones, we test all functionalities of the malicious app, including picture taking, preview window hiding, and picture sending. We let the malicious app send the stealthily taken pictures to another phone. If the receiver can successfully open and view the pictures, we regard the attack as successful. As long as the Wifi is available, if the malicious app can take a picture, it can always send the picture out.

On the phones provided by *Baidu* test platform, because we cannot physically access those phones, we only test the picture taking functionality on the test platform phones. For the convenience of test, we let the malicious app show the preview window on the screen. Therefore, to check whether a phone's screenshots (generated by the test platform) contain the preview window or not, we can verify whether the picture taking is successful or not.

As shown in Table 1, for version 4.1.1 phones from 5 vendors, the success rate of transplantation attack is 100%. For version 4.1.2 phones from 5 vendors, the success rate of transplantation attack is 75%. We also measure the success rate per vendor. As shown in Table 2, the success rate for Samsung phones is 52% (25 phones in total). The success rate for Huawei phones is 54.55% (11 phones in total). Overall, among the 69 phones, the overall success rate is 46.38%. This means nearly a half of the phone in real world would possibly suffer from this spy-on-user attack.

Table 1: Success rate of different Android versions

Android Version	Vender	Number	Success Rate
Android 4.0.3	HTC	4	0
	Huawei	3	
	LG	1	
Android 4.0.4	Google	1	12.5%
	Samsung	4	
	HTC	5	
	Huawei	1	
	Sony	1	
	Moto	4	
Android 4.1.1	Google	1	100%
	Samsung	1	
	HTC	4	
	Huawei	2	
	Meizu	2	
Android 4.1.2	Google	2	75%
	Samsung	16	
	HTC	1	
	Huawei	3	
	Sony	2	
Android 4.2.1	Samsung	1	0
Android 4.2.2	Huawei	1	40%
	Sony	3	
	LG	1	
Android 4.3	Samsung	3	0
	HTC	1	
	Huawei	1	
Total	8	69	46.38%

Table 2: Success rate of different vendors

Vendor	Google	Samsung	HTC	Huawei
Success Rate	75%	52%	33.33%	54.55%
Vendor	Sony	Meizu	LG	Moto
Success Rate	33.33%	100%	50%	0

5.2 Look into the phones where the attack is not successful

The experiment on version 4.0.3 is very confusing, so we analyze this version's picture taking workflow, and we find there is no difference between this version and other 4.x versions. All 4.0.3 version of phones are provided by *Baidu*. Since we cannot get the failure info (*adb log*) of phones from *Baidu* test platform, we cannot figure out the failure reason on version 4.0.3 as well as version 4.2.1 phones. However, we believe this is a side benefit of customization according to the failure reasons of the phones used by our labmates, which will be analyzed as follows.

Table 3: Experiment result on our labmates phones

Vender	Model	Version	Result
Google	Nexus S	4.0.4	√
	Nexus S	4.1.2	√
	Nexus 4G	4.1.1	√
	Galaxy Nexus		×
Samsung	SHV-E160S (Galaxy Note)	4.0.4	×
	GT-I8268	4.1.2	√
	GT-I9300 (Galaxy S3)	4.1.2	√
	SCH-I879	4.1.2	×
	SCH-I959 (Galaxy S4)	4.2.2	×
	SCH-N719 (Galaxy NoteII)	4.3	×
HTC	T528t (One ST)	4.0.4	×
Sony	LT29i (Xperia TX)	4.1.2	√
MeiZu	M040 (MX2)	4.1.1	√
Huawei	P6-C00 (Ascend P6)	4.2.2	√

We only analyze the failure reason phones used by our labmates. The experiment result is shown in Table 3.

The transplantation attack does not succeed on 6 phones. The failure reasons are different for each phone. To analyze each phone's failure reason, we obtain their *adb log* of taking a picture generated by the *Camera* app shipped on the test phone and by the malicious app. Here, we summarize our findings.

For Google Galaxy Nexus, we analyze its source code of picture taking workflow since this phone support AOSP (Android Open Source Project). We find that before opening the camera device, the *mediaserver* process will open the device */dev/rproc_user* first, which belongs to the *drmrpc* group. Unlike the *camera* group ID, the *drmrpc* group ID cannot be obtained by apps. Therefore, as apps cannot become a member of the *drmrpc* group, they cannot open the */dev/rproc_user* device. As a result, the attack fails.

For Samsung SHV-E160S, the difference between the *Camera* app and the malicious app is that the malicious app is "unable to find matching camera info" for the given camera ID, but the *Camera* app can. As a result, the malicious app cannot open the camera, and the error number is -1, which means "operation not permitted". As we cannot get the source code of this phone, we could only infer that it may be the vendor has modified the workflow of opening the camera device.

For Samsung SCH-I879, the error message and error number are the same as Samsung SHV-E160S, which still is "operation not permitted". Since Samsung SCH-I879's Android version is the same as Samsung GT-I8268 and Samsung GT-I9300, we compare the adb logs obtained from the three phones. However, as they use different hardware and different internal logic of picture taking, the comparison between the three phones does not help.

For Samsung SCH-I959, the log shows that the camera device is successfully initialized. But taking pictures on this phone needs to write a file (*CameraID.txt*) into the *data* partition. Otherwise, the preview cannot successfully start. As a result, the *takePicture* function fails, whose error number is -38. This error number is not defined by the AOSP, and we believe it is defined by the vendor. Since the malicious app does not have privilege to write the *data* partition, the transplantation attack cannot succeed.

For Samsung SCH-N719, when initializing the camera device, it should open the device */dev/video0*, which belongs to the *camera* group. As the malicious app is already set as a member of the *camera* group. Theoretically, it could access the device. Surprisingly, the experiment fails. To diagnose, we analyze the *adb log* and a metadata file (*uevent-d.smdk4x12.rc*), and we find the camera hardware of Samsung SCH-N719 is the same as Samsung GT-I9300 on which phone the attack is successful. The difference between the two phones is that Samsung SCH-N719's Android version is 4.3 and the SEAndroid is enabled. We will discuss the SEAndroid in Section 6.

The last one is HTC-T528t, whose error message is "cannot open OpenMAX registry file /tmp/.omxregister". The failure reason is like the Samsung SCH-I959, and this one is the malicious app does not have privilege to access the registry file. But the error number is different. On HTC-T528t, the error number is 0x80001000, which we believe is defined by the vendor as well.

Among the 6 failed phones, 3 of them (Galaxy Nexus, Samsung SCH-I959, and HTC-T528t) fail because extra device and files are involved in their picture taking workflow. We wonder if the malicious app can access the device and files, could the transplantation attack succeed? To answer this question, we do an experiment on the Galaxy Nexus phone, also because this phone supports AOSP.

We know the failure reason of this phone is that the malicious app cannot be assigned the *drmrpc* group ID. Learning from the binding between the CAMERA permission and *camera* group ID, we make the *drmrpc* group ID available to apps by binding it to a permission, e.g., binding it to the CAMERA permission. Binding them needs to modify a metadata file (*platform.xml*), which needs root privilege. After binding, the malicious app can get the *drmrpc* group ID. Then, we rerun the malicious app, and this time the malicious app succeeds in taking a picture and sending the picture out.

According to this experiment, we can infer that if the malicious app can access to the devices and files, the success rate of transplantation attack will be increased from 57.14% to 78.57% in Table 3.

5.3 Evading Antivirus

Employee phones or individual phones may be installed Antivirus (AVs). To test whether the malicious app could evade detection under AVs monitoring, we choose the top 7 **free** AVs according to the [28]'s comparison result. Among the protections they provide, we care about the Scans Phone Apps protection, the Real-Time Protection (discover harmful threads immediately), the Antispyware protection (protect users from being spied), and the Quarantine Section protection (store the suspicious thread in an isolation area). These protections could be classified into two categories: the installation time protection and the runtime protection.

In order to know whether the malicious app could evade detection at installation time, we first install the 7 AVs into 3 experiment phones, then install the malicious app. The 7

AVs' scanning result claims the app is clean, as a result, the app is successfully installed into the 3 phones. Then we run the app under the 7 AVs' monitoring to test whether the app could evade runtime detection. As expected, none of the 7 AVs detect the malicious app out. The result is shown in Table 4.

The result shows that the malicious app can successfully evade detection at both installation time and runtime. Two possible reasons are as follows. The first one is that the installation time scanning only scans the signature of an app. As the malicious app is new, it does not have signatures, yet. In addition, the AVs do not regard loading external *.so* libraries is malicious. Therefore, when the native code thread is running, the AVs do not regard the running thread as evil, either.

5.4 Evading Enterprise Device Administration

Device Administration is usually enforced in the enterprise, in which the phones are owned by companies or organizations. Android framework provides several special Android APIs, which are called Device Administration APIs. They could be used by device admin apps to configure a phone. Administrators could install the admin app on the employee's phones to, for example, disable or enable the camera device. It is designed that once the camera device is disabled by the Device Administration APIs, apps cannot access the camera device anymore.

To understand whether the transplantation attack could sustain the camera device disabling, we run the *Camera* app and the malicious app after the camera device is disabled, respectively. As expected, the *Camera* app fails in taking a picture after the camera device is disabled. However, the malicious app sustains the disabling and successfully takes a picture.

That is because the *Camera* app relies on the *mediaserver* process to take pictures. When the camera device is disabled, the value of a flag (*sys.secpolicy.camera.disabled*) is set to 1 (true). Once the flag's value is 1, the *mediaserver* process will reject any request of accessing the camera device. What is to say, all picture taking APIs cannot be called. In the transplantation attack, the malicious app does not rely on the *mediaserver* process, does not need to call those APIs, and does not execute the flag checking code in its address space, either. Therefore, the transplantation attack can evade the Device Administration as well.

6. DISCUSSION

6.1 Design Deficiency

The transplantation attack indicates that there is a subtle design/implementation deficiency of Android security management.

Since it is the *mediaserver* process in charge of talking with the camera driver, and since an app does not, we wonder whether it is necessary for Android system to put an app into the *camera* group. To answer this question, we did an experiment by removing the apps with CAMERA permission from the *camera* group. We found that the *Camera* app as well as apps relying on it (by sending an *Intent*) can take pictures even if they are not running with the *camera* group ID. The result shows that binding the CAMERA per-

Table 4: Antivirus Testing Result

AVs\Protections	Lookout	McAfee	Kaspersky	ESET	Trend	F-Secure	NetQin
Scan Phone Apps	√	√	√	√	√	√	√
Real-Time	√	√	√	√	√	√	√
Antispyware	√	√	√	NA	NA	√	√
Quarantine Section	√	NA	√	√	NA	√	NA

mission with the camera group could be a design deficiency, since this will allow the transplantation attack to succeed.

6.2 How to Defend

There may be several ways to defend the transplantation attack, but some of them may not work out. For example, forbidding the usage of system libraries may sound a good idea to defend the attack. However, as apps can ship their own copy of the required system library, this way may not work out. Here, we discuss two possible ways as follows.

6.2.1 Break the Binding Between Permissions and Group IDs.

To start transplantation attack, a malicious app should get the capability of accessing a hardware device. To gain this capability, the malicious app should be assigned with the hardware's group ID by applying corresponding permission. Noticing this, a defence is that we could break the binding between permission strings and group IDs. Taking Camera device as an example, breaking the binding between CAMERA permission and *camera* group ID will not affect the normal apps to take pictures. That is because Camera device has a daemon process (*mediaserver* process, in which Camera Service runs) in charge of taking pictures. Apps just need to send request to the daemon process, and the process will handle the picture taking work.

One weakness of this defence is that when the hardware has zero daemon process (e.g., there is no daemon process for Sdcard) or more than one daemon processes, it is possible to result in denying of services.

6.2.2 Using SEAndroid Policy.

SEAndroid enforces mandatory access control to every process (user) under a fine-grained access control policy. Every process belongs to a domain (type). Here, third-party apps are classified into the *untrusted_app* domain, which will be blocked when directly access the camera driver.

Although SEAndroid can block accessing the camera driver, it has a rather limited enforcement range. SEAndroid [27] is merged into AOSP since version 4.3 and enforced since version 4.4. According to Google's survey [16], the phones shipped with version 4.3 and 4.4 each accounts for 8.5% of the total at the beginning of May, 2014. That a phone shipped with 4.3 version of Android does not mean that the SEAndroid is enforced. So, nearly 90% of the Android phones in the wild are however not protected by SEAndroid. Among the phones used by our labmates, 93% of them without SEAndroid. It may take a long period of time before SEAndroid can be widely deployed in the wild. During this period of time, many many users may suffer from the spy-on-user attack.

Besides the distribution range limitation, SEAndroid has weakness as well. Pau Oliva shows 3 weaknesses of SEAndroid and gives out 4 ways to bypass SEAndroid [29]. We

did an experiment, in which we change SEAndroid from enforce mode to permissive mode via PC terminals. The same principle could be applied to apps. The experiment shows that SEAndroid can indeed be bypassed.

7. RELATED WORKS

A Similar Attack. Xiaoyong et. al. [35] illustrate an end-to-end attack similar to transplantation attack. Their attack can take a picture without applying CAMERA permission, and can evade API auditing as well. However, their attack has a critical premise that the camera device node (*/dev/video*) should be set as publicly readable and writable (a Linux permission of 666), which means the phone is mistakenly configured. Otherwise, their attack cannot succeed. In case of fulfilling the premise, the transplantation attack can succeed without applying CAMERA permission, too. In addition, transplantation attack can work on nearly a half of well configured phones.

Xiaoyong et. al. have implemented the whole HAL layer within their app, which is quite different from us. We just implemented a *bridge.so*, and let the *bridge.so* call the transplanted *.so* libraries of System Library layer and HAL layer. Our attack and their attack are constructed in very different ways. Obviously, our attack has much less lines of code.

Xiaoyong's work and our work share different focus, too. They mainly focus on understanding security risks in vendors' customization process; and their attack is inspired by a security flaw that vendors have mistakenly configured the camera device node with permission of 666. However, at the beginning, our focus is to construct a transplantation attack to evade API auditing.

Other Spy-on-user Attacks. Besides Camera, many ways can be applied to spy on user. TouchLogger [7], TapLogger [31], TapPrints [20], ACCessory [24], ACComplice [18], Soundcomber [26], and Screenmilker use motion sensor readings, microphone, screenshots, to work as a keylogger to spy on users' input, location hacker to trace users' driving, or sound trojan to infer users' credit card accounts, etc. Stealthy Video Capturer [30] stealthily record video to compromise users' privacy. Besides the side channels on smartphones, physical side channels like shoulder surfing, reflection of the screen from sunglass [25], and oil fingerprint [32] [4] also can be used to spy on users.

Although these works also focus on spying on user, none of their methods is carried out by transplantation attack, and they may be faced the risk of being detected out by API auditing.

Permission Escalation Attacks. Another well studied attack of Android system is permission escalation attack. To detect whether an app has unprotected interfaces that can be exploited to escalate permissions, a number of detection tools have been proposed [8] [12] [13] [3] [15]. These static analysis tools are likely to be incomplete, as they cannot completely predict the actual permission escalation attack occurring at runtime. To address this issue, some framework extension solutions [14] [10] [6] [17] [5] have been proposed.

Root Exploits Attacks. According to [36], attacks exploiting root privilege play a significant role in compromising Android security. Among the root exploiting malware, the *DroidKungFu* [22] is a typical example. Attacks exploiting root privilege could break the boundary of Android sandbox and could access resources without applying permissions. The root exploits attacks could be blocked by SEAndroid [27]. By introducing SEAndroid, processes even running with root privilege cannot access the protected files and devices.

Framework Enhancements. A large number of solutions [21] [37] [23] [9] focus on enhancing runtime permission control to restrict app's permission at runtime. These solutions aim at providing a fine-grained access control for IPC. However, the transplantation attack does not involve IPC. Therefore, the attack fails these solutions.

8. CONCLUSION

In this paper, we propose the transplantation attack, an attack which enables a malicious app to take (potentially privacy-harming) pictures at anytime without being audited by the Android API auditing. The transplantation attack, when being applied to achieve the spy-on-user goal, results in stealthiest and unnoticed picture taking. We have conducted a set of real world attacking experiments. 46.38% of the 69 smartphones (manufactured by 8 vendors) tested by us let the transplantation attack succeed. The transplantation attack also uncovers a subtle design/implementation deficiency of the Android system. Our recent analysis reveals that although on AOSP version 4.4 the deficiency is fixed, most of vendors have not fix this problem yet.

9. ACKNOWLEDGEMENTS

We would like to thank the anonymous reviewers for their valuable comments. This work is supported by Strategy Pilot Project of Chinese Academy of Sciences under Grant XDA06010702; National High Technology Research and Development Program of China (863 Program) under Grant 2013AA01A214, 2012AA013104. Peng Liu is supported by Army Research Office W911NF-09-1-0525, W911NF-13-1-0421; National Science Foundation CCF-1320605, SBE-1422215.

10. REFERENCES

[1] Baidu Mobile Test Center. Available at http://mtc.baidu.com/.

[2] Common vulnerabilities and exposures. http://cve.mitre.org/.

[3] K. W. Y. Au, Y. F. Zhou, Z. Huang, and D. Lie. Pscout: analyzing the android permission specification. In *ACM CCS*, 2012.

[4] A. J. Aviv, K. Gibson, E. Mossop, M. Blaze, and J. M. Smith. Smudge attacks on smartphone touch screens. In *Proceedings of the 4th USENIX Conference on Offensive Technologies*, WOOT'10, pages 1–7, Berkeley, CA, USA, 2010. USENIX Association.

[5] S. Bugiel, L. Davi, A. Dmitrienko, T. Fischer, and A.-R. Sadeghi. XMandroid: a new android evolution to mitigate privilege escalation attacks. *Technische Universität Darmstadt, Technical Report TR-2011-04*.

[6] S. Bugiel, L. Davi, A. Dmitrienko, T. Fischer, A.-R. Sadeghi, and B. Shastry. Towards taming privilege-escalation attacks on android. In *19th NDSS*, 2012.

[7] L. Cai and H. Chen. Touchlogger: Inferring keystrokes on touch screen from smartphone motion. In *Proceedings of the 6th USENIX Conference on Hot Topics in Security*, HotSec'11, pages 9–9, Berkeley, CA, USA, 2011. USENIX Association.

[8] E. Chin, A. P. Felt, K. Greenwood, and D. Wagner. Analyzing inter-application communication in android. In *9th MobiSys*, 2011.

[9] M. Conti, V. T. N. Nguyen, and B. Crispo. Crepe: Context-related policy enforcement for android. In *Information Security*. 2011.

[10] M. Dietz, S. Shekhar, Y. Pisetsky, A. Shu, and D. S. Wallach. Quire: Lightweight provenance for smart phone operating systems. In *USENIX Security*, 2011.

[11] T. Donegan. How your phone camera can be used to spy on you. http://cameras.reviewed.com/features/how-your-smartphone-camera-can-be-used-to-spy-on-you, 5 2014.

[12] W. Enck, M. Ongtang, and P. McDaniel. On lightweight mobile phone application certification. In *16th ACM CCS*, pages 235–245. ACM, 2009.

[13] A. P. Felt, E. Chin, S. Hanna, D. Song, and D. Wagner. Android permissions demystified. In *18th ACM CCS*, pages 627–638. ACM, 2011.

[14] A. P. Felt, H. J. Wang, A. Moshchuk, S. Hanna, and E. Chin. Permission re-delegation: Attacks and defenses. In *USENIX Security Symposium*, 2011.

[15] A. P. Fuchs, A. Chaudhuri, and J. S. Foster. Scandroid: Automated security certification of android applications. *Manuscript, Univ. of Maryland*, 2009.

[16] Google. Dashboards. http://developer.android.com/about/dashboards/index.html?utm_source=ausdroid.net\#Platform, 2014.03.

[17] M. Grace, Y. Zhou, Z. Wang, and X. Jiang. Systematic detection of capability leaks in stock android smartphones. In *19th NDSS*, 2012.

[18] J. Han, E. Owusu, L. Nguyen, A. Perrig, and J. Zhang. Accomplice: Location inference using accelerometers on smartphones. In *Communication Systems and Networks (COMSNETS), 2012 Fourth International Conference on*, pages 1–9, Jan 2012.

[19] P. Hornyack, S. Han, J. Jung, S. Schechter, and D. Wetherall. These aren't the droids you're looking for: retrofitting android to protect data from imperious applications. In *18th ACM CCS*, 2011.

[20] E. Miluzzo, A. Varshavsky, S. Balakrishnan, and R. R. Choudhury. Tapprints: Your finger taps have fingerprints. In *Proceedings of the 10th International Conference on Mobile Systems, Applications, and Services*, MobiSys '12, pages 323–336, New York, NY, USA, 2012. ACM.

[21] M. Nauman, S. Khan, and X. Zhang. Apex: extending android permission model and enforcement with user-defined runtime constraints. In *5th ACM CCS*, 2010.

[22] NC State University. Security alert: New sophisticated android malware droidkungfu found in alternative

chinese app markets. Available at `http://www.csc.ncsu.edu/faculty/jiang/DroidKungFu.html`, 2011.

[23] M. Ongtang, S. McLaughlin, W. Enck, and P. McDaniel. Semantically rich application-centric security in android. *Security and Communication Networks*, 2012.

[24] E. Owusu, J. Han, S. Das, A. Perrig, and J. Zhang. Accessory: Password inference using accelerometers on smartphones. In *Proceedings of the Twelfth Workshop on Mobile Computing Systems & Applications*, HotMobile '12, pages 9:1–9:6, New York, NY, USA, 2012. ACM.

[25] R. Raguram, A. M. W. 0002, D. Goswami, F. Monrose, and J.-M. Frahm. ispy: automatic reconstruction of typed input from compromising reflections. In Y. Chen, G. Danezis, and V. Shmatikov, editors, *ACM Conference on Computer and Communications Security*, pages 527–536. ACM, 2011.

[26] R. Schlegel, K. Zhang, X.-y. Zhou, M. Intwala, A. Kapadia, and X. Wang. Soundcomber: A stealthy and context-aware sound trojan for smartphones. In *NDSS*, volume 11, pages 17–33, 2011.

[27] S. Smalley and R. Craig. Security Enhanced (SE) Android: Bringing Flexible MAC to Android. In *NDSS*, 2013.

[28] Toptenreviews. 2014 Best Mobile Security Software Comparisons and Reviews. Available at `http://mobile-security-software-review.toptenreviews.com/`, 2014.

[29] viaForensics. Defeating SEAndroid ÍC DEFCON 21 Presentation. Available at `https://viaforensics.com/mobile-security/implementing-seandroid-defcon-21-presentation.html`, 8/3/2013.

[30] N. Xu, F. Zhang, Y. Luo, W. Jia, D. Xuan, and J. Teng. Stealthy video capturer: A new video-based spyware in 3g smartphones. In *Proceedings of the Second ACM Conference on Wireless Network Security*, WiSec '09, pages 69–78, New York, NY, USA, 2009. ACM.

[31] Z. Xu, K. Bai, and S. Zhu. Taplogger: Inferring user inputs on smartphone touchscreens using on-board motion sensors. In *Proceedings of the Fifth ACM Conference on Security and Privacy in Wireless and Mobile Networks*, WISEC '12, pages 113–124, New York, NY, USA, 2012. ACM.

[32] Y. Zhang, P. Xia, J. Luo, Z. Ling, B. Liu, and X. Fu. Fingerprint attack against touch-enabled devices. In *Proceedings of the Second ACM Workshop on Security and Privacy in Smartphones and Mobile Devices*, SPSM '12, pages 57–68, New York, NY, USA, 2012. ACM.

[33] W. Zhou, Y. Zhou, M. Grace, X. Jiang, and S. Zou. Fast, scalable detection of "piggybacked" mobile applications. In *3rd CODASPY*, 2013.

[34] W. Zhou, Y. Zhou, X. Jiang, and P. Ning. Detecting repackaged smartphone applications in third-party android marketplaces. In *2nd CODASPY*, pages 317–326. ACM, 2012.

[35] X. Zhou, Y. Lee, N. Zhang, M. Naveed, and X. Wang. The peril of fragmentation: Security hazards in android device driver customizations. In *IEEE Symposium on Security and Privacy*, 2014.

[36] Y. Zhou and X. Jiang. Dissecting android malware: Characterization and evolution. In *Security and Privacy (SP)*, pages 95–109. IEEE, 2012.

[37] Y. Zhou, X. Zhang, X. Jiang, and V. W. Freeh. Taming information-stealing smartphone applications (on android). In *Trust and Trustworthy Computing*. 2011.

On the Character of Phishing URLs: Accurate and Robust Statistical Learning Classifiers*

Rakesh Verma, Keith Dyer
Dept. of Computer Science, University of Houston
Houston, Texas, USA
rmverma@cs.uh.edu, kwdyer@uh.edu

ABSTRACT

Phishing attacks resulted in an estimated $3.2 billion dollars worth of stolen property in 2007, and the success rate for phishing attacks is increasing each year [17]. Phishing attacks are becoming harder to detect and more elusive by using short time windows to launch attacks. In order to combat the increasing effectiveness of phishing attacks, we propose that combining statistical analysis of website URLs with machine learning techniques will give a more accurate classification of phishing URLs. Using a two-sample Kolmogorov-Smirnov test along with other features we were able to accurately classify 99.3% of our dataset, with a false positive rate of less than 0.4%. Thus, accuracy of phishing URL classification can be greatly increased through the use of these statistical measures.

Keywords

Phishing URL Classification, Kolmogorov-Smirnov Distance, character distributions, Kullback-Leibler Divergence

1. INTRODUCTION

Phishing is the act of acquiring sensitive information by pretending to be a legitimate entity, through the use of electronic communications. Phishing attacks in 2006 cost victims up to $2.8 billion dollars worth of damages and affected nearly 2.3 million people, and unfortunately the incidence rate appears to be increasing, with 3.6 million people losing up to $3.2 billion dollars in 2007 [17]. Furthermore, the number of potential phishing targets is increasing as technology costs decrease allowing more areas to become fully integrated with online business. There are many methods that phishers use to distribute their attack, but all classical attacks [22] share one feature, they require a URL to direct their targets to the phishing website. Thus, we focus our efforts on URL classification, as a URL classifier will be use-

ful across any classical method of phishing attack. Another reason for focusing on URL classification is to ensure more distance between the user and the phisher as visiting the site for visual cues, as some defensive methods entail, can install malware on the user's computer.

Traditional methods to combat phishing include blacklists, or lists of websites that once identified as phishing will be blocked by DNS servers and browsers. This method can be effective, but, more recently, phishers have been hosting their attacks and luring victims within short time frames while rapidly changing domains. This ensures that their damage is done by the time their attack gets blacklisted. A potentially more robust approach to combat phishing attacks is to identify automatically which websites are phishing or not before users access it. Some research has been done using machine learning techniques to develop such a URL classification model [16], but we believe our approach is novel in its use of statistical measures such as the Kolmogorov-Smirnov test and our testing using four different real data sets is much more comprehensive. In particular, researchers in [29] report a Logistic Regression algorithm to achieve an accurate model, but their approach requires *manual* extraction of the features, whereas our statistical measures perform at the same level of accuracy with completely automatic feature extraction.

1.1 Our Contributions and Results

Our contributions include the construction of multiple machine learning classifiers comprising a short list of features, and their evaluations on *four* unique real data sets. We present the results for each feature individually, as well as our most accurate multi-feature classifier. The results were obtained by analysis on four real data sets, the first was comprised of URLs from PhishTank (reported by humans) and Alexa organization. The second and third were provided to us by authors of [29], with the second consisting of phishing URLs from APWG (live feed for members), the third consisting of phishing URLs from Huawei Digital's phishing repositories and the fourth is the DMOZ Open Directory Project data set. The second and third data sets were combined with legit URLs collected by [29]. Our contributions therefore not only indicate the value of a feature, but also the robustness of a feature, due to the real data sets being collected at different times, and through completely unique organizations (APWG, Huawei digital, Phishtank, and DMOZ). In contrast to previous work such as [16], we do not use any host-based features. In contrast to previous works such as [4] and [25], who use more than 300,000 and millions of features respectively, we show that robust and

---

*Research supported in part by NSF grants CNS 1319212 and DUE 1241772

effective classification is possible with no more than a few dozen features.

In addition to presenting the performance of each feature on multiple data sets, we present each feature evaluated using a different machine learning algorithm. We used the WEKA interface [12] to easily develop and compare multiple different machine learning algorithms for our feature sets, and we present the results for each algorithm, with each feature in isolation, and in best combinations. For all work in this paper we used WEKA stable version 3.6. This work can easily be recreated using WEKA or one of the many other popular machine learning packages.

The outline for the rest of the paper follows: Section 2 presents our hypothesis and gives a brief overview of our results. Section 3 presents our classifiers, the datasets they were trained on, the algorithms used, and covers our feature extraction process. Section 4 presents our analysis and results for our classifiers. Section 5 covers related research and comparisons. Section 6 concludes with implications of the results.

2. HYPOTHESIS

Many phishing website URLs can be identified by a trained person relatively easily, and we want to emulate this behavior automatically. Specifically, our primary question in this paper is:

1. Can statistical techniques applied to a URL be used to accurately differentiate between legitimate and phishing websites?

Specifically, we focus on the character distribution of URLs and a few other features, selected with the goal of robustness, in order to evaluate this question. To best answer this question in depth and breadth we present our results on multiple features and with multiple learning algorithms. Our results indicate that an accurate classification is possible using these methods. Additionally, we find that the use of statistical methods, together with the features selected, improves the robustness of the classifier.

3. CLASSIFIERS

3.1 Features

This section discusses our feature extraction algorithms. Prior to feature extraction "http://" and "https://" were removed from the URL, so as not to give extraneous information to the features such as number of punctuation, and to prevent URLs classified without such parts from being misclassified.

In contrast to previous work, e.g., [4, 25], we use a short list (few dozens) of URL-only features to study the effectiveness of each feature carefully and to investigate whether it is possible to design a robust and effective URL classifier with just a few features. Because we wish to design an *accurate and robust* automatic classifier, we have carefully selected a combination of new features supplemented with others that complement them or that test the claims made by previous researchers/antiphishing organizations. In the process some features will be similar to those used in previous work, since there are only so many dimensions to a URL, which is basically a string of symbols. Hence, at the outset, we wish to clarify and emphasize here the several novel aspects of our work. The first novel aspect of our work is our choice of aspects to focus on, specifically we focus on character distributions. The second, the way we extract the relevant information and construct the actual feature from the aspect of the URL is novel. The third is our use of efficient algorithms, e.g. Aho-Corasick pattern matching algorithm, for fast construction of features. Finally, our testing and validation is much more comprehensive than previous work wherein we use several machine learning algorithms and four different real data sets. Moreover, we show the generalization capability of our classifiers by training them on one data set and testing them on totally different data sets, which to our knowledge no previous work on phishing has done. This is important because it reveals how prone our models are to overfitting, and gives an idea of what kind of performance the system would have in a real scenario where phishing methodologies change rapidly.

Kolmogorov-Smirnov Distance: In [18] the authors point out that character frequencies might be a good indicator for phishing detection, but they do not explain how it might be used nor did they build a classifier. We explore several different ways in which this distribution can be converted to a feature. First, we used the two sample Kolmogorov-Smirnov test to calculate how similar the distribution of English characters are in standard English to the distributions in legitimate and in phishing URLs, we then use this metric as a feature for our machine learning classifiers.

The Kolmogorov-Smirnov distance is calculated by calculating the two-sample Kolmogorov-Smirnov (K-S) test statistic for the normalized frequency distribution of English characters in the URL and comparing that to the normalized frequency distribution of English characters in standard English text. The accepted distribution for standard English text is readily available online [19]. In order to do the calculation, we first count the number of each character in the URL, next we normalize it to construct the normalized frequency distribution. Next we construct a cumulative distribution function (CDF) for the distribution of frequencies, and then we can compare the URL CDF and the standard English CDF using the K-S test. Through experiments, we found that we got better results by comparing the standard English CDF for only the characters that were present in the candidate URL's CDF. This preserved character importance.

Kullback-Leibler Divergence: As a second metric for comparing the distribution of character frequencies in standard URLs and phishing URLs we implemented a Kullback-Leibler (KL) Divergence test [14]. We first construct the two distributions we are comparing, the distribution of normalized character frequencies for the URL, and the distribution of normalized character frequencies in Standard English. Next we compute the following distance using this formula:

$$D = \sum_{i \in Q} ln \left(\frac{P(i)}{Q(i)} \right) P(i)$$

Here D is the KL-Divergence value, P represents the distribution of characters in standard English, and Q represents the distribution of characters in the URL. Characters not in the URL are absent from set Q and therefore they contribute no value to the divergence. The final KL-Divergence value was included as a feature in our classifier.

Euclidean Distance: The Euclidean Distance is a third metric for comparing character frequencies in URLs. For Euclidean Distance we calculated the sum of the squares of the difference in normalized character frequency in standard English and in the URL. Here, we compared all English characters, regardless of whether or not they were in the URL.

Character Frequencies: We used normalized character frequencies as a collection of features. For each character, we counted the number of times that character occurred in the URL, next we divided this number by the total length of the URL, finally we used this normalized frequency as a feature in our classifier. This greatly increased the size of the feature vector, but also led to a much higher accuracy.

The remaining features are carefully devised with the goal of increasing robustness and catch the phisher who tries to adapt to our character distribution approaches or uses techniques to avoid detection from the unwary user.

Edit Distance: Edit distance is defined as the number of substitutions, insertions and deletions required to change one string of characters into another. We pulled a set of 1000 random URLs from the DMOZ, specifically different URLs than were used in our DMOZ data set. Then when training we calculate the edit distance between each URL and our set of 1000 DMOZ legitimate URLs. We then take the minimal value from those 1000 distances, and record it as a integer based feature in our classifier.

The logic behind this was that our classifier's strongest classification features are based on the character frequencies of the phishing URLs vs standard english. We suppose that if a phisher has read this paper, and attempts to construct URLs that have a character distribution that is very much like legitimate URLs they might get through our classifier. The edit distance we believe will enhance the robustness of our classifier by finding URLs that are close to standard, but off by a small amount. For example, www.paypal.com and www.paypai.com. The paypai.com URL may not be caught by our character frequency methods, but the edit distance of 1 will make it look suspicious, and might catch it, thus increasing the robustness of our methods. Specifically, we calculate the edit distance for the URL as a whole to a set of whole legitimate URLs, and calculate the edit distance of the domain to a set of legitimate domains.

From our experiments we found that there was very little improvement in going from 100 URLs to 1000 URLs in our legitimate set, but the time to classify became much slower as the legitimate set grew large. Because of this reasoning we used a set of 100 URLs for all our edit distance tests instead of the initial 1000. This implies that phishing URLs that contain a target are typically aimed at a small set of legitimate companies. The literature has evidence to support this claim [18].

Length: In [18] the authors observed that the length of the domain is longer on average for legitimate URLs when compared to phishing URLs, while the length of the total URL was longer for phishing URLs than legitimate URLs. Other works such as [16, 4, 11] have used length as a feature, but we decided that the best way to capture the observation was to use the ratio of the length of the total URL over the length of the domain. For this, phishing URLs with a long URL length, divided by a small domain would yield a high ratio. Legitimate URLs with a shorter total length, and longer domain would then yield a smaller ratio.

@ and - Symbols: Another way that phishers might attempt to emulate a valid URL is through special characters such as the @ and - symbols. The @ symbol is special because everything to the left of the @ is ignored by the browser. Phishers could potentially exploit this by hosting a URL such as www.paypal.com@phishing.com. Many people might immediately recognize paypal.com, and determine it to be a legitimate website, whereas the browser really goes directly to phishing.com. This feature is simply the sum of the occurrences of @ and - symbols in the URL.

Number of Punctuation Symbols: We counted the number of punctuation symbols in the URL and used this value as a feature in our classifier. We found that phishing URLs tend to have more punctuation symbols than legitimate URLs. In contrast to the work in [30, 11], we include more types of punctuation in our summation: { . ! # $ % & * , ; : '}

Number of Top-Level Domains (TLDs) in URL: We found that many phishing URLs would attempt to imitate a legitimate website by placing TLDs in uncommon locations in the URL in order to trick the victim into believing the URL redirected to a website they were familiar with. For example, www.xyz.com/YourBank.com.php. Specifically, we counted the number of TLDs that were in the path of the URL, and not included in the domain. We found URLs that contained TLDs in the path were very likely to be phishing.

Number of Target Words: Since APWG reports claim that 40-50% of phishing attacks are based on common legal web sites, we decided to check this and so we compiled a list of target words which included many popular phishing targets, such as Ebay and paypal [1]. We then removed the domain from the URL in question, and then searched for any occurrences of our target words. For speed and efficiency, we build an Aho-Corasick automaton to very quickly find all occurrences of targets in the remaining URL. The Aho-Corasick automaton allowed us to create a very large target list, without significantly increasing the time required to classify a URL. Finally we sum the number of targets found, and use this value as a feature for the classifiers.

IP Address: We implemented a simple algorithm that determined if the domain consisted of only numbers and punctuation, we used the value 1 for true, and 0 for false, and included it as a feature in our classifier. IP Address is a popular feature in the literature, being used by [16, 7, 4, 11, 13]. From the analysis of our data sets we find that phishing URLs encountered in the real world are many times more likely to be IP only URLs than legitimate websites. This provides the justification for us to use this feature.

Number of Suspicious Words: Examination of a small dataset of phishing URLs led to this feature, where we constructed a small list of action words, such as "login" and "account." We used many terms employed before, as other authors have already demonstrated their effectiveness. Our list included only nine words, so we did not implement any special data structures to increase speed, but if necessary the Aho-Corasick would suit this purpose if the list needed to be expanded. We summed the number of suspicious words found in each URL, and used this number as a feature. We searched for the following list of words in our implementation: {"confirm","account","secure","ebayisapi","webscr", "login","signin","submit","update"}.

3.2 Machine Learning Algorithms

We used the WEKA library to construct our models. Using the WEKA library allowed us freedom to quickly compare and contrast the different machine learning algorithms and their results without having to implement the feature extraction algorithms more than once. We used multiple different algorithmic types in our approach to ensure a large scope was covered. We examined the following tree based algorithms RandomForest and J48. We examined a rule based learner called PART which combines C4 trees and RIPPER learning. We looked at functional algorithms such as SMO, and Logistic Regression. Finally, we looked at NaiveBayes as a baseline for comparison.

PART: The PART algorithm constructs a decision list for classifying the URL. It was originally proposed in [8]. The algorithm uses separate-and-conquer methods. In each iteration it constructs a partial C4.5 decision tree and makes the "best" leaf into a rule. We used WEKA's default parameters for the classifier.

SMO: This is an implementation of Platt's sequential minimal optimization algorithm for training a support vector classifier [20]. The default SVM kernel for WEKA's implementation of Platt's SMO is the polynomial kernel:

$$K(x,y) = <x,y>^p$$

We selected the p value in the above formula by running a series of small experiments testing p values from 1 to 5. We concluded that a p value of 1 had the best combination of a low false positive rate and high accuracy rate of the set. For this experiment we constructed two data sets, set I - consisting of 1000 random phishing and legitimate URLs from our primary data set, and set II - containing 1000 random phishing and legitimate URLs from our DMOZ data set. We used the combination of all of our features for the following table.

P	Accuracy I	Accuracy II	FP-Rate I	FP-Rate II
1	99.20%	95.95%	0.1%	2.9%
2	99.25%	95.99%	0.6%	3.2%
3	99.25%	95.39%	0.6%	4.4%
4	99.25%	95.29%	0.7%	4.7%
5	97.45%	95.14%	0.8%	4.7%

Table 1: Accuracy and False-Positive Rate for small sets I and II.

All further references to the SMO algorithm correspond to p value of 1.

J48: Algorithm J48 generates a C4.5 decision tree for classification. The algorithm is discussed in [21]. We used the WEKA 3.6 default pruning threshold.

Logistic Regression: The logistic regression implementation in WEKA is a standard multinomial logistic regression model, with the addition of a ridge estimator. The original method is presented in [15]. There are a few modifications to leCessie's algorithm in the WEKA implementation, such as the addition of weighted instances [27].

NaiveBayes: These classifiers have been used quite successfully in many real-world problems, but have been shown to be less effective than more current approaches such as boosted trees [28]. The threshold values are calculated by default in the WEKA implementation, and we used these defaults for our experiments.

RandomForest: The random forest algorithm constructs a multitude of decision trees, and then during classification the algorithm returns the most often occurred class from the array of individual trees. The trees are all constructed using a random subset of features from the entire feature list. The method has been proven quite effective at classifying [28].

For values we used WEKA's default implementation of the RandomForest class. This involves ten unlimited depth trees, with a feature selection of $log\ M + 1$, where M is the total number of features.

3.3 Datasets

For our experiments we used four different real data sets. Data Set I consists of 24,545 URLs comprised of 11,271 phishing URLs from PhishTank.com, accessed on February 12, 2014. We then combined that with 13,274 legitimate URL's taken from Alexa.com on February 11, 2014. We acquired our second and third data sets thanks to authors of [29]. The second set consists of 14,920 phishing URLs provided from Huawei Digital's own phishing repository. This was paired with 14,999 of the original authors' legitimate URLs. The third data set consists of 18,395 phishing URLs acquired from APWG combined with 19,999 less popular legitimate websites gathered using the original authors' crawler. Finally, we extracted 11,275 random legitimate URLs from the DMOZ Open Directory Project [6], and paired them with the 11,271 phishing URLs we gathered from PhishTank. This is our fourth data set.

To summarize, our four data sets used legitimate URLs from Alexa.com, [29], and DMOZ. We acquired phishing URLs from PhishTank, Huawei's phishing repository, and the APWG. To demonstrate the diversity of our data we analyzed the breakdown of unique TLDs as well as unique domains in the four sets (Table 2). The main conclusion is that our datasets are diverse with one exception, the DMOZ set contains a less diverse selection of unique domains; the top 50 most popular domain names account for roughly 10% of the data for the other three groups, whereas the DMOZ-PhishTank group's top 50 domains account for nearly 25% of the URLs in the dataset.

4. ANALYSIS AND RESULTS

In this section, we present the results obtained using each of the classifiers, and each of the features. We begin by presenting each feature's results in isolation, and then expand to include our best classifiers using combinations of features. We present the comparison of features into two sections, character frequency based features, and other standard features. To save space, we omit results on different datasets that are similar (Tables 3-6 report results for Data set 1 and Tables in Sections 4.1-4.3 are for Data Sets 1 and 2 for this reason).

Character Frequency based Methods

First, we present the results for classifying using our different algorithms, based on a single feature in isolation. These values indicate the percent of accuracy achieved with classification following a 5-fold cross-validation test. We decided to use five fold cross validation as a way to evaluate the effectiveness of our models. Cross validation allows us to see how well our model generalizes to unseen data from the same domain. We originally decided on ten fold cross validation but eventually migrated our tests to five folds to reduce

Data Set Domain and TLD Diversity

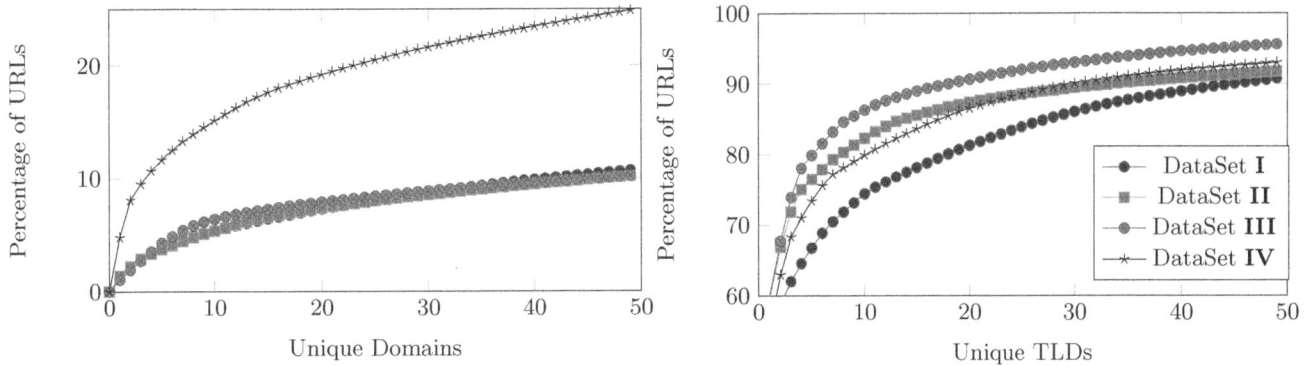

Table 2: Diversity of Data Sets I, II, III and IV. The charts represent how much of the data is contained in the top 50 domains and TLDs.

training time from ten trainings per test to five. Here we present the character frequency features, it is significant to note that KS-Distance, KL-Divergence, and Euclidean Distance are all single features, meaning the feature vector has a length of 1. The character frequencies feature result in a feature vector consisting of an individual feature for every English character found in the URL, resulting in a maximum size of 26.

Accuracy for character frequency features I

Features	Logistic	PART	SMO	J48
Euclidean	65.16%	68.08%	64.98%	68.42%
KS-Distance	92.51%	92.54%	92.49%	92.53%
KL-Divergence	94.78%	94.76%	94.78%	94.76%
Char. Frequencies	79.70%	95.65%	80.14%	95.01%
Edit Distance	87.54%	91.11%	75.88%	91.24%

Accuracy for character frequency features II

Features	RandomForest	NaiveBayes
Euclidean	76.49%	64.53%
KS-Distance	92.56%	92.48%
KL-Divergence	93.35%	94.79%
Char. Frequencies	96.30%	90.34%
Edit Distance	91.08%	87.44%

Table 3: Accuracies on Data Set I

The Euclidean distance, performs poorly across all algorithms, when compared to the other measures. The KS-Distance and the KL-Divergence are close, but the latter appears to give a slightly more accurate classification. The pure character frequencies perform well for tree and rule based learners, (PART, RandomForest, and J48) but underperformed on Logistic Regression, SMO, and NaiveBayes. From this data we can see that the statistical measures for KS-Distance and KL-Divergence provide similar classification performance as constructing a lengthy feature vector based on every unique character in the URL. Additionally, in certain learning algorithms the single feature statistical methods are better able to classify than constructing the lengthy feature vector for each character.

We define a positive occurrence to be a phishing URL. In the context of our tests then a false positive is a benign URL that was falsely classified as phishing. We chose to include false positive rate in our results because it has specific

False-Positives for character frequency features I

Features	Logistic	PART	SMO	J48
Euclidean	30.10%	21.03%	31.01%	19.31%
KS-Distance	4.37%	4.36%	4.37%	4.38%
KL-Divergence	3.18%	2.39%	2.64%	2.39%
Char. Frequencies	5.09%	3.79%	3.90%	3.49%
Edit Distance	1.13%	2.82%	1.00%	3.49%

False-Positives for character frequency features II

Features	RandomForest	NaiveBayes
Euclidean	23.79%	33.47%
KS-Distance	4.33%	4.37%
KL-Divergence	5.71%	3.22%
Char. Frequencies	1.60%	2.12%
Edit Distance	5.55%	1.16%

Table 4: False positive rates on Data Set I.

interest to the problem of phishing detection. When any software program is attempting to detect phishing attacks it is important that they have a very low false positive rate, because each false positive occurrence in a real system might mean an important message never reaches its recipient.

For character frequency based methods, the Euclidean distance feature not only has a low accuracy, but a very high false positive rate. The rule and tree based methods appeared to do a better job of keeping the false positive rate low, with PART, J48, and RandomForest all having an 8-12% lower false positive rate for the feature. The KL-Divergence algorithm had the lowest false-positive rate for four of the six experiments, and the highest accuracy for three of the six experiments. For the cases that KL-Divergence was not the best, only once was it not the second best either. This implies that on average the KL-Divergence algorithm is better than any of the three other methods for use as a feature in our classifier. In addition to these results, the KL-Divergence method has the advantage of a low dimensionality feature vector, resulting in faster training times for the chosen machine learning algorithm.

Other Methods

Here we present the features we used that were unrelated to character frequencies.

From the results in the following tables we conclude that

Accuracies for other features I

Features	Logistic	PART	SMO	J48
Length	71.11%	71.35%	71.49%	71.49%
@ and - symbols	68.11%	68.11%	68.11%	68.11%
Punctuation	84.66%	84.66%	66.65%	84.66%
TLD	83.50%	83.98%	83.50%	83.98%
Target Words	84.08%	84.08%	80.11%	84.08%
IP Address	55.60%	55.60%	55.60%	55.60%
Suspicious Words	64.81%	64.81%	64.81%	64.81%

Accuracies for other features II

Features	RandomForest	NaiveBayes
Length	71.39%	67.40%
@ and - symbols	68.11%	68.11%
Punctuation	84.66%	76.44%
TLD	83.98%	83.50%
Target Words	84.08%	80.91%
IP Address	55.60%	55.60%
Suspicious Words	64.81%	64.81%

Table 5: Accuracies for other methods. Data Set I.

punctuation, presence of target words, and number of TLDs following the domain of the URL were good features for phishing classification, with all achieving over 80% accuracy across multiple algorithms. Additionally, our results indicate that length is a decent feature, performing next best. The remaining in order of average accuracy were special symbols, suspicious words, and finally IP addresses.

Many of these features may not classify a large portion of the data set, for example the IP address feature accurately classifies only 55.6%, barely more than half, but it captures URLs that would not be correctly classified by the other features. Thus many of the low accuracy features add significant value to the final multi-feature models.

Additionally from this we conclude that there is little variability between learning algorithms for these specific features. There are two notable exceptions, firstly NaiveBayes appears to perform slightly worse for length and punctuation, and secondly, punctuation performs significantly worse for SMO, at 66.65% accuracy compared to the 84.66% that was achieved by all the other algorithms but Naive Bayes.

False-Positive rates for other features I

Features	Logistic	PART	SMO	J48
Length	17.83%	14.60%	12.67%	12.67%
@ and - symbols	4.14%	4.14%	4.14%	4.14%
Punctuation	9.50%	9.51%	0.08%	9.51%
TLD	21.45%	22.83%	21.45%	22.83%
Target Words	5.96%	5.96%	2.13%	5.96%
IP Address	0.05%	0.05%	0.05%	0.05%
Suspicious Words	0.19%	0.19%	0.19%	0.19%

Our test results indicate that IP Address, and suspicious words have a very low false positive rate. While the IP Address feature and the suspicious word feature may not classify a large number of URLs as phishing, the ones that do get classified are almost always a phishing URL. This is very good at increasing the total accuracy of the multi-feature classifier without substantially increasing the false-positive rate.

Following IP and suspicious words, we found target words and special symbols to be the next best in regards to a low false-positive rate. Target words was one of the highest ac-

False-Positive rates for other features II

Features	RandomForest	NaiveBayes
Length	14.67%	4.14%
@ and - symbols	4.14%	4.14%
Punctuation	9.50%	2.13%
TLD	22.83%	21.45%
Target Words	5.96%	18.06%
IP Address	0.05%	0.05%
Suspicious Words	0.19%	0.19%

Table 6: False-positive rates for Data Set I.

curacy features, and one of the lowest false-positive rate features in our experiments. This demonstrates that using target words to help catch phishers is especially effective.

The last three features in order of increasing false-positive rate are punctuation, length, and number of TLDs after the domain. It appears logical that these features would have a higher false-positive rate than the preceding ones. For example, the number of legitimate URLs that contains suspicious words such as "Account" or "Login" would be very few, compared to the number of legitimate URLs that might have an abnormally high number of punctuation marks, or an odd domain to url length ratio.

The TLD feature had the highest false-positive rate at over 20%. We considered removing it because of this, but when we tested it in our final multi-feature models we found that the presence of the TLD feature increased accuracy without having any significant impact on the classifiers false-positive rate.

The same trends above are present here as well. Specifically, the punctuation values for SMO are considerably different than the other algorithms. While the punctuation classification is 20% less accurate from SMO, it has an extremely low false-positive rate comparatively.

Aho-Corasick

We utilized the Aho-Corasick automaton for finding occurrences of the targets in our URLs. The Aho-Corasick data structure is a fast tree based search structure that allows searching for any of a large set of pattern strings in a large amount of text quickly. The Aho-Corasick algorithm was developed in 1975 at Bell Labs and first presented in [2]. Adopting the Aho-Corasick algorithm allowed us to expand the number of targets we were able to search for without negatively impacting classification time, or training time. We ran some experiments to demonstrate the effectiveness of using this data structure in the URL classification problem. For our targets we took the 100,000 topmost popular websites from Alexa.com, and then extracted target names from that list.

In the following table, N is the number of targets we looked for in our URLs. The columns represent how long it took to construct our feature vector for targets on Data Set I, a set of 24,545 URLs. Test A is using the Aho-Corasick, and Test B is using Java's built in function String.contains(String), which returns true or false. We indexed the numbers for readability with 100 corresponding to 2.32 seconds.

From our tests we find that by implementing the Aho-Corasick data structure for finding targets within the URLs we can look for up to 2,000 targets before we begin to see any effect on the performance. This allows us to cover nearly all possible targets without negatively impacting the perfor-

Feature Construction Time

N	Test A	Test B
20	100	100
200	100	107.32
2,000	100	202.59
20,000	123.71	782.33
100,000	166.38	4021.55

Table 7: Time to construct features with and without Aho-Corasick.

mance of our classifier in the training stage, or in real-time use of the classifier for detection of phishing URLs. Additionally, we found that increasing the target count above 2,000 had no statistical change in the accuracy or false-positive rate of the classifier.

4.1 Multi-Feature Models

In this section we combine the features into a single multi-feature classification model, and present the results for running a 5-fold cross-validation test on each of our data sets. For this data we used no feature selection, meaning we include every feature in the model. There has been some research to indicate that machine learning performance can be further improved through feature selection [3].

Features	Accuracy	False-Positive Rate
PART	98.98%	0.889%
Logistic	97.70%	2.682%
J48	99.01%	0.8286%
RandomForest	98.88%	0.512%
SMO	98.51%	0.798%
NaiveBayes	79.85%	2.192%

Table 8: Accuracy and false-positive rate for 5-fold cross-validation on Data Set I.

Features	Accuracy	False-Positive Rate
PART	95.35%	4.805%
Logistic	94.71%	4.660%
J48	94.97%	4.447%
RandomForest	95.65%	3.247%
SMO	94.79%	4.547%
NaiveBayes	83.88%	8.087%

Table 9: Accuracy and false-positive rate for 5-fold cross-validation on Data Set II.

From these results we demonstrate that these classifiers can achieve very high classification accuracy, with low false-positive rates. We found that for the most part all the learning algorithms were similarly effective at classifying the URLs, with the exception of the NaiveBayes algorithm. The NaiveBayes algorithm was significantly less effective at classification using our feature extraction techniques.

Our results indicate that the tree and rule based learners performed slightly better than SMO and Logistic Regression algorithms, but the difference is very small, and may not be statistically significant.

For DataSet II we get on average 4% lower classification results. From examining this data we attribute this difference due to the fact that the second data set consists of many normal URLs along with a small amount of randomly selected URLs from yahoo's directory. Some of these ran-

domly selected URLs are not logical URLs but perhaps redirected links. Here is an example of such a legitimate URL from this data set.

"http://www.youtube.com/results? search_query= stephenie+meyer&search_type=&aq=f"

This URL is legitimate, but isn't a typical URL one might receive in an e-mail, or type into an address bar. It is a search query for youtube, and because of that it contains many uncommon symbols and characters for regular legitimate URLs. We believe the addition of URLs similar to this one into the data set might be the reason behind a slightly lower classification percent.

Information Gain

A popular method for evaluating how effective a feature is in a multi-feature classifier is to calculate the information gain. The general definition of information gain for decision trees is:

$$IG(T, a) = H(T) - H(T|a)$$

Where IG is the information gain, T is the class, and a is the feature. The function H is entropy.

For our multi-feature model we present the information gain values for each feature as a demonstration of which of the features was most effective when used together. The information gain values are for a model trained on data set I using the RandomForest algorithm.

Information Gain by Feature

Feature	Information Gain
Punctuation	0.557
Length	0.485
Target Words	0.456
TLD	0.392
Suspicious Words	0.126
@ and - symbols	0.126
IP Address	0.016

For the set of features that are not based on the character distribution, it appears that punctuation and length gave us the most value in our classifier, followed closely by Target Words and out of place TLDs.

Information Gain by Feature

Feature	Information Gain
KL-Divergence	0.811
KS-Distance	0.725
Edit-Distance	0.534
Euclidean	0.151

For features based on character distribution, we see that KL-Divergence adds the most, followed some what closely by KS-Distance. These values coincide with our single feature experiments, KL-Divergence performed better than KS-Distance, but only by a little bit, and euclidean distance performed much worse than either other method.

Rather than list all information gain values for character frequency, we present the top three.

It is probably not a coincidence that the letters in ".com" are the three most valuable by information gain in data set I. Perhaps phishing URLs are more or less likely to use a ".com" TLD in that data set. It is worth noting that in

Information Gain for Character Frequencies

Feature	Information Gain	Feature	Information Gain
c	0.603	w	0.605
o	0.596	h	0.450
m	0.595	e	0.435

Table 10: Data Set I   **Table 11: Data Set II**

Data Set II, the letters c, o, and m are also ranked between 0.39 and 0.41. Therefore, there may be a positive or negative correlation between phishing URLs and use of a ".com" TLD.

4.2 AdaBoost

A popular method for constructing strong learners is the Adaptive Boosting or AdaBoost method first presented in [9]. Using WEKA's built in AdaBoost implementation we were able to apply adaptive boosting to our top models to build more accurate classifiers. We used the AdaBoostM1 booster to build the following models.

Base Classifier	Accuracy	False-Positive Rate
PART	99.30%	0.475%
Logistic	98.73%	1.153%
J48	99.28%	0.535%
RandomForest	99.27%	0.324%
SMO	98.53%	0.761%
NaiveBayes	79.85%	2.192%

Table 12: AdaBoosted results on Data Set I.

Base Classifier	Accuracy	False-Positive Rate
PART	96.23%	3.160%
Logistic	94.71%	4.660%
J48	96.11%	3.554%
RandomForest	96.59%	2.554%
SMO	94.80%	4.574%
NaiveBayes	91.54%	6.907%

Table 13: AdaBoosted on Data Set II.

From our experiments we found that AdaBoosting provided a significant advantage for all algorithms. All of our algorithms reported higher accuracy and lower false-positive rate on the 5-fold cross validation tests once AdaBoosting was used in the training process. Additionally, to compare the improvement of AdaBoosting with other popular enhancement methods we ran a test on Stacking classifiers.

4.3 Stacking

Another popular method of constructing a strong learning is to use stacking. In stacking multiple learners are used to provide input to a meta learner that then builds the final model. The method takes advantage of the strengths of multiple different learning algorithms. Our implementation used WEKA's stacking classifier, using the ZeroR default implementation for the meta-classifier. We stacked the following classifiers, PART, J48, SMO, RandomForest, and Logistic Regression to build our final stacked learner.

Data Set	Accuracy	False-Positive
DataSet I	99.22%	0.580%
DataSet II	96.32%	3.167%

Table 14: Stacked classifier results.

Our stacked algorithm performed comparably with our best AdaBoosted algorithms, but not statistically better. The two methods both seem to be comparable for increasing the effectiveness of our classifier.

4.4 Cross Data Set Validation

We were interested in how our models generalized from one data set to another, so we did an experiment where we trained on one data set, and then evaluated on the other three data sets. This reveals some insight into how effective the dataset was for the phishing problem, and how well our methods generalize. For this we constructed a model using the RandomForest algorithm because from our earlier results it appeared to perform fairly accurately. We might have received better results with a stacked or boosted algorithm, but we chose to use random forest for this experiment due to the quicker training and evaluation. In the follow tables the top row indicates the training set and the first column indicates the testing set.

Cross Data Set Accuracy

	Set I	Set II	Set III	Set IV
Set I	99.98%	88.64%	86.09%	81.37%
Set II	55.99%	99.64%	87.10%	85.90%
Set III	58.14%	94.87%	99.72%	91.40%
Set IV	50.11%	81.27%	79.827%	99.58%

Table 15: Accuracy for classifier tests.

Cross Data Set False-Positives

	Set I	Set II	Set III	Set IV
Set I	0.0%	0.0%	7.1%	67.8%
Set II	83.1%	0.0%	7.7%	16.4%
Set III	83.4%	3.5%	0.0%	15.9%
Set IV	100.0%	9.2%	23.2%	0.0%

Table 16: False positives for classifier tests.

From our results we conclude that training on the Alexa data set (Set I) poorly generalized to the other data sets. Alexa consists of the top most popular websites on the web, and perhaps there are some malicious websites present in this list. Additionally, many popular websites are simple domain names, such as "www.facebook.com" with no path, while most phishing URLs have some sort of path, therefore if too many of the Alexa URLs lack a path, then it would cause the model to poorly generalize to the phishing URLs. Our classifier when trained on data from the DMOZ set, Zhang's sets, and the PhishTank URLs appear to generalize better on the other datasets.

Combined Data Set. Next we report in Table 16 our results of several classifiers with and without Adaboosting on a dataset that *combined all four datasets together*, a total of 115,405 urls with 59,548 legitimate and 55,857 phishing. The second number in each box is the Adaboosted result when the experiment finished in less than 8 hours or so.

4.5 Digging Deeper

We hypothesized that the normalized character distributions of phishing URLs are different from those of legitimate URLs because of the presence of digits, special symbols and the use of words like 'login', '.php', etc., in the URLs. Next we did a count of the URLs containing special symbols, numbers, strings such as ".php," ".js" and "login." The results are

Classifier	Accuracy	False-Positive Rate
PART	93.17%	7.08%
Logistic	90.45%/90.45%	9.69%/9.69%
J48	94.00%	6.13%
RandomForest	95.24%/96.22%	4.69%/3.61%
SMO	90.79%	8.48%
NaiveBayes	77.34%/83.45%	7.76%/4.43%

Table 17: Accuracy and false-positive rate for 5-fold cross-validation on combination of all datasets.

interesting. We report a feature only if it was present in at least 5% of the URLs in each set. The word login appears in a total of 9836 phishing URLs out of a total of 9839 URLs containing the word across all 4 sets. Results for the underscore and semicolon were also interesting, but we omit them here to save space. One might wonder, why phishers persist in their use of special symbols and strings in the URL. We suspect that there are several reasons for this, including: URL obfuscation using various encoding schemes (such as escape encoding, inappropriate UTF-8 encoding, etc.), cross-site scripting attacks through URL formatting, and preset session attacks. We leave testing of this hypothesis for the future. Note that Data sets I and IV shared phishing URLs, hence the first number is the same.

Feature	Set I	Set II	Set III	Set IV
Digits	4239/4369	4358/5032	5561/6447	4239/4918
&	1457/1457	3906/3996	2967/3070	1457/1612
?	2009/2009	6204/6401	4933/5211	2009/2665
=	2030/2034	6397/6579	5213/5472	2030/2653
-	3982/4532	7395/9077	6854/9048	3982/5685
.php	2150/2162	5082/5152	6339/6425	2150/2540

Table 18: Characters in URLs. The first number is count of phishing URLs and the second is the total number of URLs containing the feature.

4.6 Security Analysis of Our Method

An adaptive phisher may try to develop techniques that get past our classification model. They could have some success, given that our most successful techniques involved comparing the normalized character frequency of phishing vs legitimate URLs, either through statistical tests such as Kolmogorov-Smirnov, the Euclidean Distance between the two character distributions, or other methods. If phishers are to construct URLs that more closely resemble legitimate URLs then they might get past this method of classification. However, the phisher will face two problems in beating our overall classifier. The first problem with constructing more legitimate seeming URLs is that domain space is limited, when phishers have valid websites for only a few days before switching domains, they quickly run out of phishing URLs that remain somewhat close to their target. For example, if the phisher is attempting to emulate PayPal, there are so many previous attempts made to phish PayPal that anything that is extremely close to PayPal's official website URL is either already a registered domain, or is blacklisted. Therefore, in order for a phisher to emulate a Paypal URL, they have to start introducing misspellings, such as www.páypal.com, or they must construct another domain name to look like PayPal, such as www.paypal.com.anotherurl.com. Alternatively, if the phisher

constructs valid URLs that emulate no target company, few people will click the URL such that the phishers work won't be profitable. The second problem is that the phisher who tries to mimic a legal URL closely in character-frequency distribution may find himself ensnared by one of our other features used in our classifiers such as edit-distance from a legal URL.

All of these phishing techniques enhance our classification methods, and help promote the robustness of our classifier. Ultimately, the end target must be fooled into clicking the URL, and therein lies the robustness of our methods.

4.7 URL Shortening Services

One of the contributions of [18] is that phishers are more frequently employing URL shortening services. Other authors have also demonstrated that this is an ever increasing problem regarding twitter, which places a maximum character count on tweets. In order to preserve characters, nearly all links that are tweeted employ a shortening service, and recently phishers have taken advantage of this.

Our work is specifically designed to analyze the lexical features of a URL, and therefore shortening services may result in mis-classifications. An improvement for our work might be to retrieve the final URL from the service, and then apply our classifier to the final URL. This is a potential tactic that might be employed in a future work.

5. RELATED RESEARCH

Many researchers have presented their work on phishing detection, so there are some similarities between our work and theirs, but also some key differences. As the astute reader will note from the presentation below, there are also several similarities among the features used by previous researchers, since the URL is basically a string of symbols.

In [18] the authors do a good job at outlining phisher modi operandi. However, they do not create a classifier nor do they indicate how one could be created. In contrast, we propose features based on statistical methods and then use machine learning to build classifiers significantly extending their observations. Specifically, we believe we are novel in our analysis of the character frequency information that [18] provides in their work.

In [10], Garera et al. divide phishing URLs into four different types, and select features based on each type. The authors use a set of suspicious words that have some overlap with the words we have used. However, unlike their work, we chose not to include features outside of lexical analysis of the URL, as our goal was to analyze the effectiveness of using only URL analysis and keep a margin of safety between users and the attackers.

After this work was completed, we discovered the work in [16], which we missed since they focus on classifying "malicious" URLs rather than phishing URLs. Ma et al. used a strict subset of the classifiers we have used (SVM, logistic regression, and a naive bayes classifier) and also their data sets are not as rich and diverse. We have seen in the results section that naive bayes and SVM are not among the strongest classifiers with our features. One of our data sets that we use is similar to theirs in the use of DMOZ data. Unfortunately, after learning of this work, we tried to find their second source for legitimate URLs, but it is no longer available. The authors did use some lexical features such as IP address and lengths of domain and URL. Unlike their work we have not used a bag-of-words feature implementation because our goal was to demonstrate the effectiveness of a carefully chosen small feature vector. It is logical to assume we might achieve better results by including a bag-of-words, but this was specifically outside the goal of our work. Moreover, we do not use features beyond URL analysis for above mentioned reasons, whereas Ma et al. do.

The work by [30, 26] has been influential in the detection of phishing websites. There is some overlap between their work and ours, specifically in their URL analysis section of their methods. We share a set of three features: presence of @ and - symbols, number of punctuation symbols, and whether or not the URL is an IP address (also used by Ma et al. and others). Although, our punctuation filter includes more than just the dots that they use. However, bigger differences between our work and theirs are that they also use content-based features and Internet search and tested their approach on smaller datasets. The filters for IP and number of dots were also employed in the related work by [7] in the author's e-mail detection work.

Recently in [4], the authors have created a system based only on URLs to detect phishing websites. The authors achieve good accuracy, but lower than ours, with a confidence weighted classifier, using a bag-of-words implementation that generates a huge set of 369,000 features. Additionally, the authors have some hand selected features that correspond to ours, such as IP detection, TLD analysis, and Length analysis. Similar in URL features is the work of [25].

In another similar work, [11], the URL problem is analyzed further. Specifically the authors attempt to evaluate how much accuracy can be acquired by semi-supervised learning, and additionally address the problem of imbalanced data. Phishing URLs are far less common in day to day activities than legitimate URLs, this creates a natural imbalanced set of data. The authors alleviate the problem with undersampling, and feature selection methods. Their work shares some similar features with ours: length of the URL, the Dot Count, IP Address, and TLD. Additionally the authors use a target based feature that looks for popular phishing targets such as PayPal and Chase Bank. However, they do not consider character frequencies, and they tried a limited set of classifiers.

The authors in [13] have constructed a system for classifying e-mails as phishing, in their system they use a series of lexical URL features, some of which we also use. They share the following features with our work: special symbols, a collection of suspicious words, IP address, and number of periods. They also use a Random Forest algorithm to classify their e-mails. Their work demonstrates that phishing e-mail classification can be significantly improved by analysis of the URL. This result coincides with our results for phishing detection. This work differs from theirs in several respects: we consider many other classifiers than they do and we analyze more lexical features, including the character distributions of the URLs. More on phishing email detection can be found in [24, 23].

The authors in [5] use an SVM with lexical features to classify for phishing URLs. The author was specifically interested in thwarting "spear-phishing", phishing attacks focus on high-valued victims. The authors share some features with our work, and the previously mentioned related works. Uniquely shared between our two works is the feature Edit-Distance. The authors use two features, one for brand-name

distance in the domain, and another from brand-name distance in the URL. Based on their performance for each individual feature, domain brand-name distance was their most effective feature. Our edit-distance implementation differs from theirs in that their method finds the minimal edit distance from all substrings in their URL to a set of a brands, or target words. Our implementation involved finding the minimal distance between the URLs as a whole and a small subset of legitimate URLs. We achieve similar results for this feature with our method. Our single feature classifiers on edit-distance have accuracies in the upper 80%, to lower 90%, while [5]'s domain edit distance achieves an accuracy of 88.44%.

The authors of [29] used a logistic regression classifier for their anti-phishing system in place. Their classifier achieves good accuracy, but lower accuracy than us, using both host and lexical based features. We get better performance on their data sets with purely lexical based classifiers. Moreover, some of their features are manually extracted whereas ours are completely automatic.

6. CONCLUSIONS

In this paper we addressed the problem of detecting phishing websites by analyzing their URLs. Phishing is a serious crime which involves stealing of information and/or funds from victims by tricking them into disclosing their information. Phishers must convince the victim that their website is a legitimate organization. Because the victim must be convinced, certain qualities are present in the phisher's URLs.

We have demonstrated that machine learning classifiers are able to classify URLs as phishing or non-phishing with a high degree of accuracy based entirely on lexical URL features. As features for our machine learning classifier we focused on character distributions and supplemented them with a carefully chosen set of features that enhance their robustness. We found that statistical tests for distributions of character frequencies yielded highly accurate classifiers. We believe this approach is novel, and as such we present the results of four different methods used to analyze character frequencies. We found that three of the four methods we proposed were able to classify URLs with above a 90% accuracy across multiple, independent, phishing data sets.

We found that, by combining features, we can reach extremely high accuracy with a very low false-positive rate for a variety of real data sets. Additionally, we found that our best models were robust enough to classify completely independent URLs without any training and still achieve a decent level of accuracy. The implication for this work is that phishing tools can be developed to be more accurate, and more time-efficient, using the methods we have presented. Thereby we provide evidence for our purpose, to demonstrate that a robust and accurate classifier for phishing detection can be created using a small number of intelligent features, based entirely on the URL.

7. REFERENCES

[1] Greg Aaron. Phishing activity trends report. http://docs.apwg.org/reports/apwg_trends_report_q1_2014.pdf, 2014.

[2] Alfred V. Aho and Margaret J. Corasick. Efficient string matching: An aid to bibliographic search. *Commun. ACM*, 18(6):333–340, June 1975.

[3] Ram B. Basnet, Andrew H. Sung, and Quingzhong Liu. Feature selection for improved phishing detection. In *Proceedings of the 25th International Conference on Industrial Engineering and Other Applications of Applied Intelligent Systems: Advanced Research in Applied Artificial Intelligence*, IEA/AIE'12, pages 252–261, Berlin, Heidelberg, 2012. Springer-Verlag.

[4] Aaron Blum, Brad Wardman, Thamar Solorio, and Gary Warner. Lexical feature based phishing url detection using online learning. In *AISec*, pages 54–60, 2010.

[5] Weibo Chu, Bin B. Zhu, Feng Xue, Xiaohong Guan, and Zhongmin Cai. Protect sensitive sites from phishing attacks using features extractable from inaccessible phishing urls. In *ICC*, pages 1990–1994. IEEE, 2013.

[6] Netscape Communications Corporation. Open directory rdf dump. http://rdf.dmoz.org/, 2004.

[7] I. Fette, N. Sadeh, and A. Tomasic. Learning to detect phishing emails. In *Proc. 16th int'l conf. on World Wide Web*, pages 649–656. ACM, 2007.

[8] Eibe Frank and Ian H. Witten. Generating accurate rule sets without global optimization. In J. Shavlik, editor, *Fifteenth International Conference on Machine Learning*, pages 144–151. Morgan Kaufmann, 1998.

[9] Yoav Freund and Robert E. Schapire. Experiments with a new boosting algorithm. In *Thirteenth International Conference on Machine Learning*, pages 148–156, San Francisco, 1996. Morgan Kaufmann.

[10] S. Garera, N. Provos, M. Chew, and A.D. Rubin. A framework for detection and measurement of phishing attacks. In *Proc. 2007 ACM workshop on Recurring malcode*, pages 1–8, 2007.

[11] Binod Gyawali, Thamar Solorio, Manuel Montes y Gómez, Brad Wardman, and Gary Warner. Evaluating a semisupervised approach to phishing url identification in a realistic scenario. In *CEAS*, pages 176–183, 2011.

[12] Mark Hall, Eibe Frank, Geoffrey Holmes, Bernhard Pfahringer, Peter Reutemann, and Ian H. Witten. The weka data mining software: An update. *SIGKDD Explor. Newsl.*, 11(1):10–18, November 2009.

[13] Mahmoud Khonji, Youssef Iraqi, and Andrew Jones. Lexical url analysis for discriminating phishing and legitimate websites. In *CEAS*, pages 109–115, 2011.

[14] S. Kullback and R. A. Leibler. On information and sufficiency. *The Annals of Mathematical Statistics*, 22(1):79–86, 03 1951.

[15] S. le Cessie and J.C. van Houwelingen. Ridge estimators in logistic regression. *Applied Statistics*, 41(1):191–201, 1992.

[16] Justin Ma, Lawrence K. Saul, Stefan Savage, and Geoffrey M. Voelker. Learning to detect malicious urls. *ACM TIST*, 2(3):30, 2011.

[17] Thomas McCall. Gartner survey shows phishing attacks escalated in 2007. http://www.gartner.com/newsroom/id/565125, 2007.

[18] D. Kevin McGrath and Minaxi Gupta. Behind phishing: An examination of phisher modi operandi. In *LEET*, 2008.

[19] Pavel Micka. Letter frequency (english). http://en.algoritmy.net/article/40379/Letter-frequency-English, 2008.

[20] J. Platt. Fast training of support vector machines using sequential minimal optimization. In B. Schoelkopf, C. Burges, and A. Smola, editors, *Advances in Kernel Methods - Support Vector Learning*. MIT Press, 1998.

[21] Ross Quinlan. *C4.5: Programs for Machine Learning*. Morgan Kaufmann Publishers, San Mateo, CA, 1993.

[22] Tanmay Thakur and Rakesh Verma. Catching classical and hijack-based phishing attacks. In Atul Prakash and R.K. Shyamasundar, editors, *Proceedings 10th International Conference on Information Systems Security*, pages 318–337. December 2014.

[23] Rakesh Verma and Nabil Hossain. Semantic feature selection for text with application to phishing email detection. In Hyang-Sook Lee and Dong-Guk Han, editors, *Proc. 16th International Conference on Information Security and Cryptology*, pages 455–468, November 2013.

[24] Rakesh Verma, Narasimha Shashidhar, and Nabil Hossain. Detecting phishing emails the natural language way. In Sara Foresti, Moti Yung, and Fabio Martinelli, editors, *Proc. 17th European Symposium on Research in Computer Security*, pages 824–841, September 2012.

[25] C. Whittaker, B. Ryner, and M. Nazif. Large-scale automatic classification of phishing pages. *Proc. of 17th NDSS*, 2010.

[26] Guang Xiang, Jason I. Hong, Carolyn Penstein Rosé, and Lorrie Faith Cranor. CANTINA+: A feature-rich machine learning framework for detecting phishing web sites. *ACM Trans. Inf. Syst. Secur.*, 14(2):21, 2011.

[27] Xin Xu. Logistic classifier. http://weka.sourceforge.net/doc.dev/weka/classifiers/functions/Logistic.html, 2009.

[28] Harry Zhang. Exploring conditions for the optimality of naïve bayes. *IJPRAI*, 19(2):183–198, 2005.

[29] Jianyi Zhang and Yonghao Wang. A real-time automatic detection of phishing urls. In *Computer Science and Network Technology (ICCSNT), 2012 2nd International Conference on*, pages 1212–1216, Dec 2012.

[30] Y. Zhang, J.I. Hong, and L.F. Cranor. Cantina: a content-based approach to detecting phishing web sites. In *Proc. 16th int'l conf. on World Wide Web*, pages 639–648. ACM, 2007.

Content Level Access Control for OpenStack Swift Storage

Prosunjit Biswas
Univ. of Texas at San Antonio
San Antonio, TX, USA
prosun.csedu@gmail.com

Farhan Patwa
Univ. of Texas at San Antonio
San Antonio, TX, USA
farhan.patwa@utsa.edu

Ravi Sandhu
Univ. of Texas at San Antonio
San Antonio, TX, USA
ravi.sandhu@utsa.edu

ABSTRACT

Swift, the object storage service from OpenStack cloud computing platform is used for storing, managing and retrieving large amounts of data. Inside Swift, uploaded files, also known as objects, are organized in containers. Objects inside a container are managed to be accessible or restricted from users through Access Control Lists (ACLs). Swift ACL, at the finest level, works on a Swift object enforcing who can or cannot access the object. Once an object is accessible to some one, he gets the full content of the object. Thus Swift ACL is an "all or nothing" approach.

In this work, we allow Swift users to specify access control at the content level of a Swift object. The content level policy describes who can access which part of a Swift object. When a request comes for downloading (i.e. read) an object, we check content level policy along with the ACL of the object. The response of the request is a partial content of the requested object based on the credential of the requester. Our prototype implementation is done on Swift objects of content type 'application/json'.

Categories and Subject Descriptors

H.4 [**Information Systems Applications**]: Miscellaneous

Keywords

Content level access control; OpenStack Swift; ACL

1. INTRODUCTION

OpenStack Swift is a highly deployed open source cloud storage solution. With its unlimited storage capacity, it is used to store any number of large or small objects. In Swift terminology, uploaded documents are called objects. A user can upload or download an object using well defined APIs or available Swift client programs. But not everyone can download (i.e. read) every object stored in Swift. In order to maintain who can or cannot access an object, Swift uses Access Control Lists (ACLs). ACL specifies who can

or cannot access an object. Unfortunately, the ACL based approach for Swift is an 'all or nothing' approach in a way that an user can either download (i.e. read) the whole object or cannot download it at all.

We propose a content level access control mechanism for objects stored in Swift. This approach lets Swift users specify who can access which part of a Swift object. To give a concrete example, consider that a hospital stores its patient records as Swift objects. These records should be accessed differently by different personnel. For example, 'doctors' can see certain part while the 'billing accountant' can see other part of the record. Our implementation would let the data publisher specify policies expressing who can see which part of the data.

Our prototype implementation is based on JSON formatted documents. We use JSON data because recently JSON has gained immense commercial popularity which is reflected by developments including JSON document database such as MongoDB supported by the OpenStack cloud platform, Twitter's latest API (v 1.1) which supports only JSON data and so on.

2. BACKGROUND

2.1 Swift

Swift is a highly available, distributed, eventually consistent object storage which can operate standalone or integrated with the rest of the OpenStack cloud computing platform. It is used to store lots of data efficiently, safely, and cheaply using a scalable redundant storage system [3]. As opposed to conventional storage architectures like file systems which manage data using file hierarchy and block storage, Swift manages data as objects. Each object typically includes the data itself, a variable amount of metadata, and a globally unique identifier.

Using its well defined RESTful API [5], users can upload or download objects to and from Swift storage. Inside Swift, objects are organized into containers which is similar to directories in a filesystem except that Swift containers cannot be nested. Again, a user is associated with a Swift account and can have multiple containers associated with the account. In order to manage user accounts, user containers and objects inside a container, Swift uses an Account Server, a Container Server and Object Servers correspondingly.

When a user corresponding to a user account requests for an object inside a container (either for uploading or downloading), the Account Server looks for the account first in its account database and finds associated containers with the account. The Container Server then checks the container database to find whether the requested object exists in the specified container and finally the Object Server looks into 'object databases' to find retrieval information about the object. In order to retrieve an object, the Proxy Server needs to know which of the Object Servers are storing the object, and path of the object in the local filesystem of that server.

2.2 Swift ACL

Once an object is stored in Swift, who can or cannot access the object is determined by Swift Access Control List (ACL). Swift has different levels of ACL—Account level ACL, and Container level ACL, for example. Container level ACL is associated with containers in term of a *read* action, or *write* action or *listing* action. If a user is authorized read action on a container through read ACL, he or she can read or download objects from the container. Similarly, write ACL enables uploading an object into a container and listing ACL enables the list operation on the container. Account ACLs, on the other hand, allow users to grant account-level access to other users. Of these two types of ACL, Container level ACL is finer grained in that different containers of a single account can be configured differently. Nonetheless, Swift ACL is limited in the following ways.

- Once an object is set accessible to someone, he or she gets the full content of the object. But there can be some sensitive information that the publisher wants to hide out.

- Swift ACL allows sharing an object with others, but it does not allow to share objects selectively at the content level.

2.3 JSON (JavaScript Object Notation)

JSON or JavaScript Object Notation is a data representation format which uses human readable text to represent data. In JSON, data is represented in one of two forms—as an *object* or as an *array of values*. A JSON object is defined as a collection of *key-value* or *attribute-value* pairs where a *key* or an *attribute*[1] is simply a string representing a name and a *value* which is either one of the following primitive types—string, number, boolean (true or false), null or another object or an array. On the other hand, an array is defined as a set of an ordered collection of *values* (as defined above) starting from index zero. The formal definition of JSON data format is given in [1]. JSON structure has following characteristics

1. A JSON document forms a hierarchical structure which is a rooted tree.

2. In the rooted tree, leaf nodes represent text data of the document and non-leaf nodes are used to give the data a name and thus organize it.

3. In the rooted tree, a node can be uniquely identified by traversing the document from the root node to the target node.

---

[1]To avoid confusion with the use of *attribute* for attribute-based access control we will exclusively use the term *key* in this paper.

```
{
    "personal_record":{
        "name":"Alice",
        "DOB": "1/1/1990",
        "identification":{
            "DL": "25526509",
            "SSN": "32433149"
        }
    },
    "employment_record":{
        "Designation": "employee",
        "salary":50000
    }
}
```

Figure 1: A sample JSON Document containing records of an employee.

3. LABEL BASED ACCESS CONTROL

In order to protect a JSON document stored as a Swift object, we assign each JSON item (i.e. value of a JSON key) an *object-label* and each user a *user-label*. Then we specify policies in the form of (*user-label* values, *action*, *object-label* values) which means that objects labeled with any of 'object-label' values are allowed to be accessed by the users labeled with any of 'user-label' values for the specific 'action'. Here we present an informal description of the model and its open source implementation is available in [4].

3.1 Model Components

In LaBAC (Figure 2), we have one attribute assigned to objects and one attribute assigned to users. Object attribute is named *object-label* and user attribute is named *user-label*. These attributes are set valued attributes and the values of the attributes may form a partial order.

Object: Object is any resource we want to protect with the model. Examples include a JSON document or items inside a JSON document.

Object-label: Object-label is the attribute assigned on the objects. The values of this attribute may form a partial order.

User and *user-label*: User-label is the attribute assigned on each user. In a simple case, user-label values can be the set of roles assigned to the user. The values of this attribute may form a partial order.

Action: Action is the list of available actions to be exercised on the objects.

Policy: A policy in this model is a tuple of (*user-label* values, *action*, *object-label* values). The policy is interpreted such that objects labeled with any of 'object-label' values are allowed to be accessed by the users labeled with any of 'user-label' values for the specific 'action'.

Attribute Hierarchy: In our model, both object-label and user-label values may form a hierarchy or more specifically a partial order. The effect of attribute hierarchy is shown in Figure 3. As we can see in the figure, if a policy allows an action for user-label l_{uj} on object-label l_{oj}, due to the attribute hierarchy, all users having a equivalent or senior label than l_{uj} can also access object-label l_{oj} or its junior labels.

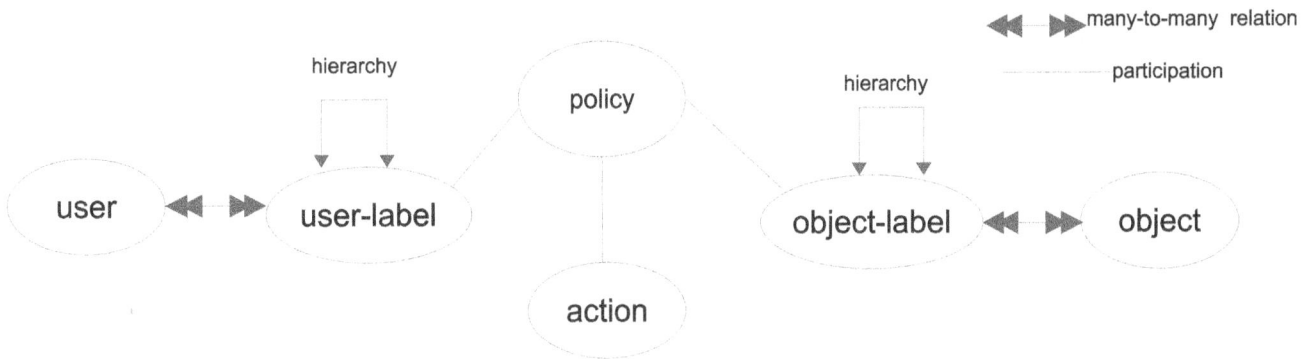

Figure 2: Label Based Access Control Model.

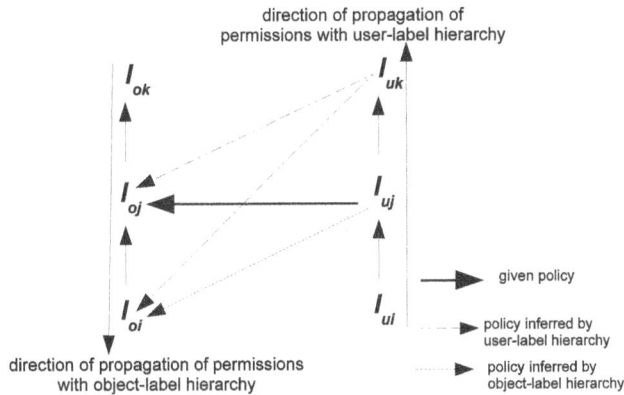

Figure 3: Propagation of permission with attribute hierarchy.

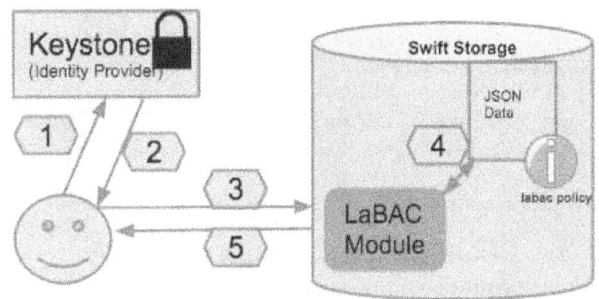

1, 2: User requests and receives Identity from Keystone.
3: User present credential to Swift.
4. LaBAC decides which JSON object is accessible.
5. User gets Partial content.

Figure 4: Required Changes in Swift Object Server for Our Extension

4. CONTENT LEVEL PROTECTION

Swift ACL specifies who can or cannot access a Swift object but it cannot specify who can access which part of the object. In order to specify security policies at the content level, Swift has to be aware of the content type and data format of the object. In our case, we addressed Swift objects of content-type *'application/json'* which is standard JSON format. How our protection mechanism works is summarized below.

- JSON items to be protected are identified using JSON-Path. For example, SSN in JSON data given in Fig. 1 is identified using JSONPath '$.personal_record.identification.SSN'.

- *object-label* values are assigned on the specified JSON item. For example, to specify that SSN is a sensitive information, we assign a label *'sensitive'* on JSONPath '$.personal_record.identification.SSN'.

- We use LaBAC policy to specify who can access (read) which *object-label*. For example, if only users with user-label 'manager' can access *sensitive* information, then we specify the LaBAC policy *('manager', read, 'sensitive')*.

When using JSONPath to identify a JSON item, one may want to specify value at the path as a condition. For example, salary information (given in Fig. 1) is sensitive only if the salary is greater than 50,000. Furthermore, it is also possible to protect one item based on value of a different item. For example, identification information (specified by JSON-Path '$.personal_record.identification') of a user is sensitive when his salary is greater than 50,000.

4.1 Labeling JSON Items

If the JSON document is large, labeling all JSON items can be tedious. In order to reduce labeling effort, we propagate label assigned on a JSON item to all its descendant items. For example, if the *personal_record* item (Fig. 1) is labeled *sensitive*, then all its descendant nodes (name, DOB, identification, DL, SSN) are also labeled *sensitive*.

5. IMPLEMENTATION

5.1 Changes in Swift Object Server

We have extended the logic of Swift Object Server. In the existing implementation, when a request comes for downloading of an object, Object Server checks the ACL and if the object is allowed by ACL, the Object Server reads the object from the disk and pass the whole content to the requester through Proxy-server.

In our implementation (see Figure 4), if the ACL denies the request, no further check is made and user gets corresponding error messages. Otherwise, we retrieve the object, content level policy (stored with the Swift Object as metadata), user credential (user-label specifically which is the roles of the user maintained by Keystone) and pass them to the LaBAC module. LaBAC module processes the requested object based on the policy and user credential, and removes unauthorized content from the object. Then only the authorized partial content of the object is returned to the requester through Swift Proxy-server.

Note that in the implementation, we have used OpenStack Keystone [2] as the identity provider and we have mapped user roles provided by the Keystone as user-label values of the requester.

5.2 Storing of Policies

In our implementation, we have two different types of policies—LaBAC policies in the form of (*user-label* values, *action*, *object-label* values) and content-level policies in the form of *(JSONPath, {Labels})*. All of these policies are stored as the metadata of the Swift object. Note that the Swift object is the JSON document itself.

One challenge of storing policies as metadata of Swift object is that Swift does not allow a single metadata item larger than 256 bytes. To circumvent this limitation, policies are stored as multiple metadata items.

5.3 Limitation of the Implementation

Our prototype implementation works only on objects of type 'application/json'. If requested object is not a JSON file or the requested object does not have content level policy set, the requester gets full content of the file.

6. PERFORMANCE

In order to analyze the performance of our implementation, we compared the download time of a Swift object enabling content policy and without enabling content policy. Our analysis (Figure 5) shows that our implementation works well for Swift object of size smaller than 100KB beyond which CLAC does not work efficiently. We believe this is because our implementation exhausts memory very soon. We conjecture that pre-labeling objects and enforcing access control in divide-and-concur fashion may improve performance.

7. RELATED WORK

There have been very few works for access control of JSON data, although JSON and XML data are very similar and lots of works has been done at the content level for XML data [7, 8]. Additionally there are prior works that apply object labels at the content level [6] for access control purposes. But, to the best of our knowledge, applying content level access control for the application context of OpenStack Swift has not yet been performed.

8. CONCLUSION

As more and more data is being uploaded in the cloud, data may contain sensitive information. With existing Swift API, one can either access the full content of an object or cannot access it at all. We propose an extension of Swift Object Server where someone can specify policies on a Swift object at the content level and let different users access different parts of it. We hope that this work would help Swift

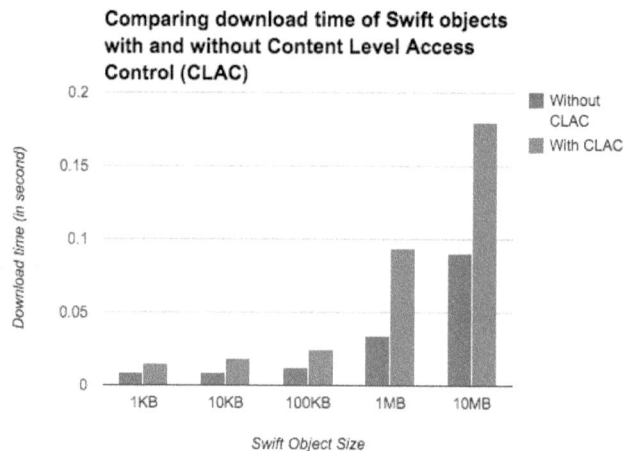

Figure 5: Performance of our Implementation

users to share objects effectively with others having more control at the content level.

Acknowledgement

The authors acknowledge the support of Rackspace for this work.

9. REFERENCES

[1] JSON Official Website. http://json.org/. [Online; accessed 09/2014].

[2] Keystone, the openstack identity service. http://docs.openstack.org/developer/keystone/. [Online; accessed 09/2014].

[3] Openstack swift offical documentation. http://docs.openstack.org/developer/swift/. [Online; accessed 09/2014].

[4] Python Package - Label Based Access Control. https://pypi.python.org/pypi/labac/0.11. [Online; accessed 09/2014].

[5] Swift API Official Documentation. http://docs.openstack.org/api/openstack-object-storage/1.0/content/. [Online; accessed 09/2014].

[6] N. R. Adam, V. Atluri, E. Bertino, and E. Ferrari. A content-based authorization model for digital libraries. *Knowledge and Data Engineering, IEEE Transactions on*, 14(2):296–315, 2002.

[7] E. Bertino, S. Castano, E. Ferrari, and M. Mesiti. Specifying and enforcing access control policies for xml document sources. *World Wide Web*, 3(3):139–151, 2000.

[8] E. Damiani, S. De Capitani di Vimercati, S. Paraboschi, and P. Samarati. A fine-grained access control system for xml documents. *ACM Transactions on Information and System Security (TISSEC)*, 5(2):169–202, 2002.

Pleco and Plectron – Two Provably Secure Password Hashing Algorithms

Bo Zhu, Xinxin Fan, and Guang Gong
Department of Electrical and Computer Engineering, University of Waterloo, Canada
{bo.zhu,x5fan,ggong}@uwaterloo.ca

ABSTRACT

We propose two practical and provably secure password hashing algorithms, PLECO and PLECTRON. They are built upon well-understood cryptographic algorithms, and combine advantages of symmetric and asymmetric primitives. By employing the Rabin cryptosystem, we prove that the one-wayness of PLECO is at least as strong as the hard problem of integer factorization. In addition, both password hashing algorithms are designed to be sequential memory-hard, in order to thwart large-scale password cracking by parallel hardware, such as GPUs, FPGAs, and ASICs. Moreover, the total computation and memory consumptions of PLECO and PLECTRON are tunable through their cost parameters.

1. INTRODUCTION

Password-based authentication may be the most widely deployed security mechanism across all information systems. However, there are two fundamental limitations of password-based authentication: 1) Users usually pick poor passwords that are subject to dictionary attacks or brute-force search; and 2) A device or server storing many passwords is a juicy target for attackers, and how to store passwords securely and minimize damages if the device or server has been breached is non-trivial. As an effective countermeasure, passwords should be obscured together with user-specific and high-entropy salts by applying a one-way function, namely *password hashing*. During authentication, the user's input is processed in the same way and then the result is compared with the one stored in the device or server.

There are several requirements that a good password hashing algorithm should fulfill:

- Similar as most cryptographic primitives, the password hashing algorithm should behave as a random function that ensures *one-wayness* and *collision resistance*.

- Different from most cryptographic primitives, the password hashing algorithm should be *heavyweight* in computation and memory usage to slow down brute-force

CODASPY'15, March 2–4, 2015, San Antonio, Texas, USA.
ACM 978-1-4503-3191-3/15/03.
http://dx.doi.org/10.1145/2699026.2699125.

attacks to a certain degree and make large-scale attacks economically difficult.

In this paper, we propose two novel password hashing algorithms, named PLECO and PLECTRON, respectively, based upon several well-studied cryptographic structures and primitives. The novelty in the designs of PLECO and PLECTRON is the combination of asymmetric and symmetric components that offers a twofold benefit: 1) Since the tools to cryptanalyzing asymmetric algorithms are quite different from those for symmetric ones, the composition of asymmetric and symmetric components will make cryptanalysis much harder. This is analogous to the designs of ARX based cryptographic primitives [1, 3] and the block cipher IDEA [5] where mixed operations are used; 2) The asymmetric component makes our scheme provably secure (the security of PLECO is as strong as the hard problem of integer factorization). In addition to describing the PLECO and PLECTRON designs in great detail, we also theoretically prove their security with respect to one-wayness and collision resistance.

2. DESIGN SPECIFICATIONS

2.1 Design Components

2.1.1 Provably One-Way Function

It is proven that the security of the Rabin public-key encryption scheme is computationally equivalent to the hard problem of integer factorization [7]. Let us define

$$\mathsf{Rabin}_n(x) = x^2 \bmod n,$$

where x is a positive integer in the multiplicative group of integers modulo n. Then computing the square roots, i.e., inverting the function $\mathsf{Rabin}_n(x)$, is proven to be computationally equivalent to factorizing the integer n.

2.1.2 Sponge-Based Hash Function

Keccak, which is designed by Bertoni *et al.* [4], is the winner of the SHA-3 hash function competition held by NIST. Keccak is based on a unique construction, namely *sponge construction*, which can *absorb* an arbitrary-length binary string as input, and then *squeeze* out a binary string of any required length as output. If not specified, default parameters of Keccak should be used, i.e., $r = 1024$ and $c = 576$.

2.1.3 Sequential Memory-Hard Construction

The password-based key derivation function scrypt was proposed by Percival in order to thwart parallel brute-force attacks using GPUs, FPGAs or ASICs on passwords [6], and has been widely used by cryptocurrencies. One of the core components of scrypt, namely ROMix, is proven to be *sequential memory-hard*. One important feature of being sequential memory-hard is that parallel algorithms cannot asymptotically achieve efficiency advantage than non-parallel ones. In other words, brute-force password search by using dedicated hardware with constrained memory, such as GPUs, FPGAs, and ASICs, would not be significantly faster than a single-core desktop computer. For a more detailed definition of sequential memory-hard, the reader is referred to [6].

2.2 Designs of Pleco and Plectron

The following notations are used in this section:

- $||$ concatenates two binary strings;

- $\mathsf{int}(\cdot)$ converts a binary string into a non-negative integer, where the little-endian convention is used, i.e., the left-most (lowest address) bit is the least significant bit of the integer;

- $\mathsf{str}_b(\cdot)$ converts a non-negative integer back to a binary string by using the same bit ordering convention as $\mathsf{int}(\cdot)$, and may append zeros to the string in order to achieve a total length of b bits;

- 0^t denotes a t-bit all-zero binary string, e.g., $0^t = \mathsf{str}_t(0)$ for $t > 0$, and 0^0 means an empty string;

- $\mathsf{len}(\cdot)$ denotes the bit-length of a binary string;

- $\mathsf{size}(\cdot)$ denotes the number of bits in the binary representation of a given non-negative integer, e.g., $\mathsf{size}(256) = 9$ and $\mathsf{size}(255) = 8$;

- Keccak_b denotes a Keccak instance that produces exactly b bits as output.

Given a modulus n, we define a new hash function

$$\mathcal{H}_n(x) = \mathsf{str}_N(\mathsf{Rabin}_n(1 + \mathsf{int}(\mathsf{Keccak}_{N-1}(x)))),$$

where $N = \mathsf{size}(n)$. To be secure, N should be at least 1024, or preferably larger than 3072, according to [2]. The modulus n can be obtained using the same approach for generating the RSA modulus $n = p \cdot q$ or chosen from a public composite number with unknown factorization as proposed in the design of SQUASH [8].

Our new password hashing algorithm PLECO is defined by Algorithm 1, which takes as input

- a modulus n,

- a 128-bit binary string *salt* as a unique or randomly generated salt,

- a variable-length ($\leq$ 128 bytes) binary string *pass* as a user password,

- a positive integer *tcost* as the time cost parameter,

- and a positive integer *mcost* as the memory cost parameter.

PLECO will produce an N-bit hash tag, but sometimes applications need to flexibly choose tag sizes, e.g., generating cryptographic keys from passphrases entered by users. We recommend applying Keccak to the output of PLECO

Algorithm 1 PLECO(n, *salt*, *pass*, *tcost*, *mcost*)

1: $L \leftarrow 8 \cdot \lceil \mathsf{size}(n)/8 \rceil - \mathsf{size}(n)$
2: $x \leftarrow salt || \mathsf{str}_{16}(\mathsf{len}(pass)) || pass || 0^{1024 - \mathsf{len}(pass)}$
3: $ctr \leftarrow 0$
4: $x \leftarrow \mathcal{H}_n(\mathsf{str}_{128}(ctr) || x)$
5: **for** $i \leftarrow 0$ to $tcost - 1$ **do**
6:     **for** $j \leftarrow 0$ to $mcost - 1$ **do**
7:         $v_j \leftarrow x$
8:         $ctr \leftarrow ctr + 1$
9:         $x \leftarrow \mathcal{H}_n(\mathsf{str}_{128}(ctr) || x)$
10:     **end for**
11:     **for** $j \leftarrow 0$ to $mcost - 1$ **do**
12:         $k \leftarrow \mathsf{int}(x) \bmod mcost$
13:         $ctr \leftarrow ctr + 1$
14:         $x \leftarrow \mathcal{H}_n(\mathsf{str}_{128}(ctr) || x || 0^L || v_k)$
15:     **end for**
16:     $ctr \leftarrow ctr + 1$
17:     $x \leftarrow \mathcal{H}_n(\mathsf{str}_{128}(ctr) || x)$
18: **end for**
19: **return** x

---

again to produce tags of required lengths. We name this modified algorithm as PLECTRON and specifies its design in Algorithm 2, where

- *hsize* denotes the desired bit-length of the hash tag.

Algorithm 2 PLECTRON(n, *salt*, *pass*, *tcost*, *mcost*, *hsize*)

1: $t \leftarrow$ PLECO(n, *salt*, *pass*, *tcost*, *mcost*)
2: **return** $\mathsf{Keccak}_{hsize}(t)$

---

3. SECURITY ANALYSIS

In what follows, we discuss security properties of PLECO and PLECTRON in detail. Due to the page limitation, we omit the proofs for our theorems. For more details, please refer to our full paper [9].

3.1 One-Wayness

One of the most important security goals of designing a password hashing scheme is one-wayness, i.e., attackers should not be able to devise any methods faster than brute-force search for inverting the hashing algorithm in order to obtain original passwords.

Formally, we give the following definition.

Definition 1. For a given function f and a pre-specified set Y containing certain outputs of f, we define the advantage of an adversary $\mathcal{A}$ finding preimages of the elements in Y (i.e., inverting f) as

$$\mathbf{Adv}_f^{\mathrm{Pre}(Y)}(\mathcal{A}) \stackrel{\text{def}}{=} \Pr[y \stackrel{\$}{\leftarrow} Y, x \leftarrow \mathcal{A}^{f,y} : f(x) = y],$$

where $y \stackrel{\$}{\leftarrow} Y$ means randomly assigning one element of Y to y.

Then we can give the theorems about the one-wayness of PLECO and PLECTRON. The preimage security of PLECO is guaranteed by Rabin_n.

THEOREM 1 (ONE-WAYNESS OF PLECO). *If PLECO and* $\mathcal{H}_n$ *use a same modulus* n, *then we have*

$$\mathbf{Adv}_{\text{PLECO}}^{\text{Pre}(S)}(\mathcal{A}) \leq \mathbf{Adv}_{\text{Rabin}_n}^{\text{Pre}(S)}(\mathcal{A}),$$

where S *is a set containing all possible outputs of* PLECO.

THEOREM 2 (ONE-WAYNESS OF PLECTRON). *If* $\mathcal{H}_n$ *and* PLECTRON *use a same modulus* n, *then we have*

$$\mathbf{Adv}_{\text{PLECTRON}}^{\text{Pre}(S)}(\mathcal{A}) \leq \mathbf{Adv}_{\text{Keccak}_{hsize}}^{\text{Pre}(S)}(\mathcal{A}),$$

where S *is a set containing all possible outputs of* PLECTRON.

3.2 Collision Resistance

Formally, we give the following security definitions.

Definition 2. For a given function f, we define the advantage of an adversary $\mathcal{A}$ to find a collision of f as

$$\mathbf{Adv}_f^{\text{Coll}}(\mathcal{A}) \overset{\text{def}}{=} \Pr[x_1, x_2 \leftarrow \mathcal{A}^f : f(x_1) = f(x_2)].$$

Definition 3. For a given function f, we define the advantage of an adversary $\mathcal{A}$ to obtain an output difference d as

$$\mathbf{Adv}_f^{\text{Diff}(d)}(\mathcal{A}) \overset{\text{def}}{=} \Pr[x_1, x_2 \leftarrow \mathcal{A}^{f,d} : f(x_1) = d - f(x_2)].$$

Definition 4. For a given positive composite integer m, we define the advantage of an adversary $\mathcal{A}$ to obtain a nontrivial factor of m as

$$\mathbf{Adv}_m^{\text{Fact}}(\mathcal{A}) \overset{\text{def}}{=} \Pr[x \leftarrow \mathcal{A}^m, 1 < x < m : x|m].$$

We give the following theorems to characterize adversaries' collision advantages on PLECO and PLECTRON.

THEOREM 3 (COLLISION RESISTANCE OF PLECO). *If the cost parameters, mcost and tcost, of* PLECO *keep unchanged, and* $\mathcal{H}_n$ *and* PLECO *use a same modulus* n, *then we have*

$$
\begin{aligned}
\mathbf{Adv}_{\text{PLECO}}^{\text{Coll}}(\mathcal{A}) \leq & \; \mathbf{Adv}_{\text{Keccak}_{N-1}}^{\text{Coll}}(\mathcal{A}) \\
& + \mathbf{Adv}_{\text{Keccak}_{N-1}}^{\text{Diff}(n)}(\mathcal{A}) \\
& + \mathbf{Adv}_n^{\text{Fact}}(\mathcal{A}).
\end{aligned}
$$

THEOREM 4 (COLLISION RESISTANCE OF PLECTRON). *If the cost parameters and output hash length, mcost, tcost and hsize, of* PLECTRON *keep unchanged, and* $\mathcal{H}_n$ *and* PLECTRON *use a same modulus* n, *then we have*

$$
\begin{aligned}
\mathbf{Adv}_{\text{PLECTRON}_n}^{\text{Coll}}(\mathcal{A}) \leq & \; \mathbf{Adv}_{\text{Keccak}_{N-1}}^{\text{Coll}}(\mathcal{A}) \\
& + \mathbf{Adv}_{\text{Keccak}_{N-1}}^{\text{Diff}(n)}(\mathcal{A}) \\
& + \mathbf{Adv}_n^{\text{Fact}}(\mathcal{A}) + \mathbf{Adv}_{\text{Keccak}_{hsize}}^{\text{Coll}}(\mathcal{A}).
\end{aligned}
$$

3.3 Thwarting Parallel Brute-Force Attacks

The hardware such as GPUs, FPGAs, and ASICs can feature thousands of cores for parallel computation, but in return each core possesses very restrained memory space. By using the structure of ROMix, the internal iteration of PLECO (Lines 6-15 in Algorithm 1) inherits scrypt's security property of being sequential memory-hard. PLECO and PLECTRON also provide a tunable memory parameter $mcost$ to increase their memory cost as desired. Although the design of PLECO is slightly different from ROMix, the security proofs of ROMix can be easily transferred to here, since in the original proofs the internal hash function is treated as a Random Oracle.

4. PERFORMANCE ANALYSIS

We have tested our initial implementations of PLECO and PLECTRON on a 2.6 GHz Intel Core i7 processor. We set $tcost = 1$ and $mcost = 2^{16}$ when profiling the software performance, which means the programs will consume 2^{16}size(n)-bit memory, i.e., around 17 MB for PLECO/PLECTRON using 2048-bit moduli. We have also tested scrypt on the same machine, using the configuration $(N = 2^{14}, r = 8, p = 1)$ that yields a similar memory usage as PLECO/PLECTRON with 2048-bit moduli, and it takes 35 ms to compute scrypt.

Table 1: Software performance (in seconds)

Modulus Size	PLECO	PLECTRON
1024	0.684	0.686
2048	2.215	2.235
3072	4.355	4.358

5. ACKNOWLEDGEMENT

The authors would like to thank Samuel Neves for bringing up the paper about RSA-UFOs.

This work is supported by NSERC Discovery Grant and ORF-RE Grant.

6. REFERENCES

[1] J. P. Aumasson and D. J. Bernstein, SipHash: a fast short-input PRF, Progress in Cryptology, INDOCRYPT 2012, LNCS 7668, pp. 489–508, 2012.

[2] E. Barker, W. Barker, W. Burr, W. Polk, and M. Smid, Recommendation for key management, part 1: general (revision 3), *NIST Special Publication 800-57*, 2012.

[3] D. J. Bernstein, The Salsa20 family of stream ciphers, *New Stream Cipher Designs*, LNCS 4986, pp. 8–97, 2008.

[4] G. Bertoni, J. Daemen, M. Peeters, and G. Van Assche, The Keccak SHA-3 submission. *Submission to NIST (Round 3)*, 2011.

[5] X. Lai and J. L. Massey, A Proposal for a New Block Encryption Standard, LNCS 473, pp. 389–404, 1991.

[6] C. Percival, Stronger key derivation via sequential memory-hard functions, *BSDCan*, 2009.

[7] M. O. Rabin, Digitalized signatures and public-Key functions as intractable as factorization, *Technical Report*, MIT, 1979.

[8] A. Shamir, SQUASH – A new MAC with provable security properties for highly constrained devices such as RFID tags, *Fast Software Encryption, FSE 2008*, LNCS 5086, pp 144-157, 2008.

[9] B. Zhu, X. Fan, and G. Gong, Pleco and Plectron – Two Provably Secure Password Hashing Algorithms, *Cryptology ePrint Archive, Report 2014/655*, 2014.

Secure Information and Resource Sharing in Cloud

Yun Zhang
Institute for Cyber Security
Univ of Texas at San Antonio
San Antonio, TX 78249
Amy.u.Zhang@gmail.com

Ram Krishnan
Dept. of Electrical and
Computer Engineering
Univ of Texas at San Antonio
San Antonio, TX 78249
Ram.Krishnan@utsa.edu

Ravi Sandhu
Institute for Cyber Security
Univ of Texas at San Antonio
San Antonio, TX 78249
Ravi.Sandhu@utsa.edu

ABSTRACT

The significant threats from information security breaches in cyber world is one of the most serious security problems. Organizations are facing growing number of sophisticated cyber-attacks every year. Efficient and secure sharing of attack and security information during cyber incident response plays increasingly significant role in fixing the problems as well as helping organizations recover fast. While traditional systems are slow and inefficient in sharing information and resources securely, cloud platform provides us a considerable convenience to facilitate the sharing. In this paper, we propose access control models for secure information and resource sharing (IARS) in cloud Infrastructure as a Service (IaaS).

Keywords

Formal models; IaaS; OpenStack; Resource sharing

1. INTRODUCTION

It has been a long history since the concept of information sharing came out in the field of information technology. The need to share information between organizations becomes significant for various reasons, such as cyber incident response, business collaboration, etc. The lacking of important attack and threat information sharing may lead to a big security breach. As organizations are moving to cloud, we explore information sharing in cloud platforms.

Traditional techniques for information sharing are lacking in three aspects, as follows.

1. Systems in different organizations are incompatible with each other, which make it impossible for one user in one organization to have access to the system in another organization.

2. Systems are lacking of mechanisms to accommodate temporary users, whereby a temporary user may only be assigned with a internal user account, which incurs a substantial risk of information leakage.

CODASPY'15, March 2–4, 2015, San Antonio, Texas, USA.
ACM 978-1-4503-3191-3/15/03.
http://dx.doi.org/10.1145/2699026.2699126.

3. Trust issues among organizations remain a big concern.

In the environment of cloud platform, systems of different organization can talk to each other under the same access control architecture. Cloud platform make is possible for users belongs to one organization have the possibility to be assigned to another organization conveniently. Cloud platform also gives the ability to define different level of users with more specific permissions, under which risk is more likely to be controlled.

Our motivation to build a secure information and resource sharing (IARS) model in IaaS came from the case of response to a cyber incident. Consider a community cyber incident response scenario where organizations that provide critical infrastructure to a community (such as a city, county or a state) share information related to a cyber incident in a controlled manner [2]. Sharing information amongst such organizations can greatly improve the resilience of increasingly cyber-dependent communities in case of coordinated cyber attacks [3]. An effective cyber incident response mechanism needs to be built up to provide organizations technical support and services to handle the problems once the cyber incident happens. The most significant part of this mechanism is how to share incident data securely and efficiently. The incident data may not only include the logs of attacks, but also the compromised machine, even the malware. With traditional ways, sharing is constrained in a manual way by means of reporting, which is slow and insufficient. In order to response to cyber attack fast and accurately, we want to share not only the report, but all related information, even a virus or a compromised machine. Cloud platform of IaaS gives us a very good option to place the sharing space, which holds the incident data. Thus, we explored various modeling ways in cloud of IaaS and formalized one of the models.

2. BACKGROUND

OpenStack is an open source cloud platform of IaaS. OpenStack software controls large pools of compute, storage, and networking resources throughout a datacenter [1]. It provides several services, including compute (Nova), identity (Keystone), block storage (Cinder), object storage (Swift), image (Glance), networking (Neutron) and Dashboard (Horizon). Nova provides computing service, like virtual machines. Keystone provides authentication and authorization services. Swift provides object storage services. In [7], the authors present a core OpenStack Access Control (OSAC) model, as shown in figure 1. The OSAC model consists of eight entities: users, groups, projects, domains, roles, services, operations, and tokens. Users represent people who

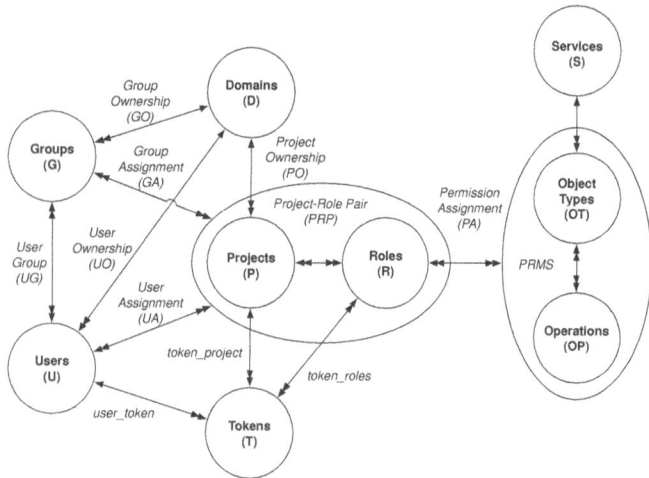

Figure 1: OpenStack Access Control (OSAC) model [7]

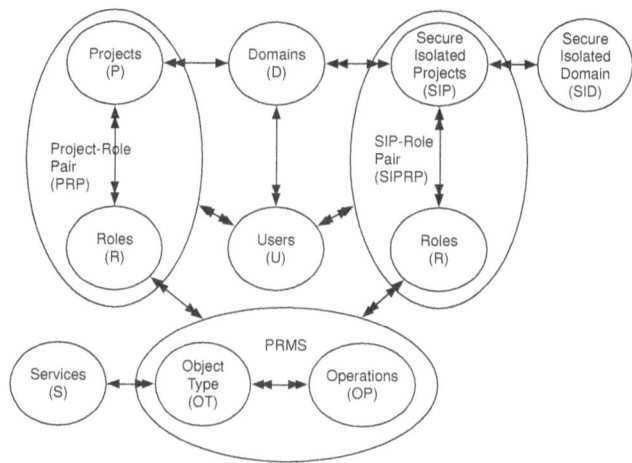

Figure 2: OpenStack Access Control (OSAC) model with SID extension(ignore group and token components)

are authenticated to access OpenStack cloud resources while a group is a set of users. Projects define a boundary of cloud resources—a resource container in which users can get access to the services the cloud provides, such as virtual machines, storages, networks, and so on. Domain is a higher level concept that equates to a tenant (customer) of the CSP. Roles are global, which are used to specify access levels of users to services in specific projects in a given domain. An object type and operation pair defines actions which can be performed by end users on cloud services and resources. Users authenticate themselves to Keystone and obtain a token which they then use to access different services. The token contains various information for a user to get permission to a project or domain.

3. OSAC-SID MODEL

In the OSAC-SID model, we assume that a user can belong to only one organization, which is consistent with the user and home-domain concept in OpenStack. We extend the OSAC model to include SID and SIP components, as shown in figure 2. For every possible combination of organizations in the cloud, we create a SID to include all SIPs that will be set up among these organizations. For each IARS event, we create a SIP within the appropriate SID.

Similar to the concept of domains which is designed to add one more layer for administration of projects, SID is a administrative concept to manage SIPs. The SID function is transparent to users. SID and SIP components are isolated from the regular domain and projects components. Unlike the concept of domains, there are no users that belong to a SID. A SID exists only for setting up SIPs. However, since a SID is formed and associated with a collection of domains, there are users who will be associated with the SID—but only under the constraint that they are from the collection of domains which are associated with that SID.

A SIP provides a secure isolated space for IARS in the cloud. In other words, SIP is another type of resources container in OpenStack, which is restricted only for IARS among domains and projects. Users who are assigned to a SIP have similar access capability to request all cloud services like users who are assigned to a project.

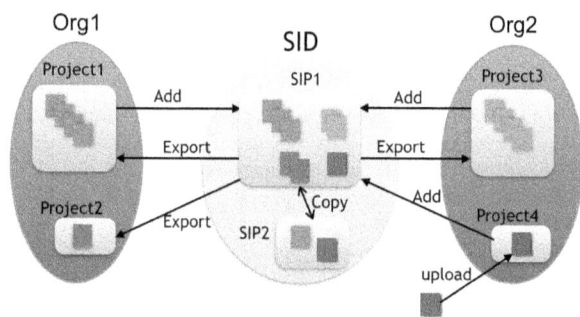

Figure 3: Establish a SID

4. IMPLEMENTATION

In this section, we discuss implementation considerations in OpenStack. Recall that Keystone is the authentication and authorization service in OpenStack. In order to deploy the model in OpenStack platform, we need to modify Keystone entity to include SID and SIP functionality in OpenStack, which facilitates features of IARS.

We assume that each domain represents an organization in OpenStack while projects inside a domain could represent a department or temporary project in the organization. In the case of collaboration, multiple organizations would form a group to create a SID. SIPs will be created inside the SID to facilitate collaboration for different reasons. Objects are exchanged among organizations and SIPs as per SID policy. Figure 3 gives a simple view of how SID is established among two organizations Org1 and Org2.

We implement the model in OpenStack Icehouse release. To establish a SID, we need to modify two parts in OpenStack: policy and Keystone. In policy file, we define that only domain admins are allowed to create a SID and only a SID admin is allowed to create a SIP inside the SID. In Keystone, we add methods to constrain the grants that a SID admin can only add users from his own home domain to the SID while a domain admin is allowed to add any users to his own home domain in OpenStack.

The SID/SIP establishment steps are as follows.

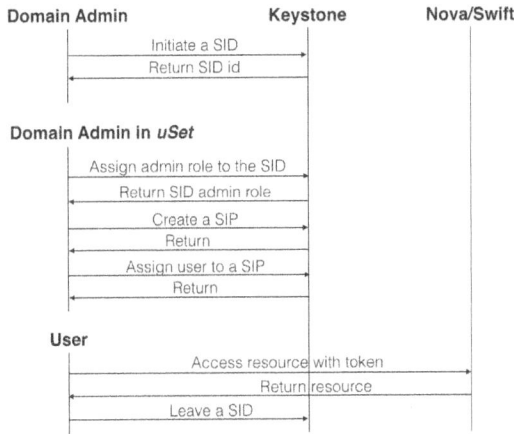

Figure 4: SID/SIP Establishment Process

1. A domain admin initiate a SID creation with parameter of *uSet* which is a set of domain admin users of domains which are willing to collaborate.

2. Domain admins who belong to uSet assign themselves the SID admin role to the SID.

3. SID admins create SIPs and assign users from their home domains to any SIPs inside the SID.

The point here is that uSet defines the set of domain admins who will be SID admins in the collaboration group. However, it doesn't mean that being in the uSet will give the domain admin the admin power over the SID. Instead, in order to complete the process of assigning domain admin to be a SID admin, the domain admin need to agree with the initiation which we implemented by allowing the domain admin to assign himself to the SID admin role. After step two, a domain admin officially becomes a SID admin. Step three allows SID admin to set up SIPs and assign their users to a specific SIP. A user does not have an access to a SIP without being assigned to it, i.e., even if a user has access to the SID, he/she can only access SIPs he/she is assigned to inside the SID. Figure 4 shows the flow to establish a SID/SIP.

After the SID/SIP is established, users can start operation inside SID/SIP as well as between SID/SIP and their home projects. We choose Swift as storage in our enforcement in OpenStack. Nova provides us the ability to create a virtual machine in a SIP. Glance helps to share virtual machine image among domains, which is very useful in case that the collaboration group need to share a virtual machine, like an attacked machine image. Currently, the access control for user accessing the resource inside a SIP is very straight forward. We use the access policy of project for a SIP. Thus, more fine-grained access control over a normal user to a SIP would be our future work.

5. RELATED WORK

There are several differences between our model and other models. First, we proposed our model in a IaaS cloud environment rather than distributed systems. Second, we don't give the collaboration group the direct access over the original data and resources in the organization s done in [6,

5]. Instead, we transfer copies to the collaboration group. Third, we don't use a separate Community Authorization Service(CAS) [5] to manage the access control policies for the collaboration group. Instead, we utilize the setting of roles, users and policies of the cloud to facilitate the access control over the collaboration group. Out approach is more like the model proposed in [4], from where we adapt the group-centric concept and relaize it in a IaaS cloud environment.

6. CONCLUSION AND FUTURE WORK

We developed and implemented a model for IARS. For the future work, we plan to investigate fine-grained access control within a SIP, such as virtual machine access control, networking access control, and so on.

7. ACKNOWLEDGMENTS

The authors would like to acknowledge the support of the LMI Research Institute's Academic Partnership Program.

8. REFERENCES

[1] http://openstack.org.

[2] K. Harrison and G. White. Information sharing requirements and framework needed for community cyber incident detection and response. In *Homeland Security (HST), 2012 IEEE Conference on Technologies for*, pages 463–469, Nov 2012.

[3] Keith Harrison and Gregory B. White. Anonymous and distributed community cyberincident detection. *IEEE Security and Privacy*, 11(5):20–27, 2013.

[4] Ram Krishnan, Ravi Sandhu, Jianwei Niu, and William Winsborough. Towards a framework for group-centric secure collaboration. In *Collaborative Computing: Networking, Applications and Worksharing, 2009. CollaborateCom 2009. 5th International Conference on*, pages 1–10. IEEE, 2009.

[5] Laura Pearlman, Von Welch, Ian Foster, Carl Kesselman, and Steven Tuecke. A community authorization service for group collaboration. In *Policies for Distributed Systems and Networks, 2002. Proceedings. Third International Workshop on*, pages 50–59. IEEE, 2002.

[6] Deborah Shands, Richard Yee, Jay Jacobs, and E John Sebes. Secure virtual enclaves: Supporting coalition use of distributed application technologies. In *DARPA Information Survivability Conference and Exposition, 2000. DISCEX'00. Proceedings*, volume 1, pages 335–350. IEEE, 2000.

[7] Bo Tang and Ravi Sandhu. Extending OpenStack access control with domain trust. In *In Proceedings 8th International Conference on Network and System Security (NSS 2014)*, October 15-17 2014.

One Thing Leads to Another: Credential Based Privilege Escalation

Peter Snyder and Chris Kanich
University of Illinois at Chicago
Chicago, Illinois, USA
{psnyde2,ckanich}@uic.edu

Abstract

A user's primary email account, in addition to being an easy point of contact in our online world, is increasingly being used as a single point of failure for all web security. Features like unlimited message storage, numerous weak password reset features and economically enticing spoils (in the form of financial accounts or personal photos) all add up to an environment where overthrowing someone's life via their primary email account is increasingly likely and damaging. We describe an attack we call credential based privilege escalation, and a methodology to evaluate this attack's potential for user harm at web scale. In a study of over 9,000 users we find that, unsurprisingly, access to a vast number of online accounts can be gained by breaking into a user's primary email account (even without knowing the email account's password), but even then the monetizable value in a typical account is relatively low. We also describe future directions in understanding both the technical and human aspects of credential based privilege escalation.

Categories and Subject Descriptors

H.3.5 [**Information Storage and Retrieval**]: On-line Information Services; J.m [**Computer Applications**]: Miscellaneous; K.4.4 [**Computers and Society**]: Electronic Commerce

Keywords

web security; web privacy

General Terms

security; privacy

1. INTRODUCTION

At the heart of most cybercrime is unauthorized access: attackers are able to transfer information, computation, and economic value (from e.g. credit cards or bank accounts)

CODASPY'15, March 2–4, 2015, San Antonio, Texas, USA.
ACM 978-1-4503-3191-3/15/03.
http://dx.doi.org/10.1145/2699026.2699127.

from victims to themselves. The value proposition for attackers is composed of two parts: gaining unauthorized access to systems or accounts, and extracting the valuable information from those stores of value. Traditional analysis of cybercrime primarily focuses on the criminal efforts as a sort of one-two punch: first gain access to a large store of e.g. credit card numbers from a retailer, then somehow monetize that information, either through selling to a third party or performing fraudulent transactions.

While the unauthorized access portion of a sophisticated cybercrime attack is likely to consist of multiple break-ins chained together—for instance an unpatched web server allows a remote exploit, after which a database server is breached from inside a corporate firewall—these attacks are typically carried out by humans and rely on exploiting the unique configuration of the network at hand. However, the current web ecosystem lends itself to a different type of multistage attack which is much more easily automated, in an attack we call credential based privilege escalation.

"Privilege escalation," as traditionally defined, allows attackers with some foothold into a system to access more resources than they were intended. Typically, this is enabled by some flaw in the software installed on the machine. However, in credential based privilege escalation, multiple factors combine to allow the attacker to gain additional privileges. These factors are largely not purely technical problems and many have a human component: passwords shared between accounts, sites that email passwords in plain text, or even account reset capabilities which are amenable to social engineering.

There is no doubt that stealing the credentials to one database server housing credit card records is far more lucrative than breaking into several trivial online accounts. However, through any of the above weaknesses, even an account as inane as a discussion forum or a mobile videogame has the potential to allow an attacker to escalate his privilege, perhaps by re-using that password to log in to the user's email account, after which the user might be able to take over several other possibly lucrative accounts. This issue is exacerbated by how email accounts have become central to users' online lives: a large portion of online accounts defer all security to the email account through "password reset" features, thus ensuring that if an attacker wants carte blanche to impersonate someone online, they need only compromise that person's email account. Indeed, the hacking of technology journalist Mat Honan showed how complete and damaging this type of privilege escalation can be if the attacker's goal is vandalism rather than personal gain [7].

Due to the homogeneity and popularity of many modern online accounts, the risk that an attack like this could be automated by a motivated attacker could greatly endanger user safety on the web.

Understanding the extent to which credential based privilege escalation is possible is an important first step to determining what steps can be taken to mitigate it on the web. As this is both a social and technical problem, approaches to defending against it must consider both the human victims and attackers, as well as the extent of the damage poor system design choices can have. Here we describe our approach to investigating both users' perceptions of these threats, along with the true extent of the damage they might cause.

2. RELATED WORK

Much work has been done documenting how cyber criminals monetize account credentials and in what volumes they are able to do so. Thomas and Martin[4] documented the diverse and specialized systems that cyber criminals use for buying, selling and monetizing a wide variety of stolen pieces of information, including online credentials. Similarly, Franklin et al[5] measured the types of information bought and sold on black market forums. They found that that the majority of traded data related to credit cards, with less than 1 percent of data being username / password values.

Others have found that the underground market for account credentials is not as active as had been previously claimed. In investigating who bore the greatest burden from financial cyber crime, Florencio and Herley [4] found that while forums were active with offers to buy and sell stolen credentials, the actual number of documented completed trades was very low, and advertised prices were heavily discounted, possibly indicating a difficulty in monetizing stolen credentials.

Other work has been done into how cyber criminals are able to acquire the account credentials they hope to monitize. Moore and Clayton[9] found that between 280,000 and 560,000 individuals have credentials stolen through phishing attacks each year, and the FBI has documented the millions of dollars stolen through credentials stolen from the Zeus Botnet[3] from [1]. Krebs [8] also found that criminals extract passwords and other account credentials where possible from breached machines. Holz et al. [6] point out that credentials are also commonly stolen from shared machines and public terminals, where many people input their credentials into a malicious devices.

3. METHODOLOGY

To evaluate credential based account escalation, we built a prototype "account theft audit" tool. The operation of our tool has been approved by the IRB of our institution. As it appears to the user, our tool provides an analysis of their personal email accounts and gives them feedback, both on how much those accounts are reported to be worth on the cybercriminal underground, as well as which accounts might be easily accessed via an attacker who gains access to their primary email account.

To build our prototype, we combined three components: first, we gather empirical information about how much access to different accounts is worth to cybercriminals. Then, we performed a survey of many popular web properties to create signatures for both their welcome email messages and

their password reset policies. Finally, we combine these information sources in our account theft audit tool through a web application. This process is a win-win for users and researchers, as users get immediate feedback about the security and value of their account, and we gain another data point regarding how prevalent risk due to credential based privilege escalation is on the web.

3.1 Underground Value

Assessing value in underground markets is a difficult proposition: by their very nature, successful underground markets shield their participants and their no doubt illegal activities from view. Even so, cybercrime researchers have been able to find price lists for several different types of accounts online [2]. While these price lists are certainly suspect, the fact that these accounts are being offered for sale when many of them can have their password reset via the email address associated with the account shows that credential based privilege escalation can allow a cybercriminal with access to a set of email accounts to amplify their earnings by selling both the email account and the accounts within it piecemeal on the cybercriminal underground.

3.2 Web Account Survey

We include the price information in the account theft audit mostly as supplementary information for the user: far more important for us is the web account survey which shows how much an attacker's access can be amplified via shared password or email-based password resets. We combined a manual analysis of English language websites which were popular hacking targets in underground markets with a list of websites that send passwords via plain text in email [10]. This information allows us to both warn a user when a shared password might be revealed to an attacker via a password reminder email, and when an attacker could amplify their access via a password reset request to a compromised email account.

3.3 Web Tool Prototype

Finally, we combine these information sources with a web-based email account analysis platform of our own design. For a previous project, we built an infrastructure which allows users to opt in to a web based experiment which gives our server temporary access to a subset of the capabilities of their Google account - specifically, their Gmail account. Importantly, this access is explicitly temporary, does not include any knowledge of the credentials needed to log in to the account, and can be revoked by the user immediately via a Google web page if they so choose (rather than being mediated by our server).

Our prototype performs a series of searches against their gmail account for messages sent from a list of popular or insecure web accounts. The prototype can scan a gmail account with over 4 gigabytes of email for these accounts in under 45 seconds, and gives the user instant feedback about both the progress of the scan and progressively adds new accounts to the report as they are found.

4. PRELIMINARY RESULTS

Through our underground market reconnaissance we have pricing information on seven different accounts, and we track account existence for 1,475 accounts. We've had 9,026 users try the service and opt in to having their information included in the study.

From the data we have collected, the average account price is \$14.17, and the maximum account price seen was \$40.05. While these prices are most likely not completely accurate in the cybercriminal underground, this average shows that several of the tracked accounts are very popular with both cybercriminals and users of our tool, showing that vulnerability to credential based privilege escalation is quite common among our study participants.

While we only have limited results now, we wish to explore several other angles to this problem which we present next in Section 5.

5. FUTURE WORK

Our prototype is currently deployed and actively collecting data. However, we have several angles we wish to explore in this space using this study and tool. While our current approach focuses on the extent to which credential based privilege escalation enables access amplification for cyber-criminals, the human component is just as interesting: can an account theft audit tool, which gives users an extremely personal reminder of both how important their email account is, improve security by giving users a "teachable moment" about protecting their accounts? Exploring this hypothesis via either value to cybercriminals or other proxies for account value like number of messages, account age, or number of accounts created via this email address might enable service providers to impress better security practices on their users.

Our current model of privilege escalation is built around password reset via email and plaintext passwords, either those stored in the account, or those sent by poorly implemented services. As seen in both the Mat Honan example and the August 2014 iCloud photo compromise, many other vectors exist for privilege escalation via social or technical means - in the Honan example it was social engineering using credit card number fragments, and in the iCloud example, one likely culprit was a non-rate-limited security question prompt for account reset.

These two privilege escalation angles each present new challenges: in the first example, evaluating the ease with which an attacker can socially engineer a customer service representative would allow us to form a more complete model of what a motivated but non-expert cybercriminal would be able to accomplish. In the second example, a more complete model of how to take over an account, beyond simple password reset via email, must be considered as well. Understanding each of these attack vectors will bring us closer to a more systematic and complete understanding how cybercriminals perform account takeover.

6. REFERENCES

[1] ANDERSON, R., BARTON, C., BÖHME, R., CLAYTON, R., VAN EETEN, M., LEVI, M., MOORE, T., AND SAVAGE, S. Measuring the cost of cybercrime. In *WEIS* (2012).

[2] DANCHEV, D. Hacked origin, uplay, hulu plus, netflix, spotify, skype, twitter, instagram, tumblr, freelancer accounts offered for sale. http://www.webroot.com/blog/2013/06/07/hacked-origin-uplay-hulu-plus-netflix-spotify-skype-twitter-instagram-tumblr-freelancer-accounts-offered-for-sale/, 2013.

[3] FEDERAL BUREAU OF INVESTIGATION. International cooperation disrupts multi-country cyber theft ring. http://www.fbi.gov/news/pressrel/press-releases/international-cooperation-disrupts-multi-country-cyber-theft-ring, October 2010.

[4] FLORENCIO, D., AND HERLEY, C. Is everything we know about password stealing wrong? *Security & Privacy, IEEE 10*, 6 (2012), 63–69.

[5] FRANKLIN, J., PERRIG, A., PAXSON, V., AND SAVAGE, S. An inquiry into the nature and causes of the wealth of internet miscreants. In *ACM conference on Computer and communications security* (2007), pp. 375–388.

[6] HOLZ, T., ENGELBERTH, M., AND FREILING, F. *Learning more about the underground economy: A case-study of keyloggers and dropzones.* Springer, 2009.

[7] HONAN, M. How apple and amazon security flaws led to my epic hacking. http://www.wired.com/2012/08/apple-amazon-mat-honan-hacking/all/, Aug 2012.

[8] KREBS, B. The scrap value of a hacked pc. http://voices.washingtonpost.com/securityfix/2009/05/the_scrap_value_of_a_hacked_pc.html, May 2009.

[9] MOORE, T., AND CLAYTON, R. Examining the impact of website take-down on phishing. In *Proceedings of the anti-phishing working groups 2nd annual eCrime researchers summit* (2007), ACM, pp. 1–13.

[10] VAN KLOETEN, O., AND TABACHNIK, I. Plain text offenders. http://plaintextoffenders.com/, 2012.

Toward De-Anonymizing Bitcoin by Mapping Users Location

Jules Dupont, Anna C Squicciarini
College of Information Sciences and Technology
Pennsylvania State University
asquicciarini@ist.psu.edu, jnd5183@psu.edu

ABSTRACT

The Bitcoin system (https://bitcoin.org) is a pseudo- anony-mous currency that can dissociate a user from any real-world identity. In that context, a successful breach of the virtual and physical divide represents a significant flaw in the Bit-coin system [1]. In this project we demonstrate how to glean information about the real-world users behind Bitcoin trans-actions. We analyze publicly available data about the cryp-tocurrency. In particular, we focus on determining informa-tion about a Bitcoin user's physical location by examining that user's spending habits.

1. ANONYMITY IN BITCOIN

Bitcoin is a cryptocurrency system designed so that users can make transactions and hold money with zero trust in any third-party organizations. In current financial systems, users must trust certain entities. For example, anyone using US dollars must trust that the Federal Reserve will act re-sponsibly and in their best interest; such trust can be prob-lematic because Federal Reserve policies are often contro-versial and tend to favor certain groups. In recent years, for instance, people who save money have been hurt by the Fed's decision to keep interest rates low.

In response to issues of trust, Bitcoin has emerged as a cryptocurrency that uses asymmetric cryptography to estab-lish ownership of funds and proof-of-work to prevent double-spending [3]. The backbone of Bitcoin is a peer-to-peer net-work that maintains a history of all transactions ever made with Bitcoin. The set of all transaction history is called the blockchain, and it is used to verify the validity of transac-tions.

Users of Bitcoin can hold funds in one or more Bitcoin addresses. Each address is secured by a cryptographic pass-word, and users can generate as many or as few addresses as desired. Addresses are not linked to a real-world iden-tity unless a user explicitly publishes information about the address.

CODASPY'15, March 2–4, 2015, San Antonio, Texas, USA.
ACM 978-1-4503-3191-3/15/03.
http://dx.doi.org/10.1145/2699026.2699128.

In order for one user to send funds to another, the sender of the funds broadcasts news of the transaction across the Bitcoin peer-to-peer network. The sender stamps the trans-action with a digital signature that arises from the crypto-graphic password securing an address; in this way, the sender proves ownership of the funds involved in the transaction. Then, nodes called "miners" compare the broadcasted trans-action to the existing transaction history. These "miners" ensure that senders cannot double-spend funds. Miners are rewarded for their efforts with transaction fees and newly generated coins from the network.

The exact functioning of the Bitcoin network is omitted from this discussion as it is not required for the purpose of this project. Whenever funds are transferred from one Bitcoin address to another, the Bitcoin system records the transaction in a public ledger called the blockchain; recorded information includes the sending address, the receiving ad-dress, the amount transferred, and the time of the trans-action. Anyone with an Internet connection can access the block chain and all of the information it contains. Addi-tionally, transactions can have multiple inputs and multiple outputs (i.e., a receiver can split funds into multiple different addresses).

2. DATA COLLECTION PROCESS

2.1 Bitcoin Blockchain

To build a reliable dataset, we downloaded the Bitcoin blockchain covering January 3, 2009 to March 31, 2014. At that point in time, the blockchain included 41,099,115 trans-actions involving 38,886,789 Bitcoin addresses.

We processed the blockchain to determine whether any Bitcoin addresses had common owners. As described above, a user can own many Bitcoin addresses. Additionally, users can use multiple addresses as inputs to a single transaction. However, as discussed by Meiklejohn [2], almost all trans-actions with multiple inputs are created by a single user; therefore, if transaction 1 has addresses A and B as inputs, we can assume that A and B have a common owner. Addi-tionally, if transaction 2 has addresses B and C as inputs, we can assume that A, B, and C all have a common owner. By applying this line of reasoning to the blockchain we down-loaded, we condense the 38,886,789 addresses involved to 17,472,156 owners.

2.2 Determining Ground Truth Data

To obtain some ground-truth data, we also collected data about the physical location of the owners of certain Bitcoin

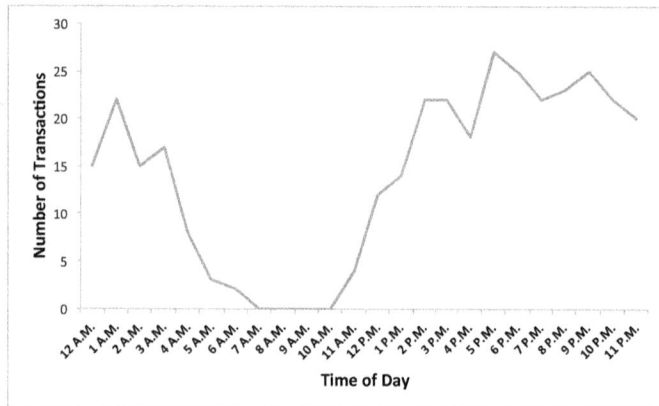

Figure 1: The time of day of a Bitcoin user's purchases, reported with the network's timezone (UTC 0).

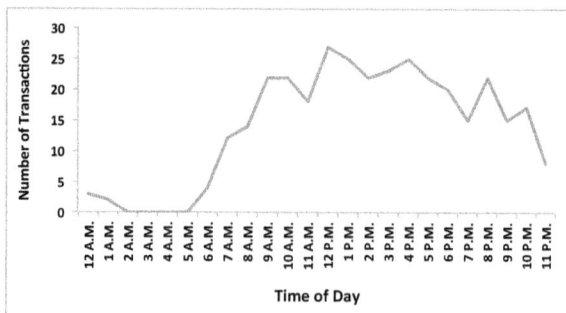

Figure 2: The time of day of a Bitcoin user's purchases, reported at the user's true local time (UTC -5).

addresses. Because charities must publish a Bitcoin address in order to accept donations, we were able to find the locations of a few "brick-and-mortar" organizations. In addition, we collected data from the public user profile pages at bitcointalk.org, one of the most popular online forums for Bitcoin users. Bitcointalk profiles give users the option of listing a real-world location and a Bitcoin address, which gave us a way of linking addresses to physical location. We found a total of 1, 800 addresses with known location data. However, not all of those addresses were suitable for our purposes. 362 had physical locations that spanned multiple timezones (e.g., a Bitcointalk user lists his location as "United States"); our algorithm focused heavily on timezones, so this data was not appropriate for our uses. Of the remaining 1438 addresses, only 518 had been used as inputs to 6 or more transactions, which was the minimum transaction history necessary for analysis.

Upon identifying the 518 addresses with appropriate physical locations and transaction history, we matched each address to the timezone of its physical location. We denoted timezones with UTC offsets, which specifies the difference in time between a certain place and UTC (Coordinated Universal Time). For example, anyone living in Eastern Standard Time on the East Coast of the US lives at a UTC offset of -5 hours during the winter, because the East Coast is 5 hours behind UTC. Because the US observes Daylight Savings Time, the UTC offset for the East Coast changes to -4 during the summer. For any locations that observe Daylight Savings Time, we recorded the UTC offset when Daylight Savings Time was not in effect.

In all, 39 UTC offsets are in use around the world, ranging from UTC -12 to UTC + 14. Certain countries have offsets of quarter-hours, such as Venezuela, which is 4 and a half hours behind UTC.

3. MAPPING BITCOIN ADDRESSES TO GEOGRAPHIC LOCATIONS

3.1 Premise

As a stepping stone towards a granular determination of location of bitcoin users, we decided to create a means for identifying the timezone of residence of Bitcoin users. Be-

cause timezones are inherently related to physical location, identifying the timezone of a Bitcoin user provides some insight about location and represents a first step towards a more precise assessment of geographic location.

The fundamental premise of our project is that people have different spending habits at different times of the day. For example, most people do not carry out financial transactions at 4 A.M., because most people are asleep at the time; conversely, most people are awake and spend money in the late afternoon [4].

Additionally, 4 A.M. in China is different from 4 A.M. in New York City. Therefore, we can expect the transaction history of a Bitcoin user to vary depending on the timezone of that user. By analyzing the times of day at which a user has made transactions, we can therefore make an informed guess as to that user's timezone of residence.

Of course, this approach is probabilistic in nature, and there will be exceptions to our premise. For example, individuals working a night-shift will probably be much more likely to spend money at night. However, our results show that our premise is still highly applicable to the users in our ground-truth data.

3.2 Methodology

To start, we consider all transactions that a given Bitcoin user provided an input for; we ignore transactions in which a user participates as a receiver because users can receive money without being actively involved in a transaction (e.g., while asleep). The blockchain records all times at UTC, without any offset.

Upon selecting all transactions to which a user was an input, we create a histogram of the times of day at which a user acted as an input to a transaction. As an example, consider Figure 1, which shows the times of day that one particular Bitcoin user engaged in transactions. Because the blockchain records times in UTC 0, the times of day are implausible. For example, the histogram would suggest that the user never made any purchases between 7 A.M. and 10 A.M., but made 15 purchases at 4 A.M. While such a set of spending habits is possible, it is improbable given normal human behavior.

Because we suspect that the histogram does not show the correct UTC offset for this Bitcoin user, we try to guess alternate offsets that are more consistent with the available evidence. Our algorithm for determining the correct offset has several steps:

First, we produce a range of possible UTC offsets by finding the 1-hour window within the histogram that has the least number of purchases. If multiple 1-hour windows have an equally low number of purchases, then we select all of the windows. In Figure 1, the results of this step would be the set {7 A.M., 8 A.M., 9 A.M., 10 A.M}. Then, we assume that the 1-hour window corresponds to 5 A.M. in the Bitcoin user's local time, and generate a list of UTC offsets that convert the 1-hour window at UTC 0 to 5 A.M. local time. For example, one of the 1-hour windows for Figure 1 is 7 A.M. In order for 7 A.M. at UTC 0 to equal 5 A.M. in local time, the UTC offset from local time would have to be UTC -2. The result of this step is a set of possible UTC offsets; any offset in the range could be a plausible time zone for the Bitcoin user. Next, we narrow down the set by eliminating offsets. Our approach is to treat each possible offset as a hypothesis, and see how consistent it is with existing evidence. If the hypothesis is inconsistent, it is discarded from the range.

To this date, we have developed two tests for consistency: analysis of half-days, and analysis of early morning.

The analysis of half-days method relies on the premise that most individuals will make more purchases between noon and midnight than between midnight and noon. Such a premise is implicitly plausible because the typical individual has more waking hours between noon and midnight than midnight and noon. When testing an offset for consistency with this premise, we assume that the offset is the user's local time. Based on that assumption, we can divide the day into two halves. If the noon to midnight half has substantially fewer purchases than the midnight to noon half, the current offset is inconsistent with available evidence of the user's behavior, and so it should be discarded from the set.

The analysis of early morning method is based on the idea that most people do not make many purchases in the early morning hours. Specifically, we assume that purchases made between 4 A.M. and 6 A.M. should constitute only a small percentage of the purchases that a user makes over the course of a day. To test an offset for consistency with this assumption, we again assume that the offset is the user's local time. Then, we use that assumption to determine the number of purchases made between 4 A.M and 6 A.M. If the percentage is too high, the offset is inconsistent, and is discarded from the set.

Upon having tested all offsets within the set, we obtain at a set of UTC offsets that are representative of the user's local time. Our ongoing work focuses on narrowing the set of timezones further and selecting one best guess from the set.

3.3 Initial Results

In order to asses the accuracy of the algorithm discussed above, we run it over our ground-truth data. For each Bitcoin address in the data, we determine a set of possible UTC offsets. If the address's true UTC offset is in the set, we count that guess as accurate; if the true offset is not in the set, then the guess is wrong.

Our best results show 72% accuracy with an average of 11 UTC offsets per guess set. Because there are 39 possible UTC offsets, the expected outcome of random guessing is only $\frac{11}{39} \approx 28\%$. Therefore, our current algorithm is more than twice as effective as random guessing. As we continue to refine the algorithm by narrowing the guess set produced, we anticipate the advantage over random guessing to increase significantly.

4. DISCUSSION

Our current results demonstrate that a Bitcoin user's participation in purchases provides some information about that user's physical location. Even though our current indicator of location is not specific, it is a first step towards extracting significant information from the pseudonymous blockchain. More importantly, timezone can be refined into a more relevant indicator of physical location, such as a Bitcoin user's country of residence.

In this respect, we are currently working on improving our algorithm for guessing timezones. So far, our refinements to the algorithm have involved adding consistency tests to the second step described above. More consistency tests will help create narrower sets with comparable accuracy. Once we have achieved relatively small sets, we will also work on selecting one best-guess from the set of possibilities.

Once we are satisfied with our algorithm for guessing timezones, we will translate timezones into a better indicator of geographic location, such as a Bitcoin user's country of residence. Some timezones are intrinsically linked to a particular country (e.g., UTC -4:30 is used only by Venezuela). Even if a Bitcoin user is in a timezone used by multiple countries, determining a country of residence is still possible because of differences in timezone implementation across countries. For example, many countries have different implementations of Daylight Savings Time (DST), ranging from not using DST at all to switching at different periods of the year By seeing which implementation of DST is most consistent with a user's spending habits, we can determine the user's most likely country of residence.

5. ACKNOWLEDGEMENT

Portions this work were supported by the Army Research Office under grant W911NF-13-1-0271.

6. REFERENCES

[1] J. Bohr and M. Bashir. Who uses bitcoin? an exploration of the bitcoin community. In *Privacy, Security and Trust (PST), 2014 Twelfth Annual International Conference on*, pages 94–101. IEEE, 2014.

[2] S. Meiklejohn, M. Pomarole, G. Jordan, K. Levchenko, D. McCoy, G. M. Voelker, and S. Savage. A fistful of bitcoins: characterizing payments among men with no names. In *Proceedings of the 2013 conference on Internet measurement conference*, pages 127–140. ACM, 2013.

[3] S. Nakamoto. Bitcoin: A peer-to-peer electronic cash system. *Consulted*, 1(2012):28, 2008.

[4] PWC. Online shopping habits, survey, 2014. http://www.pwc.com/gx/en/retail-consumer/retail-consumer-publications/global-multi-channel-consumer-survey/index.jhtml.

Epidemic Behavior of Negative Users in Online Social Sites

Cong Liao
Pennsylvania State University
University Park, PA
cxl491@psu.edu

Anna Squicciarini
Pennsylvania State University
University Park, PA
acs20@psu.edu

Christopher Griffin
Pennsylvania State University
University Park, PA
griffinch@psu.edu

ABSTRACT

With the increasing popularity of user-contributed sites, the phenomenon of "social" pollution, the presence of abusive posts has become increasingly prevalent. In this paper, we describe a novel approach to explain and predict negative behavior spreading dynamics in online social networks by using well-known epidemic models. We show how using pure and hybrid models, it is possible not only to explain the phenomenon of abusiveness in certain online commentaries, but also that it is possible to predict these behavioral patterns with properly defined hybrid models. We summarize our results on a large set of experiments on Youtube commentaries, and show how the different epidemic patterns of behavior are tied to specific interaction patterns among users.

1. INTRODUCTION

"Social" pollution, the presence of abusive or deceptive posts (generated from spammers, trolls or disgruntled users) in online, user-contributed sites, has become increasingly prevalent (e.g. [3]). Depending on the specific environment, these polluting posts may appear in the form of trolling, flaming, harassment, threats trolling, multiple accounts (cybil), shared accounts, advertising, plagiarism etc. Regardless of their character, negative behavior influences others' perspective of the community, leading to a possibly quick decay of the overall users' experience and feelings for the community.

Despite a significant amount of work on detection of social spammers, collective attention spam [6, 8, 5, 4, 7], and online vandalism, the dynamics underlying online abusive behavior remain uncertain. Toward developing a better understanding of social pollution, in this paper, we aim to build mathematical models to explain how negative comments online actually spread on large scale social networks. Our context presents several unique challenges, including the detection and labeling of negative comments, the subtle influence users may have on one another, and the possible unpredictable patterns certain users may display, which is always less systematic than an automated spammer agent. To the best of our knowledge, we are not aware of any research efforts adopting epidemic models to explain the spreading of online abusive behavior.

We specifically investigate how a Youtube commentary can be described by using well-known deterministic models for infectious diseases. The adopted deterministic models are simple enough to be operationally useful and can also help us identify persistent and common characteristics of particular classes of videos. Further, we use epidemic dynamics as predictive models, and analyze them using econometric principles in which a model is fit with all data and the next data point predicted. Using this approach, we observe a very highly accurate forecasting capability for empirical spreading dynamics. In addition, we observe clustering of model parameters in our forecasting approach suggesting *hybrid models* may be appropriate for better modeling spreading dynamics. We illustrate such hybrid models for a subset of our data.

Our experiments, carried out on a large, real world, Youtube dataset demonstrate that these dynamics exist, although more complex than a basic model can efficiently describe. Rather, hybrid models determined identified using econometric forecasting methods can be used to efficiently capture these dynamics, allowing not only to explain the trend of certain commentaries but also enabling prediction, and anticipate possible bursts of negative content on a given commentary. The results obtained from this study help us gain an understanding of information pollution dynamics on online user-contributed sites.

2. APPROACH

Typical online social network systems share similar characteristics, e.g., information posted online, whether positive or negative, can be influential and certain users are prone to be affected by abusive contents while others don't, which highlight some similarities between the spread of diseases and viruses and "negative" opinions spread over online social sites. Accordingly, we hypothesize that an epidemic model may appropriately describe the system behaviors.

2.1 Epidemic Model

We model users' behaviors according to an epidemic model. Users in the system are initially considered as *susceptible* since they bear the risk of being affected by negative source inside the system. Those who are later exposed to negative information are denoted as *exposed*. Certain *infected* users

CODASPY'15, March 2–4, 2015, San Antonio, Texas, USA.
ACM 978-1-4503-3191-3/15/03.
http://dx.doi.org/10.1145/2699026.2699129.

would spread negative content in the system. The exposed users who later join or endorse such abusive behaviors also become infected. However, some exposed users who remain unaffected or act against it are *immune*. The above process is illustrated in Figure 1.

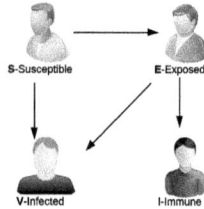

Figure 1: Epidemic Model and State Transition

The state of an individual user is dynamically changing given his behaviors over time, thus the total number of susceptible $S(t)$, exposed $E(t)$, infected $V(t)$ and immune $I(t)$ users also evolve accordingly. The dynamics of the whole system can be expressed in terms of the following differential equations:

$$dS/dt = -\lambda_p p_n S - \lambda_r p_n SV \qquad (1)$$
$$dE/dt = \lambda_r p_n SV - \lambda_p E \qquad (2)$$
$$dV/dt = \lambda_p p_n S + \lambda_p p_n E \qquad (3)$$
$$dI/dt = \lambda_p (1 - p_n) E \qquad (4)$$

where λ_p is Average posting rate by users, p_n average reading rate by users, λ_p is average probability of content posted by a user being negative.

3. EMPIRICAL ANALYSIS

3.1 Data Set

We use a data set inclusive of 800 YouTube videos, each with approximately 500 comments. For each video, the dataset provides detailed information such as unique movie id, title, data, tag names, rating, number of comments etc. With regard to each comment, information about its content, sender id, rating, etc. is included.

First, we identify abusive behaviors by labeling the comments as *positive*, *neutral* or *negative*, according to the following criteria: 1) rating score of a comment, 2) ratio of abusive terms in a comment, 3) sentimental analysis using AlchemyAPI tool [1]. We combine three labeling approaches together, to achieve a reliable classification with adequate accuracy.

Then, for each commentary, we use the labeled comments to identify users' states and their state transitions described by the model in Section 2.1. In our analysis, we discretize "time" based on comment frequency instead of clock time unit like hours for two reasons: 1) video comments display a sporadic posting time pattern and may span a long periods, 2) it matters a comments is read and visible by incoming users rather than how much earlier it is posted. We set a time epoch of 10 and update users' state status every 10 comments with the following criteria. Initially, all users are in susceptible state S. A user is moved into exposed state E if commenting a either neutral or positive comment, and the prior ten posts have at least five negative comments. A user is labeled as infected V once posting a negative comment. Finally, an immune user kept posting non-negative

comments after being exposed. We keep track of the total number of S, E, V, I at each time interval.

3.2 Model Fitting

A key step to evaluate whether epidemic model can effectively describe the behaviors of abusive users is to output a suitable set of parameters. We used the nonlinear least squares module in the optimization toolbox provided by MathWorks (Matlab) [2] to solve this nonlinear model fitting problem. The overall parameter selection process is displayed in Figure 2.

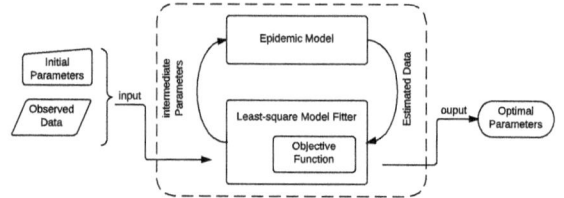

Figure 2: Parameter Selection

With the generated parameters, we applied the model to each commentary. We specifically compare estimated and observed number of infected users over time. We provide an example of model fitting to the labeled comments for a movie in Figure 3a. The fitting process for all the analyzed movies, omitted for lack of space, shows that the degree of accuracy of the yielded epidemic models to describe the abusive user behaviors differs significantly among different videos.

In particular, a higher total error is observed for Music videos; this category seems to be the least accurate category among all, whereas commentaries on Comedy are better modeled through our epidemic models. This is likely due to the nature of the comments, the videos' subject and the audience contributing to the discussion. For example music videos typically attract younger viewers, who also adopt explicit language and jargon hard to detect automatically. Comedy videos instead attract a broader audience, and comments are likely less involved and opinionated than in other categories.

3.3 Predictive Model

We also study whether our models could possibly be used for predictive purposes, i.e., given few comments on a commentary system, is it possible to predict the rate of users who will become infected and therefore will display abusive behavior. Given the inability to uniformly explain malicious behavior through a single epidemic model, we used an econometric forecasting method, that optimizes the prediction. Our methodology is as follows - upon training the model with 30% of the commentary data, we estimated the initial parameters. Next, we attempt to predict the next five time epochs in the model ($5\Delta t = 50$ comments), and compute the least squared error based on simulated and actual data. Given the predefined threshold, we either continued with the prediction for the next data points or we updated the parameters with a re-optimization on the new data. We provide one instance of the above process as shown in Figure 3b. As observed, with only one or three rounds of optimization, we obtain a drastic improvement of accuracy, compared with the fitting example of Figure 3a. The results generated from this process illustrate that the epidemic dynamic model used with an econometric forecasting approach

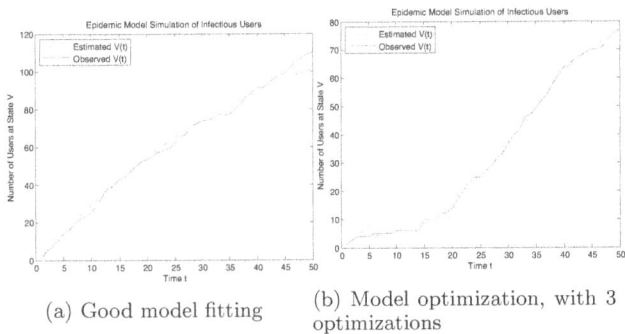

(a) Good model fitting (b) Model optimization, with 3 optimizations

Figure 3: Examples of Model Fitting and Optimization

are capable of accurately predicting future behavior of infection spread. In addition, the fact that this re-optimization approach works suggests the hybrid fitting approach, which we discuss in the sequel.

3.4 Hybrid Models

Re-optimization in the forecasting experiments implies a fitting approach with multiple epidemic models. We investigate whether such a hybrid model would be appropriate. The forecasting method generates multiple sets of parameters. Each set can be represented by a point in a 3D space. We identify a natural clustering formed around the points and each cluster corresponds to one hidden state. The overall epidemic dynamics of the system can be considered as a finite state machine, where each state is related to a epidemic model represented by the centroid of the cluster. Two examples of parameter visualization are shown in Figure 4a and Figure 4c respectively. In each figure, the temporal orders of the parameter points are labeled by a sequence of number.

Besides, the resulting examples of system modeling using hybrid model approach are presented in Figure 4b and Figure 4d. The state transitions are marked by the black stars. After each state, we explicitly compute the up-to-date R-squared (RSQ) value to evaluate the modeling process as presented in Table 1. In the first example, the RSQ value keeps increasing during state transition. While in the second example, even though we observe the effects of accumulated errors reflected by a minor decreasing of RSQ value when the system moves from the second state to the third state, the final R-squared value, compared with the one in initial state, indicates that the hybrid automata can effectively capture the overall change in epidemic dynamics.

4. CONCLUSIONS

We presented our study of abusive behavior in online user-contributed systems. We used a customized epidemic model to explain the dynamics of abusive users in these sites. Our findings indicate that, although complex, there exist significant epidemic spreading patterns in how users misbehave in these sites, and they can be properly modeled using classical and hybrid epidemic models. With the optimal model parameters, the epidemic model can be applied to explain the behaviors of infectious users.

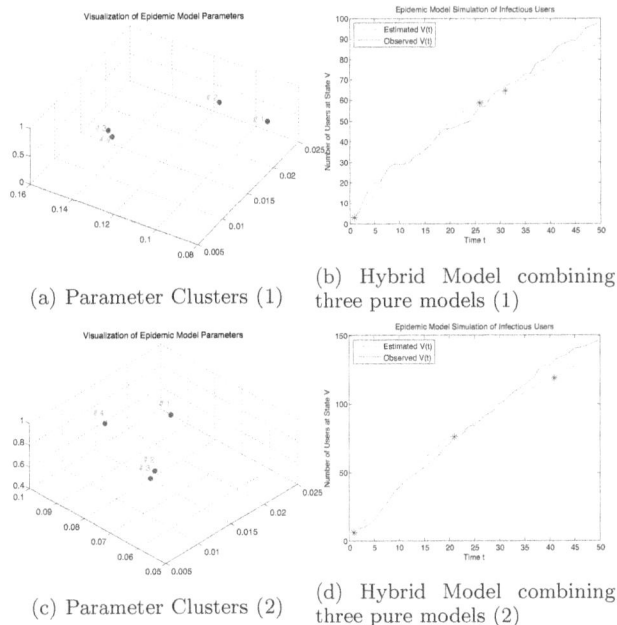

(a) Parameter Clusters (1) (b) Hybrid Model combining three pure models (1)

(c) Parameter Clusters (2) (d) Hybrid Model combining three pure models (2)

Figure 4: Parameter evolution and resulting hybrid model

State	R-squared	
	Example (1)	Example (2)
State 1	0.9226	0.7723
State 2	0.9532	0.9871
State 3	0.9607	0.9869

Table 1: Trend of R^2 Values in State Transition

5. ACKNOWLEDGEMENTS

Portions of this work were supported by the Army Research Office under grant W911NF-13-1-0271.

6. REFERENCES

[1] Alchemyapi. http://www.alchemyapi.com.
[2] lsqnonlin-mathworks. http://www.mathworks.com/help/optim/ug/lsqnonlin.html.
[3] S. L. Carty. Social networking abuse. http://socialnetworking.lovetoknow.com/Social_Networking_Abuse.
[4] X. Hu, J. Tang, Y. Zhang, and H. Liu. Social spammer detection in microblogging. In *Proceedings of the Twenty-Third International Joint Conference on Artificial Intelligence*, IJCAI'13, pages 2633–2639. AAAI Press, 2013.
[5] A. Kantchelian, J. Ma, L. Huang, S. Afroz, A. Joseph, and J. D. Tygar. Robust detection of comment spam using entropy rate. In *Proceedings of the 5th ACM Workshop on Security and Artificial Intelligence*, AISec '12, pages 59–70. ACM, 2012.
[6] K. Lee, J. Caverlee, and S. Webb. Uncovering social spammers: Social honeypots + machine learning. In *Proceedings of the 33rd International ACM SIGIR Conference on Research and Development in Information Retrieval*, SIGIR '10, pages 435–442, 2010.
[7] V. Sridharan, V. Shankar, and M. Gupta. Twitter games: How successful spammers pick targets. In *Proceedings of the 28th Annual Computer Security Applications Conference*, ACSAC '12, pages 389–398. ACM, 2012.
[8] K. Thomas, C. Grier, D. Song, and V. Paxson. Suspended accounts in retrospect: An analysis of twitter spam. In *Proceedings of the 2011 ACM SIGCOMM Conference on Internet Measurement Conference*, IMC '11, pages 243–258, New York, NY, USA, 2011. ACM.

Rapid Screening of Transformed Data Leaks with Efficient Algorithms and Parallel Computing[*]

Xiaokui Shu, Jing Zhang, Danfeng (Daphne) Yao, Wu-Chun Feng
Department of Computer Science
Virginia Tech
Blacksburg, VA, USA
{subx, zjing14, danfeng, feng}@cs.vt.edu

ABSTRACT

The leak of sensitive data on computer systems poses a serious threat to organizational security. Organizations need to identify the exposure of sensitive data by screening the content in storage and transmission, i.e., to detect sensitive information being stored or transmitted in the clear. However, detecting the exposure of sensitive information is challenging due to data transformation in the content. Transformations (such as insertion, deletion) result in highly unpredictable leak patterns. Existing automata-based string matching algorithms are impractical for detecting transformed data leaks, because of its formidable complexity when modeling the required regular expressions. We design two new algorithms for detecting long and transformed data leaks. Our system achieves high detection accuracy in recognizing transformed leaks compared to the state-of-the-art inspection methods. We parallelize our prototype on graphics processing unit and demonstrate the strong scalability of our detection solution required by a sizable organization.

Categories and Subject Descriptors

C.2.0 [**Computer-Communication Networks**]: General—*security and protection*; D.1.3 [**Programming Techniques**]: Concurrent Programming—*parallel programming*

Keywords

Data leak detection; content inspection; algorithm; sampling; alignment; dynamic programming; parallelism

1. INTRODUCTION

The number of leaked records on personal computers and organization networks increases dramatically in the last years from 95 million in 2010 to 822 million in 2013 [3]. A typical approach to minimize the exposure of sensitive data is to identify all occurrences of cleartext sensitive data in storages or communications. The detection system alerts administrators of any sensitive data exposure discovered in file systems or supervised network channels. Leaks can then be identified according to the sensitive data storage and sharing policy. Different from pattern matching techniques employed in anti-virus and intrusion detection systems, data leak detection imposes new security requirements and algorithmic challenges:

1. *Data transformation.* The exposed data in the content may be transformed or modified by users or applications, so it may no longer be identical to the original sensitive data, e.g., insertions of metadata or formatting tags, substitutions of characters, and data truncation. Thus, the detection algorithm needs to recognize variations of sensitive data patterns.

2. *Scalability.* The heavy workload of data leak screening is due to *long sensitive data patterns* and the *large amount of content*. Sensitive data (e.g., documents, source code) can be of arbitrary length (e.g., megabytes). Some types of contents may need to be scanned in a timely manner (e.g., traffic scanning).

Automata-based string matching are widely used in anti-virus and network intrusion detection systems (NIDS) where the patterns to search for are static or can be characterized by regular expressions [1]. Automata are not designed to support unpredictable and arbitrary pattern variations. In data leak detection scenarios, the transformation of leaked data (in the description of regular expression) is unknown to the detection method. Creating comprehensive automata models covering all possible variations of a pattern is infeasible. Therefore, automata approach cannot be used for detecting long and transformed data leaks.

Existing data leak detection approaches are largely based on set intersection. Set intersection between the content fragment set and sensitive data fragment set tells the amount of sensitive data fragments appearing in the content[1]. However, set intersection is *orderless*, i.e., the order information of fragments is abandoned. Thus, set-based detection generates undesirable false alerts. In addition, set intersection cannot effectively measure the likelihood of a leak when partial data is leaked. Therefore, none of the existing techniques is adequate for detecting transformed data leaks.

The key of our solution to the detection of transformed data leaks is a new sequence alignment algorithm. *The alignment is between the sampled sensitive data sequence and the sampled content being inspected.* The alignment produces a

---

[*]This work has been supported in part by Security and Software Engineering Research Center (S²ERC), a NSF sponsored multi-university Industry/University Cooperative Research Center (I/UCRC).

CODASPY'15, March 2–4, 2015, San Antonio, Texas, USA.
ACM 978-1-4503-3191-3/15/03.
http://dx.doi.org/10.1145/2699026.2699130.

---

[1]Typical units in a set are *n*-grams of a string, which preserves local features of a string and tolerates discrepancies.

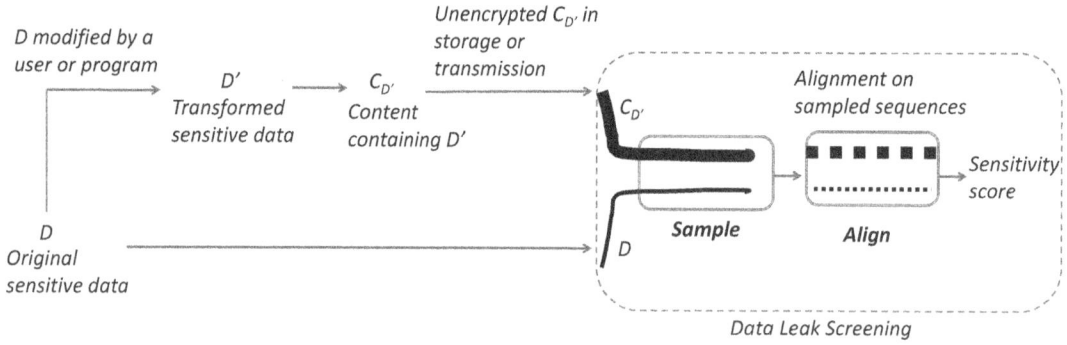

Figure 1: A schematic drawing showing the two types of sequences in our model, their relations, and the workflow of our detection.

score indicating the amount of sensitive data contained in the content. Our alignment-based solution measures the order of n-grams and handles arbitrary variations of patterns without an explicit specification of all possible variations.

In order to deal with the scalability issue, we design a pair of algorithms to perform alignment. Our solution consists of a *comparable* sampling algorithm and a *sampling oblivious* alignment algorithm. Our sampling algorithm samples both content and sensitive data sequences. It satisfies the *comparable sampling* property that the similarity of two sequences is preserved through sampling, and the samples are meaningful to be aligned. Our solution aligns sampled sequences to infer the similarity between the original sequences before sampling. The special *sampling oblivious* property differentiates our algorithm from existing ones. Experiments show that our solution achieves accurate detection with low false positive and false negative rates. It substantially outperforms set-based methods in terms of detection accuracy.

We design the pair of algorithms to be efficiently parallelized. We parallelize our prototype on a GPU, which achieves nearly 50 times of speedup over the CPU version. Our prototype reaches 400Mbps analysis throughput. This performance can support the rapid security scanning of storage and communication required by a sizable organization.

2. MODELS AND OVERVIEW

In our data leak detection model, we analyze two types of sequences: sensitive data sequence and content sequence.

- *Content sequence* is the sequence to be examined for leaks. The content may be data extracted from file systems on workstations and servers, or payloads extracted from supervised network channels[2].

- *Sensitive data sequence* is the information, e.g., proprietary documents, that needs to be protected and cannot be exposed to unauthorized parties.

Both the content and the sensitive data sequences are known to the analysis system. A data leak is detected when the detection system finds a piece of sensitive data in the content sequence (Fig. 1), but the appearance is not allowed in the sensitive data storage and sharing policy. We assume that the analysis system is secure and trustworthy. Thus, the sensitive data sequence is secure during the data leak analysis. The two assumptions can be removed when our

---

[2]Such channels are widely used for advanced NIDS where MITM (man-in-the-middle) SSL sessions are employed to handle encryption.

alignment is performed utilizing secure multi-party computation or other privacy-preserving techniques [2,4]. We do not aim at detecting stealthy data leaks that an attacker encrypt the sensitive data by herself before leaking it.

2.1 Technical Challenges

High detection specificity. In our data-leak detection model, high specificity refers to the ability to distinguish true leaks from coincidental matches, which can cause false alarms. Existing set-based detection is orderless, where the order of matched patterns (n-grams) is ignored. Orderless detection can result in false positives as shown below.

Sensitive data	abcdefg
3-grams of the sensitive data	abc, bcd, cde, def, efg
Content stream (false positive)	...efg...cde...abc...

Pervasive and localized modification. Sensitive data could be modified before it is leaked out. The modification can occur throughout a sequence (pervasive modification). The modification can also only affect a local region (local modification). We describe some modification examples:

- Character replacement, e.g., WordPress replaces every space character with a + in HTTP POST requests.
- String insertion: HTML tags inserted throughout a document for formatting or embedding objects.
- Data truncation or partial data leak, e.g., one page of a two-page sensitive document is transmitted.

2.2 Overview of Our Approach

Our work presents an efficient sequence comparison technique needed for analyzing a large amount of content for sensitive data exposure. We illustrate our workflow in Fig. 1. Our detection approach consists of a special sampling algorithm and a corresponding alignment algorithm working on preprocessed n-grams of sequences. The pair of algorithms computes a quantitative similarity score between sensitive data and content. Local alignment, as opposed to global alignment, is used to identify similar sequence segments, enabling the detection of partial data leaks.

Our workflow includes EXTRACTION, PREPROCESSING, SAMPLING, ALIGNMENT, and DECISION operations. The EXTRACTION operation collects content. The PREPROCESSING operation prepares the sequences of n-grams for both the content and sensitive data. The SAMPLING operation generates samples from both sensitive data and content sequences. The ALIGNMENT operation performs local alignment between the two sampled sequences to compute their similarity. Finally, the DECISION operation confirms and reports leaks according to the sensitive data sharing policy.

3. IMPLEMENTATION AND EVALUATION

We evaluate the accuracy of our solution with several large datasets under real-world data leak scenarios[3]. We implement a single-threaded prototype (referred to as *AlignDLD* system) and a collection intersection method as a baseline. Both systems are written in C++, compiled using g++ 4.7.1 with flag -O3. We also provide two parallel versions of our prototype for performance demonstration.

- *AlignDLD:* our sample-and-align data leak detection method with sampling parameters $N = 10$ and $|w| = 100$. 3-grams and 32-bit Rabin's fingerprints are used.
- *Coll-Inter:* a data leak detection system based on collection intersection[4], which is widely adopted by commercial tools such as GlobalVelocity and GoCloudDLP. 8-grams and 64-bit Rabin's fingerprints are used, which is standard with collection intersection.

We conduct all experiments in a virtualized network using VirtualBox. The detection system is deployed on the gateway that connects the virtual local network and the Internet. Simple leaks are performed using web and FTP file transmission. Publishing services such as WordPress modifies sensitive data when it is leaked. We test our detection system using two dataset: *A. Enron dataset* consisting of 2.6GB emails, and *B. MiscNet* consisting of 500MB Internet traffic dump with various kinds of Internet traffic.

We define the *sensitivity* $\mathbb{S} \in [0,1]$ of the content sequence in Formula 1. It indicates the similarity of sensitive data D and content $C_{D'}$ with respect to their sequences $\mathcal{S}^a$ and $\mathcal{S}^b$ after PREPROCESS. ξ is the maximum score in the alignment, and r is the reward for one-unit match in the alignment.

$$\mathbb{S} = \frac{\xi}{r \times \min\left(|\mathcal{S}^a|, |\mathcal{S}^b|\right)} \qquad (1)$$

3.1 Detecting Modified Leaks

We conduct detection accuracy experiments on three types of data leaks listed below.

1. Content without any leak, i.e., the content does not contain any sensitive data.
2. Content with unmodified leak, i.e., sensitive data appearing in the content is not modified.
3. Content with modified leaks caused by WordPress, which substitutes every space with "+" in the content.

We evaluate and compare AlignDLD and Coll-Inter. We present the distributions of all sensitivity values in Fig. 2. Both methods perform as expected in the scenarios of no-leak and unmodified leak. The solid lines in Figure 2 represent the detection results of leaks with WordPress modifications. Our AlignDLD method in Fig. 2 (a) gives much higher sensitivity scores to the transformed data leak than the Coll-Inter method. With a threshold of 0.2, **all the email messages with transformed leaks are detected and reported.** In contrast, the collection intersection method in Fig. 2 (b) has a significant overlap between messages with no leak and messages with transformed leaks. Its accuracy is much lower than that of our method, e.g., 63.8% recall and a 10 times higher false positive rate.

---

[3]We only present the most important experiments due to the limited space.
[4]Set and collection intersections are used interchangeably.

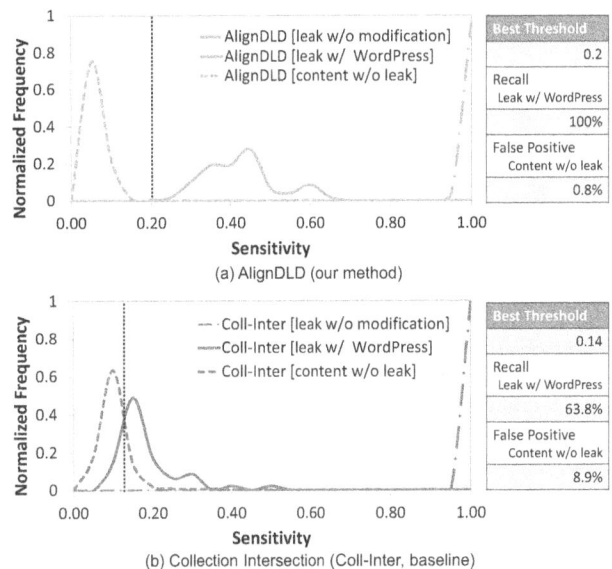

(a) AlignDLD (our method)

(b) Collection Intersection (Coll-Inter, baseline)

Figure 2: Detection comparison of leak through WordPress using AlignDLD (a) and Coll-Inter (b).

3.2 Parallelization and Scalability

In order to achieve high analysis throughput, we parallelize our algorithms on CPU as well as on general-purpose GPU platforms. The multithreaded CPU version is written in C, compiled using gcc 4.4.5 with flag -O2. The GPU version is written in CUDA compiled using CUDA 4.2 with flag -O2 -arch sm 20 and NVIDIA driver v295.41. We deploy our prototypes on a hybrid CPU-GPU machine equipped with an Intel Core i5 2400 and an NVIDIA Tesla C2050 GPU (Fermi architecture with 448 GPU cores).

Our GPU detection prototype achieves over 40 times of speedup over the CPU version on both content datasets. The prototype achieves a throughput of over 400Mbps against dataset B. This throughput is comparable to that of a moderate commercial firewall.

4. CONCLUSIONS

Despite the commercial success of data leak software and appliances, existing solutions based on set intersection have serious security drawbacks. We present new and sophisticated alignment-based algorithms to improve the accuracy detecting data leaks, e.g., high specificity (i.e., low false alarm rate). Our extensive experimental evaluations with real-world data and leak scenarios confirm that our method has much higher precision in detecting transformed data leaks than the state-of-the-art set intersection method.

5. REFERENCES

[1] A. V. Aho and M. J. Corasick. Efficient string matching: An aid to bibliographic search. *Commun. ACM*, 18(6):333–340, 1975.
[2] F. Liu, X. Shu, D. Yao, and A. R. Butt. Privacy-preserving scanning of big content for sensitive data exposure with MapReduce. In *Proceedings of ACM CODASPY*, 2015.
[3] RiskBasedSecurity. Data breach quickview: An executive's guide to 2013 data breach trends, Feb 2014.
[4] X. Shu and D. Yao. Data leak detection as a service. In *Proceedings of SecureComm*, 2012.

Information Sharing and User Privacy in the Third-party Identity Management Landscape

Anna Vapen[†]   Niklas Carlsson[†]   Anirban Mahanti[‡]   Nahid Shahmehri[†]
[†] Linköping University, Sweden, firstname.lastname@liu.se
[‡] NICTA, Australia, anirban.mahanti@nicta.com.au

ABSTRACT

Third-party identity management services enable cross-site information sharing, making Web access seamless but also raise significant privacy implications for the users. Using a combination of manual analysis of identified third-party identity management relationships and targeted case studies we capture how the protocol usage and third-party selection is changing, profile what information is requested to be shared (and actions to be performed) between websites, and identify privacy issues and practical problems that occur when using multiple accounts (associated with these services). The study highlights differences in the privacy leakage risks associated with different classes of websites, and shows that the use of multiple third-party websites, in many cases, can cause the user to lose (at least) partial control over which information is shared/posted on their behalf.

Categories and Subject Descriptors

K.6.5 [**Management of Computing and Information Systems**]: Security and Protection

Keywords

Third-party Identity Management; Cross-site Information Sharing; User Privacy

1. INTRODUCTION

Many popular web services, such as Facebook, Twitter, and Google, rely heavily on their large number of active users and the rich data and personal information these users create or provide. In addition to monetizing the high service usage and personal information, the rich user information can also be used to provide personalized and customized user experiences that add value for their users. Therefore, many other websites are partnering with these companies, often using third-party single sign-on (SSO) [1, 2] services provided by these and other popular websites.

CODASPY'15, March 2–4, 2015, San Antonio, Texas, USA.
ACM 978-1-4503-3191-3/15/03.
http://dx.doi.org/10.1145/2699026.2699131.

With SSO, a website such as Soundcloud will partner with one or more other third-party websites (e.g., Facebook and Google), which will be responsible for user authentication on behalf of Soundcloud. In this scenario, Soundcloud is referred to as a relying party (RP) and Facebook/Google is referred to as a third-party identity provider (IDP).

In addition to providing an authentication service, at the time of account creation or first login, the user is typically asked to approve an app-right agreement between the user and the RP, which (i) gives permission to the RP to read information from the user's IDP account, and (ii) authorizes the RP to perform certain actions on the IDP, such as posting information. Such permissions also place great responsibility on the RPs, and can raise significant privacy concerns for users.

The paper makes three primary contributions. First, we present a high-level characterization of the protocol and IDP usage observed in the wild (Section 2). Second, we characterize the cross-site information sharing and authorized app-rights associated with the most popular IDPs (Section 3). Third, we use targeted login and account creation tests to analyze the information sharing in scenarios in which the users have accounts with multiple IDPs (Section 4). For a complete description of our methodology, contributions, and a discussion of the above results we refer to our full paper [3]. Here, we briefly describe some high-level results.

2. PROTOCOL AND IDP SELECTION

Today's RP-IDP relationships are typically implemented using OpenID or OAuth. While OpenID was designed purely for authentication and OAuth primarily is an authorization protocol, both protocols provide an SSO service that allows the user to access the RP by authenticating with the IDP without needing local RP credentials. With OAuth, a local RP account is always linked with the user's IDP account (even though the user must not remember any such account information later), allowing information sharing between the RP and IDP. Local RP accounts are optional with OpenID.

For our analysis, we primarily focus on all RP-IDP relationships that we have manually identified on the 200 most popular websites on the Web, but will also leverage the 3,203 unique RP-IDP relationships (3,329 before removing false positives) identified using our custom designed Selenium-based crawling tool [4].

OAuth is the dominant protocol as observed in both manual and crawled datasets. For example, in Apr. 2012, 121 of 180 (67%) relationships in the manual dataset and 2,543 of 3,203 (79%) relationships in the crawled dataset are directly classified as OAuth, compared to only 20 (11%) and 180 (6%) as OpenID relationships in the two datasets. Of the remaining relationships, 39 and 441 used an IDP that supports both OpenID and OAuth. Since then, as measured in Sept. 2014, we have seen a further increase of OAuth usage (+24%) and drop in OpenID usage (-10%) among the top-200 websites.

We have found that IDP selection differs significantly depending on how many IDPs an RP selects, and some IDPs are more likely to be selected together with other IDPs. In total the top-5 ranked IDPs are responsible for 92% (33 of 36) and 90% (1,111 of 1,233) of the relationships of RPs selecting one single IDP. For RPs with 2-3 IDPs, 83% and 75% of the relationships are to the top-5, but for RPs with 4 or more IDPs only 38% and 55% are to IDPs ranked in the top-5. Facebook+Twitter is the most popular pairing with 37% (125 of 335) of all IDP pairs, Chinese QQ+Sina placing second (19%), and Facebook+Google third (12%).

3. APP RIGHTS AND INFORMATION FLOWS

We carefully recorded the app-right agreements for the RP-IDP relationships identified in the manual top-200 dataset. The app-right agreements reveal (i) the information that the RP *will obtain* from the IDP, and (ii) the actions the RP *will be allowed* to perform on the IDP, on behalf of the user.

3.1 Classification of Information

When analyzing the APIs of the three major IDPs (Facebook, Twitter and Google) and the actual app-right usage in our datasets, we have identified five different types of app rights, each with their own privacy implications. The first four classes (B, P, C, F) capture data transferred from the IDP to the RP. Class A includes actions being performed by the RP, on the IDP, on behalf of the user.

- **Basic information (B):** Relatively non-private information that the user is often asked to provide websites. This class includes unique identifiers (e.g., user name, id, or email address) to identify existing accounts, age range, language, and public user profile information.

- **Personal information (P):** This class includes personal information common in many basic "bundles" (e.g., gender, country, time zone, and friend list), but also more sensitive information such as political views, religion, and sexual orientation.

- **Created content (C):** This class contains content directly or indirectly created by the user (e.g., images, likes, and check-in history).

- **Friends' information (F):** This class consists of data of other potentially non-consenting users (e.g., friends).

- **Actions taken on behalf of the user (A):** This final class includes the right for the RP to perform *actions* on behalf of the user on the IDP. This include, for example, the right to post information about the user's actions on the RP (e.g., sharing music the user has listened to) on the user's IDP timeline.

3.2 Risk Types

Today, many IDPs bundle the information requested into larger "bundles", and RPs must select which bundle to present

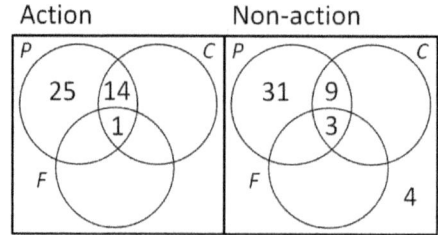

Figure 1: Number of RP-IDP relationships of different app-right types in the top-200 dataset.

Table 1: Risk types identified in dataset.

Risk type	Class combination	Risk type	Class combination
$\mathcal{A}^-$	$A \cap B$	$\overline{\mathcal{A}}^-$	$\neg A \cap B$
$\mathcal{A}$	$A \cap P$	$\overline{\mathcal{A}}$	$\neg A \cap P$
$\mathcal{A}^+$	$A \cap P \cap C$	$\overline{\mathcal{A}}^+$	$\neg A \cap P \cap C$
$\mathcal{A}^{++}$	$A \cap P \cap C \cap F$	$\overline{\mathcal{A}}^{++}$	$\neg A \cap P \cap C \cap F$

to the users. This simplifies the agreements, but reduces the control over information sharing, often resulting in the user being asked to grant permissions to share more information than the RP requires to perform the desired service.

Figure 1 summarizes all the observed app-right agreements in our Feb. 2014 dataset. We use a Venn diagram to show all relationships involving actions in the left square and all others in the right square. The small number of pure B relationships (4), suggests that there appear to be an expectation of trust in the RPs, beyond what the user typically would share publicly. Generally, RPs that are performing actions (A) on behalf of their users are more likely to request access to content (C) from the IDP. In total, 40 of the 87 classified relationships include actions (A). Of these, 14 RPs also request access to content (C). Of the 47 app-right agreements that does not request actions to be performed, only 12 (9+3) also request access to content (C).

We note that within each of the two boxes there is a clear ordering in risk types observed. In particular, class F is only used in combination with both C and P. This combination clearly has the highest privacy risks associated with it. Similarly, class C is only used in combination with P, clearly distinguishing its risks with those of sites that only request personal (P) or basic (B) information. Motivated by these observations, we identify 8 semi-ordered risk classes. Table 1 summarizes the observed classes. We note that there is a strict privacy ordering in each column (from (-) to (++)), and with regards to each row (as allowing actions implies some risk), but that further ordering is not possible without making assumptions.

3.3 RP-based Analysis

Using the above RP-IDP relationship type classification, we next compare the app rights for different classes of RPs. Among the classes with at least 10 RPs, News sites and File sharing sites are the most frequent users of actions (risk types $\mathcal{A}$ and $\mathcal{A}^+$), with 55% and 50% of their relationships including actions, respectively. Also Video sharing (67%) and Tech (63%) sites has large fraction of relationships that include action (A) permissions. The high action (A) usage is likely an effect of these sites often wanting to promote contents to friends of the user. While we express privacy concerns regarding $\mathcal{A}^+$ relationships, these sites would in

Table 2: Breakdown of relationship types for the top-three English speaking IDPs.

IDP	Tot	$\mathcal{A}^-$	$\overline{\mathcal{A}}$	$\overline{\mathcal{A}^+}$	$\overline{\mathcal{A}^{++}}$	$\mathcal{A}$	$\mathcal{A}^+$	$\mathcal{A}^{++}$	Unk
Facebook	55	0	24	5	3	13	3	1	6
Twitter	15	0	0	4	0	0	11	0	0
Google	29	4	7	0	0	12	0	0	6

fact desire that the information that their content are being read/watched to propagate across many sites.

Relationships including actions are primarily associated with RPs that have many IDPs. For example, while RPs with one IDP use actions in 33% of their relationships (all using Facebook as their only IDP), RPs with multiple IDPs use actions in 48-53% of their relationships. As with our discussion about News and File sharing sites, the many IDPs of these RPs increases the risk for cross-site leakage.

The most restrictive type ($\overline{\mathcal{A}^-}$) includes only OpenID. Even if OpenID allows some data transfer, OAuth is the primary protocol for content sharing without actions ($\overline{\mathcal{A}^+}$). Naturally, all relationships including actions use OAuth.

3.4 Head-to-Head IDP Comparison

The top-three English speaking IDPs are used relatively differently by their RPs and the usage is relatively independent of which other IDPs the RPs are using.

Table 2 breaks down the app rights for RPs using each of these three IDPs. Google is the only IDP with type $\overline{\mathcal{A}^-}$ relationships. Google's mix of OpenID-based and OAuth-based relationships share less information than Facebook. Facebook typically allows rich datasets to be imported to the RP. For Twitter, public messages and contacts are normally the only shared data. Twitter is particularly attractive for RPs wanting to perform actions on behalf of their users. RPs importing personal data (P) from Facebook, often do the same with Google (with or without actions). We also observe several cases where Google and Twitter are used together and both IDPs use actions (A) and import personal (P) data (classified as type $\mathcal{A}$). In general, there is a bias for selecting to use actions (A) with one IDP, given that actions are used with the other IDP.

4. MULTI-ACCOUNT INFORMATION

It is becoming increasingly common that users have accounts with multiple of the RP's IDPs. In addition, a local RP account may be created either before connecting the account to one of the IDPs, or when first creating the account using one of the IDPs. The use of all these accounts and their relative dependencies can complicate the situation for the end user, potentially increasing privacy risks.

We performed tests for each pairing of the three most popular English-speaking IDPs: Facebook, Twitter, and Google. For each possible IDP pairing, we allowed both IDPs in the pair to be used first in a sequence of tests. The tests were also performed both with and without first creating local accounts at the RPs. For each test sequence, we recorded all information $I_{u(\alpha\to\gamma)}$ (of type B, P, C or F) that a user u agrees that the RP γ can import from IDP α, all information $I_{u(\gamma\to\alpha)}$ that user u agrees that the RP can post on the IDP (through actions (A)), all information $I_{u(u\to\gamma)}$ that the user manually inserts into its local profile, and the information $I_{u(p)}$ which ends up in the user profile.

Information collision: Significant identity management complications can arise because of overlapping information shared by the IDPs (i.e., $I_{u(\alpha\to\gamma)}$ and $I_{u(\beta\to\gamma)}$) and the RP. We find that contact lists (26 of 42) are the most common overlap, and that regardless if there exists an initial local account or not, in 9 of 42 cases, at least some potentially conflicting information is imported to the user's RP profile from both IDPs.

Account merging and collisions: We have found that both account merging and the information transferred between accounts often are highly dependent on the order in which accounts are added. Furthermore, in many cases the user is not able to merge accounts, or control if merging should take place.

Cross-IDP information leakage Looking at the overlap $I_{u(\alpha\to\gamma)}\cap I_{u(\gamma\to\beta)}$ we observed multiple cases where cross-IDP sharing is possible, allowing information to be moved from one IDP to another IDP (via the RP). For example, six RPs allow personal (P) and/or content (C) from Facebook to be posted on Twitter, and five RPs allow basic (B) information from Facebook or Google to be transferred. We have also observed two RPs that have general posting rights on Facebook that allow transfer from Google, and two RPs that allow Facebook to transfer data from Twitter (although in this case Twitter would only transfer profile picture and name to the RPs).

5. CONCLUSIONS

Using targeted case studies on both manually and automatically identified RP-IDP relationships, this paper characterizes the cross-site information sharing and privacy risks in the third-party identity management landscape. We observe significant differences in the information leakage risks seen both across classes of RPs and across popular IDPs. Yet, for all website classes except Ads/cdn services, we find multiple high-risk sites among the top-200 websites. This includes RPs that both import private information and that are authorized to perform actions on the IDP. Furthermore, we find significant incompatibilities and inconsistencies in scenarios involving multiple IDPs. Clearly, many RPs are not designed to simply and securely use multiple IDPs. The lack of multi-IDP support can have serious negative consequences as many of these IDPs are popular services with many users, increasing the chance that users have accounts with multiple IDPs.

6. REFERENCES

[1] R. Dhamija and L. Dusseault. The seven flaws of identity management: Usability and security challenges. *IEEE Security & Privacy*, 6(2):24 – 29, Mar/Apr. 2008.

[2] S.-T. Sun, E. Pospisil, I. Muslukhov, N. Dindar, K. Hawkey, and K. Beznosov. Investigating user's perspective of web single sign-on: Conceptual gaps, alternative design and acceptance model. *ACM Trans. on Internet Technology*, 13(1):2:1–2:35, Nov. 2013.

[3] A. Vapen, N. Carlsson, A. Mahanti, and N. Shahmehri. Information sharing and user privacy in the third-party identity management landscape. Technical report, 2014.

[4] A. Vapen, N. Carlsson, A. Mahanti, and N. Shahmehri. Third-party identity management usage on the web. In *Proc. PAM*, Mar. 2014.

Practical Exploit Generation for Intent Message Vulnerabilities in Android

Daniele Gallingani
University of Illinois at Chicago
Chicago, IL
Politecnico di Milano
Milano, Italy
daniele.gallingani@mail.polimi.it

Rigel Gjomemo
University of Illinois at Chicago
Chicago, IL
rgjome1@uic.edu

V.N. Venkatakrishnan
University of Illinois at Chicago
Chicago, IL
venkat@uic.edu

Stefano Zanero
Politecnico di Milano
Milano, Italy
stefano.zanero@polimi.it

ABSTRACT

Android's Inter-Component Communication (ICC) mechanism strongly relies on Intent messages. Unfortunately, due to the lack of message origin verification in Intents, application security completely relies on the programmer's skill and attention. In this paper, we advance the state of the art by developing a method to automatically detect potential vulnerabilities and, most importantly, demonstrate whether they can be exploited or not. To this end, we adopt a formal approach to automatically produce malicious payloads that can trigger dangerous behavior in vulnerable applications. We test our methods on a representative sample of applications, and we find that 29 out of 64 tested applications are potentially vulnerable, while 26 of them are automatically proven to be exploitable.

Categories and Subject Descriptors: D.4.6 [Operating Systems]: Security and Protection

Keywords: Android, Application Security

1. Introduction

Android applications are formed by logically separated components that mainly communicate with each other through *Intents*, which carry data and request the execution of a procedure to another application. However, the Android Intent Passing mechanisms do not provide the receiving component with any information concerning the origin of an intent, thus facilitating the creation of spoofed intents with malicious input data [1, 2]. If such malicious input is not properly validated or sanitized by an application before being processed, it may subvert its state and control flow in unexpected ways. This attack vector may lead to a wide range of attacks, not only against the application itself, but also against other applications that receive and process data from the vulnerable app.

Previous research studied applications and the Android ecosystem to identify components that are exposed to receiving intents from untrusted applications and to check whether there exist dataflows from data input points to critical operations. However, this previous research is not being able to automatically verify the *practical exploitability* of the discovered dataflows [2]. This is due to two main reasons: 1) static analysis techniques approximate the behavior of programs and include additional behaviors that are not actually present and, 2) analysis techniques in state-of-the-art approaches only take into account the existence of potential suspicious paths and ignore the effect of the code along those paths, such as the use of input validation to mitigate intent spoofing vulnerabilities [1].

In this paper, we automatically develop proof-of-concept exploits against applications, to effectively prove that they are vulnerable to intent message vulnerabilities. We statically analyze the application to identify data-flows under an attacker's (indirect) control and design an analyzer that is able to follow such flows and identify Intent data that may affect either directly or indirectly the results that a component produces and sends in output. At this point, we use a constraint solver to develop concrete proof-of-concept exploits, thereby confirming the presence of the vulnerability. We test our approach on 64 popular applications from the Google Play store. Of these, 29 exhibit potential vulnerabilities, and for 26 of these, we are able to automatically generate an exploit, i.e. spoofed intents that trigger and demonstrate those vulnerabilities.

2. Problem Statement

Threat Model. In our threat model, an attacker first analyzes the manifest file to identify exposed components that can receive intent messages. An example of such a component is depicted in Listing 1, where the *onCreate* method (line 1) is called to start a component. Next, the attacker identifies statements inside those components whose execution may be subverted to the attacker' s advantage. These statements may include network operations, database operations, updates to GUI elements and so on, and their execution may be subverted by modifying their parameter values, e.g., URLs where data are sent by network operations, database queries, and the text of GUI elements (e.g., the HttpPost object creation in line 19, where the attacker may be able to modify the value of the *url*

This work was partially supported by National Science Foundation grants CNS-1065537, CNS-1069311, CNS-12416854

CODASPY'15, March 2–4, 2015, San Antonio, Texas, USA.
ACM 978-1-4503-3191-3/15/03.
http://dx.doi.org/10.1145/2699026.2699132.

variable to a domain under the attacker's control, or the statement on line 31, where the attacker may be able to modify the value of the variable p). We call such statements targeted by an attacker *sink* statements and those statements that extract intent data values *source* statements (e.g., lines 2-5).

Listing 1: Source code of a vulnerable application

```
1   void onCreate(Bundle savedInstance) {
2     Intent intent=getIntent();
3     String host = intent.getStringExtra("hostname");
4     String user = intent.getStringExtra("username");
5     String file = intent.getStringExtra("filename");
6     String url="http://www.example.com";
7     if (host.contains("example.com"))
8       url = "http://" + host + "/";
9     if (file.contains(".."))
10      file = file.replace("..", "");
11    String userId = getUserID(user);
12    if (userId != -1)
13      textView.setText(user_name);
14    String b64File = toBase64(file);
15    String httpPar = toHttpParams(b64File,user_id);
16    . . .
17    try {
18      DefaultHttpClient httpC = new DefaultHttpClient();
19      HttpPost post = new HttpPost(url+httpPar);
20      . . .
21      httpC.execute(post);
22    }
23    catch(IOException e) {
24      e.printStackTrace();
25    }
26  }
27  String toBase64(String p) {
28    if(p=null || p.equals(""))
29      p = "/data/data/com.example/defaultFile.pdf";
30    else
31      p = "/data/data/com.example/public/" + p;
32    byte[] bytes = InputStream.read(p);
33    String b = Base64Encoder.toString(bytes);
34    return b;
35  }
```

As has been recognized by previous work, to detect this type of vulnerabilities, it is important to correctly identify paths that starting from the *source* statements enable an attacker to influence the variable values at the *sink* statements. However, the existence of a path does not imply that an attack is feasible. To precisely identify exploit opportunities and prevent them, the operations performed on the variable values along that path must also be considered. In fact, these operations may include sanitizations (e.g., lines 9-10), and other business logic operations (e.g., lines 11-13) that, while allowing an attacker to influence the values at the sink statements, make exploits unfeasible. In the rest of the paper, we present a method for automatically detecting such vulnerabilities and providing exploitability proofs for them.

3. Approach

3.1 Problem Formulation and Approach Overview

We formulate the problem as follows. Let the *state* of an application at a particular point in the program be defined as a set of (variable, value) pairs $V = \{(v_1, a_1), (v_2, a_2), ..., (v_n, a_n)\}$ visible at that point during execution. To successfully launch an exploit on a specific *sink*, an attacker needs to induce a state of the attacker's choosing at that sink. We denote this state by *exploit state* and represent it with a set of (variable, value) pairs $V_E = \{(v_{e1}, b_1)(v_{e2}, b_2)..., (v_{em}, b_m)\}$, where the variables v_{ei} represent the parameters of the sink statement. Furthermore, to be able to induce state V_E at the sink, the attacker can only use the input

state at the *source* statements defined as a set of (variable, value) pairs $V_I = \{(v_{i1}, c_1), (v_{i2}, c_2)..., (v_{in}, c_n)\}$.

From a defensive and application vetting perspective, there can be many sink statements of interest to an attacker and they can be located anywhere inside the application. In addition, there can be many exploits for each sink statement. For example, if an attacker has control over the application state at a database query statement, there can be many exploit states V_E at his disposal, each performing a different type of SQL injection.

Therefore, we state the problem as follows. Given a point p in the program and an arbitrary exploit state V_E in p, can we automatically determine if there exists a state V_I at the *source* statements that induces V_E in p when the program executes? To answer this question, the relationship between the state at any point in the program and state V_I at the source statements must be made explicit. The discovery of such relationship and its modeling as a function F, such that we can automatically compute $V_I = F(V_E)$ is at the core of our approach. The steps of our approach are described next.

Paths computation. Since every program point p may be a sink statement, in this first step we compute all the paths between the *source* statements and every point in the program. Such analysis faces two main challenges. The first challenge arises due to the interprocedural nature of Android programs. In fact, the analysis must be able to deal with interprocedural data-flows and identify paths through deep sequences of method calls as well as recursive method calls. The second challenge is that of *path explosion*, which is a common problem in data flow analysis, and which becomes even more problematic in an interprocedural context.

To deal with these challenges, we first divide the methods into two sets: user-defined and libraries. Next, a control-flow supergraph of the user-defined methods is created by the data-flow analysis framework. In this supergraph, the call sites are joined with callee definitions and callees' exit sites are joined back with the call sites. We show a portion of the supergraph built for our example in Figure 1, where each node corresponds to a statement and is labeled with the line number from code listing 1. To further limit the size of the supergraph, we perform a preliminary *taint propagation* step. During this step, the nodes of the supergraph are partitioned into two sets, namely the set of statements that use values in V_I and can thus be influenced by an attacker, and the set of statements whose execution is independent from an attacker.

The taint propagation and the path computation steps are modeled as an IFDS data-flow analysis problem where taint and path information is collected inside facts associated with each point in the program [3,4].

Symbolic execution. After the path computation step, symbolic execution over the paths is performed to derive the set of constraints imposed over the variable values along those paths. At the end of this step, for every program point p, a logic formula F_p is created, whose variables correspond to program variables and whose terms correspond to the program statements that modify those variables. Thus, F_p represents the relationship between the input state V_I and the application state in p. The syntax of the symbolic formulas used in our approach is described by the pseudo-grammar shown in Figure 2, where terminal symbols are represented in bold.

In particular, the terminal symbol $solv\_stat$ represent Java statements whose operations semantics can be modeled by the solver used in the exploit generation step. In addition, these are the statements that use at least one tainted variable. Conversely, $nonsolv\_stat$ represents statements that cannot be modeled by the solver. Finally, var represents tainted variables, $constant$ represents constant strings, while the $+$ terminal represents string concatenation.

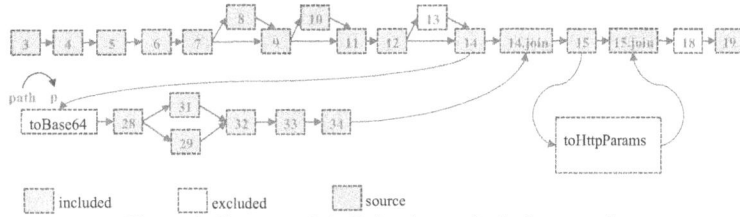

Figure 1: Supergraph built by the analysis framework.

$$
\begin{aligned}
F_p &\rightarrow F_p \vee conj \mid conj \\
conj &\rightarrow (conj \wedge term) \mid term \\
term &\rightarrow stat \mid \neg stat \\
stat &\rightarrow statement \mid \boldsymbol{var} == statement \\
statement &\rightarrow statement + single\_stat \mid single\_stat \\
single\_stat &\rightarrow \boldsymbol{var} \mid \boldsymbol{constant} \mid \boldsymbol{library\_method} \\
library\_method &\rightarrow \boldsymbol{solv\_stat} \mid \boldsymbol{nonsolv\_stat}
\end{aligned}
$$

Figure 2: Grammar of Symbolic Formula

For instance, the formula F_p related to the sink statement on line 20 of Figure 1 is derived as:

$(host.contains("example.com") \wedge url=="http://" + host + "/") \vee$
$(! \, host.contains("example.com") \wedge url=="http://www.example.com/")$

We note that each term in the symbolic formula represents a statement along the path, while each new path created by a branching statements is represented using a disjunction. Assignment operations in the code are modeled using equality constraints, in order to capture the equality conditions between two expressions.

Exploit generation. The input to this step is a program point p, the corresponding formula F_p and a set of assignments representing the exploit state V_E. The first operation of this step is the translation of the symbolic formula F_p into the solver's language. In particular, for each member of the $solv\_stat$ statements, we create a set of constraints in the language of the solver, which model the behavior of that statement. The members of the $unsolv\_stat$ statements are modeled with a particular operator in the solver's language that returns the whole domain of values for the variable.

For the implementation of this step, we chose the Kaluza solver, which provides string solving capabilities and several primitives that can model string operations [5]. Given the symbolic formula $F_p \wedge V_E$ for a particular point p, the solver provides a (possibly empty) solution containing the values of the variables in V_I, corresponding to the malicious input.

4. Results

Table 1: Experimental Results

Application	Implication
IM+	Display an arbitrary web page inside Activity && change Activity title.
Mint	Display an arbitrary web page inside an Activity
PromoQui	Load an arbitrary web page and change the common purchase process
GoSMS	Prompt to the user notification about a new message with arbitrary sender and SMS content

We evaluate our approach on 64 applications from the Google Play Store. The evaluation detected paths from sources to sinks in 29 of the 64 applications. Out of these 29 applications, the solver was able to produce exploits for 26 of them. The majority of these

exploits enable an attacker to arbitrarily change different UI components inside the applications, thus potentially leading to phishing attacks. Some of our results are summarized in Table 1, which describes the security implications for each application.

Table 2 shows different measurements of our approach. In particular, for the 64 applications under evaluation, we discovered 92 paths leading to a sink out of 537, with an average of 4.2 vulnerable paths per application. For each vulnerable path the analyzer collected an average number of 17.2 statements with an average number of 5.8 statements including API calls.

	Min	Max	Avg
Per-application execution time	2.4 min	33.2 min	12.3 min
Per-application components	3	31	24.5
Per-application vulnerable paths	2	19	4.2
Per-path statements	5	81	17.2
Per-path if-statements	0	3	0.98

Table 2: Other experimental setup

Our results show that only a few applications properly implement validation of data received from Intent messages. Most applications perform only basic checks on Intent payloads parts, such as null-checks, performed only to protect against malformed Intents data. However, such checks are not strict enough to defend application resources against more sophisticated Intent spoofing attacks.

5. Conclusions

In this paper, we provide an automated analysis framework to study vulnerabilities in Android applications arising from the lack of validation checks over Intent data. Improving over the state of the art, we provide proofs of vulnerabilities by automatically generating exploits under the form of malicious data to be sent with an Intent message. We evaluate our approach and find several vulnerabilities and exploits for those vulnerabilities. Our results confirm that a large percentage of commonly-used applications do not implement appropriate security safeguards.

6. References

[1] E. Chin, A. P. Felt, K. Greenwood, and D. Wagner, "Analyzing inter-application communication in android," in *Proceedings of the 9th international conference on Mobile systems, applications, and services*. ACM, 2011, pp. 239–252.

[2] L. Lu, Z. Li, Z. Wu, W. Lee, and G. Jiang, "Chex: Statically vetting android apps for component hijacking vulnerabilities," in *ACM Conference on Computer and Communications Security (CCS)*, 2012, pp. 229–240.

[3] "Heros ifds/ide solver," http://sable.github.io/heros/, 2013.

[4] E. Bodden, "Inter-procedural data-flow analysis with ifds/ide and soot," in *ACM SIGPLAN International Workshop on State of the Art in Java Program analysis*, ser. SOAP. ACM, 2012, pp. 3–8.

[5] "Kaluza string solver," http://webblaze.cs.berkeley.edu/2010/kaluza/, 2010.

A Network Security Game Model

Vivek Shandilya
Dept of Computer Science
University of Memphis
Memphis, TN-38152
001 9018481763
vmshndly@memphis.edu

Sajjan Shiva
Dept of Computer Science
University of Memphis
Memphis, TN-38152
001 901 678 5465
sshiva@memphis.edu

ABSTRACT

There have been attempts to model the interaction between users, both malicious and benign, and network administrators as games. Building on such works, we here present a game model which is generic enough to capture various modes of such interactions. The model facilitates stochastic games with imperfect information. The imperfect information is due to erroneous sensors leading to incorrect perception of the current state by the players. To model this error in perception distributed over other multiple states, we use Euclidean distances between inputs from the sensors.

Categories and Subject Descriptors

K.6.5 [Security and Protection]: Authentication, Invasive Software, Unauthorized access

Keywords

Game model; Security games; General Sum Games; imperfect-incomplete information; Stochastic game

1. INTRODUCTION

There is a growing attempt in the past decade to apply game theoretic approaches to the field of network security. In a network, when a user's anomalous behavior is observed by the administrator, it may not be possible to immediately decide if the user is an attacker or not. Moreover, even if the user has malicious intentions, such initial observation may not be sufficient to fully understand the motivations of the attacker. In such cases, when there is not enough information to classify a user exhibiting anomalous behavior, game theory offers a framework for interaction. [2] gives a survey of the works to model the interaction between a user and a network administrator and it provides a classification of these works based on the game models used. [1] modeled the interaction between an attacker and the administrator as a stochastic game with 14 states considering 3 types of attacks. Their game assumed perfect information. [3] presented a two state, imperfect information, zero sum, stochastic game with numerical simulation showing the advantage of considering the imperfect information. The main motivation for considering the imperfection in the information was the errors in the player's sensors. The error in the sensor makes the player believe that he may be in the states other than the state he really

CODASPY'15, March 2-4, 2015, San Antonio, Texas, USA.
ACM 978-1-4503-3191-3/15/03.
http://dx.doi.org/10.1145/2699026.2699133

is. Here we make extensions to this work. Our model has the same structure with one extension. When there are more than two states in the game, this error in sensor could make him mistakenly believe he is in any of the other states than the one he really is in. The error in perceiving the state gets distributed over the other states depending on the sensor reading's error needed to misread the state as the current state. Based on this extension in the game model, a game with five states is designed. The error in the perception of current state gets distributed over the four states other than the real state. Thus, the probability of the player 1 being deluded to be in any of the other states is proportional to the distance between the sensor readings of state defining variables of the other states from that of the current real state.

2. GAME MODEL

The model considers that a player 2 k observes the game's true state using an imperfect sensor/ a set of imperfect sensors. That means, player k can view the present state ξ_j to be any state in the information set $I^k_{\xi_j} = \{\xi_{j1}, \xi_{j2}. . . \xi_{jp}\}$ with ξ_j being an element of $I^k_{\xi_j}$. The perceived action set at this state may be expanded, i.e., player may decide to take an action which is allowed at $\xi_{ji} \neq \xi_j$ where ξ_{ji}, belongs to $I^k_{\xi_j}$. When the true state is

ξ_j, let the player k's extended action set $B^k_{\xi_j} = \bigcup_{\xi_j \in Ik\xi_j} A^k_{\xi_j}$ where $A^k_{\xi_j}$ denotes the allowed action set of player k at state is ξ_j .If the player k takes an action $\alpha^k \in B_{\xi_j}$, when the true state is ξ_j but α^k is not in A^k_j, then in terms of the influence on state transition probabilities, α^k is considered equivalent to player k taking no action at state ξ_j . However, its influence on player k's payoff α^k may not be equivalent to player k taking no action at state ξ_j depending upon the cost of the attempted execution of α^k. Formally, the model is represented by a tuple, $(S, E^1, E^2, A^1, A^2, Q, R^1, R^2, \beta)$ whose elements are defined below.

- $S = \{\xi_1, \xi_2. . . \xi_N \}$ is the set of states.

  $k=0, 1. . . K$ for one administrator and users respectively.

- $E^k = \{E^k_{\xi_1}, E^k_{\xi_2}. . . E^k_{\xi_N}\}$, $k=1,2$ where the jth,

  $0 < j < N$, set E_{ξ_j} with $E^k_{\xi_j} = \{p^k_{ji} \mid 1 \leq i \leq m_j , \sum^{mj}_{i=1} p^k_{ji} = 1, p^k_{ji} > 0. \}$, represents the error probabilities of kth player's sensor at the true state ξ_j over the corresponding information set, $I^k_{\xi_j}$. $I^k = \{I^k_{\xi_1}, I^k_{\xi_2}... I^k_{\xi_N}\}$, $k =1,2$ where the I^k_j represents the information set of player k when the true state is ξ_j , i.e., $I^k_{\xi_j} = \{\xi_{j1}, \xi_{j2}, . . . , \xi_{ji}, . . . , \xi_{imj}\}$ where $m_j =|I^k_{\xi_j}|$, $\xi_{ji} \in S$, with $m_j \leq N$ being an integer indicating the number of states that have a possibility of being considered the current state at state ξ_j with the condition that $\xi_j \in I_{\xi_j}$.

- $A^k = \{A^k_{\xi_1}, A^k_{\xi_2}. . . A^k_{\xi_N}\}$, $k = 1, 2$ is the action set of player k, where $A^k_{\xi j} = \{\alpha^k_{j1}, \alpha^k_{j1} \ldots \alpha^k_{jMk}\}$ is the action set of player k at state ξj. Let $B^k = \{B^k_{\xi 1}, B^k_{\xi 2} \ldots B^k_{\xi n}\}$, k=1,2, where $B^k_{\xi j}$ represents the action set of player k at $I^k_{\xi j}$.

That means $B^k_{\xi j} = \bigcup_{\xi j \in I k \xi j} A^k_{\xi j}$. By introducing different action sets at each state we may get distinct $B^k_{\xi j}$ at for each distinct $I^k_{\xi j}$. Let $T^k_{\xi j} = |B^k_{\xi j}|$.

• The state transition probabilities are represented by function Q: $S \times B1 \times B2 \times S \rightarrow [0\ 1]$ which maps a pair of states and a pair of actions to a real number between 0 and 1. The model assumes that for any state ξ^k_j if the player k takes an action $\alpha^k_j \in B^k_{\xi j}$, that does not belong to $A^k_{\xi j}$, then $Q(\xi_{j1}, \alpha^k_{i1}, \alpha^l_{i2}, \xi_{j2}) = Q(\xi_{j1}, \text{Normal operation}, \alpha^l_{i2}, \xi_{j2})$ where l represents the other player.

• The reward of the player k is determined by the function $R^k : S \times B1 \times B2 \rightarrow R$ which maps a state and a pair of actions to a real number.

• β, $0 < \beta < 1$ is the discount factor for discounting the future rewards in this infinite horizon game.

3. ERROR DISTRIBUTION

As E^k represents the set of error probabilities of the player k, let us consider the set of error probabilities $E^k_{\xi j}$ with the current state being ξj. Let the error of the sensor for player k at the state ξ_i is γ^k_j. $0 \leq \gamma^k_j, < 1$. The error γ^k_j is always less than 1 because the real state ξ_j is always taken as an element of the information set $I_{\xi j}$ at ξ_j. Then at the current state ξ_j, let the probabilities with which administrator perceives the current state to be ξ_1, ξ_2, ξ_3 and ξ_4 be p^k_{j1}, p^k_{j2}, p^k_{j3}, and p^k_{j4} respectively. Then the error at state ξ_j is $\gamma^k_j = (\sum_{i=1}^N p^k_{ji}) - p^k_{ji} = 1 - p^k_{ji}$. For $1 \leq i, j \leq N$, let ω^k_{ji} be the set of sensor inputs to the player k indicating the current state to be ξ_j, while the real current state is ξ_i. In practice the sensor can be a device or a collection of devices which collects values of some parameters of the system. All such parameters can be considered to form an orthogonal basis of the vector space, where some closed volume is taken to be associated with each state. All of those points in that closed region get mapped to one state. All of them have the values of the parameters which lead the player to perceive the current state to be the particular state. Let the current real state be ξ_j, where $1 \leq j \leq N$. At this state the sensor inputs at two different instances be, say ω^k_{ji} and ω^k_{jh}, where $1 \leq i, h \leq N$ due to erroneous sensors. This leads to the perception of the current state to be ξ_i and ξ_h respectively. Depending on the nature of the system, consider some representative statistical measure of central tendencies of ω^k_{ji} and ω^k_{jh}. Let Ed^k_{jih} to be the Euclidean distance between those measures. In this work, *larger errors are assumed to be less probable than the smaller errors* in sensor operations, that is, $Ed^k_{jj1} > Edkj$ implies $p^k_{ji} > p^k_{jh}$. In the following game with 5-states, the sensor error is distributed over the three states other than the real current state. This means for example, if the sensor error at ξ_1 is 0.3, then the probability with which the administrator perceives the current state to be not ξ_1 is 0.3. This could result in perceiving the current state to be ξ_1, ξ_2 and ξ_3 states respectively with probabilities of 0.15, 0.1 and 0.05. From the sensor relation, we have the sensor error at state $\xi_j | i \neq j$, $\gamma^k_j = \sum_{i=1}^N p^k_{ji}$ related to the probabilities of virtual states. The sensor outputs values of parameters which define states. Particular range of values of particular set of parameters will correspond to a state. In fact the

general way to define it, is a set of values, covering the range, for each of the parameters to correspond to a state. And if there are some parameters whose values do not affect in deciding a particular state then then range can accommodate any value.
• values corresponding to a set of parameters
• a vector space with these parameters constituting the basis
Thus we can see the state definition as follows.
• $S \rightarrow S - O$, where
– $S - O = \{S - O_0, S - O_1, S - O_2, \ldots S - O_N\}$,
– $S - O = \{s - o_{i0}, s - o_{i1}, s - o_{i2}, , \ldots, s - o_{iFi}\}$
– $s - o_{ij} = (s - o_{ij}(0), s - o_{ij}(1), s - o_{ij}(2), \ldots, s - o_{ij}(g))$ implies j^{th} g-dimensional sequence corresponding to i^{th} state, ξ_j.
– $s - o_{ij}(l)$ =a MCT, representative value of the expected range of values for the lth parameter in the jth behavior belonging to ξ_j. l *belongs to set of natural numbers, $0 \leq l \leq g$*
– g = number of parameters observed by sensors
– $0 \leq j \leq Fi$, where $Fi + 1$ disjoint ranges correspond to state ξ_j
When there is an anomaly detected, in terms of sensor values, which do not exactly fit into any particular state and there is uncertainty about to which state the current values belong to, imperfect information must be considered.
• **C**urrent observed **V**alues of parameters as anomaly $CV = (cv0, cv1, cv2, \ldots, cvg)$ = current values of g parameters
• consider the minimum of Euclidean distances with elements in each state$(\Theta_{0f0}, \Theta_{1f1}, \Theta_{1f2}, \ldots, \Theta_{1fN})$. where fi implies the fi^{th} element, $0 \leq fi \leq Fi$ has the minimum of distances between CV and $s - o_{ifi}$ element in the ith state.
• $\Theta_{1f1} = $ square root of $((\sum_{j=0}^{j=g} cv_j - (s - o_{ij})) / (g))$min
• The error in perception of states is given by $P_{ji} = (\sum_{j=0}^N \Theta_{jfi} - \Theta_{ifi}) / (\sum_{j=0}^N \Theta_{jfi})$
• Then the error at state ξ_j is given by $\gamma^k_j = \sum_{i=1}^N p^k_{ji} - p^k_{ji} = 1 - p^k_{ji}$
• **larger errors are assumed to be less probable than smaller errors**
An simple illustration to show its application can be as below. Example:
Low_Privilege State
• 8AM-6PM = {Download·2Mbps, Upload·150kbps }
This behavior is high-privilege, when manager works at his computer.

High_Privilege State
• 8AM-6PM = {Download≤2Mbps, Upload≤150kbps }
This behavior is high-privilege, when manager works at his computer.
Sensor Readings At 3:30PM there is 1.7Mbps download and 150 kbps upload.
• ((0.7+0.3)-0.7)/(0.7+0.3)=0.3 Probability in Low_Privilege State. Mean Download: 1Mbps
• ((0.7+0.3)-0.3)/(0.7+0.3) =0.7 Probability in High_Privilege State. Mean Download: 2Mbps

4. UTILITY OF THE GENERIC GAME MODEL IN SECURITY SYSTEMS

The generic game model is used as the first step in designing the architecture of the security system, which acts as an event driven system. When a set of anomalies is detected in the operation of the system the potential attacks are identified, using a taxonomical approach [5], and then using the methodology outlined in [4] another taxonomical approach is used to select the suitable game model as shown in Figure 1.

The generic game model presented here is useful to design the different game models suitable for different types of attacks. In fact even a similar type of attack in different situations need different game models as outlined in [4]. But it is not practical to

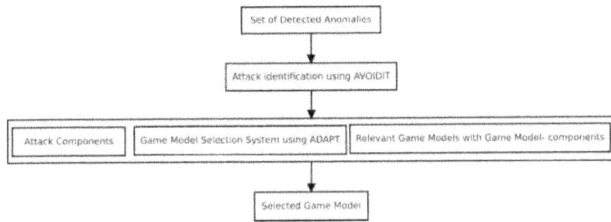

Figure 1. Event flow in the Security System.

manually design different game models. To derive it in an automated way the generic game model should be extendable to accommodate the distinct specifications needed for different types of attack. The Figure 2 shows how the generic game model will be actually useful in the finally coming up with the appropriate response to the attacks.

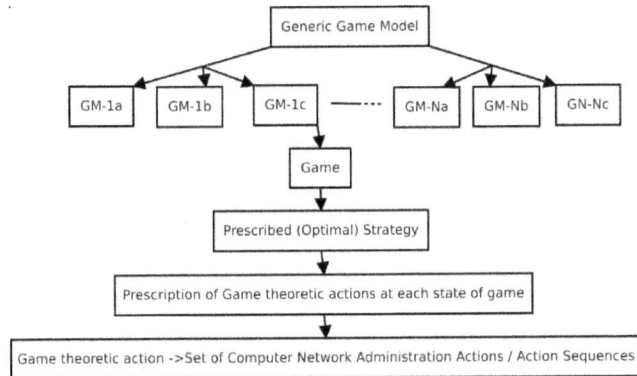

Figure 2. Generic Game Model's Utility.

5. CONCLUSION

In this short paper we present the formal game model and how the errors due to imperfect information distributed over many states can be computed. In our ongoing work we are building a generic security game based on this model, and show how to efficiently computing effective equilibria to be able to find out the preferable strategy to ensure optimal outcome.

6. REFERENCES

[1] Lye, K. and Wing, J. 2005. Game Strategies in network security. *International Journal of Information Security, vol. 4, no 1, pp. 71-86.*

[2] Roy, S., Ellis, C. , Shiva, S., Dasgupta, D., Shandilya V. and Wu. Q. . . 2010. A survey of game theory as applied to network security. *The 43rd Hawaii International Conference on system Sciences.*

[3] Shiva, S., Roy, S., Bedi, H., Dasgupta, D., and Wu. Q.. 2010. A stochastic game with imperfect information for cyber security. *The 5th International conference on i-warfare & security (ICIW), Dayton, Ohio.*

[4] Simmons, C., Shiva, S., Bedi, H., and Shandilya. V. 2013. ADAPT: A game inspired attack-defense and performance metric taxonomy. *Security and Privacy protection in Information Processing Systems, pp. 344-364. Springer Berlin Heidelberg.*

[5] Simmons, C., Shiva, S., Phan, V., Shandilya, V. and Simmons, L. 2012. IRS: An issue resolution system for cyber-attack classification and management. SAM, *Los Vegas, July.*

CryptStream: Cryptographic Access Controls for Streaming Data

Cory Thoma
corythoma@cs.pitt.edu

Adam J. Lee
adamlee@cs.pitt.edu
University of Pittsburgh
Pittsburgh, Pennsylvania
15260

Alexandros Labrinidis
labrinid@cs.pitt.edu

ABSTRACT

With data becoming available in larger quantities and at higher rates, new data processing paradigms have been proposed to handle large and fast data. Data Stream Processing is one such paradigm wherein transient data flows as streams through sets of continuous queries, only returning results when data is of interest to the querier, allowing uninteresting data to be ignored. To process these data streams, users are employing third party computational platforms or large private platforms to reduce the individual cost for querying and computing over data streams. Utilizing third parties for outsourcing computation means data being processed is available to the third party as well, which could violate the data provider's privacy. There has been research done into access control for streaming data, and these works provide a good first step, but fall short of a complete system. In this paper, we introduce CryptStream for cryptographically enforcing access controls over streaming data. CryptStream combines data providers access control policies with ones prescribed by the data consumer and the server as well. We show that CryptStream improves over earlier work in the same design space while providing smaller overheads and more flexibility.

1. INTRODUCTION

The proliferation of small powerful computing devises has led to an increase in the availability of data. Whether it be a smart phone, smart watch, sensor, or large computing clusters; data has become more available at faster speeds and greater volumes. Traditional data management paradigms lack the ability to maintain accurate and quick response to queries being executed over faster data. To combat this problem, the data streaming paradigm has been proposed as a way to efficiently and effectively manage large amounts of quick data, or data that is time sensitive. DSMSs separate the data *source* from the data *consumer* so that control no longer resides with either. As a result, control over what entities have access to data resides with the server

CODASPY'15, March 2–4, 2015, San Antonio, Texas, USA.
ACM 978-1-4503-3191-3/15/03.
http://dx.doi.org/10.1145/2699026.2699134

employed to handle queries. To bring control back to the data source, we propose *CryptStream*, a method for cryptographically enforcing access control over streaming systems. CryptStream allows a data source to describe an access control policy over their streaming data while also allowing data consumers to maximize the use of third party computing platforms through the use of special encryption schemes.

Work in the same design space as CryptStream provides a good first step. The closest work, StreamForce [1], falls short of providing a complete system. First, it limits the querying power of the data consumer by limiting it to predescribed views. It also incurs large overheads due to the use of Outsourced Attribute Based Encryption for every data tuple. In this paper, we introduce CryptStream as a system that cryptographically enforces access controls over streaming data. CryptStream aims at overcoming limitations of previous works while also providing new techniques for policy enforcement and query processing. Specifically, CryptStream makes the following contributions:

- Unlike previous work, CryptStream allows users to cryptographically enforce access control over streaming data and change their policies in real time. In CryptStream, access control is based upon the data consumer's attributes. To enforce changes in policy, CryptStream utilizes modifications to the concept of Security Punctuations [2] to enforce Attribute Based Access Control (ABAC) polices.

- CryptStream provides a built-in scheme for distributing and managing cryptographic keys based on user attributes. Using Security Punctuations, keys can be distributed via CP-ABE enforcement of ABAC policies so that only the proper data consumers can access data.

- CryptStream can combine access control policies from the data provider, data consumer, and the server while not requiring the access control framework to be the same.

- Finally, CryptStream is a system which allows data consumers to submit almost any type of query. Through the use of special encryption techniques, data consumers can execute almost any type of query so long as they were given permission by the data provider.

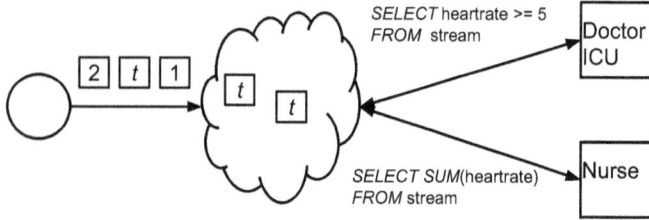

Figure 1: An example of one data provider and two clients accessing that data providers stream.

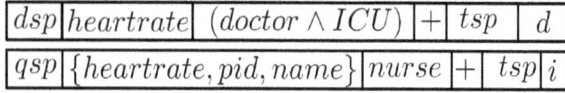

dsp	$heartrate$	$(doctor \wedge ICU)$	$+$	tsp	d
qsp	$\{heartrate, pid, name\}$	$nurse$	$+$	tsp	i

Figure 2: Two security punctuations illustrating a data provider and a querier punctuation.

Figure 3: Outsourced ABE decryption for different operators with different numbers of attributes.

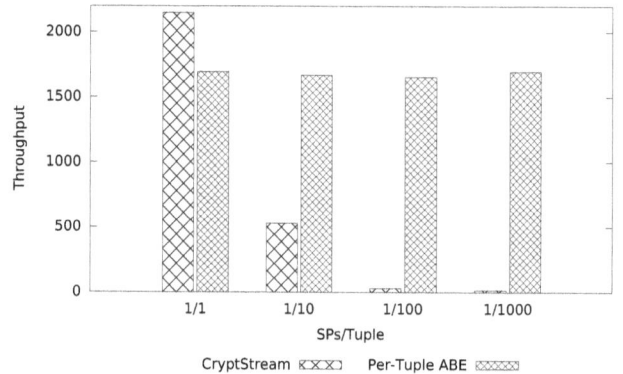

Figure 4: The frequency of Security Punctuation affects the throughput for CryptStream.

2. CRYPTSTREAM

CryptStream has three main components: *data providers*, *clients*, and *compute & route nodes*. Data providers initialize and populate streams of data which they have authored access control policies over. Clients submit queries on data streams and are the subjects for which a data provider will enforce access. The last component, the compute & route node, handles the execution of queries on data streams. The compute & route node is assumed to be untrusted with data provider data in that it should not have access to streams in plain text. Unless a data provider authors an access control policy which grants a compute & route node or a client access, they have no access to a data stream in plain-text. Figure 1 depicts the three components together. The data provider is represented by a circle, the compute & route node is represented by a cloud, and the squares with an ICU doctor and a nurse represent clients. The other components in Figure 1 will be discussed in further sections.

2.1 Background

Each client is associated with a set of attributes which are used by data providers to create *Attribute Based Access Control* (ABAC) policies for enforcing access to their streams. ABAC systems combine attributes through logical "and" and "or" statements and will only grant access if the statement is true based on a clients attributes. In order to transmit data so that the plain-text is not exposed, Attribute Based Encryption (ABE) is used. ABE is a prohibitively expensive operation, so rather than use it directly for each data tuple transmitted, ABE is only used to exchange keys for faster more functional encryption schemes as described below. This reduces the necessity of ABE to use only when creating or updating policies. A new or updated policy is disseminated via *Security Punctuations* (SPs) which are simply a special tuple injected into a data stream by the data provider containing six fields: the type of SP, the data being accessed, the policy, whether the policy is denying or granting access, a timestamp, and either immediate or deferred enforcement. For CryptStream, the type is either a data security punctuation (dsp) if it comes from a data provider, or a querier security punctuation (qsp) if it comes from a client. SPs are represented as numbers squares in Figure 1. Note that SPs are just part of the normal data stream. All data provider policies are ABAC policies enforced via ABE.

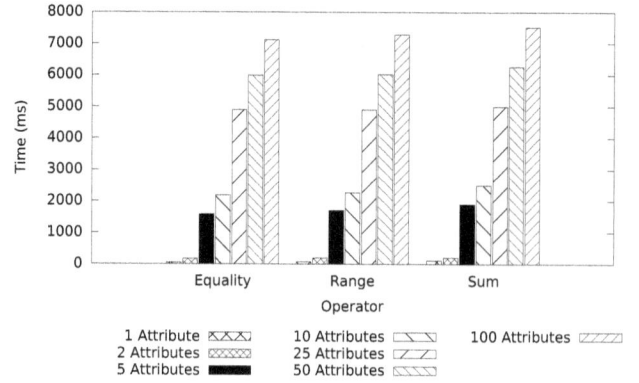

The overhead of ABE depends on the number of attributes. Figure 3 shows query types if ABE encryption is used for operating on data tuples. CryptStream avoids these overheads since ABE is only used to transmit policies. The frequency of these transmissions can also affect performance. Figure 4 shows how the frequency of security punctuations affects the throughput of CryptStream. Note that after a 2:1 ratio of data tuples to punctuations, CryptStream outperforms ABE encryption for each data tuple, and improves with less frequent policy updates.

Consider the punctuations in Figure 2. The first punctuation shows the a data security punctuation where the data provider is granting access (the "+") to the field "heartrate" for a doctor who is in the ICU. They are deferring enforcement, meaning the change in policy only affects tuples arriving after the timestamp. The second punctuation shows a querier security punctuation which only grants the role of "nurse" access to the fields "heartrate", "name" and the "pid" patient ID and is immediately enforced, meaning that it also affects a tuples currently in system or operator buffers. Notice that a qsp allows Role Based Access Controls to be used. CryptStream supports arbitrary access control policies for clients so long as the compute & route node supports it. When a data provider generates a new policy, the policy is given to CryptStream which parses it and generates the

Scheme	Type of Queries	Supported operators	Information Gained by Adversary
RND	None	None	Nothing
DET	Equality	Select, Project, Equi-Join, Count, Group By, Order by	Equality of attributes
OPE	Range	Select, Join, Count	A partial to full order of tuples
SUM	Summations	Aggregates over summations	Nothing

Table 1: Summary of what types of queries and operators are supported by each encryption scheme, as well as what each scheme could reveal to a potential adversary.

punctuations. When a data provider generates a data tuple, it is given to CryptStream which handles the encryption of fields.

2.2 Other Components

In CryptStream, compute & route nodes are unchanged since CryptStream sits on the data provider and client acting as an interface into the DSMS. On the client, this interface is tasked with decryption of data provider streams, handling the translation of queries, and gathering keys and accesses from data provider punctuations. When a punctuation is sent to compute & route nodes, any client wanting to access that stream is given the tuple. The CryptStream interface will use the ABE keys provided by a trusted third party to try decrypt the key given in the SP. If successful, the key is stored along with the attributes it is used to encrypt and the punctuation is forgotten.

Another task of the client is to translate queries. When a client wishes to access a stream, it gets the schema and a deterministic key from the data provider via a special tuple. Whenever the client wants to access a field in the tuple, the CryptStream interface will intercept the query and encrypt any field with the deterministic key so that fields can be accessed without the plain-text field name being exposed to the compute & route node. The query is then submitted to be executed. When results are returned to the client, they pass through the CryptStream interface where they are decrypted and then given to the client.

Recall that SPs are only used to transmit keys for more efficient encryption types. In order to allow computation to be done on the server, CryptStream employs four encryption types; deterministic (DET), order preserving (OPE), Homomorphic (HOM), and Random (RND). Each encryption type comes with some guarantee on what the server learns as well as a different level of functionality. These trade-offs are described in table 1. When a data provider issues a new SP, part of the description of data being accessed includes the level of access, which allows the CryptStream interface to determine which queries can run on the compute & route nodes and which need to be processed locally. Figure 5 shows the cost for each operation compared to plain-text operations and a straw-man approach. This straw-man approach simply sends all tuples to the client encrypted encrypted with the RND encryption scheme, meaning that the server gains no information about the tuple, but no functionality is provided.

Figure 1 shows two different queries. The top query requires OPE encryption in order to execute on the compute & route nodes. This means that SP 1 would have given access using the OPE encryption technique and passing the proper

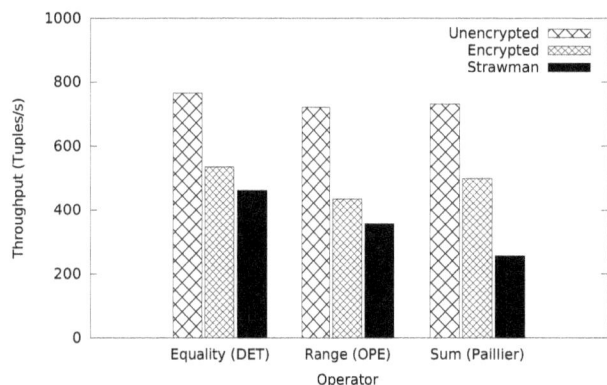

Figure 5: Throughput for each of the different operations supported for both unencrypted and encrypted streams given each encryption type.

key to decrypt them. The second query requires using addition, and therefore requires HOM levels of access. The data provider would have to generate an SP to give HOM permission to the client, but since none was provided, tuples are sent back the client for processing.

3. CONCLUSION

In this paper, we overview CryptStream for cryptographically enforced access controls on streaming data. CryptStream enables a data provider to author Attribute Based Access Control policies on their data streams. Using interfaces on both the data provider and client, CryptStream allows multiple policies to be enforced at the same time from any number of clients, data providers, and compute & route nodes. Through the use of different encryption techniques, CryptStream allows computation to be done on the compute & route node while maintaining some guarantee of confidentiality. Finally, CryptStream does not rely on third parties or off-line key distribution. Using Security Punctuations, CryptStream distributes and manages cryptographic keys online.

4. REFERENCES

[1] D. T. T. Anh and A. Datta. Streamforce: outsourcing access control enforcement for stream data to the clouds. In *Proceedings of the 4th ACM conference on Data and application security and privacy*, pages 13–24. ACM, 2014.

[2] R. Nehme, E. A. Rundensteiner, and E. Bertino. A security punctuation framework for enforcing access control on streaming data. In *Data Engineering, 2008. ICDE 2008. IEEE 24th International Conference on*, pages 406–415. IEEE, 2008.

ABSS: an Attribute-based Sanitizable Signature for Integrity of Outsourced Database with Public Cloud

Lei Xu
University of Houston
Houston, TX, USA
lxu13@uh.edu

Xinwen Zhang
Samsung
San Jose, CA, USA
xinwenzhang@gmail.com

Xiaoxin Wu
Samsung
San Jose, CA, USA
xiaoxinwu@hotmail.com

Weidong Shi
University of Houston
Houston, TX, USA
wshi3@uh.edu

ABSTRACT

Database outsourcing is an important application of cloud computing, and security is one of the most critical concerns in adopting this application model, such as data privacy, query privacy, etc. Data integrity is another essential requirement for outsourced database system. When the database is outsourced to public cloud, the situation is more complex as different users may modify the data and these users may hold different privileges for different parts of the database. Furthermore, as the cloud is in charge of the management of the database, users have to rely on the cloud to guarantee data integrity. We propose ABSS to protect the integrity of outsourced database which supports fine-grained modification policy. ABSS utilizes an attribute based sanitizable signature scheme, which combining the ingredients of attribute based encryption and sanitizable signature. ABSS enables the database owner to deploy fine-grained policy of database modification and can detect illegal modifications without trusting the cloud. We also discuss the security properties and performance of ABSS to show its practicability.

Categories and Subject Descriptors

E.3 [**Data Encryption**]: Public key cryptosystems; D.4.6 [**Security and Protection**]: Cryptographic controls

Keywords

cloud computing, cloud storage, database, integrity, access control

1. INTRODUCTION

Database-as-a-service (DaaS) is a fascinating application for cloud computing. Due to the flexible computation, storage, and communication capabilities of cloud, DaaS can meet different types of demands and save users' budget/time.

There are already some products in the market, such as Amazon's SimpleDB and Microsoft Azure SQL Database.

Integrity is an essential component of the security of outsourced database. Classical digital signatures can be implemented to guarantee data integrity, but they are not suitable for the scenario of database outsourcing because when some users modify the database, the signature has to be re-generated from scratch. Sanitizable signature proposed by Giuseppe et.al. [2] allows authorized users to modify the message without affecting the original signature. [9] extended sanitizable signature such that the message can only be modified to a predefined set of strings. These schemes partially solve the problem of integrity of outsourced database as a user is not required to re-generate the signature from scratch after modifies the database. Nonetheless, these schemes consider little about users' different rights of modification and cannot support fine-grained modification control.

In this paper, we propose attribute based sanitizable signature (ABSS) which can ensure the integrity of outsourced database and support fine-grained modification control. ABSS utilizes attribute based sanitizable signature and attribute based encryption technique. With ABSS the data owner who outsources the database can define rules using attributes such that only users satisfy the owner defined rules can modify the database while do not affect the integrity property.

2. ATTRIBUTE BASED SANITIZABLE SIGNATURE

First we describe the construction of attribute based sanitizable signature scheme. The construction utilizes ciphertext policy based encryption [5] and sanitizable signature [2].

Setup. Setup consists of three parts:

1. Classical digital signature setup. For *data owner*, a pair of public/private keys for classical signature scheme with hash-and-encode mechanism such as DSA or ECDSA is generated. Denote the key pair as (pk^{sign}, sk^{sign}). There could be multiple *data owners*, and in this case each one is given a classical signature key pair. Each *data owner* keeps his/her private key sk^{sign} secret and publishes the public key pk^{sign}. Let $Sign_{sk^{sign}}()$ and $Veri_{pk^{sign}}()$ be the classical digital signature generation and verification procedure respectively.

2. Attribute based encryption setup. Following the ciphertext policy attribute based encryption scheme proposed in [5], KDC picks a set of attributes, generates the main public parameters $PARA_{ABE}$ and the main se-

cret key MSK. KDC keeps MSK secret and publishes $PARA_{ABE}$. Each *data modifier* is attached a set of attributes, and KDC generates a *sanitization key* sk^{sanit} for him/her using his/her attributes set and MSK. Let $Enc(\mathcal{T}, msg)$ be the encryption of msg under public parameters $PARA_{ABE}$ and access structure $\mathcal{T}$, $Dec(sk^{sanit}, cipher)$ be the decryption of $cipher$ with sanitization key sk^{sanit}. The decryption will succeed only if the attributes related to sk^{sanit} satisfies the access structure of $cipher$.

3. Chameleon hash parameter setup. Following the chameleon hash scheme proposed in [3], the public parameters of the chameleon hash is established, denoted as $PARA_{CH}$. Public/private key pairs for chameleon hash are not generated at this step. Let $CH(pk^{CH}, msg, r)$ be the procedure of computing chameleon hash value of msg, where pk^{CH} is a public key for the chameleon hash scheme and r is the random value used for the construction. According to the property of chameleon hash function, with the corresponding private key sk^{CH} and a new message msg', one can find a new random value r' such that

$$CH(pk_{CH}, msg, r) = CH(pk^{CH}, msg', r').$$

Signature generation. Given a message m, the *data owner* first generates a key pair for chameleon hash under $PARA_{CH}$ at random, denoted as (pk^{CH}, sk^{CH}), and divides m into t edit units $m = m_1 || m_2 || \cdots || m_t$. Note that it is not necessary for $|m_i| = |m_j|, i \neq j$. Then *data owner* picks a random identifier ID_m for m and decides which parts of m can be modified. *Data owner* also provides an access structure $\mathcal{T}$ describes which type of *data modifiers* can modify it. The signature is computed as:

$$
\begin{aligned}
\sigma &= GenSanitSig(m, sk^{sign}, pk^{CH}, sk^{CH}, \mathcal{T}, PARA_{ABE}) \\
&= (Sign_{sk^{sign}}(ID_m || t || \mathcal{T} || C_{sk^{CH}} || \bar{m}_1 || \ldots || \bar{m}_t), C_{sk^{CH}})
\end{aligned}
$$

where

$$
\bar{m}_i = \begin{cases} CH_{\mathcal{T}}(ID_m || i || m_i, r_i), & \text{if } m_i \text{ can be modified,} \\ m_i || i, & \text{otherwise.} \end{cases}
$$

$C_{sk^{CH}} = Enc(\mathcal{T}, sk^{CH})$ is the cipher-text of sk^{CH}. r_i is a random value used in the computation of chameleon hash.

Here we use the chameleon hash scheme in [3] for $CH_{\mathcal{T}}(\cdot)$. Let $p = uq + 1$ be a prime number, q is also a prime. Let g be a generator of the subgroup of squares of order q. The private key x is selected at random from $[1, q-1]$, and the public key is $y = g^x$. Let $\mathcal{H}$ be a hash function, $CH_{\mathcal{T}}(m) = \rho - (y^e g^\delta \mod p) \mod q$, where $r = (\rho, \delta) \in \mathbb{Z}_q \times \mathbb{Z}_q$ and $e = \mathcal{H}(m, \rho)$. In order to verify the signature, r_i should be stored with message m_i.

Signature sanitization. For a signature σ of message m with access structure $\mathcal{T}$, a *data modifier* with sanitization private key sk^{sanit} runs $Dec(sk^{sanit}, C_{sk^{CH}})$. If the attributes of the *data modifier* matches the access structure $\mathcal{T}$, the decryption will succeed and the *data modifier* will receive sk^{CH}, the plain-text of $C_{sk^{CH}}$, otherwise the *data modifier* gets nothing. Recall that sk^{CH} is the private key for the underline chameleon hash scheme. So for a message segment m_i that designed to allow modification, *data modifier* can chose a new message m_i' at will and compute the corresponding random value r_i' such that $CH(pk_{CH}, m_i, r_i) = CH(pk_{CH}, m_i', r_i')$. It can be seen easily that the σ is still a valid signature of the modified message m.

Signature verification. Given a signature σ for a message m, the *verifier* who wants to verify σ has to do the following:

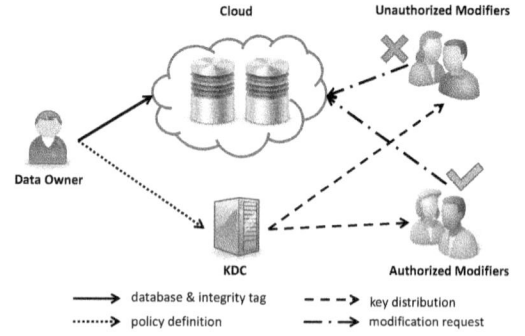

Figure 1: Overall framework. The date owner outsources the database to the cloud and sends the modification policy to KDC. The data owner also includes an integrity signature with the database. KDC distributes keys to different users according to the modification policy. When a user tries to modify the database, he/she needs to do some computation with his/her key and the integrity signature. Only if the modification made by the user is consistent with the data owner defined policy, the integrity signature will not be damaged.

1. For each edit unit m_i, the verifier calculates the chameleon hash value of this unit with corresponding random value and public key;
2. The verifier concatenates all the chameleon hash values and essential parts such as the access structure, and finally get the input to the classical signature scheme, denoted as *message*;
3. The verifier checks whether σ is a valid signature of *message*. If the verification succeed, then the sanitizable signature is accepted. Otherwise, the sanitizable signature is rejected.

The proposed scheme achieves fine grained modification control and unforgeability. Due to the limitation of space, we omit the detailed analysis.

3. APPLYING ABSS TO OUTSOURCED DATABASE

In this section we discuss applying ABSS to protect the integrity of the outsourced database where multiple users with different authorities may modify the database. Queries such as *select* will not change the data saved in the database, and we focus on the operations such as *modification, insertion,* and *deletion*. Here we consider the integrity of a table, or relation. The integrity of a database is guaranteed if all the tables' integrity is protected.

System overview. For an outsourced database, it usually works in one-create-many-modify manner. Specifically, there is one user uploads the database, and sets up modification policy. Then many users may modify the database. In this process, we also need other parties that are in charge of database storage and key distribution. Figure 1 depicts the overall framework and relationships between different participants.

Data layout and initialization. In order to utilize ABSS for integrity of outsourced database, the basic edit unit should be decided. One nature idea is to take tuples as the basic edit unit (in fact some database system such as Accumulo already supports this level of access control [1]). Figure 2 depicts the data layout for this case. For each tuple of the database, *data owner* generates a key pair for chameleon

attribute 1	attribute 2	......	attribute t	random numbers	hash value	access policy
data$_{11}$	data$_{21}$	......	data$_{t1}$	r_1	h_1	policy$_1$
data$_{12}$	data$_{22}$	......	data$_{t2}$	r_2	h_2	policy$_2$
......	......	......	......	......	......	......
ABSS signature value						

Figure 2: Outsourced database with attribute based sanitizable signature. Each tuple is given a policy and related information is stored together with original data.

hash at random and calculates a hash value for this tuple. The hash value and corresponding random values are saved with the tuple. *Data owner* also has a policy attached to the tuple, which decides what type of *data modifier* can edit this tuple legally. The policy is expressed by encrypting the chameleon hash private key with CP-ABE using a designated access structure. Finally, *data owner* collects all the chameleon hash values and generates a classical digital signature with his/her private key for signature. This classical digital signature is for the whole table. Note that ABSS scheme does not depend on specific attribute based encryption scheme, so we can replace the CP-ABE scheme we uses here with other ABE schemes to realize other policy definitions.

Supporting database operations. We consider four types of operations with ABSS: tuple modification, tuple insertion, tuple deletion and integrity verification. The detailed description is given in the full version of the paper.

4. RELATED WORK

The security of outsourced database has been studied a lot in the past. Research in this area can be roughly divided into two categories, database privacy and database integrity.

Outsourced database privacy. It is a challenge to protect the data privacy while enabling the cloud to perform queries. Hacigümüş et al. proposed a method for secure SQL processing by adding secure indices to each tuple in the database [7]. In [4] the authors proposed a hardware based solution for database privacy.

Outsourced database integrity. Different methods are proposed to guarantee the integrity of the query result, e.g., adding another round of interaction between the end user and the cloud [10], verifying the query process itself using cryptographic proof [11], utilizing dual-encryption [12], etc.

People also studied the integrity of the database itself. Hacigümüş et al. proposed a integrity protection scheme using record integrity codes and incremental signature [8]. Zhu et al. given a method for integrity verification utilizing random sampling and index-hash table [13]. Another line of research related to outsourced database integrity is remote file integrity checking [6]. Our solution is different from these related works by supporting fine-grained modification policy.

5. CONCLUSION AND FUTURE WORK

This paper proposes ABSS for integrity protection of outsourced database. Attribute based sanitizable signature scheme is a key component of ABSS which integrates sanitizable signature with attribute based encryption. Compared with previous techniques, ABSS is more flexible and scalable from two aspects: (1) It allows multiple users to modify the same tuple; (2) Data owner can define fine-grained policy for database modification. We discuss how to apply ABSS

to support database operations such as modification, insertion, and deletion. However, there are some technique issues that need to be addressed. For both data layouts we proposed in this work, the storage cost is still high. The scheme will be more practical if we could make the extra storage cost constant. Integration of such work into the present ABSS framework requires further investigation.

6. REFERENCES

[1] Apache. Accumulo https://accumulo.apache.org/.
[2] G. Ateniese, D. H. Chou, B. de Medeiros, and G. Tsudik. Sanitizable signatures. In S. D. C. di Vimercati, P. F. Syverson, and D. Gollmann, editors, *European Symposium on Research in Computer Security - ESORICS 2005*, volume 7459 of *LNCS*, pages 159–177. Springer-Verlag, 2005.
[3] G. Ateniese and B. de Medeiros. On the key exposure problem in chameleon hashes. In C. Blundo and S. Cimato, editors, *Security in Communication Networks - SCN 2004*, volume 3352 of *LNCS*, pages 165–179. Springer-Verlag, 2004.
[4] S. Bajaj and R. Sion. TrustedDB: A trusted hardware-based database with privacy and data confidentiality. *IEEE Transactions on Knowledge and Data Engineering*, 26(3):752–765, 2014.
[5] J. Bethencourt, A. Sahai, and B. Waters. Ciphertext-policy attribute-based encryption. In *IEEE Symposium on Security and Privacy - S&P 2007*, pages 321–334. IEEE Computer Society, 2007.
[6] Y. Deswarte, J.-J. Quisquater, and A. Saïdane. Remote integrity checking. In *Integrity and Internal Control in Information Systems VI*, pages 1–11. Springer, 2004.
[7] H. Hacigümüş, B. R. Iyer, C. Li, and S. Mehrotra. Executing sql over encrypted data in the database-service-provider model. In M. J. Franklin, B. Moon, and A. Ailamaki, editors, *Proceedings of the ACM International Conference on Management of Data - SIGMOD 2002*, pages 216–227. ACM, 2002.
[8] H. Hacigümüş, B. Iyer, and S. Mehrotra. Ensuring the integrity of encrypted databases in the database-as-a-service model. In *Data and Applications Security XVII*, pages 61–74. Springer, 2004.
[9] M. Klonowski and A. Lauks. Extended sanitizable signatures. In M. S. Rhee and B. Lee, editors, *Information Security and Cryptology - ICISC 2006*, volume 4296 of *LNCS*, pages 343–355. Springer-Verlag, 2006.
[10] M. Narasimha and G. Tsudik. Dsac: integrity for outsourced databases with signature aggregation and chaining. In *Proceedings of the 14th ACM international conference on Information and knowledge management*, pages 235–236. ACM, 2005.
[11] R. Sion. Query execution assurance for outsourced databases. In *Proceedings of the 31st international conference on Very large data bases*, pages 601–612. VLDB Endowment, 2005.
[12] H. Wang, J. Yin, C.-s. Perng, C.-s., and P. S. Yu. Dual encryption for query integrity assurance. In *Proceedings of the 17th ACM conference on Information and knowledge management*, pages 863–872. ACM, 2008.
[13] Y. Zhu, H. Wang, Z. Hu, G.-J. Ahn, H. Hu, and S. S. Yau. Dynamic audit services for integrity verification of outsourced storages in clouds. In *Proceedings of the 2011 ACM Symposium on Applied Computing*, pages 1550–1557. ACM, 2011.

BigGate: Access Control Framework for Outsourced Key-Value Stores

Erman Pattuk
The Univ. of Texas at Dallas
800 West Campbell Road
Richardson, Texas, 75080
erman.pattuk@utdallas.edu

Murat Kantarcioglu
The Univ. of Texas at Dallas
800 West Campbell Road
Richardson, Texas, 75080
muratk@utdallas.edu

Huseyin Ulusoy
The Univ. of Texas at Dallas
800 West Campbell Road
Richardson, Texas, 75080
huseyin.ulusoy@utdallas.edu

ABSTRACT

Due to its scalable design, key-value stores have become the backbone of many large-scale Internet companies that need to cope with millions of transactions every day. It is also an attractive cloud outsourcing technology: driven by economical benefits, many major companies like Amazon, Google, and Microsoft provide key-value storage services to their customers. However, customers are reluctant to utilize such services due to security and privacy concerns. Outsourced sensitive key-value data (e.g., social security numbers as keys, and health reports as value) may be stolen by third-party adversaries and/or malicious insiders. Furthermore, an institution, who is utilizing key-value storage services, may naturally desire to have access control mechanisms among its departments or users, while leaking as little information as possible to the cloud provider to preserve data privacy. We believe that addressing these security and privacy concerns are crucial in further adoption of key-value storage services. In this paper, we present a novel system, BigGate, that provides secure outsourcing and efficient processing of encrypted key-value data, and enforces access control policies. We formally prove the security of our system, and by carefully implemented empirical analysis, show that the overhead induced by BigGate can be as low as 2%.

Categories and Subject Descriptors

H.2 [**Database Management**]; H.2.7 [**Database Administration**]: Security, integrity, and protection

Keywords

Key-Value Stores; Security and Privacy; Access Control; Outsourcing; Cloud Computing; Searchable Encryption

1. INTRODUCTION

Exponential increase in the volume of data generated and collected every day forced large-scale Internet companies to invent more efficient data management solutions. When

existing relational databases failed to scale, pioneered by Google's BigTable [11] and Amazon's Dynamo [14], *Key-Value Stores* emerged as a popular choice to store and mine the so-called *Big Data*. In addition to popular services such as *Platform-as-a-service* [18] and *Software-as-a-service* [25], many major companies (e.g., Google's BigTable, Amazon's SimpleDB [2], Microsoft's Azure [8]) added *key-value storage services* to their repertoire to allow customers to leverage the efficiency of key-value stores.

On the customer side, it is extremely tempting to adopt key-value storage services (i) to gain economical benefits by reducing IT related costs, and (ii) to mitigate the burden of IT management and devote more time to core business tasks. However, handing out possibly sensitive data to a distant location inherently introduces security and privacy challenges. One of those critical challenges is securing outsourced key-value pairs against different attacks (e.g., [19, 23]), while providing efficient query processing capabilities such as searching and retrieving key-value pairs. Another challenge is to provide access control for key-value pairs, while leaking minimal information to unauthorized parties. Addressing these challenges is crucial, since multiple users or departments inside the customer organization may be utilizing the same storage service, and access to sensitive data may need to be controlled to prevent any misuse.

Although there are some recent works trying to address above challenges separately, to our knowledge, none of them addresses the aforementioned challenges simultaneously for key-value stores. For example, *BigSecret* aims to secure outsourced key-value data in a multiple cloud setup, but does not consider multi-tenant utilization, in which access control is a necessity [22]. Apache's *Accumulo* is a successful open-source key-value store implementation that provides fine-grained access control in a multi-tenant setup. However, it necessitates that the cloud provider, who runs the Accumulo instance, is *fully trusted*. In a real-world scenario, this means that the cloud provider learns all private outsourced information, since it has the control to peek in and read key-value pairs. Furthermore, Accumulo is an *extension* to BigTable-like key-value stores, with own specific implementation. However, what we need is a generic framework that is easily applicable to all key-value stores with minimal effort. On the other hand, nearly all remaining popular key-value store implementations lack even basic security mechanisms, such as encryption of data at rest, simple access control among the users [20]. Finally, it is not possible to directly combine a scheme like *Accumulo* with *BigSecret* to address the aforementioned challenges since creating private access control mechanisms over encrypted key-value stores may require a complete redesign.

A naive approach to propose secure and efficient solutions for key-value stores would be to directly apply off-the-shelf cryptographic techniques or existing solutions for relational databases. Attribute based encryption (ABE) is one such technique that can be employed to enforce access control policies on outsourced encrypted data [10]. However, as shown in Sect. 4, ABE application on key-value stores introduces extremely high overhead. For instance, average latency to execute a query takes $20s$ and average throughput drops down to $17opt/s$, while a plain setup with no security features has $5ms$ average latency and $1000opt/s$ throughput in most cases. Hence, developing secure and efficient systems for key-value stores requires tailored solutions. That is why solutions such as CryptDB may not necessarily be an efficient solution for key-value stores [24]. CryptDB focuses on relational data and addresses traditional SQL queries. Since relational databases are not designed to efficiently handle key-value data, new tools such as Apache HBase [7] are developed. Similarly, the processing of encrypted key-value data using encrypted relational data management system such as CryptDB is not scalable due to the underlying storage assumptions and lack of distributed processing.

To address the aforementioned challenges, we propose a novel security framework for key-value stores, BigGate, that (i) enables secure and efficient outsourcing of key-value pairs, and (ii) enforces two different modes of access control mechanisms in a multi-tenant setup. BigGate's generic design achieves easy integration with nearly all key-value store implementations, while providing provable security, efficiency, and access control.

1.1 Overview of BigGate

The entities in our work are (i) the cloud provider CP, which supplies key-value storage services to its customers; (ii) the set of users $\mathcal{U} = \{u_1, \ldots, u_k\}$, who benefit from the CP's services; (iii) the proxy PR, which acts as a mediator between $\mathcal{U}$ and CP, and is responsible for the management of outsourced encrypted data; (iv) the system administrator, whose only responsibility is to allow new users into the system by creating credentials, and to keep the master secret; and (v) the adversary that aims to learn private information of any user. In particular, PR is equipped with the BigGate implementation to secure outsourced data, to handle requests from multiple users efficiently, and to enforce access control policies.

To clarify the role of entities play in a real-life case, assume that a university, consisting of multiple departments, starts using BigGate. The users are separate departments, each having its own (potentially) private dataset; while the system administrator will be the IT department, welcoming new users into the system, and storing secrets. IT will acquire cloud storage services from a third-party cloud provider (e.g., Amazon, Microsoft), which is denoted as the CP in BigGate. Over time, IT may start utilizing services from another cloud service provider due to various reasons (e.g., to reduce costs). In such a case, the whole process of changing the service provider should be transparent to users. Hence, the users communicate with the collection of hardware that is setup by the IT, which we refer to as the proxy. The proxy is not necessarily located within the physical reach of the IT department; it may be a static resource on another cloud

service provider. In any case, the adversary (e.g., a hacker outside the campus domain) tries learning private data of the users, and may capture PR or CP. For brevity, the system administrator is referred to as the *admin*, whereas CP and BigGate may be used interchangeably.

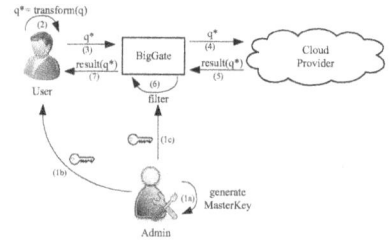

Figure 1: An overview of BigGate

Figure 1 shows an overview of the proposed system. The admin creates a master secret, which is used to derive all other cryptographic keys (step-1a). Each user is given a set of secret information (e.g., access rank, a set of labels, a set of cryptographic keys, etc.), once they are approved to utilize CP's services by the admin (step-1b). Finally, the admin creates the secret keys for the proxy, and instantiates BigGate implementation on PR (step-1c).

The users are allowed to execute several different query types, which are discussed thoroughly in Sect. 3, by communicating with BigGate. In case a user $u_i \in \mathcal{U}$ aims to execute a query q on the outsourced data, u_i employs an initial pre-processing on q (step-2) to hide private information. u_i uses its cryptographic keys to *encipher* private data in q, and sends the transformed query (i.e., q^*) to BigGate (step-3). BigGate checks the credentials of u_i to see if it is allowed to execute q, and sends q^* to CP (step-4). CP runs the transformed query, and returns the result to Big-Gate (step-5), which is post-processed for further eligibility and false positive filtering (step-6). The final set of result is handed over to u_i, who performs decryption, and acquires the actual result (step-7).

1.2 Adversarial Model

The adversary aims to learn the private information of a single or multiple users by, including but not limited to, capturing secret keys, stealing outsourced data, or eavesdropping communications. On the other hand, the goal of BigGate is to enforce access control policies, while mitigating possible *privacy loss* that may occur due to data theft and data processing. While we assume that the secret keys are kept hidden from the adversary, we note that the problem of protecting a secret key is orthogonal to this work. Furthermore, there exist many security protocols (e.g., *Secure Sockets Layer* [17, 16], *Transport Layer Security* [21, 15]) to establish encrypted and authenticated channels between two entities. Thus, we assume that inter-entity channels are created using any of those protocols, and are secure.

We model the adversary as *semi-honest*, i.e., it obeys the specifications of any protocol, while trying to infer as much private information as possible. Hence, the cloud provider and the proxy are semi-trusted by any user, since they could possibly get captured by the adversary. This choice of adversarial modeling is appropriate, since the outsourced data is encrypted, and the administrator or a user would eventually notice an unauthorized modification due to incorrect query results. Furthermore, the cloud provider may inquire to learn a user's private information, but may not be allowed to *modify* it, due to *service level agreements*; which makes the semi-honest model realistic. On the other hand, the users do not trust to each other, and hide personal data and secret keys from each other.

1.3 Contributions

In this paper, we make the following contributions:

- We present BigGate, a novel system that enables secure and efficient outsourcing in key-value stores, while providing two different access control models suitable for multi-tenant environments.

- We provide a formal security proof for BigGate, and show that our system is secure, even when CP and PR are captured by a semi-honest adversary.

- As a proof-of-concept, we implement a prototype of BigGate; and empirically show that it is applicable to real-world scenarios with overhead as low as 2%.

1.4 Outline

We start by providing background information in Sect. 2, about the cryptographic primitives used in BigGate. It is followed by the proposed system in Sect. 3. Sect. 4 shows the results of the empirical analysis performed. In Sect. 5, we provide a formal security proof of BigGate. Finally, we explain the related work in Sect. 6, and conclude the work in Sect. 7.

2. BACKGROUND

In this section, we describe the cryptographic primitives that form the basis of our construction in BigGate.

A symmetric encryption scheme `SKE:=(Gen, E, D)` is composed of three polynomial-time algorithms:

1. `Gen`:$1^l \rightarrow \{0,1\}^k$ takes a security parameter 1^l, and returns a secret key $K \in \{0,1\}^k$.

2. `E`:$\{0,1\}^k \times \{0,1\}^n \rightarrow \{0,1\}^n$ encrypts a plaintext message $p \in \{0,1\}^n$ with a secret key $K \in \{0,1\}^k$.

3. `D`:$\{0,1\}^k \times \{0,1\}^n \rightarrow \{0,1\}^n$ decrypts a ciphertext $c \in \{0,1\}^n$ using a secret key $K \in \{0,1\}^k$.

A *secure* symmetric encryption scheme implies that a ciphertext gives no information about the corresponding plaintext or the key, and is computationally indistinguishable from random strings [13].

A pseudo-random function (PRF) is a polynomial-time computable function, whose output is indistinguishable from a random function by any polynomial-time adversary. A `PRF:=(Gen, H)` is composed of two functions:

1. `Gen`:$1^l \rightarrow \{0,1\}^k$ takes a security parameter 1^l, and returns a secret key $K \in \{0,1\}^k$.

2. `H`:$\{0,1\}^k \times \{0,1\}^* \rightarrow \{0,1\}^n$ calculates the digest of a plaintext message $m \in \{0,1\}^*$ with a secret key $K \in \{0,1\}^k$.

A *secure* PRF implies computational indistinguishability, *pre-image*, *second pre-image*, and *collusion* resistance.

A pseudo-random generator (PRG) is a polynomial-time computable function, whose output is indistinguishable from a random number generator by any polynomial-time adversary. A PRG is composed of a single function `PRG:=(G)`:

1. `G`:$\{0,1\}^n \rightarrow \{0,1\}^{2n}$ takes a seed $s \in \{0,1\}^n$ and produces a pseudo-random number $c \in \{0,1\}^{2n}$.

3. BigGate FRAMEWORK

BigGate has two types of access control policy enforcement mechanisms, namely *multi-level* and *attribute-based*. In the first mode, different access hierarchies are defined, whose secret keys are derived from a master secret owned by the admin. Each user is assigned an *access level*, and given the corresponding secret key. In this mode, a user that has access to level i can also access all encrypted data that is secured by a secret key of level j, where $i < j$. On the other hand, the second mode enforces attribute-based access control policies, in which each key-value pair is associated with a boolean expression, such that a user has access to a given key-value pair provided that user's credentials satisfy the expression. Each user is given a set of labels and the corresponding set of keys, which allows her to decrypt and learn the actual outsourced data.

BigGate supports three basic operations (i.e., *Store*, *Retrieve*, and *Remove*) that are inherently provided in all key-value store implementations. This property makes BigGate more generic and allows easy integration with numerous NoSQL systems. In this section, we describe each BigGate mode in detail and clarify (i) which entity possesses what secret information, (ii) what are the protocols for processing each query type.

3.1 Multi-Level (ML) Mode

As discussed before, each user is given an access level i, where $i > 0$, and $i = 1$ is the top access level; and the corresponding secret key that is used to encrypt the outsourced data. In this mode of operation, the smaller the access level, the more priority that user has.

The system is initialized by the admin, who creates the master secret key MK uniformly at random from the key space $\mathcal{K}$ using `Gen` method of `SKE`. Next, it chooses two random PRF keys $key_{\mathcal{U}}^{prf}$ and key_{CP}^{prf}, which are used by the set of users and the cloud provider to index outgoing key elements, respectively, by `Gen` method of `PRF`. Using these PRF keys, the users and the cloud provider manage a *cryptographic index* on the outsourced data, such that the number of false positives (i.e., a key-value pair that is not in the actual result list of a query, but is returned by CP due to collusion in indexing) is minimized. Finally, the admin chooses a secret key key_{PR}^{enc} uniformly at random from the key space for the proxy using `SKE.Gen`.

In the next step, the admin authorizes new users to benefit from the CP's key-value storage services. When a new user u_i is added to the authorized users list, it is given an access level $x > 0$ and the corresponding symmetric secret key key_x^{enc}. Given a pseudo-random generator `PRG:=(G)` and `left(.)` is the left half of the given input, level x key is calculated as x iterations of `G` function calls[1]:

$$key_x^{enc} \leftarrow \text{left}(\text{G}(key_{x-1}^{enc})), \text{ where } key_0^{enc} \leftarrow MK \quad (1)$$

[1]We remark that the input and output size of the PRG is adjusted to match the required key size for the SKE.

This mechanism allows a user at level x to calculate the secret keys for levels $i > x$, while forbidding it from the secret keys for $j < x$ due to the security of the pseudo-random generator.

Finally the proxy, where BigGate is running, is given what we refer to as the *access list* (AL) that shows, which user has what level of access. Using the given list, the proxy can check if a query originated from a user with access level x has the privileges to execute the query. Table 1 shows the summary of secret information possessions among the entities. It can be seen that the cloud provider receives only the encrypted key-value pairs, which does not reflect any information about the plaintext data.

Entity			
Admin	**User**	**Proxy**	**CP**
MK	$key_{\mathcal{U}}^{prf}$	key_{PR}^{prf}	Outsourced Data
	Access level x	key_{PR}^{enc}	
	key_x^{enc}	AL	

Table 1: Possession table for multi-level mode

As will be clear in the query execution protocols, a user encrypts any sensitive data, before handing it to the proxy. Hence, data privacy is protected, even if the proxy and the cloud provider are under the control of the semi-trusted adversary. Furthermore, the proxy learns no sensitive information, even if it misbehaves and does not enforce the access control policies as specified.

3.1.1 Store Query

Given a secure symmetric encryption scheme `SKE:=(Gen, E, D)`, and a secure pseudo-random function `PRF:=(Gen, H)`, the processing of a store query is as follows:

1. User $u \in \mathcal{U}$, with the access level x, holds a key-value pair (k, v) that will be stored on CP. (k, v) will be stored for the access level $x' \geq x$.

2. Using `SKE.Gen`, u generates a random key k_r^{enc}.

3. u calculates (k', v'), where $k' \leftarrow \mathtt{H}(key_{\mathcal{U}}^{prf}, k)$ and $v' \leftarrow \mathtt{E}(key_r^{enc}, k\|v)\|\mathtt{E}(key_{x'}^{enc}, k_r^{enc})\|x'$.

4. Proxy retrieves (k', v') from u.

5. Proxy checks if u is eligible to insert this pair for the access level x'. It proceeds to the next step if $x \leq x'$.

6. It calculates (k'', v''), where $k'' \leftarrow \mathtt{H}(key_{PR}^{prf}, k')$ and $v'' \leftarrow \mathtt{E}(key_{PR}^{enc}, k'\|v')$.

7. CP retrieves and stores (k'', v'')

To store a key-value pair, the user and the proxy, both, perform pre-processing on the outsourced data. As shown in step-3, u protects its private information from the proxy, simply by encrypting the concatenated sensitive elements with a randomly generated encryption key, while that key is encrypted with the access level key. Since the encryption scheme is secure, v' and v'' reflect no information about the plaintext key-value pair (k, v). Furthermore, it is impossible to invert H, and calculate k from k' or k''. Even though u encrypts its input prior to sending it to the proxy, the proxy re-encrypts the input (k', v') to hide the access level information from the cloud provider. By doing so, CP is inhibited from learning any information about the users' private data.

Prior to sending the transformed key-value pair to the cloud provider, BigGate checks if u is authorized to execute the *Store* query for the access level x', since u may be requesting to store this pair for a *higher* access level (e.g., u has access level 3, but the pair has access level 2). In case $x' < x$, BigGate filters out the request, and does not allow u to store such a pair, since u does not have the symmetric key for the access level x'.

The overhead of a store query in BigGate, with respect to an insecure implementation, is 1 PRF and 2 encryption calls for u; 1 PRF and 1 encryption calls for the PR.

3.1.2 Retrieve Query

Once the data is outsourced, the users will aim to execute retrieve queries to read data from CP. Now that the data is encrypted under an access level secret key, it will be read by only those who can calculate the decryption key:

1. User $u \in \mathcal{U}$, with the access level x, aims to read the value element of a particular key element k.

2. u calculates $k' \leftarrow \mathtt{H}(key_{\mathcal{U}}^{prf}, k)$.

3. Proxy gets the retrieve query for k'.

4. It calculates $k'' \leftarrow \mathtt{H}(key_{PR}^{prf}, k')$.

5. CP returns the corresponding (k'', v'') pair to proxy, if k'' is stored previously.

6. Proxy decrypts v'', and gets the access level x'.

7. By looking at the access list, proxy checks if u is eligible to read this key-value pair (i.e., if $x \leq x'$). If so, it returns (k', v') to u, where $v' \leftarrow \mathtt{D}(key_{PR}^{enc}, v'')$.

8. u calculates key_x^{enc}, retrieves the randomly generated key key_r^{enc} using decryption with key_x^{enc}, and uses key_r^{enc} to get v.

Once again, the user u and the proxy collaborate to perform a retrieve query on the outsourced data. The user u never reveals the queried key element k, since the proxy only observes the hashed value k'. Moreover, the proxy and the cloud provider learns nothing about the value element v during the execution. Once u retrieves encrypted version of the requested data, it first decrypts the prefix of v' and learns the random key key_r^{enc}. Then, that random key is used to decrypt the remaining part of v' and get v. The overhead of a retrieve query in BigGate is 1 PRF and 1 decryption calls for the proxy; 1 PRF and 2 decryption calls for u.

Although the query specifications require PR to enforce policies, it is critical to attain data privacy even if the adversary and a malicious user collaborate to expose sensitive data. Suppose an unauthorized user $u_A \in \mathcal{U}$ with access level x aims to read a key-value pair, which is encrypted with the secret key for access level $x' < x$ (i.e., with a stricter access level key). u_A collaborates with the adversary, who has already captured PR, and retrieves the encrypted key-value pair, even though she is not authorized to. Even under such circumstances, the security of that encrypted key-value pair is assured, since u_A cannot calculate the key for the access level $x' < x$ due to the security of PRG and SKE.

3.1.3 Remove Query

Processing a remove query is very similar to the processing of a retrieve query, except the very last step, where the user decrypts the resulting key-value pair. In detail, the execution is composed of the following stages:

1. User $u \in \mathcal{U}$, with the access level x, aims to remove the key-value pair of a particular key element k.

2. u calculates $k' \leftarrow \mathtt{H}(key_{\mathcal{U}}^{prf}, k)$.

3. Proxy gets the remove query for k'.

4. It calculates $k'' \leftarrow \mathtt{H}(key_{PR}^{prf}, k')$.

5. Then, proxy gets the key-value pair (k'', v'') from CP.

6. It decrypts v'' to get the access level for this entry, and checks if u is eligible to execute this operation.

7. If so, proxy requests to remove k'' from CP.

The querying user u should be eligible to remove the key-value pair. To check if that is the case, the proxy PR performs a retrieve query for the transformed key element k'. Once the result is received, it decrypts the value element, and checks if u has the appropriate access level. If u satisfies this condition, then PR requests a remove operation on the transformed key element k''. The overhead of this operation is 1 PRF for u; 1 PRF and 1 decryption for PR.

3.2 Attribute-Based (AB) Mode

In this mode of operation, each user is given a set of labels, which are in turn used to check if a boolean expression is satisfied for the queried key-value pair. In the system initialization phase, the admin uses $\mathtt{PRF.Gen}$ and generates the master secret MK. Next, it creates the set of ordered labels $\mathcal{L} = \{L_1, \ldots, L_n\}$, and n secret keys $key_{L_i}^{enc}$ for each label $L_i \in \mathcal{L}$ by $\mathtt{H}(MK, L_i)$. Then, it creates the common PRF key $key_{\mathcal{U}}^{prf}$ for the users, the PRF key_{PR}^{prf} and encryption keys key_{PR}^{enc} for the proxy using $\mathtt{PRF.Gen}$ and $\mathtt{SKE.Gen}$.

Once the initialization phase is over, the admin starts authorizing new users into the system. A new authorized user u_i is given the set of labels that she has access to (i.e., $L_{i_1}, \ldots, L_{i_k}$), and the corresponding keys for the labels (i.e., $key_{L_{i_1}}^{enc}, \ldots, key_{L_{i_k}}^{enc}$).

When BigGate enforces fine-grained policies, a boolean expression for a key-value pair is always processed in its *disjunctive normal form* (DNF). In particular, a boolean expression b is disjunction of a set of components $c_1, \ldots, c_m$, where each component is conjunction of a set of literals:

$$b := c_1 \bigvee \ldots \bigvee c_m, \text{ where } c_i := L_{i_1} \bigwedge \ldots \bigwedge L_{i_k} \quad (2)$$

Finally the proxy is given the updated *access list* showing which user holds which labels. Using the given list, the proxy can check if the user u with the set of labels $\mathcal{L}_u$ has the privileges to execute a given query. Table 2 gives a summary of secret information possessions among the entities. It can be seen that CP receives only the encrypted key-value pairs, which reflects no information about the plaintext data.

Given a component c_i of the boolean expression b, the user calculates the secret key $key_{c_i}^{enc}$ by concatenating all

Entity			
Admin	**User**	**Proxy**	**CP**
MK	$key_{\mathcal{U}}^{prf}$	key_{PR}^{prf}	Outsourced Data
	Set of labels $\mathcal{L}_u$	key_{PR}^{enc}	
	$key_{L_i}^{enc} \; \forall L_i \in \mathcal{L}_u$	AL	

Table 2: Possession table for attribute-based mode

label encryption keys of c_i in ascending order and hashing the result with $key_{\mathcal{U}}^{prf}$:

$$key_{c_i}^{enc} \leftarrow \mathtt{H}(key_{\mathcal{U}}^{prf}, key')$$
$$\text{where } key' \leftarrow key_{L_{i_1}}^{enc} \| \ldots \| key_{L_{i_k}}^{enc} \quad (3)$$

3.2.1 Store Query

Given a secure symmetric encryption scheme $\mathtt{SKE} := (\mathtt{Gen}, \mathtt{E}, \mathtt{D})$, and a secure pseudo-random function $\mathtt{PRF} := (\mathtt{Gen}, \mathtt{H})$, the processing of a store query is as follows:

1. User $u \in \mathcal{U}$, with the set of labels $\mathcal{L}_u$, holds a key-value pair (k, v) that will be stored on CP. The boolean expression for this key-value entry will be $b := c_1 \bigvee \ldots \bigvee c_m$, where u satisfies each $c_i \in b$.

2. Using $\mathtt{SKE.Gen}$, u generates a random key k_r^{enc}.

3. For $i = 1$ to $i = m$, u encrypts the random key with the component key $key_{c_i}^{enc}$ to get $v_i' \leftarrow \mathtt{E}(key_{c_i}^{enc}, k_r^{enc})$.

4. User calculates $v_0' \leftarrow \mathtt{E}(key_r^{enc}, k \| v)$.

5. Finally, u sends b and (k', v') to the proxy, where $k' \leftarrow \mathtt{H}(key_{\mathcal{U}}^{prf}, k)$ and $v' \leftarrow v_0' \| \ldots \| v_m'$.

6. Proxy calculates (k'', v''), where $k'' \leftarrow \mathtt{H}(key_{PR}^{prf}, k')$ and $v'' \leftarrow \mathtt{E}(key_{PR}^{enc}, k' \| v' \| b)$.

7. CP retrieves and stores (k'', v'').

Unlike the multi-level mode, the size of the ciphertext v' linearly increase with the number of components in the boolean expression b. For each single component c_i in b, u calculates the component key and encrypts the randomly generated key, which is used to encrypt the actual key-value pair (k, v). Since the encryption scheme is secure, v' reflects no information about the plaintext key-value pair (k, v). Furthermore, it is impossible to invert $\mathtt{H}$ and calculate k from k' or k''. Once again, the proxy performs re-encryption of the outsourced data to hide b from CP. The proxy sends the resulting key-value pair (k'', v'') to CP and terminates.

The overhead of a store query in BigGate, with respect to an unmodified insecure implementation, is $m + 1$ PRF and $m + 1$ encryption calls for the user, 1 PRF and 1 encryption calls for the proxy, where m is the number of DNF components in the boolean expression.

3.2.2 Retrieve Query

Executing a retrieve query in the attribute-based mode is quite similar to the processing in the multi-level mode, except the way the proxy checks the eligibility of the user. Rather than a simple access level check, BigGate has to calculate if the querying user u satisfies the boolean expression. Satisfying even one of the DNF components implies that u has enough set of labels to *read* the key-value pair. Processing of a retrieve query is composed of the following steps:

1. User $u \in \mathcal{U}$, with the set of labels $\mathcal{L}_u$, aims to read the value element of a particular key element k.

2. u calculates $k' \leftarrow \mathtt{H}(key_{\mathcal{U}}^{prf}, k)$.

3. Proxy gets the retrieve query for k'.

4. Proxy calculates $k'' \leftarrow \mathtt{H}(key_{PR}^{prf}, k')$.

5. It retrieves v'' from CP and decrypts it to get the boolean expression b.

6. By looking at the access list, proxy checks if u is eligible to read this key-value pair (i.e., if u's labels satisfy b).

7. If so, it returns v' and b to u.

8. u calculates a component key $key_{c_i}^{enc}$ that can be satisfied by its labels, decrypts v'_i to get the random encryption key key_r^{enc}, and gets $v \leftarrow \mathtt{D}(key_r^{enc}, v'_0)$.

Once again, the user u and the proxy PR collaborate to perform a retrieve query. u never reveals the queried key element k, since PR only observes the hashed value k'. Moreover, PR and CP learns nothing about the value element v during the execution. Only PR sees the boolean expression for the queried key-value pair, while CP learns nothing about the raw data. The overhead of a retrieve query in the attribute-based mode is 1 PRF and 2 decryption call for u, and 1 PRF and 1 decryption calls for PR.

The security guarantees in the previous mode is also provided while enforcing attribute-based access control policies. Let's assume that the adversary, who controls the proxy, does not follow the retrieve query specifications, and gives an encrypted key-value pair to a collaborating malicious user. That user cannot decrypt the key-value pair, since she cannot generate the SKE keys. Hence, data privacy is protected, even if the proxy does not enforce the policies.

3.2.3 Remove Query

To issue a remove query for a key element k, the user u is required to satisfy at least one component of the boolean expression b. BigGate checks if this condition is met, simply by looking at its access list. Specifically, the following steps are performed to execute a remove query:

1. User $u \in \mathcal{U}$, with the set of labels $\mathcal{L}_u$, aims to remove the key-value pair of a particular key element k.

2. u calculates $k' \leftarrow \mathtt{H}(key_{\mathcal{U}}^{prf}, k)$.

3. Proxy gets the remove query for k'.

4. It calculates $k'' \leftarrow \mathtt{H}(key_{PR}^{prf}, k')$.

5. Then, proxy retrieves (k'', v'') from CP.

6. It decrypts v'' to get b for the queried key element k, and checks if u is eligible to execute the operation.

7. If so, proxy requests to remove k'' from CP.

The overhead of this operation is 1 PRF for the user; 1 PRF and 1 decryption calls for the proxy.

4. EXPERIMENTAL EVALUATION

In this section, we will discuss the experimental setup and show the evaluation results.

4.1 Experimental Setup

As it is challenging to exhaustively implement and test BigGate to support each existing key-value store, our current implementation supports only Apache HBase [7]. HBase is an open source, distributed key-value store implementation, based on Google's BigTable [11]. It is a persistent, and strictly consistent storage system using Hadoop Distributed File System (HDFS) [6] for data storage.

We have developed a multi-threaded proxy server application written in Java that handles incoming requests as described in Sect. 3. It queues the incoming requests from the users, and processes them in order using the *thread pool architecture*. In addition to the proxy application, we have developed a thick client library in Java, which performs preprocessing and post-processing on the user's requests transparently. The keys for BigGate modes are given to each user by the system administrator, which in turn are used while communicating with the proxy.

As the *cloud provider* entity, we used a cluster of 6 nodes, which is located in our university campus network. Each node in the cluster has an Intel Xeon E5 at 1.90 GHz with 1TB disk space and 16GB of main memory. On the other hand, our proxy implementation is executed on an IBM x3500 m3 server with 16GB of main memory, and 4 quad-core CPUs at 2.4 GHz. Finally, *Yahoo! Cloud Serving Benchmark* (YCSB) v0.1.4 [12] is employed to generate user queries, which is executed on a separate machine with the same configuration as the proxy. Both machines are located in the university campus, and all three entities (i.e., the users, the proxy, and the cloud provider) communicate with each other via campus network of 1 Gbps. The performance metrics that are measured in this paper are as follows:

- Average latency (ms): It is the average time spent in milliseconds to issue a query and get the result on the user-side. Our aim is to observe if running BigGate (with ML or AB) introduces a further delay for the query execution from the user's perspective. Increased latency implies that a user waits more to finalize an operation.

- Average time spent in user-proxy communication (ms): This metric shows the average time spent in milliseconds for the network communication between a user and the proxy, which includes sending a query (e.g., sending the key and value elements), and getting the result (e.g., getting a value element).

- Average time spent in proxy-cloud communication (ms): This metric is the average time spent for the proxy-cloud network communication, which is basically the time between the proxy sending the query, and getting the result from the cloud provider.

- Throughput (opt/s): It is simply the number of queries executed per second, which will potentially increase as the number of concurrent users increase.

We measure the average latency and throughput using the results from the YCSB tool, while the other two metrics are measured within our implementation. Each experiment runs for 5 minutes, and repeated 5 times, where the average value is represents the final result.

The number of users, who concurrently send queries to the proxy, changes exponentially between 1 to 300, in order

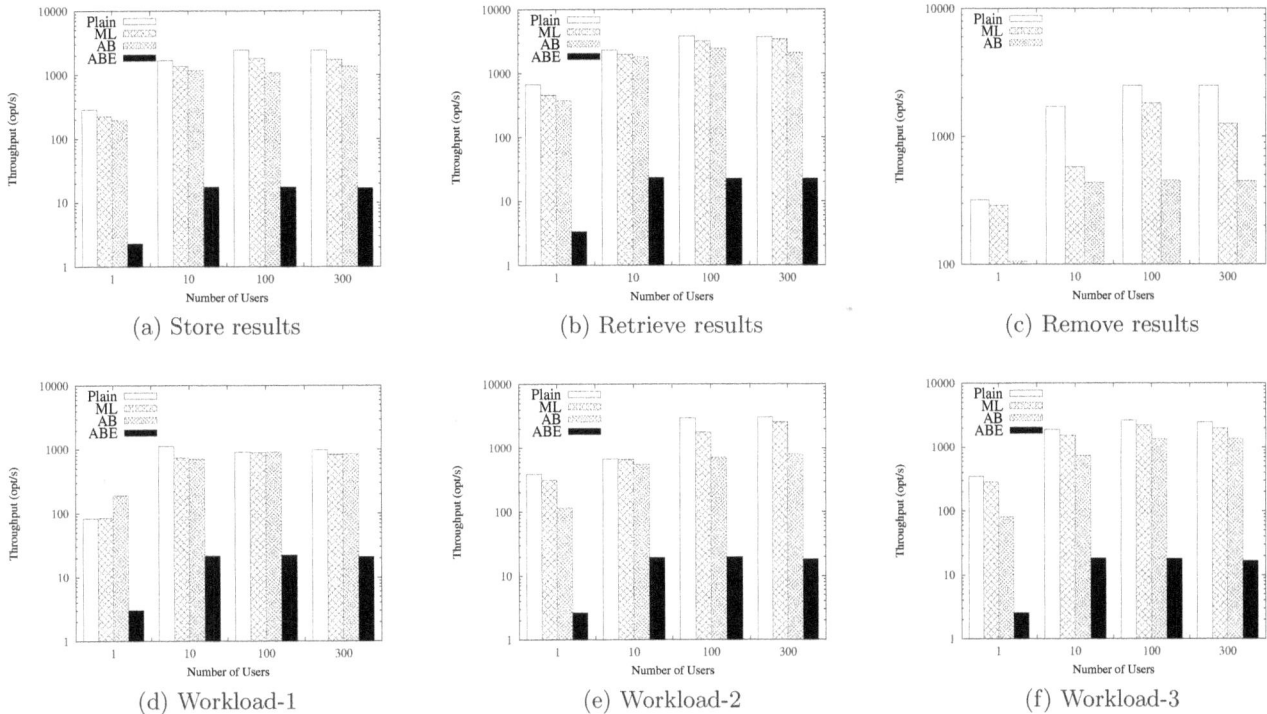

(a) Store results   (b) Retrieve results   (c) Remove results

(d) Workload-1   (e) Workload-2   (f) Workload-3

Figure 2: Throughput results for micro-benchmarking and workload experiments

to observe the performance with increased load. The upper limit of 300 users is based on the limitations of using a single machine to send queries from, and several reports (e.g., [3, 1]), which show that the average number of web page views for most popular web sites is nearly 37 billion per year (i.e., nearly 1100 per second). Furthermore, we believe the number 300 is enough to mine rules about the performance of BigGate. Throughout the experiments, we used SHA-512 as the pseudo-random function, and AES-256 in CTR mode as the symmetric key encryption mechanism; while the size of a key-value pair is 1.1KB in total (a key element is 100 bytes, and a value element is 1 KB).

We tested two modes of BigGate (i.e., Multi-Level (ML) and Attribute-Based (AB)), and the *Plain* setup, which includes no protection at all. In the plain setup, the proxy simply relays the information from a user to the cloud proxy, and does not employ any security mechanism. The purpose of having such a setup is to observe the effects of security mechanism overhead by BigGate. To compare and show that applying off-the-shelf techniques to key-value stores is inadequate, we implemented and tested ciphertext-policy attribute-based encryption (ABE) scheme of Bethencourt et al. [10]. In this mode, the users encrypt data with ABE prior to outsourcing with their attribute keys, and can only decrypt retrieved data if they can satisfy the boolean expression associated with the key-value pair.

We start by executing a micro benchmarking, in which we measure the average performance for each query type. Our aim in that set of experiments is to extrapolate rules about the overhead induced by BigGate. It is followed by separate realistic experiments, where we measure the behavior under three different *workloads*. The three workloads are:

- Workload 1: This is the retrieve intensive workload, with 75% retrieve and 25% store queries. This type of workload resembles newspaper web sites, in which insertions are rare in compare to read requests, since each user would like to read the latest news.

- Workload 2: The rate of retrieve and store queries are equal (i.e., 50%) in this workload. An example for this workload would be a social web site, where the users update their information through feeds, and read the data of their *friends*.

- Workload 3: This is the store intensive workload, with 25% retrieve and 75% store queries. Auditing applications would be a nice example for this type of workload.

4.2 Micro Benchmarks

Table 3 shows the latency results for the store query, augmented with the average time spent on *user-proxy* and *proxy-cloud* network communication. We observe that the latency values are mainly dominated by the proxy-cloud network communication for 1 and 10 concurrent users, which is approximately 65% of the average latency. The communication between the set of users and the proxy is nearly negligible, since the interaction is limited to sending the query and retrieving the final result. We observe that as the number of concurrent users exceeds 100, the latency values increase dramatically. This is natural, in the sense that the proxy has to queue the incoming requests, since it cannot handle each request (e.g., 300 at maximum) at the same time. Creating an execution thread for each incoming request and actually processing them at the same time would result in resource consumption and race condition among the threads. That is simply the reason behind increased latency values, while other two metrics (i.e., user-proxy and proxy-cloud) are almost the same.

		Number of concurrent users			
		1	10	100	300
Plain	Total	3.511	5.986	40.970	207.35
	User-Proxy	0.036	0.037	0.038	0.038
	Proxy-Cloud	2.674	5.125	4.006	4.059
ML	Total	4.404	7.404	55.319	289.737
	User-Proxy	0.188	0.055	0.051	0.052
	Proxy-Cloud	3.057	6.391	5.315	5.574
AB	Total	5.079	8.495	92.402	371.705
	User-Proxy	0.233	0.103	0.068	0.056
	Proxy-Cloud	3.635	7.305	8.942	7.172
ABE	Total	438.729	576.916	5731.8	29040.4
	User-Proxy	429.043	550.15	551.361	572.647
	Proxy-Cloud	7.772	23.188	23.885	14.324

Table 3: Average latency in *ms* for *Store* query

We see that BigGate in ML mode behaves very similar to the Plain setup, while overhead of BigGate in AB gets slightly high as the number of users exceed 100. On the other hand, even for 1 concurrent client, we see that applying existing attribute-based encryption techniques to key-value stores introduces huge overheads, increasing the average latency to $438ms$.

Figure 2a shows the average throughput values for a store query, in which BigGate gives very close results to the Plain setup. However, the number of operations performed for ABE drops down to 17 in almost all cases. The reason for having such huge overhead is the amount of work that is done in a single encryption using ABE. Clients have to perform a lot of work prior to outsourcing a single key-value pair, leading to such low performance values.

On the other hand, we see that the throughput values increase sharply as the number of concurrent users increase from 1 to 10. However, the throughput stays within a certain bound for all three setups (i.e., Plain, ML, and AB). The throughput values do not increase further as the users increase, due to the cloud provider being already saturated with enough requests. To improve the throughput, the cloud provider should horizontally scale by adding new nodes to the cluster.

Table 4 shows the results for the retrieve query type. We see that the latency values for the Plain setup and BigGate modes are quite similar due to the PRF and encryption mechanisms introduced by BigGate[2]. In terms of throughput, as shown in Fig. 2b, the difference between the Plain setup and BigGate drops down to 10%. On the contrary, ABE setup is very inefficient, mostly giving $16opt/s$. Such values prove that key-value stores require light-weight operations, rather than complicated cryptographic techniques.

Table 5 and Fig. 2c show the average latency and average throughput results for the remove query type. We observe that BigGate introduces approximately 40% overhead in both modes, mainly due to sequential structure of a remove query. As described in Sect. 3, the proxy has to check if the querying user is allowed to complete the remove operation. To do so, the proxy should first perform a retrieve operation for the queried key-value pair. Remove query is executed if the user satisfies this requirement, giving us a two-step execution.

---

[2]We note that the latency values include user-side processing as well (e.g., encryption of value element, hashing of key element).

		Number of concurrent users			
		1	10	100	300
Plain	Total	1.464	4.265	26.149	130.871
	User-Proxy	0.034	0.040	0.045	0.043
	Proxy-Cloud	0.633	3.356	2.510	2.564
ML	Total	2.128	4.976	30.968	144.601
	User-Proxy	0.055	0.047	0.050	0.050
	Proxy-Cloud	0.888	3.894	2.887	2.704
AB	Total	2.611	5.537	40.226	236.531
	User-Proxy	0.050	0.055	0.055	0.062
	Proxy-Cloud	1.475	4.385	4.385	4.502
ABE	Total	294.756	418.652	4048.7	10935.7
	User-Proxy	0.189	0.169	1.105	1.800
	Proxy-Cloud	3.233	2.640	2.164	2.006

Table 4: Average latency in *ms* for *Retrieve* query

		Number of concurrent users			
		1	10	100	300
Plain	Total	3.101	5.724	39.858	197.473
	User-Proxy	0.030	0.030	0.037	0.038
	Proxy-Cloud	2.275	4.908	3.885	3.891
ML	Total	3.369	16.831	54.579	393.777
	User-Proxy	0.040	0.040	0.042	0.043
	Proxy-Cloud	2.358	15.891	5.281	7.750
AB	Total	9.392	22.679	220.28	1116.78
	User-Proxy	0.036	0.040	0.043	0.044
	Proxy-Cloud	8.441	21.717	21.875	22.189

Table 5: Average latency in *ms* for *Remove* query

4.3 Workload Experiments

Tables 6 to 8 show the average latency values for 3 different workloads, while Fig. 2d to Fig. 2f show the average throughput values.

		Number of concurrent users			
		1	10	100	300
Plain	Total	12.065	8.900	109.933	507.525
	User-Proxy	0.049	0.044	0.046	0.046
	Proxy-Cloud	11.216	7.993	10.905	10.066
ML	Total	11.773	13.445	112.912	599.534
	User-Proxy	0.101	0.055	0.059	0.080
	Proxy-Cloud	10.549	12.383	11.081	11.774
AB	Total	5.238	14.201	109.863	591.305
	User-Proxy	0.104	0.069	0.065	0.064
	Proxy-Cloud	4.078	13.060	10.759	11.579
ABE	Total	330.841	452.888	4298.4	20296.0
	User-Proxy	116.084	146.983	434.164	435.118
	Proxy-Cloud	2.403	3.130	3.148	3.784

Table 6: Average latency in *ms* for Workload-1

For the retrieve-intensive workload (i.e., workload-1), we observe that BigGate in both modes perform almost the same as the plain setup in terms of throughput. We observe a slight overhead around 10% only when the number of concurrent client is 10. In remaining three cases, we observe that the maximum overhead is around 2%. On the other hand, we see that applying ABE to key-value stores performs almost with 99% overhead for the retrieve-intensive workload. The main reason is the amount of work that a client has to perform during the execution of a single retrieve or store query when using ABE technique. Although the underlying infrastructure (i.e., the hardware) can handle up to 1000 operations per second as shown in the plain setup, client cannot finish encrypting/decrypting data, and do not saturate the infrastructure enough. Our results for throughput coincide with the latency results in workload-1. We see that even when the number of concurrent clients is

		Number of concurrent users			
		1	10	100	300
Plain	Total	2.537	14.666	33.102	159.815
	User-Proxy	0.034	0.042	0.039	0.040
	Proxy-Cloud	1.707	13.779	3.220	3.158
ML	Total	3.127	14.954	54.456	188.587
	User-Proxy	0.143	0.062	0.057	0.065
	Proxy-Cloud	1.920	13.920	5.365	3.620
AB	Total	8.595	18.041	140.690	627.832
	User-Proxy	0.155	0.079	0.067	0.074
	Proxy-Cloud	7.394	16.944	13.845	12.311
ABE	Total	377.670	496.526	4642.8	20204.0
	User-Proxy	240.184	278.406	474.869	485.495
	Proxy-Cloud	3.456	4.868	6.269	6.688

Table 7: Average latency in ms for Workload-2

		Number of concurrent users			
		1	10	100	300
Plain	Total	2.865	5.143	37.773	199.395
	User-Proxy	0.034	0.036	0.039	0.039
	Proxy-Cloud	2.2024	4.290	3.655	3.948
ML	Total	3.436	6.251	44.414	247.853
	User-Proxy	0.183	0.063	0.059	0.063
	Proxy-Cloud	2.237	5.257	4.230	4.783
AB	Total	12.293	13.512	73.529	360.540
	User-Proxy	0.193	0.086	0.063	0.074
	Proxy-Cloud	10.847	12.439	7.111	6.964
ABE	Total	392.090	530.206	5067.9	24457.2
	User-Proxy	299.068	408.751	520.162	559.392
	Proxy-Cloud	3.935	12.558	11.987	6.367

Table 8: Average latency in ms for Workload-3

300, there is only $90ms$ difference between the plain setup and BigGate modes.

When the rate of store queries increase, as in workload-2, we observe that BigGate AB mode gets to have more overhead with respect to its performance in workload-1. This happens mainly due to the increased CPU dependency to process a store query in AB mode. Since, the number of operations that the client should perform linearly increase with the size of the boolean expression, executing a store query may degrade performance slightly in a real-world workload. On the other hand, we see that BigGate in ML mode has almost identical performance with respect to the plain setup in terms of throughput with at most 20% overhead for 100 concurrent clients, and 5% in remaining cases. The reason stems from the simplicity of operations in ML mode in comparison to the operations in AB mode. Once again, we observe that ABE gives the least performance with approximately $17opt/s$ and almost $20s$.

Finally, for the store-intensive workload (i.e., workload-3), we see that increased store query rate affects BigGate in AB mode negatively. The overhead increases up to 40% in terms of throughput and to 50% in terms latency for Big-Gate in AB mode. As stated previously, store query processing of the AB mode heavily affects the performance. On the contrary, we see that BigGate in ML mode performs with at most 20% overhead. However, ABE is still the slowest technique that is absolutely not applicable to any real-world scenario in key-value stores domain.

5. SECURITY

To prove the security of BigGate, we should first consider what are the possible adversarial setups. Since, we have two entities that the adversary can take control of (e.g., the proxy and the cloud provider), there are 3 possible adversarial setups: (i) the proxy and the cloud provider are cap-tured, (ii) only the cloud provider is captured, or (iii) only the proxy is captured. We will investigate only the worst case, in which both the proxy and the cloud provider are captured by the semi-honest adversary, since doing so will also prove the security in the other two cases.

In this work, we adapt the simulation based adaptive semantic security definition in [13] to prove that BigGate is secure. Proving security using this definition is almost a standard in searchable symmetric encryption schemes, in which the data owner (i.e., the set of users in our setup) encrypts and outsources data management to a third party (i.e., the cloud provider) with efficient searching capabilities. We base our proof on the simulation based approach, since BigGate is, in fact, a searchable symmetric encryption scheme that is specifically designed for key-value stores. Before proceeding to the actual proof, we have to make some definitions for formalization.

5.1 Multi-Level Mode

We assume that a user $u \in \mathcal{U}$ with access level x holds a set of key-value pairs $\mathcal{D} := \{(k_1, v_1), \ldots, (k_n, v_n)\}$, and wants to outsource them to a cloud provider using BigGate. It uses a secure pseudo-random function $\texttt{PRF} := (\texttt{Gen}, \texttt{H})$, a secure symmetric encryption scheme $\texttt{SKE} := (\texttt{Gen}, \texttt{E}, \texttt{D})$, and a pseudo-random generator $\texttt{PRG} := (\texttt{G})$ as mentioned in Sect. 2. Furthermore, it holds $K := (key_{\mathcal{U}}^{prf}, key_x^{enc})$ hidden from the proxy and the cloud provider, where the first and second is u's PRF and symmetric encryption keys, respectively. Once the data is outsourced to the cloud provider, u will query q key elements $\mathcal{W} := \{w_1, \ldots, w_q\}$.

DEFINITION 1. *A q-query history over $\mathcal{D}$ is a sequence $H_q := (\mathcal{D}, w_1, \ldots, w_q)$ that includes the outsourced key-value pairs, and q queried key elements.*

DEFINITION 2. *The search pattern induced by the q-query history $H_q := (\mathcal{D}, w_1, \ldots, w_q)$ is the q-by-q symmetric matrix $\sigma(H_q)$, such that $\sigma[i,j] := 1$ if $w_i = w_j$, and 0 otherwise.*

DEFINITION 3. *Given a q-query history $H_q := (\mathcal{D}, w_1, \ldots, w_q)$, the adversary's view of H_q under the secret cryptographic key pair of u, $K := (key_{\mathcal{U}}^{prf}, key_x^{enc})$, is the sequence $V_K(H_q) := (\texttt{E}(key_x^{enc}, k_1 \| v_1), \ldots, \texttt{E}(key_x^{enc}, k_n \| v_n), \texttt{H}(key_{\mathcal{U}}^{prf}, k_1), \ldots, \texttt{H}(key_{\mathcal{U}}^{prf}, k_n), \texttt{H}(key_{\mathcal{U}}^{prf}, w_1), \ldots, \texttt{H}(key_{\mathcal{U}}^{prf}, w_q), x).$*

The view is the information that the adversary observes during the execution of our protocol. First of all, the adversary is given the encrypted key-value pairs by the user, which is simply the set $(\texttt{H}(key_{\mathcal{U}}^{prf}, k_j), \texttt{E}(key_x^{enc}, k_j \| v_j))$ for $1 \leq j \leq n$. Moreover, the adversary will observe the set of queried key elements, which is $\texttt{H}(key_{\mathcal{U}}^{prf}, w_j)$ for $1 \leq j \leq q$; and the access level of u, which is simply x.

DEFINITION 4. *Given a q-query history $H_q := (\mathcal{D}, w_1, \ldots, w_q)$, the trace of H_q under the secret cryptographic key pair of u, $K := (key_{\mathcal{U}}^{prf}, key_x^{enc})$, is the sequence $\tau(H_q) := (\sigma(H_q), |k_1 \| v_1|, \ldots, |k_n \| v_n|, x).$*

The trace is actually what the user allows the adversary to see, i.e., what the adversary is limited to see, throughout the execution. In another way, the adversary is not allowed to see anything more than the search pattern, access level of the user, and the size of each concatenated key-value pair. We assume that the size of the PRF used by the user is a public information, so the adversary knows $(\mathtt{H}(key_{\mathcal{U}}^{prf}, k_j)$ for any $1 \le j \le n$.

Given the definitions, we define what a secure outsourcing mechanism is, as in [13], which tolerates the leakage of search pattern to an adversary.

DEFINITION 5. *A symmetric searchable encryption scheme is adaptively semantically secure, if there exists a probabilistic polynomial time simulator S that can adaptively simulate an adversary's view of the history from the trace with probability negligibly close to 1. More formally, for any polynomial size distinguisher D, for all polynomials poly and a large r:*

$$Pr[D(V_K(H_q)) = 1] - Pr[D(S(\tau(H_q))) = 1] < \frac{1}{poly(r)}$$

where probabilities are taken over H_q, and the internal coins of key generation and encryption.

THEOREM 1. *Let $\mathtt{PRG:=(G)}$ be a pseudo-random generator, $\mathtt{PRF:=(Gen,H)}$ be a secure PRF, and $\mathtt{SKE:=(Gen,E,D)}$ be a semantically secure symmetric encryption scheme, then BigGate in multi-level mode satisfies Definition 5, and is adaptively semantically secure, when the proxy and the cloud provider are captured by a semi-honest adversary.*

PROOF. It suffices to show the existence of a polynomial size simulator S that creates a simulated view from the given trace (i.e., $S(\tau(H_q))$) indistinguishable from the real view $V_K(H_q)$.

- For the jth key-value pair $(1 \le j \le n)$: S chooses three random strings a_j, b_j, c_j, where $|b_j\|c_j| = |k_j\|v_j|$, and the length of a_j is the PRF's output length. The PRF is computationally indistinguishable, thus a_j is indistinguishable from $\mathtt{H}(key_{\mathcal{U}}^{prf}, k_j)$. Furthermore, since the symmetric encryption scheme is semantically secure, $\mathtt{E}(key_x^{enc}, k_j\|v_j)$ is computationally indistinguishable from $|b_j\|c_j|$.

- For the jth queried key element w_j for $1 \le j \le n$: if w_j was not asked before, S randomly creates a string $w_j^* \leftarrow d$, and simulate the actual queried key element $\mathtt{H}(key_{\mathcal{U}}^{prf}, w_j)$, where the length of d is the output size of the PRF. If w_j was asked before, then S simply reads the already assigned random string $w_j^* \leftarrow w_m^*$, where $\sigma[m, j] \leftarrow 1$ and $m < j$. S can check if a key element was asked before simply by looking at the search pattern, which is already given to the adversary. Since the PRF is secure, the simulated key elements are computationally indistinguishable from the actual queried key elements.

We conclude by stating that BigGate in multi-level mode is secure, since the generated view from the trace is computationally indistinguishable from the real view by any polynomially bounded adversary. □

5.2 Attribute-Based Mode

Proving security of the attribute-based mode is very similar to the case in multi-level mode, except a few changes in the view and trace definitions.

DEFINITION 6. *Given a q-query history $H_q := (\mathcal{D}, w_1, \ldots, w_q)$, the adversary's view of H_q under the secret cryptographic key pair of u, $K := (key_{\mathcal{U}}^{prf}, key_x^{enc})$, is the sequence*

$$V_K(H_q) := (E(key_x^{enc}, k_1\|v_1), \ldots, E(key_x^{enc}, k_n\|v_n), \mathtt{H}(key_{\mathcal{U}}^{prf}, k_1), \ldots, \mathtt{H}(key_{\mathcal{U}}^{prf}, k_n), b_1, \ldots, b_n, \mathtt{H}(key_{\mathcal{U}}^{prf}, w_1), \ldots, \mathtt{H}(key_{\mathcal{U}}^{prf}, w_q)).$$

In addition to the view definition in Def. 3, the adversary observes the boolean expression b_1 to b_n for each outsourced key-value pair.

DEFINITION 7. *Given a q-query history $H_q := (\mathcal{D}, w_1, \ldots, w_q)$, the trace of H_q under the secret cryptographic key pair of u, $K := (key_{\mathcal{U}}^{prf}, key_x^{enc})$, is the sequence $\tau(H_q) := (\sigma(H_q), |k_1\|v_1|, \ldots, |k_n\|v_n|, b_1, \ldots, b_n)$.*

The trace for the attribute-based mode is simply the search pattern, the size and boolean expression of each concatenated key-value pair.

THEOREM 2. *Let $\mathtt{SKE:=(Gen,E,D)}$ be a semantically secure symmetric encryption scheme, $\mathtt{PRG:=(G)}$ be a pseudorandom generator, and $\mathtt{PRF:=(Gen,H)}$ be a secure PRF, then BigGate in attribute-based mode satisfies Definition 5, and is adaptively semantically secure, when the proxy and the cloud provider are captured by a semi-honest adversary.*

PROOF. Once again, it suffices to show the existence of a polynomial size simulator S that creates a simulated view from $S(\tau(H_q))$ indistinguishable from the real view $V_K(H_q)$. Behavior of the simulator S is exactly the same as in the previous proof. If the request is new, simulator creates random strings that are indistinguishable from ciphertexts and hashed values. An adversary that distinguishes such random strings from ciphertexts or digests implies that $\mathtt{SKE}$ and $\mathtt{PRF}$ schemes are insecure, which contradicts our initial assumption. Hence, BigGate in attribute-based mode adheres to Definition 5 and is secure. □

6. RELATED WORK

Security and privacy issues in Key-Value Stores are still in its infancy. Rather than proposing more secure solutions, the priority is to achieve better scalability and efficiency. It is well-known that many popular implementations (e.g., Apache's Cassandra [5], MongoDB [9]) do not even encrypt data at rest [20].

Apache's Accumulo is one of the few examples that provide access control on the stored data [4]. It assigns a boolean expression to each key-value pair, which a user has to satisfy with the labels she possesses to get access to. Our work differs from Accumulo in terms of trust issues. A server running Accumulo should be *fully-trusted*, since the server has the privileges to access the outsourced data. However, such a requirement is not acceptable in a real-world scenario, where the cloud provider may have intentions to behave as a semi-honest adversary to learn users' private information.

Peekabo is one of the first protocols to protect privacy in key-value stores [26], in which the key and value elements are stored on different servers separately. By doing so, the the authors claim that an adversary cannot learn any useful information, as long as both key and value servers are captured. In the basic model of the protocol, a client uses public key cryptography to execute queries, which results in high overhead in latency. Then, they propose to use symmetric encryption scheme to process a *retrieve* query, where the key server and the value server learn only the queried key element and returned value respectively. In addition to the encryption mechanism, they employ simple access control mechanisms by assigning a set of users to a key-value pair. The key-server checks if a user is allowed to get the queried key-value pair, thus achieves a basic level of access control. Unlike our work, Xie et al. does not provide a formally proven security, but rely on the assumption that the adversary cannot infer any information from the separated key and value elements.

BigSecret is one framework that is similar to our proposed system [22]. It uses cryptographic tools to encrypt and index outsourced data, and performs an optimization on the overall efficiency by distributing data and workload on a *multi-cloud* setup. It assumes that the cloud is utilized by one user (or multiple users of the same entity), thus does not protect a user from one another. Our work differs from BigSecret in terms of multi-tenancy, cloud setup, access control capabilities, and set of supported queries.

Finally, *Attribute-Based Encryption* (ABE) based solutions may be considered as a candidate to handle access control problem in key-value stores. There exist some works (e.g., [27, 29, 28]) that focused on enforcing access-control policies in cloud storage. However, those works differ from our work with respect to the considered setup. We particularly investigate key-value stores, in which achieving low latency is critical. Unfortunately, as shown in Sect. 4, straightforward application of ABE techniques to key-value stores result in extremely high latency values, making it inapplicable and inefficient for the problem that we investigate.

7. CONCLUSION

In this work, we propose BigGate, a secure and efficient framework that is specially designed for key-value stores and enables (i) secure outsourcing of key-value pairs, and (ii) two different modes of access control enforcement mechanisms in a multi-tenant setup. We detail two, simple yet effective, modes of operations namely the multi-level (ML) and attribute-based (AB) modes. Via formal proof, we show that BigGate is secure, even when both the proxy and the cloud provider are controlled by a semi-honest adversary. We execute empirical analysis on BigGate, and observe that the overhead due to securing outsourced data and providing access control in key-value stores can be as low as 2%.

8. ACKNOWLEDGMENTS

This work is partially supported by the following grants: Air Force Office of Scientific Research FA9550-12-1-0082, National Institutes of Health Grants 1R01LM009989 and 1R01HG006844, National Science Foundation (NSF) Grants Career CNS-0845803, CNS-1111529, CNS-1228198 and Army Research Office Grant W911NF-12-1-0558.

9. REFERENCES

[1] Us web statistics released for may 2012: which sites dominate, and where do we go for online news? http://www.theguardian.com, 2012.

[2] Amazon simpledb, 2013. http://aws.amazon.com/simpledb.

[3] Internet 2012 in numbers, 2013. http://royal.pingdom.com.

[4] Apache accumulo, 2014. http://accumulo.apache.org.

[5] Apache cassandra, 2014. http://cassandra.apache.org.

[6] Apache hadoop, 2014. http://hadoop.apache.org.

[7] Apache hbase, 2014. http://hbase.apache.org.

[8] Microsoft azure, 2014. https://azure.microsoft.com.

[9] Mongodb, 2014. http://www.mongodb.org.

[10] J. Bethencourt, A. Sahai, and B. Waters. Ciphertext-policy attribute-based encryption. In *IEEE Symposium on Security and Privacy*, pages 321–334, 2007.

[11] F. Chang, J. Dean, S. Ghemawat, W. C. Hsieh, D. A. Wallach, M. Burrows, T. Chandra, A. Fikes, and R. E. Gruber. Bigtable: a distributed storage system for structured data. In *Operating Systems Design and Implementation*, pages 205–218, 2006.

[12] B. F. Cooper, A. Silberstein, E. Tam, R. Ramakrishnan, and R. Sears. Benchmarking cloud serving systems with ycsb. In *Proceedings of the 1st ACM symposium on Cloud computing*, pages 143–154. ACM, 2010.

[13] R. Curtmola, J. A. Garay, S. Kamara, and R. Ostrovsky. Searchable symmetric encryption: improved definitions and efficient constructions. In *ACM Conference on Computer and Communications Security*, pages 79–88, 2006.

[14] G. Decandia, D. Hastorun, M. Jampani, G. Kakulapati, A. Lakshman, A. Pilchin, S. Sivasubramanian, P. Vosshall, and W. Vogels. Dynamo: amazon's highly available key-value store. In *ACM Symposium on Operating Systems Principles*, pages 205–220, 2007.

[15] T. Dierks and C. Allen. The TLS Protocol Version 1.0. 1998.

[16] A. Freier, P. Karlton, and P. Kocher. The ssl protocol version 3. 1996. http://ci.nii.ac.jp/naid/10015295976.

[17] K. Hickman and T. Elgamal. The ssl protocol. *Netscape Communications Corp*, 501, 1995.

[18] E. Keller and J. Rexford. The platform as a service model for networking. In *Proceedings of the 2010 internet network management conference on Research on enterprise networking*, volume 4. USENIX Association, 2010.

[19] A. Matthews. Vodafone hacked: 2 million clients' data stolen, 2013. http://www.cnbc.com/id/101028261.

[20] L. Okman, N. Gal-Oz, Y. Gonen, E. Gudes, and J. Abramov. Security Issues in NoSQL Databases. 2011.

[21] R. Oppliger. *SSL and TLS: Theory and Practice*. Artech House, 2009.

[22] E. Pattuk, M. Kantarcioglu, V. Khadilkar, H. Ulusoy, and S. Mehrotra. Bigsecret: A secure data management framework for key-value stores. In *Proceedings of the 2013 IEEE Sixth International Conference on Cloud Computing*, CLOUD '13, pages 147–154. IEEE Computer Society, 2013.

[23] C. Placek. Personal data of 4 million advocate patients stolen, 2013. http://www.dailyherald.com.

[24] R. A. Popa, C. Redfield, N. Zeldovich, and H. Balakrishnan. Cryptdb: protecting confidentiality with encrypted query processing. In *Proceedings of the Twenty-Third ACM Symposium on Operating Systems Principles*, pages 85–100. ACM, 2011.

[25] R. Prodan and S. Ostermann. A Survey and Taxonomy of Infrastructure as a Service and Web Hosting Cloud Providers. In *Grid Computing, 2009 10th IEEE/ACM International Conference on*, pages 17–25, 2009.

[26] Y. Xie, M. K. Reiter, and D. R. O'hallaron. Protecting Privacy in Key-Value Search Systems. In *Annual Computer Security Applications Conference*, pages 493–504, 2006.

[27] K. Yang, X. Jia, K. Ren, and B. Zhang. Dac-macs: Effective data access control for multi-authority clud storage systems. In *INFOCOM Proceedings IEEE*, pages 2895–2903, 2013.

[28] S. Yu, C. Wang, K. Ren, and W. Lou. Achieving secure, scalable, and fine-grained data access control in cloud computing. In *INFOCOM, 2010 Proceedings IEEE*, pages 1–9. Ieee, 2010.

[29] S. Yu, C. Wang, K. Ren, and W. Lou. Attribute based data sharing with attribute revocation. In *Proceedings of the 5th ACM Symposium on Information, Computer, and Communications Security*, pages 261–270, 2010.

Virtual Resource Orchestration Constraints in Cloud Infrastructure as a Service

Khalid Bijon
Institute for Cyber Security
Univ of Texas at San Antonio
khalid.bijon@utsa.edu

Ram Krishnan
Institute for Cyber Security
Univ of Texas at San Antonio
ram.krishnan@utsa.edu

Ravi Sandhu
Institute for Cyber Security
Univ of Texas at San Antonio
ravi.sandhu@utsa.edu

ABSTRACT

In an infrastructure as a service (IaaS) cloud, virtualized IT resources such as compute, storage and network are offered on demand by a cloud service provider (CSP) to its tenants (customers). A major problem for enterprise-scale tenants that typically obtain significant amount of resources from a CSP concerns orchestrating those resources in a secure manner. For instance, unlike configuring physical hardware, virtual resources in IaaS are configured using software, and hence prone to misconfigurations that can lead to critical security violations. Examples of such resource orchestration operations include creating virtual machines with appropriate operating system and software images depending on their purpose, creating networks, connecting virtual machines to networks, attaching a storage volume to a particular virtual machine, etc. In this paper, we propose attribute-based constraints specification and enforcement as a means to mitigate this issue. High-level constraints specified using attributes of virtual resources prevent resource orchestration operations that can lead to critical misconfigurations. Our model allows tenants to customize the attributes of their resources and specify fine-grained constraints. We further propose a constraint mining approach to automatically generate constraints once the tenants specify the attributes for virtual resources. We present our model, enforcement challenges, and its demonstration in OpenStack, the *de facto* open-source cloud IaaS software.

Categories and Subject Descriptors

K.6.5 [**Management of Computing and Information Systems**]: Security and Protection

General Terms

Security

Keywords

Cloud IaaS, Virtual-Resource Orchestration, Constraints, Configuration Policy, Security Policy Mining

1. INTRODUCTION

Enterprises are increasingly driven by economics and flexibility to use computing resources provided by cloud IaaS [23]. In cloud IaaS the physical resources in a datacenter are logically arranged by the cloud service provider (CSP), while computing resources are virtualized and hosted on those logical collections of physical resources. This is illustrated in figure 1 where, for example, a rack is a collection of a specific set of physical servers and network hosts. Other resources such as physical storages may be associated with those compute hosts in the rack. This is shown as physical resource to physical resource mapping (PR-to-PR) in the figure. The single and double-headed arrows indicate the usual "one-to" and "many-to" mappings respectively. In cloud IaaS, enterprises or tenants obtain a number of separate pieces of virtual computing resources (or simply virtual resources or resources), e.g. virtual machines (VMs), virtual networks (NETs), etc., from the CSP, where a physical resource is shared by multiple virtual resources for maximizing utilization and reducing cost. IaaS providers allow multi-tenancy which multiplexes virtual resources of multiple enterprises upon same hardware. This includes co-location of VMs from different tenants on a single (physical) host, sharing of VM images in a repository, etc. This is illustrated as virtual resource to physical resource mapping in figure 1. This raises many security and performance considerations for a tenant's workload in the cloud. For instance, a tenant's VMs can be attacked by co-located malicious VMs of an adversary tenant. Such issues that arise due to multi-tenancy of virtual resources on physical resources have been extensively investigated in the past (see for example [19, 22, 28, 29, 32, 33]).

Another major issue arises from the fact that, for a given tenant with large-scale, heterogeneous virtual resources in IaaS, orchestrating those resources in a secure manner is cumbersome. Virtual to virtual resource mapping relations are also shown in figure 1. Here, orchestration refers to resource management issues such as creating networks, designing network layouts, applying appropriate images to VMs, etc. Since, in IaaS resource orchestration operations are performed in software (unlike in the case of physical resources where, for instance, servers are physically connected via Ethernet cables), they are highly prone to misconfigurations that can lead to security issues or increased exposure. For instance, a web-facing VM can be accidentally connected

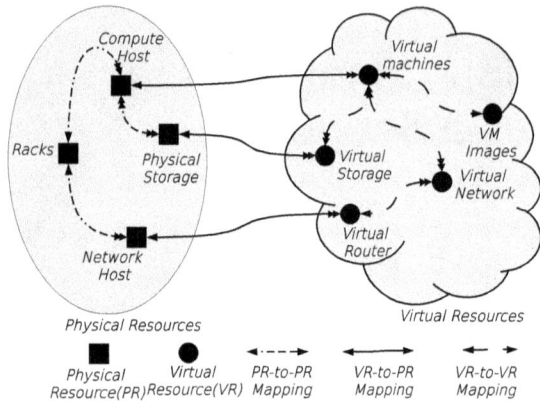

Figure 1: Cloud Resources Mapping Relation

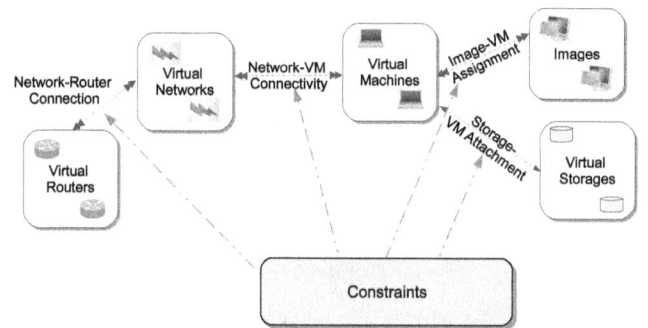

Figure 2: Constraints on Virtual Resources Arrangement Configurations

to a sensitive internal network or a low-assurance image may be applied to a VM that is expected to be security-hardened.

In this paper, we present the design, implementation, and evaluation of attribute-based CVRM (constraint-driven virtual resource management) as an approach to mitigate such concerns in cloud IaaS. Constraints in access control theory are effective ways of risk mitigation. A classic example is separation of duty in RBAC [24] where certain roles such as accounts manager and purchase manager conflict with each other and hence should never be assigned to the same user. Our developed CVRM enables tenants to express several essential properties of cloud resources as their attributes and specify constraints on resource mappings (VR-to-VR in figure 1) based on those attributes. We expect such constraints to be specified by a tenant administrative user or the CSP administrator. We provide a number of examples illustrating the utility of this technique in practical situations, such as configuring a Hadoop Cluster and a 3-tier business application in cloud IaaS. The CSP can then algorithmically enforce such constraints specified by all of its tenants when a virtual resource is mapped with another. We have implemented a prototype of CVRM in the widely-deployed OpenStack, the *de facto* open-source IaaS cloud software. We also propose an algorithm for mining the constraints in CVRM where the tenants specify the necessary attributes according to their business specifications and the algorithm automatically constructs the required constraints.

2. MOTIVATION

Migrating line-of-business applications to IaaS can be disastrous rather than beneficial for the tenants if their virtual resources are not properly configured. A misconfigured system not only hinders expected performance but also poses several security threats to a tenant. These threats include (i) malicious image insertion and inadvertent leakage of sensitive information through snapshot, (ii) sensitive information passing from a virtual machine to malicious virtual networks, and (iii) flow of information from a highly sensitive virtual network to a malicious or less sensitive one. However, present commercial cloud IaaS providers, including Amazon and Rackspace, offer at best rudimentary capabilities for such configuration management. For instance, AWS-IAM [1] offers a tenant to specify policies that can restrict resource-level permissions for certain users where the

permissions include snapshot a VM, create a virtual storage with specific capacity, etc. On the other hand, Rackspace provides a fixed mechanism for isolation management where cloud resources and administrative users of a tenant, also referred as admin-users, can be grouped into different projects where admin-users can only configure the resources in their assigned projects. These fixed approaches lack the generality to capture diverse enterprise-specific requirements for configuring virtual resources. Moreover, in these user-driven configuration management setups, completely relying on the admin-users increases the risk of possible misconfiguration since admin-users may inadvertently create incorrect configurations. It also elevates potential for insider threats.

Motivated by this scenario, we aim to develop CVRM that offers a tenant to specify various constraints for configuring the required arrangements of virtual resources. We address the fact that security concerns due to misconfiguration will vary across line-of-business applications of the tenants. For instance, 3-tier business application will be concerned about protecting unauthorized disclosure of data, while hadoop cluster configurations will seek to ensure integrity and availability of the resources. CVRM is designed to address tenant-specific constraints where the constraints are enforced on user-operations that affect the configurations of virtual resources. Constraints specified by a tenant can be enforced on operations performed by the tenant's admin-users during regular operations or by CSP's admin-users in case of exceptions and troubleshooting. We believe that, in addition to any access control mechanism implemented in this system, CVRM provides resource management capability that prevents misconfiguration caused by admin-users.

Figure 2 shows conceptual view of constraint driven virtual resource management. Constraints can be specified for a specific mapping relation (or simply relation) between two virtual resources. We describe these mapping relations and possible misconfiguration issues. We also provide examples for 3-tier application and hadoop cluster configurations. Note that, 3-tier aims to isolate computational requirements of an organization by three different tiers—presentation (PS), application (APP), and database (DB), for better security and scalability. Hadoop is a master-slave architecture for faster analysis of big-data where security issues include integrity and availability of the resources.

- **IMG-VM Compatibility Relations:** As shown in figure 2, a virtual machine image, also referred as IMG, can be used by multiple VMs and also from a VM multiple snapshots can be imaged. This process provides quick replication of a VM into large numbers of VMs, and also quick migration of a VM to another server. However, incorrect usage of IMG can critically affect the security and performance in the system. For instance, in 3-tier, VMs running the application of each tier require separate IMGs since VMs in different tiers perform different operations. Thus, an IMG created for DB-tier is not to be used for VMs of PS-tier, since PS-tier VMs are web-facing and the IMG may expose critical information about DB-tier. Similarly, in hadoop, each type of VMs such as nameNode and taskTracker have different functionalities, whereby improper use of IMG can hamper performance and availability.

- **NET-VM Connectivity Relations:** A group of VMs, connect to a network NET, so as to internally communicate. However, a wrong VM connected to a NET may hamper communication in NET and availability of information. For instance, in 3-tier application, APP-tier VMs can be connected to each other for faster communications, however, accidental assignment of VMs from other tiers can hamper the flow. Similarly, the taskTracker VMs performing reduce jobs should be connected with each other and no other VMs should connect to this network.

- **RT-NET Connection Relations:** Using a virtual router (RT), VMs of two selected NETs can communicate. In 3-tier application, VMs of APP-tier and PS-tier should communicate, however, PS-tier should not directly communicate with DB-tier. Also, connection to the external internet is only authorized for tier-1 VMs. Similarly, in hadoop, a NET for nameNode VMs should only connect to the NET of jobTracker VMs.

- **STR-VM Attachment Relations:** A persistent virtual storage (STR), is like a hard-disk drive which can be attached and detached to multiple VMs, but one at a time, until it is destroyed. Note that, a STR attached to a VM stores data from the VM. Later, if the STR is detached and re-attached to another VM without deleting its data, the new VM will get access to the data of the previous VM.

3. DESIGN OF CVRM

Intuitively, an attribute captures a property of an entity in the system, expressed as a name:value pair. For instance, clearance can be a user attribute and values of clearance could be 'top-secret', 'secret', etc. In the context of cloud IaaS, various useful properties of the virtual resources, such as VMs and NETs, can be captured by associating attributes to them. For instance, attributes can represent a VM's different properties including owner tenant, operational purpose, workloads sophistication, and connected networks. In CVRM, given that the properties of the virtual resources are represented by their attributes, a constraint is enforced while mapping (i.e., connecting) two virtual resources by comparing the specific attributes of the virtual resources.

In this section, we formally define CVRM that includes representation of the basic elements, relations among virtual resources and the constraint specification language. Then, we instantiate CVRM for 3-tier architecture in cloud IaaS.

3.1 Formal Specification

The basic elements of CVRM include representation of existing tenants and virtual resources in a cloud IaaS system where each virtual resource belongs to a particular tenant. A virtual resource is also mapped to a particular class of virtual resource such as VM, NET, IMG, RT, and STR. Formally, we have the following.

- VR is the set of all existing virtual resources in CSP.

- CLS is the set of all classes of virtual resources that are supported by the CSP.

- $rCls$: VR → CLS, is a function that maps each virtual resource to its class.

- TENANTS is the finite set of existing tenants in CSP.

- $tenant$: VR → TENANTS, is a function that maps each virtual resource to the tenant that owns it.

- VR_{tnt} is the set of virtual resources that are owned by the tenant tnt. Formally,
  $VR_{tnt} = \{v \in VR \mid tenant(v) = tnt\}$.

Here, VR_{tnt} contains the virtual resources of a tenant tnt and these virtual resources are partitioned into different sets based on their class. We define such sets of the virtual resources of each tenant as follows,

- $VR_{tnt.c}$ is the set of virtual resources of class c that are owned by the tenant tnt. Formally,
  $VR_{tnt.c} = \{v \in VR_{tnt} \mid rCls(v) = c\}$.

In a tenant, a particular class of virtual resources can have specific type of mapping relations to virtual resources of another class. For instance, virtual resources of class VM can have connection-mapping and attachment-mapping relations with virtual resources of class NET and STR respectively. We can define the relations between elements of every two classes of virtual resources in a tenant as follows,

- $\mathcal{R}_{tnt,c_i,c_j}$ is the relation between virtual resources of class c_i and c_j in a tenant tnt. Formally,
  $\mathcal{R}_{tnt,c_i,c_j} \subseteq VR_{tnt,c_i} \times VR_{tnt,c_j}$.

However, CVRM restricts the following type of relations,

1. Relations between virtual resources of same class cannot be specified (i.e., $\mathcal{R}_{tnt,c_i,c_i}$ cannot be specified).

2. For two classes $c_i \neq c_j$ we can define $\mathcal{R}_{tnt,c_i,c_j}$ or $\mathcal{R}_{tnt,c_j,c_i}$ but not both.

CVRM provides two operations called Add and $\mathcal{R}M$ respectively to add and remove tuples to a relation, where each operation is a function that takes as inputs the relation and two virtual resources of appropriate classes. Each operation also evaluates a specific constraint with respect to these two virtual resources as discussed below. Formally they are defined as follows (the notation for defining these operations is similar to the notation of schema used in NIST RBAC [25]),

$Add(\mathcal{R}_{tnt,c_i,c_j}, vr_1, vr_2) \triangleleft$
$vr_1 \in VR_{tnt,c_i} \wedge vr_2 \in VR_{tnt,c_j} \wedge consEval(\delta^{Add}_{tnt,c_i,c_j}, vr_1, vr_2)$
$\mathcal{R}_{tnt,c_i,c_j}' = \mathcal{R}_{tnt,c_i,c_j} \cup \{<vr_1, vr_2>\} \triangleright$

$$RM(\mathcal{R}_{\text{tnt},c_i,c_j},\text{vr}_1,\text{vr}_2) \lhd$$
$$\text{vr}_1 \in VR_{\text{tnt},c_i} \wedge \text{vr}_2 \in VR_{\text{tnt},c_j} \wedge consEval(\delta^{RM}_{\text{tnt},c_i,c_j},\text{vr}_1,\text{vr}_2)$$
$$\mathcal{R}_{\text{tnt},c_i,c_j}' = \mathcal{R}_{\text{tnt},c_i,c_j} - \{<\text{vr}_1,\text{vr}_2>\}\rhd$$

Here, $\delta^{Add}_{\text{tnt},c_i,c_j}$ and $\delta^{RM}_{\text{tnt},c_i,c_j}$ are constraints that are respectively specified for adding and removing a tuple to the relation $\mathcal{R}_{\text{tnt},c_i,c_j}$. A successful execution of an operation is allowed if the constraint is satisfied for the particular virtual resources vr_1 and vr_2. Both Add and RM call the constraint evaluation function $consEval$ with vr_1, vr_2 as inputs along with the relevant constraint. Evaluation of the constraint is a simple evaluation of a logical formula to true or false.

Basically, a constraint compares different properties assigned to the virtual resources vr_1 and vr_2 which are evaluated by $consEval$ to make a decision. In CVRM, there are attributes of each class of virtual resource that characterize different properties of the resources and are modeled as functions. For each attribute function, there is a set of finite constant values that represents the possible values of that attribute. We assume values of attributes to be atomic,[1] therefore, for a particular element of that resource, the name of the attribute function maps to one value from the set. For convenience attribute functions are simply referred to as attributes. Formally, we have the following.

- $ATTR^{c_i}_{\text{tnt}}$ is the set of attribute functions of a virtual resource class c_i in tenant tnt. Here, for a function $att \in ATTR^{c_i}_{\text{tnt}}$, the domain of the function is the virtual resources VR_{tnt,c_i} and the codomain is the values of att written as $SCOPE_{att}$ which is a set of atomic values. Formally, $att : VR_{\text{tnt},c_i} \rightarrow SCOPE_{att}$ where $att \in ATTR^{c_i}_{\text{tnt}}$.

Now, for each $\mathcal{R}_{\text{tnt},c_i,c_j}$, at most two constraints can be specified for the operations Add and RM respectively. Each constraint is used to verify if assigned values of specific attributes of two virtual resources vr_1 and vr_2 of class c_i and c_j respectively satisfy certain conditions. CVRM uses the grammar below to specify constraints,

```
<Quantifier>:= ∀(vr1,vr2) ∈ R_<Cls>,<Cls> . <Stmt>
<Stmt>:= <Stmt> <connector><Stmt> | (<rule>)
<rule>:= <Token> → <Token>
<Token>:= (<Token> <connector> <Token>)|(<Term>)
<Term>:= <Attribute>(<resource>) <comparator> <Scope>
<Attribute>::= <letter> | <digit> | <Attribute>
<Scope>::= <letter> | <digit> <Scope>
<connector>::= ∧ | ∨
<comparator>::= = | ≠
<Cls>::= c_1 | c_2 | ... | c_n
<resource> ::= vr1 | vr2
<digit>::= 0|1|2| ...|8|9
<letter>::= a|b|...|y|z|A|B|...|Y|Z
```

The constraint specification grammar syntax is given in Backus Normal Form (BNF). Each constraint statement contains single or multiple small expressions in the form of implication, A→B, joined by logical connectors. The small expression is also referred to as constraint-rule or just rule.

---

[1] As given in section 2, in 3-tier application, an example of such constraints is to restrict communication between VMs of APP-tier and DB-tier. Here, if the attribute is called *tier* and the possible values are presentation, application and database, a vm can only get one of the three values. However, there might be constraints that require set-valued attributes where the virtual resources get multiple values. CVRM is not currently designed to express such constraints, however, can be easily extended to set-valued attributes.

Both A and B in a rule A→B contain one or more predicates connected by logical connectors, where a predicate contains an attribute function of a specific class of virtual resource and the function returns the assigned value to the attribute of a specific instance of that class and, then, the predicate compares the value with a particular value of the attribute. Basically, a rule, A→B, verifies that if assigned attribute values of a virtual resource vr1 meets the conditions specified in A then assigned attribute values of vr2 should satisfy the condition in B in order to insert vr1 and vr2 into a relation.

Note that, the grammar is also weakly typed since in each predicate <Attribute> and <Scope> are replaced by arbitrary names. To this end, we develop a simple static type-checking system that ensures valid constraint expression. For each predicate of a constraint, it checks if the value, specified after the <comparator> sign of the predicate, belongs to the scope of the attribute name specified before the <comparator>. It is formally defined as follows.

Predicate format:
attribute(<Resource>) <comparator> attribute-value

Type-Checking Rule:
If attribute-value $\in SCOPE_{\text{attribute}}$ *Then*
  return *true*
Else
  return *error*

3.2 Instantiation

In this section, we instantiate CVRM for an example of 3-tier business application setup. Another example of hadoop cluster setup is given in the appendix. We focus on the tenant called 3-tier. The classes of virtual resources supported by the CSP are VM, NET, RT, STR and IMG and 3-tier supports relations from VM-to-NET, NET-to-RT, VM-to-IMG and VM-to-STR which are written as $\mathcal{R}_{\text{3-tier},VM,NET}$, $\mathcal{R}_{\text{3-tier},NET,RT}$, $\mathcal{R}_{\text{3-tier},VM,STR}$ and $\mathcal{R}_{\text{3-tier},VM,IMG}$ respectively.

Attributes are defined for the instances of each class of virtual resources that characterize different properties necessary to capture the requirements to run 3-tier application in cloud. Figure 3-A identifies the attributes of the virtual resources of tenant 3-tier. It also shows the mapping relation among virtual resources (represented by arrow-headed lines). Figure 3-B gives the scopes of these attributes. For instance, in A, a VM attribute *tier* represent the tier-operations a VM performs and B shows the scope of *tier* which is presentation, application, database. For each vm, *tier* assigns a value from the scope to the vm. An example attribute assignment for a vm that performs as a database server is: *tier*(VM)= database. Other two attributes of VM called *versionVM* and *status* represent the version of a VM in specific tier and the activity status respectively. Similarly, IMG also has attributes called *tier* and *versionIMG* that represnts the tier and version respectively for which an IMG is created. For 3-tier, we also create a NET attribute called *netType* that specifies the layer for which a NET is created for the communication. For instance, a NET with *netType* value psNet should only carry presentation layer data. Figure 3-A and 3-B also defines attributes and their scopes for RT and STR respectively.

Generally, in CVRM, tenants can specify attributes for their virtual resources to capture specific organizational re-

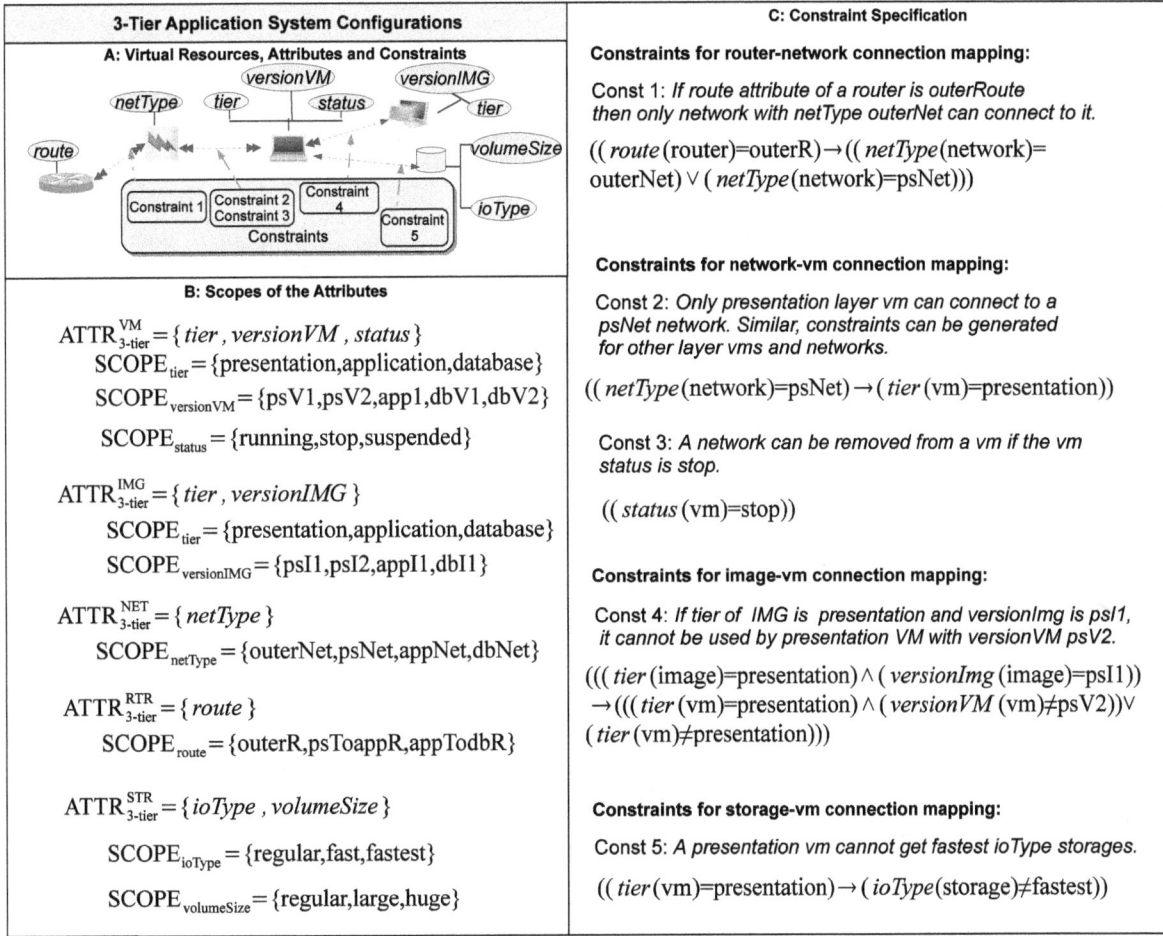

Figure 3: Constraints Specification for 3-Tier Application System

quirements. Also, resources can have certain general properties irrespective of organizational diversities of the tenants. CVRM categorizes attributes in two types: one that captures the general properties across all the tenants (referred as inter-tenant attributes) and the other that captures tenant-specific properties (referred to as intra-tenant attributes).

For a 3-tier application, the tenant specifies VM attribute called *tier*, as shown in figure 3-A, for their operational purpose. Here, *tier* is intra-tenant attribute since this attribute does not capture anything in other applications such as hadoop. However, *volumeSize* attribute of STR represents the size of the volume and this attribute is required by virtual storage regardless of operational objectives of different tenants, and is thereby an inter-tenant attribute

In this setup, proper administration of the attributes is necessary where administration process should include creation and deletion of the attributes and their scopes as well as assigning correct attribute values to the virtual resources. Creation and deletion of inter-tenant attributes and their scopes should be managed by the CSP's admin-users, while, the attribute value assignment to virtual resources are performed by CSP's or tenant's admin-users or by the IaaS system as appropriate. Attribute administration is beyond the scope of this paper. However, there is literature on attribute administration [18] that might apply in this context.

Followed by attribute specification of the resources, the tenant 3-tier specifies at most two constraints for the relations of every two classes. Some example constraints with high level descriptions are shown in figure 3-C. For instance, constraint $\delta_{\text{3-tier,VM,NET}}^{\text{Add}}$ applies to the $\mathcal{A}dd$ operation where it checks if a vm is connecting to an appropriate virtual network by comparing their attributes. Another constraint called $\delta_{\text{3-tier,VM,NET}}^{\text{RM}}$ applies to $\mathcal{R}M$ operation of same relation where it checks if the a vm is in stop state to disconnect it from a virtual network. Figure 3-C also shows example constraints for other relations.

4. CVRM ENFORCEMENT

We describe a CVRM enforcement in OpenStack cloud platform. Then, we analyze some security issues of CVRM.

4.1 Enforcement in OpenStack

Figure 4 shows conceptual picture of CVRM enforcement process in IaaS. This process includes a constraint specifier and constraint enforcer components. Constraint specifier specifies necessary attributes and their scopes for the virtual resources in IaaS. It also specifies the constraints for the operations that add/remove configuration-relations between two virtual resources. When users execute the operations, respective constraints are enforced. As shown in the figure, after getting each request from users, the constraint evalua-

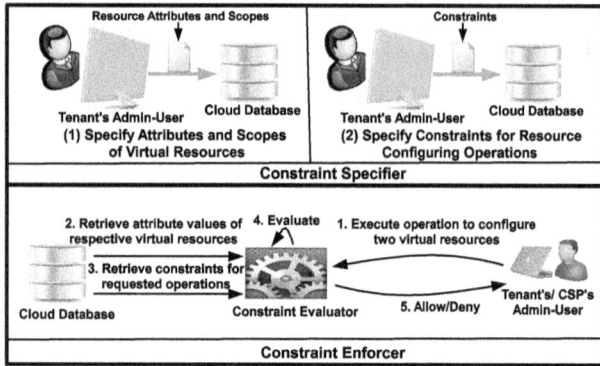

Figure 4: Components of CVRM Enforcement Process in a Service of OpenStack

tor retrieves the attributes of the virtual resources and the respective constraints from cloud database and evaluate the constraints to make decision.

4.1.1 OpenStack Overview

OpenStack comprises various service components that provide functionalities for managing different virtual resources. For instance, it has compute service called nova that offers operations for the management of VMs where the operations include create, delete, start and stop virtual machines. nova also has operations for arranging other virtual resources to VMs, e.g., connect VMs with NETs, attach STRs to VMs, etc. In OpenStack, each resource is a member of a specific project. A user is authorized to exercise a service operation to virtual resources of a project if she is a member of the project and has the role called *project-admin*. There is also a notion in OpenStack called domain where a domain consists multiple projects. A user who is a member of a domain and assigned to the role called *domain-admin* is responsible to create/delete projects in that domain as well as add/remove users to specific projects. We can consider such users of a domain and its projects as the super and regular admin-users of a tenant respectively. There is also a fixed domain called admin whose members are the CSP's admin-users. Members of the admin domain are responsible to create other domains and also add/remove users to them. Generally, in OpenStack, if a user requests a virtual resource configuration-operation, the authorization service which is called keystone provides a token that contains user authorization information including the projects where the user is a member. The operation is allowed if the project of respective virtual-resources are same as the requesting user.

Figure 5 shows execution steps of an user-operation (*volume-attach*) in OpenStack that attaches a STR to a VM. When a user in a project tries to execute the operation, the OpenStack client program retrieves the token for the user from keystone. Then, it forwards the token along with respective VM and STR names to nova since nova manages *volume-attach*. nova verifies validity of the token and collects the tenant information of VM and STR from database and it approves if the given user, VM and STR are in same tenant.

4.1.2 Constraint Specifier

Our designed constraint specifier component can be included in each service in OpenStack. The specifier extends

respective service operations by adding functionalities for the creation and management of the attributes and their scopes for respective virtual resources. In a tenant (domain), managing such functionalities are only authorized for the users having *domain-admin* role in the domain. Specifier also provides operations for constraint specification. Each constraint is mapped to an operation-name to which it applies. Operations that specify constraints are also authorized only to users having *domain-admin* role. Attributes, their scopes and constraints are stored in database-tables of respective service. Entries in a database-table across tenants (domains) are isolated by specific domain ids and admin-users of a domain cannot access other domains' information.

Figure 6 shows a nova operation of the constraint-specifier component that specifies VM attributes. Database of nova contains tables for storing attributes and constraints. When a user tries to create an attribute, the token of the user is verified to check if the user has *domain-admin* role in order to make a decision. The component also contains similar operations that specify constraints.

4.1.3 Constraint Enforcer

Similar to constraint specifier, an enforcer component is included in every service in OpenStack. When a user executes a service operation that affects a relation between two virtual resources, enforcer verifies the respective constraint which is already specified by constraint specifier. This process retrieves attributes of the virtual resources and the constraint expression from service database. It implements an evaluator to evaluate the constraint for making a decision. Note that, in OpenStack, these operations are authorized only for project admin-users.

Figure 7 shows extended view of figure 5 for the execution of *volume-attach*. Besides, comparing the project information of the VM, storage and user, the enforcer component now retrieves the attributes for VM and STR and constraint for *volume-attach* and evaluates the constraints by considering the VM and STR attributes.

4.2 Security Analysis

We present different security issues for enforcing CVRM in practice.

4.2.1 Constraint Specifications Process

- **Constraints, Attribute and Scope:** CVRM aims to restrict privileges of admin-users in order to mitigate misconfiguration issues of a tenant. Therefore, constraints specification and modification process should be restricted to the majority of admin-users and only selected admin-users of a tenant should be authorized to specify constraints, attributes of the virtual resources and their scope. In OpenStack, there are three types of admin-users: CSP-admin, domain-admin and project-admin. In our developed constraint enforcement in OpenStack we only authorize domain-admins to manage the constraints, attributes and their scopes where the specified constraints are applied to all three type of admin-users. A more formal isolation management scheme is given in [8] that can also be applied here.

- **Attribute Value Assignments:** An admin-user who can create virtual-resources should also assign values to their attributes. In CVRM, the project-admin users

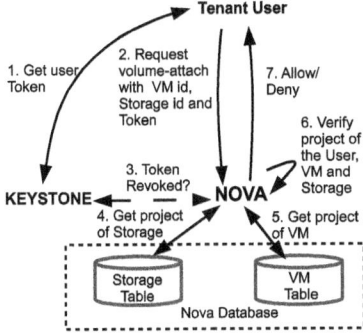

Figure 5: Operation *volume-attach* in Nova

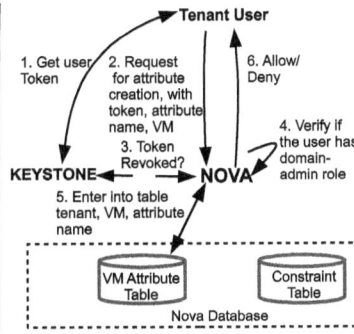

Figure 6: Constraint Specifier in Nova

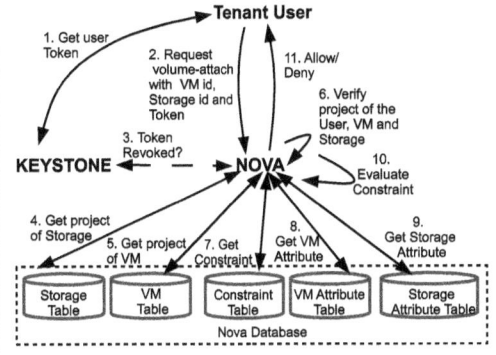

Figure 7: Constraint Enforcement for *volume-attach*

can assign values to the attributes. However, one needs to make sure that the admin-users can only assign appropriate values. For instance, a project-admin can create VMs and assign only her project-id to those VMs (not ids of other projects). In this paper we do not focus on such access control system, however, existing mechanisms such as [8] might be useful.

- **Generalized Enforcement Engine with Data Isolation:** For scalability, one generalized enforcement engine should be designed for the evaluations of the constraints of all the tenants. In our developed enforcement engine in OpenStack, constraints are stored in the database separated according to the domain-id of a tenant and only respective admin-users can have access to their constraints.

4.2.2 Issues on Constraint Structure

- **Contradictory Constraint:** The sub-expressions of a constraint can be of two types. One restricts the relation of virtual resources of two different classes when values of their attributes are mutual exclusive. Another one forces relation when the values of the attributes are congruent. A constraint containing both type of sub-expressions for same combination of values of the attributes generates contradictory decisions for a relation. We call these constraints as contradictory constraints and they need to be avoided.

- **Deadlock Constraints:** In a constraint, a value, let's say, val_x of an attribute att_p of the virtual resources of specific class c_i can have mutual exclusion relation with all the values of an attribute att_q of the virtual resources of class c_j. Then, the virtual resources of class c_i with assigned value val_x cannot be arranged with any resources of c_j. These constraints are deadlock constraints and tenants need to handle them properly.

- **Redundant CVRM Expressions:** In CVRM, an expression is redundant if it specified multiple times. Redundant expression unnecessarily increases the runtime complexity since it requires evaluation of the same expression more than once. One such example of a redundant expression is the multiple occurrences of same sub-expression in a constraint expression.

4.3 Prototype Implementation

We describe the implemented prototype of CVRM enforcement process. We leverage the DevStack cloud framework [2], a quick and stand-alone installation of OpenStack, for the implementation and analysis. We choose DevStack as it provides all components of the open source cloud platform OpenStack. We installed DevStack in a physical server that has 4 cores and 3GB RAM. We implemented the CVRM components for nova. The implemented component can specify attributes and their scopes for VMs and NETs which are stored in the database. It also has a process to specify and evaluate constraints for VM-NET connection. Our python-based implementation of constraint specifier, that includes API design to enable users to declare attributes and constraints which require tables creation into DevStack database (MySQL), has 190 lines of sqlalchemy code. The constraint enforcer that includes the constraint parser has 257 lines. The parser returns true or false value based on a constraint expression by considering assigned attribute values for a VM and NET which need to be connected.

5. CONSTRAINT MINING IN CVRM

In this section, we consider approaches for mining CVRM constraints from already specified relations among the instances of two classes of virtual resources. Basically, this process generates a collection of restricted rules, also refereed as min_rule, where a min_rule is an implication, a→b, in which both a and b are single predicates. Note that, the actual rule in the form of A→B as defined in section 3.1 allows both A and B to be collections of predicates connected by ∧ and/or ∨. Now for a given $\mathcal{R}_{tnt,c_i,c_j}$, $\delta^{Add}_{\mathcal{R}_{tnt,c_i,c_j}}$ and $\delta^{RM}_{\mathcal{R}_{tnt,c_i,c_j}}$, a min_rule can be generated by following grammar,

```
<Quantifier>:= ∀(vr1,vr2) ∈ R<Cls>,<Cls> . <Stmt>
<Stmt>:= <Stmt> <connector><Stmt> | (<min_rule>)
<min_rule>:= <Token> → <Token>
<Token>:= <Attribute>(<resource>)<comparator><Scope>
<Attribute>::= <letter> | <digit> | <Attribute>
<Scope>::= <letter> | <digit> <Scope>
<connector>::= ∧ | ∨
<comparator>::= = | ≠
<Cls>::= c₁ | c₂ | ... | cₙ
<resouce> ::= vr1 | vr2
<digit>::= 0|1|2| ...|8|9
<letter>::= a|b|...|y|z|A|B|...|Y|Z
```

Each min_rule is restricted to specify a comparison between only two attributes of virtual resource classes c_i and c_j. Now let us say $\mathcal{R}_{tnt,c_i,c_j}$ is a given set of tuples that specifies the relation between instances of the two classes

c_i and c_j. The min_rule mining problem is to construct all possible min_rules. For given $\mathcal{R}_{\mathrm{tnt},c_i,c_j}$, $\mathsf{ATTR}_{\mathrm{tnt}}^{c_i}$, $\mathsf{ATTR}_{\mathrm{tnt}}^{c_j}$, $att_p \in \mathsf{ATTR}_{\mathrm{tnt}}^{c_i}$, $att_q \in \mathsf{ATTR}_{\mathrm{tnt}}^{c_j}$, SCOPE_{att_p} and SCOPE_{att_q}, min_rules can be of four following formats, where each val has to belong to the appropriate attribute SCOPE_{att}.

- a→b where a≡(att_p(vr1)=val_x) $\wedge$ b≡(att_q(vr2)=val_y).

- a→$\overline{\mathrm{b}}$ where a≡(att_p(vr1)=val_x) $\wedge$ $\overline{\mathrm{b}}$≡(att_q(vr2)$\neq$$val_y$).

- $\overline{\mathrm{a}}$→b where $\overline{\mathrm{a}}$≡(att_p(vr1)$\neq$$val_x$) $\wedge$ b≡(att_q(vr2)=val_y).

- $\overline{\mathrm{a}}$→$\overline{\mathrm{b}}$ where $\overline{\mathrm{a}}$≡(att_p(vr1)$\neq$$val_x$) $\wedge$ $\overline{\mathrm{b}}$≡(att_q(vr2)$\neq$$val_y$).

For simplicity, we provide a mining algorithm for the format a→$\overline{\mathrm{b}}$ which is also referred as mutual exclusive min_rule. Similar algorithms can be generated for other formats. We choose mutual exclusive min_rule format because we develop mining algorithm on top of a constraint mining algorithm for role based access control [20] where they also mine mutual exclusive roles, so it is feasible to compare mutual exclusive min_rule to mutual exclusive roles.

5.1 Overview: Mining Constraints in RBAC

Mining association rules has become a fundamental problem in data mining, and it has been studied extensively. Many algorithms such as FP-growth, Apriori, and Eclat [4] have been developed to solve this problem in databases containing transactions. Recently, a constraint mining algorithm, called anti-Apriori, is proposed for role-based access control (RBAC) [20] which is developed on top of the Apriori algorithm [4]. In RBAC, U and R contains set of users and roles in the system. A function *user_roles* maps each user to a set of roles that are assigned to the user. Now the mutual exclusive constraint for RBAC is defined as follows.

A mutual exclusive RBAC constraint between roles $\in$ R is an implication of the form R1→$\overline{\mathrm{R2}}$ where R1 $\subset$ R and R2 $\subset$ R and R1 $\cap$ R2=$\emptyset$ and *user_roles*(u) $\subseteq$ R1 $\rightarrow$ *user_roles*(u) $\cap$ R2 = $\emptyset$ for each user u $\in$ U. Let D be a set of user-role assignments, the constraint R1→R2 has confidence c if c% of users in U that are assigned a role in R1 do not have any role from R2, and it has support s if s% users are assigned a role in R1. The constraint R1→$\overline{\mathrm{R2}}$ holds for D if it has certain user-specified minimum support and confidence.

5.2 Mining min_rule in CVRM

In this section, we discuss the mining approaches for mutual exclusive min_rule. We first utilize the anti-Apriori algorithm [20] for mining min_rules. Then, we customize the anti-Apriori algorithm, which we call CVRM-Apriori, for min_rule mining in order to get better performance.

5.2.1 Reduction to RBAC constraint mining

In this approach, we identify inputs of a mutual exclusive min_rule mining algorithm and reduce them to the inputs of anti-Apriori. Then, we collect the outputs from anti-Apriori algorithm and construct min_rules.

Inputs of a min_rule mining algorithm: In CVRM, each mutual exclusive min_rule is restricted to specify a mutual exclusive relation between one value of an attribute of virtual resources of a particular class with another value of an attribute of virtual resources of another class. For given $\mathcal{R}_{\mathrm{tnt},c_i,c_j}$, $\mathsf{VR}_{\mathrm{tnt},c_i}$, $\mathsf{VR}_{\mathrm{tnt},c_j}$, and for each $att_p \in \mathsf{ATTR}_{\mathrm{tnt}}^{c_i}$ and for each $att_q \in \mathsf{ATTR}_{\mathrm{tnt}}^{c_j}$, the inputs for a mutual exclusive

min_rule algorithm are $\mathsf{VR}_{\mathrm{tnt},c_i}$, $\mathsf{VR}_{\mathrm{tnt},c_j}$, $\mathcal{R}_{\mathrm{tnt},c_i,c_j}$, att_p, att_q, SCOPE_{att_p} and SCOPE_{att_q}.

Inputs of anti-Apriori: The inputs of the anti-Apriori algorithm are U, R, the user-role assignment matrix M (M is a u×r dimension boolean matrix where u and r is the size of U and R and for each $u_i \in$ U and $r_j \in$ R, $M[u_i][r_j]$=1 if $r_j \in$ *user_roles*(u_i) and 0 otherwise), matrix O where O=$\overline{\mathrm{M}}$, minconf (minimum confidence) and minsup (minimum support). The inputs of the min_rule mining algorithm are reduced to the anti-Apriori algorithm as follows.

1. U = $\mathsf{VR}_{\mathrm{tnt},c_i}$×$\mathsf{VR}_{\mathrm{tnt},c_j}$ and R = SCOPE_{att_p} $\cup$ SCOPE_{att_q}. Without loss of generality, we assume the values in SCOPE_{att_p} and SCOPE_{att_q} are disjoint.

2. M is a |U| × |R| dimensional boolean matrix where, for each u$\in$U and for each r $\in$ R, M[u][r]=1 where (vr1,vr2)=u and att_p(vr1)=r or att_q(vr2)=r. Also, O=$\overline{\mathrm{M}}$.

3. minconf and minsup are the values specified by the users.

Now, anti-Apriori generates constraints in following steps,

1. Scan M to find all combinations of $R_i \subseteq$ R in a set F where the support of R_i is greater than minsup.

2. Scan O to find all combinations of $R_i \subseteq$ R in a set $\overline{\mathrm{F}}$ where the support is greater than minsup.

3. For each $R_i \in$ F and for each $\overline{R}_j \in \overline{\mathrm{F}}$, generate mutual exclusive rules in the format of R_i→$\overline{R}_j$ if its confidence is greater than minconf and store R_i→$\overline{R}_j$ in Rules.

min_rule Creation from Output of anti-Apriori algorithm: Output of anti-Apriori is a set of mutual exclusive rules from which the min_rules are constructed as follows, for each R_i→$\overline{R}_j \in$ Rules, each $val_x \in R_i$ and $val_y \in \overline{R}_j$ construct a min_rule att_p(v1)=val_x $\rightarrow$ att_q(v2)$\neq$$val_y$ where $val_x \in \mathsf{SCOPE}_{att_p}$ and $val_y \in \mathsf{SCOPE}_{att_q}$.

Although, this approach constructs min_rules, it lacks scalability for the following reasons.
(1) Size of the input parameter U is multiplicative with respective to the virtual resources of two different class since it is created by the cross product of each pair of virtual resources. It thereby makes the size of matrix M and O very large, increasing the run-time complexity.
(2) Algorithm anti-Apriori is designed to identify relations among all possible subset of roles, therefore, it needs multiple scans to database which is very costly. However, for mining the min_rules should require much simpler approach since it only needs to identify relations between every two values of two different attributes of the virtual resources.

5.2.2 Anti-Apriori for min_rule mining (CVRM-Apriori)

We customize the anti-Apriori algorithm for mining mutual exclusive min_rules. For a given $\mathsf{VR}_{\mathrm{tnt},c_i}$, $\mathsf{VR}_{\mathrm{tnt},c_j}$, for each $att_p \in \mathsf{ATTR}_{\mathrm{tnt}}^{c_i}$ and for each $att_q \in \mathsf{ATTR}_{\mathrm{tnt}}^{c_j}$, a mutual exclusive min_rule between each $val_x \in \mathsf{SCOPE}_{att_p}$ and $val_y \in \mathsf{SCOPE}_{att_q}$ holds for an already specified $\mathcal{R}_{\mathrm{tnt},c_i,c_j}$ if it satisfies certain user-specified minsup and minconf. The support and confidence of a min_rule is calculated as follows,

- We define a function called $insideR_{tnt,c_i,c_j}^{att_p}$ that returns a set of elements in $\mathcal{R}_{tnt,c_i,c_j}$ that has a value val_x of an attribute $att_p \in \mathsf{ATTR}_{tnt}^{c_i}$. Formally, $insideR_{tnt,c_i,c_j}^{att_p}(val_x) = \{(vr1,vr2) \mid (vr1,vr2) \in \mathcal{R}_{tnt,c_i,c_j} \wedge att_p(vr1)=val_x\}$.

- Another function called $outsideR_{tnt,c_i,c_j}^{att_q}$ returns the set of elements in $\mathcal{R}_{tnt,c_i,c_j}$ that does not have a value val_y of an attribute $att_q \in \mathsf{ATTR}_{tnt}^{c_j}$. Formally, $outsideR_{tnt,c_i,c_j}^{att_q}(val_y) = \{(vr1,vr2) \mid (vr1,vr2) \in \mathcal{R}_{tnt,c_i,c_j} \wedge att_q(vr2) \neq val_y\}$.

- Now, a function called $support_{tnt,c_i,c_j}^{att_p}$ calculates support of a value val_x of an attribute $att_p \in \mathsf{ATTR}_{tnt}^{c_i}$. Formally,
$$support_{tnt,c_i,c_j}^{att_p}(val_x) = \frac{|insideR_{tnt,c_i,c_j}^{att_p}(val_x)|}{|\mathcal{R}_{tnt,c_i,c_j}|},$$
that calculates the ratio of the number of tuples in $\mathcal{R}_{tnt,c_i,c_j}$ that contain val_x of the attribute $att_p \in \mathsf{ATTR}_{tnt}^{c_i}$ with all tuples in $\mathcal{R}_{tnt,c_i,c_j}$.

- Similarly, $support_{tnt,c_i,c_j}^{att_q}(val_y) = \frac{|outsideR_{tnt,c_i,c_j}^{att_q}(val_y)|}{|\mathcal{R}_{tnt,c_i,c_j}|}$, is another function that calculates the ratio of the number of tuples in $\mathcal{R}_{tnt,c_i,c_j}$ that do not contain val_y of the attribute $att_q \in \mathsf{ATTR}_{tnt}^{c_j}$ with all tuples in $\mathcal{R}_{tnt,c_i,c_j}$.

- Finally, a function called $confidence_{tnt,c_i,c_j}^{att_p,att_q}$ calculates the confidence which is the ratio of the number of elements in $\mathcal{R}_{tnt,c_i,c_j}$ that have a value val_x of an attribute $att_p \in \mathsf{ATTR}_{tnt}^{c_i}$, but, simultaneously, do not have a value val_y of an attribute $att_q \in \mathsf{ATTR}_{tnt}^{c_j}$ with the total number of elements in $\mathcal{R}_{tnt,c_i,c_j}$ that have a value val_x of an attribute $att_p \in \mathsf{ATTR}_{tnt}^{c_i}$. Formally,
$$confidence_{tnt,c_i,c_j}^{att_p,att_q}(val_x,val_y) =$$
$$\frac{|insideR_{tnt,c_i,c_j}^{att_p}(val_x) \cap outsideR_{tnt,c_i,c_j}^{att_q}(val_y)|}{|insideR_{tnt,c_i,c_j}^{att_p}(val_x)|}$$

Now, for a given $\mathcal{R}_{tnt,c_i,c_j}$, for each $att_p \in \mathsf{ATTR}_{tnt}^{c_i}$ and for each $att_q \in \mathsf{ATTR}_{tnt}^{c_j}$, user specified $min\_sup_{tnt,c_i,c_j}^{att_p,att_q}$ and $min\_conf_{tnt,c_i,c_j}^{att_p,att_q}$, algorithm 1 constructs the min_rules. In algorithm 1, procedure Identify_ Frequency identifies each attribute value $val_x \in \mathsf{SCOPE}_{att_p}$ and each attribute value $val_y \in \mathsf{SCOPE}_{att_q}$ whose supports satisfy $min\_sup_{tnt,c_i,c_j}^{att_p,att_q}$ and returns them in sets F and $\overline{\mathrm{F}}$ respectively. Now, the Gen_min_rule procedure takes the sets F and $\overline{\mathrm{F}}$ and for each $val_x \in \mathrm{F}$ and for each $val_y \in \overline{\mathrm{F}}$ constructs the min_rules that satisfy the value of $min\_conf_{tnt,c_i,c_j}^{att_p,att_q}$. This algorithm overcomes the scalability issues of anti-Apriori algorithm since it only identifies relations between two values instead of two subset of values of attributes, and F and $\overline{\mathrm{F}}$ are specified separately from the scopes of two different attributes.

5.3 Implementation and Analysis

We compare the performance of anit-Apriori and CVRM-Apriori algorithms. We implemented and evaluated both the mining algorithms, which are defined in 5.2, to construct min_rules for the add operation for VM-NET connectivity relations. We define three attributes for VM and two attributes for NET. The value of each attribute of the virtual

---

Algorithm 1 Apriori Algorithm for min_rule Mining

1: **procedure** IDENTIFY_FREQUENCY(SCOPE_{att_p}, SCOPE_{att_q}, $min\_sup_{tnt,c_i,c_j}^{att_p,att_q}$)
2:     F = {}, $\overline{\mathrm{F}}$={}
3:     **for all** $val \in \mathsf{SCOPE}_{att_p}$ **do**
4:         **if** $support_{tnt,c_i,c_j}^{att_p}(val) \geq min\_sup_{tnt,c_i,c_j}^{att_p,att_q}$ **then**
5:             *Insert val into F*
6:         **end if**
7:     **end for**
8:     **for all** $val \in \mathsf{SCOPE}_{att_q}$ **do**
9:         **if** $support_{tnt,c_i,c_j}^{att_q}(val) \geq min\_sup_{tnt,c_i,c_j}^{att_p,att_q}$ **then**
10:            *Insert val into $\overline{\mathrm{F}}$*
11:         **end if**
12:     **end for**
13:     *Return F and $\overline{\mathrm{F}}$*
14: **end procedure**
15: **procedure** GEN_min_rule(F, $\overline{\mathrm{F}}$, $min\_conf_{tnt,c_i,c_j}^{att_p,att_q}$)
16:     **for all** $val_x \in \mathrm{F}$ and $val_y \in \overline{\mathrm{F}}$ **do**
17:         **if** $confidence_{tnt,c_i,c_j}^{att_p,att_q}(val_x,val_y) \geq$
18:         $min\_conf_{tnt,c_i,c_j}^{att_p,att_q}$ **then**
19:            Create_min_rule(min_rule$_i$, val_x, val_y)
20:         **end if**
21:     **end for**
22: **end procedure**

---

resources is specified in their 'meta' information. We randomly connect 10 NETs to VMs where each VM is assigned to at-least 3 NETs. Then, we collect logs of VM-NET connection from the nova database of DevStack and evaluate both algorithms.

Our first experiment verifies scalability of the algorithms when number of VMs increases. We gradually increase VMs from 50 to 500 with a fixed size of scope of each attribute to 10 from which we randomly assign a value for each attribute of VMs and NETs. Then, for each VM attribute and NET attribute pair we separately execute both algorithms and record time. We repeated this process 10 times for each algorithm. Figure 8 shows the average execution time of both algorithms where time of anti-Apriori is very high while CVRM-apriori gives much better performance. For instance, for 50 VMs the average time of anti-Apriori is 1.3s where it is 14.2s for 500 VMs. On the other hand, in CVRM-Apriori, it is 0.23s and 1.2s. The reason is that the size of U of anti-Apriori is multiplicative with increasing number of VMs where in CVRM-Apriori it is only additive.

In second experiment, we fixed the VMs to 100, however, increase the scope of each VM attribute from 10 to 20 and executed both algorithms. We also executed each of them 10 times and recorded the time. Figure 9 shows the evaluation results. Note that, like experiment one, anti-Apriori gives very poor performance with compare to CVRM-Aprior. For instance, from 10 to 20 values in scope the required time of anti-Apriori increases 1.3s where, in CVRM-Apriori, it remains almost constant. The reason behind this is that anti-Apriori calculates mutual exclusive relations for all the combination of the values of two attributes which unnecessarily increases time since min_rule only needs to capture separate relations between each two values of attributes.

In general, CVRM-Apriori behaves similar to the 2-frequent Apriori algorithm which requires exactly 2 scans over the database, hence, the required run-time complexity of CVRM-

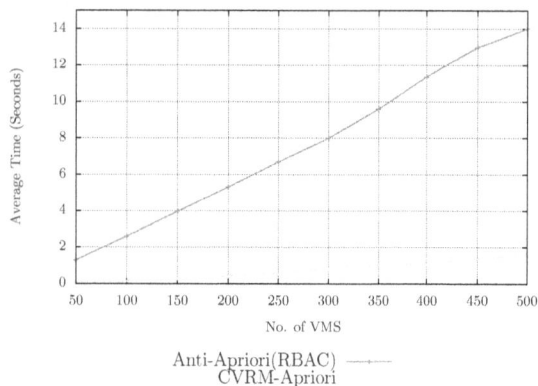

Figure 8: Mining Time with Increasing No. of VMs

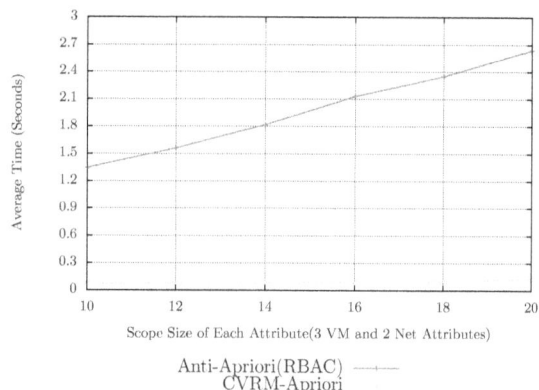

Figure 9: Mining Time with Increasing Scopes

Apriori is as good as FP-growth algorithm, which is an efficient Apriori algorithm with FP-tree data structure. Also, the accuracy of CVRM-Apriori is exactly same of the general Apriori algorithm since it does not discard any items from database for calculating the support and confidence.

6. RELATED WORK

Providing functionality to clients for resource-level permission management has started to receive more attention recently from cloud IaaS providers. However, this is primarily for managing user or group privileges to access their virtual resources. AWS Identity and Access Management (IAM) policies [1] now can construct fine-grained policies to control users' access to Subnets, VPCs, Security Groups and also type of virtual machines they can create. Also, the open source cloud platform OpenStack [3] has developed service called Keystone to manage users privilege to access cloud resources using some type of role-based access control. However, both platforms lack suitable mechanism so that clients can systematically specify policy to manage their virtual resources towards building a desired computing environment that addresses security, scale, hpc, etc. This increases various security threats for the running workloads from different tenants in cloud IaaS system. For instance, Shieh at al [26] shows that arbitrary sharing of network, in cloud, may cause denial of service attack and performance interferences. Wei et al [30] shows that uncontrolled snapshots and uses of images cause security risk for both creator and user of images. Sivathanu et al [27] presents an experimental analysis on I/O performance bottleneck when virtual storages are placed arbitrarily in physical storage and shared by random vms. Hence, different performance and security issues exist in cloud IaaS for unorganized multiplexing of resources and lack of controls, several of which are summarized in [14, 16, 17]. Hashizume et al [16] discuss and enumerates the security threats in cloud IaaS arising due to sharing physical machine, using images from public repository, sharing networks and storage, and also lack of proper resource control mechanism. Recently, for improving these scenarios, several efforts have been conducted by different groups of researchers. For instance, several improvements on shared network performance management have been proposed [5, 6, 26]. CloudNaas [6] provides better management of application-specific address spaces, middlebox traversal, bandwidth reservation, etc. Shieh at al [26] gives a bandwidth allocation scheme that allows infrastructure providers to define bandwidth sharing in cloud network with multiple tenants. Sivathanu et al [27] identifies four different factors that affects storage I/O performance and provides guidelines and their experimental analysis to minimize I/O overhead. Developing proper virtual machine placement algorithm also recently drew attention from research community [10, 11, 13, 15, 21, 31] for improving different aspects, e.g. high performance and load balancing. Present literature also contains several processes on users authorization and access control models for cloud IaaS that includes different RBAC models for cloud IaaS [9, 12].

Our contribution, in this paper, is unique and different than above described efforts. We aim to provide flexible mechanism to capture different requirements of the tenants to manage their virtual resources. Trusted virtual data center (TVDc) [7] is closely related to our work, where they assign virtual resources and users different colors where resources with similar colors can be combined to build a computing environment. Note that, color can be represented by an attribute, hence, CVRM is a generalization of TVDc in which resources are managed by multiple attributes.

7. CONCLUSIONS

We presented CVRM, the very first constraint specification process that enables tenants to specify several virtual resource management policies needed for production enterprise applications to run in IaaS clouds. CVRM can be specified as part of a cloud deployment, and are installed in the every cloud service provided by the IaaS providers.

We also identified that virtual-resource management policies can be discovered and constructed from log-file where it is similar to the well-known frequent-itemsets mining problem in database system. We demonstrated a constraint mining algorithm for CVRM where the algorithm leverages standard Apriori algorithm from the data mining literature. However, in this paper, we consider that the log-file is static and noise-free. Also, we do not analyze whether the mined constraints preserve semantic meaning with respective to the configuration requirements of the tenant. An obvious future work would be to identify various factors in IaaS that helps mining the rule with semantic meaning. Also, it will be interesting to determine noise in this system and develop a more dynamic mining algorithm that can eliminate such noises from the mining data.

8. ACKNOWLEDGEMENT

This research is partially supported by NSF Grants (CNS-1111925 and CNS-1423481). The authors thank Farhan Patwa and the anonymous reviewers for their helpful suggestions.

9. REFERENCES

[1] AWS identity and access management. *https://aws.amazon.com/iam/*.

[2] Devstack. *https://wiki.openstack.org/wiki/DevStack*.

[3] Openstack. *http://docs.openstack.org/*.

[4] R. Agrawal, T. Imieliński, and A. Swami. Mining association rules between sets of items in large databases. In *Proceedings of International Conference on Management of Data*, pages 207–216. ACM, 1993.

[5] H. Ballani, P. Costa, T. Karagiannis, and A. I. Rowstron. Towards predictable datacenter networks. In *Procedings of The ACM Special Interest Group on Data Communication*, pages 242–253, 2011.

[6] T. Benson et al. Cloudnaas: a cloud networking platform for enterprise applications. In *Proceedings of the 2nd Symposium on Cloud Computing*. ACM, 2011.

[7] S. Berger et al. Security for the cloud infrastructure: Trusted virtual data center implementation. *IBM Journal of Research and Development*, 53(4):6–1, 2009.

[8] K. Bijon, R. Krishnan, and R. Sandhu. A formal model for isolation management in cloud infrastructure-as-a-service. In *Proceedings of the 8th International Conference on Network and System Security (NSS)*. 2014.

[9] S. Bleikertz et al. Secure cloud maintenance - protecting workloads against insider attacks. In *Proceedings of the ACM Symposium on Information, Computer and Communications Security*, 2012.

[10] N. Bobroff et al. Dynamic placement of virtual machines for managing SLA violations. In *Proceedings of the International Symposium on Integrated Network Management*. IEEE, 2007.

[11] N. M. Calcavecchia, O. Biran, E. Hadad, and Y. Moatti. Vm placement strategies for cloud scenarios. In *Procedings of The International Conference on Cloud Computing*. IEEE, 2012.

[12] J. M. A. Calero et al. Toward a multi-tenancy authorization system for cloud services. *IEEE Security & Privacy*, 8(6):48–55, 2010.

[13] L. Cherkasova et al. Comparison of the three cpu schedulers in xen. *SIGMETRICS Performance Evaluation Review*, 35(2):42–51, 2007.

[14] W. Dawoud, I. Takouna, and C. Meinel. Infrastructure as a service security: Challenges and solutions. In *Procedings of International Conference on Informatics and Systems*, pages 1–8, 2010.

[15] A. Gupta et al. Hpc-aware vm placement in infrastructure clouds. In *IEEE Intl. Conf. on Cloud Engineering*, volume 13, 2013.

[16] K. Hashizume et al. An analysis of security issues for cloud computing. *Journal of Internet Services and Applications*, 4(1):1–13, 2013.

[17] A. Jasti, P. Shah, R. Nagaraj, and R. Pendse. Security in multi-tenancy cloud. In *Proceedings of the International Carnahan Conference on Security Technology (ICCST)*, pages 35–41. IEEE, 2010.

[18] X. Jin, R. Krishnan, and R. Sandhu. A role-based administration model for attributes. In *Proceedings of the International Workshop on Secure and Resilient Architectures and Systems*. ACM, 2012.

[19] E. Keller, J. Szefer, J. Rexford, and R. B. Lee. Nohype: virtualized cloud infrastructure without the virtualization. In *ACM SIGARCH Computer Architecture News*, volume 38, pages 350–361, 2010.

[20] X. Ma, R. Li, Z. Lu, and W. Wang. Mining constraints in role-based access control. *Mathematical and Computer Modelling*, 55(1):87–96, 2012.

[21] K. Mills, J. Filliben, and C. Dabrowski. Comparing vm-placement algorithms for on-demand clouds. In *Procedings of The International Conference on Cloud Computing Technology and Science*. IEEE, 2011.

[22] T. Ristenpart et al. Hey, you, get off of my cloud: exploring information leakage in third-party compute clouds. In *Proceedings of The ACM Conference on Computer and Communications Security*, 2009.

[23] J. Rivera. Gartner identifies the top 10 strategic technology trends for 2014. *http://www.gartner.com/newsroom/id/2603623*, 2013.

[24] R. Sandhu, E. Coyne, H. Feinstein, and C. Youman. Role-based access control models. *IEEE Computer*, 29(2):38–47, 1996.

[25] R. Sandhu, D. Ferraiolo, and R. Kuhn. The NIST model for role-based access control: towards a unified standard. In *ACM workshop on Role-based access control*, volume 2000, 2000.

[26] A. Shieh et al. Sharing the data center network. In *Proceedings of the 8th USENIX conference on Networked systems design and implementation*, 2011.

[27] S. Sivathanu, L. Liu, M. Yiduo, and X. Pu. Storage management in virtualized cloud environment. In *Procedings of The International Conference on Cloud Computing*, pages 204–211. IEEE, 2010.

[28] J. Szefer et al. Eliminating the hypervisor attack surface for a more secure cloud. In *Proceedings of The ACM Conference on Computer and Communications Security*, pages 401–412. ACM, 2011.

[29] V. Varadarajan et al. Resource-freeing attacks: improve your cloud performance (at your neighbor's expense). In *Proceedings of The ACM Conference on Computer and Communications Security*, pages 281–292, 2012.

[30] J. Wei et al. Managing security of virtual machine images in a cloud environment. In *Procedings of the ACM workshop on Cloud computing security*, 2009.

[31] C.-T. Yang et al. A dynamic resource allocation model for virtual machine management on cloud. In *Grid and Distributed Computing*. Springer, 2011.

[32] F. Zhang et al. Cloudvisor: Retrofitting protection of virtual machines in multi-tenant cloud with nested virtualization. In *Proceedings of the ACM Symposium on Operating Systems Principles*, pages 203–216, 2011.

[33] Y. Zhang et al. Cross-vm side channels and their use to extract private keys. In *proceedings of the 19th ACM Conference on Computer and Communications Security*, 2012.

Hadoop Cluster Configurations

A: Virtual Resources, Attributes and Constraints

route   netType   nodeType

Constraint 1   Constraint 2
Constraints

B: Scopes of the Attributes

$\mathbf{ATTR}_{\mathbf{hadoop}}^{\mathbf{VM}} = \{nodeType\}$

$\mathbf{SCOPE}_{\mathbf{nodeType}} = \{clientNode, nameNode, jobTracker, mapTask, reduceTask\}$

$\mathbf{ATTR}_{\mathbf{hadoop}}^{\mathbf{NET}} = \{netType\}$

$\mathbf{SCOPE}_{\mathbf{netType}} = \{outerNet, clientNet, nameNet, jobNet, mapNet, reduceNet\}$

$\mathbf{ATTR}_{\mathbf{hadoop}}^{\mathbf{RT}} = \{route\}$

$\mathbf{SCOPE}_{\mathbf{route}} = \{outerRoute, nameRoute, jobRoute, taskRoute\}$

C: Constraint Specification

Constraints for router-network connection mapping:

Constraint 1: *If route attribute of a router is outerRoute then only network with netType outerNet and clientNet can connect to it and if If route attribute is taskRoute then it cannot be connected with nameNet, outerNet and clientNet.*

$((route\,(router) = outerRoute) \rightarrow$
$((netType\,(network) = outerNet) \vee (netType\,(network) = clientNet)))$
$\wedge ((route\,(router) = taskRoute) \rightarrow$
$(((netType\,(network) \neq nameNet) \wedge (netType\,(network) = outerNet))$
$\wedge (netType\,(network) = clientNet)))$

Constraints for network-vm connection mapping:

Constraint 2: *In a nameNet network only nameNode and jobTracker vm can be connected.*

$((netType\,(network) = nameNet) \rightarrow$
$((nodeType\,(vm) = nameNode) \vee (nodeType\,(vm) = jobTracker)))$

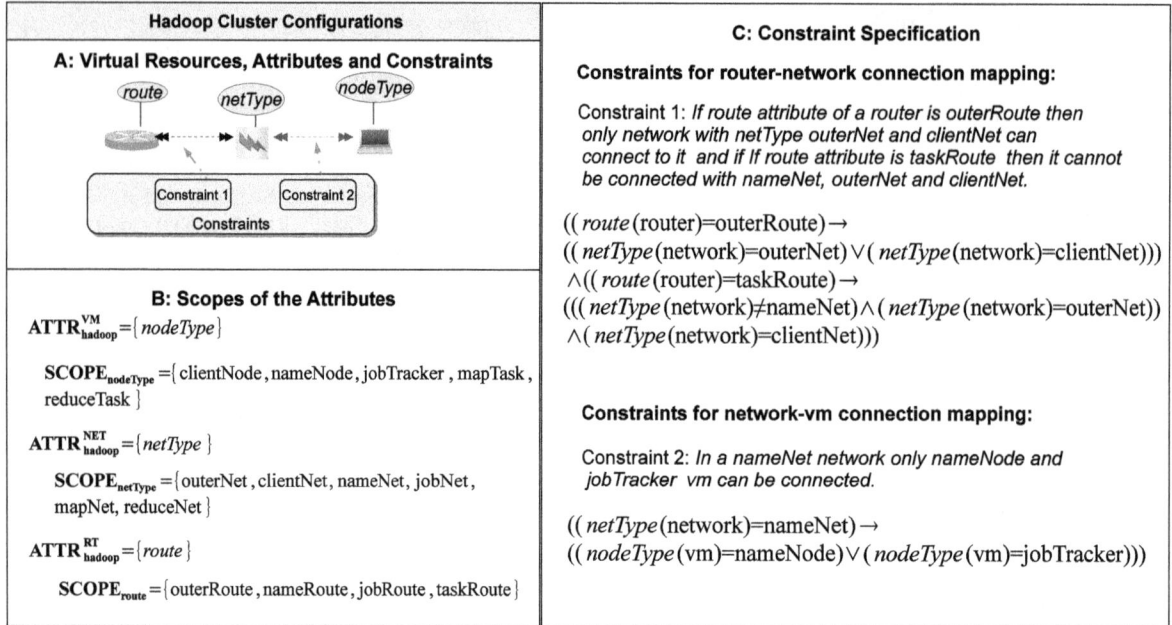

Figure 10: Constraints Specification for Hadoop Cluster

Appendix: CVRM for Hadoop Cluster Setup

We discuss the CVRM instantiation for a simple hadoop cluster setup. The set TENANTS contains the tenant hadoop. The classes of the virtual resources supported by CSP are VM, NET, and RT and specified relations are between VM-to-NET and NET-to-RT. The relations are represented as $\mathcal{R}_{hadoop,VM,NET}$ and $\mathcal{R}_{hadoop,NET,RT}$.

In this simple hadoop setup, we only define one attribute for each virtual resources (shown in figure 10-A). Here, a VM attribute *nodeType* represent the type of operations a vm performs in hadoop cluster and figure 10-B shows the scope of *nodeType* that is clientNode, nameNode, job-Tracker, mapTask, reduceTask. Similarly, two attributes *netType* and *route* are defined for NET and RT respectively. Note that, other attributes can also defined for more complex hadoop configuration management.

Followed by attribute specification of the resources, we show two constraints for adding elements in each of the relations (shown in figure 10-C). Here, for instance, constraint $\delta_{hadoop,NET,RT}^{Add}$ applies to the *Add* operation where it restricts all the NETs except outerNet and clientNet to connect a RT which has value outerRoute in *route* attribute. This constraint only allows clientNet to connect to outer internet.

Privacy-Preserving Scanning of Big Content for Sensitive Data Exposure with MapReduce[*]

Fang Liu, Xiaokui Shu, Danfeng (Daphne) Yao and Ali R. Butt
Department Computer Science
Virginia Tech
Blacksburg, VA, USA
{fbeyond, subx, danfeng, butta}@cs.vt.edu

ABSTRACT

The exposure of sensitive data in storage and transmission poses a serious threat to organizational and personal security. Data leak detection aims at scanning content (in storage or transmission) for exposed sensitive data. Because of the large content and data volume, such a screening algorithm needs to be scalable for a timely detection. Our solution uses the MapReduce framework for detecting exposed sensitive content, because it has the ability to arbitrarily scale and utilize public resources for the task, such as Amazon EC2. We design new MapReduce algorithms for computing collection intersection for data leak detection. Our prototype implemented with the Hadoop system achieves 225 Mbps analysis throughput with 24 nodes. Our algorithms support a useful privacy-preserving data transformation. This transformation enables the privacy-preserving technique to minimize the exposure of sensitive data during the detection. This transformation supports the secure outsourcing of the data leak detection to untrusted MapReduce and cloud providers.

Categories and Subject Descriptors

C.2.0 [**Computer-Communication Networks**]: General—*security and protection*; C.2.4 [**Computer-Communication Networks**]: Distributed System—*distributed applications*

Keywords

Data leak detection; MapReduce; Scalability; Collection intersection

---

[*]This work has been supported in part by Security and Software Engineering Research Center (S^2ERC), a NSF sponsored multi-university Industry/University Cooperative Research Center (I/UCRC), and ARO YIP W911NF-14-1-0535.

1. INTRODUCTION

The exposure of sensitive data is a serious threat to the confidentiality of organizational and personal data. Reports showed that over 800 million sensitive records were exposed in 2013 through over 2,000 incidents [13]. Reasons include compromised systems, the loss of devices, or unencrypted data storage or network transmission. While many data leak incidents are due to malicious attacks, a significant portion of the incidents are caused by unintentional mistakes of employees or data owners.

There exist several approaches for detecting data exfiltration, e.g., enforcing strict data-access policies on a host (e.g., storage capsule [7]), watermarking sensitive data sets and tracking data flow anomalies (e.g., DBMS-layer [2]) and inspecting outbound network traffic for anomalies. In the last category, the analysis proposed by Borders and Prakash [6] detects changes in network traffic patterns by searching for unjustifiable increase in HTTP traffic-flow volume, that indicates data exfiltration. The technique proposed by Shu and Yao [32] performs deep packet inspection to search for exposed outbound traffic that bears high similarity to sensitive data. Set intersection is used for the similarity measure. The intersection is computed between the set of n-grams from the content and the set of n-grams from the sensitive data.

This similarity-based detection is versatile, capable of analyzing both text and some binary-encoded context (e.g., Word or .pdf files). A naive implementation requires $O(nm)$ complexity, where n and m are sizes of the two sets A and B, respectively. If the sets are relatively small, then a faster implementation is to use a hashtable to store set A and then testing whether items in B exist in the hashtable or not, giving $O(n + m)$ complexity.

However, if A and B are both very large (as in our data-leak detection scenario), a naive hashtable may have hash collisions that slow down the computation. Increasing the size of the hashtable may not be practical due to memory limitation and thrashing.[1] One may attempt to distribute the dataset into multiple hashtables across several machines and coordinate the nodes to compute set intersections for leak scanning. However, such a system is nontrivial to implement from scratch and has not been reported in the literature.

In this paper, we present a data-leak detection system in MapReduce. MapReduce [14] is a programming framework for distributed data intensive applications. It has been

---

[1]We experimentally validated this on a single host. The results are shown in Table 3 in the appendix.

used to solve security problems such as spam filtering [9, 10], Internet traffic analysis [20] and log analysis [4, 21, 36]. MapReduce algorithms can be deployed on nodes in the cloud or in local computer clusters.

However, none of these work addressed the privacy requirement of sensitive data, especially when it is outsourced to a third party for analysis. The reason is that the MapReduce nodes may be compromised or owned by semi-honest adversaries, who may attempt to gain knowledge of the sensitive data. For example, researchers demonstrated the possibility of exploring information leakage across VMs through side channel attacks in third-party compute clouds (e.g., Amazon EC2) in [30].

Although private multi-party set intersection methods exist [18], the high computational overhead is a concern for time-sensitive security applications such as data-leak detection.

In this work, we present a new MapReduce-based system to detect the occurrences of plaintext sensitive data in storage and transmission. The detection is distributed and parallel, capable of screening massive amount of content for exposed information. We address an important data privacy requirement. **In our privacy-preserving data-leak detection, MapReduce nodes scan content in data storage or network transmission for leaks without learning what the sensitive data is.**

Specifically, the data privacy protection is realized with fast one-way transformation. This transformation requires the pre- and post-processing by the data owner for hiding and precisely identifying the matched items, respectively. Both the sensitive data and the content need to be transformed and protected by the data owner, before it is given to the MapReduce nodes for the detection. In the meantime, such a transformation has to support the equality comparison required by the set intersection. This technique provides strong privacy guarantee for the data owner, in terms of the low probability for a MapReduce node to recover the sensitive data.

Besides the privacy guarantee, another advantage of our data leak solution is its scalability. Because of the intrinsic $\langle key, value \rangle$ organization of items in MapReduce, the worst-case complexity of our algorithms is correlated to the size of the leak (specifically a $\gamma \in [0, 1]$ factor denoting the size of the intersection between the content set and the sensitive data set). This complexity reduction brought by the γ factor is significant, because the value is extremely low for normal content without leak. In our algorithm, items not in the intersection (non-sensitive content) are quickly dropped without further processing. Therefore, the MapReduce-based algorithms have a lower computational complexity when compared to the traditional set-intersection implementation. Our contributions in this paper are as follows.

- We present a series of new MapReduce parallel algorithms for distributedly computing the sensitivity of content based on its similarity with sensitive data patterns. The similarity is based on collection intersection (a variant of set intersection that also counts duplicates). The MapReduce-based collection intersection algorithms are useful beyond the specific data leak detection problem.

- Our detection provides the privacy enhancement to preserve the confidentiality of sensitive data during the

outsourced detection. Because of this privacy enhancement, our MapReduce algorithms can be deployed in distributed environments where the operating nodes are owned by third-party service providers. Applications of our work include data leak detection in the cloud and outsourced data leak detection.

- We implement our algorithms using the open source Hadoop framework. Our prototype outputs the degree of sensitivity for the content, and pinpoints the occurrences of potential leaks in the content. Higher sensitivity values indicate that the content is more likely to contain sensitive information. Our implementation has very efficient intermediate data representations, which significantly minimizes the disk and network I/O overhead. We performed two sets of experimental evaluations, one on Amazon EC2 and one on a local computer cluster, using large-scale email data. We achieved 225 Mbps throughput for the privacy-preserving data leak detection when processing 74 GB of content.

Our MapReduce algorithms reduce the worst-case computation complexity of set intersection by a factor of γ, where $\gamma \in [0, 1]$ is the average set intersection rate of the inputs. Because data leak is a low likelihood event, γ is usually very small in normal content, making this reduction a significant improvement.

2. THREAT MODEL AND DESIGN OVERVIEW

There are two types of input sequences in our data-leak detection model: content sequences and sensitive data sequences.

- *Content* is the data to be inspected for any occurrences of sensitive data patterns. The content can be extracted from file system and network traffic. The detection needs to partition the original content stream into **content segments**.

- *Sensitive data* contains the sensitive information that cannot be exposed to unauthorized parties, e.g., customers' records, proprietary documents. Sensitive data can also be partitioned to smaller **sensitive data sequences**.

2.1 Threat Model and Security Goal

In our model, two parties participate in the large-scale data leak detection system: data owner and data-leak detection (DLD) provider.

- *Data owner* owns the sensitive data and wants to know whether the sensitive data is leaked. It has the full access to both the content and the sensitive data. However, it only has limited computation and storage capability and needs to authorize the DLD provider to help inspect the content for inadvertent data leak.

- *DLD provider* provides detection service and has unlimited computation and storage power when compared with data owner. It can perform offline inspection without real time delay. However, the DLD provider is honest-but-curious (aka semi-honest). That is, it follows the prescribed protocol but may attempt to gain knowledge of sensitive data. The DLD provider is not given the access to the plaintext content. It can perform dictionary attack on the signature of sensitive data records.

Our goal is to offer DLD provider solutions to scan massive content for sensitive data exposure and minimize the possibility that the DLD provider learns about the sensitive information.

- **Scalability**: the ability to process content at a variety of scales, e.g., megabytes to terabytes, enabling the DLD provider to offer on-demand content inspection.

- **Privacy**: the ability to keep the sensitive data confidential, not disclosed to the DLD provider or any attacker breaking into the detection system.

- **Accuracy**: the ability to identify all leaks and only real leaks in the content, which implies low false negative/positive rates for the detection.

Our framework is not designed to detect intentional data exfiltration, during which the attacker may encrypt or transform the sensitive data.

2.2 Computation Goal

Our detection is based on computing the similarity between content segments and sensitive data sequences, specifically the intersection of two collections of n-grams. n-grams captures local features of a sequence and have also been used in other sequence similarity methods (e.g., web search duplication [8]). Following the terminology proposed by Broder *et al.* [8], we also refer to n-gram as *shingle*.

One collection consists of shingles obtained from the content segment and the other collection consists of shingles from the sensitive sequence. Collection intersection differs from set intersection, in that it also records duplicated items in the intersection, which is illustrated in Figure 1. Recording the frequencies of intersected items achieves more fine-grained detection. Thus, collection intersection is preferred for data leak analysis than set intersection.

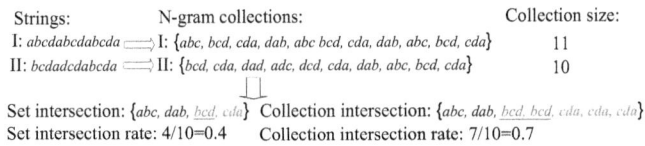

Strings: N-gram collections: Collection size:

I: *abcdabcdabcda* ⟹ I: {*abc, bcd, cda, dab, abc bcd, cda, dab, abc, bcd, cda*}   11

II: *bcdadcdabcda* ⟹ II: {*bcd, cda, dad, adc, dcd, cda, dab, abc, bcd, cda*}   10

Set intersection: {*abc, dab, bcd, cda*} Collection intersection: {*abc, dab, bcd, bcd, cda, cda, cda*}

Set intersection rate: 4/10=0.4   Collection intersection rate: 7/10=0.7

Figure 1: An example illustrating the difference between set intersection and collection intersection in handling duplicates for 3-grams.

Notation used in our algorithms is shown in Table 1, including collection identifier CID, size CSize (in terms of the number of items), occurrence frequency *Snum* of an item in one collection, occurrence frequency *Inum* of an item in an intersection, and intersection rate *Irate* of a content collection with respect to some sensitive data.

Formally, given a content collection C_c and a sensitive data collection C_s, our algorithms aim to compute the intersection rate $Irate \in [0, 1]$ defined in Equation 1, where $Inum$ is the occurrence frequency of an item i in the intersection $C_s \cap C_c$ (defined in Table 1). The sum of frequencies of all

items appeared in the collection intersection is normalized by the size of the sensitive data collection, which yields the intersection rate *Irate*. The rate represents the percentage of sensitive data that appears in the content. *Irate* is also referred to as the *sensitivity score* of a content collection.

$$Irate = \frac{\sum\limits_{i \in \{C_s \cap C_c\}} Inum_i}{|C_s|} \qquad (1)$$

Syntax	Definition
CID	An identifier of a collection (content or sensitive data)
CSize	Size of a collection
Snum	Occurrence frequency of an item
Inum	Occurrence frequency of an item in an intersection
CSid	A pair of CIDs $\langle CID_1, CID_2 \rangle$, where CID_1 is for a content collection and CID_2 is for a sensitive data collection
Irate	Intersection rate between a content collection and a sensitive data collection as defined in Equation 1. Also referred to as the sensitivity score of the content.
ISN	A 3-item tuple of a collection ⟨identifier *CID*, size *CSize*, and the number of items in the collection⟩
CSS	An identifier for a collection intersection, consisting of a ID pair *CSid* of two collections and the size of the sensitive data collection *CSize*

Table 1: Notation used in our MapReduce algorithms.

2.3 Confidentiality of Sensitive Data

Naive collection-intersection solutions performing on *shingles* provide no protection for the sensitive data. The reason is that MapReduce nodes can easily reconstruct sensitive data from the shingles. Our detection utilizes several methods for the data owner to transform shingles before they are released to the MapReduce nodes. These transformations, including specialized hash function, provide strong-yet-efficient confidentiality protection for the sensitive information. In exchange for these privacy guarantees, the data owner needs to perform additional data pre- and post-processing operations.

In addition to protecting the confidentiality of sensitive data, the pre-processing operations also need to satisfy following requirements:

- **Equality-preserving**: the transformation operation should be deterministic so that two identical shingles within one session are always mapped to the same item for comparison.

- **One-wayness**: the function should be easy to compute given any shingle and hard to invert given the output of a sensitive shingle.

Our collection intersection (in Section 3) is computed on one-way hash values of n-grams, specifically Rabin fingerprints. Rabin fingerprint is a fast one-way hash function, which is computational expensive to invert.

Specifically, Rabin fingerprint of a n-bit shingle is based on the coefficients of the remainder of the polynomial modular operation with an irreducible polynomial $p(x)$ as the modulo as shown in Equation 2, where c_{n-i+1} is the i-th bit in the shingle.

$$f \;=\; c_1 x^{n-1} + c_2 x^{n-2} + ... + c_{n-1} x + c_n \; mod \; p(x) \;(2)$$

Section 4 presents the security analysis of our approach especially on the confidentiality of sensitive data.

2.4 Workload Distribution

The details on how the workload is distributed between data owner and DLD provider is as follows and shown in Figure 2:

1. Data owner has m sensitive sequences $\{S_1, S_2, \cdots, S_m\}$ with average size $\mathcal{S}'$ and n content segments $\{C_1, C_2, \cdots, C_n\}$ with average size $\mathcal{C}'$. It obtains shingles from the content and sensitive data respectively. Then it chooses the public parameters $(n, p(x), L)$, where n is the length of shingle, $p(x)$ is the irreducible polynomial and L is the fingerprint length. The data owner computes Rabin fingerprints with Equation 2 and releases the sensitive collections $\{C_{S1}, C_{S2}, \cdots, C_{Sm}\}$ and content fingerprint collections $\{C_{C1}, C_{C2}, \cdots, C_{Cn}\}$ to the DLD provider.

2. DLD provider receives both the sensitive fingerprint collections and content fingerprint collections. It deploys MapRecuce framework and compares the n content collections with the m sensitive collections using our two-phase MapReduce algorithms. By computing the intersection rate of each content and sensitive collections pair, it outputs whether the sensitive data was leaked and reports all the data leak alerts to data owner.

3. Data owner receives the data leak alerts with a set of tuples $\{(C_{Ci}, C_{Sj}), (C_{Ck}, C_{Sl}), \cdots\}$. The data owner maps them to suspicious content segments and the plain sensitive sequences tuples $\{(C_i, S_j), (C_k, S_l), \cdots\}$. The data owner consults plaintext content to confirm that true leaks (as opposed to accidental matches) occur in these content segments and further pinpoint the leak occurrences.

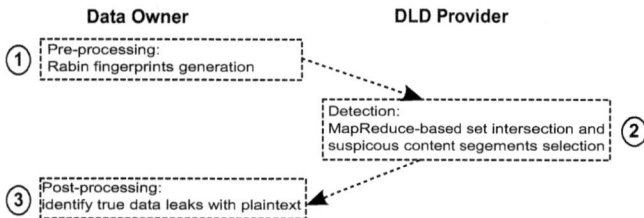

Figure 2: Workload distribution for DLD provider and data owner.

2.5 MapReduce-Based Design and Challenges

MapReduce is a programming model for processing large-scale data sets on clusters. A MapReduce algorithm has two phases: `map` that supports the distribution and partition of inputs to nodes, and `reduce` that groups and integrates the nodes' outputs. MapReduce data needs to be in the format of $\langle key, value \rangle$ pair, where key serves as an index and the value represents the properties corresponding to the key/data item. A complex problem may require several rounds of map and reduce operations, requiring redefining and redistributing $\langle key, value \rangle$ pairs between rounds.

There exist several MapReduce-specific challenges when realizing collection-intersection based data leak detection.

1. **Complex data fields** Collection intersection with duplicates is more complex than set intersection. This requires the design of complex data fields for $\langle key, value \rangle$ pairs and a series of `map` and `reduce` operations.

2. **Memory and I/O efficiency** The use of multiple data fields (e.g., collection size and ID, shingle frequency) in $\langle key, value \rangle$ pairs may cause frequent garbage collection and heavy network and disk I/O.

3. **Optimal segmentation of data streams** While larger segment size allows the full utilization of CPU, it may cause insufficient memory problem and reduced detection sensitivity.

Our data-leak detection algorithms in MapReduce addresses these technical challenges in MapReduce framework and achieves the security and privacy goals. We design structured-yet-compact representations for data fields of intermediate values, which significantly improves the efficiency of our algorithms. Our prototype also realizes an additional post-processing partitioning and analysis, which allows one to pinpoint the leak occurrences in large content segments. We experimentally evaluate the impact of segment sizes on detection throughput and identify the optimal segment size for performance.

2.6 Detection Workflow

To compute the intersection rate of two fingerprint collections $Irate$, we design two MapReduce algorithms, DIVIDER and REASSEMBLER, each of which has a `map` and a `reduce` operation. Map and reduce operations are connected through a redistribution process. During the redistribution, outputs from map (in the form of $\langle key, value \rangle$ pairs) are sent to reducer nodes, as the inputs to the reduce algorithm. The key value of a record decides to which reducer node the it is forwarded. Records with the same key are sent to the same reducer.

1. DIVIDER takes the following as inputs: fingerprints of both content and sensitive data, and the information about the collections containing these fingerprints. Its purpose is to count the number of a fingerprint's occurrences in a collection intersection (i.e., $Inum$ in Equation 1) for all fingerprints in all intersections.

   In `map` operation, it re-organizes the fingerprints to identify all the occurrences of a fingerprint across multiple content or sensitive data collections. Each `map` instance processes one collection. This reorganization traverses the list of fingerprints. Using the fingerprint as the key, it then emits (i.e., redistributes) the records with the same key to the same node.

In `reduce`, for each fingerprint in an intersection the algorithm computes the *Inum* value, which is its number of occurrences in the intersection. Each `reduce` instance processes one fingerprint. The algorithm outputs the tuple $\langle CSS, Inum \rangle$, where *CSS* is the identifier of the intersection (consisting of IDs of the two collections and the size of the sensitive data collection[2]). Outputs are written to MapReduce file system.

2. REASSEMBLER takes as inputs $\langle CSS, Inum \rangle$ (outputs from Algorithm DIVIDER). The purpose of this algorithm is to compute the intersection rates (i.e., *Irate* in Equation 1) of all collection intersections $\{C_{c_i} \cap C_{s_j}\}$ between a content collection C_{c_i} and a sensitive data collection C_{s_j}.

In `map`, the inputs are read from the file system, and redistributed to reducer nodes according to the identifier of an intersection *CSS* (key). A reducer has as inputs the *Inum* values for all the fingerprints appearing in a collection intersection whose identifier is *CSS*. At `reduce`, it computes the intersection rate of *CSS* based on Equation 1.

In the next section, we present our algorithms for realizing the collection intersection workflow with one-way Rabin fingerprints. In Section 4, we explain why our privacy preserving technique is able to protect the sensitive data against semi-honest MapReduce nodes and discuss the causes of false alarms and the limitations.

3. COLLECTION INTERSECTION IN MAPREDUCE

We present our collection-intersection algorithm in the MapReduce framework. The algorithm computes the intersection rate of two collections as defined in Equation 1. Each collection consists of Rabin fingerprints of n-grams generated from a sequence (sensitive data or content).

RECORDREADER is a (standard) MapReduce class. We customize it to read initial inputs into our detection system and transform them into the $\langle key, value \rangle$ format required by the `map` function. The initial inputs of our RECORDREADER are content fingerprints segments and sensitive fingerprints sequences. For the DIVIDER algorithm, the RECORDREADER has two tasks: *i)* to read in each `map` split (e.g., content segment) as a whole and *ii)* to generate $\langle CSize, fingerprint \rangle$ pairs required by the `map` operation of DIVIDER algorithm.

3.1 DIVIDER **Algorithm**

DIVIDER is the most important and computational intensive algorithm in our system. Pseudocode of DIVIDER is given in Algorithm 1. In order to count the number of a fingerprint's occurrences in a collection intersection, the map operation in DIVIDER goes through the input $\langle CSize, fingerprint \rangle$ pairs, and reorganizes them to be indexed by fingerprint values. For each fingerprint in a collection, map records its origin information (e.g., *CID*, *CSize* of the collection) and *Snum* (fingerprint's frequency of occurrence in the collection). These values are useful for later intersection-rate computation.

[2]The sensitive data collection is typically much smaller than the content collection.

Algorithm 1 DIVIDER: To count the number of a fingerprint's occurrences in a collection intersection for all fingerprints in all intersections.

Input: Output of RECORDREADER in a format of $\langle CSize, Fingerprint \rangle$ as $\langle key, value \rangle$ pair.
Output: $\langle CSS, Inum \rangle$ as $\langle key, value \rangle$ pair, where *CSS* contains content collection ID, sensitive data collection ID and the size of the sensitive data collection. *Inum* is occurrence frequency of a fingerprint in the collection intersection.

```
 1: function DIVIDER::MAPPER(CSize, Fingerprint)
 2:     ▷ Record necessary information for the collection.
 3:     ISN ← CID, CSize and Snum
 4:     Emit⟨Fingerprint, ISN⟩
 5: end function
 1: function DIVIDER::REDUCER(Fingerprint, ISNlist[c₁,...,cₙ])
 2:     j = 0, k = 0
 3:     ▷ Divide the list into a sensitive list and a content list
 4:     for all cᵢ in ISNlist do
 5:         if cᵢ belongs to sensitive collections then
 6:             SensList[++j] ← cᵢ
 7:         else
 8:             ContentList[++k] ← cᵢ
 9:         end if
10:     end for
11:     ▷ Record the fingerprint occurrence in the intersection
12:     for all sens in SensList do
13:         for all content in ContentList do
14:             Size ← sens.CSize
15:             Inum ← Min(sens.Snum, content.Snum)
16:             CSS ← ⟨content.CID, sens.CID, Size⟩
17:             Emit ⟨CSS, Inum⟩
18:         end for
19:     end for
20: end function
```

Steps of our MapReduce algorithms are illustrated with a running example (with four MapReduce nodes) in Figure 3. The example has two content collections C_1 and C_2, and two sensitive data collections S_1 and S_2. The sizes of their corresponding collections are 3, 4, 3 and 3, respectively. E.g., in node 1 of Figure 3, map outputs the pair $\langle a, (C_1, 3, 1) \rangle$, indicating fingerprint (key) a is from content collection C_1 of size 3 and occurs once in C_1.

The advantage of using the fingerprint as the key in the map's outputs is that it allows the reducer to quickly identify non-intersected items. After redistribution, entries having the same fingerprint are sent to the same reducer node as inputs to the reduce algorithm. E.g., in Figure 3, all occurrences of fingerprint a are sent to node 1, including two occurrences from content collections C_1 and C_2, one occurrence from sensitive data collection S_1.

Reduce algorithm is more complex than map. It partitions the occurrences of a fingerprint into two lists, one list (*ContentList*) for the occurrences in content collections and one for sensitive data (*SensList*). It then uses a double for-loop to identify the fingerprints that appear in intersections, e.g., a. Non-intersected fingerprints are not analyzed, significantly reducing the computational overhead. This reduction is reflected in our computational complexity analysis in Table 2, specifically the $\gamma \in [0,1]$ reduction factor representing the size of intersection.

The for-loops also compute the occurrence frequency *Inum* of the fingerprint in an intersection. E.g., for node 3 in Figure 3, d appears once in $C_1 \cap S_1$ and once $C_1 \cap S_2$. The output

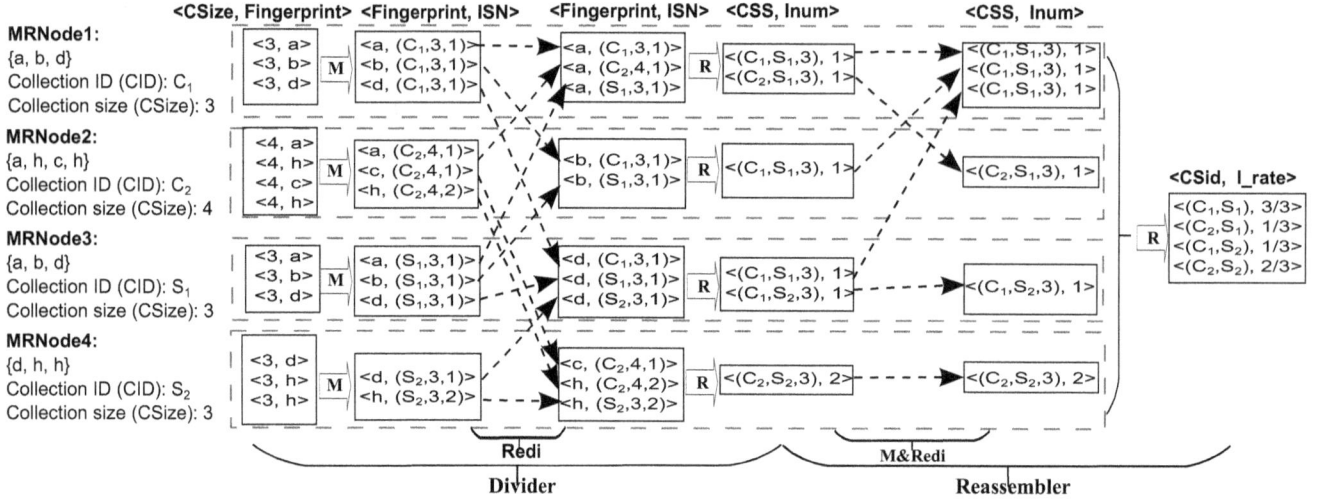

Figure 3: A Running example illustrating DIVIDER and REASSEMBLER algorithms, with four MapReduce nodes, two content collections C_1 and C_2, and two sensitive data collections S_1 and S_2. **M**, **R**, **Redi** stand for map, reduce, and redistribution, respectively. $\langle key, value \rangle$ of each operation is shown at the top.

of the algorithm is the $\langle CSS, Inum \rangle$ pairs, indicating that a fingerprint occurs $Inum$ number of times in a collection intersection whose identifier is CSS.

3.2 REASSEMBLER Algorithm

Algorithm 2 REASSEMBLER: To compute the intersection rates $Irate$ of all collection intersections $\{C_{c_i} \cap C_{s_j}\}$ between a content collection C_{c_i} and a sensitive data collection C_{s_j}.

Input: Output of DIVIDER in a format of $\langle CSS, Inum \rangle$ as $\langle key, value \rangle$ pairs.
Output: $\langle CSid, Irate \rangle$ pairs where $CSid$ represents a pair of a content collection ID and a sensitive collection ID, while $Irate$ represents the intersection rate between them

1: **function** REASSEMBLER::MAPPER(CSS, $Inum$)
2:     Emit$\langle CSS, Inum \rangle$
3: **end function**

1: **function** REASSEMBLER::REDUCER(CSS, $Inum[n_1, \ldots, n_n]$)
2:     $intersection \leftarrow 0$
3:     ▷ Add up all the elements in $Inum[]$
4:     **for all** n_i in $Inum[]$ **do**
5:         $intersection \leftarrow intersection + n_i$
6:     **end for**
7:     $CSid \leftarrow CSS.CSid$
8:     ▷ Compute intersection rate
9:     $Irate \leftarrow \frac{|intersection|}{CSS.CSize}$
10:     Emit $\langle CSid, Irate \rangle$
11: **end function**

The purpose of REASSEMBLER is to compute the intersection rates $Irate$ of all collection-and-sensitive-data intersections. Pseudocode of REASSEMBLER is in Algorithm 2. The map operation in REASSEMBLER emits (i.e., redistributes) inputs $\langle CSS, Inum \rangle$ pairs according to their key CSS values to different reducers. The reducer can then compute the intersection rate $Irate$ for the content and sensitive data collection pair. I.e., this redistribution sends all the intersected

items between a content collection C_{c_i} and a sensitive data collection C_{s_j} to the same reducer. E.g., in Figure 3, all the pairs with $(C_1, S_1, 3)$ as key are sent to MapReduce node 1. In node 1, the total number of fingerprints shared by C_1 and S_1 is 3. The intersection rate is 1.

Complexity Analysis The computational and communication complexities of various operations of our algorithm are shown in Table 2. We denote the average size of a sensitive data collection by $\mathcal{S}$, the average size of a content collection by $\mathcal{C}$, the number of sensitive data collections by m, the number of content collections by n, and the average intersection rate by $\gamma \in [0, 1]$. Without loss of generality, we assume that $|\mathcal{S}| < |\mathcal{C}|$ and $|\mathcal{S}m| < |\mathcal{C}n|$. We do not include post-processing in complexity analysis. Our total communication complexity $O(\mathcal{C}n + \mathcal{S}mn\gamma)$ covers the number of records ($\langle key, value \rangle$ pairs) that all operations output. For a hashtable-based (non-MapReduce) approach, where each content collection is stored in a hashtable (total n hashtables of size $\mathcal{C}$ each) and each sensitive data item (total $\mathcal{S}m$ items) is compared against all n hashtables, the computational complexity is $O(\mathcal{C}n + \mathcal{S}mn)$.

4. SECURITY ANALYSIS AND DISCUSSION

MapReduce nodes that perform the data-leak detection may be controlled by honest-but-curious providers (aka semi-honest), who follow the protocol, but may attempt to gain knowledge of the sensitive data information (e.g., by logging the intermediate results and making inferences). We analyze the security and privacy guarantees provided by our MapReduce based data leak detection system. The privacy goal of our system is to prevent the sensitive data from being exposed to DLD provider or untrusted nodes.

Privacy guarantee Let f_s be the Rabin fingerprint of sensitive data shingle s. Using the algorithms in Section 3, a MapReduce node knows fingerprint f_s but not shingle s of the sensitive data. We assume that attackers are not able to

Algorithm	Comp.	Comm.
Our Pre-processing	$O(\mathcal{C}n + \mathcal{S}m)$	$O(\mathcal{C}n + \mathcal{S}m)$
Our Divider::M.	$O(\mathcal{C}n + \mathcal{S}m)$	$O(\mathcal{C}n + \mathcal{S}m)$
Our Divider::R.	$O(\mathcal{C}n + \mathcal{S}mn\gamma)$	$O(\mathcal{S}mn\gamma)$
Our Reassembler::M.	$O(\mathcal{S}mn\gamma)$	$O(\mathcal{S}mn\gamma)$
Our Reassembler::R.	$O(\mathcal{S}mn\gamma)$	$O(mn)$
Our Total	$O(\mathcal{C}n + \mathcal{S}mn\gamma)$	$O(\mathcal{C}n + \mathcal{S}mn\gamma)$
Hashtable	$O(\mathcal{C}n + \mathcal{S}mn)$	N/A

Table 2: Computation and communication complexity of each phase in our MapReduce algorithm and that of the conventional hashtable-based approach. We denote the average size of a sensitive data collection by $\mathcal{S}$, the average size of a content collection by $\mathcal{C}$, the number of sensitive data collections by m, the number of content collections by n, and the average intersection rate by $\gamma \in [0, 1]$.

infer s in polynomial time from f_s. This assumption is guaranteed by the one-way Rabin fingerprinting function [29].

In addition, the data owner chooses a different irreducible polynomial $p(x)$ for each session. Under this configuration, the same shingle is mapped to different fingerprints in multiple sessions. The advantage of this design is the increased randomization in the fingerprint computation, making it more challenging for the DLD provider to correlate values and infer preimage. This randomization also increases the difficulty of dictionary attacks. Other cryptographic mechanisms, e.g., XORing a secret session key with content and sensitive data before fingerprinting, achieve similar security improvement. Because the transformation needs to preserve equality comparison (in Section 2.3), the configuration needs to be consistent within a session.

Collisions Two types of collisions are involved in our detection framework: fingerprint collisions and coincidental matches. Fingerprint collisions rarely happen as long as the length of fingerprint is sufficiently long (64 bits fingerprints are sufficient long with the collision probability being less than 10^{-6}, according to the study by Broder [8]). Coincidental match occurs when some shingles in content happens to mach some in sensitive data. These shingle matches may be due to shorter shingles, large content segment or sensitive data containing widely used patterns. With proper shingle length and threshold setting, the detection accuracy would not be affected by the coincidental matches. We perform accuracy experiment in Section 5.4, which shows that the intersection rate for normal leak is much higher than that caused by coincidental matches.

Our data leak detection framework is designed to detect accidental data leaks in content, instead of intentional data exfiltration. In intentional data exfiltration, which cannot be detected by deep packet inspection, an attacker may encrypt or transform the sensitive data.

5. IMPLEMENTATION AND EVALUATION

We implement our algorithms with Java in Hadoop, which is an open-source software system implementing MapReduce. We set the length of fingerprint and shingle to 8 bytes (64 bits). This length was previously reported as optimal for robust similarity test [8], as it is long enough to preserve some local context and short enough to resist certain

transformations. Our prototype implements an additional IP-based post-processing analysis and partition focusing on the suspicious content. It allows the data owner to pinpoint the IPs of hosts where leaks occur. We output the suspicious content segments and corresponding hosts.

We make several technical measures to reduce disk and network I/O. We use (structured) SequenceFile format as the intermediate data format. We minimize the size of $\langle key, value \rangle$ pairs. E.g., the size of *value* after `map` in DIVIDER is 6 bytes on average. We implement COMBINATION classes that significantly reduce the amount of intermediate results written to the distributed file systems (DFS). This reduction in size is achieved by aggregating same $\langle key, value \rangle$ pairs. This method reduces the data volume by half. We also enable Hadoop compression, which gives as high as 20-fold size reduction.

We deploy our algorithms in two different 24-node Hadoop systems, a local cluster and Amazon Elastic Compute Cloud (EC2). For both environments, we set one node as master node and the rest as slave nodes.

- *Amazon EC2:* 24 nodes each having a c3.2xlarge instance with 8 CPUs and 15 GB RAM.

- *Local cluster:* 24 nodes each having two quad-core 2.8 GHz Xeon processors and 8 GB RAM.

We use the Enron Email Corpus, including both email header and body to perform the performance experiments. The entire dataset is used as content and a small subset of it as the sensitive data. For the accuracy experiment, we use 10 academic research paper as the sensitive data and transformed Enron emails as content (insert `</br>` at each new line).

Our experiments aim to answer the flowing questions.

1. How does the size of content segment affect the analysis throughput? (Section 5.1)

2. What is the throughput of our analysis on Amazon EC2 and the local clusters? (Section 5.2)

3. How does the size of sensitive data affect the detection performance? (Section 5.3)

4. What is the detection accuracy of our data leak detection system? (Section 5.4)

Suppose we have n content segments with s of them containing sensitive sequences ($s < n$). During the detection, the content segments with intersection rates above the threshold t raise alerts in our detection algorithms. Suppose m content segments raise the alerts and s' of them are true leak instances. Then, we define the following metrics:

- detection rate as $\frac{s'}{s}$.

- false positive rate as $\frac{m-s'}{n-s}$.

5.1 Optimal Size of Content Segment

Content volume is usually overwhelmingly larger than sensitive data, as new content is generated continuously in storage and in transmission. Thus, we evaluate the throughput of different sizes and numbers of content segments in order to find the optimal segment size for scalability. A content segment with size $\hat{C}$ is the original sequence that is used to

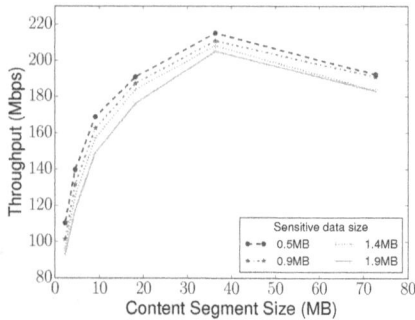

Figure 4: Throughput with different sizes of content segments. For each setup (line), the size of the content analyzed is 37 GB.

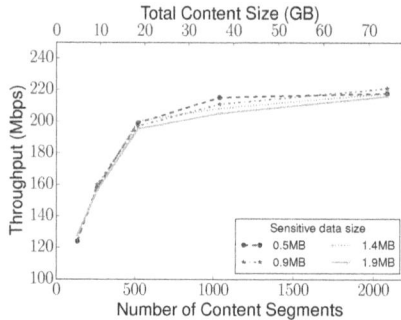

Figure 5: Throughput with different amount of content workload. Each content segment is 37 MB.

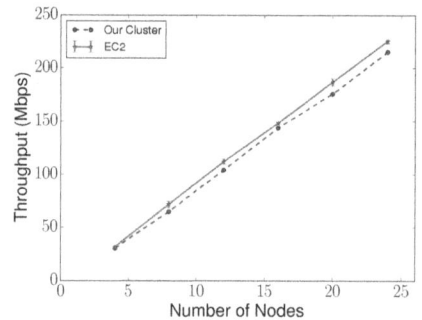

Figure 6: Throughput with different number of nodes on a local cluster or Amazon EC2.

generate the n-gram content collection. A sensitive sequence with size $\hat{S}$ is the original sequence that is used to generate the n-gram sensitive collection.

The total size of content analyzed is 37 GB, which consists of multiple copies of Enron data. Detection performance under different content segment sizes (from 2 MB to 80 MB) is measured. We vary the size of sensitive data from 0.5 MB to 2 MB. The results are shown in Figure 4.

We observe that when $\hat{C} < 37$ MB, the throughput of our analysis increases with the size $\hat{C}$ of content segment. When $\hat{C}$ becomes larger than 37 MB, the throughput begins to decrease. The reason for this decrease is that more computation resources are spend on garbage collection with larger $\hat{C}$. There are over 16 processes running at one nodes at the same time. We assign 400 MB memory for each process to process 37x8 MB shingles. Thus, we set the size of content segments to 37 MB for the rest of our experiments. This size also allows the full utilization of the Hadoop file system (HDFS) I/O capacity without causing out-of-memory problems.

We also evaluate the throughput under a varying number of content segments n, i.e., workload. The results are shown in Figure 5, where the total size of content analyzed is shown at the top X-axis (up to 74 GB). Throughput increases as workload increases as expected.

In both experiments, the size of sensitive data is small enough to fit in one collection. Larger size of sensitive data increases the computation overhead, which explains the slight decrease in throughput in both Figures 4 and 5.

5.2 Scalability

For scalability evaluation, we processed 37 GB content with different numbers of nodes, 4, 8, 12, 16, 20, and 24. The experiments were deployed on both on the local cluster and on Amazon EC2. Our results are shown in Figure 6. The system scales well, as the throughput linearly increases with the number of nodes. The peak throughput observed is 215 Mbps on the local cluster and 225 Mbps on Amazon EC2. EC2 cluster gives 3% to 11% performance improvement. This improvement is partly due to the larger memory. The standard error bars of EC2 nodes are shown in Figure 6 (from three runs). Variances of throughputs on the local cluster are negligible.

We break down the total overhead based on the DIVIDER and REASSEMBLER operations. The results are shown in

Figure 7 with the runtime (Y-axis) in a log scale. DIVIDER algorithm is much more expensive than REASSEMBLER, accounting for 85% to 98% of the total runtime. With increasing content workload, DIVIDER's runtime increases, more significantly than that of REASSEMBLER.

These observations are expected, as DIVIDER algorithm is more complex. Specifically, both `map` and `reduce` in DIVIDER need to touch *all* content items. Because of the large content volume, these operations are expensive. In comparison, REASSEMBLER algorithm only touches the intersected items, which is substantially smaller for normal content without leaks. These experimental results are consistent with our complexity analysis in Table 2.

5.3 Performance Impact of Sensitive Data

We reorganize the performance results in Figure 4 so that the sizes of sensitive data are shown at the X-axis. The new figure is Figure 8, where each setup (line) processes 37 GB data and differs in their size for content segment. There are a few observations. First, smaller content segment size incurs higher computational overhead, e.g., for keeping tracking the collection information (discussed in Section 5.1).

The second observation is that the runtime increases as the size of sensitive data increases, which is expected. Experiments with the largest content segment (bottom line in Figure 8) have the smallest increase, i.e., the least affected by the increasing volume of sensitive data.

This difference in intercept is explained next. The total computation complexity is $O(\mathcal{C}n + \mathcal{S}mn\gamma)$ (Table 2). In $O(\mathcal{C}n + \mathcal{S}mn\gamma)$, $n\gamma$ serves as the coefficient (i.e., intercept), as the total size $\mathcal{S}m$ of sensitive data increases, where n is the number of content segments. When 37 GB content is broken into small segments, n is large. A larger coefficient magnifies the increase in sensitive data, resulting in more substantial overhead increase. Therefore, the line at the bottom of Figure 8 represents our recommended configuration with a large 37 MB content segment size.

5.4 Detection Accuracy

We used Enron emails as content and 10 academic papers as sensitive data. We pre-processed the content into four types: content not containing sensitive data (C_c), content containing sensitive data (C_s), transformed content not containing sensitive data (T_c) and transformed content containing sensitive data (T_s). We transformed the content data by

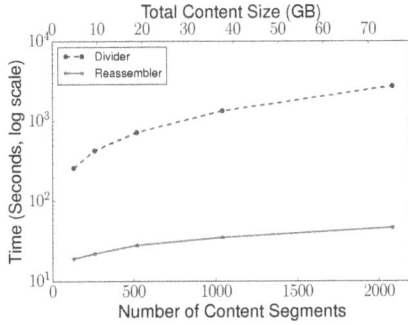

Figure 7: Runtime of DIVIDER and RE-ASSEMBLER algorithms. The DIVIDER operation takes 85% to 98% of the total runtime. The Y-axis is in 10 based log scale.

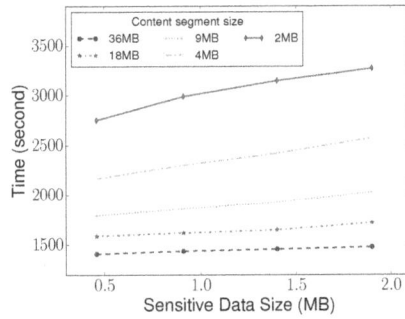

Figure 8: Runtime with a vary size of sensitive data. The content volume is 37.5 GB for each setup. Each setup (line) has a different size for content segments.

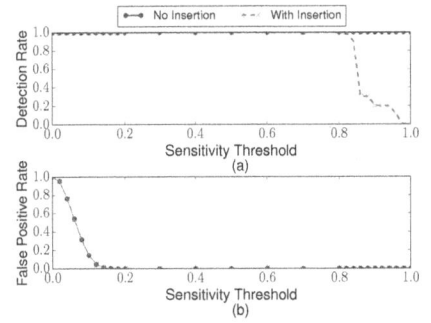

Figure 9: Detection accuracy with different threshold. The detection rate is 1 with very low false positive rate when the thresholds ranges from 0.18 to 0.8. In Figure (b), the false positive rates of the two lines are very close.

inserting `</br>` at each new line. Detection rates are computed from C_s and T_s. If alerts are raised by the segments from these two types of data, the alerts are true positives. The false positive rates are computed from C_c and T_c. If alerts are are raised by segments from these two types of data, the alerts are false positives. Our results on false positive rates and detection rates are shown in Figure 9.

With sensitivity threshold ranging from 0.18 to 0.82, the detection rate is 1, with 0 false positive rate for both the transformed leak and the non-transformed leak. The false positive rates of transformed data leak and non-transformed data leak are very close (the two lines mostly overlap). The false positive rate of the transformed data leak is on average 2.55% lower than that of the non-transformed leak, when the sensitivity threshold is smaller than 0.18. When the sensitivity threshold ranges from 0.3 to 0.7, our detection rate is 1 and false positive rate is 0.

Summary We summarize our experimental findings below.

1. Our MapReduce-based data leak detection algorithms linearly scale with the number of nodes. We achieved 225 Mbps throughput on Amazon EC2 cluster and a similar throughput on our local cluster. *Divider* algorithm accounts for 85% to 98% of the total runtime.

2. We observed that larger content segment size $\hat{C}$ (up to 37 MB) gives higher performance. This observation is due to the decreased amount of bookkeeping information for keeping track of collections, which results in significantly reduced I/O overhead associated with intermediate results.

   When the content segment size $\hat{C}$ is large (37 MB), we observed that the increase in the amount of sensitive data has a relatively small impact on the runtime. Give the content workload, larger $\hat{C}$ means fewer number of content segments, resulting in a smaller coefficient.

3. We validated that our detection system has high detection accuracy for some transformed data leaks. By setting the threshold to be a proper value, our algorithms can detect the leaks with low false alerts.

4. *Limitations* Our method is designed for detecting accidental data exposure in content, but not for inten-

tional data exfiltration, which typically uses strong encryption. Detecting malicious data leaks, in particular those by insiders, is still an active research area. Coincidental matches may generate false positives in our detection, e.g., an insensitive phone number in the content happens to match part of a sensitive credit card number. A possible mitigation is for the data owner to further inspect the context surrounding the matching shingles and interpret its semantics.

6. RELATED WORK

One may adopt network-based and/or host-based approaches to prevent personal or organizational sensitive information from being leaked. Solutions from both paradigms are necessary, and complementary to each other.

Borders and Prakash [6] presented a network-analysis approach for estimating information leak in the outbound traffic. The method identifies anomalous and drastic increase in the amount of information carried by the traffic. The method was not designed to detect small-scale data leak. In comparison, our technique is based on intersection-based pattern matching analysis. Thus, our method is more sensitive to small and stealthy leaks than the approach in [6]. In addition, our analysis can also be applied to content in data storage (e.g., data center), besides network traffic.

Croft and Caesar [12] compared two logical copies of network traffic to control the movement of sensitive data. The work by Papadimitriou and Garcia-Molina [26] aims at finding the agents that leaked the sensitive data. Shu and Yao [32] presented privacy-preserving methods for protecting sensitive data in a non-MapReduce based detection environment. Shu *et al.* [33] further proposed to accelerate screening transformed data leaks using GPU. Blanton *et al.* [5] proposed a solution for fast outsourcing of sequence edit distance and secure path computation, while preserving the confidentiality of the sequence.

Examples of host-based approaches include Auto-FBI [43] and Aquifer [23]. Auto-FBI guarantees the secure access of sensitive data on the web. It achieves this guarantee by automatically generating a new browser instance for sensitive content. Aquifer is a policy framework and system. It helps prevent accidental information disclosure in OS.

MapReduce framework was used to solve problems in data mining [41], machine learning [25], database [4, 35], and bioinformatics [22]. MapReduce algorithms for computing document similarity (e.g., [1, 15, 39]) involve pairwise similarity comparison. Similarity measures may be Hamming distance, edit distance or Jaccard distance. MapReduce was also used by security applications, such as log analysis [19, 36], spam filtering [9, 10] and malware and botnet detection [17, 28, 42] for scalability. The security solutions proposed by Bilge *et al.* [3], Yang *et al.* [36] and Yen *et al.* [37] analyzed network traffic or logs with MapReduce, searching for malware signatures or behavior patterns. Our MapReduce-based data leak detection problem is new, which none of the existing MapReduce solutions addresses. In addition, our detection goal differs from the aforementioned solutions.

Several techniques have been proposed to improve the privacy protection of MapReduce framework. Such solutions typically assume that the cloud provider is trustworthy. For example, Pappas *et al.* [27] proposed a data-flow tracking method in cloud applications. It audits the use of the sensitive data sent to cloud. Roy *et al.* [31] integrates mandatory access control with differential privacy in order to manage the use of sensitive data in MapReduce computations. Yoon and Squicciarini [38] detected malicious or cheating MapReduce nodes by correlating different nodes' system and Hadoop logs. Squicciarini *et al.* [34] presented techniques that prevent information leakage from the indexes of data in the cloud. In comparison, Our work has a different security model. We assume that MapReduce algorithms are developed by trustworthy entities, yet the MapReduce provider may attempt to gain knowledge of the sensitive information.

There exist MapReduce algorithms for computing the set intersection [4, 35]. They differ from our collection intersection algorithms, as explained in Section 2. Our collection intersection algorithm requires new intermediate data fields and processing for counting and recording duplicates in the intersection. Several techniques were developed for monitoring or improving MapReduce performance, e.g., to identify nodes with slow tasks [11], GPU acceleration [16] and efficient data transfer [21]. These advanced techniques can be applied to further speed up our prototype.

7. CONCLUSIONS AND FUTURE WORK

Our work is motivated by the increasing number of accidental data leak issues in organizational personal environments. We presented a MapReduce system for detecting the occurrences of sensitive data patterns in massive-scale content in data storage or network transmission. Our system provides privacy enhancement to minimize the exposure of sensitive data during the outsourced detection. We deployed and evaluated our prototype with the Hadoop platform on Amazon EC2 and a local cluster, and achieved 225 Mbps analysis throughput. For future work, we plan to explore the deployment of our detection system to hybrid cloud environments, which consist of private machines owned by the data owner and public machines owned by the cloud provider. The use of hybrid cloud infrastructure will likely improve the efficiency of our detection system. We also plan to explore the use of hybrid cloud (e.g., [24, 40]) for the collection-intersection computation.

8. ACKNOWLEDGEMENTS

The authors acknowledge the open access subvention fund from Virginia Tech. The authors thank Michael Wolfe for his support and feedback on the work.

9. REFERENCES

[1] Ranieri Baraglia, Gianmarco De Francisci Morales, and Claudio Lucchese. Document similarity self-join with MapReduce. In *Data Mining (ICDM), 2010 IEEE 10th International Conference on*, pages 731–736. IEEE Computer Society, 2010.

[2] Elisa Bertino and Gabriel Ghinita. Towards mechanisms for detection and prevention of data exfiltration by insiders: Keynote talk paper. In *Proceedings of the 6th ACM Symposium on Information, Computer and Communications Security*, ASIACCS '11, pages 10–19, New York, NY, USA, 2011. ACM.

[3] Leyla Bilge, Davide Balzarotti, William Robertson, Engin Kirda, and Christopher Kruegel. Disclosure: Detecting botnet command and control servers through large-scale netflow analysis. In *Proceedings of the 28th Annual Computer Security Applications Conference*, ACSAC '12, pages 129–138, New York, NY, USA, 2012. ACM.

[4] Spyros Blanas, Jignesh M. Patel, Vuk Ercegovac, Jun Rao, Eugene J. Shekita, and Yuanyuan Tian. A comparison of join algorithms for log processing in MapReduce. In *Proceedings of the 2010 ACM SIGMOD International Conference on Management of Data*, SIGMOD '10, pages 975–986, New York, NY, USA, 2010. ACM.

[5] Marina Blanton, Mikhail J. Atallah, Keith B. Frikken, and Qutaibah M. Malluhi. Secure and efficient outsourcing of sequence comparisons. In *Computer Security - ESORICS 2012 - 17th European Symposium on Research in Computer Security, Pisa, Italy, September 10-12, 2012. Proceedings*, pages 505–522, 2012.

[6] Kevin Borders and Atul Prakash. Quantifying information leaks in outbound web traffic. In *IEEE Symposium on Security and Privacy*, pages 129–140. IEEE Computer Society, 2009.

[7] Kevin Borders, Eric Vander Weele, Billy Lau, and Atul Prakash. Protecting confidential data on personal computers with storage capsules. In *USENIX Security Symposium*, pages 367–382. USENIX Association, 2009.

[8] Andrei Z. Broder. Identifying and filtering near-duplicate documents. In *Combinatorial Pattern Matching, 11th Annual Symposium*, volume 1848 of *Lecture Notes in Computer Science*, pages 1–10. Springer, 2000.

[9] Godwin Caruana, Maozhen Li, and Hao Qi. SpamCloud: A MapReduce based anti-spam architecture. In *Seventh International Conference on Fuzzy Systems and Knowledge Discovery*, pages 3003–3006. IEEE, 2010.

[10] Godwin Caruana, Maozhen Li, and Man Qi. A MapReduce based parallel SVM for large scale spam filtering. In *Eighth International Conference on Fuzzy*

Systems and Knowledge Discovery, pages 2659–2662. IEEE, 2011.

[11] Qi Chen, Cheng Liu, and Zhen Xiao. Improving MapReduce performance using smart speculative execution strategy. *Computers, IEEE Transactions on*, 63(4):954–967, April 2014.

[12] Jason Croft and Matthew Caesar. Towards practical avoidance of information leakage in enterprise networks. In *6th USENIX Workshop on Hot Topics in Security, HotSec'11*. USENIX Association, 2011.

[13] Data Loss DB. http://datalossdb.org/statistics.

[14] Jeffrey Dean and Sanjay Ghemawat. MapReduce: simplified data processing on large clusters. *Commun. ACM*, 51(1):107–113, 2008.

[15] Tamer Elsayed, Jimmy J. Lin, and Douglas W. Oard. Pairwise document similarity in large collections with MapReduce. In *ACL (Short Papers)*, pages 265–268. The Association for Computer Linguistics, 2008.

[16] Wenbin Fang, Bingsheng He, Qiong Luo, and Naga K. Govindaraju. Mars: Accelerating MapReduce with graphics processors. *IEEE Trans. Parallel Distrib. Syst.*, 22(4):608–620, 2011.

[17] Jérôme François, Shaonan Wang, Walter Bronzi, Radu State, and Thomas Engel. BotCloud: Detecting botnets using MapReduce. In *IEEE International Workshop on Information Forensics and Security*, pages 1–6. IEEE, 2011.

[18] Michael J. Freedman, Kobbi Nissim, and Benny Pinkas. Efficient private matching and set intersection. In *Advances in Cryptology - EUROCRYPT 2004, International Conference on the Theory and Applications of Cryptographic Techniques*, volume 3027 of *Lecture Notes in Computer Science*, pages 1–19. Springer, 2004.

[19] Xiaoyu Fu, Rui Ren, Jianfeng Zhan, Wei Zhou, Zhen Jia, and Gang Lu. LogMaster: Mining event correlations in logs of large-scale cluster systems. In *IEEE 31st Symposium on Reliable Distributed Systems*, pages 71–80. IEEE, 2012.

[20] Youngseok Lee, Wonchul Kang, and Hyeongu Son. An Internet traffic analysis method with MapReduce. In *Network Operations and Management Symposium Workshops (NOMS Wksps), 2010 IEEE/IFIP*, pages 357–361, April 2010.

[21] Dionysios Logothetis, Chris Trezzo, Kevin C. Webb, and Kenneth Yocum. In-situ MapReduce for log processing. In *USENIX Annual Technical Conference*. USENIX Association, 2011.

[22] Andréa M. Matsunaga, Maurício O. Tsugawa, and José A. B. Fortes. Cloudblast: Combining MapReduce and virtualization on distributed resources for bioinformatics applications. In *eScience*, pages 222–229. IEEE Computer Society, 2008.

[23] Adwait Nadkarni and William Enck. Preventing accidental data disclosure in modern operating systems. In *ACM Conference on Computer and Communications Security*, pages 1029–1042. ACM, 2013.

[24] Kerim Yasin Oktay, Vaibhav Khadilkar, Bijit Hore, Murat Kantarcioglu, Sharad Mehrotra, and Bhavani Thuraisingham. Risk-aware workload distribution in hybrid clouds. In *Proceedings of the 2012 IEEE Fifth International Conference on Cloud Computing*, CLOUD '12, pages 229–236, Washington, DC, USA, 2012. IEEE Computer Society.

[25] Biswanath Panda, Joshua S. Herbach, Sugato Basu, and Roberto J. Bayardo. Planet: Massively parallel learning of tree ensembles with MapReduce. *Proc. VLDB Endow.*, 2(2):1426–1437, August 2009.

[26] Panagiotis Papadimitriou and Hector Garcia-Molina. Data leakage detection. *IEEE Trans. Knowl. Data Eng.*, 23(1):51–63, 2011.

[27] Vasilis Pappas, VasileiosP. Kemerlis, Angeliki Zavou, Michalis Polychronakis, and AngelosD. Keromytis. Cloudfence: Enabling users to audit the use of their cloud-resident data. In *Research in Attacks, Intrusions, and Defenses*, volume 8145 of *Lecture Notes in Computer Science*, pages 411–431. Springer Berlin Heidelberg, 2013.

[28] Niels Provos, Dean McNamee, Panayiotis Mavrommatis, Ke Wang, and Nagendra Modadugu. The ghost in the browser: Analysis of web-based malware. In *First Workshop on Hot Topics in Understanding Botnets*. USENIX Association, 2007.

[29] Michael O. Rabin. Fingerprinting by random polynomials. Technical Report TR-15-81, Harvard Aiken Computation Laboratory, 1981.

[30] Thomas Ristenpart, Eran Tromer, Hovav Shacham, and Stefan Savage. Hey, you, get off of my cloud: Exploring information leakage in third-party compute clouds. In *Proceedings of the 16th ACM Conference on Computer and Communications Security*, CCS '09, pages 199–212, New York, NY, USA, 2009. ACM.

[31] Indrajit Roy, Srinath T. V. Setty, Ann Kilzer, Vitaly Shmatikov, and Emmett Witchel. Airavat: Security and privacy for MapReduce. In *Proceedings of the 7th USENIX Symposium on Networked Systems Design and Implementation*, pages 297–312. USENIX Association, 2010.

[32] Xiaokui Shu and Danfeng (Daphne) Yao. Data leak detection as a service. In *SecureComm*, volume 106 of *Lecture Notes of the Institute for Computer Sciences, Social Informatics and Telecommunications Engineering*, pages 222–240. Springer, 2012.

[33] Xiaokui Shu, Jing Zhang, Danfeng (Daphne) Yao, and Wu-Chun Feng. Rapid screening of transformed data leaks with efficient algorithms and parallel computing. In *Proceedings of the 5th ACM Conference on Data and Application Security and Privacy*, CODASPY '15, New York, NY, USA, 2015. ACM.

[34] Anna Cinzia Squicciarini, Smitha Sundareswaran, and Dan Lin. Preventing information leakage from indexing in the cloud. In *IEEE International Conference on Cloud Computing, CLOUD 2010, Miami, FL, USA, 5-10 July, 2010*, pages 188–195. IEEE, 2010.

[35] Rares Vernica, Michael J. Carey, and Chen Li. Efficient parallel set-similarity joins using MapReduce. In *Proceedings of the 2010 ACM SIGMOD International Conference on Management of Data*, SIGMOD '10, pages 495–506, New York, NY, USA, 2010. ACM.

[36] Shun-Fa Yang, Wei-Yu Chen, and Yao-Tsung Wang. ICAS: An inter-VM IDS log cloud analysis system. In

Cloud Computing and Intelligence Systems (CCIS), 2011 IEEE International Conference on, pages 285–289, Sept 2011.

[37] Ting-Fang Yen, Alina Oprea, Kaan Onarlioglu, Todd Leetham, William Robertson, Ari Juels, and Engin Kirda. Beehive: Large-scale log analysis for detecting suspicious activity in enterprise networks. In *Proceedings of the 29th Annual Computer Security Applications Conference*, ACSAC '13, pages 199–208, New York, NY, USA, 2013. ACM.

[38] Eunjung Yoon and A Squicciarini. Toward detecting compromised mapreduce workers through log analysis. In *Cluster, Cloud and Grid Computing (CCGrid), 2014 14th IEEE/ACM International Symposium on*, pages 41–50, May 2014.

[39] Peisen Yuan, Chaofeng Sha, Xiaoling Wang, Bin Yang, Aoying Zhou, and Su Yang. XML structural similarity search using MapReduce. In *Web-Age Information Management, 11th International Conference*, volume 6184 of *Lecture Notes in Computer Science*, pages 169–181. Springer, 2010.

[40] Chunwang Zhang, Ee-Chien Chang, and R.H.C. Yap. Tagged-mapreduce: A general framework for secure computing with mixed-sensitivity data on hybrid clouds. In *Cluster, Cloud and Grid Computing (CCGrid), 2014 14th IEEE/ACM International Symposium on*, pages 31–40, May 2014.

[41] Weizhong Zhao, Huifang Ma, and Qing He. Parallel *k*-means clustering based on MapReduce. In *Cloud Computing, First International Conference, CloudCom 2009*, volume 5931 of *Lecture Notes in Computer Science*, pages 674–679. Springer, 2009.

[42] Li Zhuang, John Dunagan, Daniel R. Simon, Helen J. Wang, Ivan Osipkov, and J. Doug Tygar. Characterizing botnets from Email spam records. In *First USENIX Workshop on Large-Scale Exploits and Emergent Threats, LEET '08*. USENIX Association, 2008.

[43] Mohsen Zohrevandi and Rida A. Bazzi. Auto-FBI: A user-friendly approach for secure access to sensitive content on the web. In *Proceedings of the 29th Annual Computer Security Applications Conference*, ACSAC '13, pages 349–358, New York, NY, USA, 2013. ACM.

APPENDIX

A. PERFORMANCE OF A SINGLE HOST

To verify that one host alone cannot perform large-scale data leak detection, a single host version of the similarity-based detection algorithm was implemented and tested on one machine containing two quad-core 2.8 GHz Xeon processors and 8 gigabytes of RAM.

We tested the performance with different size of content and sensitive data and monitored the system. The performance is shown in Table 3.

This single machine-based detection system crashes with large content or sensitive data because of lacking sufficient memory. Thus, when the content or sensitive data are large, a single host is not capable of completing the detection due to memory limitation and thrashing. This experiment confirms the importance of our parallel data leak detection framework with MapReduce.

Sensitive Content	0.9 MB	1.4 MB	1.9 MB
588 MB	22.08	20.81	*
1229 MB	24.21	*	*
2355 MB	25.7	*	*
4710 MB	*	*	*

Table 3: Detection throughput (Mbps) on a single host with different content size and sensitive data size. * indicates that the system crashes before the detection is finished.

Identifying and Understanding Self-Checksumming Defenses in Software

Jing Qiu
Harbin Institute of Technology
Harbin, China
topmint@hit.edu.cn

Babak Yadegari
The University of Arizona
Tucson, USA
babaky@cs.arizona.edu

Brian Johannesmeyer
The University of Arizona
Tucson, USA
bjohannesmeyer
@cs.arizona.edu

Saumya Debray
The University of Arizona
Tucson, USA
debray@cs.arizona.edu

Xiaohong Su
Harbin Institute of Technology
Harbin, China
sxh@hit.edu.cn

ABSTRACT

Software self-checksumming is widely used as an anti-tampering mechanism for protecting intellectual property and deterring piracy. This makes it important to understand the strengths and weaknesses of various approaches to self-checksumming. This paper describes a dynamic information-flow-based attack that aims to identify and understand self-checksumming behavior in software. Our approach is applicable to a wide class of self-chesumming defenses and the information obtained can be used to determine how the checksumming defenses may be bypassed. Experiments using a prototype implementation of our ideas indicate that our approach can successfully identify self-checksumming behavior in (our implementations of) proposals from the research literature.

1. INTRODUCTION

Self-checksumming is widely used in software anti-tampering defenses [3,5,6,8,9,14,18]. The idea is to compute a hash value from the instructions of the program (or something closely related to those instructions) and ensure that the program continues to function correctly if and only if the computed hash has the expected value. This can be used to protect software against piracy, since any attempt to tamper with the code, e.g., to disable or remove a license check, will be detected during checksumming. This makes it important to understand the strengths and weaknesses of different approaches to self-checksumming.

This paper describes a dynamic information-flow-based attack that aims to identify and understand a large class of self-checksumming behavior in software. Our analysis provides a wide range of information about the checksumming code, such as: whether self-checksumming is being car-

ried out and, if so, the location(s) of the code performing the checksumming; the origin of the checksum code (if it is created or modified dynamically); the checksum values computed; the locations of the code checking these checksum values; the mechanism by which the tamper-response is triggered (e.g., via a conditional jump, indirect jump, or through an unpacking key computed from the checksum); whether or not the instruction(s) triggering the tamper response are shared with any non-checksumming code; and so on. From an attacker's perspective, such information can provide a great deal of insight into the checksumming code and indicate how the self-checksumming can be bypassed or defeated. From the defender's perspective, such information can illuminate weaknesses in the self-checksumming code and possibly suggest remedies.

Our approach makes the following assumptions:

1. **Self-containedness.** The software performs its own integrity checking. This excludes systems, like Conqueror [14], that involve an external entity for verification.

2. **Observability.** The attacker has complete access to the host and is able to observe the program as it executes, including the instructions executed and the values of registers and memory.

Unlike the earlier work of Wurster *et al.* [22, 24], the work described here is a pure-software approach that does not rely on hardware assistance. To the best of our knowledge, this is the first such pure-software attack against self-checksumming systems. In terms of relative power, our approach does not seem directly comparable with that of Wurster *et al.*: on the one hand, our approach is unaffected by techniques, such as self-modifying code, that can defeat Wurster *et al.*'s attack [8]; on the other hand, programs that do not satisfy the assumptions listed above cannot be handled using our approach but may be susceptible to Wurster *et al.*'s attack.

The remainder of this paper is organized as follows. Section 2 provides background on self-checksumming; Section 3 describes our approach to detection of self-checksumming; Section 4 gives evaluation results for a prototype implementation of our ideas; Section 5 discusses limitations and future work; Section 6 discusses related work; and Section 7 concludes.

2. BACKGROUND

Self-checksumming is widely used in anti-tampering mechanisms that aim to ensure that software that is going to be executed on an untrustworthy host has not been modified in unauthorized ways [3,5,6,8,9]. The idea is to compute a checksum or a hash value over appropriate portions of the program's code and use this value in the subsequent computation in such a way that the program executes as expected if and only if the hash value computed is the expected one. Compared to other proposals for software integrity protection, which require additional special-purpose hardware [21] or continuous connection with a remote "authentication server" [14], self-checksumming has the advantage of being implementable using commodity hardware and software. In particular, since self-checksumming does not require access to an authentication server, it is readily usable on mobile devices, such as smartphones and laptops, that may not always have network connectivity.

Horne *et al.* [9] divide this approach into two categories: *static* checksumming, which checks the static code of the program prior to execution; and *dynamic* checksumming, which checks the software as it executes.

2.1 Static Self-Checksumming

Static self-checksumming verifies the integrity of the software once, generally at the beginning of execution, to ensure that the disk image of the software has not been tampered with. This is typically done by accessing the bytes of the program file (whose name is usually passed to the executing process as an argument by the operating system), either by reading the file into memory or by mapping the file into the process's address space. Once the contents of the executable file are available for access, some or all of the code can be checksummed in a straightforward way.

2.2 Dynamic Self-Checksumming

While static self-checksumming can detect changes made to the program executable, it cannot detect changes made to the memory image of the program's code during the course of its execution. Dynamic self-checksumming addresses this problem by periodically checking the memory image of the program as it executes. The process of dynamic self-checksumming can be thought of, conceptually, as consisting of three components: (1) *checksum code insertion*, which inserts the code for computing the checksum into the program (if necessary); (2) *checksum computation*; and (3) *verification and tamper response*, which checks whether the checksum value computed matches the expected value and responds appropriately if it does not.

In many cases, no separate insertion component is necessary because the code that performs the checksum computation is compiled as part of the program's code and does not have to be inserted separately. An alternative approach, which aims to make the checksum code harder to identify, is to unpack or import the checksum code into the program at unpredictable intervals and/or locations in memory.

The checksum may be computed either on the code that is actually executed, or on non-executable memory locations containing a packed version the code (see Figure 1). The checksum computation may, but need not, encompass all of a program's code. First, the checksum computation may be limited in scope to some specific sensitive code modules whose integrity has to be enforced. Second, the overall

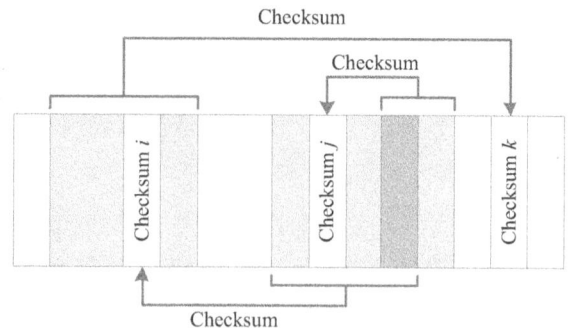

Figure 2: Program protected using multiple guards

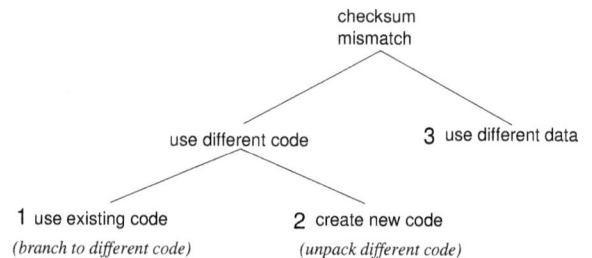

Figure 3: Tamper response: design choices

checksum computation may, in general, be carried out by a collection of distinct code snippets working together, with each snippet computing a checksum on some limited range of code. This makes possible a powerful self-checksumming model that uses a network of different checksumming routines that protect each other [6,9]. Figure 2 shows an example of such approach. In this example the program has three checksumming routines each of which compute a checksum over the area of the code marked as grey and compares it with the pre-computed checksummed accordingly. As shown in Figure 2, checksum routines can have overlaps, meaning that they verify each others' integrity as well as the integrity of the code. To attack such a protection mechanism, the attacker has to detect all of the checksumming routines and disable them all at once; this is likely to be significantly more challenging than identifying and disabling a single guard.

The final step in self-checksumming is to check that the computed checksum matches the expected value and to activate a tamper response, where the program's execution behavior deviates from the normal, if it does not. Figure 3 illustrates the design choices for this step: in order for program behavior to deviate from normal, either the code or the data have to be different than for normal execution; and the execution of different code can be done either by branching to existing code, or by creating (unpacking) code that is different than what would normally have been created. Accordingly, the tamper response can be activated in one of three ways (the numbers in the list below correspond to those in Figure 3):

1. The program can branch to code that activates the tamper response. This can be done using either (*i*) straightforward compare-and-conditional-branch logic; or (*ii*) using the checksum value to compute the tar-

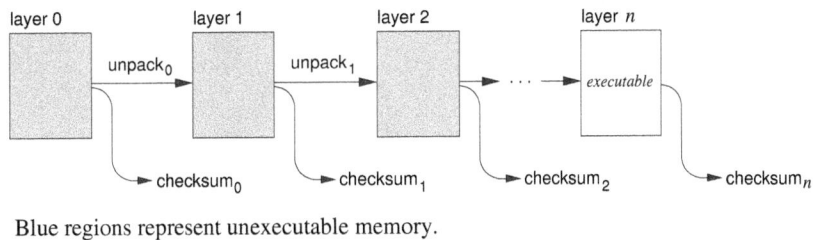

Blue regions represent unexecutable memory.

Figure 1: Checksumming combined with multiple layers of unpacking.

get of an indirect jump such that the correct target address is computed if and only if the checksum value computed is the expected one. For example, Tan *et al.* describe a scheme where a checksum mismatch causes control to be transferred to code that corrupts the program state by setting some pointers to NULL; the program then eventually crashes when this corrupted pointer is dereferenced [19].

2. The checksum value can be used to change the result of code unpacking: e.g., by using the checksum value to affect either (*i*) the value of the decryption key for some dynamically unpacked code [5,23]; and/or (*ii*) the value of one or more bytes that subsequently get unpacked and executed. In this case, an incorrect checksum value silently produces and executes incorrect/garbage code.

3. The checksum value can be incorporated into the logic of the computation in such a way that an incorrect checksum value causes the program to silently produce incorrect output. The following simple example illustrates this approach: the variable **p** is initialized to the correct value, 1, if and only if the computed checksum is equal to the expected value of **0x1234**.

```
int factorial(int n) {
    int cksum = compute_checksum();
    // expected checksum = 0x1234

    int p = 1 + (cksum ^ 0x1234);
    while (n > 0) {
        p *= n--;
    }
    return p;
}
```

Since programs interact with their execution environments through system calls, this approach requires that an incorrect checksum should affect the argument(s) to some output system call.

The discussion in this paper focuses primarily on dynamic checksumming.

3. SELF-CHECKSUMMING DETECTION

3.1 An Overview of Our Approach

Intuitively, checksumming involves two kinds of computation:

1. computing a value from the contents of locations that either contain code (i.e., are executed) or are used to create code (e.g., through unpacking); and

2. using the value so computed (or a value derived from it) to affect the code the program executes and/or the output(s) it produces.

The key insight behind our approach is that both these computations can be identified using (different kinds of) taint propagation. Since many software protection tools use run-time code unpacking (e.g., Obsidium [1], Themida [16], VM-Protect [2]), we do not rely on static analysis, which is unable to examine dynamically created code; instead, we use dynamic analysis.

Fig. 4 gives an overview of our approach. It consists of the following steps:

1. **Execution tracing**. The only input of our approach is an instruction trace of the target program. This can be done by using tools such as Intel Pin [13] or Ether [7].

2. **Backward taint analysis**. This step identifies memory locations that are either code (i.e., instructions or parts of instructions) or which are used to create code. We first walk through the trace and collect the addresses of executed memory locations. We then propagate taint in a backward direction, i.e., from uses to definitions, to identify locations that may have been used to create the executed code.

3. **Forward taint analysis**. This step identifies the flow of values computed from code locations to instructions that affect the code executed by the program. This is done by starting from the locations tainted in the backward taint analysis step and then propagating taint forwards (i.e., from definitions to uses).

4. **Checksumming detection**. This step identifies the checksum verification instructions. It looks for instructions I in the execution trace satisfying any of the following:

   (a) I is a control transfer instruction with one or more tainted operands; or

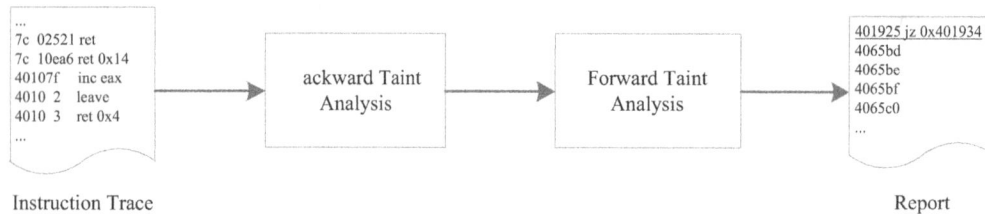

Figure 4: Overview of our approach

(b) I writes a tainted value to a location that is subsequently executed; or

(c) I passes a tainted value to an output system call.

Once the checksum verification instructions have been identified, further analysis can be performed, starting from these verification instructions, to obtain additional details about the checksumming code for the program.

The combination of backward and forward taint computation is necessary because it is possible to set up the checksum computation so that it considers, not the locations that are actually executed, but locations from which the instructions at those executed locations were created. For example, a piece of sensitive code—say, a license check or anti-analysis defense—may be stored in encrypted form in a memory region R, and decrypted as needed into some other memory region S from which it is executed; meanwhile the checksum computation can be applied to the memory region R, which is not itself executed. The backward taint analysis starts with the executed code in S, goes backward to taint R, then propagate this taint forward to the instruction(s) that perform checksum verification.

We use the following notation and terminology in the discussion that follows. Given an instruction I, $\mathsf{addr}(I)$ denotes the memory address of I; $\mathsf{length}(I)$ denotes its length in bytes; and $\mathsf{Read}(I)$ and $\mathsf{Write}(I)$ denote, respectively, the sets of locations read and written by I. An instruction I is tainted if $\mathsf{Read}(I)$ and/or $\mathsf{Write}(I)$ is tainted.

3.2 Taint Analysis

We perform byte-level taint analysis on instruction traces. Taint can be propagated in either a forward direction (i.e., the same direction as control flow) or backward (i.e., opposite to control flow). In forward taint propagation, the destination bytes of an instruction are tainted if and only if they are affected by the tainted bytes of the source; in backward taint propagation, source operand bytes are tainted if they affected the tainted bytes of the destination. Our current prototype handles taint propagation for the following instructions: data movement instructions, including string operations, push and pop instructions, and the `lea` instruction; arithmetic and logical instructions; shift and rotate instructions; and instructions that access the EFLAGS register. For instructions whose result does not depend on the source operands, e.g., "`xor eax, eax`" or "`sub eax, eax`", the result of the operation—in these examples, the contents of register `eax`—is marked as untainted.

Backward taint analysis is used to identify locations that are either executed or used to create/modify locations that are executed. Since this phase is used to identify locations that are used to create or modify code at runtime, it only propagates taint through data locations but not through the condition codes (the EFLAGS register) of the underlying x86 platform. Taint is propagated backward from a location ℓ at some point in the execution trace if and only if ℓ is live at that point. This means that when propagating taint across a data movement instruction I whose destination operand is tainted, at the point immediately before I the source operand of I will be tainted and the destination will be marked as untainted (since the destination is not live at the point right before I).

In forward taint analysis, taint is propagated through both data locations and condition code flags. For the instructions that use flags of EFLAGS, such as ADC (Add with Carry), the flag(s) read by the instruction are considered as source operands: if a flag read by the instruction is tainted, the destination will be tainted.

3.3 Identifying Self-Checksumming

Algorithm 1 gives a high level overview of the self-checksumming detection algorithm. The algorithm consists of three steps:

1. The first step is locating the source of the executed code using backward taint analysis on the program's execution trace (Algorithm 2). However, the locations in the source of the executed code will be excluded if they are not read or written by any other instruction (Algorithm 1 lines $4-6$).

2. Next we perform forward tainting on the execution trace, starting using the tainted locations from the backward taint phase as the taint source, to identify instructions with tainted operands that can affect the program's observable behavior (Algorithm 3). As part of this computation, as a "pre-forward-taint" step to accelerate the forward tainting step, we check whether any instruction reads or writes any tainted locations (Algorithm 3 lines $3-11$): if there are none, then the program does not do any self-checksumming and the algorithm exits. Otherwise, for each such instruction, we collect together the range of memory locations it checksums (Algorithm 3 lines $12-22$).

3. Finally, those instructions in this set for which the range of locations exceeds a (user-definable) threshold θ_{min} are identified as the checksum verification instructions (Algorithm 1 lines $9-13$).

In x86, a functions call is translated to a combination of `push` instructions and a `call` instruction. Such call instructions often do not read or write tainted memory locations. Thus, a call instruction that invokes an output system call with a tainted parameter will be regarded as a tainted instruction as well (Algorithm 3, lines $7-9$). So we can detect

Algorithm 1: Algorithm for detecting code check-summings. θ_{min} and θ_{max} are (user-definable) thresholds used to control the granularity of checksum reporting.

Input: T: Instruction trace $(I_0, I_1, \ldots, I_N)$
Output: R: Code self-checksum information

1   $R \longleftarrow \emptyset$;
   // Step 1: Backward taint analysis
2   $M, AccessedM = \texttt{BackwardTaintAnalysis}(T)$;
3   $ExecutedMem \longleftarrow M$;
4   $M \longleftarrow M \cap AccessedM$;
5   **if** $M == \emptyset$ **then**
6 | **return** R;

   // Step 2: Forward taint analysis
7   $RS = \texttt{ForwardTaintAnalysis}(T, M, ExecutedMem)$
   // Step 3: Summarize the result
8   $Ignored \longleftarrow 0$;
9   **foreach** $<I, Locations>$ *in* RS **do**
10 | **if** $Locations.size() > \theta_{min}$ **then**
11 | | $R \longleftarrow R \cup \{<I, Locations>\}$;
12 | **else**
13 | | $Ignored \mathrel{+}= Locations.size()$;

14 **if** $Ignored > \theta_{max}$ **then**
15 | WARNING("no. of ignored locations exceeds θ_{max}");

16 **return** R;

Algorithm 2: Backward taint analysis procedure

---

1 **Function** $\texttt{BackwardTaint}(T)$
2 | $M \longleftarrow \emptyset, AccessedM \longleftarrow \emptyset$;
3 | **foreach** *Instruction* I *in* T **do**
4 | | **for** $i \longleftarrow 0$ **to** $\text{length}(I)$ **do**
5 | | | $M \longleftarrow M \cup \{\text{addr}(I) + i\}$;
6 | | $AccessedM \longleftarrow AccessedM \cup \text{Read}(I) \cup \text{Write}(I)$;

    // Backward taint
7 | **for** $i = N$ **to** 0 *Step* -1 **do**
8 | | Backward taint $T[i]$ and update M accordingly;
9 | **return** $M, AccessedM$

---

the checksumming that its checksum flows to an output system call.

We use the threshold θ_{min} (step 3) to filter out false positives that occasionally arise in executables that use file compression to reduce their size. The issue is that if a file compressor finds the same byte sequence in multiple places within a file (some of which may be code while the other occurrences are unrelated data), this byte sequence is extracted out for compression purposes; during decompression (i.e., unpacking), this can cause bytes to be copied from an executed location to a non-executed location, in order to restore the multiple occurrences of that sequence. Our algorithm then marks the non-executed destination location as tainted during forward taint propagation, and any subsequent use of those locations, e.g., in a conditional branch, is flagged as being potentially a checksum verification. Our experience has been that the number of bytes involved in such coincidental matches is usually quite small. We therefore use the threshold θ_{min} to filter out matches involving only small regions of memory: in our prototype implementation, we set $\theta_{min} = 16$ bytes. We note that an attacker can try to defeat our algorithm using a collection of different checks, each of which covers fewer than θ_{min} bytes of memory but which collectively cover a significant amount of memory. To handle this, we add a global threshold θ_{max} on the number of memory bytes that can be ignored in this way. If the total memory size of the ignored regions exceeds θ_{max} the algorithm produces a warning to this effect (Algorithm 1 lines 14 − 15).

As described in Figure 1, a program can have many layers of unpacking,[1] and self-checksumming can be performed at

---

[1]Some software protection tools produce executables with dozens or hundreds of layers of runtime code unpacking [10].

any point(s) in the unpacking sequence. Algorithm 1 can detect self-checksumming performed at any layer of unpacking. To see this, suppose at the ith level, function ϕ_i transforms data C_{i-1} to C_i, i.e. $C_i = \phi_i(C_{i-1})$. Suppose that there are n levels of unpacking and the resulting executable code is C_n. $CHECK(C_i)$ denotes a checksumming that verifies the integrity of C_i. The execution trace has the structure

$$C_1 = \phi_1(C_0)$$
$$\ldots$$
$$C_2 = \phi_2(C_1)$$
$$\ldots$$
$$C_n = \phi_n(C_{n-1})$$
$$\ldots$$
$$C_n$$

In the first step of the algorithm, all executed locations are collected and used as the taint source; this includes the instruction addresses in C_n as well as the code for all of the ϕ_i. Since ϕ_n reads C_{n-1}, the locations for C_{n-1} will become tainted. It is a straightforward induction to show that, proceeding in this way, all of the C_i as well as ϕ_i will be backward tainted; these locations will then be the taint source of the forward taint analysis. Now suppose that checksumming occurs before the kth unpacking step ($1 \leq k \leq n$), and the set of locations checksummed is $C'_{k-1} \subseteq C_{k-1}$.

Suppose that the checksummed locations C'_{k-1} originated in some set of locations C'_0 in the original packed representation. The backward taint analysis will mark C'_0 as tainted, and therefore the locations C'_{k-1} read by the checksumming code $CHECK(C_{k-1})$, as well as the values involved in the checksum computation itself, will be marked as tainted during the forward taint propagation from C'_0. As a result the values flowing into the checksum verification will be tainted and so the self-checksumming will be detected.

3.4 Understanding Self-Checksumming

Once the checksum verification instruction(s) have been identified, the taint information gathered from the forward taint propagation step can be used, possibly in conjunction with some additional analysis of the execution trace, to extract a variety of information about the self-checksumming protections deployed by the program under study. This information can be useful in guiding efforts to defeat or bypass the program's self-checksumming anti-tamper defenses. This section briefly describes some of the information that can be obtained in this way.

Algorithm 3: Forward taint analysis procedure

```
1  Function ForwardTaintAnalysis(T, TaintedMem,
       ExecMem)
2      map<Instruction, set<Location> > RS;
3      M ⟵ TaintedMem, T' ⟵ ∅, Calls ⟵ ∅;
4      foreach Instruction I in T do
5          if (Write(I) ∪ Read(I)) ∩ M ≠ ∅ then
6          └   T'.push_back(I);
7          else if I invokes an output system call C
8                   ∧ A parameter of C is tainted then
9          └   T'.push_back(I), Calls ⟵ Calls ∪ {I};
10         └  Forward taint I and update M accordingly;
11     if T' == ∅ then return RS ;
12     foreach Location L in TaintedMem do
           // Forward taint L
13         M ⟵ {L};
14         foreach Instruction I in T' do
15             if I ∉ Calls then
16                 Forward taint I and update M
                   accordingly;
17                 if (Write(I) ∪ Read(I)) ∩ M ≠ ∅ then
18                     if I is a control transfer instruction
19                         ∨ Write(I) ∩ ExecMem ≠ ∅ then
20                     └   RS[I].insert(L);
21             else if  A parameter of the call I invokes is
                   tainted then
22                 └   RS[I].insert(L);
23     return RS
```

I. Checksum Computation.

To obtain the pieces of code that compute checksums, we can compute a backward dynamic slice [12] from the operands of each occurrence of a set of checksum verification instructions in the execution trace. There are two points to note here. First, the slicing algorithm has to take into account the unstructured nature of executable code [11]. Second, the control flow graph of the program may not be readily available: in this case, we use the execution trace to construct a control flow graph for the portions of the code that were executed. Since the program under consideration may use dynamically unpacked code (possibly with many layers of unpacking), the same memory address can contain different instructions at different points in the program, so an instruction cannot be identified by its memory address alone, but requires an additional parameter indicating how many times it has been modified. The reason we compute these slices at each dynamic occurrence of a checksum verification instruction is that it is possible for different checksum computation codes to share the same verification code. Note that sharing verification code in this way may not be a good idea since it can reduce the overall security of the system; our point here is simply that, even if the verification code is shared between many different checksum computations, our analysis can tease them apart. This approach can also tease apart different checksum computations even if their execu-

tions overlap (e.g., due to being run in different threads) and so are interleaved in the trace.[2]

The dynamic slice computation also provides information about the origin of the checksum computation code (see Section 2). Specifically, if any of the locations that are executed during the checksum computation are modified prior to execution (via memory writes), then the checksum code is created/unpacked dynamically. In this case, attempts to disable the checksum computation (e.g., by having it returns a precomputed checksum value, which is in fact available in the execution trace) may prefer to focus on the source of the unpacked code (which is also available in the dynamic slice) rather than the unpacked code itself.

Finally, the dynamic slice can be used to identify violations of the self-containedness assumption of Section 1. If any component of the checksum computation—either the checksum computation code or a seed for the checksum value —is obtained from an external source (e.g., a remote server), some components of the slice will be seen as originating from network reads; if the checksum computed by the program is communicated to an external entity for verification, then a tainted value will be seen as an argument to a network write. This can be used to understand the behavior of anti-tamper systems such as Conqueror [14].

II. Checksum Verification.

An attacker may try to bypass the self-checksumming defenses by altering the checksum verification code, e.g., by inserting an unconditional jump to the "normal execution" code. Knowing the conditions under which such an attack will or will not work can be helpful for guiding the attacker in selecting an attack. This can be done using information from the taint analysis. This simple attack may not work under the following conditions:

1. the tamper response is invoked using a control transfer instruction I, where some executions of I in the trace have a tainted operand (indicating a checksum computation) and other executions of I have no tainted operands (indicating a non-checksum computation); or

2. a forward-tainted value is written to a backward-tainted location (indicating that the value of the computed checksum is used to create or modify code that is subsequently executed), or loaded as an argument to an output operation in the program (e.g., a `write` operation).

The situation described in the first of these conditions can arise in virtualization-obfuscated code (e.g., we observed it in code protected using Themida [16]). This kind of obfuscation embeds the program logic in the byte-code of a custom virtual machine; the executable code for the program consists of the emulator for this virual machine. The emulator uses a handler for each different operation of the virtual machine, e.g.:

```
handle_if_EQ:  /* if_EQ op1, op2, target */
    op1 = fetch_op1();
    op2 = fetch_op2();
    target = fetch_op3();
    ip = (op1 == op2)? target : (ip + 1);
    goto emulator_dispatch;
```

[2]In order to distinguish between instructions from different threads, the execution trace has to record a thread-id for each instruction.

Thus, the code fragment shown above will be executed whenever an "if_EQ" operation is encountered in the byte code, including for example the checksum verification (if the verification is done using an "if_EQ" operation). Thus, the conditional branch that performs the checksum verification (in which case the operands are tainted) is shared with other non-checksum-computations (in which case the operands are not tainted). Naively altering the operation of this code will therefore alter the behavior of all such conditional branches in the byte code, not just the checksum verification code.

3.5 Examples

This section illustrates our approach using three simple examples.

EXAMPLE 3.1. This example illustrates "standard self checksumming", which refers to programs that do not have any code unpacking or runtime code generation and which use explicit control transfers to branch to the tamper response.[3]

```
/* compute checksum */        checksum = 0
checksum = 0;                 checksum += buf[0]
for (i = 0; i < N; i++){      checksum += buf[1]
    checksum += buf[i];       ...
}                             checksum += buf[N-1]
                              cmp checksum, V
/* verify checksum */         jnz tamper_response
if (checksum != V) {
    // tamper response
}
```

(a) Self-checksumming code   (b) Trace (fragment)

Suppose buf points to the executed code section being checksummed: then the locations buf+i are used as taint sources during backward taint propagation, and the locations buf+0, buf+1, ..., buf+N-1 are therefore tainted during this phase. Forward tainting from the locations buf+i, through the fragment of the trace shown above, will then cause the location checksum to become tainted. This will then cause the condition code flags to be tainted after the instruction "cmp checksum, V". Since the condition code flags are used as inputs to the conditional branch instruction "jnz tamper_response", our analysis will identify this conditional branch as taking tainted inputs (Algorithm 3, line 17) and therefore flag it as a tamper response instruction.

EXAMPLE 3.2. This example considers the situation where a checksum for one piece of code is used as the decryption key for a second piece of code: any tampering with the first code region results in the wrong decryption key being used for the second code section, resulting in the generation of garbage code by the unpacker. This approach to self-checksumming-based anti-tampering has been proposed by Cappaert et al. [5] and Wang et al. [23].

Suppose that, in the code fragment shown below, buf points to executed code and buf2 points to packed code that is unpacked using the checksum value for buf as the decryption key:

---
[3]The "tamper response" here may simply involve setting a flag to indicate a checksum mismatch, with further actions delayed to enhance stealth, e.g., as suggested by Tan et al. [19].

```
/* compute checksum */        checksum = 0
checksum = 0;                 checksum += buf[0]
for (i=0; i < N1; i++) {      checksum += buf[1]
    checksum += buf[i];       ...
}                             checksum += buf[N1-1]
                              buf2[0] ^= checksum
/* decrypt code */            buf2[1] ^= checksum
for (i=0; i < N2; i++) {      ...
    buf2 ^= checksum;         buf2[N2-1] ^= checksum
}
                              ...
/* execute code */            jmp buf2
...
```

(a) Self-checksumming code   (b) Trace (fragment)

Since buf and buf2 point to executed code locations, the memory regions buf+0, ..., buf+N1-1 and buf2+0, ..., buf2+N2-1 are tainted during backward taint propagation. During forward taint propagation, the taint on buf+0, ..., buf+N1-1 causes checksum to become tainted. Since buf2+0, ..., buf2+N2-1 are also tainted, this then causes our analysis detects that, in the assignments to buf2, tainted values are written to an executed location and therefore flags this code as a tamper response (Algorithm 3, line 18).

EXAMPLE 3.3. This example shows that a checksum can be used for initializing a variable. The variable is taken in a computation whose result is finally displayed to the screen.

```
/* compute checksum */        checksum = 0
checksum = 0;                 checksum += buf[0]
for (i=0; i < N; i++) {       checksum += buf[1]
    checksum += buf[i];       ...
}                             checksum += buf[N1-1]
                              p = 1+ checksum^0x1234
int p=1+checksum^0x1234;      p *= n
while (n > 0) p *= n--;       n -= 1
printf("%d\n", p);            cmp n, 0
                              jnz loop
                              ...
                              push p
                              ...
                              call printf
```

(a) Self-checksumming code   (b) Trace (fragment)

Suppose buf points to an executed code section. Forward tainting buf+i, the system call "printf" will be identified as a tamper response instruction because its second parameter p is tainted (Algorithm 3, lines 20 − 21).

3.6 Implementation Considerations

The space and time costs of processing large traces can potentially be a concern for offline dynamic analyses such as ours. Trace compression techniques can significantly mitigate the storage and I/O costs of processing large traces: e.g., Bhansali et al. [4] describe a trace compression scheme that results in roughly 0.5 bits of trace data per dynamic instruction instance.

Additionally, we use two optimization techniques to speed up taint propagation, which is at the heart of our analysis: (i) reducing the number of instructions that have to be examined for taint propagation; and (ii) reducing the overall cost of forward taint propagation using parallelism.

Eliminating irrelevant instructions.

In order to reduce the number of instructions processed during forward taint propagation, we use a pre-tainting phase to propagate taint information and identify a sub-trace of

213

the original trace that contains all the relevant instructions for forward taint propagation (Algorithm 3, lines 3 − 9). We can prove that forward taint propagation from this sub-trace is equivalent to forward tainting from the entire original trace. This can produce significant improvements in performance because the sub-trace obtained from this pre-tainting phase is usually significantly smaller than the original trace. As an example of the performance improvements obtained, for Media Player Classic the total time drops from 480 secs to 240 secs; while for the 50-guards program the total processing time improves by more than fourfold, going from 6,282 secs to 1,352 secs.[4]

Second, to avoid processing irrelevant instructions, we only trace instructions executed after the target program reaches its entry point. This avoids tracing and recording process startup code.

Exploiting concurrency.

We use multi-threading to parallelize forward taint propagation step. Since the trace is a read-only input for forward taint propagation, it can be processed in parallel without locking overheads. We partition the locations tainted during the backward-taint step into a fixed number of subsets and for each subset create a thread to perform forward tainting.

4. EVALUATION

4.1 Setup

This section discusses our experiences with using a prototype tool we developed to evaluate our ideas. Execution tracing is carried out using an Intel Pin tool [13]. The data presented here were obtained on a 2.67GHz Intel Xeon E5640 processor (12 MB L1 cache) with 96 GB of main memory running Ubuntu 12.04. Our tool was run with 16 parallel threads. The threshold θ_{min} and θ_{max} in Algorithm 1 are set to 16 and 512, respectively.

We used two sets of test programs to evaluate our tool. In each case, the test program we used is an MD5 computation program obtained from http://people.csail.mit.edu/rivest/Md5.c, executed with a text file of Abraham Lincoln's Gettysburg Address as input.

- Group 1 consists of seven widely used open source programs: Media Player Classic 1.7.6; Notepad++ 6.6.7; FileZilla 3.7.0; WinMerge 2.14.0; DOSBox 0.74; VLC 2.0.5; and 7-Zip 9.20. We used the source code for these programs to verify that none of them were performing any self-checksumming. This was used as a baseline to check that there were no false positives reported by our tool.

- Group 2 consists of a set of programs we wrote to implement advanced self-checksumming schemes for which we could not find any third-party tools.[5] In each case,

---

[4]These timings refer to single-threaded execution time. The performance data given in Section 4 refer to multi-threaded execution times.

[5]In order to evaluate our algorithm on state-of-the-art commercial software anti-tampering systems, we also approached two commercial vendors who market anti-tampering systems that are based on peer-reviewed research

we modified the MD5 program mentioned above to incorporate the self-checksumming mechanism. The checksumming schemes we tested were as follows:

(i) Programs with multiple self-checksumming guards, as described by Chang *et al.* [6] and Horne *et al.* [9]. The objective was to test whether our approach can correctly identify multiple overlapping guards checking each other. We implemented and tested programs with one, four, ten, and fifty guards; in the results given below, we refer to these as *1-guard*, *4-guards*, *10-guards*, and *50-guards* respectively.

(ii) Self-checksumming programs that use the value of the checksum as a code decryption key, as described by Cappaert *et al.* [5] and Wang *et al.* [23]. The objective was to test whether our approach can detect self-checksumming schemes where the checksum verification and tamper response step uses dynamic code modification instead of an explicit control transfer. In the results below, we refer to this program as *decrypt-key*.

(iii) Checksumming combined with runtime code unpacking, as illustrated in Figure 1. The objective was to test whether our approach could detect self-checksumming when the locations being checksummed are not themselves executed, but are used to create code that is executed. We tested a program with 100 layers of unpacking, with checksumming carried out after each even-numbered unpacking layer for a total of 50 different checksum computations. In the results given below, refer to this program as *100-layers*.

(iv) The checksum is used for generating a MD5 initialization constant. The MD5 value is output to the screen by $printf()$. In the results given below, we refer to this program as *chksum-md5*.

These programs tested the precision and recall of our approach. The source code for these programs, as well as the executables obtained from them that we used in our tests, are available at http://www.cs.arizona.edu/projects/lynx/Samples/Self-checksumming/.

We validated the results obtained from our analysis as follows.

- For programs in Group 1, we compile their source code and generate debug information files. The debug information is a representation of the relationship between the executable program and the original source code. With these debug information, we validate the result of programs in Group 1 using a debugger to monitor the execution of each program.

- For Group 2, we instrumented the programs we constructed to report, at runtime, each address range that was checksummed each time a checksum was computed. This was then compared with the results reported by our tool.

---

publications on software self-checksumming. The vendors declined to provide access to their protection tools; one vendor cited concerns about the potential for adverse publicity resulting from our work.

Table 1: Evaluation result

Program	Trace Size		No. of Tainted Instructions	No. of Taint Sources	No. of Guards		Analysis Time (sec)
	Mbytes	Instructions			Found	Ground Truth	
1-guard	11	179,339	60,298	3,394	1	1	5
4-guards	13	209,926	71,885	3,641	4	4	6
10-guards	22	375,563	142,483	4,916	10	10	16
50-guards	160	2,780,558	1,760,264	4,855	50	50	237
100-layers	92	1,600,653	1,083,861	2,335	50	50	53
decrpt-key	9	166,581	72,422	2,352	1	1	4
chksum-md5	17	297,068	118,526	2,353	1	1	5

4.2 Evaluation Results

The result of the evaluation is given in Table 1. The "Number of Taint Sources" column gives the total number of locations tainted during backward tainting; the "No. of Tainted Instructions" column gives the total number of instructions tainted during forward tainting. We did not find any false positives in the programs in Groups 1 and 2.

4.2.1 Precision of Analysis

Group 1.

We have checked the source code of programs in Group 1, and no checksumming is found in the source code. Our prototype tool does not find any code checksumming as expected. In the processing of most programs except Media Player Classic (MPC), our approach exit early after backward taint analysis because no instruction reads or writes the executed locations. MPC employs a third party library to hook system APIs. It writes an unconditional jump instruction at the head of the hooked API. The source of the bytes written is discovered by the backward taint analysis. But no checksumming is found in MPC as expected.

Group 2.

In Group 2, for programs with multiple guards, our approach successfully identifies all designed checksummings. However, the code coverage issues of dynamic analysis manifest themselves (see Section 5): for a specific input, not all of the protected code is executed at runtime, and since our approach starts the analysis with the set of executed locations, not all checksummed locations (i.e., the set of protected memory locations associated with each checksum verification instruction) are identified by our approach. Thus, for some of the checksum guards our tool reports a smaller range of checksummed locations than is in fact the case because some checksummed locations were not executed.

In the program with 100 layers unpacking, all checksummings are identified by our approach. Our tool reports that these checksummings have the same protected code range. That is because in the source code of this program, the checksummed code is transformed and checksummed in one layer, and then it is passed into next unpacking layer.

Our approach also successfully identifies the checksumming in the program that the computed checksum is used as a decryption key. The code of the checksumming is as follows.

```
checksum = compute_checksum(CODE);
```

```
for(i = 0; i < size; i++)
    CODE[i] -= checksum;
```

Instructions "CODE[i] -= checksum" and the range of CODE are reported by our tool.

The checksumming in "chksum-md5" is identified as well. The checksum is used for generating a MD5 initialization constant. If the protected code is tampered, the computed MD5 value is incorrect. The code is as followings.

```
int cksum = compute_checksum(CODE);
...
//This value should be 0x67452301;
mdContext->buf[0] = chksum + 0x6740E9CB;
...
printf("%s", md5_str);
...
```

The instruction "call printf" and the code range checksummed are reported by our tool.

The result of this group indicates that no matter how a checksum is used in an execution, the activity that computing a checksum over code will always be discovered by our approach.

4.2.2 Effects of Performance Optimization

Suppose there are L_1 instructions in an instruction trace and after backward taint analysis, there are L_2 locations; that forward tainting L_2 locations produce L_3 tainted instructions; and the implementation uses N threads. Define the *workload* of our approach be the total number of instructions processed. The number of instructions processed in the backward taint propagation phase is $2 * L_1$, while the total number of instructions processed during forward taint propagation is $L_2 * L_3$ without multi-threading and $L_2 * L_3/N$ with multi-threading. Thus, the unoptimized and optimized workloads are given by $2 * L_1 + L_2 * L_3$ and $2 * L_1 + L_2 * L_3/N$ respectively. The effect of multi-threading is to significantly reduce the workload for the forward taint propagation phase.

Table 2 shows that the optimization sharply decreases the work load. In Group 1, most programs' analysis exit early because we found that no instruction reads or writes executed locations. Thus, the optimization is not worked and the work load is $2 * L_1$. In the analysis of the reset programs, the optimized approach only processes average 2.92% instructions of the un-optimized approach while obtaining the same result. It indicates that excluding irrelevant instructions and the parallel processing technology make our approach more practical to real world binary analysis. When dealing with the trace file of a large scale program, just simply split the work load and assign them to more processors. The more processors join, the less time will take.

Table 2: Work load of the approach without and with optimizations. The work load is defined as the number of processed instructions.

Program	Without ($\times 10^6$)	With ($\times 10^6$)	With/Without (%)
1-guard	609	13	2.16
4-guards	727	16	2.20
10-guards	1,847	45	2.41
50-guards	13,505	540	4.00
100-layers	3,740	161	4.31
decrpt-key	392	11	2.80
chksum-md5	693	18	2.58

4.3 A Case Study

As a case study of our ideas, we applied our prototype tool to a well-known and widely used Internet communication application. Our initial experiments use an execution trace up to the point where the application's splash screen appears (approx. 62.6 million instructions).

After the program begins execution, it unpacks some code (this is done *in situ* rather than generating code into some fresh memory region) using the following unpacking logic:

```
SEED = 0x135a936d;
unsigned char* CODE = &SOME_CODE_SECN; // 0x5bc1f0
for(int i = 0; i < 0x16160; ++i) {
    if (i == 0x15f08) i += 0x28; // Skip 0x28 bytes
    CODE[i] ^= SEED & 0xFF;
    rol(SEED, 3);  // rotate left
}
```

Somewhat later in the execution the application executes self-checksumming code that is part of the code unpacked earlier. The checksum computation and validation code has the following logic:

```
unsigned int chksum = 0x0A9C35B72;
unsigned char* CODE = &SOME_CODE_SECN; // 0x5bc1f0
for (i = 0; i < 0x16160; i++) {
    chksum = (chksum >> 4) + CODE[i];
    chksum2 = chksum & 0x0f000000;
    if (chksum2 != 0) {
        chksum ^= (chksum2 << 0x18);
    }
    chksum &= ~chksum2;
}

f = BIT_MASK ^ chksum;
...
call f;      // validation!
...
return;
```

The validation code in this case does not explicitly compare the computed checksum against an expected value, but rather uses it to compute the target of an indirect call (indicated above by the comment 'validation!'): an incorrect checksum value simply transfers control to the wrong address and results in an incorrect execution.

The for-loop that computes the checksum in the code shown above contains an if-statement that checks whether the variable checksum2 is nonzero. Since this is a conditional branch that tests the value of a checksum value, our tool flags this as a possible validation check. Since this if-statement is executed each time around the loop, our tool reports a series of different code regions $C_0, C_1, \ldots, C_i, \ldots$

that are "checked" by this test, such that each C_i is a proper prefix of each C_j for $j > i$. It would be straightforward to modify our tool to detect these overlapped regions and collapse them into a single reported region, however this is a reporting issue orthogonal to that of detecting and identifying self-checksumming.

5. DISCUSSION AND FUTURE WORK

While the dynamic analysis-based approach we use has the advantage of being able to deal transparently with anti-analysis defenses such as runtime code self-modification, it has the disadvantage of limited code coverage. The code coverage problem can be mitigated using multi-path exploration techniques [15].

A second problem with offline dynamic analysis is the potential for large trace files, which can incur significant storage and processing costs. This issue can be mitigated using trace compression techniques, e.g., Bhansali *et al.* [4] describe a trace compression scheme that results in roughly 0.5 bits of trace data per dynamic instruction instance.

Finally, while the offline analysis used by our approach can identify self-checksumming and provide a great deal of information about the specific defenses being used by a given program, it does not automatically translate into a straightforward way to disable the checksumming. In the experimental evaluation of our prototype, we manually validate the correctness of detection results. This can be tricky if the checksumming code is created dynamically at unpredictable locations in memory.

Our current prototype implementation does not currently incorporate trace compression or multi-path exploration: we plan to do so as part of future work to improve execution performance and code coverage. We also plan to explore online analysis algorithms and to extend our analysis to other kinds of anti-analysis defenses such as timing-based tracing detection.

The discussion in this paper focuses on dynamic checksumming and does not consider static checksumming. It is not difficult, in principle, to adapt our approach to handle static checksumming: all we need to do is to keep track of library/system calls to identify any access the program file, either through explicit file I/O or by mapping the file into the process's virtual address space. Once this has been done, it is not too difficult to parse the file structure and identify operations that read from locations within the file that correspond to code. Incorporation of such logic into our prototype implementation is the subject of future work.

6. RELATED WORK

There is a considerable body of work on anti-tampering defenses for software. Much of this work focuses on self-contained defenses based on code self-checksumming that meet our assumptions as described in Section 1. Aucsmith [3] introduced an implementation of a self-checking mechanism based on multiple self-modifying and self-decrypting code blocks that check the validity of the code as it is running. Chang *et al.* [6] and Horne *et al.* [9] discuss self-checksumming systems that use a network of guards such that each guard is protected by multiple other guards. Disabling this kind of protection requires all the guards be disabled at once which makes it non-trivial for the attacker. Tsang *et al.* use a large number of small size protectors capable of giving non-pre-programmed tamper responses, and use multiple versions of a function for creating non-deterministic execution [20]. Wang *et al.* [23] and Cappaert *et al.* [5] propose the use of checksum values as a key to decrypt the encrypted code that is going to be executed, such that any tampering causes the code to be decrypted with the wrong key and silently produces incorrect code. Tan *et al.* discuss stealthy tamper response techniques that make it difficult for an attacker to tie the tamper response back to the checksum verification code [19]. By and large these works assume a threat model based on pure static analysis; their self-checksumming defenses can be clearly identified by our dynamic analysis-based approach. There has also been some work on anti-tampering defenses where the checksum verification is performed by an external verifier on a trusted remote server [14, 18]. These approaches do not use self-contained self-checksumming defenses, as discussed in Section 1, and so fall outside the scope of this work.

The only other work we know of that looks at attacks on self-checksumming code is that of Wurster *et al.* [22, 24], who exploit an assumption underlying self-checksumming approaches that the same byte values will be retrieved from a virtual memory address range regardless of whether it is retrieved as code or data. They show that an adversary hardware assisted techniques to violate this assumption and bypass the self-checksumming defense. Giffin *et al.* show that self-modifying code can be used to detect this attack [8]. Unlike Wurster *et al.*'s attack, the work we describe is a pure-software approach that does not rely on hardware assistance. To the best of our knowledge, this is the first such pure-software attack against self-checksumming systems. In terms of relative power, our approach does not seem directly comparable with that of Wurster *et al.*: on the one hand, our approach is unaffected by techniques, such as self-modifying code, that can defeat Wurster *et al.*'s attack [8]; on the other hand, programs that do not satisfy our self-containedness assumption (see Section 1) cannot be handled using our approach but may be susceptible to Wurster *et al.*'s attack.

There is a wide body of literature on various forms of taint analysis and their applications to software analysis, e.g., see [17]. To the best of our knowledge none of these works apply taint analysis to the problem of detecting or understanding self-checksumming.

Wang *et al.* proposed a fuzzing tool for software vulnerabilities detection. They use taint analysis to detect checksumming on the input data of a program. The checksumming is similar to ours but there two big differences. First, they identify data checksumming while we focus on code checksumming. Second, they identify the hot bytes which are checksummed bytes in the input data such that only the checksumming with classic verifier can be identified by their approach. Instead, our approach focus the identification of checksumming verifiers such that more kinds of checksumming can be identified by our approach.

7. CONCLUSION

This paper describes an information-flow-based attack against software anti-tampering defenses based on self-checksumming; to the best of our knowledge it is the first pure-software attack against such defenses. Our approach is based on dynamic analysis: it uses backward taint propagation to identify memory locations that are either executed or which are used to compute the values of locations that are executed, followed by a forward taint propagation that identifies checksum computations on the code. Experiments using a prototype implementation show that our approach can effectively identify a wide range of self-checksumming behaviors, including a number of proposals for self-checksumming that described in the research literature.

Acknowledgments

This research was supported in part by the Air Force Office of Scientific Research (AFOSR) under grant no. FA9550-11-1-0191; the National Science Foundation (NSF) under grants CNS-1115829, CNS-1145913, III-1318343, and CNS-1318955; and the US Department of Defense under grant no. FA2386-14-1-3016. The work of Jing Qiu was supported by National Natural Science Foundation of China (NSFC) 61173021. The opinions, findings, and conclusions expressed in this paper are solely those of the authors and do not necessarily reflect the views of AFOSR, NSF or NSFC.

8. REFERENCES

[1] Obsidium software protection system. http://www.obsidium.de/show/home/en.

[2] VMProtect – New-generation software protection. http://www.vmprotect.ru/.

[3] D. Aucsmith. Tamper resistant software: An implementation. In *Information Hiding*, pages 317–333. Springer, 1996.

[4] S. Bhansali, W.-K. Chen, S. de Jong, A. Edwards, R. Murray, M. Drinić, D. Mihočka, and J. Chau. Framework for instruction-level tracing and analysis of program executions. In *Proceedings of the 2Nd International Conference on Virtual Execution Environments*, VEE '06, pages 154–163, 2006.

[5] J. Cappaert, B. Preneel, B. Anckaert, M. Madou, and K. De Bosschere. Towards tamper resistant code encryption: Practice and experience. In *Information Security Practice and Experience*, pages 86–100. Springer, 2008.

[6] H. Chang and M. J. Atallah. Protecting software code by guards. In *Security and privacy in digital rights management*, pages 160–175. Springer, 2002.

[7] A. Dinaburg, P. Royal, M. Sharif, and W. Lee. Ether: malware analysis via hardware virtualization extensions. In *Proceedings of the 15th ACM conference on Computer and communications security*, pages 51–62. ACM, 2008.

[8] J. T. Giffin, M. Christodorescu, and L. Kruger. Strengthening software self-checksumming via self-modifying code. In *Computer Security Applications Conference, 21st Annual*, pages 10–pp. IEEE, 2005.

[9] B. Horne, L. Matheson, C. Sheehan, and R. E. Tarjan. Dynamic self-checking techniques for improved tamper resistance. In *Security and privacy in digital rights management*, pages 141–159. Springer, 2002.

[10] M. G. Kang, P. Poosankam, and H. Yin. Renovo: A hidden code extractor for packed executables. In *Proc. Fifth ACM Workshop on Recurring Malcode (WORM 2007)*, Nov. 2007.

[11] B. Korel. Computation of dynamic program slices for unstructured programs. *IEEE Transactions on Software Engineering*, 23(1):17–34, Jan. 1997.

[12] B. Korel and J. Laski. Dynamic program slicing. *Inf. Process. Lett.*, 29(3):155–163, Oct. 1988.

[13] C.-K. Luk, R. Cohn, R. Muth, H. Patil, A. Klauser, G. Lowney, S. Wallace, V. J. Reddi, and K. Hazelwood. Pin: building customized program analysis tools with dynamic instrumentation. *ACM Sigplan Notices*, 40(6):190–200, 2005.

[14] L. Martignoni, R. Paleari, and D. Bruschi. Conqueror: tamper-proof code execution on legacy systems. In

Detection of Intrusions and Malware, and Vulnerability Assessment, pages 21–40. Springer, 2010.

[15] A. Moser, C. Kruegel, and E. Kirda. Exploring multiple execution paths for malware analysis. In *SP '07: Proceedings of the 2007 IEEE Symposium on Security and Privacy*, pages 231–245, 2007.

[16] Oreans Technologies. Themida: Advanced windows software protection system, Sept. 2008. http://www.oreans.com/themida.php.

[17] E. J. Schwartz, T. Avgerinos, and D. Brumley. All you ever wanted to know about dynamic taint analysis and forward symbolic execution (but might have been afraid to ask). In *IEEE Symposium on Security and Privacy*, pages 317–331, 2010.

[18] A. Seshadri, M. Luk, E. Shi, A. Perrig, L. van Doorn, and P. Khosla. Pioneer: verifying code integrity and enforcing untampered code execution on legacy systems. *ACM SIGOPS Operating Systems Review*, 39(5):1–16, 2005.

[19] G. Tan, Y. Chen, and M. H. Jakubowski. Delayed and controlled failures in tamper-resistant software. In

Information Hiding, volume 4437 of *Lecture Notes in Computer Science*, pages 216–231. Springer, 2006.

[20] H.-C. Tsang, M.-C. Lee, and C.-M. Pun. A robust anti-tamper protection scheme. In *Availability, Reliability and Security (ARES), 2011 Sixth International Conference on*, pages 109–118. IEEE, 2011.

[21] J. Tygar and B. S. Yee. Dyad: A system for using physically secure coprocessors. 1991.

[22] P. C. Van Oorschot, A. Somayaji, and G. Wurster. Hardware-assisted circumvention of self-hashing software tamper resistance. *Dependable and Secure Computing, IEEE Transactions on*, 2(2):82–92, 2005.

[23] P. Wang, S. Kim, and K. Kim. Tamper resistant software through dynamic integrity checking. In *Proc. 2005 Symposium on Cryptography and Information Security (SCIS2005)*, Jan. 2005.

[24] G. Wurster, P. Van Oorschot, and A. Somayaji. A generic attack on checksumming-based software tamper resistance. In *Security and Privacy, 2005 IEEE Symposium on*, pages 127–138. IEEE, 2005.

Robust Fingerprinting for Relocatable Code

Irfan Ahmed, Vassil Roussev, Aisha Ali Gombe
Department of Computer Science
University of New Orleans
2000 Lakeshore Dr.
New Orleans LA USA - 70148
irfan.ahmed@uno.edu, vassil@cs.uno.edu, aaligomb@my.uno.edu

ABSTRACT

Robust fingerprinting of executable code contained in a memory image is a prerequisite for a large number of security and forensic applications, especially in a cloud environment. Prior state of the art has focused specifically on identifying kernel versions by means of complex differential analysis of several aspects of the kernel code implementation.

In this work, we present a novel technique that can identify *any* relocatable code, including the kernel, based on inherent patterns present in relocation tables. We show that such patterns are very distinct and can be used to accurately and efficiently identify known executables in a memory snapshot, including remnants of prior executions. We develop a research prototype, codeid, and evaluate its efficacy on more than 50,000 sample executables containing kernels, kernel modules, applications, dynamic link libraries, and malware. The empirical results show that our method achieves almost 100% accuracy with zero false negatives.

Categories and Subject Descriptors

K.6 [**Management Of Computing And Information Systems**]: Security and Protection; D.4.6 [**Operating Systems**]: Security and Protection—*Invasive software, Security kernels, Verification*

Keywords

code fingerprinting; codeid; memory analysis; virtual machine introspection; cloud security; malware detection

1. INTRODUCTION

Identifying executable binary code–operating system (OS) kernels, libraries, applications, malicious code (*malware*)–is the main focus of almost all (proactive) security monitoring, and (reactive) forensic analysis applications. For instance, fingerprinting of the OS kernel enables memory forensic tools (such as Volatility [18, 5]) to parse the memory with the data structures pertinent to the kernel version; fingerprinting of

malware is at the core antivirus applications. Most incident response and deep forensics techniques rely heavily on the ability to recognize the exact code being executed on the target system.

In an *Infrastructure-as-a-service* (IaaS) *cloud* environment, (executable) code fingerprinting is a critical tool that enables a large number of automated services, such as patch management and host intrusion detection/prevention. More generally, the trend is towards cloud providers providing ever more sophisticated security-related services for their tenants. Indeed, providers who monitor a large population of virtual machines (VMs) are in a much better position to track attacks in progress, and proactively identify and shield other vulnerable VMs. This applies not only to network services, but also to client code in virtualized workstations.

All such services are reliant on their ability to gather an inventory of running code inside the VMs. Although it is possible to obtain some of this information indirectly by network scanning, or by examining the file system, such approaches are inherently incomplete as most applications do not provide a network service, and tenants routinely encrypt file system content. Thus, the only reliable approach is to directly examine the physical memory of the VM.

In this paper, we present *CodeIdentifier* (codeid)–a new fingerprinting technique and tool for relocatable code that identifies memory-resident code based on the content of relocation tables. *CodeIdentifier* divides an executable file into memory-page size blocks, and generates signatures for the blocks. A block signature consists of two components: 1) relocations (or pointers) in the code of the block identified by relocation table, and 2) the offset values of the relocations from the start of the block. The signatures are then used to identify the exact in-memory pages represented by the signatures. We have exhaustively evaluated codeid signatures on more than 50,000 sample executables (of kernel, kernel modules, applications, libraries, and malware), and established that the signatures are quite unique and are able to distinguish close versions of the code. The empirical results show that codeid detects in-memory code pages with almost 100% accuracy, and no false negatives.

The *main contribution* of this work is the development of codeid, which is a) *accurate*–it yields precise results, even for closely related code; b) *robust*–it works with partial information and can perform remnant detection; c) *performant*–the resulting tool is fast enough to be of practical use in scanning live VMs; and d) *fully automated*–it requires no human in the loop to generate and use new signatures.

The rest of the discussion is organized as follows: Section 2 provides a brief summary of related work; Section 3 presents the main concepts and techniques used in our solutions; Section 4 contains the experimental validation of the proposed approach; and Section 5 summarizes our findings and conclusions.

2. RELATED WORK

Prior work on executable fingerprinting techniques–apart from malware detection, which is outside the scope of this discussion–focus primarily on operating system (OS) kernel version detection.

2.1 Deep analysis techniques

Deep analysis approaches parse and (partially) interpret the memory capture with the express goal of finding unique implementation traits that separate different kernels.

Gu *et al.* [3] propose *OS-Sommelier*, which extensively parses and analyses memory dump for kernel version identification, such as virtual-to-physical address translation, and disassembling the code. In order to create a signature of a kernel, the tool takes a snapshot of the memory that contains the kernel, and then processes the snapshot in three main steps.

First, it searches the entire snapshot and identifies the page global directory (PGD) for virtual-to-physical address translation. Second, it identifies the kernel code–the PGD is used to make clusters of the similar read-only pages, assuming that the kernel-code pages are read-only for code protection. Next, the *cluster* which contains core-kernel code is identified; this is necessary since the same module can be loaded with different kernel versions. The authors use two particular instructions that are empirically identified as being used only by the core kernel, and not by modules.

Third, the tool generates the signatures, which are the cryptographic hashes of the kernel pages. Since the kernel code contains pointers whose values change when the kernel loads in different locations in the memory, this step is preceeded by zeroing out of all such pointer values before computing the hashes. To identify the locations of the pointers, the code is (partially) disassembled. Thus, a kernel signature consists of the obtained set of page hashes. Finally, when a kernel version needs to be identified in a memory image, the same steps are repeated on the target to create signatures, which are then compared with the known signatures. We discuss *OS-Sommelier*'s performance in more detail in our evaluation section.

Lin *et al.* [8] propose *Siggraph*, which relies on identifying in-memory kernel data structures. Since data structure definitions vary across operating systems, *Siggraph* can be used for OS fingerprinting. The main limitation is that well-known data structures tend to be stable across at least minor version releases. More generally, data structures changes are unpredictable and require manual reverse engineering effort whenever a new version comes out.

Christodorescu *et al.* [2] employ the *interrupt descriptor table* (IDT) for kernel version identification. The table is an array of interrupt vectors containing pointers to interrupt handler code. Since interrupt handler code tends to change over time, the authors compute the cryptographic hash of handler code, and use them as signatures to identify different kernels. Since this approach requires the value of the *IDTR* register to locate the IDT, it can only work on a live system.

Volatility [18] is a popular framework for deep forensic analysis of memory images. Since knowing the precise kernel version is critical for a lot of its functions, it maintains the profiles of kernel version for parsing memory captures and applying the correct set of data structure definitions. Volatility provides the `imageinfo` [4] tool to identify the various *MS Windows* versions. The tool scans the whole memory dump using predetermined signatures to find kernel debugging symbols table, which also contains the exact kernel version information. The Volatility approach has two main drawbacks: a) it is fragile in that the signature values can be altered to make Volatility not to find the table; and b) it is not fully automated and requires an expert analyst to drive the discovery process.

2.2 Other fingerprinting techniques

Quynh [13] proposes UFO–a kernel code-independent OS fingerprinting technique, which uses CPU register states for kernel version identification. UFO utilizes the fact that the protected mode of the Intel platform enforces few constraints on how OS is implemented. Thus, different OS versions use different ways of setting up low-level data structures and other details, such as global and interrupt descriptor tables (GDT and IDT) [15] [9] differently. As a results, the values of some registers, such as base and limit values of GDTR and IDTR, are different. UFO uses a fuzzy matching approach and looks for the closest match, giving different weights to each parameter in a signature. While matching signatures, it computes the sum of the weights of each parameter matched and the signature with highest weight represents the kernel version. In [3], Gu *et al.* evaluated UFO on different versions of Linux and Windows kernel and concluded that it does not work well on many *MS Windows* kernels and close versions of Linux kernel. Importantly, UFO is restricted to work only on a live system and cannot be used on memory captures.

Historically, there are a number of network fingerprinting tools (such as *nmap* [10] and *Xprobe2* [20]) that remotely identify the kernel version of a target system based on the packets being exchanged. Since the TCP/IP stack is implemented differently by operating systems, the differences in the reply of the crafted packets can be used to identify the OS versions. Such an approach is not relevant to our scenario and is, generally, inherently unreliable.

One accurate approach to identify the kernel version is to examine the file system on the hard disk of target system and, for instance, maintain a database of the file hashes for different version of the kernel. *Virt-inspector* [17] is a tool that provides the capability to identify the kernel version on hard disk, USB, CD etc. It uses libguestfs [6] library to examine the file system on any non-volatile media. The main constraint here is the requirement to access non-volatile media, which in our case is not given.

3. RELOCATION-BASED CODE FINGER-PRINTING

3.1 Problem statement & requirements

Given a physical memory capture, our goal is to identify the presence of a known piece of code in it, which is running at an arbitrary location. Indeed, modern operating systems routinely use *address space layout randomization* (ASLR) and purposefully choose a random starting address. This

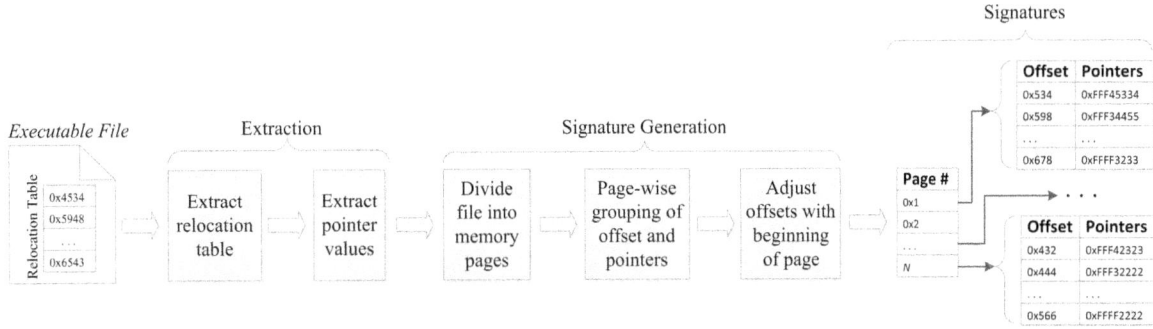

Figure 1: *CodeIdentifier* signature generation process

means that code must be able to execute regardless of its starting address. This property can be accomplished in one of two principle ways: a) by generating position-independent code–resulting in a *position-independent executable* (PIE)– that can be loaded at any address with no modifications to the code; b) by generating *relocatable code*–resulting in a *portable executable* (PE)–whose absolute addresses are adjusted at load time using the chosen base address value.

For PIEs, since no tranformations are applied to the code at load time, there is a direct mapping between the contents of the file containing the binary and the corresponding contents of RAM pages during execution. This leads to a straighforward approach to identifying the executable in memory: first, generate the (cryptographic) hash of all code pages for the binary, then compare the set to the hashes of all RAM pages of the target.

Therefore, in this work, we assume that the target code is in PE format, which is the case for nearly all kernel modules, libraries, and applications for the *MS Windows* platform.

Given our motivating problem of supporting security and management services in a large-scale virtualized environment, any practical solution should address at least three basic requirements:

Accuracy. The solution must have very low false positive/negative rates, and must be sensitive enough to distinguish among different version releases of the same executable.

Robustness. The solution should be able to work with partial information in order to accommodate paging effects and remnant detection from completed executions.

Throughput. The solution must have high throughput and low overhead to facilitate fast response and low implementation cost.

3.2 Overview

Recall that relocation is the process of assigning load addresses to the different program components and adjusting the code in the loaded program, correspondingly. The relocations are the pointers in the code that need to be adjusted depending on where the executable is loaded into memory. An executable file contains a relocation table, which lists the locations of the pointers in the code as offsets from the beginning of the file. The table itself is only needed at load time, and is subsequently discarded.

As it turns out, the combination of the location and the value of pointers naturally provide unique signatures for the pages of an executable file that we can use as a basis for a fingerprint. For that purpose, codeid 1) extracts the reloca-

Table 1: Example: Pointer difference.

Pointer location	In-memory pointer (α)	In-file pointer (β)	Difference
0x16	0xF8CC24E0	0x000104E0	0xF8CB2000
0x3B	0xF8CC2490	0x00010490	0xF8CB2000
0x40	0xF8CC2500	0x00010500	0xF8CB2000
0x5A	0xF8CC2584	0x00010584	0xF8CB2000

tion table from the file; 2) divides it into page-sized blocks; and 3) uses the relocations to create separate signatures for each page. The signature itself consists of a list of offsets to pointers from the beginning of a page, and the corresponding pointer values. Figure 1 illustrates the process. Given a set of codeid signatures, the memory capture is split into pages and each one is compared (as explained below) with every page signature in the set. Matches are tallied per known executable to determine the best match.

3.3 Design Rationale

As outlined above, signatures are created from the executable file but are compared to live memory pages, and creates several challenges we need to overcome. The first one is ASLR.

When an executable file is created, it is assigned a notional base address and all absolute addresses of pointers in the code are given relative to the base address. If the file is loaded into the memory at the notional base address, then all pointers could be used as is, and there would be a one-to-one correspondance between on-disk and in-memory representations of the code page; the comparison would be trivial. However, due to ASLR, the file is loaded with a randomized base address, rendering a direct comparison meaningless.

Figure 2 illustrates the difference in pointer values when the file is not loaded at its pre-determined base address. It shows two code snapshots of a *hello world* kernel driver for *MS Windows*. The first snapshot is taken from the memory when the driver is loaded at the memory location 0xF8CC2000. The second snapshot is obtained from the driver file, whose pre-determined base address is 0x00010000. Since the base addresses are different, the pointer values are also different.

However, as shown on the diagram, if we subtract the pointer values from the base address, the resulting *offset* values are the same in both cases. This means that, instead of directly using pointer values in signatures, we can compute and use offset values in the signatures. To compute

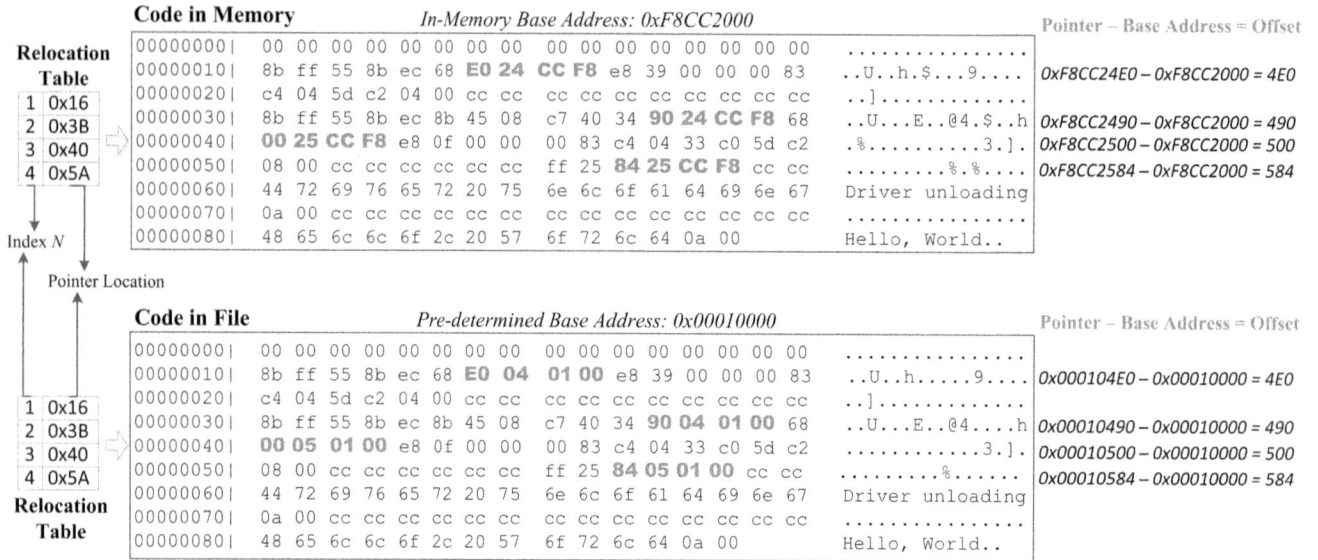

Figure 2: Example: ASLR impact on pointer values, and consistency in offsets

the base address, we use a *cross-pointer differential technique*. Since all pointers are derived from the base address, the difference between any pointer's value in its on-disk and in-memory representations is equal to the difference of base addresses of code in file and memory.

The difference of base addresses of kernel module in memory and file (from the last example) is 0xF8CC2000 - 0x00010000 = 0xF8CB2000. The relocation table has four elements and, as shown in Table 1, the pointer difference is always equal to the difference in base addresses.

More formally, given n relocation in a code page, we denote each relocation in memory by $\alpha(i)$ and in file by $\beta(i)$, respectively ($0 \leq i < n$). Then a successful match is equivalent to the following predicate:

$$\forall 0 \leq i < n, \alpha(i) - \beta(i) = \alpha(i+1) - \beta(i+1) \qquad (1)$$

Computing base address of in-memory code. By using the relative pointer differences, we avoid the need to know the base in-memory address B_m. However, knowing the base address is useful for other purposes, such as the creation of more robust signatures for data structure (e.g. *EPRO-CESS*). Therefore, we extend the technique to derive it. Let B_f be the base address of the in-file code. Then,

$$B_m = \alpha(i) - \beta(i) + B_f, \text{for any } i : 0 \leq i < n. \qquad (2)$$

(It should be clear that this technique is *not* an attack on ASLR–an attacker would need access to RAM *before* running the calculation.)

Paging Considerations. The effectiveness of codeid is clearly dependent on the number of pages actually present in main memory. For the *MS Windows* kernels we found that about 25% are marked *nonpaged*, which makes them a reliable target. Kernel modules (drivers) are also nonpaged by default. For user applications our observations show that, under normal conditions, the effects are negligible for the applications we observed. (Further work would be needed to study the behavior under memory shortage conditions.)

Algorithm 1 Single page signature match

page_match(P, S) : *boolean*
$diff = uint32(P[S[1].offset]) - S[1].ptr$
for $j = 2$ to $|S|$ **do**
  if $(uint32(P[S[j].offset]) - S[j].ptr) \neq diff$ **then**
    return $false$
return $true$

We use a *majority-wins* approach, which in practice eliminates (Section 4.4) much of the paging-related noise. One further refinement is to ignore pages marked as discardable (about 13% of the kernel) as they have almost no chance of being in memory.

Correct *page alignment* between in-file and in-memory pages for the executable is another potential problem. Fortunately, our study found that these are always aligned so no additional effort is necessary.

3.4 Signature Comparison

Recall that a (page) signature consists of a list of offset-pointer (O-P) pairs (<*offset, ptr*>), and that a file fingerprint consist of a list of such signatures. More formally, let F be a file fingerprint, $|F|$ be the number of page signatures it contains, and $S_k, k = 1..|F|$ be the individual signatures.

Let $|S_k|, k = 1..|F|$ be the length (number of O-P pairs) of each constituent signature, and $S_i[j], i = 1..|F|, j = 1..|S_i|$ be the individual <*offset, ptr*> O-P pairs. Also, denote by $|M|$ the size of the memory image in pages, and by $P_k, k = 1..|M|$ the content of individual pages (byte arrays), each of which is of size $|P|$. We use the function $uint32(P_k[j]), j = 0..|P| - 3$ to denote the extraction of a 32-bit value from page P_k, starting at location j.

We express the *page_match* predicate from equation (1) between a raw memory *page* P and a *signature* S in the algorithm 1. Thus, a match between fingerprint F consisting of signatures $S_1, ..., S_{|F|}$ and memory image M consisting of pages $P_1, ..., P_{|M|}$ returns the number of signatures matched

Algorithm 2 Count page signature matches

$match\_count(F, M) : int$
$\quad count = 0$
$\quad$**for** $i = 1$ to $|M|$ **do**
$\quad\quad$**for** $j = 1$ to $|F|$ **do**
$\quad\quad\quad$**if** $signature\_match(P_i, S_j)$ **then**
$\quad\quad\quad\quad count = count + 1$
$\quad$**return** $count$

Algorithm 3 Best fingerprint match(es)

$best\_match(RS, M) : int$
$\quad m = 0, result = \varnothing,$
$\quad match[1..|RS|] = \{0, ..., 0\}$
$\quad$**for** $i = 1$ to $|RS|$ **do**
$\quad\quad match[i] = fingerprint\_match(RS_i, M)$
$\quad\quad m = max(m, match[i])$
$\quad$**for** $i = 1$ to $|RS|$ **do**
$\quad\quad$**if** $match[i] == m$ **then**
$\quad\quad\quad result = result \cup RS_i$
$\quad$**return** $result$

Algorithm 4 Creating a filter table.

$filter = new$ **hashtable**$()$
for $i = 1$ to $|RS|$ **do**
$\quad$**for** $j = 1$ to $|S_i|$ **do**
$\quad\quad key = S_i[j].offset \mid (uint32(S_i[j].ptr) $ & $ \texttt{0x0FFF})$
$\quad\quad value = filter.lookup(key)$
$\quad\quad$**if** $value ==$ **nil then**
$\quad\quad\quad value = new$ **set**$()$
$\quad\quad value = value \cup S_i$
$\quad\quad filter.put(key, value)$

Algorithm 5 Signature matching with O-P filtering.

$\quad$**for** $i = 1$ to $|M|$ **do**
$\quad\quad$**for** $j = 1$ to $|P| - 4$ **do**
$\quad\quad\quad key = j \mid (uint32(P_i) $ & $ \texttt{0x0FFF})$
$\quad\quad\quad candidates = filter.lookup(key)$
$\quad\quad\quad$**for** S in $candidates$ **do**
$\quad\quad\quad\quad$**if** $signature\_match(P_i, S)$ **then**
$\quad\quad\quad\quad\quad result = result \cup S$
$\quad$**return** $result$

(Algorithm 2). The result of matching *all* the signatures in a reference set *RS* would simply return the identities of those signatures that are equal to the highest fingerprint match (Algorithm 3). There are some optimizations that can be done in practice to improve the computation but, fundamentally, the complexity is proportional to $|M| \times |RS|$. Scanning through all of memory is unavoidable (in the general case) but the reference set could potentially be preprocessed to speed up the computation.

The key insight in this respect is the recognition that the least significant 12 bits in a pointer value (for a 4KiB page) remain constant after load-time adjustments (Table 1, Figure 2). One way to take advantage of this property is to create a hashtable that uses the concatenation of 12-bit page offset and 12-bit pointer value as a key. The corresponding value includes the set of all signatures that contain that particular O-P combination. During the match process, the

Table 2: Test data used in evaluations

Dataset	#1	#2	#3	#4	Total
Files	20	17,010	26	34,014	51,070

table serves as a filter that limits the matching process to signatures that contain the given O-P pair.

The process of creating the filter is illustrated by Algorithm 4, where the "|" sign stands for concatenation and the "&" sign for the *bitwise AND* operation. Algorithm 5 shows a modified version of the baseline approach that incorporates filtering. Once the results are obtained, it is trivial to pick out the best match(es).

Conceptually, the filtering does not alter the asymtpotic complexity—in the worst case, all signatures could end up in the same set. However, under the assumption of relatively uniform distribution of the O-P keys (which we have observed empirically), it does reduce the number of signature comparisons by a substantial constant factor. As our experimental results in the following section show, this makes a big difference for larger sets, which is the most important case.

4. EVALUATION

We have developed a proof-of-concept implementation in *C* and used to evaluate our technique. The current version of `codeid` is approximately 1,000 lines of code and works with 32-bit *MS Windows* executables.

4.1 Test Data

We used four datasets (Table 2) with a total of 51,070 executable files: Dataset #1 (*OS Kernels*) contains the kernels for *MS Windows* 2000 Server, XP SP1 (service pack 1), SP2 and SP 3, Vista with SP0 (initial release), SP1, and SP2, Windows 7 SP0 and SP1, and Windows 8 and 8.1. Since we are only evaluating 32-bit Windows executables, we also consider the kernel version (`ntkrnlpa.exe`) that has physical address extension (PAE) support, in addition to `ntoskrnl.exe` that has no PAE support.

Dataset #2 (*MS Windows system libraries and executables*) consists of the application (`.exe`) and library (`.dll`) files of `system32` folder from 11 different versions of *MS Windows* (2000 Server, XP, Vista, 7, and 8).

Dataset #3 (*popular applications*) contains recent versions of eight popular *MS Windows* applications:

Adobe Reader (`AcroRd32.exe`), *AVG antivirus* (`avgui.exe`), *Google Chrome* (`chrome.exe`), *Command Prompt* (`cmd.exe`), *Firefox* (`firefox.exe`), *Internet Explorer* (`iexplore.exe`), *Windows Media Player* (`wmplayer.exe`), *WinRAR Archiver* (`WinRAR.exe`). We also obtained the old versions of the applications[1], installed them, and extracted the executable files that get loaded into memory.

Dataset #4 (*malware*) consists of a sampling of malware executables obtained from the *VX Heaven* public repository [19]. The samples are already split into several different categories—backdoor, constructor, exploit, flooder, packed, rootkit, trojan, virus, and worm.

4.2 Relocation Prevalence & Code Coverage

The first obvious questions to study are the *prevalance* of relocations in executable files–how many relocations *per page*

---

[1] From `http://www.oldapps.com/`

Table 3: Set #1 (kernels) relocation prevalence and coverage.

Version	Prevalance (P_1)	Coverage (C_1) (%)
2000 Server	66.26	85.90
XP SP1	59.97	88.02
XP SP2	60.12	88.50
XP SP3	56.26	88.08
Vista SP0	56.25	84.61
Vista SP1	55.25	85.99
Vista SP2	55.31	85.79
Win 7 SP0	54.28	86.04
Win 7 SP1	54.05	86.14
Win 8	51.64	91.89
Win 8.1	51.64	91.89

Table 4: Set #2 (system) relocation prevalence and coverage.

Version	Files	P_2	C_2
2000 Server	811	99.77	73.51
XP SP1	923	98.91	72.90
XP SP2	928	94.98	74.39
XP SP3	1,023	95.01	74.25
Vista SP0	1,623	99.66	70.96
Vista SP1	1,641	99.58	70.99
Vista SP2	1,657	99.98	70.60
Win 7 SP0	1,787	101.05	70.63
Win 7 SP1	1,987	101.95	70.21
Win 8	2,259	116.73	71.68
Win 8.1	2,371	116.36	72.43
Weighted Avg		104.12	71.72

can we expect to find–and (code) *coverage*–what fraction of the pages in the executable contain relocations.

Specifically, we define $P_i, i = 1..4$ to be the mean number of relocations per page (for each version/category) of dataset i. Similarly, $C_i, i = 1..4$ is the percentage of pages containing relocations (per version/category).

Tables 3 through 6 present a summary of our findings. In all cases we found the minimum number of relocations, if present, to be at least *four*, which is above the minimum of *two* necessary to build a page signature.

4.3 Collisions & Signature Overlap

Clearly, the accuracy of the `codeid` matching process depends critically on the uniqueness of the page and file signatures. In this section, we study the collision rates of signatures across different executables in our dataset.

Recall that each file signature is a set of page signatures with the latter consisting of a sequence of *offset-relocation* (O-R) pair elements. For the rest of this section, we quantify the level of O-R collisions among page signatures.

Let the total number of O-R pairs in a page signature be r_j and let c_j be the number of collisions (matching pairs in another signature) for page j. We define the *overlap rate* O_j for page j as $O_j = c_j/r_j, j = 1..N$ (N is the total number of pages).

Tables 7 through 10 present the distribution of O-R collisions per page by quantile, as well as the special cases of 0% and 100% collisions (a blank cell indicates zero, while

Table 5: Set #3 (applications) relocation prevalence and coverage.

Application	P_3	C_3
Adobe Reader 9.4	75.67	7.41
10.1.4	75.66	72.05
11.0.03	79.92	90.60
AVG 2012	119.48	93.37
2013	106.87	94.18
2014	107.04	94.08
Chrome 33.0.1750.146	58.96	66.16
33.0.1750.154	58.98	65.83
34.0.1857.116	57.91	68.56
cmd 6	96.12	70.21
6.1	93.88	90.95
6.2	107.91	83.33
Firefox 23	127.33	4.69
24, 25	78.00	3.17
27, 28	79.00	3.17
IExplorer 7	109.57	9.27
8	142.60	6.21
9	98.33	3.35
10	89.50	2.20
Media Player 11	88.00	5.13
12	108.00	5.13
WinRAR 3.91	108.60	77.22
4.2	105.48	77.65
5.01	99.10	78.45

Table 6: Set #4 (malware) relocation prevalence and coverage.

Category	Files	P_4	C_4
Backdoor	8,654	372.00	71.57
Constructor	106	316.08	66.95
Exploit	140	258.00	66.51
Flooder	136	220.59	72.84
Packed	43	343.00	60.65
Rootkit	562	258.00	60.62
Trojan	22,744	464.60	71.78
Virus	398	310.67	71.88
Worm	1,231	340.00	74.29
Weighted Avg		428.87	71.59

Table 7: Set #1 signature overlap distribution.

Version	0%	20%	40%	60%	80%	99%	**100%**
Win2000	100						
WinXP	100						
WinVista	25.30	72.18	1.89	0.16	0.21	0.26	
Win7	65.91	33.88	0.21				
Win8	100						

0.00 means a rate of less than 0.001%). For example, in Table 7 the row for *Vista* shows that 25.3% of the pages had no overlap, 72.2% had between 1 and 20 percent overlap, 1.89% had between 21 and 40 percent overlap, and so on. (The results are aggregated by major version, but *all* pairs of page signatures were compared across the set.)

Recall that, in practical terms, the only collisions that truly matter are the 100% ones–the rest of the columns are presented for completenes. As long as there is at least one

Table 8: Set #2 signature overlap distribution.

Version	0%	20%	40%	60%	80%	99%	100%
Win2000	76.66	22.80	0.47	0.04	0.01	0.02	
WinXP1	78.40	21.20	0.36	0.02		0.01	0.00
WinXP2	86.27	13.59	0.13		0.00	0.01	0.00
WinXP3	94.50	4.67	0.31	0.19	0.14	0.16	0.03
WinVista	99.93	0.06	0.01	0.00			
Win7	99.81	0.17	0.01				0.01
Win8	99.83	0.17	0.00				0.00

Table 9: Set #3 signature overlap distribution.

Application	0%	20%	40%	60%	80%	99%	100%
AVG 2012	12.68	61.97	21.75	3.50	0.11		
2013	13.77	69.96	12.15	4.01		0.11	
2014	100						
Chrome							
33.0.1750.146	38.93	61.07					
34.0.1857.116	36.84	63.16					
IExplorer 7	42.86	50.00	7.014				
8	100						
9	100						
10	50.00	50.00					

Table 10: Set #4 signature overlap distribution.

Category	0%	20%	40%	60%	80%	99%	100%
Backdoor	61.02	10.47	00.48	00.17	00.16	00.54	**27.16**
Constructor	98.75	01.20	00.01	00.03		00.01	
Exploit	88.42	11.29	00.24		00.02	00.02	
Flooder	96.29	02.77	00.10	00.12	00.20	00.39	**00.14**
Packed	92.11	07.89					
Rootkit	95.14	03.12	00.07		00.09	00.56	**01.01**
Trojan	79.80	10.48	00.72	00.34	00.32	00.63	**07.70**
Virus	95.17	04.64	00.02		00.01	00.02	**00.13**
Worm	99.45	00.24	00.04	00.07	00.10	00.07	**00.03**

unique O-R pair in the page signature, the *page_match* predicate (Algorithm 1) would return *false* so no confusion will take place.

For the set #1 experiments (Table 7), we generated signatures for a total of 20 kernel files (both with and without PAE support), resulting in 11,472 page signatures and 641,636 O-R pairs. Clearly, the main result is that no two pages completely overlap; that is, *all page signatures are unique*. Further, on most versions, there is no O-R overlap at all.

Set #2–17,000 *system* files–present a very similar picture (Table 8), with the additional trend of decreasing overlap from older to newer versions. We are not in a position to definitively explain the trend; one possibility is that newer compiler optimizations lead to less stable O-R configurations in response to minor code changes.

Popular applications (set #3) further confirm the uniqueness of relocations. Five out of the eight applications–*Adobe Reader*, *cmd*, *Firefox*, *Media Player*, and *WinRAR* contain *only non-overlapping* page signatures. This is a particularly important property for applications like *Firefox* and *Media Player* that have only 2-5 page signatures per file. It is notable also that the five *Firefox* versions cover a release period of only eight months (Aug 2013–Apr 2014). The overlap for the remaining three applications (Table 9) stays almost completely in the lowest quantile.

Although malware detection/classification is *not* the main target application of this work codeid can do a thorough job of finding *known* malware executables. Table 10 shows

a summary of our study of set #4 (976,754 page signatures). Almost all the signatures are quite distinct; the only major exceptions are the *backdoor* and (to a lesser degree) *trojan* categories, where full signature overlap is observed in 27.12% and 7.67% of the cases, respectively.

Using similarity hashing [14] and the sdhash tool [16] on the files reveals that the *backdoor* set contains 964 closely related versions of Backdoor.Win32.Hupigon (similarity score 95 out of 100), and it is the main reason for signature collisions. Using the same approach we find that Trojan-Downloader.Win32.Banload contributes 718 near-identical versions accounting for 4.4% of the samples (and collisions) in the category.

In summary, our collision study finds ample evidence for the assertion that page relocation tables provide a set of characteristic attributes for almost any *MS Windows* executable. The only exceptions we found are binaries that are nearly identical, as determined by static analysis.

4.4 Accuracy Analysis

In this section, we measure the effectiveness of codeid on page and file level in both kernel and user space against actual memory captures. We use VMware's VM snapshot mechanism to obtain the RAM targets, which are 2GB in size.

4.4.1 Page-level accuracy

Our first study quantifies the false positive (FP) and false negative (FN) rates for page signatures. For that purpose, we need a method for establishing the ground truth, and due to the uncertainty of paging, simply loading/running the binary is not enough to assume that all pages would be in memory. We need a method to *ascertain* which *individual* pages are *physically* present in memory.

Establishing ground truth. To establish a baseline, we analyze the memory image using *libvmi* [7, 11] library (which is an outgrowth of the earlier work on XenAccess [1]). Unlike our approach, *libvmi* finds and interprets the relevant kernel data structures, such as LDR_DATA_TABLE_ ENTRY, EPROCESS, PEB, and PEB_LDR_DATA. Using this information, it can identify the virtual base address and size of kernel, as well as other executables, including dynamic link libraries (.DLL), applications (.EXE), and kernel modules (.SYS).

Specifically, we employ *libvmi* to map the running processes to a set of physical pages. Using the map, we define specific page targets for codeid; that is, we expect the tool not only to show a match for the correct executable, but also to point to a page owned by the respective process.

Under this definition of the ground truth, we define the four possible experimental outcomes as follows:

- *True Positive* (TP): codeid has identified the correct (memory page) signature *and* the page belongs to the correct process.

- *False Positive* (FP): codeid has identified the wrong signature *or* the page does *not* belong to the correct process.

- *True Negative* (TN): codeid yields *no* match *and* the memory image does *not* contain the target binary.

- *False Negative* (FN): codeid yields *no* match *and* the memory image *does* contain the target binary.

Table 11: Page-level accuracy: kernel modules

Version	Pages	FPR	FNR	Accuracy
XP1	1,517	0.0000	0.0000	1.0000
XP2	2,001	0.0020	0.0000	0.9980
XP3	1,922	0.0000	0.0000	1.0000
Vista0	3,267	0.0083	0.0000	0.9917
Vista1	3,342	0.0009	0.0000	0.9991
Vista2	3,454	0.0026	0.0000	0.9974
Win7	3,790	0.0000	0.0000	1.0000
Win7.1	3,717	0.0016	0.0000	0.9984
Win8	5,193	0.0029	0.0000	0.9871
Win8.1	5,336	0.0002	0.0000	0.9998
Overall	33,539	0.0019	0.0000	0.9981

Table 12: Page-level accuracy:non-kernel processes

Version	Pages	FPR	FNR	Accuracy
XP1	4,992	0.0048	0.0000	0.9952
XP2	5,962	0.0002	0.0000	0.9998
XP3	5,359	0.0011	0.0000	0.9989
Vista0	14,298	0.0034	0.0000	0.9966
Vista1	15,117	0.0064	0.0000	0.9936
Vista2	15,382	0.0000	0.0000	1.0000
Win7	16,232	0.0025	0.0000	0.9975
Win7.1	17,426	0.0007	0.0000	0.9993
Win8	26,128	0.0010	0.0000	0.9990
Win8.1	28,452	0.0039	0.0000	0.9961
Overall	149,348	0.0024	0.0000	0.9976

As it turns out, the criteria are in need of some refinement. The first adjustment is for FP results–in addition to the page mapped to the address space of the running process, `codeid` would also find the original page in the file cache (if present) regardless of whether the process is still running. (From the point of view of `codeid`, it looks as if the binary was loaded exactly at the nominal base address.) This special case can be detected by simply keeping a crypto hash of the page, and–depending on use case–turn hash-based page matches on/off. Therefore, we exclude identical page matches from the FP results.

The second adjustment is necessary for classifying FN outcomes. Upon inspecting preliminary results, we realized that in some cases, although the page is mapped, it contains only `0x00` or `0xFF` bytes. Clearly, such an outcome is a *true* negative–although it trivially satifies equation (1)–so we filter out from the FN set all pages with precisely zero (Shannon) entropy.

For these experiments, we split all the processes found in the memory capture into kernel and non-kernel, and Tables 11 and 12 summarize our respective observations. The first column shows the *MS Windows* version, followed by the total number of pages extracted, the FP rate, the FN rate, and the standard measure of accuracy:

$$Accuracy = \frac{TP + TN}{TP + TN + FP + FN}.$$

The first important observation is that the there are *zero false negatives*. This is to be unexpected–if the page is indeed in memory, it must satisfy the *page_match* predicate.

The presented false positive rate is a conservative estimate and can be further improved–manual examination of a sampling of the false positive results indicate that they are triggered primarily by low (but not zero) entropy pages that could further be filtered out.

Overall, the accuracy–which in the absense is false positives is equal to the *TPR*–is consistently high across both sets. By aggregating the results, we conclude that the overall *page-level* accuracy is 0.9977.

4.4.2 File-level accuracy

For evaluating the file-level accuracy, which would be the user-experienced performance, we considered two case studies–kernel modules and applications.

Kernel accuracy. First, we focus on the classification error across 10 different versions of the kernel modules. The main rationale here is that, unlike other executables, we can clearly attribute the modules to different versions.

There are a total of 182 different (by name) modules across the ten *MS Windows* distributions. Of these, only 26 are ideal targets as they are present in *all* versions. Since that is too small a set, we expanded it to include all modules that occur in at least three versions, which brings our evaluation set to 157.

Table 13 shows the results of matching the memory images (columns) vs. the corresponding file-derived `codeid` signatures (rows); blank cells indicate zeroes. The *GT* column represents the ground truth–the total number of binaries present in the image, as per kernel data structures. The *TPR* column is the TP rate–the ratio of the diagonal element to GT. Thus, the ideal confusion matrix would consist of the diagonal elements matching the corresponging *GT* value, and all other elements set to zero.

The evaluation procedure emulates what our tool does–for each file fingerprint, we match all the page signatures against the memory capture and count the total number of matches. All fingerprints that have signature matches equal to the maximum number of matches are declared a file match. Since more than one version may match the file, row numbers may add up to more than the *GT*.

Based on page-level results, we would expect near-perfect true positive rates across the sets; indeed, with one exception, the rates range from 0.95 to 1.0. The difference in performance is accounted for by differences in the fraction of pages *actually loaded* by the page system. The overall fraction of pages not loaded for all 10 images was only 2.2%–773 out of 33,539; however, the *VistaSP1* image alone had 434 pages (out of 3,342) missing, or 13%. (The latter is probably the result of a snapshot taken too soon after boot.)

Further examination showed that missing pages tend to be clustered, typically in the form of entire modules having no valid pages in memory. Thus, their effects are amplified in our statistics (e.g., a missing module with a 3-page signature represents only 0.1% of the page signatures for *VistaSP1* but a full 1% of the number of kernel modules).

Conceptually, such lapses are not the fault of `codeid` (or any other comparable method) simply because the data to be detected is not present. This underscores the importance of page-level detection, and suggests that page-level performance is a cleaner measure of algorithmic potential, as it excludes the (unpredictable) effects of paging.

The use of *VMware* memory snapshots also presented us with an additional (unplanned) test case–the detection of

Table 13: Kernel modules confusion matrix

	WinXP			Vista			Win7		Win8		GT	TPR
WinXP	60	10	5								61	.9836
	9	79	19								82	.9634
	5	20	74								74	.9600
Vista				95	7						95	1.000
				21	75	45					97	.7732
				15	19	95					95	1.000
Win7							102	57			102	1.000
							58	103			103	1.000
Win8									110		110	1.000
										109	109	1.000

Table 14: *Firefox* 23–29 confusion matrix

Version	23	24	25	26	27	28	29	GT
Firefox 23	3							3
24		2						2
25			2	2				2
26			2	2				2
27					2	1		2
28					1	2	1	2
29						1	2	2

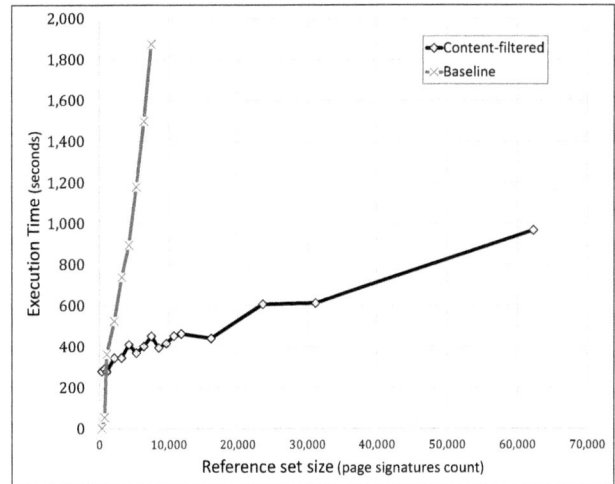

Figure 3: Algorithm speed performance: baseline vs. content-filtered

VMware's own drivers in the image. Since they are identical across all cases, the matches were excluded from Table 13. However, in the initial results, they appeared as background noise in the form of 2-5 additional file matches across *all* cases. The result were illustrative in that page detection per module was either 100%, or 0%, which corresponds to the driver being either loaded, or not.

Application accuracy. In the previous section, we saw that applications tend to have no page signature collisions, which makes the testing of file-level matches a rather trivial pursuit. Therefore, we focused on testing across the different versions of a single application. In an attempt to construct a difficult target, we picked seven consecutive version of *Firefox*–23 through 29–and performed the same analysis as with the kernel case. Recall that *Firefox* has no more than three pages with relocations, and individual releases come every six weeks. Taken together, these present among the most difficult challenges, as we would expect the executable to change only incrementally and a large amount of commonality to be present across the binaries.

Nonetheless, the results in Table 14 show that `codeid` is successful in identifying *all* the pages of the correct executable, and only two neighboring versions (25 and 26) are tied.

4.5 Throughput

Recall that in Section 3.4 we proposed two versions of the fingerprint matching algorithm. Both scan the given memory image page-by-page and match them against the reference set of signatures obtained from the files. The difference between the two is that the first one compares all signatures with each page of memory, whereas the second one scans memory byte-by-byte, reading 32-bits at a time, and identifies more relevant signatures that can be matched with the page. Thus, we would expect the second approach to be more efficient for working with a large number as it shifts the *primary* dependence of processing time from the number of signatures to the size of pages.

We ran our PoC implementations on a 2.6GHz Intel Core i7 CPU using a 2GB target (33,554,432 pages), and normal-ized results to represent time per GB of RAM processed. Initially we use Windows XP SP2 memory dump to search the page signatures of *ntoskrnl.exe* (381 in number) and then later start using the 1,074 signatures of Windows 8.1 kernel.

Figure 3 depicts the throughput of the algorithms as a function of the number of signatures. As we would expect, processing time for both algorithms grows linearly. The baseline version starts much lower but rises at a much steeper angle than the second algorithm, which filters the candidate signatures before comparison; the crossover point is around 1,000 signatures.

Another way to look at the relative performance it to consider throughput in terms of of page-signature matches per second that each version can perform. For the baseline, the relevant number is 2.1–2.5 million for sets of 1,000+, whereas the content-filtered version starts at a comparable 2 million for the 1,074-signature set but steadily rises to 33.8 million for the last set with 62,292 signatures. We should emphasize that our reference implementation is not, of yet, optimized for throughput. There are numerous opportunities to speed up the processing, such as filtering out of pages based on location and/or content, sampling of the signatures, further indexing of the reference set, cache optimization, and concurrent processing. These are beyond the scope of this work, which is primarily targeted at evaluating feasibility and suitability of the proposed technique.

4.6 Comparison with prior work

Recall that prior work focuses on the *specific* problem of identifying OS kernels, and not of identifying code in general. Indeed, the approaches taken have focused on kernel specific privileged instructions, the content of kernel data structures, and special CPU registers, and *cannot* be extended to applications. Thus, for an apples-to-apples comparison, we limit ourselves to identifying kernel versions.

Particularly, we used *MS Windows* kernels for evaluation since they have relocatable code. The Linux kernel, on the other hand is PIE and does not lie within the scope of the paper. Furthermore, we have already argued that finding PIE code is not a difficult problem as we can exactly compute

Table 15: Head-to-head comparison of `codeid` **and** *OS-Sommelier*

Windows Version	*OS-Sommelier*		`codeid`	
	VMware	QEMU	VMware	QEMU
Win Server 2000	✓	✓	✓	✓
Win XP SP1	×	×	✓	✓
Win XP SP2	✓	×	✓	✓
Win XP SP3	✓	✓	✓	✓
Win Vista SP0	✓	✓	✓	✓
Win Vista SP1	✓	✓	✓	✓
Win Vista SP2	×	×	✓	✓
Win 7 SP0	✓	✓	✓	✓
Win 7 SP1	×	×	✓	✓
Win 8	×	×	✓	✓
Win 8.1	×	×	✓	✓

hash of code pages (from the kernel image file) and find them in RAM. Indeed, such an approach would be much simpler and more robust than prior work, and would also cover any other PIE code.

In [3], the authors have performed an extensive evaluation showing that *OS-Sommelier*'s detection capabilities are strictly better than prior approaches based on profiling the kernel implementation using CPU (special) register values, and the contents of the IDT [2].

Therefore, we consider *OS-Sommelier* to be the best representation of the prior state of the art, and the most relevant benchmark for our own work. The authors gracefully provided us with their code so we could perform a head-to-head comparison.

We used both QEMU [12] and VMware to perform the evaluation of `codeid` and *OS-Sommelier* in order to see how sensitive they are. Recall that *OS-Sommelier* needs a memory snapshot of the kernel to generate its signature. We used one set of RAM captures for the signature generation phase, and a different one to perform the actual experiments. Table 15 summarizes the results. As the results show, `codeid` performed perfectly, whereas *OS-Sommelier* encountered a variety of problems, eventually succeeding on only five of the eleven versions tested. Below we briefly summarize our experience with *OS-Sommelier*.

Positive results. The tool was able to successfully generate and recognize both QEMU and VMware images for the following versions: Windows Server 2000, Windows XP SP1 and SP3, Windows Vista SP0 and SP1, Windows 7 SP0.

Inconsistent results. *Windows XP SP2*: The tool was unable to disassemble the pages extracted from QEMU image, which resulted in an "Unknown OS" error both during generation and comparison attempts. However, image from VMware causes no such problems.

Vista SP2 If QEMU image is used to generate signatures, then a VMware-acquired image always gets identified as Vista SP1. Similarly, if VMware image is used as the base, then the corresponding QEMU gets misidentified as Vista SP1.

No results. The tool was unable to generate signatures for Windows 7 SP1, Windows 8, and 8.1. The specific cause of the failure is that the tool cannot find a specific byte pattern–`0f 20 d8 0f 22 d8`–which leads to a crash.

The main takeaway is that the approach taken by *OS-Sommelier* is too complicated and inherently fragile; it needs human input with every new version of the OS. Even more problematic is the high sensitivity to the hypervisor as in an IaaS environment, multiple hypervisor options are the norm.

In contrast, our approach is robust since it only needs the file of the executable (no memory image) to generate the signature and works seemlessly across kernel and application versions. Our technique looks at the code as data and its performance would not be affected by minute details on how the image was acquired. Our method generates perfectly unique signatures for the kernels (Table 7) and detects the exact kernel versions with 100% accuracy.

5. CONCLUSIONS

In this work we considered the problem of identifying known executable code in memory images and proposed a new solution based on using relocation tables as the key identifying characteristic. We showed that relocation tables tend to be quite distinct and, therefore, are an excellent basis for building a unique fingerprint. We demonstrated how the in-file and in-memory version of the pages with relocations can be related as they get transformed by ASLR. In the process, we developed a simple method to calculate the base address of executable.

Unlike prior work, which relies heavily on deep manual analysis and results in fragile methods that are not guaranteed to work on newer versions, *CodeIdentifier* presents a fully automated solution that is fast, accurate, and robust. Our approach is not narrowly focused on kernel version identification but works for any executable, with the kernel being a special use case; the only input required to generate a signature is the file containing the executable. No knowledge of kernel data structures, or any interpretation of the memory capture is necessary.

Our experimental evaluation showed that we can pinpoint individual memory pages as belonging to a known executable with *zero false negatives* and with 99.77% accuracy. We can find trace evidence of prior executions in the file cache and can distinguish them from pages belonging to active processes. *CodeIdentifier* identified perfectly all 11 kernels tested and, in addition, can correctly map kernel modules to their respective *MS Windows* version with a TP rate between 0.96 and 1.00. We showed that our method performs well in distinguishing application with small signatures and close versions. Specifically we demonstrated successful detection and identification of seven consecutive versions of *Firefox*–the most difficult application in our test set.

We have developed a scalable page-signature matching algorithm, which can perform 33.8 million page-signature matches per second (on a sigle core) with a reference set containing over 62,000 page signatures. We expect future work to speed this by at least a factor of 10 by preprocessing the reference set and the memory image.

The main limiting factor to the presented method is the unpredictability of the paging system; our experience shows that, under normal workloads, this is not a notable impediment. Most importantly, the zero false negative rate of our method ensures that, if the target code is in memory, it will be found.

Finally, although not specifically targeted at malware detection, `codeid` can be reliably used for ad-hoc malware signature generation and in-memory scans. This is useful for newly discovered samples (during incident response) before a more succinct signature is derived and incorporated into the security monitoring infrastructure.

6. REFERENCES

[1] W. L. Bryan D. Payne Martim D. P. de A. Carbone. Secure and flexible monitoring of virtual machines. In *Proceedings of the Annual Computer Security Applications Conference*, 2007.

[2] M. Christodorescu, R. Sailer, D. L. Schales, D. Sgandurra, and D. Zamboni. Cloud security is not (just) virtualization security: A short paper. In *Proceedings of the 2009 ACM Workshop on Cloud Computing Security*, CCSW '09, pages 97–102, New York, NY, USA, 2009. ACM.

[3] Y. Gu, Y. Fu, A. Prakash, Z. Lin, and H. Yin. OS-Sommelier: Memory-only operating system fingerprinting in the cloud. In *Proceedings of the Third ACM Symposium on Cloud Computing*, SoCC '12, pages 5:1–5:13, New York, NY, USA, 2012. ACM.

[4] *imageinfo.* https://code.google.com/p/volatility/wiki/CommandReference#imageinfo.

[5] N. L. P. Jr., A. Walters, T. Fraser, and W. A. Arbaugh. Fatkit: A framework for the extraction and analysis of digital forensic data from volatile system memory. *Digital Investigation*, 3(4):197–210, 2006.

[6] *libguestfs.* http://libguestfs.org/.

[7] *libvmi.* http://code.google.com/p/vmitools/.

[8] Z. Lin, J. Rhee, X. Zhang, D. Xu, and X. Jiang. Siggraph: Brute force scanning of kernel data structure instances using graph-based signatures. In *NDSS*, 2011.

[9] R. Love. *Linux Kernel Development.* Addison-Wesley Professional, third edition, 2010.

[10] *nmap.* http://nmap.org/.

[11] B. D. Payne. Simplifying virtual machine introspection using libvmi, 2012. Sandia Report SAND2012-7818, http://prod.sandia.gov/techlib/access-control.cgi/2012/127818.pdf.

[12] *qemu.* http://qemu.org.

[13] N. A. Quynh. Operating system fingerprinting for virtual machines. In *DEFCON 18*, 2010. http://www.defcon.org/images/defcon-18/dc-18-presentations/Quynh/DEFCON-18-Quynh-OS-Fingerprinting-VM.pdf.

[14] V. Roussev. Data fingerprinting with similarity digests. In *Advances in Digital Forensics VI*, pages 207–226. Springer, 2010.

[15] M. E. Russinovich, D. A. Solomon, and A. Ionescu. *Windows Internals: Including Windows Server 2008 and Windows Vista.* Microsoft Press, fifth edition, 2009.

[16] *sdhash.* http://sdhash.org.

[17] *virt-inspector.* http://libguestfs.org/virt-inspector.1.html.

[18] *Volatility.* https://code.google.com/p/volatility/.

[19] *VX Heaven.* http://vxheaven.org.

[20] *Xprobe2.* http://sourceforge.net/projects/xprobe/files/xprobe2/.

Software-Based Protection against Changeware

Sebastian Banescu
Alexander Pretschner
Technische Universität München, Germany
{banescu,pretschn}@cs.tum.edu

Dominic Battré, Stéfano Cazzulani
Robert Shield, Greg Thompson
Google Inc.
{battre,stefanoc,robertshield,grt}@google.com

ABSTRACT

We call *changeware* software that surreptitiously modifies resources of software applications, e.g., configuration files. Changeware is developed by malicious entities which gain profit if their changeware is executed by large numbers of end-users of the targeted software. *Browser hijacking* malware is one popular example that aims at changing web-browser settings such as the default search engine or the home page. Changeware tends to provoke end-user dissatisfaction with the target application, e.g. due to repeated failure of persisting the desired configuration. We describe a solution to counter changeware, to be employed by vendors of software targeted by changeware. It combines several protection mechanisms: white-box cryptography to hide a cryptographic key, software diversity to counter automated key retrieval attacks, and run-time process memory integrity checking to avoid illegitimate calls of the developed API.

Categories and Subject Descriptors

K.6.5 [**Security and Protection**]: Invasive software

Keywords

Software protection; Malware defense; Integrity protection; White-box cryptography; Obfuscation; Software Diversity

1. INTRODUCTION

Some malware surreptitiously attacks the integrity of specific software assets, not their confidentiality or availability. An attack is successful if malware is able to automatically change specific assets of a target software in accordance with the attacker's wishes, when executed on a large number of victims' devices. We call this type of malware *changeware* throughout the remainder of this paper. The typical changeware attack scenario involves three types of participants: (1) The *software vendor* and distributor of a software called X that consists of both read-only binaries (signed by the OS vendor) and editable assets (e.g., configuration files) that

must be modifiable by X; (2) *end-users* of X (victims of changeware) who we assume numerous (thousands to hundreds of millions) and who download X from the Internet; and (3) *changeware developers* who gain a monetary or other advantage proportional to the number of remote systems of legitimate X end-users they successfully attack.

The goal of the changeware developer is to attack a large number of legitimate end-users of X by: (1) creating an automated attack in the form of a computer program (i.e., changeware) and (2) tricking end-users into executing it. Changeware is less complex than other types of malware, because it does not contain exploits to gain root privileges. This is because it does not need such privileges for a successful attack. Therefore, we assume that changeware does not have root privileges during its execution.

If an end-user executes changeware, all *editable* software resources (assets) associated with X, i.e., not protected by the underlying operating system (OS) code signature verification mechanism, are subject to unsolicited modification because changeware has the same privileges as the currently authenticated OS user. Note that modification of non-editable software assets such as application binaries signed by the OS vendor are detected and signaled to the end-user by the OS. However, applications generally also need editable resources (e.g. configuration files), which are prone to unsolicited modification attacks. One popular example is browser-hijacking if X is a web-browser.

These attacks have become popular nowadays because of the possibility of bundling changeware with benign software into the same executable installer. The end-user (victim) is tricked into installing a seemingly legitimate software (i.e., digitally signed by a trusted vendor) which also installs changeware transparently for the victim. The high success-rate of this social-engineering step of the attack is appealing to changeware developers since it eliminates the task of bypassing network and operating-system security mechanisms (e.g. firewalls, authentication).

Unfortunately, changeware is not detected by most commercial anti-virus software, as a consequence of its seemingly legitimate behavior. Changeware modifies software assets belonging to the same OS user under whose privileges the attacked software is also running. Since access control in OSs like Microsoft Windows, Linux, Mac OS, etc. is user-centric and not application-centric, changeware has the right to edit assets that belong to other applications.

Changeware can also write the memory of any other process running under the same OS user privileges. Several OSs (see Section 3.4.1) even offer the possibility to start a thread

CODASPY'15, March 2–4, 2015, San Antonio, Texas, USA.
ACM 978-1-4503-3191-3/15/03.
http://dx.doi.org/10.1145/2699026.2699099 .

inside a process, which executes code that was previously written to (*injected into*) the process memory by changeware. To make things more difficult, on Windows OSs, code injection, in the form of dynamic-link library (DLL) injection, is also executed by benign software (e.g. anti-virus applications) and therefore not considered malicious.

Leveraging a *trusted entity* such as additional hardware (e.g. the Trusted Platform Module[30], smart-cards), to protect the integrity of software assets is possible. Such trusted entities contain a hardware protected secret-key which can be used to compute a message authentication code of software asset values. However, such a trusted entity implies additional costs for end-users, usage or setup inconvenience and possibly privacy concerns. Another approach for defending against changeware would be to re-authenticate the end-user via the OS password prompt, whenever changes to software assets occur. This way, writing to software assets is done by the OS kernel, which only performs the changes if the user confirms the changes via re-authentication. However, this would negatively impact user experience and may become too tedious for practical use. Therefore, a solution which is transparent to the end-user is preferable.

This paper addresses the problem of how to protect editable software assets and makes the following contributions:

1. A novel software-only solution against changeware that (a) can be directly employed by the targeted software vendor; (b) is transparent to the end-user; and (c) does not require communication with trusted entities. The solution leverages three distinct protection mechanisms: *white-box cryptography* [5], *software diversity* [13], and *run-time process memory invariant checking*.

2. A set of data obfuscation transformations at the level of source code. These hide the position of white-box cryptographic ciphers inside the data segment of an executable binary.

3. An inter-process run-time checking mechanism via code injection. This verifies that synchronous function calls are the ones intended by the software vendor. Verification is performed against a white-list of fixed-size precomputed OS version-dependent signatures of the call-stack of the calling thread and its associated code.

4. An implementation and evaluation of our solution in the form of a case-study on protecting the Chromium web-browser user preference against browser hijacking.

The remainder of this paper is structured as follows. After briefly presenting related work (Section 2), we describe our solution in Section 3, the core of this paper. We evaluate and discuss guarantees and limitations in Sections 4 and 5. Finally, conclusions and directions for future work are presented in Section 6.

2. RELATED WORK

Since our candidate solution encompasses white-box cryptographic primitives, software diversity and run-time integrity checking, we structure related work accordingly.

2.1 White-Box Cryptography

White-box cryptography (WBC) was pioneered by Chow *et al.* [6, 5], who proposed the first white-box DES, respectively white-box AES (WB-AES) ciphers in 2002. The goal of white-box cryptography is the secure storage of secret keys (used by cryptographic ciphers), in software, without hardware keys or trusted entities. Instead of storing the secret key of a cryptographic cipher separately from the actual cipher logic, white-box cryptography embeds the key inside the cipher logic. For instance, for AES ciphers, the key can be embedded by multiplication with the T-boxes of each encryption round [12]. However, simply embedding the key in the T-boxes of AES is prone to key extraction attacks since the specification of AES is publicly known. Therefore, WB-AES implementations use complex techniques to prevent key extraction attacks, e.g., wide linear encodings [32], perturbations to the cipher equations [2] and dual-ciphers [21].

The idea behind the white-box approach in [5] is to encode the internal AES cipher logic (functions) inside lookup tables (LUTs). One extreme and impractical instance of this idea is to encode all plaintext-ciphertext pairs corresponding to an AES cipher with a 128-bit key, as a LUT with 2^{128} entries, where each entry consists of 128-bits. Such a LUT would leak no information about the secret-key but exceed the storage capacity of currently available devices. However, this LUT-based approach also works for transforming internal AES functions (e.g. XOR functions, AddRoundKey, SubBytes and MixColumns [12]) to table lookups, which can be divided such that they have a smaller input and output size. Moreover, LUTs can also be used to encode random invertible bijective functions, which are used to further obfuscate the LUTs representing internal AES functions. This leads to an implementation which is much more compact in terms of storage, in the order of megabytes. However, it is also less resilient to cryptanalysis attacks than the single huge LUT instance mentioned before. Nonetheless, such a white-box cryptographic cipher still requires a higher workfactor (i.e. $\leq 2^{22}$ [24]), relative to attacks on systems which store the encryption key separately from the cipher logic [27].

The last decade has seen many new and improved white-box cipher proposals [2, 25, 32, 21]. Several research efforts have also been focused on key extraction of proposed white-box ciphers via cryptanalysis [1, 31, 26, 10, 9]. However, these attacks assume that the location and structure of the LUTs used by the white-box ciphers is known or can be easily recovered from its binary file. Changeware writers must create software, which executed with no administrator privileges can: (1) automatically extract the secret keys from *a large number* of white-box cipher instances one of which is deployed on any victim's machine; and (2) use the corresponding secret keys to change the values of assets on the corresponding machines. In order to counter such automated attacks against white-box ciphers, we employ software diversity, presented in Section 2.2.

2.2 Software Diversity

The intuition behind software diversity stems from biology where biodiversity implicitly serves as a species survival mechanism against disease and viruses [33]. Similarly, it has been shown that software diversity is able to neutralize attacks tailored for a particular software instance, when applied to diverse software instances [13].

Software diversity comes in different flavors, e.g. N-version programming [4], system configuration diversity [17], automated software transformations [14], etc. In our work we use automated software transformations, because they offer a good trade-off between the effectiveness against auto-

232

mated secret key extraction attacks against white-box cryptographic ciphers and the cost of generating diverse cipher instances (e.g. N-version programming of white-box cryptographic ciphers would have much higher costs).

The seminal work of Forrest *et al.* [13] shows how software diversity can protect against some stack-based attacks (e.g. code-injection). Modern operating systems implement a variant of the ideas introduced in [13], called *address space layout randomization* (ASLR), which diversifies the base addresses of large program objects (e.g. code segment, data segment). However, ASLR cannot counter changeware, which directly changes user editable software assets and uses legitimate OS APIs to inject code into the target software process. Section 3.3 presents the software transformations we employed to generate diverse WB-AES cipher instances, in order to withstand changeware attacks.

2.3 Run-time Integrity Checking

Software self-checking augments code so that it can protect itself against unauthorized modifications. This protection is useful for software which includes functionality that an illegal user may want to circumvent, e.g. license checking. Self-checking is performed by *guards* [3] or *testers* [18]. As the program executes code guards/testers read a range of instructions from memory and compare their hash against a precomputed value. Such techniques are effective against attacks which hot-patch the target software, however they are not effective against changeware which injects code into a process and starts a remote thread.

Jacobson *et al.* [19] define *conformant program execution* as a set of run-time checks on program states, where a state represents elements of a machine that are affected by program execution (e.g. registers and memory). The two elements which characterize the program state are the program counter (PC) and the call stack (currently active stack frames). They dynamically construct a *call multigraph* (CMG) for a target binary, where nodes represent procedures and arcs represent procedure calls. The CMG is constructed at load time via disassembly, afterwards the program's execution is monitored. At every system-call, their run-time monitor checks for inconsistencies: (1) between the call stack and the CMG and (2) between the PC and the valid program instructions, which are recovered during disassembly. If the procedure call sequence on the stack is not a path in the CMG or if the PC does not point to a valid instruction, then the program execution is non-conformant and it is terminated to prevent code-reuse attacks such as return- and jump-oriented programming.

In contrast, our technique does not construct a CMG for the target binary at load-time. Instead, a subgraph of the CMG is constructed by the vendor before installation on the end-user system. The CMG subgraph can hence be constructed directly from source code, which eliminates the problem of incomplete or incorrect x86 disassembly [11, Chapter 1]. This CMG subgraph only involves the paths which end with procedures that modify software assets. During execution of the target program our checks do not require code disassembly, because they operate directly on the binary. Hence, we do not check if each PC points to a valid program instruction, but instead we compute a single hash of all code segments where each PC points to, and compare this to a value pre-computed by the vendor. Our run-time integrity check arguably has a lower impact on program performance because it is only executed when changes are made to software assets.

3. APPROACH

The scenario in the introduction assumes X to be used by huge numbers of end-users and targeted by changeware developers. In the following we assume that X has in the order of 100 MBs or more of read-only binaries, and that X needs to modify its editable assets at most once per second. We further assume that the code for the modification of the editable assets consists of a fixed set of non-recursive call sequences, i.e. there are no unpredictable call sequences that modify assets. This assumption will be crucial for our authentication approach presented in Section 3.4.2.

Our goal is to protect the integrity of a set of software assets associated with an application targeted by changeware. One straightforward solution is to use a (secret) key to compute a message authentication code (MAC) of the software asset values on the end-user system, whenever they are changed by the target application. This requires embedding the key inside the application binary which is shipped to the end-user. Because cryptographic keys are small chunks of high-entropy data (e.g., an AES key has 128 bits) and application code has lower entropy, the keys can be extracted automatically in linear time with respect to the size of the binary file of the target application [27].

3.1 Protect Key with White-Box AES

To counter entropy-based key extraction attacks, we use the WB-AES technique of Chow et al. [5], which embeds the key into a network of LUTs (Section 2.1). This key is used to compute message authentication codes (MACs) for integrity checking, and to compute encrypted assets for restoration purposes (Section 3.4).

MAC verification requires that the secret key of the WB-AES cipher be persisted between shut-down and start-up of X. This is the case when using WB-AES with an embedded key. Unfortunately, the WB-AES cipher which is stored in a binary located on the end-user system is prone to automated key-extraction attacks [1, 24]. However, these attacks assume that the location and structure of the LUTs of the WB-AES cipher inside the target binary are known. This is a fair assumption given that WB-AES LUTs are large in size and have a high entropy. Nevertheless, a LUT based WB-AES instance consists of thousands of LUTs with different structures and high entropy, which are each used at a specific point (round) of the cipher operation. Therefore, a practical attack would also require identifying which LUTs from the target binary have which function in the white-box cipher [29]. To increase the work-factor for WB-AES LUT identification, in Section 3.2 we present how several *syntactically different* and *semantically equivalent* binary instances of X can be automatically generated using software diversity through randomized obfuscation transformations.

3.2 Prevent Automated Attacks with Diversity

Software diversity can be used to generate a different binary instance for each end-user or generate different instances for groups of end-users (see below). Since the changeware developer does not know which end-user has which binary, s/he must develop an attack effective against all diverse instances of X. We argue that such a universally effective changeware must take a *trial-and-error* approach towards extracting the WB-AES key from a binary, due to the randomized obfuscation transformations applied to every diverse binary instance. Therefore, even if the changeware developer is fully aware of the obfuscation transformation types which are applied, due to randomness of transformation parameters s/he has to search through several possible WB-AES LUT configurations and run a cryptanalysis attack [1, 24] on each configuration. The correctness of every key extracted by a cryptanalysis attack must be checked by using it to encrypt the legitimate settings with a plain AES cipher and verifying that the the ciphertext matches the one computed by the WB-AES cipher.

However, software diversity raises the following concerns:

- *Storage and distribution costs* increase proportionally with the number of diverse release builds of X.

- *Differential updates* are harder to generate and push to end-users, because different instances require different update patches. Moreover, these updates become larger in size, because diverse instances contain many differences relative to each other.

- *Crash analysis servers* run by the software vendor must store the debugging symbols of every existing version of X. Upon receiving a *crash report* containing a snapshot of X's memory, the crash analysis servers must map this report to the corresponding debugging symbols, to perform a correct analysis.

- *Time-stamping binary signatures* is necessary to preserve the validity of the signature for X, even after the signing certificate expires [16]. However, time-stamping requires use of a limited rate Internet service offered by the OS vendor, which is the main bottleneck in case thousands of instances of X require time-stamping their digital signatures.

To address these concerns, we propose to separate the WB-AES cipher code from the source code of X. Therefore, X runs in a separate process from the WB-AES cipher, which will be referred to as *WBCrypto* throughout the remainder of this paper. It can be signed by the vendor of X rather than the vendor of the OS, and it acts as a gateway to any legitimate persistent modifications of assets associated with X, i.e., all asset change requests will be delegated to WBCrypto. We call *WBCrypto proxy* the functions of X which delegate the asset change requests to WBCrypto, i.e., the functions which call the WBCrypto API directly and pass it a string command indicating what changes should be made to which assets.

Yet, even though we now have overcome the above concerns, remember that we assumed X to have huge numbers of users. Generating one WBCrypto instance per user then is prohibitive because of time, storage and electric energy requirements. And even if generating different binaries for such a huge user-base was feasible, it would raise privacy concerns because each end-user could now be uniquely identified by the vendor of X. An improvement of this approach is to generate a smaller number (m) of diverse instances (e.g. several thousands) each being indexed from 0 to $m-1$. A WBCrypto instance with index $i \in \{0, ..., m-1\}$ is distributed to an end-user if the unique system identifier (id) of his machine (e.g. file-system UUID [23], Windows SID [15]) satisfies the following relation: $id \bmod m = i$. This leads to m groups of thousands of end-users having the same binary, which offers anonymity of an end-user in the group of

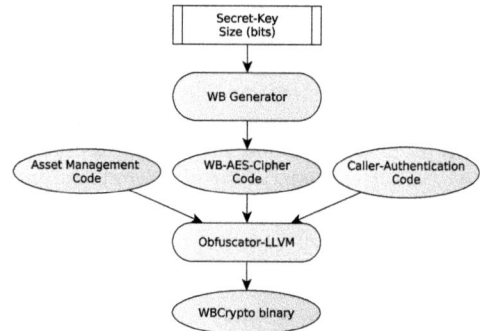

Figure 1: Server-side work-flow

users which have the same key [28] and still raises the bar for changeware.

The life-cycle of WBCrypto can be described in two stages. The first stage occurs before WBCrypto is distributed to end-users. It consists of generating diverse WBCrypto instances and occurs on trusted build-servers owned by the software vendor. The second stage occurs after WBCrypto is distributed to end-users. It consists of the operation of WBCrypto on a local system of an end-user.

3.3 Server-Side Generation of WBCrypto

We have implemented a C++ code generator which we call the *WB Generator*. It is hosted on trusted-build servers of the software vendor and can produce white-box AES cipher instances using the LUT-based technique introduced by Chow *et al.* [5]. The WB generator employs both *key-diversity* and *software-diversity*. Key-diversity implies generating different random keys, to mitigate the impact of successful key extraction from one application instance. Specifically, if an attacker extracts the key embedded in his/her WB-AES instance, s/he will not be able to use the same key to manipulate software assets of all other end-users of X (or, if keys are created for groups of users, to manipulate assets in different groups). Software-diversity is employed via data and control-flow obfuscation transformations which increase the attacker's effort for extracting the position and structure of the WB-AES LUTs from any binary instance. Specifically, if an attacker is able to reverse engineer his own copy of WBCrypto and extracts the offset values of the WB-AES LUTs, s/he will not be able to use the same offsets to extract the LUTs from (all) other instances of WBCrypto.

Our current WB generator implementation is limited to the AES cipher with various key sizes (128, 192, 256 bits). In future work we plan to incorporate different block ciphers (e.g. DES, Blowfish) and other WBC techniques [2, 25, 32, 21]. The WB Generator is OS independent and can be used to generate diverse WB-AES ciphers.

Figure 1 shows the work-flow for generating a WBCrypto module on the server-side. The upper part shows the WB generator, which takes as input the key size of the AES cipher. The WB generator first generates a random key and subsequently the LUTs of the WB-AES cipher for the corresponding key. Finally, the WB generator writes the LUTs and instructions for WB-AES en-/de-cryption to a C++ source file. Remember that there is one key, and hence one WBCrypto instance, per group of users.

In order to prevent automatic retrieval of LUTs and thus automatic extraction of the secret key, a second step is to obfuscate the source code using the transformations presented in the following paragraphs. The output of the WB generator is a C++ source file which must be compiled together with *asset management* code and *caller authentication* code (see Section 3.4). The outputs of the server-side work-flow from Figure 1 are diverse WBCrypto binaries which are shipped to random groups of end-users.

Randomization of Unused Nibbles.

WBCrypto instances contain over a thousand LUTs which represent randomly encoded versions of the XOR function, which have an 8-bit input and a 4-bit output. For efficiency reasons, the possible output values are stored in 1 byte chunks instead of packing two 4-bit values inside of one byte. This means that such lookup tables may be easily identified in the data segment of the WBCrypto binary because they contain values of the form 0x0?, i.e. only the lowest nibble is used. An attacker could use this pattern to automatically identify the position of the XOR tables in a WBCrypto binary, with high probability of success. Therefore, we obfuscate the representation of these LUTs by transforming their high-nibble from zeros to random values.

Interleave LUTs with Random Data.

In the C++ output of the WB generator, a WB-AES LUT is represented by a statically initialized multi-dimensional array. This means that the bytes corresponding to LUTs are placed in the data segment of the compiled binary. Therefore, they are not affected by ASLR. Hence the LUTs will always be loaded at the same virtual address, relative to the base address of WBCrypto's process memory. An attacker who finds these offsets can use them to extract the LUTs from any WBCrypto binary instance.

We employ an obfuscation technique that adds randomly sized statically initialized arrays containing garbage data in between the initialization of the LUTs used by the WB-AES cipher. Due to the high entropy of the LUTs used by the WB-AES cipher, the added garbage arrays cannot be distinguished from the WB-AES LUTs using entropy analysis. This obfuscation technique enlarges the search space of the attacker directly proportional to the number and size of the garbage arrays. This leads to a trade-off between the size of the WBCrypto binary and the size of the search space of the attacker, which we discuss in Section 4.

Control-Flow Obfuscation.

For the purpose of control-flow obfuscation we employ *instruction substitution* [7], *opaque predicate insertion* [8] and *control-flow flattening* [22] techniques. These techniques are implemented by the open-source compile-time obfuscation engine *Obfuscator-LLVM* [20] (lower green-rounded-rectangle in Figure 1). These obfuscation transformations change the form of references to the WB-AES LUTs inside the code segment of WBCrypto. We also employ anti-disassembly techniques [11, Chapter 21], to prevent changeware from disassembling the WBCrypto binary and extracting the address of the WB-AES LUTs from assembly code.

3.4 Client-Side Operation of WBCrypto

WBCrypto computes and stores a MAC and possibly the ciphertext of software assets upon installation and whenever these values are *written* by X. On start-up, or more generally, whenever the asset is *read*, WBCrypto computes a new MAC for comparison purposes. For restoration purposes,

it may also compute the ciphertext of the current values of X's software assets. If the MACs differ, then changes were made to its assets while X was offline or, more generally, in-between the last read and write operations on assets, and the end-user is notified. If the end-user does not agree with the changes, then s/he can restore the previous version of the assets by decrypting the last good known version. If changeware repeatedly changes the assets, each modification will lead to a notification, which is likely to quickly annoy the user. Therefore, the replacement with the known good value can also be done automatically. If there is only a MAC but no known good version, then default settings can be restored. It is also possible to retrieve any last good known version of the assets if a backup copy of that version of the encrypted software assets has been stored on cloud storage by the end-user. Because they are encrypted, asset values are not disclosed to the cloud service provider. Such a backup also ensures that software assets can be restored even if changeware deletes the ciphertext from local storage.

Remember that having WBCrypto as a self standing software module has several advantages compared to integrating the WB-AES code inside X's binary. WBCrypto is relatively small in size (a few MBs) compared to X and can therefore be built, shipped and updated separately. The crash analysis process is unaffected since only WBCrypto is diversified, not X itself. Since WBCrypto is only used by X, its authenticity can be ensured by a digital certificate signed by the vendor of X and not by the OS vendor. The WBCrypto code verification key—which is not the secret-key embedded in WBCrypto—can therefore be hard-coded inside X's binary, which eliminates the need for time-stamping the binary signature of all the diverse instances of WBCrypto by the service of the OS vendor which is a potential bottleneck. We may thus assume that X is able to verify the integrity of the WBCrypto binary.

3.4.1 Malicious Calls to WBCrypto

However, separating the WB-AES cipher and X into distinct binaries also has disadvantages. Most importantly, it opens up another attack vector. The interface of WBCrypto, which previously was only internally accessible to X, is now accessible by changeware. To prevent calls performed by changeware to the WBCrypto interface, we need a run-time checking mechanism which can discriminate between calls intended by the software vendor (*benign calls*) and other calls which we consider to be *malicious calls*.

One approach towards authenticating the caller of the WBCrypto interface is to simply check if the calling process has several characteristics of X, e.g. the loaded library modules are those which are supposed to be loaded by X. However, not all calls originating from a particular process are necessarily benign. Consider a simple defense mechanism which merely checks whether or not the calling process is in a set of benign processes. On Microsoft Windows OSs, such a defense mechanism is vulnerable to the attack illustrated in Figure 2, where a malicious process (M) injects code into the benign process (e.g. X) and then starts a remote thread which surreptitiously calls WBCrypto proxy functions. In this case the call will appear to come from a benign process, however it should not be executed by WBCrypto, because it is not the behavior intended by the vendor of X.

Code injection and remote thread creation do not require exploiting a vulnerability in X, because the Windows API

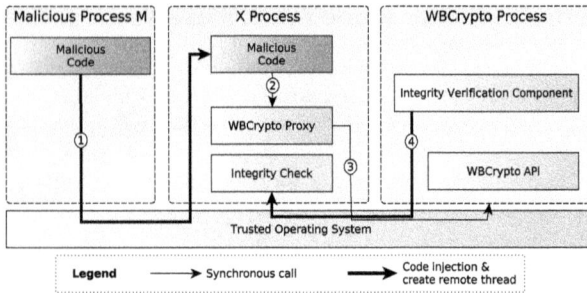

Figure 2: Malicious Call-Path and Caller Authentication

offers functions which can perform such actions on any process running under the same OS user, i.e. `WriteProcessMemory` and `CreateRemoteThread`.[1]

3.4.2 Caller Authentication

A skillful attacker could develop changeware such that it has the same call-stack structure as X, i.e. the return addresses on the call-stack of changeware point to the same code offsets as the return addresses on the call-stack of X. On the other hand, an attacker could also develop changeware such that its code pages would contain the code pages of X, yet its call-stack structure would be different. However, if both the code and the call-stack structure of changeware are the same as in X, then the changeware can be considered equivalent to X, hence benign software. Moreover, we do not exclude changeware which tampers with the code of X after it is loaded in process memory if that code page is writable. Therefore, we compare precomputed *known good values* with both (1) the call-stack structure and (2) the code to where the return addresses on the call-stack point to. This allows us to effectively detect malicious calls to the WBCrypto API as described in Section 3.4.1.

We define a *call-path* as a chain of (synchronous, blocking) function calls (possibly across thread or process boundaries) such that the last function in this chain is a WBCrypto proxy function. A call-path is uniquely identified by a fixed size hash value computed from the concatenation of all the relative return addresses on the call-stacks of the execution threads which performed the function calls, and the memory pages to which the return addresses on the stacks point to.

The set of all *benign call-paths*, representing the intended behavior of X, is fixed by its vendor before deployment on the end-user systems. This set is distributed as a read-only white-list signed by the software vendor, created by:

1. Generate the call-graph of X, e.g., by using the Callgrind tool of Valgrind (http://valgrind.org/);

---

[1]This kind of attack is also possible on current Debian Linux and was also possible on Ubuntu Linux before August 2011, via the `ptrace` system call, which is generally used by debuggers. Current Ubuntu Linux versions use a system flag called `ptrace_scope`, which by default allows a non-root process to attach via `ptrace` only to its child processes or children of the debugger, see https://wiki.ubuntu.com/Security/Features#ptrace. Nonetheless, this default setting is often changed by a root user to enable operation of some applications, e.g. Mono applications, Qt Creator, GNU Debugger, etc. Moreover, we do not exclude buffer overflow exploits for X, which aim at changing the control flow of X such that it calls the WBCrypto API in order to surreptitiously change the values of software assets.

2. Select the paths in the call-graph which end in a call to the WBCrypto API, i.e. WBCrypto proxy functions;

3. Compute and store hash values of invariants of all selected paths (see below).

Any call-path hash value not included in this white-list is considered to be a *malicious call-path*.

At runtime, the *caller authentication code* of WBCrypto (mid-right blue-oval in Figure 1), computes the call-path hash for every API call it gets from a process P, to the function which sets the value of a software asset. If the call-path hash value is in the white-list, then WBCrypto executes the API call it received from P, otherwise it discards it. This guarantees that all of the attacks presented in Section 3.4.1 will be unsuccessful in surreptitiously changing the values of the software assets.

The caller authentication implementation consists of 3 phases, executed whenever any process (denoted P) makes a call to the WBCrypto API, sending it a string command v, which indicates persistent changes to software assets should be made. Fighting fire with fire, in the first phase WBCrypto injects an *integrity check* routine into the calling process X, using the API of the trusted OS, i.e. step 4 in Figure 2. In the second phase, the previously injected code is executed in a dedicated execution thread ($T1$) inside P. This thread performs the following steps:

1. To compute the hash value of the current call path, which we will later compare to the precomputed legal paths, we first need to identify the thread ($T2$) inside the process memory of P which called any known WBCrypto proxy function, from software X's binary. This is done by traversing the stack of each thread in P, searching for a return address pointing inside any WBCrypto proxy function (denoted S), having a pointer to the string command v on the same stack frame as the return address to S. This guarantees that $T2$ ends with a synchronous call to the WBCrypto proxy function with argument v (i.e. $S(v)$), corresponding to the command received by WBCrypto, which triggered caller authentication. If $T2$ is found, we continue with step 2, otherwise if $T2$ is not found, caller authentication stops and denies the authentication.

2. If $T2$ is identified, then this is the thread which made the call to the WBCrypto API for persistent asset changes. We extract the *absolute* return addresses from each stack frame by iterating over $T2$'s stack one word at a time, starting from the stack base address. On each stack frame we will find the value of the previous frame pointer (EBPs), which we recognize because it points to lower memory addresses on the same stack. The value of the absolute return addresses is the first double-word under the EBP.

3. The *relative* return address is obtained by subtracting the base address of the dynamic library module where the relative address points to, from the absolute return address. The relative return address is relevant because it is invariant with regard to different executions of the target software on the same OS version.

4. We compute a hash: (a) of the code pages where each absolute return address points to and (b) of the relative return address values. This hash uniquely identifies

236

the stack structure with relative return addresses and the code associated with $T2$'s stack.

5. Because call-paths may cross thread boundaries, we recurse on step 1. This time, instead of searching for a WBCrypto proxy function, we search for functions which may have triggered the WBCrypto API call of $T2$. These functions are known by the vendor of X because they constitute the intended behavior of X. If we did not consider call-paths which span over different threads, an attacker could take advantage of this and trigger a call to the WBCrypto API via a legitimate thread $T2$, which would be seen as a benign call by WBCrypto.

The output of this algorithm is a hash of the concatenated hash values from all threads in one call-path.

In the third phase, WBCrypto waits for thread $T1$ to finish and retrieves its return value, i.e. the call-path hash value. It is subsequently compared to white-list entries.

3.4.3 Message Authentication

We have implemented *caller authentication* described in Section 3.4.2 for the Chromium open-source web-browser, where changeware attacks are represented by hijacking browser user preferences. Our implementation is specific to Microsoft Windows OSs, for which browser hijacking changeware often comes pre-packed with other software such as toolbars and are therefore installed by mistake by end-users.

Our implementation detects if a malicious thread directly/synchronously calls the WBCrypto proxy functions in Chromium. However, if changeware is able to asynchronously post a call to WBCrypto via a legitimate call-path, then the caller authentication will consider this call benign and it will execute it. This problem occurs for asynchronous (non-blocking) function calls, which break a call-path in separate synchronous parts. This causes every call before and including the last asynchronous function call to be discarded from the call-path, which is verified via caller authentication. We call this problem *message authentication*, because the asynchronous function calls may be seen as messages which are sent/posted from callers to callees.

We envision an attack where a malicious thread can surreptitiously change asset values by delegating this task to a legitimate thread, via asynchronous message passing. In the first step of this attack, changeware injects code into the target process. Subsequently this injected code posts a message to a legitimate thread, hence delegating a call to the WBCrypto proxy functions.

We acknowledge that asynchronous inter-thread communication is frequently encountered in applications, because such an architecture offers better performance and UI responsiveness. Therefore, we also implemented a proof-of-concept mechanism for message authentication.

The motivation for message authentication is the need to verify that only legitimate threads possibly asynchronously posted the message which led to a WBCrypto API call. For this purpose, legitimate threads are identified via application internal IDs, instead of via OS assigned thread IDs. To query if a legitimate thread sent a message which led to a WBCrypto API call, we add a private data structure (Θ_x) to the thread local storage of each browser thread (T_x). The memory address of thread local storage is assumed to be unknown by other threads, because it is randomly chosen by

the OS kernel. A malicious thread hence cannot locate and modify Θ_x belonging to a legitimate thread T_x. Θ_x stores *only* those messages (denoted θ) posted by this thread that contain API calls to WBCrypto.

To notify WBCrypto about which Chromium thread made the call, we modify the WBCrypto proxy functions to send the internal ID indicated by the thread (T_x) which posted the message. Note that this ID value can be spoofed by a malicious thread, which does not have this ID such that a message appears to have been posted by a benign thread.

Due to message asynchronicity each hash value in the call-path white-list needs to be associated with a set of benign threads, which are allowed to perform the corresponding call-path. In our implementation we only allow the Chromium *main thread* to post messages containing API calls to WBCrypto. We ensure this by only including hashes corresponding to legitimate call-paths in the white-list.

The last step enables WBCrypto to compute the call-path hash value only if T_x is associated with any call-path in the white-list. Using the previous modifications, the integrity checking module in our caller-authentication thread inside the Chromium process can post a message to T_x "asking" if it sent θ. A malicious thread will never be "asked" anything, because Chromium uses internal IDs (not OS assigned thread IDs) to identify special browser threads such as the main thread. Using a whitelist of internal thread IDs, we can ensure that only threads which have an internal ID are allowed to post messages which call WBCrypto proxy functions. T_x receives the "question" from the integrity checking module and replies affirmative only if θ is in its local Θ_x. If T_x replies affirmative, then the integrity check thread continues to compute the call-path hash value as in the original caller authentication algorithm, otherwise is returns an invalid hash value to WBCrypto.

4. EVALUATION

4.1 Performance Evaluation

4.1.1 WB Generator

We tested the WB generator on an average system with 2 CPU cores and 8 GB of RAM. We generated thousands of WB-AES instances having distinct key sizes and different numbers of random tables of various sizes added to them. The maximum and median sizes of the C++ files and compiled WB-AES instances are shown in Table 1 as a function of the cipher key size. The sizes are larger than the tens of kilo-bytes needed by a standard AES implementation. Compressing them would only negligibly reduce their size, because of the LUTs' high entropy. However, compared to the total size of Chromium binaries, it is roughly 2.5%. The size of the WB-AES instances in fact motivated our respective general space assumption in Section 1.

The maximum and median times to generate and compile the C++ WB-AES instances are shown in Table 2 as a function of the key size. We believe it is possible to significantly improve the median generation and compilation time (ca. 1 min.) by a multi-threaded implementation of the WB generator, which we leave to future work.

We also measured the run-time performance of all the generated WB-AES instances. The time needed to WB encrypt a file grows linearly with the size of the plaintext. The average time needed to WB encrypt 1 mega-byte of data using

	Max C++	Max bin	Med C++	Med bin
AES-128	115	20	15	2.6
AES-192	164	27	18	4.5
AES-256	166	26	20	4.8

Table 1: Size (**mega-bytes**) of C++ and binary WB-AES instances (Chromium binaries ≈100MBs)

	Max Gen	Max Cpl	Med Gen	Med Cpl
AES-128	475	154	40	12
AES-192	1075	326	37	16
AES-256	1049	239	32	22

Table 2: Time (**seconds**) to generate C++ WB-AES instances

AES-128, AES-192 and AES-256 is 3.25 seconds, 3.56 seconds, respectively 4.11 seconds. This average is significantly slower than using the latest version of *openssl* to encrypt the same file, which takes 25, 27, respectively 30 milliseconds. This does not pose any problems if we use our approach to check integrity breaches (compute and compare MACs), but not necessarily repair them (compute and compare encrypted files), see Section 3.4. Moreover, this does not pose serious problems under the assumption of Section 1 that asset files are rarely written. Both clearly is the case for our Chromium case-study where (1) we encrypt only a few kilo-bytes, or even far less if we use our approach solely to compute a MAC; and (2) settings files are changed rarely.

4.1.2 WBCrypto

Our PoC implementation only influences executions which trigger a call to the WBCrypto API. Other executions are not impacted, which keeps resource consumption minimal.

We have measured the time needed to perform both caller authentication and message authentication on a machine having an Intel Xeon E5645 CPU with 6 cores running at a frequency of 2.4 GHz. The Microsoft Windows 7 OS load has been set to an average value of 100 running processes containing over 1000 threads in total. The results showed that caller authentication execution time averages at 134 milliseconds after a few hundred runs, with a maximum time of 145 milliseconds. Computing the hash over the code pages to where the return address points to is linear with respect to the code size and takes about 48% of the total execution time. Iterating over the portable executable (PE) relocation table and setting the indicated offsets to a constant fixed value takes about 42% of the total execution time. This step is necessary to ensure that hashes computed over the code pages do not contain random addresses set by ASLR. The remaining 10% of the execution time is required for finding the thread which made the call to the WBCrypto API, and iterating over its call-stack. The execution time difference between message authentication and caller authentication varies between 19 and 50 milliseconds.

Since user preference changes are an infrequent event in every-day browser usage, even such a delay arguably does not have negative impact on the end-user experience, because it does not freeze the browser UI and it is small enough to pass until the user gets a chance to notice it.

4.2 Security Evaluation

The attack tree in Figure 3 shows the attack space for a changeware developer. The root of the tree represents the goal to persistently change the values of software assets without being detected. Effective changeware may: (1) use the secret key to re-compute asset MAC values after modifying

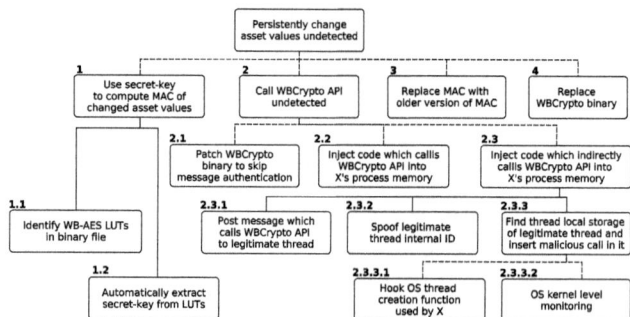

Figure 3: Attack Tree (dashed OR-edges, solid AND-edges)

them, (2) call the WBCrypto API such that it is not detected by the integrity check of message authentication, (3) replace the asset value and its MAC with an older value which fits the attacker's interest or (4) replace the WBCrypto binary with a rogue or cracked version. The following sub-sections present each of these attacks in detail.

4.2.1 LUT Search-Space Increase

Assume that a browser-hijacking changeware writer is able to reverse-engineer the WBCrypto instance on his local system such that s/he knows: (1) WBCrypto uses the WB-AES cipher of Chow *et al.* [5] (2) the size and structure of the useful LUTs and (3) the additional obfuscation transformations described in Section 3.3. Even with this knowledge the changeware developer must, for each instance of WBCrypto, implement a search algorithm to identify the memory offset of the LUTs in the data segment of the WBCrypto binary (node 1.1 in Figure 3). Let n be the total size of the added garbage LUTs in bytes and let k be the number of useful LUTs of the WB-AES cipher. On average, changeware has to perform a key-extraction attack $(n+k)!/2$ times, because the garbage LUTs are randomly interleaved with the useful LUTs. Therefore, there is a trade-off between security and size: increasing n will also increase the size of WBCrypto. In our PoC implementation we group the 3008 WB-AES LUTs together according to the 4 types of LUTs presented in [5]. Half of these LUTs are used for encryption, while the other half are used for decryption. Therefore, the C++ output by our WB Generator always contains $k = 8$ statically initialized arrays which group together all the WB-AES LUTs, plus a random number of randomly sized garbage arrays.

Setting the total size of the garbage arrays to $n = 100$ bytes, an attacker has to execute the WB-AES cryptanalysis attack of [24] for $(100+8)!/2$ different configurations of the WB-AES LUTs. Even if a changeware search algorithm would be improved such that it could locate the WB-AES LUTs in logarithmic time, this would still require over 166 days on a 2,4 GHz CPU. For our experiment described in Section 4.1.1 we have generated WB-AES instances with the values of n up to 100 MBs, which would require hundreds of thousands of years of execution time on the above CPU.

4.2.2 Malicious Calls to WBCrypto

If a changeware developer believes that the protection offered by the obfuscation and diversity techniques are difficult to attack, s/he may attempt to develop changeware that calls the WBCrypto API without this being detected as coming from a malicious origin.

Changeware could be built such that it patches the WB-Crypto binary to skip the message authentication integrity check (node 2.1). This attack is detected by the signature verification performed by X before it launches WBCrypto as its child process. Remember that in Section 3.4 the WBCrypto binary is signed by the vendor of X and the signature verification key is embedded in X's binary.

Another attack would be to inject code inside of X's process memory, which then calls the WBCrypto proxy functions as described in Section 3.4 (node 2.2). This attack is detected by our caller authentication algorithm (see Section 3.4.2), because the hash of the malicious call-path will not be in the white-list of WBCrypto. Moreover, any (a) synchronous call originating directly from a malicious process will also be detected, because the return value of the integrity check will not be in the set of benign call-paths. We have implemented the direct (synchronous) and indirect (asynchronous) calls to WBCrypto as demonstrator changeware examples using the Windows native API. These samples are able to surreptitiously change Chromium user preferences if caller authentication is not performed. They are all detected by caller authentication, with the exception of changeware which asynchronously posts a message to a legitimate thread of X (node 2.3). However, such changeware is detected by message authentication (see Section 3.4.3) even if it spoofs its internal thread ID (node 2.3.2).

Message authentication relies on the fact that attribute values stored in the thread local storage of one thread are not accessible by other threads. Therefore a malicious thread cannot directly add a task to the locally stored task list of a legitimate Chromium thread (node 2.3.3).

To overcome this mechanism, the changeware would need to monitor the inter-thread communication inside the Chromium browser process. One possible way of monitoring would be at the OS kernel level (node 2.3.3.1). However, that would require changeware to have root privileges, which was excluded in Section 1. If changeware had root privileges it could directly modify the Chromium binaries and disable the OS code signature verification "alarms." For instance, changeware with root privileges could disable *User Account Control* in the Microsoft Windows OS, which notifies the user if a binary signature is valid.

Another possible attack is to hook the thread creation system calls (e.g. `BaseThreadInitThunk` from kernel32.dll) and insert functionality which would leak the desired information (i.e. Θ_x's address) from the legitimate thread of X (node 2.3.3.2). However, the integrity check performed via *caller authentication* would detect this hook, via the call-stack inspection of the legitimate thread, because this change would return an invalid hash value to the WBCrypto module.

4.2.3 Replay Attacks

Usually, some asset values change more frequently than others. We partition an asset file into a set $\{p_0, p_1, \ldots, p_n\}$, $n \geq 0$ and compute a ciphertext for each part $c_i = \epsilon_k(p_i)$. This partition can be as fine grained as needed by the application. *Replay attacks* (node 3) in this context consist of changeware installed on an end-user system: (1) recording several asset values and their corresponding MAC values and (2) eventually replacing a current asset value and its MAC with a previously recorded value.

For instance if p_i is set by the target software as a legitimate asset value, then changeware interested in keeping this value records its MAC (c_i). Later if the end-user decides to switch the asset value to p_i', changeware can surreptitiously change this asset value back to p_i. To prevent such replay attacks, we use the WB-AES cipher to compute one single MAC value of the concatenation of: (1) all ciphertexts and (2) the time-stamp when the asset file was last modified. The MAC is computed as $h = H(\epsilon_k(c_0 \mid c_1 \mid \ldots \mid c_n \mid time))$, where H is a hash function such as SHA-256. Since changeware does not have root privileges it cannot tamper with the modification time of a file, which is managed by the OS.

4.2.4 Replace WBCrypto Binary

Replacement of the WBCrypto binary with a rogue binary, which mimics the behavior of WBCrypto, is prevented by the code signature of the vendor of X (see Section 3.4). Nonetheless, an attacker could semi-automatically cryptanalyze the WBCrypto binary instance deployed on his own machine and extract the secret key. Afterwards, he can build changeware which replaces the WBCrypto of any end-user of X, with his cracked version for which the secret key was extracted. This attack is prevented due to WBCrypto binary binding to end-user devices via the unique identifier (id) provided by the OS. As described in Section 3.2, the WBCrypto module instances are indexed from 0 to m and an instance is deployed only if its index i is congruent to the end-users' id modulo m. On startup, X first performs a system call to retrieve the id and then checks whether the signature of WBCrypto is valid for the hash of the current WBCrypto binary concatenated with id mod m. Therefore, the attacker can replace WBCrypto instances only on end-user devices that have the same id. However, the WBCrypto instances on devices with the same id are identical, hence there is no benefit in replacing them. Moreover, an attacker does not know which end-users have the same id as him.

5. DISCUSSION AND LIMITATIONS

5.1 Applicability of Results

Our solution does not aim to defend against changeware which performs changes in the process memory of the target software, i.e., against changeware that makes dynamic but not persistent changes to software assets. However, we believe that caller authentication (see Section 3.4.2) and message authentication (see Section 3.4.3) can be integrated into the target software in order to protect against such non-persistent changes to process memory.

One example of non-persistent changes to process memory, which can be detected by caller authentication, is an *import address table* (IAT) patching attack which is frequently employed by malware to portable executables on MS Windows. IAT entries can be seen as pairs of function name and pointer to function code. IAT patching replaces the legitimate pointers to function code by pointers to injected (malicious) code. It is detected by message authentication because the hash of the call-path involving any patched function would not match the hash from the white-list.

One limitation of the caller authentication mechanism is its dependency on the code of the libraries needed for benign call-path hash computation. The benign call-path hash values included in a white-list are specific to the version of the libraries where functions on the call-path are defined. Since a part of these libraries are provided by the OS vendor and others by the vendor of the target software (X), the

239

white-list must be updated for each update of the OS or of X, i.e. around twice per month. This means that there is not one unique white-list for all end-users. Instead there is a white-list specific to each compatible version of libraries of the OS and the libraries of X. Whenever X starts up, it checks if the library file versions associated with the white-list have changed due to updates. If so it will request an update of the white-list to the current library versions. The white-list is a read-only asset and is signed by the vendor of X and distributed/updated separately from WBCrypto. Therefore, WBCrypto is not updated every time the white-list is updated. WBCrypto simply checks if the white-list was tampered with by verifying its signature using the public verification key of vendor X, and then uses the contents of the white-list during caller and message authentication.

5.2 Alternative Solutions

An alternative to our solution is implemented by modifying the OS kernel. We avoided this approach because we want our solution to function without changes to the underlying infrastructure on which the target software runs. However, if changing the OS kernel is possible, we argue that WBC and software diversity are no longer needed, because the kernel can protect secret-keys under root privileges such that they are not accessible to changeware.

In order to ensure that each application installed on the OS has a different key, the kernel would generate a unique random secret-key, which is persistently stored under root/administrator privileges, i.e. not accessible to changeware and is permanently associated only with this application. An application does not directly get access to its unique key, but instead the OS offers a cryptographic API (similar to the one offered by WBCrypto), which an application has to provide the data for which to compute a MAC value. The OS verifies which binary was used to launch the process calling this API and uses the secret-key associated with it to compute the MAC. To prevent changeware attacks by code injection and remote thread creation (as described in Section 3.4), the OS kernel performs caller authentication of any thread which calls this API. The white-list of benign call-paths is safely hard-coded in the target software binary signed by the OS vendor before distribution to end-users.

Another alternative solution is to augment the OS access-control mechanism such that upon installation certain software assets can be marked as editable only by a set of applications, i.e. not by any application running under the same OS user. This kind of application-centric access control would also be able to prevent changeware from writing to another process' memory, i.e., code injection.

These solutions would eliminate the generation, storage and distribution costs for the target software vendor. Moreover, the run-time performance would be improved by using a classical cryptographic cipher implementation instead of a diversified white-box version of the same cipher.

6. CONCLUSIONS AND FUTURE WORK

We have presented a novel software-based solution against changeware, i.e. malware with no root/administrator privileges, which performs surreptitious persistent changes to software assets which are not protected by the OS code signature verification mechanism. Our solution combines techniques from the fields of software obfuscation, software diversity and run-time checking. The solution can be applied by the vendor of software targeted by changeware; its function is transparent to end-users. This solution is effective under the assumption that it is unfeasible for an attacker to manually construct attacks for a large set of diverse instances of the target software, i.e. for a large part of its user base. Additionally we require the code for the modification of the editable assets to be a fixed set of non-recursive routine call sequences, i.e. there are no unpredictable call sequences that modify assets.

Performance of the target software is slightly affected due to additional time needed to perform caller authentication and white-box encryption. However, this performance overhead is in the order of a fifth of a second, which is acceptable assuming that persistent changes to software assets occur rather infrequently. Moreover, our solution requires non-negligible production and distribution resources for WBCrypto, on the software vendor's side. However, the size of WBCrypto is under 5 MBs and poses a much smaller overhead than re-distribution of the entire target application which we assumed to be in the order of 100s of MBs. We also assumed a huge user base because otherwise changeware developers are unlikely to invest into an attack.

The software diversity and obfuscation transformations offered by the WB Generator, used to generate WBCrypto are application and OS independent. The caller authentication algorithm can be applied to any application if: (1) the OS allows code injection and execution of this code in the target's process memory and (2) the target application permits blocking function calls for the period needed to perform caller authentication. Currently Microsoft Windows OSs allow code injection via system calls. This is not allowed on all Linux distributions. The message authentication mechanism can be implemented for applications which mandate that asset values should be changed only via special threads which can be internally identified, without using the OS assigned thread ID.

Caller- and message-authentication were necessary because the WBCrypto code could not be directly integrated in the code of the target application due to technical and organizational concerns such as: storage and distributions costs, differential updates, crash analysis and most importantly time-stamping binary signatures. If we had taken a less specific approach in our work, such concerns would not have been considered, which means that integrating an obfuscated and diversified WB-AES cipher into the target software would have been a viable solution. Our work shows that such a viable solution is not applicable in practice if it cannot be easily integrated in the existing software engineering processes of the target software. Therefore, we adapted the solution such that it is practicable.

There are several possible future research directions for the current work. The WB generator can be improved by adding additional diversity dimensions, such as *cipher diversity*, i.e. implementing additional block ciphers (e.g. DES, Blowfish, etc.) and more WBC techniques [2, 25, 32, 21]. The performance overhead of caller authentication can be improved by tuning the memory integrity checks or finding cheaper substitutes for the most costly operations. The performance of the WB Generator can be improved such that it offers faster builds and smaller sized WBCrypto instances. Finally, the most interesting problem we are currently working on is quantification of the attacker effort added by software diversity and obfuscation in this context.

7. REFERENCES

[1] O. Billet, H. Gilbert, and C. Ech-Chatbi. Cryptanalysis of a white box AES implementation. In *Selected Areas in Cryptography*, number 3357 in Lecture Notes in Computer Science, pages 227–240. Springer Berlin Heidelberg, Jan. 2005.

[2] J. Bringer, H. Chabanne, and E. Dottax. White box cryptography: Another attempt. *located at, last visited on Jul*, 22(2011):14, 2006.

[3] H. Chang and M. J. Atallah. Protecting software code by guards. In *Security and privacy in digital rights management*, pages 160–175. Springer, 2002.

[4] L. Chen and A. Avizienis. N-version programming: A fault-tolerance approach to reliability of software operation. In *Proc. 8th IEEE Int. Symp. on Fault-Tolerant Computing (FTCS-8)*, pages 3–9, 1978.

[5] S. Chow, P. Eisen, H. Johnson, and P. C. V. Oorschot. White-box cryptography and an AES implementation. In *Selected Areas in Cryptography*, number 2595 in Lecture Notes in Computer Science, pages 250–270. Springer Berlin Heidelberg, Jan. 2003.

[6] S. Chow, P. Eisen, H. Johnson, and P. C. Van Oorschot. A white-box DES implementation for DRM applications. In *Digital Rights Management*, pages 1–15. Springer, 2003.

[7] F. B. Cohen. Operating system protection through program evolution. *Computers & Security*, 12(6):565–584, Oct. 1993.

[8] C. Collberg, C. Thomborson, and D. Low. A taxonomy of obfuscating transformations. Technical report, Department of Computer Science, The University of Auckland, New Zealand, 1997.

[9] Y. De Mulder, P. Roelse, and B. Preneel. Cryptanalysis of the Xiao-Lai white-box AES implementation. In *Selected Areas in Cryptography*, pages 34–49, 2013.

[10] Y. De Mulder, B. Wyseur, and B. Preneel. Cryptanalysis of a perturbated white-box AES implementation. In G. Gong and K. C. Gupta, editors, *Progress in Cryptology - INDOCRYPT 2010*, number 6498 in Lecture Notes in Computer Science, pages 292–310. Springer Berlin Heidelberg, Jan. 2010.

[11] C. Eagle. *The IDA pro book: the unofficial guide to the world's most popular disassembler*. No Starch Press, 2011.

[12] P. FIPS. 197: Advanced encryption standard (aes). *National Institute of Standards and Technology*, 2001.

[13] S. Forrest, A. Somayaji, and D. Ackley. Building diverse computer systems. In *Operating Systems, 1997., The Sixth Workshop on Hot Topics in*, pages 67–72, 1997.

[14] M. Franz. E unibus pluram: massive-scale software diversity as a defense mechanism. In *Proceedings of the 2010 workshop on New security paradigms*, NSPW '10, pages 7–16, New York, NY, USA, 2010. ACM.

[15] S. Govindavajhala and A. W. Appel. Windows access control demystified. Technical report, Department of Computer Science, Princeton University, 2006.

[16] S. Haber and W. S. Stornetta. How to time-stamp a digital document. In *Proceedings of the 10th Annual International Cryptology Conference on Advances in Cryptology*, CRYPTO '90, pages 437–455, London, UK, UK, 1991. Springer-Verlag.

[17] M. A. Hiltunen, R. D. Schlichting, C. A. Ugarte, and G. T. Wong. Survivability through customization and adaptability: The cactus approach. In *DARPA Information Survivability Conference and Exposition, 2000. DISCEX'00. Proceedings*, volume 1, pages 294–307. IEEE, 2000.

[18] B. Horne, L. Matheson, C. Sheehan, and R. E. Tarjan. Dynamic self-checking techniques for improved tamper resistance. In *Security and privacy in digital rights management*, pages 141–159. Springer, 2002.

[19] E. R. Jacobson, A. R. Bernat, W. R. Williams, and B. P. Miller. Detecting code reuse attacks with a model of conformant program execution. In *International Symposium on Engineering Secure Software and Systems (ESSoS)*, pages 1–18. Springer Berlin Heidelberg, 2014.

[20] P. Junod, J. Rinaldini, and J. Wehrli. Obfuscator-LLVM. https://github.com/obfuscator-llvm/obfuscator, 2014. GitHub repository.

[21] M. Karroumi. Protecting white-box AES with dual ciphers. In K.-H. Rhee and D. Nyang, editors, *Information Security and Cryptology - ICISC 2010*, number 6829 in Lecture Notes in Computer Science, pages 278–291. Springer Berlin Heidelberg, Jan. 2011.

[22] T. László and Á. Kiss. Obfuscating c++ programs via control flow flattening. *Annales Universitatis Scientarum Budapestinensis de Rolando Eötvös Nominatae, Sectio Computatorica*, 30:3–19, 2009.

[23] P. Leach, M. Mealling, and R. Salz. A Universally Unique IDentifier (UUID) URN Namespace. RFC 4122 (Proposed Standard), July 2005.

[24] T. Lepoint, M. Rivain, Y. De Mulder, P. Roelse, and B. Preneel. Two Attacks on a White-Box AES Implementation. In *Selected Areas in Cryptography–SAC 2013*, pages 265–285. Springer, 2014.

[25] W. Michiels and P. Gorissen. Mechanism for software tamper resistance: an application of white-box cryptography. In *Proc. ACM workshop on Digital Rights Management*, pages 82–89, 2007.

[26] W. Michiels, P. Gorissen, and H. D. L. Hollmann. Cryptanalysis of a generic class of white-box implementations. In R. M. Avanzi, L. Keliher, and F. Sica, editors, *Selected Areas in Cryptography*, number 5381 in Lecture Notes in Computer Science, pages 414–428. Springer Berlin Heidelberg, Jan. 2009.

[27] A. Shamir and N. Van Someren. Playing 'hide and seek' with stored keys. In *Financial cryptography*, pages 118–124, 1999.

[28] L. Sweeney. k-anonymity: A model for protecting privacy. *International Journal of Uncertainty, Fuzziness and Knowledge-Based Systems*, 10(05):557–570, 2002.

[29] SysK. Practical cracking of white-box implementations. In *Phrack Magazine*. Phrack Inc., 2012. Volume 0x0e, Issue 0x44, Phile #0x08 of 0x13.

[30] Trusted Computing Group. Trusted Platform Module (TPM) Specifications. Online at https://www.trustedcomputinggroup.org/developers/

`trusted_platform_module/specifications`. Accessed on: 14-07-2014.

[31] B. Wyseur, W. Michiels, P. Gorissen, and B. Preneel. Cryptanalysis of white-box DES implementations with arbitrary external encodings. In C. Adams, A. Miri, and M. Wiener, editors, *Selected Areas in Cryptography*, number 4876 in Lecture Notes in Computer Science, pages 264–277. Springer Berlin Heidelberg, Jan. 2007.

[32] Y. Xiao and X. Lai. A secure implementation of white-box AES. In *2nd International Conference on Computer Science and its Applications, 2009. CSA '09*, pages 1–6, 2009.

[33] S. Yachi and M. Loreau. Biodiversity and ecosystem productivity in a fluctuating environment: the insurance hypothesis. *Proceedings of the National Academy of Sciences*, 96(4):1463–1468, 1999.

Aligning Security and Business Objectives for Process-Aware Information Systems

Günter Karjoth
Lucerne University of Applied Sciences and Arts
karjoth@acm.org

Abstract

Enterprises are increasingly subject to compliance rules that originate from corporate guidelines, industry sector standards, and laws. The goal of access control is not only to protect against unauthorized users but also against threats that often reside within organizations where authorized users may misuse system resources. Although access control is fundamental in protecting information systems, it can pose an obstacle to achieving business objectives. Today, security policies have to be aligned with the business goals and are not anymore a purely technical issue. Business processes are therefore of special interest. When described by workflows, they define the causal dependencies between a set of tasks, whose execution constitutes a business objective. Already in 1999, Bertino, Ferrari and Atluri showed how to specify and enforce authorization constraints in workflow management systems [1]. But only in recent years, triggered by the raise of high-level modeling languages such as the Business Process Model and Notation (BPMN), business processes were enhanced with compliance requirements in terms of process annotations, tying the control objectives into the execution flow.

This talk will look at recent research results in this area, including approaches to scope authorization constraints within workflows with loops and conditional execution [2],

ACM Classification

D.4.6 [Security and Protection]: Access controls;
H.4.1 [Office Automation]: Workflow management

Author Keywords: Access control; Separation of Duty; business process; workflow; compliance; enforcement; obstruction; cost-minimizing authorization policy

CODASPY'15, March 2–4, 2015, San Antonio, Texas, USA.
ACM 978-1-4503-3191-3/15/03.
http://dx.doi.org/10.1145/2699026.2699028

to capture the effects of enforcement on business objectives [3], and to select the optimal between multiple authorization policies satisfying the given constraints [4].

This work was mainly done in collaboration with Samuel Burri, when we both were at IBM Research – Zurich, and David Basin from ETH Zurich.

REFERENCES

[1] E. Bertino, E. Ferrari, and V. Atluri. The specification and enforcement of authorization constraints in workflow management systems. ACM Trans. Inf. Syst. Secur. 2, 1 (February 1999), 65-104.

[2] D. Basin, S.J. Burri, and G. Karjoth. Dynamic enforcement of abstract separation of duty constraints. ACM Transactions on Information and System Security (TISSEC) , 15, 3, Article 13 (2012).

[3] D. Basin, S.J. Burri, and G. Karjoth. Obstruction-free authorization enforcement: Aligning security and business objectives. Journal of Computer Security (JCS). Vol. 22, 661–698 (2014).

[4] D. Basin, S.J. Burri, and G. Karjoth. Optimal Workflow-aware Authorizations. In 17th ACM Symposium on Access Control Models and Technologies (SACMAT '12), pages 93–102. ACM Press, 2012.

Short Bio

Günter Karjoth studied computer science at the University of Stuttgart (Germany) followed by a doctorate. Prior to joining the Lucerne University of Applied Sciences and Arts (School of Business) in 2013, he worked at IBM Research – Zurich. Over the past thirty-five years, his research interest ranged from identity and access management, enterprise privacy, middleware and mobile agent security to protocol engineering. He taught at the ETH Zurich between 2005 and 2013 on "Privacy in the Electronic Society". He is an ACM Distinguished Scientist (2013) and received IBM Outstanding Achievement Awards for his work on Privacy for RFID (2006) and on the Enterprise Privacy Architecture (2005).

A Dynamic Approach to Detect Anomalous Queries on Relational Databases

Mohammad Saiful Islam
Computer Science
Department
University of Texas at Dallas
saiful@utdallas.edu

Mehmet Kuzu
Computer Science
Department
University of Texas at Dallas
mehmet.kuzu@utdallas.edu

Murat Kantarcioglu
Computer Science
Department
University of Texas at Dallas
muratk@utdallas.edu

ABSTRACT

Protecting sensitive datasets from insider and outsider attacks has been a major concern over the years. Relational Database Management System (RDBMS) has been the de facto standard to store, retrieve and manage large datasets efficiently in the last few years. However, as surprising as it seems, not a lot of works can be found in the literature which protect databases from anomalous accesses. In this paper, we present a novel Intrusion Detection System (IDS) for relational databases. Our primary objective is to protect databases from both insider and outsider threats by detecting anomalous access patterns using Hidden Markov Model (HMM). While most of the previous notable works in this area focus on query syntax to detect anomalous access, our approach takes into account the amount of sensitive information a query result contains to detect a potential intrusion. Finally, our empirical evaluation on the publicly available TPC-H dataset shows that our IDS can detect anomalous query access with a high degree of accuracy.

Categories and Subject Descriptors

H.2 [**Database Management**]: Database Administration—*Security, Integrity, and Protection*; K.6.5 [**Management of Computing and Information Systems**]: Security and Protection—*Unauthorized Access*

Keywords

RDBMS; Intrusion Detection; Anomaly Detection; Hidden Markov Model

1. INTRODUCTION

Intrusion detection system (IDS) is considered as a very important component of any security solution. The primary objective of an intrusion detection system is to identify an intrusion in its early stage and mitigate the cost and risk associated with such an intrusion. Although, quite a lot of research has been done to build intrusion free information

systems, intrusion detection system still remains an integral part of any security solution for the following reasons.

First of all, it is often extremely difficult to realize *provably secure* information systems [6]. It is the role of the intrusion detection systems to bridge the gap between the ideal, but sometimes unattainable security mechanisms and the existing, rather handicapped security mechanisms.

Secondly, a recent *Mandiant M-Trends* threat report [15] mentions that most attackers use valid credentials to attack software systems. Conventional intrusion prevention mechanisms fail miserably if an attacker possesses valid credentials. For example, according to a Wall Street Journal article, hackers stole electronic credential from a vendor and used that credential to cause the recent data breach [20] in the American reatiling company `Target`.

Finally, a recent U.S. Secret Service/CERT/Microsoft E-Crime report states that 34% of all the surveyed attacks were insider attacks [16]. Therefore, intrusion detection systems can play a vital role in thwarting insider attacks.

There is a plethora of intrusion detection systems proposed in the literature to date (e.g., [8, 23] etc.). Almost all of the proposed intrusion detection systems can be classified into either *host based* or *network based* depending on the input data and the scope of operation [7].

1. *Host Based Intrusion Detection Systems, HIDS.* Presence of a subsequence of anomalous system calls in the Operating System (OS) calls traces works as evidence of an intrusion to a host for these systems.

2. *Network Based Intrusion Detection Systems, NIDS.* Network-based systems, on the other hand, use network traffic data to detect an intrusion to the network.

Intrusion detection systems mentioned in the preceding paragraph identify intrusions from different perspective. However, over the last few years, a significant portion of information systems run on an underlying database system. It has been argued in [11] that database intrusions may not always be reflected as intrusion on the OS or network level. That is why, *host based* and *network based* IDS may often fail to detect database intrusions. To counteract this threat, a few intrusion detection systems have been proposed in the literature that specifically focuses on database intrusion (e.g., [5,11,16] etc.). There are two mainstream approaches of database specific intrusion detection systems in the literature: *query syntax centric* and *data centric*. *Query syntax centric* ID approaches use SQL queries to create normal usage profiles and use these profiles to detect an intrusion. *Data centric* approaches, on the other hand, use the actual data accessed by an user to detect intrusions. Since relational database model has become the de facto standard over the last few years, almost all of these approaches are tailor made for RDBMS.

In this paper, we present a new data centric anomaly detection technique for RDBMS. Motivations behind our work are presented in the following section.

1.1 Motivation

Most of the notable works in *Database Intrusion Detection Systems* (DIDS) (e.g., [5, 11] etc.) use query syntax to build regular usage profiles. However, an intruder can modify a regular query ever so slightly and retrieve a significantly different resultset. In such cases, query syntax based approaches can not detect these intrusions. To further inspect this point, let us assume that a bank cashier provides one to one service to bank clients. As a part of the service, the cashier submits a SQL query to retrieve the account record that belongs to a particular customer.

Valid Query	Intrusive Query
select *Name, AcctBal* from *Account* where *AcctNum* = 123456789	select *Name, AcctBal* from Account where *AcctNum* ≠ −1

Table 1: **Valid and Intrusive queries with similar syntax.**

The query on the left side of Table 1 presents a valid cashier query. Now, let us assume that an intruder wants to access all the records in the *Account* relation. With that objective, she can submit a query presented on the right side of Table 1. This query would return all the records in the *Account* table to the intruder. Interestingly, the syntax of these two queries are similar. Furthermore, syntax based ID systems such as [11] would extract exactly the same set of features for both queries. Therefore, these two queries would seem identical to such intrusion detection systems and the intrusive query would remain undetected. However, the results for these two queries would be significantly different. The valid query would fetch only one record, while the intrusive query may fetch millions of records depending on the size of the Account table. Therefore, this example clearly indicates that most of the syntax based approaches are not able to detect these types of intrusions.

Again, almost all the proposed approaches in the literature, both query centric and data centric, evaluates the validity of a given query in isolation. That is, previously submitted queries do not affect the detection process of a given query. However, we argue that it is imperative to take into account the previously submitted queries to accurately detect an intrusive query. We further explain this argument with the following hypothetical example.

Let us consider a customer representative (e.g., Jane) of an online shopping company who provides phone service to its customers. As a part of her service, she helps a customer to choose various products from the list of available products. If she is able to convince her customer to purchase any particular product, she helps the customer to buy that particular product. During the whole process, Jane submits one or more queries to access the product data, followed by a customer account query. Now, let us assume that an intruder makes repeated queries to the customer account table in order to steal sensitive information such as credit card information. Any of these intrusive queries would remain undetected if they are evaluated in isolation. This is because, it is usual for Jane to submit queries to retrieve customer account information. However, these queries would be easily detected if they are evaluated with respect to the context they are submitted to the database. That is, they would be detected by a DIDS which takes into account the previously submitted queries. More specifically, it is highly unusual for Jane to make repeated queries to retrieve the customer account information. This clearly indicates that a DIDS should take into account the context as well as the query itself to detect a potential intrusion.

In fact, the inability of detecting intrusions described in the above scenario can be attributed to the fact that none of the query syntax centric and data centric approaches takes into account the data sensitivity values of the query results. As a result, these techniques implicitly assume that each and every tuple in a database is equally sensitive. However, most of the contemporary databases store data with different levels of sensitivity.[1] An intruder has more incentive to access sensitive data such as credit card information, Social Security Number (SSN) etc. Therefore, an intruder is expected to access only the sensitive parts of the database. A valid user, on the other hand, have incentives to access both sensitive and insensitive parts of the database. Therefore, a database intrusion detection system, when equipped with the knowledge of data sensitivity values, is more likely to distinguish a sequence of anomalous database accesses from sequences of valid accesses. In this paper, we propose a new anomaly detection techniques for RDBMS that uses query sensitivity scores to train a Hidden Markov Model and use this model to detect anomalous query accesses.

1.2 Our Contributions

In this paper, we propose a new data centric anomaly detection systems for relational database model. In our proposed scheme, sensitivity scores are assigned by domain experts to each attribute in the database schema. These scores are used to assign a sensitivity score to each query result. During the training phase, clean query sensitivity scores are used to train Hidden Markov Models (HMM) which represents the normal user behavior. In the detection phase, each query is assigned an anomaly score by the HMM depending on the query sensitivity score as well as the query trace for the session. The strengths of our proposed scheme are given as follows.

Data Centric Anomaly Detection. Since we do not use information on known attacks, our approach is more likely to succeed to detect unknown newer attack types. Again, instead of query syntax, we take into account the sensitivity score of the dataset accessed through a query. Since, an adversary is more likely to issue SQL queries to retrieve sensitive records, our approach have the better probability of catching them.

---

[1]For example, an online retailing company may contain publicly accessible non-sensitive data that describes product features. At the same time, this company is expected to contain extremely sensitive data such as customer's credit card information.

Context Aware Detection. Our proposed scheme evaluates a particular query w.r.t. the entire query session. This makes it harder for an adversary to masquerade as a valid user. Therefore, we argue that our approach can detect wider variety of intrusions since each query is evaluated w.r.t. its context.

Adaptive. Our proposed scheme does not depend on the underlying database schema. Furthermore, our scheme can be periodically updated to match the dynamically changing user behavior. Since our scheme logs each query in the audit logs, a DBA can use a sanitize query trace and modify HMM parameters according to the query trace.

The rest of this paper is organized as follows. We provide a brief survey of background information and related work in §2. A short primer on HMM is presented in §3. We describe our approach in details in §4. In §5, we present a thorough empirical evaluation of our proposed scheme by using the publicly available TPC-H benchmark. Finally, we conclude this paper with §6.

2. RELATED WORK

Since the seminal work done by Denning et al. [7], Intrusion Detection Systems (IDS) has followed one of the two well known paradigms [8]. *Signature based methods* such as [23] use a set of attack signatures provided by human experts to detect an ongoing attack. *Data Mining based methods*, on the other hand, leverage the generalization ability of data mining techniques and thus have the ability to detect newer attack types [8].

Data Mining methods themselves can be dichotomized into two broad classes [13]. In *misuse detection systems* [5, 17], a dataset consists of both labeled normal and intrusive instances is used to train a learning algorithm. *Anomaly detection systems* [9], on the other hand, use historical data to build profiles of normal behavior. Intrusion is detected by identifying behavior pattern that deviates from these known profiles. These approaches are not particularly vulnerable against previously unknown types of attacks.

Most of the intrusion detection systems proposed in the literature are either *host based* or *network based*. However, often times intrusions on the database level are not properly reflected in the network or OS level [11]. Therefore, a few intrusion detection systems have been proposed that uses the database audit trails (i.e., SQL query trace) to identify an intrusion against the underlying DBMS.

Liu et al. proposed intrusion tolerant database system architectures in [14]. Similarly, Wenhui et al. proposed a two layer architecture to protect web-based database systems against possible intrusions [24]. Although, none of these works present a concrete ID system, they establish the necessity of such systems.

There are two mainstream approaches of database specific intrusion detection systems in the literature. *Query syntax centric* ID approaches use SQL queries to create normal usage profiles and use these profiles to detect an intrusion. *Data centric* approaches, on the other hand, use the actual data accessed by an user to detect intrusions.

Chung et al. proposed a query syntax based misuse detection system called *Demids* in [5]. In *Demids*, query audit logs are used to establish a working set of a particular user which consists of a set of attributes that are accessed together along with some values. Kamra et al. proposed a similar anomaly detection system in [11]. In training phase, features are extracted from queries of each role in the database to train a *Naive Bayes Classifier*.

Alternatively, there is a few data centric approaches proposed in the literature [16, 19]. Mathew et al. proposed a data centric approach to detect insider attacks in [16]. In this work, features (e.g., maximum value, minimum value, average value for numerical attributes) are extracted from the resultset of a query and machine learning techniques are used to train a learning algorithm. Again, Spalka et al. presents an anomaly detection system for RDBMS in [19]. In this work, anomaly is detected by monitoring basic statistics of a relation from time to time.

Each of these data centric approaches does not take into account the data sensitivity values of the query results. However, the query access pattern of an intruder largely depends on data sensitivity. Therefore, an IDS should take into account data sensitivities to isolate intrusive queries from the valid ones. Again, all the existing database ID systems consider queries as stand alone units. That is, they implicitly assume that given a partial query session $q = \langle q_1, \cdots q_{i-1} \rangle$ for any given user, the probability distribution of the ith query is independent of q. That is, $Pr[q_i = p \mid q] = Pr[q_i = r \mid q]$ for any two queries $p, r \in Q$, where Q is the set of all possible queries. However, this oversimplifies query distribution in real world databases. In fact, an attacker might take advantage of this oversimplification and only issues queries to sensitive data which a valid user submits from time to time. Therefore, an effective IDS should consider a query as a part of a session, not an independent individual entity. We find Hidden Markov Model to be a wonderful machine learning tool that takes into account query context to detect anomalous query.

In this paper, we propose a data-centric anomaly detection system for RDBMS that detects intrusion based on data sensitivity with respect to the ongoing user query session. In our approach, we assign sensitivity values to each query result and use Hidden Markov Model to detect query anomaly. It should be noted that Harel et al. proposed a notion of *Misuseability Weight* in [10]. This *Misuseability weight* is very similar in concept to our sensitivity score.

3. HIDDEN MARKOV MODEL

Hidden Markov Model (HMM) is an extremely powerful tool to model temporal sequence information. It has been widely used in temporal pattern recognition problems (e.g., speech recognition, bioinformatics, gesture recognition) due to its high detection rate [18]. HMMs has also been used in the general area of intrusion detection by some notable works (e.g., [4]). Since we model database intrusion as a temporal sequence of observable query sensitivity scores in our work, we find HMM to be an effective tool to detect intrusions. We present a brief primer on Hidden Markov Model in the following paragraph. Furthermore, We use the same set of notations as [18] in our discussion on HMM.

An HMM is formally defined as an ordered tuple $\lambda = (N, M, A, B, \pi)$.

1. *Number of states, N.* The number of states in the HMM is denoted by N. The set of states are denoted by $S = \{S_1, S_2, \cdots, S_N\}$. Again, the state at time interval t is denoted by q_t.

2. *Discrete alphabet size, M*. Size of the discrete alphabet size for each state in the HMM is denoted by M. The alphabet set is denoted by $V = \{v_1, \cdots v_M\}$.

3. *State transition probability distribution, A*. The state transition probability matrix is denoted by $A = \{a_{i,j}\}$.

$$a_{i,j} = Pr\left[q_{t+1} = S_j \mid q_t = S_i\right], \quad 1 \le i, j \le N.$$

4. *Symbol probability distribution, B*. The discrete probability distribution function for any state i is denoted by $B = \{b_i(j)\}$. That is,

$$b_i(j) = Pr\left[v_j \text{ at t } \mid q_t = S_i\right], \quad 1 \le i \le N, \ 1 \le j \le M.$$

5. *Initial state distribution, π*. The initial state distribution is denoted by $\pi = \{\pi_i\}$ where $\pi_i = Pr\left[q_0 = S_i\right]$ for $1 \le i \le N$.

4. OUR APPROACH

In this section, we describe the proposed anomaly detection system. In essence, we use hidden Markov models to build usage profiles. These profiles are used in the detection phase to identify a potential intrusion.

4.1 Building Profiles

We argue that building separate profiles for each individual user does not scale well for databases with big user base. Besides, often times than not, many users of a database system exhibits common pattern in their database usage. Therefore, individual user profiles would incur unnecessary space and computational overhead. For example, it is expected that all the tellers in a banking system are expected to have a similar database access pattern.

Again, Kamra et al. proposed role profiles in [11] when the underlying RDBMS has *Role Based Access Control* (RBAC) in place. We also propose role based profiles for the following reasons.

1. RBAC has become quite standard among relational database models these days. By definition of roles, users in a particular role are expected to share the same usage pattern. Therefore, building profiles for roles seems well justified.

2. Even when there is no role information present in the database, *Role Mining* algorithms such as [12,22] etc. can be used to assign users to artificial roles. Profiles of these artificial roles are then built by the anomaly detection engine and used to detect anomalous queries.

Throughout the rest of the paper, we assume that the underlying database system has well defined roles and therefore we build usage profiles for each defined roles.

4.2 Sensitivity Score

In our model, we indicate the sensitivity of a piece of data by an associated sensitivity score. This sensitivity score can be known a priori from domain knowledge, or sensitive information can be inferred dynamically using various pattern matching techniques. Again, there might be different granularity of sensitivity levels.

1. *Relation Level Scoring*. In the coarse level, we can attach sensitivity score to each relation in a RDBMS.

That way, a relation that stores publicly available product information for an online merchant (e.g., Amazon) can have zero sensitivity score. A relation that stores credit card information of the clients, on the other hand, would have high sensitivity score.

2. *Attribute Level Scoring*. Again, we can attach sensitivity score to each attribute of a relation. In this case, each cell value of that attribute would share the same sensitivity value. For example, the credit card number attribute of a payment relation can have high sensitivity score, while the name column of that same relation may have a much lower sensitivity score.

3. *Cell Level Scoring*. Finally, we can associate sensitivity score to each individual cell of relational tables. In this scheme, values for the same attribute may have different sensitivity score depending on the tuple they are representing. For example, the online purchase story of President Barrack Obama might have higher sensitivity score than that of an ordinary citizen John Smith from the state of Alabama.

It should be noted that, although cell level and attribute level scoring is more logical, they incur a higher space overhead when compared to relation level scoring. However, regardless of the scoring system used, each individual cell in a RDBMS has a sensitivity score in our model. In relation level scoring, each cell in a table has the same score, while in the attribute level scoring each cell in the same column has the same value.

4.3 Tuple Sensitivity

Let $\mathcal{A}$ be the set of all possible attributes of a given database schema. Let us assume that $R(A)$ presents the relation that consists of the attribute set A s.t. $A \subseteq \mathcal{A}$. Let t be a tuple of $R(A)$ such that $t = \langle t_1, t_2, \cdots, t_k \rangle$. *Tuple sensitivity score* of t, denoted by TS_t, is defined as follows.

$$TS_t = mf(A) \times \sum_i^k S_{t_i}. \qquad (1)$$

Here, S_{t_i} is the individual sensitivity score of the cell t_i. Furthermore, $mf : \mathcal{P}(\mathcal{A}) \longmapsto \mathcal{R}_{\ge 1}$ represents the magnification function that maps an attribute set to a corresponding *magnification factor*. Quite naturally, the domain of mf is the power set of $\mathcal{A}$ and the range is the set of all real numbers greater than or equal to 1. It should be noted that a good magnification function should reflect the correlative sensitivity among a set of attributes. For example, if we are considering a relation that represents the demographic information of a person, only knowing the name value or the address may not be considered as sensitive information. However, when both of these values are known, they might be considered as sensitive. The same thing stands for date of birth too. The date of birth itself is not sensitive at all, however when it is combined with name and address, it becomes significantly more sensitive. Therefore, $mf(\texttt{name}, \texttt{address}, \texttt{dob})$ may have a value greater than 1. This ensures that a tuple consisting of these attribute values has a sensitivity score greater than the summation of the individual cell sensitivity scores.

It should be noted that the purpose of the *magnification function* is to incorporate domain knowledge into the process of calculating tuple sensitivity score by an expert. A constant function of $mf(A) = 1$ might be used as default to nullify the effect of the magnification function. However, a realistic estimate of the magnification fucntion can greatly improve the effectiveness of the proposed IDS.

4.4 Sensitivity Score of a Query

In our proposed model, we assign a sensitivity score to each query submitted to the database. Query sensitivity score indicates the sensitivity level the resultset of a given query conveys directly and indirectly. A query resultset may convey sensitive information directly to a query issuer by containing sensitive information in its resultset. On the other hand, a query result also conveys significant amount of sensitive information indirectly (e.g., through omission). We explain this point by the following two examples.

1. Let us assume that a user submits a query to retrieve all the employee records in the `Employee` relation with the selection condition $salary \geq \$80,000$. Now, the user learns that any employee records not contained in the resultset must have a salary value of less than $80,000$. Therefore, the query is conveying significant sensitive information to a user by omitting a tuple in its resultset.

2. More appropriately, let us assume that a user has issued an aggregate query such as the average salary value of all the employees. Now, the resultset of this query would contain only one tuple, and therefore may not have a large sensitivity value. But, this average value is an important statistics regarding all the employee records in the relation `Employee`.

Therefore, these two examples clearly indicates that considering only the tuple sensitivity scores of a query resultset is not an adequate measure for the query sensitivity. Rather, we also have to consider the total set of tuples on which a particular query was run to adequately measure its sensitivity.

Definition 1. Let q be a query which resultset can be represented by R.[2] Query sensitivity score of q, denoted as QS_q, is a two dimensional vector $[SR_q,\ ST_q] \in \mathcal{R}^2$ such that

1. If $R = \pi_{proj\_atts}(\sigma_{sel\_atts}(R_1 \times R_2 \times \cdots \times R_k))$, i.e., R be the relation represented by the resultset of query q, the result query sensitivity score of q is defined as follows.

$$SR_q = \sum_{r \in R} TS_r \qquad (2)$$

2. Again, if $R' = (R_1 \times R_2 \times \cdots \times R_k)$, the touched query sensitivity score of query q is defined as follows.

$$ST_q = \sum_{r \in R'} TS_r \qquad (3)$$

[2]Extended relational algebra operators might be used to express complex queries, we do not incorporate them for the sake of simplicity. Furthermore, we intentionally omit the `Sorting` and `Grouping` operators since ordering does not affect the sensitivity of a dataset according to our definitions. However, in real life, ordering might be considered as significant information, especially for the large datasets.

In Definition 1, π and σ represents the relational algebra operators *projection* and *selection* respectively. Furthermore, $R_i \times R_j$ denotes the *Cartesian product* of R_i and R_j.

4.5 Methodology

In this section, we describe the overview of the ID process of the proposed scheme. The proposed anomaly detection scheme works in two phases: the training phase and the detection phase.

4.5.1 Training Phase.

For each role in the RDBMS, we train a Hidden Markov Model using a set of observation sequence. Each observation sequence in the training set represents a chronologically ordered sequence of query sensitivity scores taken from a valid query session of the associated role. Again, the training set should be carefully chosen to reflect all possible usage patterns of the users for that role. For example, for a managerial role, observation should be taken from query sessions in the middle of the month and also from the end of the months. This is because managers may have to perform some additional tasks during the end of the months to create summary reports and therefore may submit specific queries. we like to underscore that the training observation sequence should be intrusion free. In practice, outlier detection algorithms such as [1] are used to clean training data from intrusions.

Let us assume O be a training observation sequence such that $O = \{O_i\}$. Here, each O_i is a sequence of query sensitive scores from valid user sessions for the associated role. Therefore, our objective is to build a HMM that best describes the observation sequence O. However, it should be noted that there is no efficient solution to choose a HMM given a set of training observation sequence. However, there exists iterative procedures such as Baum-Welch method [2,3] to choose a HMM $\lambda = (A, B, \pi)$ such that $Pr[O \mid \lambda]$ is locally maximized.

4.5.2 Testing Phase.

After the training phase, we use this HMM to calculate an anomaly score for each new sequence of test queries. If the anomaly score is greater than a particular threshold, we flag an anomaly. Otherwise, we mark the query as normal and return the resultset to the user.

Definition 2. Let $Q = \langle q_1, q_2, \cdots, q_k \rangle$ be the sequence of queries submitted by an user U with role R in a particular query session. Let $O = \langle S_1, S_2, \cdots, S_k \rangle$ be the sequence of corresponding query sensitivity values. Let us define the partial observation O_i such that $O_i = \langle S_1, \cdots, S_i \rangle$ for $1 \leq i \leq k$. If λ_R be the HMM trained for role R in the training phase, the anomaly score for query q_i is defined as follows:

$$\texttt{Anomaly\_Score}(q_i) = \begin{cases} \text{Max Value} & : \text{if } Pr[O_i \mid \lambda_R] = 0 \\ \frac{1}{Pr[O_i \mid \lambda_R]} & : \text{if } Pr[O_i \mid \lambda_R] > 0 \end{cases} \qquad (4)$$

In Definition 4, *Max Value* refers to the maximum value of the programming language container (e.g., `double`, `float` etc.) used to hold the anomaly score. Again, $Pr[O_i \mid \lambda_R]$ can be efficiently computed by well known algorithms such as *Forward-Backward Algorithm* [18]. If this anomaly score is greater than a role threshold τ_R, an intrusion is detected.

Role Threshold, τ_R. Choosing an appropriate role threshold τ_R is very important for the appropriate behavior of the proposed scheme. If the threshold is too high, there would be more *false negatives*. Again, smaller threshold might give away to higher *false positive* rate. Unfortunately, there is no analytical way to choose an appropriate threshold index which would work for all database schema. Role threshold values greatly depend on the query behavior of the users of the corresponding role. Therefore, we propose the following heuristic-based threshold generation in this paper.

After a particular role HMM λ_R is trained, a sequence of p valid observations are chosen where each of these observations contains p query sensitivity score sequence. For each of these observations, we select the maximum anomaly score from the p individual query sensitivity score sequence. Finally, from these p maximum anomaly scores, we choose the ith minimum value as our role threshold τ_R. We denote this choice of i as the *Threshold Index*. In all our experiments (except for §5.2.3), we have used the median as the threshold index. There is a positive correlation between *Threshold Index* and false negative rate (FN) of the proposed scheme. Again, a smaller threshold index might incur higher false positive value. Therefore, threshold index should be chosen appropriately depending on the desired ratio of false positives and false negatives.

Figure 1 depicts the overall detection mechanism by our proposed intrusion detection system.

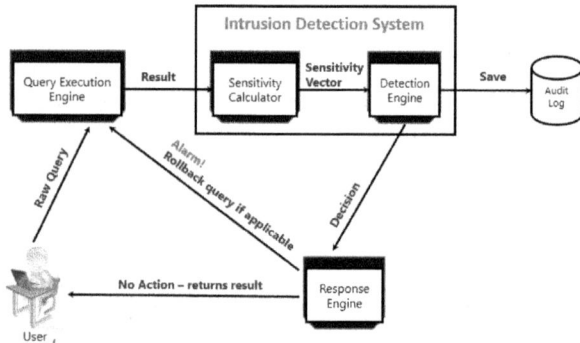

Figure 1: Anomalous query detection process.

Here, a user submits a raw query to the relational database. Query Execution Engine executes the query and the result is passed onto our intrusion detection system. The Sensitivity Calculator calculates the query sensitivity and the Detection Engine determine whether the given query is an anomaly for the given role or not. If the decision is an anomaly, the Response Engine tries to undo the effect of the query execution and raises an alarm to the appropriate authority such as DBA. If the decision is a valid query, the result is passed onto the user.

5. EXPERIMENT AND RESULT

In this section, we empirically demonstrate the efficacy of our proposed IDS on publicly available TPC-H benchmark [21]. In our evaluation, we view intrusion detection as a binary classification problem. The input to our classification engine is a sequence of query sensitivity scores from a particular user. We detect an intrusion if the classification

result is positive. Alternatively, we mark a query sequence valid if the classification output is negative. Our empirical result exhibits that the proposed Intrusion Detection system has a very high classification accuracy.

5.1 Experimental Setup

5.1.1 Dataset Used.

We use the TPC Benchmark^{TM} H (TPC-H) [21] for all the experiments reported in this paper. TPC-H benchmark has been designed by the Transaction Processing Performance Council (TPC) to have industry wide relevance. With the default SF value of 1, TPC-H dataset contains almost ten million data rows distributed across eight relational tables. TPC-H benchmark also comes with 22 decision support queries. Since each of these queries are diverse in nature, they do not conform to any fixed pattern. Therefore, this query set is ill-suited for our purpose. That is why, we do not use TPC-H queries to evaluate the proposed Intrusion Detection System.

5.1.2 Adding Sensitivity.

In our empirical evaluation, we assume cell level sensitivity score. Since TPC-H dataset does not incorporate data sensitivity, we add sensitivity score to this dataset. We tentatively assign a sensitivity score $SC_i \in \{0, 1, \cdots, s\}$ to each table T_i in the TPC-H dataset according to the Zipfian distribution with exponent 1 [25].[3] More specifically, the probability of table T_i to have a sensitivity score SC_i equals to j is given by the following equation.

$$Pr\left[SC_i = j\right] = \frac{(j+1)^{-1}}{N_s} \qquad 0 \leq j \leq m \qquad (5)$$

Here, N_s is the normalization factor $\sum_{t=1}^{s+1} \frac{1}{t}$. This assigned sensitivity score indicates the overall sensitivity level of the corresponding table.

We assign a sensitivity score $CL_j^i \in \{0, 1, \cdots, SC_i\}$ to the jth column of the ith table according to the Zipfian distribution. We believe that most of the columns of even a highly sensitive table would have low sensitivity scores. For example, a personnel table in an enterprise database system is likely to contain one or two highly sensitive columns (e.g., SSN). We use Zipfian distribution to assign column sensitivity score to simulate this real world observation.

Finally, we assign sensitivity score to an individual cell belonging to a column with sensitivity score CL_j^i according to a Gaussian distribution $\mathcal{N}(\mu, \sigma)$ with mean $\mu = CL_j^i$ and standard deviation $\sigma = CL_j^i/3$. In real world database tables, we expect most of the cells to have sensitivity scores located near the mean. We choose the mean and the standard deviation of the normal distribution such a way that 99.7% of the values are expected to fall into the range $\left[0, 2 \times CL_j^i\right]$. We replace a negative sensitivity score with a zero value.

5.1.3 Generating Roles.

The roles in our empirical evaluation is defined by the following two characteristics.

1. *Table Partition.* We assume that a user belonging to a role queries on a fixed set of tables denoted as Table Partition.

---

[3]Here, s is a positive integer. We have used $s = 3$ in all our experiments reported in this paper.

2. *Query Preference.* Each role issues queries according to a probability distribution over different types of queries.

Table Partition and *Query Preference* collectively defines a particular role. Each defined role has a Table Partition size of four. Furthermore, each partition is constructed such a way that each table in the partition is related to at least another table in the partition through a foreign key constraint. Again, roles in our implementation submit queries according to the Query Preference.

5.1.4 Generating Queries.

We focus on equality, range and aggregate queries in our implementation. We purposefully leave Group By and Order By clauses from our queries since tuple reordering in query result does not change the sensitivity score according to our definitions. Let us assume that $\mathcal{TP}$ is the table partition for a given role $\mathcal{R}$. We generate our queries in such a way that any query on $\mathcal{TP}$ is equally likely. Therefore, our query generation procedure is unbiased.

5.1.5 Building Hidden Markov Model.

We assume that each role in our RDBMS has its own Hidden Markov Model (HMM). We use a publicly available library to build and train HMM in our implementation[4]. To build each HMM, we use a observation sequence $O = \langle O_1, O_2, \cdots O_n \rangle$ of n observations. Each of these individual observations $O_i = \langle O_i^1, \cdots, O_i^m \rangle$ consists of m query sensitivity scores. Although, each of the two components of query sensitivity score can be characterized as continuous signal, as opposed to discrete symbols. However, we quantize these continuous signals into discrete symbols through a protected version of the mathematical `log` function defined in (6). As defined in 6, $plog_t : \mathcal{R}_{\geq 0} \longmapsto \mathcal{N}_t$ maps a non-negative sensitivity value into a non-negative integer $i \in \mathcal{N}_t$. Here, $\mathcal{N}_t$ is the set of non-negative integers less than or equal to t. That is, $\mathcal{N}_t = \{x \mid (x \in \mathcal{N}) \wedge (x \leq t)\}$. The quantization approach enables us to use discrete probability density functions in the HMM states. In our empirical analysis, we have used $t = 5$.

$$plog_t(x) = \min\{\lceil \log_{10}(x+1) \rceil, t\} \quad (6)$$

5.1.6 Experiment Design.

In all of the experiments presented in this paper, we uniformly pick a role $\mathcal{R}$. Again, we pick a role $\mathcal{R}'$ s.t. the probability of $(\mathcal{R} = \mathcal{R}')$ is $\frac{1}{2}$. We generate a test observation sequence using queries generated by role $\mathcal{R}'$ and use the HMM of role $\mathcal{R}$ to obtain the anomaly score for the generated test observation. If $(\mathcal{R} = \mathcal{R}')$, we consider the observation sequence is correctly classified as a valid query if and only if the anomaly score is less than or equals to the role threshold. Similarly, if $(\mathcal{R} \neq \mathcal{R}')$, we consider the test sequence is correctly classified as an intrusion if and only if the anomaly score is greater than the role threshold. Finally, if p test sequences are correctly classified out of q number of total sequences, we compute the accuracy according to the following equation.

$$Accuracy\ (\%) = \frac{p}{q} \times 100\% \quad (7)$$

---

[4]http://code.google.com/p/jahmm/

5.2 Experiment Results

We present our experimental results in this section. For each of the experiments presented in this section, we use 100 test observation sequences. Furthermore, we use the following values as default parameters. Number of training observation sequence: 200, number of training observation size: 70, number of HMM states: 7, threshold estimation parameter: 7, threshold selection index: 4 and finally we choose test observation size value of 4. We use these default values in all our experiments if not stated otherwise.

5.2.1 Accuracy for different number of HMM states

Figure 2(a) presents the accuracy of our proposed anomaly detection model for different number of HMM states. It is quite evident from Figure 2(a) that even a simple HMM with only 2 states correctly classifies more than 80% of the test observation sequence. HMMs with more number of states (e.g., 4), on the other hand, can classify more than 90% of the test observation sequences correctly.

5.2.2 Accuracy for different test observation size

Figure 2(b) presents the accuracy of the proposed anomaly detection model for different number of test observation size. Here, we choose test observation sequence of different size and investigate its effect on classification accuracy. As can be seen from Figure 2(b), accuracy rises as we increase test observation size from 1 to 4. Beyond that point, accuracy does not change significantly. More importantly, Figure 2(b) clearly demonstrates that our model can successfully classify more than 80% of the test observations of length 1.

5.2.3 Accuracy for different threshold index

In this section, we report the effect of choosing different threshold index on the accuracy of the proposed anomaly detection model. Figure 2(c) presents the accuracy for different threshold index. It is evident the accuracy suffers for smaller values of threshold index. However, it rises once the index hits the value $3 - 4$. Finally, it takes a dip for bigger indices.

6. CONCLUSIONS

Network or Operating System level intrusion detection systems are not sometimes enough to catch database intrusions. Database IDS can play a vital role in catching those previously uncaught intrusions. In this paper, we present a data centric anomaly detection system for relational databases. Our proposed scheme uses hidden markov model to build normal usage profiles based on the query sensitivity values. These profiles are later used to detect query anomaly in the context of a user query session. Our empirical analysis with a real world dataset shows that the proposed scheme can detect query anomaly with high accuracy.

7. ACKNOWLEDGMENTS

This work was partially supported by Air Force Office of Scientific Research FA9550-12-1-0082, National Institutes of Health Grants 1R0-1LM009989 and 1R01HG006844, National Science Foundation (NSF) Grants Career-CNS-0845803, CNS-1111529, CNS-1228198 and Army Research Office Grant W911NF-12-1-0558.

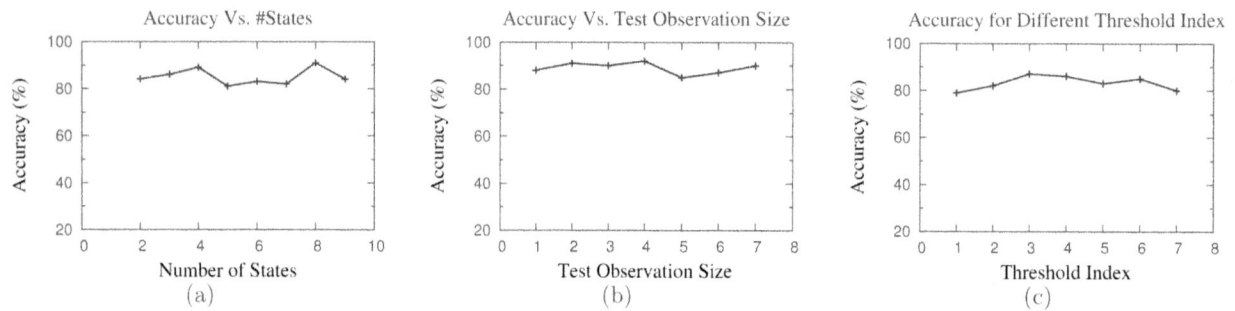

Figure 2: Accuracy for various a) Number of states. b) Test observation size. c) Threshold index.

8. REFERENCES

[1] C. C. Aggarwal and P. S. Yu. Outlier detection for high dimensional data. In *ACM Sigmod Record*, volume 30, pages 37–46. ACM, 2001.

[2] L. E. Baum and T. Petrie. Statistical inference for probabilistic functions of finite state markov chains. *The annals of mathematical statistics*, pages 1554–1563, 1966.

[3] L. E. Baum, T. Petrie, G. Soules, and N. Weiss. A maximization technique occurring in the statistical analysis of probabilistic functions of markov chains. *The annals of mathematical statistics*, pages 164–171, 1970.

[4] S.-B. Cho and S.-J. Han. Two sophisticated techniques to improve hmm-based intrusion detection systems. In *Recent Advances in Intrusion Detection*, pages 207–219. Springer, 2003.

[5] C. Y. Chung, M. Gertz, and K. Levitt. Demids: A misuse detection system for database systems. In *Integrity and Internal Control in Information Systems*, pages 159–178. Springer, 2000.

[6] H. Debar, M. Dacier, and A. Wespi. Towards a taxonomy of intrusion-detection systems. *Computer Networks*, 31(8):805–822, 1999.

[7] D. E. Denning. An intrusion-detection model. *Software Engineering, IEEE Transactions on*, (2):222–232, 1987.

[8] E. Eskin, A. Arnold, M. Prerau, L. Portnoy, and S. Stolfo. A geometric framework for unsupervised anomaly detection. In *Applications of data mining in computer security*, pages 77–101. Springer, 2002.

[9] A. K. Ghosh, J. Wanken, and F. Charron. Detecting anomalous and unknown intrusions against programs. In *Proceedings. of 14th Annual Computer Security Applications Conference, 1998.*, pages 259–267. IEEE, 1998.

[10] A. Harel, A. Shabtai, L. Rokach, and Y. Elovici. M-score: estimating the potential damage of data leakage incident by assigning misuseability weight. In *Insider Threats*, pages 13–20. ACM, 2010.

[11] A. Kamra, E. Terzi, and E. Bertino. Detecting anomalous access patterns in relational databases. *The VLDB Journal*, 17(5):1063–1077, 2008.

[12] M. Kuhlmann, D. Shohat, and G. Schimpf. Role mining-revealing business roles for security administration using data mining technology. In *Proceedings of the eighth ACM symposium on Access control models and technologies*, pages 179–186. ACM, 2003.

[13] A. Lazarevic, L. Ertöz, V. Kumar, A. Ozgur, and J. Srivastava. A comparative study of anomaly detection schemes in network intrusion detection. In *SDM*. SIAM, 2003.

[14] P. Liu. Architectures for intrusion tolerant database systems. In *Proceedings of the 18th Annual Computer Security Applications Conference*, pages 311–320. IEEE, 2002.

[15] Mandiant. Attack the security gap. M Trends 2013 Threat Report.

[16] S. Mathew, M. Petropoulos, H. Q. Ngo, and S. Upadhyaya. A data-centric approach to insider attack detection in database systems. In *Recent Advances in Intrusion Detection*, pages 382–401. Springer, 2010.

[17] P. G. Neumann and P. A. Porras. Experience with emerald to date. In *Workshop on Intrusion Detection and Network Monitoring*, pages 73–80, 1999.

[18] L. Rabiner. A tutorial on hidden markov models and selected applications in speech recognition. *Proceedings of the IEEE*, 77(2):257–286, 1989.

[19] A. Spalka and J. Lehnhardt. A comprehensive approach to anomaly detection in relational databases. In *Data and Applications Security XIX*, pages 207–221. Springer, 2005.

[20] The Wall Street Journal. Target hackers used stolen vendor credentials.

[21] TPC Benchmark^{TM} H (TPC-H). Benchmark specification. http://www.tpc.org.

[22] J. Vaidya, V. Atluri, and Q. Guo. The role mining problem: finding a minimal descriptive set of roles. In *SACMAT*, pages 175–184. ACM, 2007.

[23] G. Vigna, S. T. Eckmann, and R. A. Kemmerer. The stat tool suite. In *DARPA Information Survivability Conference and Exposition, 2000. DISCEX'00. Proceedings*, volume 2, pages 46–55. IEEE, 2000.

[24] S. Wenhui and T. Tan. A novel intrusion detection system model for securing web-based database systems. In *25th Annual International Computer Software and Applications Conference, COMPSAC 2001*, pages 249–254. IEEE, 2001.

[25] G. Zipf. *Selected studies of the Principle of Relative Frequency in Language*. Harvard U.P., 1932.

Password Meters and Generators on the Web: From Large-Scale Empirical Study to Getting It Right

Steven Van Acker
iMinds-DistriNet, KU Leuven,
3001 Leuven, Belgium

Daniel Hausknecht
Chalmers University of
Technology, Sweden

Wouter Joosen
iMinds-DistriNet, KU Leuven,
3001 Leuven, Belgium

Andrei Sabelfeld
Chalmers University of
Technology, Sweden

ABSTRACT

Web services heavily rely on passwords for user authentication. To help users chose stronger passwords, *password meter* and *password generator* facilities are becoming increasingly popular. Password meters estimate the strength of passwords provided by users. Password generators help users with generating stronger passwords.

This paper turns the spotlight on the state of the art of password meters and generators on the web. Orthogonal to the large body of work on password metrics, we focus on getting password meters and generators right in the web setting. We report on the state of affairs via a large-scale empirical study of web password meters and generators. Our findings reveal pervasive trust to third-party code to have access to the passwords. We uncover three cases when this trust is abused to leak the passwords to third parties. Furthermore, we discover that often the passwords are sent out to the network, invisibly to users, and sometimes in clear. To improve the state of the art, we propose SandPass, a general web framework that allows secure and modular porting of password meter and generation modules. We demonstrate the usefulness of the framework by a reference implementation and a case study with a password meter by the Swedish Post and Telecommunication Agency.

Categories and Subject Descriptors

K.6.5 [**Security and Protection**]: Unauthorized access

Keywords

web security; passwords; sandboxing

1. INTRODUCTION

The use of passwords is ubiquitous on the Internet. Although a variety of authentication mechanisms have been proposed [6], password-based authentication, i.e. matching the combination of username and password against credentials stored on the server, is still a widespread way of authen-

ticating on the Internet. Databases with user credentials are often leaked after a website has been compromised [59]. Password storage best practices [40] prescribe organizations to store the passwords hashed with a cryptographically strong one-way hashing algorithm and a credential-specific salt.

Password cracking. Motivated attackers will nevertheless try to reverse the stored hashes into plaintext password by *cracking* the hashes with special tools such as John The Ripper [38]. To crack a password hash, password crackers generate hashes of candidate passwords and compare them to the original hash. If a match is found, the original password was recovered or at least a password that results in the same hash value.

For short enough passwords, it is possible to enumerate passwords of a given length and store all the hashes in a database. This database, known as a *rainbow table* [37], can be used to speedup the cracking of hashes of short-length passwords. To avoid this, passwords can be combined with a *salt* [34] before hashing. Adding a salt to a hash makes rainbow tables less practical because they would have to contain all the hashes of passwords combined with all salts.

With the knowledge that users often select passwords that are based on dictionary words [25], a good strategy for a password cracker is then to use a dictionary of words as the basis for input for the cracker. This practice is known as a *dictionary attack* [34] and is used by the popular CrackLib [10] library to verify the strength of passwords entered by users. Password hashes can often be cracked despite newest hashing algorithms, although it may require a significant amount of time and resources if the plaintext password is well chosen [8].

Password meters and generators. It is thus of vital importance that users pick "strong" passwords, i.e, passwords that are not easily guessable or crackable by cracking tools. However, picking a sufficiently strong password is a difficult task for a typical user [65]. To help users with this task, tools have emerged that both evaluate the strength of user-chosen passwords and generate strong passwords using heuristics. These tools are called *password meters* and *password generators*, respectively.

Although password meters and password generators can help to select stronger passwords [56], they bring a new breed of security problems if designed or implemented carelessly. In the web setting, they are an immediate subject to all the ailments of web applications.

Passwords meters and generators on the web. This paper turns the spotlight on the state of the art of password meters and generators on the web. Orthogonal to the large body of work on password metrics [8, 7, 44, 64, 23], we focus on getting password meters and generators right in the web setting.

Browser extensions, as BadPass [5], to indicate password strength, avoid some security problems by running separately from the code on web pages, but they have the obvious inconvenience of requiring users to install an extension. The abundance of web pages with password meters and generators (analyzed in Section 2) speaks for the popularity of these services in the form of web services, which justifies our focus.

Threat model. First, we are interested in the *passive network attacker* [20] that sniffs the traffic on the network. This attacker might be able to get hold of passwords that are transmitted on the network in clear. Second, we are interested in the *web attacker* [2] that controls certain web sites. Of particular concern are *third-party web attackers* that might harvest passwords when a script from the attacker-controlled web site is included in a password meter or generator service. Also of concern are *second-party web attackers* that are in control of stand-alone password meter and generator services. It is undesirable to pass the actual passwords to such services. Although a password meter might not have the associated username, current fingerprinting techniques facilitate uniquely tracking browsers, allowing the identification of users [14]. A number of techniques such as autocomplete features open up for programmatically determining the usernames.

State of the art. The first part of our work is an analysis of the state of the art of password meters and generators on the web. We report on the state of affairs via an empirical study of password meters and generators reachable from the Bing search engine and top Alexa pages.

Unfortunately, the state of the art leaves much to be desired. Most strikingly, we find that the majority of password meters and generators lend their trust to third-party scripts. The current practice suffers from abusing the privileges of the script inclusion mechanism [36]. A recent real-life example is the defacement of the Reuters site in June 2014 [49], attributed to "Syrian Electronic Army", which compromised a third-party widget (Taboola [52]). This shows that even established content delivery networks risk being compromised, and these risks immediately extend to all web sites that include scripts from such networks.

77.9% of standalone password meters, 76.8% of standalone password generators, and 96.5% of password meters on service signup pages include third-party code (which runs with the same privileges as the main code). Figure 1 depicts the danger with trusting third-party code. A script from a third party has both access to the password and access to network communication to freely leak the password. Our findings (detailed in Section 2) include three websites that send passwords to such third-party sites as ShareThis [51] and Tynt [55].

Another unsettling finding is that password meters commonly send passwords over the network. This is unnatural because the purpose is to help the user with estimating the strength of such sensitive information as passwords. The principle of least privilege [50] calls for restricting the computation to the browser. Nevertheless, we observe that 16.35% of standalone password meters, 26.02% of standalone password generators, and 59.3% of password meters on service signup pages send the password over the network, of which 76.47%, 96.08%, and 3.92% send the password in cleartext

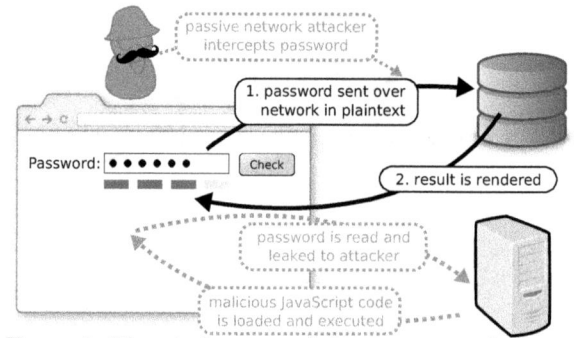

Figure 1: Threats for state-of-the-art password meters

(over HTTP). Figure 1 illustrates the possible attacks. When HTTP is used, the passive network attacker might get hold of the password by sniffing the network traffic. When HTTPS is used, the second-party server (standalone password meter or generator) gets hold of the password, an undesired situation for the first-party service associated with the tested password.

Astonishingly, only one service from all the web services from our empirical study sends hashed passwords to the server. We will come back to this important point in the space of design choices.

Getting it right. With the identified shortcomings of the state of the art at hand, we argue for a *sandboxed client-side* framework and implementation for password meters and generators on the web. From the point of security, such an implementation honors the principle of least privilege: the password stays with the client with password strength estimation/generation executed by JavaScript within the browser. The sandboxing guarantees that the JavaScript code does not access the network. From the point of usability, this enables users to test their actual passwords rather than being forced to distort the original passwords (see the discussion below in the context of the case study). Finally, from the performance point of view, this allows entirely dispensing with client-server round trips for each request. This enables substantial speedup for processing password strength estimation.

Clearly, sending the password to the server can be reasonable for the password meters on service signup pages, where the implementations require that user passwords are stored on the server anyway. However, when it comes to standalone password meters and generators, we make a case for client-side deployment. One possible argument for involving the server in password strength estimation is that the server can check passwords against a dictionary of common words/passwords or a known database of leaked passwords. However, this only makes sense if the size of such a dictionary/database is significant (in which case the secure way to implement the service is to send salted and hashed passwords over HTTPS). We argue that commonly-used password meter libraries, such as CrackLib [10] and zxcvbn [67], are based on dictionaries of size that is susceptible to client-side checking.

Likewise, a reason to generate a password on the server side, is that JavaScript's built-in random number generator is not cryptographically secure on all browsers. The Web Cryptography API [63] will remedy this when it is standardized. In the meantime, there are JavaScript libraries, such as CryptoJS [12], that provide secure cryptographic algorithms to generate random numbers.

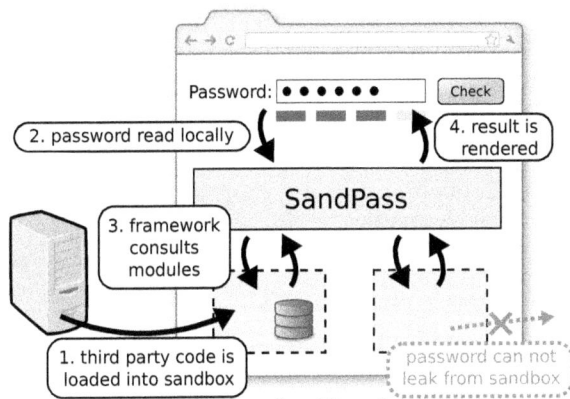
Figure 2: Secure SandPass framework

Generic framework for sandboxing. As a concrete improvement of the state of the art, we propose SandPass, a general web framework that allows secure and modular porting of password meter and generation modules. The framework provides a *generic technique for secure integration of untrusted code* that operates on sensitive data, while stripped of capabilities of leaking it out. We show how to run password meter/generator code in a separate iframe while disabling outside communication and preventing possible password leaks. Figure 2 illustrates the security of the framework. Third-party code is loaded in isolated sandboxes without network access. The framework reads the password locally and consults the modules to score the password strength. Any databases with commonly used passwords or hashes are loaded into the isolated sandboxes as well. We demonstrate the usefulness of the framework by a reference implementation, where we show how to port such known password meter modules as CrackLib [10].

Case study. Following responsible disclosure, we have contacted the web sites that send out passwords and pointed out the vulnerability. One of our reports has resulted in a subsequent case study of a service by the *Swedish Post and Telecommunication Agency (Post- och telestyrelsen, PTS)* [45], a state agency that oversees electronic communications in Sweden. The case study is based on PTS' *Test Your Password* service *(Testa lösenord)* [54]. A quick Internet search of pages linking the service suggests that this service is often recommended by the Swedish organizations, including universities, and the media when encouraging users to check the strength of their passwords. According to PTS, over 1,000,000 passwords have been tested with the service [46].

On the positive side, PTS' service avoids including third-party scripts. However, it sends (over HTTPS) the actual passwords to the server. PTS realizes that this might be problematic, which is manifested by encouraging the users on the web page *not to use their actual passwords* [46]. Not only does this make the service insecure (the users' passwords or their derivatives are leaked to PTS) but also severely limits its utility (the users are forced to distort their passwords and guess the outcome for the real passwords). In addition, the performance of the service is affected by communication round trips to the server on each request.

To help PTS improve the service, and with our reference implementation as the baseline, we have implemented a service that improves the security, utility, and performance of the Test Your Password service. The security is improved as already illustrated by Figure 2 in contrast to Figure 1. The utility is improved by enabling the users to test their real passwords. We have also made the service more interactive, providing feedback on every typed character instead of the original service where the users type the entire password and press a submit button. Due to the volume of JavaScript, our load-time performance increases with the order of 2.5x (unnoticeable for user experience). However, the speedup for the actual password processing is in the order of 34x because it is unnecessary to communicate with the server.

Contributions. A brief summary of the contributions is:

- Bringing much needed attention of the security community to the problem of design and implementation of password meters and generators on the web.

- The first large-scale empirical study of security of web password meters, password generators, and account registration pages.

- Uncovering unsatisfactory state of the art: we point out unnecessary trust to third-party servers, second-party services, and the network infrastructure.

- Development of a generic sandboxing framework that allows code to operate on sensitive data while not allowing leaks out of the sandbox.

- Design and implementation of SandPass, a secure modular password meter/generator framework. We demonstrate security with respect to both the web and passive network attacker.

- Case study with a password meter by the Swedish Post and Telecommunication Agency to improve the security, utility, and performance for a widely used service.

The code for SandPass and case study are available online [58].

2. STATE OF THE ART

To gain insight in password meters and password generators, we performed an extensive Internet search to find standalone instances of them. In addition to occurrences in the wild, they also occur on account signup pages. Since no instances of password generators were observed on signup pages, we do not consider those.

All experiments are based on a common setup which, besides the Firefox browser, also incorporates PhantomJS and mitmproxy.

PhantomJS [4] is a headless browser based on WebKit, scriptable through a JavaScript API. PhantomJS will load a page, render text and images, and execute JavaScript as any regular browser. Interaction with a loaded page can be scripted through a JavaScript API, allowing a user to automate complicated interactions with a web application and process the response. In our experiments, PhantomJS was used to render screenshots of websites once they were loaded and had their JavaScript code executed.

Mitmproxy [3] is a man-in-the-middle proxy which can be used to log, intercept, and modify all HTTP and HTTPS requests and responses passing through it. A CA SSL certificate can be installed in browsers making use of mitmproxy, allowing it to also intercept and modify encrypted traffic without the browser noticing. Python scripts can register hooks into mitmproxy, which are triggered on requests and responses, and which can perform custom actions not originally implemented into mitmproxy. In our experiments, we use mitmdump, a version of mitmproxy without a UI, together with custom hooks that trigger certain actions when a special URL is visited.

The typical workflow of any of our manual experiments is driven by a control-loop which launches a clean Firefox instance and opens an URL to investigate. All traffic is monitored and logged while the user interacts with the loaded webpage. Bookmarklets [35] are used to log information about the visited webpage and transfer that information from Firefox through mitmproxy into the control-loop.

2.1 Stand-alone password meters

Setup. We queried Bing for typical keywords associated with password meters, e.g. "password strength checker", "website to test password strength", "how secure is my password", ... and stored the top 1000 returned URLs for each set of keywords. This resulted in a total dataset of 5900 unique URLs. A number of these webpages are related to password meters in some way, but do not actually contain a functional password meter. To filter those from the dataset, we rendered screenshots for all URLs using PhantomJS, classified them manually and only retained the functional password meters.

Each of the password meters was visited manually using the common setup, and interacted with to input a 20 character password. The response of the webpage was observed to determine whether visual feedback about the strength of the given password was given. During this interaction, all HTTP and HTTPS network traffic was intercepted and logged by mitmdump.

This traffic was then analyzed to see whether any form of the password was transmitted over network. Because some forms might truncate the entered password to a shorter length, we searched for the first 8 to 20 characters of the password. To make sure the password was not sent in an encoded form, we also looked for the MD5, SHA1, SHA224, SHA256, SHA384, SHA512 hashes as well as the Base64 encoding of the different versions of the password.

Results. In the set of 5900 URLs returned by Bing, we found 104 functional password meters. Of those 104, 98 included JavaScript of which 88 were over an insecure HTTP connection, and 81 included JavaScript from a third-party host, with 73 over HTTP. 86 password meters gave visual feedback about the strength of the given password without the user having to press a submit button.

While interacting with the password meters, 17 sent out the password over the network and 13 did so over an unencrypted HTTP connection. Of those 17, 15 required a submit button to be pressed, but two did not and sent the password to a server in the background. Only one of those 17 (`http://www.check-and-secure.com/passwordcheck/`) after having pressed submit, sent the password in a hashed format over the network instead of in plaintext, using both the MD5 and SHA256 hash formats.

None of the observed password meters submitted the password to a third-party host.

2.2 Stand-alone password generators

Setup. We again queried Bing, this time for keywords associated with password generators, e.g. "password generator", "passphrase creator", "create password online", ... and stored the top 1000 returned URLs for each set of keywords. This resulted in a total dataset of 8150 unique URLs.

Just as with the raw "password meter" dataset, this set of URLs contained a number of pages related to, but not containing a password generator. We again rendered screenshots for all URLs and classified them manually.

Each password generator was then visited using our common setup, and interacted with to generate a

Figure 3: Example password generator

password. As Figure 3 suggests, users often have to interact with a password generator to customize its parameters and generate a strong password. The generated password was logged through a bookmarklet so its presence could be detecting in incoming or outgoing network streams. Again, all network traffic generated during each of the visits was logged with mitmproxy.

The network traffic captured during the visit of each password generator was then analyzed to see whether the password, or any truncated or encoded form of it, was transmitted over network either in the requests or their responses.

Results. In the set of 8150 URLs returned by Bing, we found 392 functional password generators. Of those 392, 117 did not require user input to generate a password. In total, 351 of them included JavaScript, of which 332 were over an unencrypted HTTP connection, and 301 included JavaScript from a third-party host, of which 283 were over an unencrypted HTTP connection.

We have contacted the owners of several password generators in order to determine how often their service is used. The three replies we received indicate between 50 and 115 page views on average per day.

After interacting with the password generators, 100 of them generated a password on the server side and transmitted it back to the browser. 96 of those responses happened over an unencrypted HTTP connection.

Surprisingly, six password generators also transmitted the generated password over the network from the client side. Two of those had generated the password locally, while the remaining four received it from a server. While three of the six sent the password back to a server in their own top-level domain, the other three sent the password to two popular JavaScript widgets which enable and track content-sharing on webpages: ShareThis [51] and Tynt [55].

2.3 Password meters on registration pages

Setup. For each domain in the Alexa top 250, we visited the topmost webpage (e.g. `http://example.com` for example.com) and searched for an account signup form by following links and instructions on that webpage. If a signup page was found, and it allowed us to signup for an account freely and easily (e.g. without having to enter a social ID, a credit card number, waiting for an invitation e-mail or other), the URL of the signup page was kept as being usable for this experiment.

We then visited each usable signup page manually using our common setup and typed in a strong 20 character password in

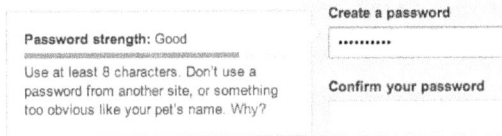

Figure 4: Example password meter from Google

the password field, but we did not click the submit button to complete the signup procedure. Figure 4 shows the password meter in action during our visit to the Google signup page, without having to click a submit button. Again, all HTTP and HTTPS network traffic generated during the visit was logged with mitmproxy.

The network traffic of each visit was analyzed to see whether the password, or any truncated or encoded form of it, was transmitted over network.

Results. From the top 250 Alexa domains we included in our experiment, we discovered 186 usable signup forms. Of the 186 signup pages, 86 use a password meter to give instant visual feedback to the registering user about the strength of the chosen password. Of those 86 signup pages with a password meter, 83 include third-party JavaScript code and 51 transmitted the entered password to a remote server in the background. Of those last 51 password-transmitting password meters on signup pages, two sent the password over unencrypted HTTP.

None of the signup pages sent the password to a host on a third-party domain.

2.4 Discussion

The most insightful results from the previous experiments with regard to our threat model, are summarized in Figure 5, Figure 6, and Figure 7.

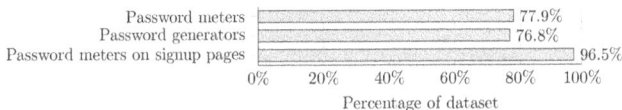

Figure 5: Fraction of dataset including 3rd party JS

Third-party web attacker. Figure 5 shows that the majority of webpages in all three datasets include third-party JavaScript in a JavaScript environment that has access to the password field: 77.9% of standalone password meters, 76.8% of standalone password generators and 96.5% of password meters on account signup pages.

The inclusion of third-party JavaScript can pose a real threat when that JavaScript is under the control of a *third-party web attacker* [36]. Even if the author of third-party JavaScript code is not malicious, the host on which this code is located might be compromised. In that case nothing prevents the attacker from creating JavaScript to read all entered passwords and leak them to the Internet.

Nikiforakis et al. [36] show that close to 70% of the top 10,000 Alexa domains include Google Analytics. We believe that our similar result does not diminish our findings because it indicates that the developers of password meters and generators are unaware of the security implications of including third party JavaScript code.

Although we did not observe any malicious scripts that are actively intercepting and stealing passwords, we have found three cases of standalone password generators from which the

generated passwords are leaked by third-party JavaScript designed to monitor content sharing.

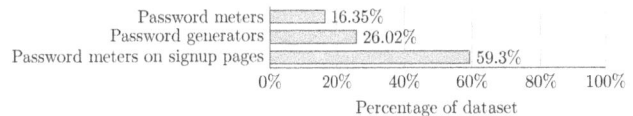

Figure 6: Fraction of dataset transmitting the password

Second-party web attacker. Figure 6 shows that 16.35% of standalone password meters, 26.02% of standalone password generators and 59.3% of password meters on account signup pages transmit passwords over the network to a remote server. This behavior is not isolated to lesser-known websites, but also occurs in highly Alexa-ranked domains. E.g. the password meter on Google's account signup page transmits the password over the network when this password exceeds seven characters.

Despite the availability of client-side solutions for the implemented services, there is a significant fraction that opts to send the password over the network and either check it on a remote server, or generate it on a remote server. It is hypothetically possible that these services use resource-intensive computations that are impractical to implement in client-side JavaScript. However, it is just as well possible that these services have been implemented by *second-party web attackers* with the purpose of tricking visitors into revealing their password and logging them. Nothing distinguishes these two possibilities for the user.

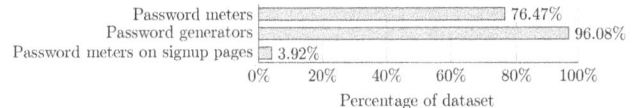

Figure 7: Fraction of password transmissions in the clear

Network attacker. Assuming that a second-party web attacker is not involved, there may be a need to send the password over the network. However, it would be unwise to send these passwords over the network in plaintext, without using encryption via HTTPS. Yet, as Figure 7 shows, the majority of standalone password meters and generators (respectively 76.47% and 96.08%) do not use encryption when transmitting the password. On the other hand, only 3.92% of the account signup pages, with a password meter, from the top 250 Alexa domains transmit the password without encryption. This data shows that a 96.1% majority of the Alexa top 250 website providers, in contrast to the providers of the standalone password meters and generators, better understand the dangers in sending password over an unencrypted connection. The handful of account signup pages in our dataset that do not use encryption when transmitting a password, can have their user's passwords intercepted by a *passive network attacker.*

3. CLIENT-SIDE FRAMEWORK

3.1 Framework

Based on our observations in the web and the attacker model, we identify requirements for the implementation of secure password meters/generators. To support web developers to fulfill these requirements in practice, we design SandPass, a JavaScript framework for secure client-side password meters/generators.

Requirements. The current state of the art for password meters and generators is vulnerable to attacks as described in our threat model in Section 1. The wide use of unencrypted HTTP connections, especially when transmitting passwords in plain text, allows for passive network attacks. But even with encrypted connections, second- and third-party web attackers can be successful by stealing the password from the webpage or tricking the client to send data over the network. However, completely banning third party code from a web page is usually not a realistic option. Also, preventing a website from sending any data over the network at all proves impractical. For example, a registration page with an integrated password meter must be able to send the user credentials to the server to complete the registration process.

It is therefore desirable to have a client-side service which on the one hand allows the inclusion of existing third party solutions for password metering and password generation, while on the other hand restricting the code's capabilities so that it cannot leak any password information. The concrete requirements for a framework to support such a service are as follows:

Client-side only: To prevent a password from being leaked, the password meter/generator does not require server access in order to provide the service. Thus, all password meter/-generator related code must be executed on the client side.

Small code base: The framework code is as small as possible to allow easy revision by web developers integrating the framework in their web page.

Code inclusion: The framework allows the inclusion of third-party code for password metering/generation.

Code isolation: To prevent JavaScript code from interfering with code of other modules or the main page, each module is isolated from the rest of the web page.

No network access: Included JavaScript code cannot send or leak password information over the network.

Result validation: The results of each module are validated before they are used in the main page to avoid content injection attacks.

Safe integration: The framework follows the current best practice for secure web implementations (e.g. the guidelines given by OWASP [39]), i.e. the framework is not the "weakest link" in an otherwise securely programmed web page.

Architecture. The architecture of SandPass is general enough to use it for both password meters and password generators.

For password meters, we assume a setting as illustrated in Figure 2. A user can type in the password in an input field on the main page which the framework then passes to the password meter code for analysis. For password generators, we assume a similar setting with the difference that the user can specify password generator options instead of supplying a password to be tested. SandPass then passes the generator options to the password generator code.

The result of the password/generator is then shown to the user on the same web page. The framework code itself is directly included in the main page and handles the collection of the input data, running the password meter/generator code, and calling the routines for updating the web view (steps 2–4 in Figure 2). These steps are executed every time a password has to be checked or generated.

The program code which actually performs the password metering/generation is downloaded by the framework and integrated in the web page as so called *modules* (step 1 in Figure 2). The purpose of modules is to isolate the third-party code from the web page as well as to restrict its network access.

3.2 Reference implementation

The reference implementation of SandPass respects the requirements and uses the architecture as described in the previous section. Additionally, we avoid using non-standard libraries to prevent dependencies on third-party code which could open security breaches in the framework. Instead, Sand-Pass uses only standard browser features and JavaScript APIs as specified for HTML5 [62].

Standard browser features. The HTML5 *iframe* [17] element allows the embedding of web pages within others. Browsers limit access between iframes according to the *Same-Origin Policy* (SOP). With the `sandbox` attribute set, a browser assigns a unique origin to the iframe, strengthening the SOP access restrictions. By default, the sandbox attribute also disables scripts, forms and popups, which can be re-enabled using the respective keywords.

The JavaScript browser API method `postMessage` [43] provides a cross-origin communication channel for sending data between browser contexts, e.g., an iframe and its host page. A browser context can add an event listener for receiving and handling messages. Besides the actual data, the message contains a `source` attribute which can be used for sending response messages to the dispatcher.

The *Content Security Policy* (CSP) [9] specifies the sources a web page is allowed to access and which protocols to use. The main purpose of CSP is to mitigate the risks of content injection attacks. It therefore prohibits by default inline scripts and the JavaScript `eval` function. These restrictions can be lifted by using the keywords `"unsafe-inline"` and `"unsafe-eval"`, respectively. Though usually defined on the server side, the policies are enforced completely in the client's browser.

```
1  <!-- fetch framework code from server -->
2  <script language="javascript" src="pwdmeter.js" />
3
4  <script language="javascript" />
5    /* respective callback functions */
6    function resultHandler(res) { ... };
7
8    /* module inclusions */
9    include("http://example.com/m.js", resultHandler, "
        check");
10
11   /* running a password strength analysis */
12   runSandPass("myPassword");
13 </script>
```

Listing 1: Example code for including SandPass

SandPass is fully implemented in JavaScript. After downloading the framework and module scripts, all code is executed in the browser without any further server interaction.

The framework can be added to the main web page through common JavaScript inclusion techniques, e.g., through the HTML script element. Listing 1 shows an example web page snippet including the framework in line 2.

SandPass provides an `include` function for the inclusion of modules. The function parameters are a list of all URLs of the script file included in the same module, the result handler function, and the name of the module's main function, i.e. the function called to later execute the module. When `include` is called, the framework fetches the module code from the given sources and creates the respective module.

The *result handler* is a JavaScript function which is called after the associated module returns a result. Its main purpose is to present the result to the user by updating the main web page. Since the demands for the result handler vary for each individual page design, the web developer is completely free to implement this function as she sees fit. The example in Listing 1 defines a result handler in line 6 which is used in line 9 when including modules in the framework.

The framework's `runSandPass` function triggers the password metering or generation (line 12 in Listing 1). The function does not implement any metering/generation logic itself but uses the `postMessage` to call the respective main function of the included modules and to provide the necessary data, e.g. the password.

When a module returns a result to the main page, the framework calls the respective result handler for providing feedback to the user.

Modularity. SandPass modules are implemented as iframes which create a new and secure execution context for included JavaScript code. Each iframe enables the `sandbox` attribute which limits the access permissions to the *Document Object Model* (DOM) of the sandboxed code to its own unique browser context. Since the purpose of a module is to run JavaScript code, the framework also uses the `"allow-scripts"` keyword to re-enable scripts in the sandbox.

Each module contains a basic HTML document which defines the most restrictive CSP rule, prohibiting access to any network resource from within the iframe.

The framework core and a module communicate through the `postMessage` API function. A module therefore contains a message receive handler. On receiving a message, it calls the modules main function and sends its result back to the framework, again using `postMessage`.

The framework imposes no restrictions on the included JavaScript code, i.e. a web developer can include code from any source as she sees fit in the sandbox. This allows SandPass to be utilized for both password meters and password generators.

4. CASE STUDY

The case study is based on the password meter by the Swedish Post and Telecommunication Agency (PTS). Their password meter web page, shown in Figure 8, contains an input field in which a user can type the password. When the submit button ("Testa!") is clicked, the password is sent to PTS for the actual checks. The

Figure 8: PTS passwordmeter

reply is an updated web page with feedback based on the results of the algorithms run on server side.

Besides syntactical checks, e.g. for the usage of upper- and lower-case letters, PTS uses the open-source library *CrackLib*. CrackLib checks if a password is somehow derivable from any word within a given dictionary. It applies transformations to the given password and checks the result for existence in the dictionary. For example, CrackLib substitutes all digits in "p455w0rd" with their respective *leet speak* [26] counterparts and transforms it to "password" which can be found in a common English dictionary.

CrackLib is fully written in C. For inclusion as a module in SandPass it has therefore been necessary to translate it to JavaScript. Additionally, we've implemented a separate script for the syntactic checks. We have then modified the PTS service to include SandPass, replacing the transmit action of the submit button with the `runSandPass` function of the framework. To provide the same results as the server-side approach, the JavaScript version of CrackLib and the script for syntactic checks have been included as modules. The respective result handler functions have been implemented to update the web page to match the layout of the original service.

As a positive side effect, the good performance of SandPass has allowed us to enable checks on every keystroke made by the user and we have therefore even improved the user experience through immediate feedback. Before, the password had had to be sent to the server first for feedback.

5. EVALUATION

SandPass implements the general requirements and architecture presented in Section 3.1. We have evaluated the framework to see how it prevents the attacks from the attacker model, i.e. the passive network attacker and the second- and third-party web attacker. We've also looked at the practical implications of SandPass for security and performance.

5.1 Security evaluation

Security guarantees. SandPass is a framework which is designed to support the implementation of fully client-side password meters and password generators. Client-side code execution renders leaking a password for analysis to the server or requesting password generation from the server redundant. In fact, the framework defines a CSP rule for included code which completely forbids any network traffic. As an implication, no password information can be leaked to a second party web attacker. Additionally, a passive network attacker cannot sniff for transmitted passwords, which is in particular the case when data is sent over only HTTP.

The framework modules are implemented as sandboxed iframes which are treated by browsers as if their content comes from a unique origin. This behavior in combination with the SOP, implemented and enforced by browsers, prevents the code of a module from accessing the DOM of the main page or even other modules. Therefore, the JavaScript code included in a module is isolated and cannot tamper with the rest of the web page. As mentioned before, the framework prevents communication with external resources by implementing the most restrictive CSP for each module, i.e. it forbids any network traffic from within a module. Therefore, a module cannot leak a password to a server. As a result, modules mitigate the threat imposed by third party web attackers and a web developer can include untrusted scripts as modules without compromising the web page's security. Note that our policy for modules affects only modules but not the rest of the web page and a web developer retains all freedom in its design.

Security considerations. Though SandPass comes with the above security guarantees, there are some security considerations which must be addressed when using web frameworks in general.

Firstly, the administrators of a web server must ensure and maintain the security properties for their servers. For Sand-Pass this means that the integrity of the framework's source code must be guaranteed. Otherwise, an attacker can easily disable security features or even replace the framework code entirely. For password meter/generator scripts, *Cross-Origin Resource Sharing* (CORS) [60] must be allowed to permit web pages of other domains to download the source codes and include them as modules. Otherwise, the scripts will be blocked by the SOP enforcement mechanism in the client's browser.

Secondly, the integrity of the framework code must not only be ensured on the server side, but also during the transmission over the network. To limit the risks of attacks there, the server can be configured to always use encrypted connections, i.e. to use HTTPS.

```
1 function evilFun(pwd) {
2   return "<img src='evil.com/img.png?"+pwd+"' />";
3 }
```

Listing 2: Example script code for malicious module

```
1 ...
2 <script language="javascript" />
3   function resHandler(result) {
4     document.getElementById("myElem").innerHTML =
         result;
5   }
6   include("http://example.com/m1.js", resHandler, "
         evilFun");
7 </script>
8 <p id="myElem"></p>
9 ...
```

Listing 3: Example code vulnerable to code injection

Thirdly, since CSP restricts the modules' network access, it is important that a module can not simply navigate its containing iframe to a page without such a restriction by e.g. manipulating `document.location`. To prevent this, the web page in which SandPass is integrated, must restrict the contents of the module iframes by setting the `child-src` CSP directive to e.g. `self` or `none`.

Finally, though every module is isolated through a sandboxed iframe, the framework allows data to flow to the main page through calls of the `postMessage` function. On receiving the data, the framework runs the respective result handler function, i.e. the handler is executed in the context of the main page. Thus, malicious modules can attack the main page through content injections if the result values are not verified properly. Listing 2 shows a possible attack scenario in which a module's main function named `evilFun` returns a string containing HTML code for an `img` element. In Listing 3, the module's result handler directly assigns the returned value to the element `myElem` on the main page. When executed, this creates a `img` element inside the web page's body. On loading the image source, the password is leaked to `evil.com` as part of the URL. This attack can be avoided by, e.g., validating the return value in the result handler or by assigning the return value to the safer HTML element property `textContent` [61] instead of `innerHTML`.

Besides that a wary administrator considers most of the above security issues for all of the services, using SandPass has the benefit that the code for the modules does not need to be hosted, analyzed for malware, updated, or otherwise maintained. The SandPass consists of a small trusted code base (76 LOC), which can be easily reviewed. The modules can be included safely from third parties in a similar way as it is common practice for libraries such as jQuery.

5.2 Performance evaluation

Our performance evaluation [58] indicates a 106ms overhead in loading time over the baseline of 72ms, mostly due to Cracklib's built-in dictionary. The microbenchmark indicates a factor 34x improvement over the delay experienced during a single password check in our PTS use case, and still a factor 2.5x improvement when the server-side password meter is on localhost. Because loading the password meter only needs to happen once, and will be cached by the browser afterwards, the load time delay is negligible. Combined with the results from the microbenchmarks and security evaluation, using a client-side password meter is beneficial for both security and performance.

6. RELATED WORK

Service providers encourage users to select stronger passwords by guidelines to improve the password entropy [16, 31]. The general problem of defining password strength is addressed by a large body of work, based on both estimating password entropy [8, 7] and on empirical password-guessing techniques and tools [44, 64, 23] that might have access to passwords that have been leaked in the past.

Egelman et al. [15] have studied the impact of password meters on password selection in experiments with user groups. The conclusion is that password meters are most useful when users are forced to change passwords.

de Carné de Carnavalet and Mannan [13] analyze password strength meters on popular web sites. They mention a classification of web sites into client-side, server-side, and hybrid meters, but the focus of their study is the password strength metrics and consistency of outcomes. As mentioned earlier, determining password strength is orthogonal to the goals in this paper. Our focus is on secure deployment of password meters and generators in the web setting.

Among the password meters we discuss in Section 2, a popular one is Dropbox's client-side password meter [67] that includes a number of syntactic and dictionary checks but provides no modular architecture or code isolation. It can be easily plugged into SandPass as a module. Another noteworthy project is Telepathwords [48] that attempts guessing the next character of a password as the user types it.

Language-subset JavaScript sandboxing techniques as [28, 11, 42] require the JavaScript code to be written in a safe subset of JavaScript. Such sandboxes place restrictions on JavaScript code, which third-party code providers are often hesitant to follow. Other JavaScript sandboxing techniques [33, 19, 32, 47, 22] require remote JavaScript code to be rewritten or instrumented on the server. These assume that a developer has access to an execution environment on the server, on which to perform the rewriting. Yet other JavaScript sandboxing techniques as [30, 57, 27] require modifications to the browser, which is a drawback for such a dynamic environment as the Internet, without tight control over browser vendors and versions.

There are approaches to JavaScript sandboxing [53, 41, 29, 1, 18, 24, 66, 21] that require neither server-side modification of code nor specially added client-side support. Instead, they use existing security features available in the browser. Some of these [53, 24, 66, 21] do not offer any means to block network traffic generated by the sandboxed JavaScript, and might allow data to leak out this way. Those sandboxes that can restrict network traffic [41, 29, 1, 18] introduce wrapper code around basic DOM functionality, which can be controlled by a fine-grained control mechanism. SandPass does not require such custom fine-grained control over basic DOM functionality, and uses standard browser functionality instead: the modules execute in a sandboxed iframe with a unique origin and CSP blocks all network traffic. Because of the usage of standard browser functionality, SandPass's codebase is small and can easily be code-reviewed.

7. CONCLUSION

We have presented a large-scale study of web-based password meters and generators. To our knowledge, this is the first such study that addresses secure deployment of password meters and generators on the web. It is alarming that services that are trusted to handle sensitive password information take the liberty to extend the trust to third-party web sites. We find that the vast majority of password meters and generators are open to third-party attacks. Further, we show that some password generators actually leak passwords to third-party web sites via JavaScript. We also find that online password meters are not widely adopted on account registration pages, but most of them also follow unsafe practices allowing credentials to leak away. Another finding is that a substantial fraction of password meters sends passwords to the network, sometimes in plaintext.

As a concrete step to advance the state of the art, we have designed and implemented SandPass, a modular and secure web framework for password meters and generators. By appropriately tuning the CSP policy for iframes, we achieve code isolation for password meter/generator code, enabling security, usability, and performance improvements. We show the usefulness of the framework with a reference implementation that indicates that client-side deployment is advantageous even in cases when password meters include dictionary checks. To further demonstrate the benefits of the framework, we perform a successful case study that allows improving the security, usability, and performance of the password strength meter provided by PTS.

SandPass enables a general technique for modular and secure sandboxing of untrusted code. There is a number of independently interesting applications scenarios for this type of sandboxing. For example, a loan or tax calculator needs access to users' private financial information, which the users might not like to leave the browser.

On the side of practical impact, we are currently in contact with PTS to help improve the current service [54] with our case study as the base.

Acknowledgements. This work was partly funded by the European Community under the ProSecuToR and WebSand projects and the Swedish research agencies SSF and VR. It was also partially funded by the Research Fund KU Leuven, and by the EU FP7 project NESSoS. With the financial support from the Prevention of and Fight against Crime Programme of the European Union (B-CCENTRE).

8. REFERENCES

[1] P. Agten, S. Van Acker, Y. Brondsema, P. H. Phung, L. Desmet, and F. Piessens. JSand: complete client-side sandboxing of third-party JavaScript without browser modifications. In *ACSAC*, 2012.

[2] D. Akhawe, A. Barth, P. E. Lam, J. C. Mitchell, and D. Song. Towards a formal foundation of web security. In *CSF*, 2010.

[3] Aldo Cortesi. mitmproxy. http://mitmproxy.org.

[4] Ariya Hidayat. PhantomJS. http://phantomjs.org.

[5] Badpass: password strength indicator. https://addons.mozilla.org/en-US/firefox/addon/badpass/.

[6] J. Bonneau, C. Herley, P. C. van Oorschot, and F. Stajano. The quest to replace passwords: A framework for comparative evaluation of web authentication schemes. In *S&P*, 2012.

[7] W. E. Burr, D. F. Dodson, W. T. Polk, and D. L. Evans. Electronic authentication guideline. In *NIST Special Publication*, 2004.

[8] L. S. Clair, L. Johansen, W. Enck, M. Pirretti, P. Traynor, P. McDaniel, and T. Jaeger. Password exhaustion: Predicting the end of password usefulness. In *ICISS*, 2006.

[9] Content security policy 1.0. http://www.w3.org/TR/CSP/.

[10] CrackLib. http://cracklib.sourceforge.net/.

[11] D. Crockford. ADsafe – making JavaScript safe for advertising. http://adsafe.org/.

[12] CryptoJS. https://code.google.com/p/crypto-js/.

[13] X. de Carné de Carnavalet and M. Mannan. From very weak to very strong: Analyzing password-strength meters. In *NDSS*, 2014.

[14] P. Eckersley. How unique is your web browser? In *PET*, 2010.

[15] S. Egelman, A. Sotirakopoulos, I. Muslukhov, K. Beznosov, and C. Herley. Does my password go up to eleven?: The impact of password meters on password selection. In *SIGCHI*, 2013.

[16] Google password help. https://accounts.google.com/PasswordHelp.

[17] Html - living standard: The iframe element. http://www.whatwg.org/specs/web-apps/current-work/multipage/the-iframe-element.html.

[18] L. Ingram and M. Walfish. TreeHouse: JavaScript sandboxes to help web developers help themselves. In *USENIX ATC*, 2012.

[19] Jacaranda. Jacaranda. http://jacaranda.org.

[20] C. Jackson and A. Barth. Forcehttps: protecting high-security web sites from network attacks. In *WWW*, 2008.

[21] C. Jackson and H. J. Wang. Subspace: secure cross-domain communication for web mashups. In *WWW*, 2007.

[22] T. Jim, N. Swamy, and M. Hicks. Defeating Script Injection Attacks with Browser-Enforced Embedded Policies. In *WWW*, 2007.

[23] P. Kelley, S. Komanduri, M. Mazurek, R. Shay, T. Vidas, L. Bauer, N. Christin, L. Cranor, and J. Lopez. Guess again (and again and again): Measuring password strength by simulating password-cracking algorithms. In *S&P*, 2012.

[24] F. D. Keukelaere, S. Bhola, M. Steiner, S. Chari, and S. Yoshihama. Smash: secure component model for cross-domain mashups on unmodified browsers. In *WWW*, 2008.

[25] D. V. Klein. Foiling the cracker: A survey of, and improvements to, password security. *USENIX Security*, 1990.

[26] Leet. http://en.wikipedia.org/wiki/Leet.

[27] T. Luo and W. Du. Contego: capability-based access control for web browsers. In *TRUST*, 2011.

[28] S. Maffeis and A. Taly. Language-based isolation of untrusted Javascript. In *CSF*, 2009.

[29] J. Magazinius, P. Phung, and D. Sands. Safe wrappers and sane policies for self protecting JavaScript. In *Nordsec*, 2010.

[30] L. Meyerovich and B. Livshits. ConScript: Specifying and enforcing fine-grained security policies for Javascript in the browser. In *S&P*, 2010.

[31] Create strong passwords. https://www.microsoft.com/security/pc-security/password-checker.aspx.

[32] Microsoft Live Labs. Live Labs Websandbox. http://websandbox.org.

[33] M. S. Miller, M. Samuel, B. Laurie, I. Awad, and M. Stay. Caja - safe active content in sanitized JavaScript. Technical report, Google Inc., June 2008.

[34] R. Morris and K. Thompson. Password security - a case history. *Commun. ACM*, 22(11):594–597, 1979.

[35] Mozilla. Use bookmarklets to quickly perform common web page tasks. https://support.mozilla.org/en-US/kb/bookmarklets-perform-common-web-page-tasks.

[36] N. Nikiforakis, L. Invernizzi, A. Kapravelos, S. Van Acker, W. Joosen, C. Kruegel, F. Piessens, and G. Vigna. You are what you include: large-scale evaluation of remote javascript inclusions. In *CCS*, 2012.

[37] P. Oechslin. Making a faster cryptanalytic time-memory trade-off. In *CRYPTO*, 2003.

[38] Openwall. John the ripper password cracker. http://www.openwall.com/john/.

[39] OWASP. HTML5 Security Cheat Sheet. https://www.owasp.org/index.php/HTML5_Security_Cheat_Sheet.

[40] OWASP. Password storage cheat sheet. https://www.owasp.org/index.php/Password_Storage_Cheat_Sheet.

[41] P. H. Phung, D. Sands, and A. Chudnov. Lightweight self-protecting JavaScript. In *ASIACCS*, 2009.

[42] J. G. Politz, S. A. Eliopoulos, A. Guha, and S. Krishnamurthi. ADsafety: type-based verification of JavaScript Sandboxing. In *USENIX Security*, 2011.

[43] Html - living standard: Posting messages. http://www.whatwg.org/specs/web-apps/current-work/multipage/web-messaging.html.

[44] R. W. Proctor, M.-C. Lien, K.-P. L. Vu, E. E. Schultz, and G. Salvendy. Improving computer security for authentication of users: influence of proactive password restrictions. *BRMIC*, 34(2):163–9, 2002.

[45] Swedish Post and Telecommunication Agency. http://www.pts.se/.

[46] A million tested passwords. http://www.pts.se/en-GB/News/Press-releases/2012/A-million-tested-passwords/.

[47] C. Reis, J. Dunagan, H. J. Wang, O. Dubrovsky, and S. Esmeir. BrowserShield: vulnerability-driven filtering of dynamic HTML. In *OSDI*, 2006.

[48] M. Research. Telepathwords: Preventing weak passwords by reading your mind. https://telepathwords.research.microsoft.com/.

[49] Syrian Electronic Army uses Taboola ad to hack Reuters (again). https://nakedsecurity.sophos.com/2014/06/23/syrian-electronic-army-uses-taboola-ad-to-hack-reuters-again/.

[50] J. H. Saltzer and M. D. Schroeder. The protection of information in computer systems. *IEEE*, 1975.

[51] Sharethis. http://www.sharethis.com/.

[52] Taboola. https://www.taboola.com/.

[53] M. Ter Louw, K. T. Ganesh, and V. Venkatakrishnan. AdJail: Practical Enforcement of Confidentiality and Integrity Policies on Web Advertisements. In *USENIX Security*, 2010.

[54] Test your password (testa lösenord). https://testalosenord.pts.se/.

[55] Tynt. http://www.tynt.com/.

[56] B. Ur, P. G. Kelley, S. Komanduri, J. Lee, M. Maass, M. L. Mazurek, T. Passaro, R. Shay, T. Vidas, L. Bauer, N. Christin, and L. F. Cranor. How does your password measure up? the effect of strength meters on password creation. In *USENIX Security*, 2012.

[57] S. Van Acker, P. De Ryck, L. Desmet, F. Piessens, and W. Joosen. WebJail: least-privilege integration of third-party components in web mashups. In *ACSAC*, 2011.

[58] S. Van Acker, D. Hausknecht, and A. Sabelfeld. Password meters and generators on the web: From large-scale empirical study to getting it right – full version and code. http://www.cse.chalmers.se/~andrei/SandPass/.

[59] Verizon. 2014 data breach investigations report. http://www.verizonenterprise.com/DBIR/2014/.

[60] W3C. Cross-Origin Resource Sharing. http://www.w3.org/TR/cors/.

[61] W3C. Document Object Model Core – textContent. http://www.w3.org/TR/DOM-Level-3-Core/core.html#Node3-textContent.

[62] W3C. W3C Standards and drafts - JavaScript APIs. http://www.w3.org/TR/#tr_JavaScript_APIs.

[63] Web Cryptography API. http://www.w3.org/TR/WebCryptoAPI/.

[64] M. Weir, S. Aggarwal, M. P. Collins, and H. Stern. Testing metrics for password creation policies by attacking large sets of revealed passwords. In *CCS*, 2010.

[65] J. J. Yan, A. F. Blackwell, R. J. Anderson, and A. Grant. Password memorability and security: Empirical results. *S&P*, 2004.

[66] S. Zarandioon, D. Yao, and V. Ganapathy. Omos: A framework for secure communication in mashup applications. In *ACSAC*, 2008.

[67] zxcvbn: realistic password strength estimation. https://tech.dropbox.com/2012/04/zxcvbn-realistic-password-strength-estimation/.

Database Fragmentation with Confidentiality Constraints: A Graph Search Approach*

Xiaofeng Xu
Emory University
400 Dowman Dr.
Atlanta, GA 30322
xiaofeng.xu@emory.edu

Li Xiong
Emory University
400 Dowman Dr.
Atlanta, GA 30322
lxiong@mathcs.emory.edu

Jinfei Liu
Emory University
400 Dowman Dr.
Atlanta, GA 30322
jinfei.liu@emory.edu

ABSTRACT

Database fragmentation is a promising approach that can be used in combination with encryption to achieve secure data outsourcing which allows clients to securely outsource their data to remote untrusted server(s) while enabling query support using the outsourced data. Given a set of confidentiality constraints, it vertically partitions the database into fragments such that the set of attributes in each constraint do not appear together in any one fragment. The optimal fragmentation problem is to find a fragmentation with minimum cost for query support. In this paper, we propose an efficient graph search based approach which obtains near optimal fragmentation. We model the fragmentation search space as a graph and propose efficient search algorithms on the graph. We present static and dynamic search strategies as well as a novel level-wise graph expansion technique which dramatically reduces the search time. Extensive experiments showed that our method significantly outperforms other state-of-the-art methods.

1. INTRODUCTION

Data security is widely recognized as a major barrier to cloud computing and other data outsourcing arrangements. Users are reluctant to place their sensitive data in the cloud due to concerns about data disclosure to potentially untrusted cloud providers and other malicious parties. The problem of secure data outsourcing or secure Data-As-a-Service (DAS) has received increasing attention in recent years [14]. The goal is to allow a client to securely outsource their data on remote untrusted server(s) while enabling computations or query support using the outsourced data [4, 21].

A common approach for secure DAS is to store entirely encrypted data on the server. Fully homomorphic encryption scheme [11, 12, 25] allows a user to store fully encrypted data while enabling arbitrary computations on the

*This research is supported by the AFOSR DDDAS program under grant FA9550-12-1-0240.

Table 1: Sample relation and confidentiality constraints

(a) PATIENT

SSN	Name	Occup	Sickness	ZIP
485-95-5671	A.Hellman	Nurse	Obesity	30322
456-32-8672	B.Dooley	Nurse	Obesity	30322
634-34-5776	C.McKinley	Clerk	Obesity	30307
675-96-3284	B.Dooley	Lawyer	Celiac	30322
546-46-2755	E.Taylor	Manger	Latex al.	30332
784-38-6673	F.White	Designer	Pollen al.	30396

(b) Constraints

C_0 {SSN}
C_1 {Name, Occup}
C_2 {Name, Sickness}
C_3 {Occup, Sickness, ZIP}

encrypted data, however, its computation cost is prohibitive in practice. Many works have focused on supporting specific queries on encrypted data using specialized encryptions (e.g. [5, 19, 20, 24]). They often require weaker forms of encryptions for complex queries. It is difficult for encryption alone to support versatile and efficient computation on the outsourced data with assurances of data confidentiality and data privacy.

Rekatsinas et.al. [22] recently formalized the problem of *privacy-aware data partitioning*, where a sensitive dataset is partitioned among untrusted parties. Even earlier, database fragmentation [6, 7] has already been proposed as a promising approach that can be used in combination with encryption to achieve secure DAS. In many scenarios, the confidentiality requirements can be represented as a set of *confidentiality constraints* specifying the sensitive attributes and sensitive associations among attributes that need to be protected. Table 1(a) shows a sample database relation PATIENT with 5 attributes. Table 1(b) shows an example set of confidentiality constraints on relation PATIENT. Singleton constraints involving a single attribute such as C_0 states that the attribute itself is sensitive. Association constraints involving multiple attributes such as C_1, C_2 and C_3 state that the associations among these attributes are sensitive, i.e. the attributes should not be visible together. The rationale for constraints such as C_3 is that the combination of *Occup* and *ZIP* may form a quasi-identifier [23] which will allow linking and re-identification attacks and lead to attribute association disclosure of *Sickness* with individual identities. While many works have focused on inference control on the databases [10] which can be useful for defining such confidentiality constraints, we assume, in this paper, the set of constraints are defined by the data owner and study the fragmentation techniques to enforce such association constraints.

Singleton constraints can be enforced via encryption of the attribute. Association constraints can be enforced via *fragmentation* which vertically partitions the database into

Table 2: Physical fragments

(a) Enc_F_1

salt	enc	Name
s_1	α	A.Hellman
s_2	β	B.Dooley
s_3	γ	C.McKinley
s_4	δ	B.Dooley
s_5	ϵ	E.Taylor
s_6	ζ	F.White

(b) Enc_F_2

salt	enc	Occup
s_7	η	Nurse
s_8	θ	Nurse
s_9	ι	Clerk
s_{10}	κ	Lawyer
s_{11}	λ	Manager
s_{12}	μ	Designer

(c) Enc_F_3

salt	enc	Sickness	ZIP
s_{13}	ν	Obesity	30322
s_{14}	ξ	Obesity	30322
s_{15}	π	Obesity	30307
s_{16}	ρ	Celiac	30322
s_{17}	σ	Latex al.	30332
s_{18}	τ	Pollen al.	30396

fragments, such that the attributes in the same constraint will not appear together in any fragment as cleartext. A fragmentation that satisfies all confidentiality constraints is called a *safe fragmentation*. Table 2 shows a possible safe fragmentation over PATIENT. Design of the physical fragments Enc_F_i will be explained later in Section 3. The fragmented database can be then outsourced to distributed servers. It is important to note that collusion attacks are also prevented in this mechanism. When multiple servers collude, even though they have the attributes together, they cannot link them with the same tuple, in other words, the association between attributes is still protected.

Not surprisingly, the fragmented data will introduce overhead for processing queries that involve attributes from multiple fragments. Given a cost model that measures the query processing overhead, the *optimal fragmentation problem* is to find a safe fragmentation with minimum cost. The optimal fragmentation problem has been shown to be NP-Hard [7, 22]. The size of the search space for the problem of n attributes is the nth Bell number, $Bell(n)$, which exponentially grows with n (e.g. $Bell(32) = 1.2806 \times 10^{26}$). Thus when n is relatively large, even one time operation of exhaustive search will take several years. The fragmentation problem can also be considered as constrained clustering problem with set constraints (association constraints). However, existing constrained clustering methods only consider pairwise *must-link* and *cannot-link* constraints [27].

Several heuristic methods regarding fragmentation with confidentiality constraints have been proposed. Ciriani et al. proposed the heuristic search method [6] which constructs a fragmentation tree consisting of all possible fragmentations and searches the fragmentation tree with some heuristic pruning strategies. They proposed another hierarchical clustering algorithm [7] based on nearest joins. However, these methods tend to result in suboptimal solutions due to their greedy search strategies. Improving the performance of heuristic method for the optimal fragmentation problem is the main contribution of this paper.

Contributions. In this paper, we propose an efficient graph search based approach for database fragmentation with confidentiality constraints. We model the search space as a graph where each vertex represents a possible solution (fragmentation) and each edge represents a transformation from one solution to another. We propose efficient search algorithms based on the general approach of local search [8] and guided local search [26] which are metaheuristic methods for solving computationally hard optimization problems. We present static and dynamic greedy search strategies as well as a novel level-wise graph expansion technique which dramatically reduces the search time. Extensive experiments showed that our method significantly outperforms other state-of-the-art methods.

The rest of this paper is organized as follows. Section 2 presents the related work. Section 3 gives an overview of the fragmentation problem. Section 4 presents our proposed graph search models and algorithms. Section 5 presents the experimental results. In Section 6, we conclude this paper and propose some future work.

2. RELATED WORK

In this section, we review some related work about secure data outsourcing and privacy-aware fragmentation.

2.1 Secure Data Outsourcing

In attempting to enhance the security of data outsourcing, a number of different approaches based on encryption have been proposed. Techniques for supporting specific operations or search on encrypted data developed in the cryptographic community [5, 24] provide strong security guarantees. The break-through of the fully homomorphic encryption scheme [11, 12, 25] bears the potential to allow a cloud user to store fully encrypted data while enabling arbitrary computations on the encrypted data. The recently developed *CryptDB* system provides a promising on-the-fly approach that explores different layers of encryption to provide confidentiality over a database system while supporting database operations [19, 20]. Other works, for example [5, 13, 24], require weaker forms of encryptions for complex queries such as joins or other queries which are costly for medium-size to very large scale data. The most essential limitation, for encryption-based methods, is that the computation cost on encrypted data is prohibitive in practice.

The literature following the seminal work on k-anonymity [16, 17] adopts syntactic privacy notions by considering specific attacks and assuming the attacker has limited background knowledge [10]. Differential privacy [9] is a strong semantic notion for guaranteeing privacy with arbitrary background knowledge for statistical data release. These methods typically only allow aggregation or perturbed statistics to be released and do not support transaction query processing that involve individual records.

2.2 Privacy-Aware Fragmentation

Recently, Rekatsinas et al. [22] formalized the problem of *privacy-aware data partitioning*, where a sensitive dataset is partitioned among untrusted parties, and proposed a general method which considered both vertical and horizontal fragmentation. A key assumption for this work is that the fragmentation servers do not collude with each other. In contrast, we focus on vertical fragmentation which is resistant to collusion. Moreover, the utility defined in [22] is the general information value in the partitioned datasets by assuming the fragments cannot be joined with each other, while our work considers the utility of query support by the fragmented data, which can be joined by trusted mediators to answer queries, in the form of data transmission cost during query processing. Below we review the works on combining vertical fragmentation and confidentiality constraints, which consider the same problem setting and are most closely related to our work.

Vertical fragmentation has been used in combination with encryption to ensure confidentiality constraints for secure data outsourcing problems. By partitioning the data into several fragments, the method of fragmentation avoids introducing perturbation or noise to the original data and supports query processing. Several heuristic methods have been proposed recently regarding the optimal fragmentation problem with confidentiality constraints. The heuristic search method [6] is based on the monotonicity of the predefined query cost and a well-designed fragmentation tree which covers the whole search space. The fragmentation tree is designed such that any offspring of an unsafe fragmentation is unsafe. Consequently, the sub-tree rooted from an unsafe fragmentation will be pruned during the search. When the volume of confidentiality constraints is sufficiently large, the pruning strategy will dramatically reduce the executing time of query processing. The hierarchical clustering method [7] for database fragmentation is based on *nearest joins*. In each iteration, two attributes with highest attribute affinity are joined if the join will not violate the confidentiality constraints. The algorithm terminates when no pair of attributes can be joined.

Different from these works, our approach models the search space as a *fragmentation graph*. Our search strategy allows dynamic navigation through the graph, guided by the confidentiality constraints, instead of a rigid top-down search strategy, and hence dramatically increases the chance to reach the optimal solution.

3. PROBLEM SETUP AND OVERVIEW

We first provide some preliminary definitions and present a formal problem setting.

3.1 Fragmentation

Definition 3.1 (Fragmentation [7]) *Given a relation scheme R and a set $A \subset R$ of attributes to be fragmented, a fragmentation of R on A is a set of fragments $\mathcal{F} = \{F_1, \cdots, F_k\}$ such that: 1) (Validity) $\forall F_i \in \mathcal{F}, F_i \subset A$; 2) (Completeness) $\forall a \in A, \exists F_i \in \mathcal{F} : a \in F_i$; and 3) (Disjointness) $\forall F_i, F_j \in \mathcal{F}, i \neq j : F_i \cap F_j = \varnothing$.*

As shown in Table 2, each fragment $F_i \in \mathcal{F}$ is physically stored in a relation, denoted Enc_F_i, called *physical fragment*. It is defined on the set $\{\underline{salt}, enc, a_{i_1}, \cdots, a_{i_n}\}$, where $a_{i_1}, \cdots, a_{i_n}$ are the attributes in F_i in clear form and enc is the encrypted values of all other attributes in R except $a_{i_1}, \cdots, a_{i_n}$, XOR'ed with the *salt*, which is a random value different for each tuple used for preventing frequency-based attacks over the encrypted values. Sensitive attributes such as SSN are encrypted in enc. In short, the data are replicated in each physical fragment with the attributes corresponding to the fragment in clear form while other attributes in encrypted form. The physical fragments can be distributed at different servers. Replicated data fragments enjoy two major advantages: 1) *availability* - failure of any fragment containing relation R does not result in unavailability of R in other fragments. Although some attributes in the fragments are encrypted, the completeness of the relation is still guaranteed within any single fragment; 2) *reduced data transfer* - relation R is available locally at each site containing a replica of R, thus only the fragment with minimum intermediate result contributes to the overall data transfer. Data transfer is closely relevant to the query cost of distributed database systems, which will be discussed later in this section. Note that the system combining fragmentation and encryption has been proved to be confidentiality preserving in [2] and [3].

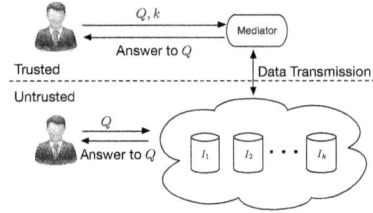

Figure 1: Query processing model

3.2 Cost Model

Figure 1 illustrates the query processing model we considered in this paper for supporting user queries using the encrypted and fragmented data. An untrusted user submits queries directly to the server that stores the fragment containing the cleartext contents to be queried, and receive the results from the corresponding server. A trusted user who is authorized to access both the cleartext and the encrypted content submit the query Q together with the key k needed for decrypting the data to a trusted query mediator. The mediator transforms query Q for each physical fragment with a subset of the queried attributes $\{a_{i_j}\}$ that overlaps with the attributes in each corresponding fragment. Each physical fragment then processes the query locally and the fragment with least amount of result data transfers the result to the mediator. The mediator then decrypts the encrypted attributes using the key provided by the user, discards spurious tuples, and finally returns the query result to the user.

The cost of distributed querying systems can be expressed with respect to the response time, consisting of two parts: local processing cost and data transfer cost. However, data transfer cost is the dominant time factor in wide networks such as the Internet [18]. Next we describe the transfer cost in our query processing model.

Let $\mathcal{Q} = \{Q_1, \cdots, Q_q\}$ be a set of queries that access relation R with attributes $A = \{a_1, \cdots, a_n\}$. Each query has an executing frequency $freq(Q_i)$ with $0 < freq(Q_i) < 1, \forall 1 \leq i \leq q$ and $\sum_{1 \leq i \leq q} freq(Q_i) = 1$. A query Q_i is formed as "*select* $a_{i_1}, \cdots, a_{i_n}$ *from* R *where* $\bigwedge_{l=1}^{n}(a_l \in V_l)$", where V_l is a set of values in the domain of attribute a_l. For a query Q_i and a fragment F_j, the query cost is calculated as $Cost(Q_i, F_j) = S(Q_i, F_j) \cdot |R| \cdot size(t_j)$, where $S(Q_i, F_j)$ is the *selectivity* of the query, $|R|$ is the number of records in relation R, and $size(t_j)$ is the length of queried tuple. The selectivity of an attribute a_l is the ratio of the tuples satisfying the querying condition for a_l, i.e. $\frac{|V_l|}{|R|}$, where $|V_l|$ is the size of V_l. We assume the values of different attributes are distributed independently of each other, the selectivity $S(Q_i, F_j)$ is then the product of the selectivity for all attributes. If attribute a_l does not appear in F_j the selectivity for a_l is set to 1. Since only the fragment with the smallest query result set returns the result back to the mediator, the final query cost of Q_i is calculated as the minimum of the query cost for all fragments, $Cost(Q_i, \mathcal{F}) = \min_{1 \leq j \leq k} Cost(Q_i, F_j)$. Thus given a fragmentation $\mathcal{F}$ and the query set $\mathcal{Q}$, the query cost for the fragmentation is $Cost(\mathcal{F}) = \sum_{1 \leq i \leq q} Cost(Q_i, \mathcal{F}) \cdot freq(Q_i)$. This definition of query cost is first introduced in [6]. Here we give a simple example of computing the query cost for a single query.

Example 3.1 *Given a query* Q: *"select * from PATIENT where Sickness = Obesity and Occup = Nurse", a fragmentation* $\mathcal{F}=\{F_1, F_2, F_3\}$ *with* $F_1=\{Name\}$, $F_2=\{Occup\}$, $F_3=\{Sickness, ZIP\}$, *the number of records* $|R| = 6$, *and* $size(t_j) = 1$ *for each fragment, the query cost* $Cost(Q, F_1) = 1 \cdot 6 \cdot 1 = 6$, $Cost(Q, F_2) = \frac{1}{3} \cdot 6 \cdot 1 = 2$, $Cost(Q, F_3) = \frac{1}{2} \cdot 6 \cdot 1 = 3$. *So* $Cost(Q, \mathcal{F}) = min\{6, 2, 3\} = 2$.

Note that the definition of query cost can change according to the query processing model and the network environment and that our method is a generic method which applies to any formula of query cost.

3.3 Confidentiality Constraints

In this subsection, we formally present some definitions including *confidentiality constraint* and *safe fragmentation*, and based on which, the optimal fragmentation problem is defined.

Definition 3.2 (Confidentiality constraint [7]) *Given a set* A *of attributes, a confidentiality constraint* C *over* A *is 1) a singleton set* $\{a\}$, *stating that the value of the attribute is sensitive; or 2) a subset* $C \subset A$, *stating that the association between values of the given attributes is sensitive.*

Singleton constraints can only be solved by encryption; the method of fragmentation only solves non-singleton constraints. Since the satisfaction of a constraint C_i implies the satisfaction of any constraint C_j if $C_i \subset C_j$, we consider a *well defined* set of constraints $\mathcal{C} = \{C_1, C_2, \cdots, C_m\}$, i.e. $\forall C_i, C_j \in \mathcal{C}$ and $i \neq j$, we have $C_i \subsetneq C_j$.

Definition 3.3 (Safe fragmentation [7]) *Given a relation schema* R, *a set* $\mathcal{C} = \{C_1, C_2, \cdots, C_m\}$ *of well defined constraints over* R, *and a set* A *of attributes to be fragmented, a fragmentation* $\mathcal{F} = \{F_1, \cdots, F_k\}$ *is safe iff* $C_i \subsetneq F_j, \forall 1 \leq i \leq m, 1 \leq j \leq k$.

Definition 3.4 (Optimal fragmentation) *Given a relation schema* R, *a set* $\mathcal{C}$ *of well defined constraints over* R, *a set* A *of attributes to be fragmented. The fragmentation* $\mathcal{F}$ *is optimal iff 1)* $\mathcal{F}$ *is a safe fragmentation of* R *on* A; *and 2)* $\forall \mathcal{F}^\star$ *and* $\mathcal{F}^\star$ *is safe, we have* $Cost(\mathcal{F}^\star) \geq Cost(\mathcal{F})$.

We formulate the optimal fragmentation problem as the following constrained optimization problem:

$$\arg \min_{\mathcal{F} \in \mathcal{U}} \{\mathcal{F} \in \mathcal{O} : Cost(\mathcal{F})\}$$

where $\mathcal{U}$ is the universal search space, $\mathcal{O} \subset \mathcal{U}$ is the feasible space consisting of all safe fragmentations.

4. ALGORITHMS

In this section, we present our graph search approach which achieves near optimal solutions for the above constrained optimization problem.

4.1 Graph Search Method

We represent the search space for the optimization problem as a fragmentation graph, denoted as $\mathcal{G}(\mathcal{U}, \mathcal{E})$, which is a graph constructed by representing the fragmentations as a set of vertices $\mathcal{U}$ and transformations between fragmentations as a set of edges $\mathcal{E}$. A fragmentation in the fragmentation graph is also called a *state*; a safe (unsafe) fragmentation is called a safe (unsafe) state. Two states x_i

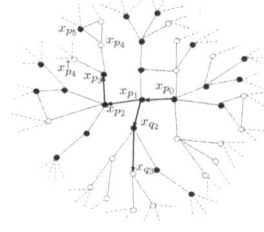

Figure 2: An example of fragmentation graph

and x_j are neighbors, i.e. connected by an edge, denoted as (x_i, x_j), if and only if they can transform to each other through an *atomic operation*. Here we consider *jump* as the atomic operation.

Definition 4.1 (Jump) *Given a fragmentation* $\mathcal{F} \in \mathcal{U}$ *and* $\mathcal{F}=\{F_1, \cdots, F_k\}$, *a source* F_s *and a destination* F_d *where* $1 \leq s, d \leq k$ *and* $s \neq d$, *an attribute* $a \in F_s$,

$$Jump(\mathcal{F}, a, d) = \{F_1, \cdots, F_s \setminus \{a\}, \cdots, F_d \bigcup \{a\}, \cdots F_k\}.$$

A *jump* operation transforms one fragmentation to another by moving an attribute from one fragment to another. For example, fragmentation $\{\{NSO\}\{Z\}\}$ can *jump* to $\{\{NS\}\{OZ\}\}$ by moving O from the first fragment to the second. *Jump* is not the only valid atomic operation for our method. If we consider *join* (joining two fragments into one) as the atomic operation, the graph will degrade to a hierarchical tree and our method becomes a reincarnation of the hierarchical clustering method [7].

The fragmentation graph forms the universal search space, which contains all possible fragmentations and links. Our graph search method greedily discovers a path towards the (nearly) optimal solution on the fragmentation graph.

Definition 4.2 (Solution path) *Given a fragmentation graph* $\mathcal{G}(\mathcal{U}, \mathcal{E})$, *a solution path* $p_x : \mathcal{U} \to \{x_{p_0}, x_{p_1}, x_{p_2}, \cdots\}$ *is a sequence of states defined in* $\mathcal{U}$. *The **search strategy** ρ decides the next state in a solution path, i.e.* $x_{p_{i+1}} = \rho(x_{p_i})$.

A solution path terminates when it cannot be extended by the corresponding search strategy. The terminating state of the solution path is the result state obtained by our graph search method. Figure 2 briefly illustrates the model of our graph search method. The solid dots and circles represent the safe states and unsafe states respectively while neighbors are connected by the lines. $\{x_{p_0}, x_{p_1}, x_{p_2}, x_{p_3}\}$ in Figure 2 shows a solution path starting from the initial state x_{p_0} and terminating at x_{p_3}. For example, a solution path could be $\{NSOZ\} \to \{\{NSO\}\{Z\}\} \to \{\{NS\}\{OZ\}\} \to \{\{N\}\{SOZ\}\}$ in the fragmentation graph for PATIENT.

Definition 4.3 (Dominance) *Given two states* x_i *and* x_j *in a fragmentation graph,* x_i *dominates* x_j, *denoted as* $x_i \succ x_j$, *iff* $\sigma(x_i) < \sigma(x_j)$. $\sigma : \mathcal{U} \to \mathbb{R}$ *is a **scoring metric** for each fragmentation.*

Next we propose the static and dynamic search strategies based on dominance.

4.2 Static Search Strategy

A straightforward search strategy is to use the query cost of a fragmentation as the scoring metric and greedily pick a neighbor fragmentation with the minimum cost at each step. Such search strategy is called static search strategy since it is invariant with the number of steps in a solution path.

Algorithm 1: $GSM(A, \mathcal{C}, \mathcal{Q}, \mathcal{F}_0)$

```
1  i ← 1; F ← F₀;                                  // initialization
2  while true do
3  │   Min ← F;
4  │   forall the (F, F*) in E do
5  │   │   if σ¹(F*) < σ¹(Min) and SatCon(C, F*) = true then
6  │   │   └   Min ← F*;
7  │   if Min = F then
8  │   └   return Min;
9  │   F ← Min; i ← i+1 ;                           // step on
```

The corresponding scoring metric and dominance relation are called static scoring metric and static dominance relation, respectively. We denote $\sigma^1(x) = Cost(x)$ as the static scoring metric, and $\succ^1$ as the corresponding dominance relation, thus the corresponding static search strategy ρ^1 is defined as

$$x_{p_{i+1}} = \rho^1(\succ^1, x_{p_i}) = \min_{x \succ^1 x_{p_i}} \{x \in \mathcal{O}, (x_{p_i}, x) \in \mathcal{E} : \sigma^1(x)\}$$

Note that, with search strategy ρ^1, the scoring metric of the selected state is lower than that of the previous state.

Algorithm 1 shows the pseudocode of function GSM, which implements our graph search method with static search strategy. GSM requires $A = \{a_1, \cdots, a_n\}$ (set of attributes to be fragmented), $\mathcal{C} = \{C_1, \cdots, C_m\}$ (set of well defined non-singleton constraints), $\mathcal{Q}$ (set of queries) and $\mathcal{F}_0$ (the initial state) as the parameters and returns Min which is the result fragmentation obtained by our algorithm. This algorithm first initializes the step counter $i = 1$ and sets the current state $\mathcal{F}$ as the initial state $\mathcal{F}_0$, then enters the main loop. At each step, the algorithm sets Min as previous selected state, $\mathcal{F}$, then visits each of its safe neighbors. The neighbor enjoying lowest scoring metric and dominates $\mathcal{F}$ is stored in Min. If such neighbor does not exist i.e. $Min = \mathcal{F}$, the algorithm returns Min as the result. Otherwise, let $\mathcal{F}$ equal Min and the step counter i increase by 1. The function $SatCon(x)$ checks whether the state x satisfies all the confidentiality constraints. It is important to note that static search strategies require safe initial states, i.e. $\mathcal{F}_0 \in \mathcal{O}$. Next we propose the dynamic search strategy which does not require a safe initial state.

4.3 Dynamic Search Strategy

Fragmentation graph with static search strategy may suffer from the problem of dead-end. Figure 2 shows an example of dead-end in our graph search method. In Figure 2, the solution path $p_x = \{x_{p_0}, x_{p_1}, x_{p_2}, x_{p_3}\}$ terminates at x_{p_3}, since all its two neighbors x_{p_4} and $x_{p_4}^\dagger$ are unsafe. However, it is possible that one of their neighbors x_{p_5} is safe and enjoys even lower query cost than x_{p_3}. The search strategy ρ^1 fails to detect this situation.

We solve the dead-ends by applying the theory of guided local search [26]. At the early stage, we treat the states in the fragmentation graph as *transparent* states, i.e. we consider the confidentiality constraints as *soft constraints* which can be violated with a *penalty*. The confidentiality constraints will become *harder* as the algorithm proceeds and eventually becomes *hard constraints* which enforces the algorithm to terminate at a safe state. We use a dynamic search strategy to represent the softness of the confidentiality constraints. A scoring metric σ is dynamic if and only if it varies with the number of steps in a solution path. We denote a dynamic scoring metric as $\sigma = [\sigma_0, \sigma_1, \sigma_2, \cdots]^T$, σ_i is applied at the ith step. The corresponding dominance relation $\succ$, denoted as $\succ = [\succ_0, \succ_1, \succ_2, \cdots]^T$, is a dynamic dominance relation and the corresponding search strategy ρ, denoted as $\rho(\succ, x) = [(\succ_0, x), (\succ_1, x), (\succ_2, x), \cdots]^T$, is a dynamic search strategy.

Intuitively, our dynamic strategy also greedily picks the neighbor solution with lowest scoring metric. However, different from the static strategy, it will allow an unsafe neighbor to be picked which helps to avoid the dead-end problem. On the other hand, to guarantee the safeness of the final solution, the scoring metric will include penalties for unsafe states and the penalties increase following a function of the number of steps. Formally, our dynamic search strategy ρ^2 is defined as

$$x_{p_{i+1}} = \rho^2(\succ_i^2, x_{p_i}) = \min_{x \succ_i^2 x_{p_i}} \{x \in \mathcal{U}, (x_{p_i}, x) \in \mathcal{E} : \sigma_i^2(x)\}$$

where $\sigma_i^2(x) = \frac{Cost(x)-\alpha}{\mu-\alpha} + i \cdot \gamma \cdot \frac{Penalty(x)-\beta}{\omega-\beta}$ is a dynamic scoring metric. $Penalty(x)$ is the penalty penalizing the fragmentation x for violating the confidentiality constraints in $\mathcal{C}$. γ is the *relaxation coefficient*. $\frac{Cost(x)-\alpha}{\mu-\alpha}$ and $\frac{Penalty(x)-\beta}{\omega-\beta}$ are the normalized query cost and penalty, respectively. The penalty function is defined as

$$Penalty(x) = \sum_{C_i \in \mathcal{C}} \delta(C_i, x)$$

where $\delta(\cdot)$ is the indicating function, which equals 1 when constraint C is violated in x and 0 otherwise. According to the cost model defined in Section 3.2, the fragmentation $\mathcal{F}^\top = \{\{a_1\}, \{a_2\}, \cdots, \{a_n\}\}$ and $\mathcal{F}^\perp = \{\{a_1, a_2, \cdots, a_n\}\}$ enjoys the highest and lowest query cost, respectively. On the other hand, $\mathcal{F}^\perp$ violates all the confidentiality constraints, thus suffers the highest penalty while $\mathcal{F}^\top$ satisfies all the confidentiality constraints, thus enjoys zero penalty. Accordingly, the regularization coefficients are set as $\mu = Cost(\mathcal{F}^\top)$, $\alpha = Cost(\mathcal{F}^\perp)$, $\omega = Penalty(\mathcal{F}^\perp)$, and $\beta = 0$.

At early stage of the search, i is small so that it guarantees the softness of the confidentiality constraints. However, i increases during the procedure thus the softness of the confidentiality constraints reduces concurrently. Specifically, when $i \geq \lceil \frac{\omega-\beta}{\gamma} \rceil$, penalty will dominate the scoring metric, i.e. fragmentations with higher penalty will be assigned higher scoring metrics regardless of their query costs, thus the solution path will be forced to extend towards states with lower penalty. Different from ρ^1, ρ^2 does not require safe initial states.

However, with search strategy ρ^2, a solution path may terminate at an unsafe state, which we call a *fake-end*.

Definition 4.4 (Fake-end) *Given a fragmentation graph* $\mathcal{G}(\mathcal{U}, \mathcal{E})$, *and a search strategy* ρ, *a solution path* $p_x = \{x_{p_0}, x_{p_1}, \cdots, x_{p_r}\}$ *enters a fake-end* x_{p_r} *if* p_x *terminates at* x_{p_r} *and* $x_{p_r} \notin \mathcal{O}$.

For example, in Figure 2, the solution path $\{x_{p_0}, x_{p_1}, x_{q_2}, x_{q_3}\}$ terminates at a fake-end x_{q_3}. Fortunately, fake-end can be easily solved by shifting the dynamic scoring metric.

Definition 4.5 (Shift) *Given a dynamic scoring metric* σ, $\sigma_i \leftarrow \sigma_{i+1}, \forall i > K, K \in \mathbb{N}$, *is a shift of* σ.

The shift essentially moves the scoring metric to the next step and allows the search to continue beyond a fake-end.

```
Algorithm 2: GSM*(A,C,Q,F₀)
```

1	$i \leftarrow 1; \mathcal{F} \leftarrow \mathcal{F}_0;$	// initialization
2	**while** *true* **do**	
3	$\quad Min \leftarrow \mathcal{F};$	
4	$\quad$ **forall the** $(\mathcal{F}, \mathcal{F}^\star)$ *in* $\mathcal{E}$ **do**	
5	$\quad\quad$ **if** $\sigma_i^2(\mathcal{F}^\star) < \sigma_i^2(Min)$ **then**	
6	$\quad\quad\quad Min \leftarrow \mathcal{F}^\star;$	
7	$\quad$ **if** $Min \neq \mathcal{F}$ **then**	
8	$\quad\quad \mathcal{F} \leftarrow Min; i \leftarrow i+1;$	// step on
9	$\quad\quad$ **continue**;	
10	$\quad$ **if** $SatCon(Min)=true$ **then**	
11	$\quad\quad$ **return** Min;	
12	$\quad i \leftarrow i+1$;	// shift

```
Algorithm 3: EGSM*(A,C,Q,F₀)
```

1	$i \leftarrow 1; k \leftarrow 2; \mathcal{F} \leftarrow \mathcal{F}_0;$	// initialization
2	**while** *true* **do**	
3	$\quad Min \leftarrow \mathcal{F};$	
4	$\quad$ **forall the** $(\mathcal{F}, \mathcal{F}^\star)$ *in* $\mathcal{E}_k$ **do**	
5	$\quad\quad$ **if** $\sigma_i^2(\mathcal{F}^\star) < \sigma_i^2(Min)$ **then**	
6	$\quad\quad\quad Min \leftarrow \mathcal{F}^\star;$	
7	$\quad$ **if** $Min \neq \mathcal{F}$ **then**	
8	$\quad\quad \mathcal{F} \leftarrow Min; i \leftarrow i+1;$	// step on
9	$\quad\quad$ **continue**;	
10	$\quad$ **if** $SatCon(Min)=true$ **then**	
11	$\quad\quad$ **return** Min;	
12	$\quad i \leftarrow i+1;$	// shift
13	$\quad$ **if** $ReqExp(\mathcal{F})=true$ **then**	
14	$\quad\quad k \leftarrow k+1;$	// expand

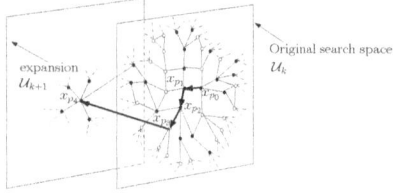

Figure 3: An example of graph expansion

Below we show that there exists a $K \in \mathbb{N}$ so that we can escape fake-ends by executing at most K shifts on σ^2. Suppose a solution path enters a fake-end x and $x = \mathcal{F} = \{F_1, \cdots, F_k\}$ where k is the number of fragments. First we claim $k < n$. Otherwise if $k = n$, the fragmentation can only be $\mathcal{F}^\top = \{\{a_1\}, \{a_2\}, \cdots, \{a_n\}\}$, it has been justified that $\mathcal{F}^\top$ is safe. Thus $\mathcal{F} \neq \mathcal{F}^\top$, and accordingly $k < n$. Consider that $\mathcal{F}$ violates the confidentiality constraint $C = \{a_1, \cdots, a_l\}$, i.e. there exists a fragment F_j with $C \subset F_j$. Let $\mathcal{F}^\star = Jump(\mathcal{F}, a_i, k+1), 1 \leq i \leq l$, $\mathcal{F}^\star$ is a neighbor of $\mathcal{F}$ and C is solved in $\mathcal{F}^\star$. Thus $Penalty(\mathcal{F}) - Penalty(\mathcal{F}^\star) \geq 1$. Let $K > \lceil \frac{\omega - \beta}{\gamma} \rceil$ and $c_1 = Cost(\mathcal{F})$, $c_2 = Cost(\mathcal{F}^\star)$, $p_1 = Penalty(\mathcal{F})$, $p_2 = Penalty(\mathcal{F}^\star)$. $\sigma_K^2(\mathcal{F}) - \sigma_K^2(\mathcal{F}^\star) = \frac{c_1 - c_2}{\mu - \alpha} + K \cdot \gamma \cdot \frac{p_1 - p_2}{\omega - \beta}$. Since $|\frac{c_1 - c_2}{\mu - \alpha}| \leq 1$, $p_1 - p_2 \geq 1$, and $K > \lceil \frac{\omega - \beta}{\gamma} \rceil$, we have $\sigma_K^2(\mathcal{F}) - \sigma_K^2(\mathcal{F}^\star) > 0$, i.e. $\mathcal{F}^\star \succ_K^2 \mathcal{F}$. Thus we can solve fake-ends by executing at most K shifts on σ^2.

Algorithm 2 shows the pseudocode for our graph search method with dynamic search strategy. Similar to function GSM, $GSM^\star$ visits all neighbors of the current state and find the fragmentation which enjoys lowest scoring metric and dominates $\mathcal{F}$. If $GSM^\star$ enters a fake-end, it executes a shift on the scoring metric and moves on to the next iteration.

4.4 Graph Expansion

The above methods can result in high computation cost due to large graph size. In this subsection, we propose a level-wise graph expansion technique which dramatically reduces the executing time of our graph search method. The basic idea is to start by considering only fragmentation solutions with a maximum number of fragments, and then expand to other solutions with more fragments as needed.

Consider the constrained optimization problem

$$\arg \min_{\mathcal{F} \in \mathcal{U}_k} \{\mathcal{F} \in \mathcal{O}_k : Cost(\mathcal{F})\}$$

where $\mathcal{O}_k$ ($\mathcal{U}_k$) is a subset of $\mathcal{O}$ ($\mathcal{U}$) with the maximum number of fragments k. $\mathcal{E}_k$ is the edge set responding to $\mathcal{U}_k$.

Our graph expansion technique starts from searching the subspace $\mathcal{U}_k$, instead of the universal search space $\mathcal{U}$, and gradually expands the subspace if needed. Since the number of neighbors of each state in $\mathcal{U}_k$ is much smaller, the executing time of the algorithm will be dramatically reduced. However, some of the fake-ends cannot be solved by shifts in the subspace searching, since the solution path will not automatically reach a state out of the subspace by *jump*s. To solve this issue, we manually expand the search space by increasing k.

Figure 3 shows the scheme of our graph expansion technique. In Figure 3, we start with the original search space $\mathcal{U}_k$ (right) with fragmentations with at most k fragments. When we detect that the solution path cannot terminate within the original search space, we expand the search space to $\mathcal{U}_{k+1}$ (left) where fragmentations can contain at most $k+1$ fragments. It is important to note that, the initial state x_0 in $\mathcal{U}_k$ is not guaranteed to be safe, thus graph expansion technique can not be used with static search strategies.

Algorithm 3 shows the pseudocode for our graph search method with graph expansion. This algorithm is quite similar to Algorithm2 except that it conducts the search in $\mathcal{U}_k$. For simplicity, we originally set $k = 2$. The $ReqExp$ function decides whether an expansion is required by checking the penalty of the current state $\mathcal{F}$, returning *true* if $\mathcal{F}$ has lower penalty than all its neighbors, otherwise returning *false*.

5. EXPERIMENTAL STUDY

In this section, we evaluate our graph search method, in comparison with other state-of-the-art fragmentation algorithms including heuristic search [6] and hierarchical clustering [7]. We also compare some of the results with the optimal solution obtained from exhaustive search.

Below we list the algorithms in our comparison which include the different versions of our proposed algorithms as well as the two state-of-the-art algorithms and the optimal solution: 1) GSM - graph search method with *jump* operation and static search strategy ρ^1 (initial state $\mathcal{F}^\top$); 2) GSM* - graph search method with *jump* operation and dynamic search strategy ρ^2 (initial state randomly generated in $\mathcal{U}$); 3) EGSM* - GSM* with graph expansion technique (initial state randomly generated in $\mathcal{U}_2$); 4) Hierarchical clustering (HC) [7] - a nearest join algorithm based on attribute affinity, which can be derived from the query set [18]; 5) Heuristic search (HS) (d=x, ps=y) [6] - a search algorithm on the fragmentation tree with the complete visited subtree

Table 3: Default settings

Parameters	Description	Default value
n	Number of attributes	10
m	Number of constraints	10
L	Length of constraints	3
γ	Relaxation coefficient	0.1

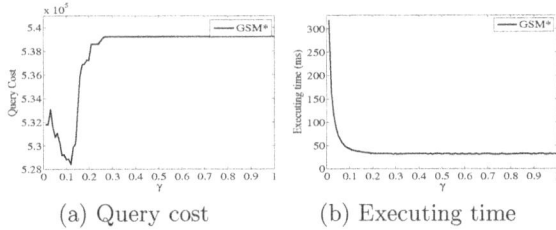

(a) Query cost   (b) Executing time

Figure 4: Impact of relaxation coefficient

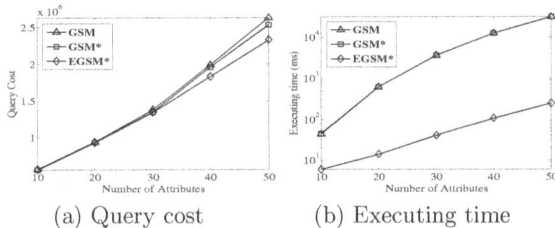

(a) Query cost   (b) Executing time

Figure 5: Compare GSMs

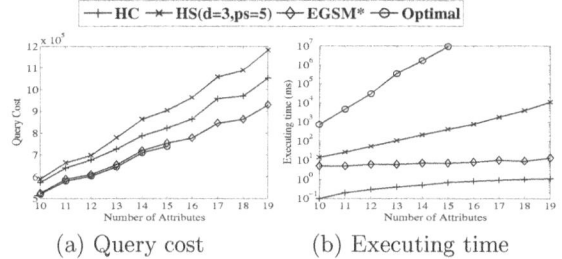

(a) Query cost   (b) Executing time

Figure 6: Impact of number of attributes

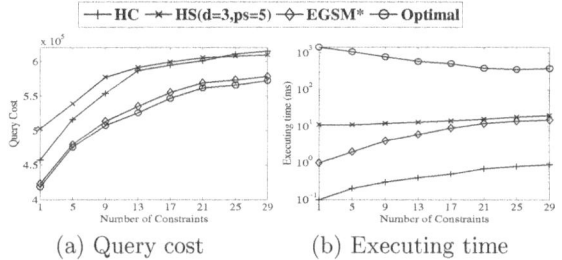

(a) Query cost   (b) Executing time

Figure 7: Impact of number of constraints

of depth x and y best solutions selected in each iteration. Generally, greater values of x and y lead to better solution but longer executing time. We set $x = 3$ and $y = 5$ in our experiments; and 6) Optimal solution - exhaustive search on the fragmentation tree [6].

We consider query cost and executing time as the criteria to evaluate the performance of the algorithms. Our experiments are implemented in Java and executed on 64-bit Red Hat Linux with 8 cores Intel(R) Core(TM) i7-2600 CPU at 3.40GHz. All experimental results are the average values of 30 independent trials. We conduct experiments on both synthetic and benchmark data sets.

5.1 Synthetic Data

We randomly generated 100 queries over synthetic data sets with 30K records. Without loss of generality, the size of each attribute is set to 1. The confidentiality constraints are randomly generated in this experiment. Table 3 shows the default settings of the parameters in our experiments. The following shows the experimental results with varying values of these parameters.

We first study the impact of relaxation coefficient γ in dynamic search strategy ρ^2. Figure 4(a) show the relation between query cost and different values of γ. Figure 4(b) illustrates the convergence rates by recording the executing time. From the figures, we find that roughly the range of [0.05, 0.15] for the γ value enjoys the best balance between effectiveness and efficiency. Thus $\gamma = 0.1$ is chosen as the default value for the remaining experiments.

Secondly we compare our GSM algorithms including GSM, GSM*, and EGSM*. The results are shown in Figure 5. We can see that GSM* gains lower query cost than GSM at similar time and the graph expansion technique not only reduces the query cost considerably but also dramatically saves com-

puting time. In the remaining experiments, we compare the EGSM* with other state-of-the-art methods.

In the third experiment, we study the impact of the number of attributes. Figure 6(a) and 6(b) show the experimental results. Figure 6(a) show that our EGSM* enjoys better performance than HC or HS. Figure 6(b) shows that HC is most time efficient, followed by EGSM*, HS, and exhaustive search. We also find that EGSM* obtains near optimal results in terms query cost.

Next we study the impact of the number of confidentiality constraints. Figure 7(a) and 7(b) show the experimental results. Figure 7(a) shows that increase of number of confidentiality constraints raises the query cost due to the fact that a large number of confidentiality constraints will likely result in highly fragmented data. Figure 7(b) compares the corresponding executing time. It can be seen from the figures that EGSM* enjoys better performance than both HC and HS in changes of number of confidentiality constraints.

Finally, we conduct experiments with different average lengths of the confidentiality constraints. The experimental results can be found from Figure 8(a) and 8(b). Figure 8(a) shows the impact of average length of the confidentiality constraints on query cost. Generally speaking, longer constraints result in lower query cost since the data is less fragmented. Experimental results regarding executing time can be found in Figure 8(b). Again, our EGSM* outperforms other methods.

5.2 Benchmark Data

In this subsection, we conduct experiments with the Adult data set from UCI benchmark[1]. We choose 10 privacy concerning attributes (including age, race, sex etc.) and prune the records with missing values.

The confidentiality constraints is usually specified by the data custodians in practice. However, for the purpose of this experiment, we generated the confidentiality constraints

---

[1]http://archive.ics.uci.edu/ml/datasets.html

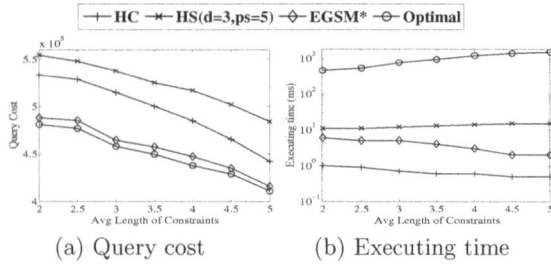

(a) Query cost   (b) Executing time

Figure 8: Impact of average length of constraints

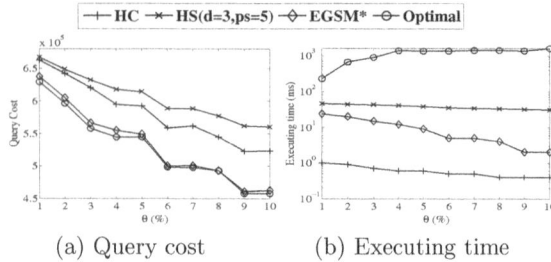

(a) Query cost   (b) Executing time

Figure 9: Impact of uniqueness threshold

for the Adult data set by considering the unique associations between the attributes. Given a relation R and its attribute set A. The *uniqueness* of an association of attributes $S = \{a_1, a_2, \ldots, a_r\} \subset A$, denoted as $U(S)$, is the number of tuples in R which have distinct values on S. If $\frac{U(S)}{|R|}$ is greater than or equal to a threshold θ, we consider S as a confidentiality constraint. It is important to note that, we do not need to search all attribute associations in the relation to find the confidentiality constraints. We can exploit the Apriori property [1] of the confidentiality constraints, i.e. the supersets of confidentiality constraints are also confidentiality constraints. Thus, efficient pruning approaches can be applied to accelerate the computation of generating confidentiality constraints.

Figure 9(a) and 9(b) show the experimental results of the Adult data set from UCI benchmark by varying the threshold θ from 1% to 10%. Generally speaking, lower threshold result in higher query cost. That is because lower threshold indicates more strict privacy requirements, which reduces the utility concurrently. Again, our EGSM* significantly outperforms both HC and HS.

6. CONCLUSIONS AND FUTURE WORK

Based on the theory of local search and guided local search, we proposed the graph search method for the fragmentation problem with confidentiality constraints. By modeling the optimal fragmentation problem as path finding problem in a graph, we avoid the issue of dead-end in traditional constrained clustering algorithms. We also propose the fragmentation graph expansion technique which dramatically reduces the time complexity of our method.

In our future work, we will consider fragmentations with overlaps and soft confidentiality constraints. Moreover, we will explore other techniques, such as *simulated annealing* [15], to search optimal solutions on the fragmentation graph. Finally, we will also apply graph search method to solve other constrained clustering problems.

7. REFERENCES

[1] R. Agrawal and R. Srikant. Fast algorithms for mining association rules in large databases. In *VLDB*, pages 487–499, 1994.

[2] J. Biskup and M. Preuß. Database fragmentation with encryption: Under which semantic c5nstraints and A priori knowledge can two keep a secret? In *DBSec*, pages 17–32, 2013.

[3] J. Biskup, M. Preuß, and L. Wiese. On the inference-proofness of database fragmentation satisfying confidentiality constraints. In *ISC*, pages 246–261, 2011.

[4] F. Bonchi, B. Malin, and Y. Saygin. Recent advances in preserving privacy when mining data. *Data Knowl. Eng.*, 65(1):1–4, 2008.

[5] D. Boneh, G. Crescenzo, R. Ostrovsky, and G. Persiano. Public key encryption with keyword search. In *EUROCRYPT*, pages 506–522, 2004.

[6] V. Ciriani, S. D. C. di Vimercati, S. Foresti, S. Jajodia, S. Paraboschi, and P. Samarati. Fragmentation design for efficient query execution over sensitive distributed databases. In *ICDCS*, pages 32–39, 2009.

[7] V. Ciriani, S. D. C. di Vimercati, S. Foresti, S. Jajodia, S. Paraboschi, and P. Samarati. Combining fragmentathon and encryption to protect privacy in data storage. *ACM Trans. Inf. Syst. Secur.*, 13(3), 2010.

[8] Y. Crama, A. W. J. Kolen, and E. Pesch. Local search in combinatorial optimization. In *Artificial Neural Networks: An Introduction to ANN Theory and Practice*, pages 157–174, 1995.

[9] C. Dwork. Differential privacy: A survey of results. In *TAMC*, volume 4978 of *Lecture Notes in Computer Science*, pages 1–19. Springer, 2008.

[10] B. C. M. Fung, K. Wang, R. Chen, and P. S. Yu. Privacy-preserving data publishing: A survey of recent developments. *ACM Comput. Surv.*, 42(4), 2010.

[11] C. Gentry. Fully homomorphic encryption using ideal lattices. In *STOC*, pages 169–178, 2009.

[12] C. Gentry. Computing arbitrary functions of encrypted data. *Commun. ACM*, 53(3):97–105, 2010.

[13] H. Hacigümüs, B. Iyer, C. Li, and S. Mehrotra. Executing sql over encrypted data in the database-service-provider model. In *SIGMOD*, pages 216–227, 2002.

[14] M. Hay, K. Liu, G. Miklau, J. Pei, and E. Terzi. Privacy-aware data management in information networks. In *SIGMOD*, pages 1201–1204, 2011.

[15] S. Kirkpatrick, C. D. Gelatt, M. P. Vecchi, et al. Optimization by simmulated annealing. *science*, 220(4598):671–680, 1983.

[16] J. Liu, J. Luo, and J. Z. Huang. Rating: Privacy preservation for multiple attributes with different sensitivity requirements. In *ICDMW*, pages 666–673, 2011.

[17] A. Machanavajjhala, J. Gehrke, D. Kifer, and M. Venkitasubramaniam. l-diversity: Privacy beyond k-anonymity. In *ICDE*, page 24, 2006.

[18] M. T. Özsu and P. Valduriez. *Principles of Distributed Database Systems, Third Edition*. Springer, 2011.

[19] R. A. Popa, C. M. S. Redfield, N. Zeldovich, and H. Balakrishnan. Cryptdb: protecting confidentiality with encrypted query processing. In *SOSP*, pages 85–100, 2011.

[20] R. A. Popa, C. M. S. Redfield, N. Zeldovich, and H. Balakrishnan. Cryptdb: processing queries on an encrypted database. *Commun. ACM*, 55(9):103–111, 2012.

[21] C. M. Procopiuc and D. Srivastava. Efficient table anonymization for aggregate query answering. In *ICDE*, pages 1291–1294, 2009.

[22] T. Rekatsinas, A. Deshpande, and A. Machanavajjhala. A SPARSI: partitioning sensitive data amongst multiple adversaries. *PVLDB*, 6(13):1594–1605, 2013.

[23] P. Samarati. Protecting respondents' identities in microdata release. *IEEE Trans. Knowl. Data Eng.*, 13(6):1010–1027, 2001.

[24] D. X. Song, D. Wagner, and A. Perrig. Practical techniques for searches on encrypted data. In *IEEE Symposium on Security and Privacy*, pages 44–55, 2000.

[25] M. van Dijk, C. Gentry, S. Halevi, and V. Vaikuntanathan. Fully homomorphic encryption over the integers. In *EUROCRYPT*, pages 24–43, 2010.

[26] C. Voudouris and E. P. K. Tsang. Guided local search and its application to the traveling salesman problem. *European Journal of Operational Research*, 113(2):469–499, 1999.

[27] K. Wagstaff and C. Cardie. Clustering with instance-level constraints. In *AAAI*, page 1097, 2000.

Distributed Search over Encrypted Big Data

Mehmet Kuzu
Department of Computer
Science
University of Texas at Dallas
Richardson, TX, USA
mehmet.kuzu@utdallas.edu

Mohammad Saiful Islam
Department of Computer
Science
University of Texas at Dallas
Richardson, TX, USA
saiful@utdallas.edu

Murat Kantarcioglu
Department of Computer
Science
University of Texas at Dallas
Richardson, TX, USA
muratk@utdallas.edu

ABSTRACT

Nowadays, huge amount of documents are increasingly transferred to the remote servers due to the appealing features of cloud computing. On the other hand, privacy and security of the sensitive information in untrusted cloud environment is a big concern. To alleviate such concerns, encryption of sensitive data before its transfer to the cloud has become an important risk mitigation option. Encrypted storage provides protection at the expense of a significant increase in the data management complexity. For effective management, it is critical to provide efficient selective document retrieval capability on the encrypted collection. In fact, considerable amount of searchable symmetric encryption schemes have been designed in the literature to achieve this task. However, with the emergence of big data everywhere, available approaches are insufficient to address some crucial real-world problems such as scalability.

In this study, we focus on practical aspects of a secure keyword search mechanism over encrypted data. First, we propose a provably secure distributed index along with a parallelizable retrieval technique that can easily scale to big data. Second, we integrate authorization into the search scheme to limit the information leakage in multi-user setting where users are allowed to access only particular documents. Third, we offer efficient updates on the distributed secure index. In addition, we conduct extensive empirical analysis on a real dataset to illustrate the efficiency of the proposed practical techniques.

Categories and Subject Descriptors

H.2.7 [**Database Administration**]: Security, integrity, and protection; H.3.3 [**Information Search and Retrieval**]: Search process

General Terms

Security, Experimentation, Performance

CODASPY'15, March 2–4, 2015, San Antonio, Texas, USA.
Copyright © 2015 ACM 978-1-4503-3191-3/15/03 ...$15.00.
http://dx.doi.org/10.1145/2699026.2699116.

Keywords

Privacy, Security, Searchable Encryption

1. INTRODUCTION

In recent years, advances in cloud computing has led to a rapid transition in information systems. Cloud services remove the burden of large scale data management in a cost-effective manner. Hence, it is quite common for individuals and organizations to outsource their documents. At the same time, storage of sensitive information in untrusted cloud environment raises serious privacy concerns. To resolve such concerns, one approach is to transfer documents in their encrypted form. Encrypted storage protects sensitive information at the expense of a significant reduction in the data processing capability. Among potential computations on the remote encrypted collection, selective retrieval is highly critical. In fact, a substantial amount of research effort has been invested to enable its efficient execution.

Searchable symmetric encryption (SSE) schemes are the most common tools for searchable and secure cloud storage [5, 6, 7, 12, 17]. Available SSE schemes enable selective document retrieval over encrypted collection. However, they do not address some practical problems of real systems such as scalability since they are mainly designed to run on a single server. With the emergence of big data everywhere, scalability becomes a fundamental requirement for cloud systems. Fortunately, this challenge is resolved by an effective design principle that enforces distribution of both data and computation to multiple commodity hardwares. In fact, old storage systems are increasingly replaced with the ones that suits well to this distributed paradigm such as HBase [1]. Accordingly, it is critical to design a SSE scheme that can easily be distributed to many machines to handle very large amounts of documents. Another important practical aspect is to consider the access rights of distinct users during the retrieval. Data owners generally share limited amount of documents with other users. To prevent excessive information leakage to the remote servers, integration of authorization into the search scheme is crucial.

In this study, we propose a distributed secure index along with a parallelizable search mechanism. This secure index is further vertically partitioned among multiple servers to enable simultaneous decryption of large index payloads during the search process. Proposed approach is highly scalable. Our empirical evaluations indicate that search operation can be performed in a few seconds for approximately 30,000,000 documents on an HBase cluster of twelve machines. We also integrate authorization into the search to restrict the information leakage of the scheme according to user access rights. Finally, we propose a secure update mechanism on the distributed index.

2. RELATED WORK

Over the years, various protocols and security definitions have been proposed for searchable symmetric encryption (SSE)([5, 6, 7, 12, 15, 17, 3, 16]). They selectively leak information (e.g., access pattern) to enable practical schemes. The first of such approaches was provided in [15]. Later on, Goh et al. proposed a security definition to formalize the security requirements of SSE in [7]. Similarly, Chang et al. introduced a slightly stronger definition in [5]. However, both definitions do not consider adaptive adversaries. This shortcoming has been addressed in [6], where Curtmola et al. presented adaptive semantic security definition.

The most computationally efficient SSE schemes that are compatible with the adaptive semantic security definition are presented in [17], [12] [11], [3] and [16]. In [17], inverted bit vector indices are generated for each unique keyword. Then bit vectors are masked with a secure encryption. The construction of [17] requires interaction with the user during the search process and its pure bit vector index structure is not efficient in terms of storage. To enable a single-round search through a more compact index along with an update mechanism, dynamic SSE scheme was proposed in [12]. Search mechanism of this construction necessitates sequential tracing on the encrypted list which hinders parallelizable search. To resolve the sequential tracing problem, a scheme that is based on red-black trees was proposed in [11]. In this construction, multiple-processors could apply decryption on distinct branches of the tree but the whole tree resides in a single machine which is not compatible with the big data design principles. In [4], a SSE scheme with support for conjunctive queries was proposed. Although this scheme could be parallelized in theory, it does not provide an update mechanism. The scheme of [3] is both dynamic and parallezible. However, this scheme does not reclaim space after deletions and applies complete re-encryption of the data periodically. Hence, it is not appropriate for applications with high deletion rates. The scheme of [16] is also dynamic and achieves sublinear search time. On the other hand, their scheme is not distributed and hierarcical index structure associated with the scheme make it challenging to adapt it in a distributed setting. Also, these schemes leak access pattern without considering user access-rights.

3. SECURE KEYWORD SEARCH

In this part, we present our secure keyword search scheme that is based on a distributed index structure. Its security analysis is presented in the full version of this paper [13].

3.1 Secure Index Construction

The proposed secure index is formed in three main phases:

1. Plain Index Generation: In this phase, each keyword is associated with a set of documents. Specifically, suppose $\{D_1, ..., D_n\}$ is a set of documents with contents $\{W(D_1), ..., W(D_n)\}$, $id(D_j)$ is the identifier of D_j and $\{w_1, ..., w_z\}$ represents the set of keywords. Then an inverted index $\{(w_1, L_{w_1}), ..., (w_z, L_{w_z})\}$ is formed such that $id(D_j) \in L_{w_i}$ if and only if $w_i \in W(D_j)$.

After inverted index construction, a plain payload is generated for each keyword in the form of a bit vector or a list. Payload type of a keyword is identified according to its frequency with the goal of minimizing storage cost. Here, both payload types should have a fixed size to hide keyword frequency. In fact, each bit vector consists of n bits where n represents the number of documents in the corpus. Similarly, each list consists of Υ identifiers where Υ is a constant. During the construction, if the frequency of a keyword is more than Υ, its payload is represented as a bit vector. Otherwise, it is represented as a list. In this setting, suppose $\Delta = \{f_1, ..., f_z\}$ represents expected frequency distribution of the keywords, $|id|$ is the identifier bit length and $I(.)$ is an indicator function. Then expected storage cost denoted as $E(\Upsilon, \Delta, n)$ can be computed as follows:

$$E(\Upsilon, \Delta, n) = \sum_{i=1}^{z} I(f_i > \Upsilon) \cdot n + (1 - I(f_i > \Upsilon)) \cdot \Upsilon \cdot |id|$$

To identify optimal Υ for minimal storage without leaking information, we use Zipf's law [14] which states that frequency of keywords are inversely proportional to their frequency based rank in a natural language corpus. In our construction, payloads of top-t ranked keywords are put into bit vector form and the others are represented as lists.

More formally, suppose $H(N)$ represents N^{th} harmonic number, $p(x; 1, N)$ represents the Zipfian distribution with exponent 1 such that $p(x) = x^{-1} \cdot H(N)^{-1}$ and z is the number of keywords in the corpus. Then a padded list will have $\Upsilon = \lceil p(t) \cdot n \rceil$ members and the expected storage cost can be computed as follows:

$$E(\Upsilon, p, n) = t \cdot n + (z - t) \cdot p(t) \cdot n \cdot |id|$$

THEOREM 3.1. *Optimal member size for a padded list denoted as* Υ *with respect to the expected storage cost* $E(\Upsilon, p, n)$ *is* $\lceil (|id| \cdot H(z) \cdot z)^{-0.5} \cdot n \rceil$.

PROOF. $arg\,min_t\ E(\Upsilon, p, n) \Rightarrow$

$\frac{dE(\Upsilon, p, n)}{dt} = \frac{d}{dt}[t \cdot n + (z - t) \cdot t^{-1} \cdot H(z)^{-1} \cdot n \cdot |id|] = 0$

$arg\,min_t\ E(\Upsilon, p, n) = \sqrt{\frac{|id| \cdot z}{H(z)}}$

$\Upsilon = \lceil p(arg\,min_t\ E(\Upsilon, p, n)) \cdot n \rceil = \lceil (|id| \cdot H(z) \cdot z)^{-0.5} \cdot n \rceil$ □

Note that Υ is identified using public distribution. Hence it does not leak any information regarding the dataset. Once Υ is identified, a plain payload P_{w_i} is generated for each keyword w_i. Specifically, suppose $\{(w_1, L_{w_1}), ..., (w_z, L_{w_z})\}$ is an inverted index where L_{w_i} is a list of identifiers for the documents that contain w_i. Here, each identifier is an integer from 1 to n where n is the number of the documents in the corpus. Then P_{w_i} is in the form of an n-bit vector if $|L_{w_i}| > \Upsilon$ such that $P_{w_i}[j] = 1$ for each $j \in L_{w_i}$ and $P_{w_i}[j] = 0$ otherwise. If $|L_{w_i}| \leq \Upsilon$, P_{w_i} is in the form a list such that P_{w_i} is generated by inserting $\Upsilon - |L_{w_i}|$ fake identifiers (i.e., $id = 0$) to the original list L_{w_i}.

2. Index Encryption: Plain index construction step results in an inverted index with fixed size bit vector or list payloads. In this step, this index is subject to encryption. Specifically, suppose $\{(w_1, P_{w_1}), ..., (w_z, P_{w_z})\}$ is a plain index, Φ_{K_t} and Ψ_{K_p} are pseudo-random functions with secret keys K_t and K_p, $O_S : \{0,1\}^\kappa \times \{0,1\}^* \mapsto \{0,1\}^\kappa$ is a random oracle[1]. Then encrypted index $\{(E_w(w_1), E_p(P_{w_1})), ..., (E_w(w_z), E_p(P_{w_z}))\}$ is generated as follows:

- Generate $E_w(w_i)$ such that $E_w(w_i) = \Phi_{K_t}(w_i)$.

- Generate a random oracle key $K(w_i)$ for the encryption of payload P_{w_i} such that $K(w_i) = \Psi_{K_p}(w_i)$.

- Construct payload encryption blocks.

1) Suppose P_{w_i} is an n-bit vector and κ is the output length of the random oracle. Then divide P_{w_i} into κ bit blocks $B^1_{w_i}$, ..., $B^\ell_{w_i}$ such that $\ell = \lceil n/\kappa \rceil$ and $B^j_{w_i} = P_{w_i}[(j-1) \cdot \kappa + 1]$ ... $P_{w_i}[(j-1) \cdot \kappa + \kappa]$. Here, $P_{w_i}[k]$ is the kth bit of P_{w_i} for $1 \le k \le n$ and zero otherwise.

2) Suppose P_{w_i} is a list of identifiers with Υ elements such that $P_{w_i} = \{id_{w_i}(1), ..., id_{w_i}(\Upsilon)\}$, $|id|$ is the bit length of the identifiers and κ is the output length of the random oracle. Then each encryption block can host $cp = \lfloor \kappa / |id| \rfloor$ identifiers. Accordingly, divide Υ members into blocks $B^1_{w_i}$, ..., $B^\iota_{w_i}$ such that $\iota = \lceil \Upsilon/cp \rceil$ and $B^j_{w_i} = id_{w_i}((j-1) \cdot cp + 1)$ ... $id_{w_i}((j-1) \cdot cp + cp)$. Here, $id_{w_i}(k)$ is the kth identifier in P_{w_i} for $1 \le k \le \Upsilon$ and zero otherwise.

- Suppose $K(w_i)$ is the random oracle key, $B^1_{w_i}$, ..., $B^r_{w_i}$ are the encryption blocks for P_{w_i}, $O_S(K(w_i), j)$ denotes the output of random oracle O_S with key $K(w_i)$ when it is applied on input j and $\oplus$ represents the xor operator. Then generate encryption of P_{w_i} denoted as $E_p(P_{w_i})$ as follows[2]:

$$E_p(P_{w_i}) = \{\pi_{w_i}[1], ..., \pi_{w_i}[r]\}$$
$$\pi_{w_i}[j] = (B^j_{w_i} \oplus O_S(K(w_i), j), \, j)$$

3. Index Partitioning: After the construction of encrypted index, it is transferred to the cloud. In cloud environment, encrypted index is split among multiple servers to parallelize the decryption of large index payloads during the keyword search phase. Specifically, encrypted payloads are divided into multiple regions which are further distributed to the region servers. In this study, we utilize the features of a distributed key-value store known as HBase [1] for index partitioning. In HBase, key-value pairs can be split into distinct regions according to their keys. To construct such regions, region bound keys R_1, R_2, ..., R_m are generated such that $R_1 < R_2 < ... < R_m$. After bound initialization, key-value pairs are mapped to the regions according to relative position of their keys with respect to these bounds. Specifically, suppose (k_i, v_i) is a pair that will be hosted in the store. Then it is placed into the jth region provided that $R_j \le k_i < R_{j+1}$. To form partitions on encrypted index $\{(E_w(w_1), E_p(P_{w_1})), ..., (E_w(w_z), E_p(P_{w_z}))\}$, we convert it into key-value pairs and map them into m distinct regions as follows:

- Suppose α is the bit length for the encrypted keywords such that $\alpha = |E_w(w_i)|$, m is the number of regions, 0^α represents a bit string of α zeros and $||$ is concatenation operator. Then generate region bound keys $R_1 = 1||0^\alpha$, $R_2 = 2||0^\alpha$, ..., $R_m = m||0^\alpha$.

- Suppose $(E_w(w_i), E_p(P_{w_i}))$ is an encrypted keyword, payload pair where $E_p(P_{w_i})$ consists of r encrypted blocks such that $E_p(P_{w_i}) = \{\pi_{w_i}[1], \pi_{w_i}[2], ..., \pi_{w_i}[r]\}$. Then m key-value pairs are constructed on $(E_w(w_i), E_p(P_{w_i}))$. Specifically, $1||E_w(w_i), 2||E_w(w_i), ..., m||E_w(w_i)$ are the keys and value for key $j||E_w(w_i)$ is an encrypted block set $\{\pi_{w_i}[j], \pi_{w_i}[j+m], ..., \pi_{w_i}[j + m \cdot \lfloor r/m \rfloor]\}$. Here, $\pi_{w_i}[k]$ is the kth block of $E_p(P_i)$ for $1 \le k \le r$ and empty otherwise.

- Each key-value pair $(j||E_w(w_i), \{\pi_{w_i}[j], \pi_{w_i}[j+m], ..., \pi_{w_i}[j + m \cdot \lfloor r/m \rfloor]\})$ is stored in HBase. Value for row-key $j||E_w(w_i)$ is distributed to $\lceil r/m \rceil$ distinct columns. In this setting, pair with key $j||E_w(w_i)$ is stored in the jth region by the construction. This is because $j||E_w(w_i)$ lies between region bound keys $R_j = j||0^\alpha$ and $R_{j+1} = (j+1)||0^\alpha$.

3.2 Secure Search Mechanism

Once secure index is constructed and distributed to the cloud region servers, data users can perform search on them with the help of the secrets they own. During this setup, data owner also transfers the encrypted document collection into the cloud along with the index. In this setting, encrypted collection denoted as $\{C_1, ..., C_n\}$ is obtained by applying secure encryption (e.g., AES in CTR mode of operation [8]) on the document collection. Suppose $Enc_{K_{coll}}$ represents the secure encryption with key K_{coll} and D_i is the ith document in the collection. Then $C_i = Enc_{K_{coll}}(D_i)$. After the transfer of encrypted collection, it is stored in the distributed file system of the cloud service provider. Search process is conducted in three main steps.

1) Trapdoor Generation: Trapdoor for retrieving documents that contain keyword w_i denoted as T_{w_i} is formed using secret keys K_t and K_p. Specifically, let Φ_{K_t} and Ψ_{K_p} be pseudo-random functions with secret keys K_t and K_p. Then $T_{w_i} = (E_w(w_i), K(w_i))$ such that $E_w(w_i) = \Phi_{K_t}(w_i)$ and $K(w_i) = \Psi_{K_p}(w_i)$. Once T_{w_i} is formed, it is sent to the cloud master server by the user.

2) Region Search: Upon reception of $T_{w_i} = (E_w(w_i), K(w_i))$, master directs it to the region servers to find the identifiers of the documents that contain w_i. Then the server that hosts j^{th} region generates row-key $j||E_w(w_i)$. If $(j||E_w(w_i), \{\pi_{w_i}[j], \pi_{w_i}[j+m], ..., \pi_{w_i}[j + m \cdot \lfloor r/m \rfloor]\})$ is a member of key-value store, server applies decryption on the encrypted payload blocks. In this setting, each block $\pi_{w_i}[k]$ is in the form of $(B^k_{w_i} \oplus O_S(K(w_i), k), k)$ by the construction where O_S is a random oracle and $B^k_{w_i}$ represents the kth plain payload block for w_i. To obtain $B^k_{w_i}$, server performs decryption using $K(w_i)$ as follows:

$$B^k_{w_i} = (B^k_{w_i} \oplus O_S(K(w_i), k)) \oplus O_S(K(w_i), k)$$

After decryption, server extracts document identifiers from each block $B^k_{w_i}$. Note that, each plain block is in the form of a bit vector or a list. If a block is in the bit vector form, identifiers are obtained from the bit locations with value one. If the block is in the list form, identifiers are obtained by decoding the encoded integers in it. Here, some decoded integers represent fake identifiers (i.e., $id = 0$) and they are eliminated by the region server at this phase.

3) Document Transfer: In this step, master receives partial results from each region server and merges them to finalize the search. Finally, encrypted documents, identifiers of which are included in the final set, are sent to user.

---

[1]Cryptographic keyed hash functions such as HMAC-SHA256 could be utilized as a random oracle [12].

[2]This encryption construct is derived from the random oracle based searchable encryption construction of [12].

3.3 Authorization-Aware Keyword Search

Almost all efficient searchable symmetric encryption schemes leak some information for efficiency. Although this leakage varies among schemes, access pattern leakage is common. That is, untrusted server learns which documents are included in the result set of an issued trapdoor without observing their contents. More formally, suppose $D[q_i]$ represents the identifiers of the documents that are in the result set of query q_i. Then access pattern for q_i denoted as $A_p(q_i)$ is a set such that $A_p(q_i) = D[q_i]$. Unfortunately, access pattern leakage may subject to some adversarial analysis [10] and it is critical to restrict it in an efficient way [3].

In real-world, it is highly likely that data owner shares only subset of documents with users through an authorization mechanism. Accordingly, if a user issues a query q_i, he/she may have access to only some of the documents, identifiers of which are included in $A_p(q_i)$. However, available schemes do not consider access rights of the users and leak $A_p(q_i)$ as it is during the search. In the context of this study, we form a secure search scheme with basic authorization as a first step toward search schemes with more sophisticated authorization techniques. Specifically, we utilize traditional file system access control lists (ACLs) [9]. In ACLs, each file is included in a single access group and each user is assigned to multiple groups. Then, users are allowed to access only the files in their respective groups. More formally, suppose documents in the collection $D = \{D_1, ..., D_n\}$ are mapped to a group from the set $G = \{G_1, ..., G_p\}$ with function $g : D \mapsto G$. Similarly, user U_i is assigned to a set of groups denoted as $G(U_i)$ such that $G(U_i) \subseteq G$. Then U_i has access to document with identifier $id(D_j)$ if and only if $g(id(D_j)) \in G(U_i)$. Here, suppose $A_p(q_j)$ denotes the identifiers of the documents that are in the result set of query q_j and $D(G_i)$ represents the identifiers of the documents that are in group G_i. Then restricted access pattern for q_j and group G_i denoted as $A_p(q_j, G_i)$ is a set such that $A_p(q_j, G_i) = A_p(q_j) \cap D(G_i)$.

The main objective of authorization-aware keyword search is to restrict the access leakage according to the user access rights. Specifically, suppose U_k issues a query q_i and $G(U_k)$ denotes the groups that involves U_k. Then proposed scheme leaks only $A_p(q_i, G_\iota)$ for each $G_\iota \in G(U_k)$ instead of $A_p(q_i)$. To achieve this goal, we extend both secure index generation and search scheme of Sections 3.1 and 3.2.

1) Authorization-Aware Secure Index Construction: In the basic index construction of Section 3.1, each keyword w_i is associated with encryption blocks $B_{w_i}^1$, ..., $B_{w_i}^r$, each of which contains the identifiers of the documents that include w_i. Then, these blocks are encrypted with the help of secret payload key K_p. In the extended version, we utilize multiple secret group keys K_{G_1}, ..., K_{G_p}. The main goal of this design is to encrypt each document identifier with the key of its group. By this way, only the users that hold the corresponding group keys could generate a valid trapdoor for their decryptions. After key generation, blocks are encrypted as follows:

- If $B_{w_i}^j$ is a list block, it consists of concatenated document identifiers $id_1 || id_2 ... || id_z$. Here, suppose $g(id_x)$ is the group of document with identifier id_x, K_{G_i} is the secret

key for group G_i, $\Psi_{K_{G_i}}$ is a pseudo-random function with key K_{G_i}, $K(w_i, g(id_x))$ denotes random oracle key for pair $(w_i, g(id_x))$, $|id|$ is the bit length of an identifier and $e(V, \iota, \upsilon)$ is a function that extracts the block of bits between indices ι and υ from bit vector V. Then encryption of $B_{w_i}^j$ denoted as $\pi_{w_i}^j$ is formed as follows:

$$K(w_i, g(id_x)) = \Psi_{K_{g(id_x)}}(w_i)$$
$$\pi_{w_i}^j = (id_1 \oplus e(O_S(K(w_i, g(id_1)), j), 1, |id|) \quad || \quad ...$$
$$|| \ id_z \oplus e(O_S(K(w_i, g(id_z)), j), (z-1) \cdot |id| + 1, z \cdot |id|), \ j)$$

- If $B_{w_i}^j$ is a bit vector of length k, it consists of bits each of which represent a document identifier denoted as $id_{j,1}$, $id_{j,2}$, ..., $id_{j,k}$ respectively. Here, suppose $G(B_{w_i}^j)$ is the set of groups for the identifiers in block $B_{w_i}^j$ such that $G(B_{w_i}^j) = g(id_{j,1}) \cup ... \cup g(id_{j,k})$ where $g(id_{j,\rho})$ represents the group of document with identifier $id_{j,\rho}$. Then bit vector is initially encrypted with each group key K_{G_ι} where $G_\iota \in G(B_{w_i}^j)$ to form encrypted bit vector $\pi_{w_i}^j(G_\iota)$:

$$K(w_i, G_\iota) = \Psi_{K_{G_\iota}}(w_i)$$
$$\pi_{w_i}^j(G_\iota) = B_{w_i}^j \oplus O(K(w_i, G_\iota), j)$$

Once encrypted bit vector is generated for each group in $G(B_{w_i}^j)$, final encrypted bit vector denoted as $\pi_{w_i}^j$ is formed by group oriented bit selection. Specifically, suppose $id_{j,1}$, ..., $id_{j,k}$ are the identifiers that is represented by bits 1, ..., k. Then ρ^{th} bit of $\pi_{w_i}^j$ is set to ρ^{th} bit of $\pi_{w_i}^j(g(id_{j,\rho}))$ where $g(id_{j,\rho})$ is the group of document with identifier $id_{j,\rho}$.

For authorization-aware construction, documents in the collection are also encrypted according to their groups. Specifically, suppose $K_{G_\iota}^C$ is a secret collection key for group G_ι, $g(id(D_i))$ denotes the group of D_i, Enc_K is a secure encryption scheme with key K and C_i is the encrypted form of D_i. Then $C_i = Enc_{K_{g(id(D_i))}^C}(D_i)$.

2) Authorization-Aware Search Mechanism:

Authorization-aware search is an extension of the search mechanism that is presented in Section 3.2. This extension integrates user-access rights into the search. For protocol execution, data owner shares secure index and group function g which maps document identifiers to access groups with cloud service provider. Service provider will further use this group information during the search to identify correct result set against user trapdoors. Then owner shares keyword encryption key K_t, group keys K_{G_j}, $K_{G_j}^C$ for $G_j \in G(U_k)$ with user U_k. Here, $G(U_k)$ represents the groups that involves user U_k. Once necessary information is shared with the participants, trapdoor generation and region search are performed as follows:

1) Trapdoor Generation: Trapdoor for retrieving documents that contain keyword w_i denoted as T_{w_i} is formed with secret keys K_t and K_{G_j} for each $G_j \in G(U_k) = \{G_{k,1}, ..., G_{k,f}\}$. Specifically, let Φ_{K_t} and Ψ_K be pseudo-random functions with secret keys K_t and K. Then $T_{w_i} = (E_w(w_i), \{[G_{k,1}, K(w_i, G_{k,1})], ..., [G_{k,f}, K(w_i, G_{k,f})]\})$ where $E_w(w_i) = \Phi_{K_t}(w_i)$ and $K(w_i, G_{k,j}) = \Psi_{K_{G_{k,j}}}(w_i)$. Once T_{w_i} is formed, it is sent to the cloud master server.

2) Region Search: Upon reception of $T_{w_i} = (E_w(w_i), \{[G_{k,1}, K(w_i, G_{k,1})], ..., [G_{k,f}, K(w_i, G_{k,f})]\})$, master directs

---

[3] Although access pattern leakage can be eliminated completely with oblivious RAM, it is not practical enough to scale well for big data.

it to the region servers. Then each server locates the encrypted blocks using $E_w(w_i)$ as in the basic search scheme. Once they are located, decryption is applied as follows:

- If $\pi_{w_i}^j$ is a list block, it consists of concatenated encrypted document identifiers $\omega_{id_{j,1}}||\omega_{id_{j,2}}...||\omega_{id_{j,z}}$. In this setting, suppose $e(V, \iota, v)$ is a function that extracts the block of bits between indices ι and v from bit vector V and $|id|$ is the bit length of an identifier. Then, for each oracle key $K(w_i, G_{k,\iota})$ in T_{w_i}, server performs the following operation:

$$id_{j,\rho}^* = \omega_{id_{j,\rho}} \oplus e(O_S(K(w_i, G_{k,\iota}), j), (\rho - 1) \cdot |id| + 1, \rho \cdot |id|)$$

Note that, legitimate document identifiers are integers between 1 and n and $g(id_{j,\rho})$ represents the group of the document with identifier $id_{j,\rho}$. In this setting, if $1 \leq id_{j,\rho}^* \leq n$ and $g(id_{j,\rho}^*) = G_{k,\iota}$, then $id_{j,\rho}^*$ is included in the search result set. Otherwise it is discarded by the server. It is clear that equality of $g(id_{j,\rho})$ and $G_{k,\iota}$ implies the equality of $id_{j,\rho}^*$ and $id_{j,\rho}$. On the other hand, decryption with a wrong group key will result in a random value.

- If $\pi_{w_i}^j$ is a bit vector block of length k, it consists of encrypted bits each of which represent document identifiers $id_{j,1}, ..., id_{j,k}$. Here, suppose $G(B_{w_i}^j)$ is the set of groups for this block such that $G(B_{w_i}^j) = g(id_{j,1}) \cup ... \cup g(id_{j,k})$ and $G(U_k)$ is the set of groups that involves user U_k who issued the trapdoor. Then bit vector is initially decrypted with each oracle key $K(w_i, G_{k,\iota})$ for $G_{k,\iota} \in (G(B_{w_i}^j) \cap G(U_k))$:

$$V_{w_i}^j(G_{k,\iota}) = \pi_{w_i}^j \oplus O(K(w_i, G_{k,\iota}), j)$$

Once bit vector is decrypted for each group in $G(B_{w_i}^j) \cap G(U_k)$, final vector denoted as $V_{w_i}^j$ is formed by group oriented bit selection. Specifically, suppose $id_{j,1}, ..., id_{j,k}$ are the identifiers that are represented by bits 1, ..., k. Then ρ^{th} bit of $V_{w_i}^j$ is set to ρ^{th} bit of $V_{w_i}^j(g(id_{j,\rho}))$ if $g(id_{j,\rho}) \in G(U_k)$ and set to zero otherwise. Finally, if ρ^{th} bit of $V_{w_i}^j$ is one, $id_{j,\rho}$ is included in the search result. Note that, correct decryption of each bit can only be obtained with correct group key. Otherwise, decrypted bit will be random.

After region servers identify document identifiers in their payloads, they transfer them to the master. Master merges the partial lists and sends the corresponding encrypted documents along with their groups to the user. In this setting, suppose (C_i, G_ι) is included in the result set. Then user decrypts C_i with secret collection key $K_{G_\iota}^C$ to obtain its plain version.

4. SECURE INDEX UPDATE

Real document storage systems are highly dynamic in their nature. Accordingly, data owner should be able to modify the encrypted collection. To achieve this goal, we extend our protocol and index structure to enable document deletion and addition.

4.1 Document Deletion

Removal of a document from the cloud storage necessitates the elimination of the references against it. To keep track of these references, we construct an update index. This new index stores the cell addresses of the search index that are connected to a particular document and it is generated through three steps.

1. **Plain Index Construction:** During the search index setup, encryption blocks are constructed for each keyword in such a way that they consist of some slots, each of which contains or represents a particular document identifier. For any document D_i, 'update index' stores these block and slot locations for the keywords that are included in D_i. More formally, suppose D_i contains keyword set denoted as $W_i = \{w_{i_1}, ..., w_{i_\ell}\}$, $E_w(w_{i_j})$ is the encrypted form of w_{i_j}, $name(D_i)$ is the unique filename of D_i, $block(w_{i_j}, D_i)$ and $slot(w_{i_j}, D_i)$ denote the block and slot order of D_i's identifier in the encryption blocks of w_{i_j}. Then address list for D_i denoted as $A(D_i)$ is a set such that $A(D_i) = \{E_w(w_{i_1}) \ || \ block(w_{i_j}, D_i) \ || \ slot(w_{i_j}, D_i), ..., E_w(w_{i_\ell}) \ || \ block(w_{i_\ell}, D_i) \ || \ slot(w_{i_\ell}, D_i)\}$. Finally, $\{(name(D_1), A(D_1)), ..., (name(D_n), A(D_n))\}$ constitutes plain 'update index'.

2. **Document and Index Padding:** Note that, address list corresponding to document D_i in plain 'update index' contains ℓ cells provided that D_i contains ℓ keywords. To hide the actual number of keywords included in a document, we apply padding on the document itself or its address list prior to their encryption. Suppose $avg_{|w|}$ is a parameter that indicates the unit bit length of a keyword, $|D_i|$ is the bit length of D_i, $A(D_i)$ is the address list for D_i in the plain 'update index'. Then D_i is expected to contain $\xi(D_i) = \lceil |D_i|/avg_{|w|} \rceil$ keywords. In this setting, if $A(D_i)$ contains less than $\xi(D_i)$ keywords, we apply padding on the address list. Specifically, we insert $|A(D_i)|$ - $\xi(D_i)$ fake cells (e.g., $E_w(fake)|| -1|| -1)$ to $A(D_i)$. If $A(D_i)$ contains more than $\xi(D_i)$ keywords, we pad document itself with empty spaces until $\xi(D_i) = \lceil |D_i|/avg_{|w|} \rceil$.

3. **Index Encryption:** Suppose $\{(name(D_1), A(D_1)), ..., (name(D_n), A(D_n))\}$ is a padded plain 'update index', Φ_{K_D} and Ψ_{K_A} are pseudo-random functions with secret keys K_D and K_A, O_D is a random oracle. Then encrypted 'update index' denoted as $\{(E_D(D_1), E_A(A_{D_1})), ..., (E_D(D_n), E_A(A_{D_n}))\}$ is generated as follows:

- Generate $E_D(D_i)$ such that $E_D(D_i) = \Phi_{K_D}(name(D_i))$.

- Generate a random oracle key $K(D_i)$ for the address list encryption of $A(D_i)$ such that $K(D_i) = \Psi_{K_A}(name(D_i))$.

- Suppose $K(D_i)$ is the random oracle key, $A_{D_i}^1, ..., A_{D_i}^r$ are members of $A(D_i)$, $O_D(K(D_i), j)$ denotes the output of random oracle O_D with key $K(D_i)$ when it is applied on input j and $\oplus$ represents xor operator. Then generate encryption of $A(D_i)$ denoted as $E_A(A(D_i))$ as follows:

$$E_A(A(D_i)) = \{\pi_{D_i}^1, ..., \pi_{D_i}^r\}$$
$$\pi_{D_i}^j = (A_{D_i}^j \oplus O_D(K(D_i), j), j)$$

Once encrypted 'update index' is generated, it is transferred to the cloud and stored in the key-value store. In this setting, for any document D_i, $(E_D(name(D_i))$ is a key and $E_A(A(D_i))$ is the corresponding value. 'Update index' enables data owner to delete documents from the remote servers. Deletion process is executed as follows:

1. **Deletion Token Generation:** Token for deleting document with filename $name(D_i)$ denoted as $T_D(D_i)$ is formed using secret keys K_D and K_A. Specifically, suppose Φ_{K_D} and Ψ_{K_A} are pseudo-random functions with keys K_D and K_A. Then $T_D(D_i) = (E_D(D_i), K(D_i))$ such that $E_D(D_i) = \Phi_{K_D}(name(D_i))$ and $K(D_i) = \Psi_{K_A}(name(D_i))$. Once $T_D(D_i)$ is formed, it is sent to the cloud master.

2. Address Extraction: Upon reception of $T_D(D_i) = (E_D(D_i), K(D_i))$, master fetches the value corresponding to row-key $E_D(D_i)$ from the key-value store. Suppose $\{\pi_{D_i}^1, ..., \pi_{D_i}^r\}$ is the value for $E_D(D_i)$. Then master decrypts the encrypted addresses as follows:

$$A_{D_i}^k = \pi_{D_i}^k \oplus O_D(K(D_i), k)$$

After decryption, master obtains the address set for the search index cells which include reference to the document to be deleted. Note that, encrypted address list contains some fake entries by the construction. These fake entries are eliminated by the master at this phase. Final address list $\{A_{D_i}^1, ..., A_{D_i}^\rho\}$ is utilized for adjusting the search index.

3. Search Index Update: Encrypted index blocks of the search index are distributed among m distinct regions. To update search index, master retrieves the necessary blocks from the region servers according to the address list $\{A_{D_i}^1, ..., A_{D_i}^\rho\}$. Note that, each address in the list is in the form of $E_w(w_j) \parallel block(w_j, D_i) \parallel slot(w_j, D_i)$. Here, $E_w(w_j)$ is the encrypted form of keyword w_j which is included in D_i, $block(w_j, D_i)$ and $slot(w_j, D_i)$ are the block and slot locations that holds the identifier for D_i.

By the search index construction, block with location $v_j^i = block(w_j, D_i)$ is stored in the kth region where $k = v_j^i \bmod m$. Specifically, it is the value corresponding to column v_j^i of row-key $k \parallel E_w(w_j)$. Master retrieves this value denoted as $\pi_{w_j}[\rho]$ from the corresponding region server and applies update on it according to its type as follows:

- Suppose $\pi_{w_j}[\rho]$ is a bit-vector block. Then master updates its ιth bit where $\iota = slot(w_j, id(D_i))$ such that $\pi_{w_j}[\rho][\iota] = \pi_{w_j}[\rho][\iota] \oplus 1$. Note that applied xor operation flips the bit to indicate the non-existence of keyword w_j in D_i. Hence, further search results for w_j will not include $id(D_i)$.

- Suppose $\pi_{w_j}[\rho]$ is a list block. Then master extends the block with signal array denoted as $S_{w_j}[\rho]$ if there is no previous update on the block. Otherwise master updates the existing $S_{w_j}[\rho]$. In this setting, signal array is an η bit vector where η is the number of slots in a list block and each bit indicates the validity of the corresponding slot. If a deletion request is issued for the ιth slot where $\iota = slot(w_j, D_i)$, ι^{th} bit is updated to invalidate this slot such that $S_{w_j}[\rho][\iota] = 1$.

With signal array, query evaluation on the search index is slightly different. During the search, region servers check the signal array prior the decryption of the slots in a list block. If $S_{w_j}[\rho][\iota] = 1$, then identifier that will be obtained from the decryption of ιth slot is not included in the result.

4.2 Document Addition

To add a set of new documents to the encrypted collection, we propose a two-round protocol. In the first round, data owner sends the number of slots that will be added to the search index corresponding to a set of keywords. According to these numbers, master transfers back the encrypted blocks with available slots. In the second round, data owner updates received blocks or generate some new blocks if available slots are not sufficient. Then, he forms the 'update index' entries for the new documents. Finally, adjusted search index blocks and the new entries for the 'update index' along with the encrypted documents are sent to the cloud.

During the setup, search index consists of encrypted blocks which are in the bit-vector or list form. Since bit-vector form represents constant number of documents, we utilize only blocks of type list during the addition process. Hence, all blocks that will be inserted into the search index will be in the list form. To facilitate the addition, master keeps an 'addition helper index'. Note that, list blocks consist of slots, each of which contains a document identifier. Some of these slots are invalidated during the deletion. In fact, helper index keeps track of these slots along with the random oracle input counter for each encrypted keyword.

Addition Helper Index: Suppose $E_w(w_1), ..., E_w(w_z)$ are the encrypted forms of keywords $w_1, ..., w_z$, η is the number of slots in list blocks, c_{w_i} denotes a counter for the blocks that are stored in search index payload for $E_w(w_i)$, $\delta_{w_i}^j$ is a set of block locations with j available slots. Then, value for helper index key $E_w(w_i)$ denoted as H_{w_i} is a pair such that $H_{w_i} = ([\delta_{w_i}^1, ..., \delta_{w_i}^\eta], c_{w_i})$. During search index setup, suppose n_{w_i} encryption blocks are formed for keyword w_i. Then $c_{w_i} = n_{w_i}$ and each $\delta_{w_i}^j$ for $1 \leq j \leq \eta$ is empty. Later, if j slots of a list block for $E_w(w_i)$ are invalidated during the deletion, location of this block is stored in $\delta_{w_i}^j$. This indicates the availability of j slots for the block.

Addition operation is performed in five main steps:

1. Generation of addition request: Suppose $D_U = \{D_1^U, ..., D_v^U\}$ is a collection of new documents with contents $\{W(D_1^U), ..., W(D_v^U)\}$, $\{w_1^u, ..., w_\ell^u\}$ is a set of all keywords that are included in the new documents, $id(D_i^U)$ is the identifier of D_i^U and Φ_{K_t} is a pseudo-random function with secret key K_t. Then data owner generates an inverted index $\{(w_1^u, L(w_1^u)), ..., (w_v^u, L(w_v^u))\}$ such that $id(D_j^U) \in L(w_i^u)$ if and only if $w_i^u \in W(D_j^U)$. Once inverted index is constructed, addition request denoted as $T_A(D_U)$ is generated for the collection. Specifically, $T_A(D_U) = \{(E_w(w_1^u), |L(w_1^u)|), ..., (E_w(w_\ell^u), |L(w_\ell^u)|)\}$ where $E_w(w_j^u) = \Phi_{K_t}(w_j^u)$ and $|L(w_j^u)|$ is the number of identifiers in $L(w_j^u)$ respectively. Finally $T_A(D_U)$ is sent to the cloud master server.

2. Block transfer: Once master receives addition request, it utilizes 'addition helper index' to locate blocks with available slots. If the number of slots is not sufficient, new blocks are generated by the user which we elaborate later.

Suppose $(E_w(w_i^u), |L(w_i^u)|)$ is included in $T_A(D_U)$ which implies that data owner needs $|L(w_i^u)|$ slots for $E_w(w_i^u)$ to store new document identifiers. Then, master initially retrieves the value of $E_w(w_i^u)$ denoted as $H_{w_i^u} = ([\delta_{w_i^u}^1, ..., \delta_{w_i^u}^\eta], c_{w_i^u})$ from the 'addition helper index'. Then starting from $\delta_{w_i^u}^\eta$ to $\delta_{w_i^u}^1$, server extracts block locations from them until the total number of extracted slots reaches to $|L(w_i^u)|$. Note that, each block location that is extracted from $\delta_{w_i}^j$ contains j slots. After this traversal, if the total number of slots does not reach to $|L(w_i^u)|$, data owner will generate new blocks. Specifically, if r_i more slots are necessary, owner will generate $\lceil r_i/\eta \rceil$ new blocks where η denotes the number of slots in a single block.

Once block locations are extracted, they are removed from the helper index and corresponding blocks are retrieved from the search index. Finally retrieved blocks for $E_w(w_i^u)$ denoted as $\Delta(w_i^u)$ along with the counter in helper index denoted as $c_{w_i^u}$ are sent back to the data owner.

3. Generation of new search index entries: Suppose data owner receives block sets $\Delta(w_1^u), ..., \Delta(w_\ell^u)$ against addition request. In this setting, $\Delta(w_i^u)$ consists of ρ_i blocks, each of which contains some available slots to store new document identifiers. In this setting, each block in $\Delta(w_i^u)$ is in the form of $\pi_{w_i^u}[\iota] \parallel S_{w_i^u}[\iota]$ where $\pi_{w_i^u}[\iota]$ is the ιth encrypted block in the search index for keyword w_i^u and $S_{w_i^u}[\iota]$ is the signal array that keeps the invalid slot locations in it. Initially, data owner decrypts each block $\pi_{w_i^u}[\iota]$ to obtain plain identifier list denoted as $id_{\iota,1} \parallel ... \parallel id_{\iota,\eta}$. Then identifiers in invalid slots of the blocks are replaced with new identifiers according to $S_{w_i^u}[\iota]$. Specifically, suppose $L(w_i^u)$ is the identifier list for the new documents that contain w_i^u. Then, provided that $S_{w_i^u}[\iota][v] = 1$, a random member of $L(w_i^u)$ is removed from it and inserted into the vth slot of the plain block. If $L(w_i^u)$ is not empty after the identifier replacement on the retrieved blocks, owner forms new blocks, slots of which are filled with the remaining member of $L(w_i^u)$. Finally both old and new blocks which we call update blocks are subject to encryption.

Suppose $c_{w_i^u}$ is the block counter for w_i, $id_{j,1}^u \parallel ... \parallel id_{j,\eta}^u$ is the content of jth plain block among the update blocks, Ψ_{K_p} is a pseudo-random permutation with key K_p and $O_S(K(w_i^u), j)$ is the output of random oracle O_S with key $K(w_i^u)$ when it is applied on input j. Then encrypted form of the block denoted as $\pi_{w_i^u}[j]$ is generated as follows[4]:

$$K(w_i^u) = \Psi_{K_p}(w_i^u)$$
$$\pi_{w_i^u}[j] = ((id_{j,1}^u \parallel ... \parallel id_{j,\eta}^u) \oplus O_S(K(w_i^u), c_{w_i^u} + j), c_{w_i^u} + j)$$

After the encryption of the update blocks, their signal arrays are cleared to zero to indicate that all slots in them are valid and new block counter for w_i is set to $c_{w_i^u} + n_i$ where n_i is the number of update blocks for w_i.

4. Generation of new update index entries: Note that, we keep 'update index' for update operations. This index stores the cell addresses of the search index that are connected to a particular document. Once identifiers corresponding to new documents are placed into the search blocks as explained in step 3, 'update index' entries are generated according to these placements. More formally, suppose new document D_i^u contains keyword set $\{w_{i_1}, ..., w_{i_z}\}$, $E_w(w_{i_j})$ is the encrypted form of w_{i_j}, $block(w_{i_j}, D_i^u)$ and $slot(w_{i_j}, D_i^u)$ denotes the block and slot locations that hosts the identifier of D_i^u in the update blocks that are generated for w_{i_j}. Then address list for D_i^u denoted as $A(D_i^u)$ is a set such that $A(D_i^u) = \{E_w(w_{i_1}) \parallel block(w_{i_j}, D_i^u) \parallel slot(w_{i_j}, D_i^u), ..., E_w(w_{i_z}) \parallel block(w_{i_z}, D_i^u) \parallel slot(w_{i_z}, D_i^u)\}$. In this setting, if update block is an old block that is received from the server, its location is its previous location. Otherwise, its location is equal to the block counter that is utilized during its encryption. Once address lists are formed for each new document, padding and encryption is applied on them as described in Section 4.1.

5. Application of the updates: At the final stage, new entries for 'update index' and 'search index' along with the encrypted documents are sent to the cloud. Updated old search index blocks are placed into their previous locations and new blocks are uniformly distributed to the regions.

5. EXPERIMENTAL ANALYSIS

In this section, we provide an empirical analysis of the proposed scheme. To perform our evaluation, we utilized public Enron dataset [2]. We selected all 30109 emails included in

---

[4]If authorization is enabled, each document identifier is encrypted through its group key as described in Section 3.3.

the sent-mail folder of all users. The corpus consists of approximately 77000 keywords. We also generated a corpus of approximately 30,000,000 emails by data replication for scalability test. To simulate a real cloud environment, we formed a HBase cluster of twelve machines.

We evaluate the computationally efficiency of search scheme with distinct settings. Storage type threshold (Υ), dataset size (n), number of regions for index partitioning (m), and number of user groups ($|G(U)|$) are the parameters. Default values for these parameters are as follows: $\Upsilon = 6$, $n = 30109$, $m = 1$, $|G(U)| = 1$. To investigate the influence of distinct parameters, we modified a single parameter at a time and used the default values for the others.

In this study, we propose an inverted index where payloads are in the form of a encrypted bit vector or list during the setup. Payload type depends on a threshold Υ. Our empirical analysis indicate that default Υ (i.e., $\Upsilon = 6$) that is computed according to Theorem 3.1 provides considerable storage savings in compare to pure bit vector or list payloads as depicted in Figure 1-a.

To investigate the effect of distinct parameters on the search performance, we measured the time between the query request and identification of search results. To do so, we generated 1000 trapdoors by randomly drawing a keyword among all keywords. Reported timing results are the averages for the issued trapdoors. The search time is almost linear in the number of documents as depicted in Figure 1-b. This is because, the number of encrypted payload blocks is proportional to the number of documents in the corpus. Figure 1-c demonstrates the influence of the number of regions generated on the HBase cluster. Increase in the number of regions decrease the unit load of each machine due to parallelized search. In this study, we proposed authorization-aware keyword search protocol. During its execution, users are requested to issue a trapdoor component for each group that they are involved in. Hence, the necessary computations is linearly proportional to the number of groups that a user is involved in as depicted in Figure 1-d.

To evaluate the scalability of the proposed scheme, we replicated the emails in our corpus 1000 times. After the replication, we generated secure index on a corpus of 30,109,000 emails. Note that replication results in increase in the numer of documents while the index of words stays at the same size. This leads to much larger index payloads which necessiate more cryptographic operations during the search. Figure 2 demonstrates the average search time for the issued 1000 random search requests. Search operation could be performed in a few seconds according to our analysis.

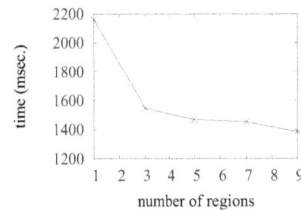

Figure 2: Scalability Evaluation

To evaluate the efficiency of the update operations, we measure the time between the request and completion of modifications on the indices. We generated update requests for documents with distinct amount of keywords. Specif-

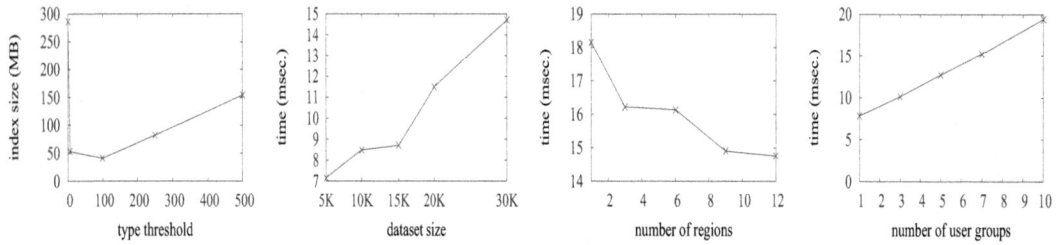

Figure 1: Influence of Protocol Parameters on Search Performance

ically, we selected 10 random emails from the corpus for each distinct keyword size (e.g., 50, ..., 250) and we issued a token for deletion and addition of the selected emails. Reported timing results are the averages over 10 executions. Figure 3 depicts the update time for deletion and addition of a document with distinct keyword size. With increasing number of keywords, update times increase since the number of operations both on the search and update index are linearly proportional to the number of keywords.

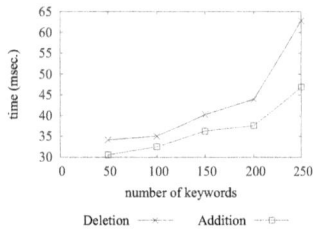

Figure 3: Update Evaluation

6. CONCLUSION

In this paper, we propose a search scheme over encrypted documents for real cloud infrastructures. Proposed design is based on a distributed secure index which allows parallel execution among many machines. To restrict information leakage according to the user access rights, proposed approach integrates authorization into the design. In addition, we also propose an effective update mechanism for distributed search index. Extensive empirical evaluations indicate the practical nature of the proposed scheme.

In this study, we provide a vertically partitioned index to enable simultaneous decryption of large payloads. In future work, we plan to design a hybrid architecture that consists of both vertically and horizontally partitioned segments to utilize resources according to query workload.

7. ACKNOWLEDGEMENTS

This work was partially supported by Air Force Office of Scientific Research FA9550-12-1-0082, National Institutes of Health Grants 1R0-1LM009989 and 1R01HG006844, National Science Foundation (NSF) Grants Career-CNS-0845803, CNS-1111529, CNS-1228198 and Army Research Office Grant W911NF-12-1-0558.

8. REFERENCES

[1] Apache hbase. http://hbase.apache.org, 2013.
[2] Enron dataset. http://www.cs.cmu.edu/enron, 2013.
[3] CASH, D., J., J., JARECKI, S., JUTLA, C., KRAWCZYK, H., ROSU, M., AND STEINER, M. Dynamic searchable encryption in very-large databases: Data structures and implementation. In NDSS'14 (2014).
[4] CASH, D., JARECKI, S., JUTLA, C., KRAWCZYK, H., ROSU, M., AND M., S. Highly-scalable searchable symmetric encryption with support for boolean queries. In Cryptology ePrint Archive, Report 2013/169 (2013).
[5] CHANG, Y., AND MITZENMACHER, M. Privacy preserving keyword searches on remote encrypted data. In Proc. of ACNS'05 (2005), pp. 442–455.
[6] CURTMOLA, R., GARAY, J., KAMARA, S., AND OSTROVSKY, R. Searchable symmetric encryption: Improved definitions and efficient constructions. Journal of Computer Security 19, 5 (2011), 895–934.
[7] GOH, E. Secure indexes. In Cryptology ePrint Archive, Report 2003/216 (2003).
[8] GOLDWASSER, S., AND BELLARE, M. Lecture Notes on Cryptography. http://cseweb.ucsd.edu/ mihir/papers/gb.html, 2008.
[9] GRUNBACHER, A. Posix access control lists on linux. In USENIX Annual Technical Conference'03 (2003).
[10] ISLAM, M. S., KUZU, M., AND KANTARCIOGLU, M. Access pattern disclosure on searchable encryption: Ramification, attack and mitigation. In NDSS'12 (2012).
[11] KAMARA, S., AND PAPAMANTHOU, C. Parallel and dynamic searchable symmetric encryption. In FC'13 (2013).
[12] KAMARA, S., PAPAMANTHOU, C., AND ROEDER, T. Dynamic searchable symmetric encryption. In CCS'12 (2012), pp. 965–976.
[13] KUZU, M., ISLAM, M. S., AND KANTARCIOGLU, M. A distributed framework for scalable search over encrypted documents. CoRR abs/1408.5539 (2014).
[14] NEWMAN, M. E. Power laws, pareto distributions and zipf's law. Contemporary Physics 46 (2005), 323–351.
[15] SONG, D., WAGNER, D., AND PERRIG, A. Practical techniques for searches on encrypted data. In Proc. of the IEEE S&P'00 (2000), pp. 44–55.
[16] STEFANOV, E., PAPAMANTHOU, C., AND SHI, E. Practical dynamic searchable encryption with small leakage. In NDSS'14 (2014).
[17] VAN LIESDONK, P., SEDGHI, S., DOUMEN, J., HARTEL, P. H., AND JONKER, W. Computationally effcient searchable symmetric encryption. In SDM'10 (2010), pp. 87–100.

Big Data Security and Privacy

Dr. Bhavani Thuraisingham

The University of Texas at Dallas

ABSTRACT

This paper describes the issues surrounding big data security and privacy and provides a summary of the National Science Foundation sponsored workshop on this topic held in Dallas, Texas on September 16-17, 2014. Our goal is to build a community in big data security and privacy to explore the challenging research problems.

1. INTRODUCTION

Database systems technology has advanced a great deal during the past four decades from the legacy systems based on network and hierarchical models to relational and object database systems. Database systems can also now be accessed via the web and data management services have been implemented as web services. Due to the explosion of web-based services, unstructured data management and social media and mobile computing, the amount of data to be handled has increased from terabytes to petabytes and zetabytes in just two decades. Such vast amounts of complex data have come to be known as Big Data. Not only does big data have to be managed efficiently, such data also has to be analyzed to extract useful nuggets to enhance businesses as well as improve society. This has come to be known as Big Data Analytics.

Storage, management and analysis of large quantities of data also results in security and privacy violations. Often data has to be retained for various reasons including for regulatory compliance. The data retained may have sensitive information and could violate user privacy. Furthermore, manipulating such big data, such as combining sets of different types of data could result in security and privacy violations. For example, while the raw data removes personally identifiable information, the derived data may contain private and sensitive information. For example, the raw data about a person may be combined with the person's address which may be sufficient to identify the person.

Different communities are working on the Big Data Challenge. For example, the systems community is developing technologies for massive storage of big data. The network community is developing solutions for managing very large networked data. The data community is developing solutions for efficiently managing and analyzing large sets of data. Big data research and development is being carried out both in academia, industry and government research labs. However, little attention has been given to security and privacy considerations for Big Data. Security cuts across multiple areas including systems, data and networks. We need the multiple communities to come together to develop solutions for Big Data Security and Privacy.

CODASPY'15, March 2–4, 2015, San Antonio, Texas, USA.
ACM 978-1-4503-3191-3/15/03.
http://dx.doi.org/10.1145/2699026.2699136

2. BIG DATA MANAGEMENT AND ANALYTICS

Big data management and analytics research is proceeding in three directions. They are:

(i) Building infrastructure and high performance computing techniques for the storage of big data;

(ii) Data management techniques such as integrating multiple data sources (both big and small) and indexing and querying big data;

(iii) Data analytics techniques that manipulate and analyze big data to extract nuggets.

We will briefly review the progress made in each of the areas. With respect to building infrastructures, technologies such as Hadoop and MapReduce as well as Storm are being developed for managing large amounts of data in the cloud. In addition, main memory data management techniques have advanced so that a few terabytes of data can be managed in main memory. Furthermore, systems such as HIVE and Cassandra as well as NoSQL databases have been developed for managing petabytes of data.

With respect to data management, traditional data management techniques such as query processing and optimization strategies are being examined for handling petabytes of data. Furthermore, graph data management techniques are being developed for the storage and management of very large networked data.

With respect to data analytics, the various data mining algorithms are being implemented on Hadoop and MapReduce based infrastructures. Additionally, data reduction techniques are being explored to reduce the massive amounts of data into manageable chunks while still maintaining the semantics of the data.

In summary, big data management and analytics techniques include extending current data management and mining techniques to handle massive amounts of data as well as developing new approaches including graph data management and mining techniques for maintaining and analyzing large networked data.

3. SECURITY AND PRIVACY

The collection, storage, manipulation and retention of massive amounts of data has resulted in serious security and privacy considerations. Various regulations are being proposed to handle big data so that the privacy of the individuals is not violated. For example, even if personally identifiable information is removed from the data, when data is combined with other data, an individual can be identified. This is essentially the inference and aggregation problem that data security researchers have been exploring for the past four decades. This problem is exacerbated with the management of big data as different sources of data now exist that are related to various individuals.

In some cases, regulations may cause privacy to be violated. For example, data that is collected (e.g., email data) has to be retained for a certain period of time (usually 5 years). As long as one keeps such data, there is a potential for privacy violations. Too many regulations can also stifle innovation. For example, if there is a regulation that raw data has to be kept as is and not manipulated or models cannot be built out of the data, then corporations cannot analyze the data in innovative ways to enhance their business. This way innovation may be stifled.

Therefore, one of the main challenges for ensuring security and privacy when dealing with big data is to come up with a balanced approach towards regulations and analytics. That is, how can an organization carry out useful analytics and still ensure the privacy of individuals. Numerous techniques for privacy-preserving data mining, privacy-preserving data integration and privacy-preserving information retrieval have been developed. The challenge is to extend these techniques for handling massive amounts of often networked data.

Another security challenge for big data management and analytics is to secure the infrastructures. Many of the technologies that have been developed including Hadoop, MapReduce, Hive, Cassandra, PigLatin, Mahout and Storm do not have adequate security protections. The question is, how can these technologies be secured and at the same time ensure high performance computing?

Next the big data management strategies such as access methods and indexing and query processing have to be secure. So the question is how can policies for different types of data such as structured, semi-structured, unstructured and graph data be integrated? Since big data may result from combining data from numerous sources, how can you ensure the quality of the data?

Finally, the entire area of security, privacy, integrity, data quality and trust policies has to be examined within the context of big data security. What are the appropriate policies for big data? How can these policies be handled without affecting performance? How can these policies be made consistent and complete?

This section has listed just some of the challenges with respect to security and privacy for big data. We need a comprehensive research program that will identify the challenges and develop solutions for big data security and privacy. Security cannot be an afterthought. That is, we cannot incorporate security into each and every big data technology that is being developed. We need to have a comprehensive strategy so that security can be incorporated while the technology is being developed. We also need to determine the appropriate types of policies and regulations to enforce before big data technologies are employed by an organization. This means researchers in multiple disciplines have to come together to determine what the problems are and explore solutions. These disciplines include high performance computing, data management and analytics, network science, and policy management.

4. BIG DATA ANALYTICS FOR SECURITY APPLICATIONS

While the challenges discussed in Section 3 deal with securing big data and ensuring the privacy of individuals, big data management, and analytics techniques can be used to solve security problems. For example, an organization can outsource activities such as identity management, email filtering and intrusion detection to the cloud. This is because massive amounts of data are being collected for such applications and this data has to be analyzed. Cloud data management is just one example of big data management. The question is, how can the developments in big data management and analytic techniques be used to solve security problems?

5. COMMUNITY BUILDING IN BIG DATA SECURITY AND PRIVACY

Recently a few workshops and panels have been held on Big Data Security. Examples include the ACM CCS workshop on Big Data Security, ACM SACMAT and IEEE Big Data Conference panels. These workshops and panels have been influenced by different communities of researchers. For example, the ACM CCS workshop series is focusing on Big Data for security applications while the IEEE Big Data Conference is focusing on cloud security issues. Furthermore, these workshops and panels mainly address a limited number of the technical issues surrounding big data security. For example, the ACM CCS workshop does not appear to address the privacy issues dealing with regulations or the security violations resulting from data analytics.

To address the above limitations, we organized a workshop on Big Data Security and Privacy on September 16-17, 2014 in Dallas Texas sponsored by the National Science Foundation (NSF) [1]. The participants of this workshop consisted of interdisciplinary researchers in the fields of higher performance computing, systems, data management and analytics, cyber security, network science and policy and social sciences who came together and determined the strategic direction for big data security and privacy. NSF has made substantial investments both in cyber security and big data. It is therefore critical that the two areas work together to determine the direction for big data security. We made a submission based on the workshop results to the National Privacy Research Strategy [2] and will have a final workshop report during the first quarter of 2015. We hope that this effort will help toward building a community in Big Data Security and Privacy.

REFERENCES

[1] NSF Workshop on Big Data Security and Privacy, http://csi.utdallas.edu/events/NSF/NSF%20workshop%20201 4.htm

[2] Big Data Security and Privacy, Submission to the National Privacy Research Strategy, https://www.nitrd.gov/cybersecurity/nprsrfi102014/BigData-SP.pdf

Towards Server-side Repair for Erasure Coding-based Distributed Storage Systems *

Bo Chen
Computer Science Department
Stony Brook University
bochen1@cs.stonybrook.edu

Anil Kumar Ammula, Reza Curtmola
Department of Computer Science
New Jersey Institute of Technology
{aa654, crix}@njit.edu

ABSTRACT

Erasure coding is one of the main mechanisms to add redundancy in a distributed storage system, by which a file with k data segments is encoded into a file with n coded segments such that any k coded segments can be used to recover the original k data segments. Each coded segment is stored at a storage server. Under an adversarial setting in which the storage servers can exhibit Byzantine behavior, remote data checking (RDC) can be used to ensure that the stored data remains retrievable over time. The main previous RDC scheme to offer such strong security guarantees, HAIL, has an inefficient repair procedure, which puts a high load on the data owner when repairing even one corrupt data segment.

In this work, we propose RDC-EC, a novel RDC scheme for erasure code-based distributed storage systems that can function under an adversarial setting. With RDC-EC we offer a solution to an open problem posed in previous work and build the first such system that has an efficient repair phase. The main insight is that RDC-EC is able to reduce the load on the data owner during the repair phase (i.e., lower bandwidth and computation) by shifting most of the burden from the data owner to the storage servers during repair. RDC-EC is able to maintain the advantages of systematic erasure coding: optimal storage for a certain reliability level and sub-file access. We build a prototype for RDC-EC and show experimentally that RDC-EC can handle efficiently large amounts of data.

Categories and Subject Descriptors

H.3.2 [**Information Storage and Retrieval**]: Information Storage

General Terms

Security, Theory, Design, Performance

Keywords

Cloud storage; remote data integrity checking; server-side repair; erasure coding

---

*The full version of this paper is available as a technical report [10].

1. Introduction

Remote data checking (RDC) [4, 24, 27, 7, 3] allows data owners to check the integrity of data stored at an untrusted server, thus enabling data owners to audit whether the server fulfills its contractual obligations. Long-term storage usually imposes certain reliability guarantees, such that the data remains retrievable over time. To achieve this guarantee, a distributed storage system usually stores data redundantly at multiple servers which are geographically spread throughout the world. In a benign setting where the storage servers are trusted, this basic approach would be sufficient to handle server failure due to natural faults. However, in an adversarial setting where the storage servers are untrusted and may behave maliciously, the basic approach may not be able to provide the desired reliability guarantee over time. In an adversarial setting, RDC can be used to ensure that valuable data is retrievable over time even if the storage servers are malicious.

When a distributed storage system is used in tandem with remote data checking, we distinguish several phases throughout the storage system's lifetime: Setup, Challenge, and Repair. During Setup, the data owner stores data redundantly at multiple storage servers. During Challenge, the data owner checks periodically each storage server to ensure the data stored at each server remains intact. If the data at one of the servers is found corrupted, the Repair phase is activated and the data owner repairs the data at the corrupted server using data from the healthy servers, such that the desired redundancy level in the system is restored. The Challenge and Repair phases will alternate over the lifetime of the storage system.

In a benign setting, the methods for storing data redundantly at multiple servers fall under three categories: *replication*, *erasure coding*, and *network coding*. We give an overview of these methods in Sec. 2, but we make here a few important observations. From a storage perspective, erasure coding is optimal since it can achieve the same reliability as replication at only a fraction of the storage cost. However, from the perspective of communication overhead in the repair phase, network coding is optimal as it incurs only a fraction of the communication imposed by erasure coding. Still, network coding has a major drawback which limits its applicability: small portions cannot be read without reconstructing the entire file. The fact that network coding does not support sub-file access to data makes it unsuitable for applications in which data read is a frequent operation.

Current RDC schemes designed for replication (MR-PDP [16]), erasure coding (HAIL [7]), and network coding (RDC-NC [15]) incur storage and communication costs as described in Table 1. We can see that these RDC schemes (approximately) preserve in an adversarial setting the storage and communication parameters that characterize a benign setting. Yet, we notice that if we were to use HAIL (*i.e.*, the RDC scheme which minimizes the storage cost

	MR-PDP [16]	HAIL [7]	RDC-NC [15]	RDC-EC (proposed approach)
Coding method	replication	erasure coding	network coding	erasure coding
Total server storage	$O(n\|F\|)$	$O(\frac{n\|F\|}{k})$	$O(\frac{2n\|F\|}{k+1})$	$O(\frac{n\|F\|}{k})$
Communication (repair phase)	$O(\|F\|)$	$O(\frac{n\|F\|}{k})$	$O(\frac{2\|F\|}{k+1})$	$O(\frac{\|F\|}{k})$
Total server computation (repair phase)	$O(1)$	$O(1)$	$O(\ell)$	$O(k)$
Support for sub-file access	yes	yes	no	yes

Table 1: A comparison of RDC schemes for distributed storage systems. A file $\mathbf{F}$ of $|\mathbf{F}|$ bits has originally k segments and is encoded into n segments. For the repair phase, the costs are for the case when one storage server fails. For RDC-NC, the client retrieves data from ℓ servers during Repair.

and allows sub-file access), then we would have to pay the highest communication cost during the Repair phase: Repairing data at one corrupted server requires the data owner to retrieve all the data at all the storage servers, reconstruct the entire data and then recompute the corrupted segment. This process may put a high burden on the data owner. In fact, the design of an RDC scheme for erasure coding-based distributed storage systems with low-bandwidth repair was posed as an open problem [7] and remained unsolved.

In this work, we provide a solution to this open problem by designing RDC-EC, a distributed storage system which functions under an adversarial setting and achieves both the storage benefits of erasure coding and the repair bandwidth benefits of network coding. RDC-EC has the following properties:

− Minimizes the storage cost (to achieve a certain reliability level).
− Allows efficient sub-file access.
− Incurs low repair bandwidth between the data owner and the storage servers.
− Functions properly under an adversarial setting.

Table 1 compares the performance of our scheme (RDC-EC) with previous RDC schemes.

1.1 Solution Overview

Our starting point is the HAIL scheme [7], which views the original data (e.g., a file) as a collection of k segments and encodes it into a collection of n segments. The n coded segments are stored at n storage servers (one segment per server). HAIL is designed to withstand a Byzantine and mobile adversary which can corrupt at most b servers in any time interval (i.e., an *epoch*). Because, in time, all the n storage servers could be corrupted, the servers are periodically challenged to provide a proof that they continue to store data. If a server is found faulty, then a repair procedure is triggered in order to bring back the system to a state in which all data is recoverable. Whereas HAIL is designed to withstand attacks while minimizing overall storage costs and communication costs during the Challenge phase, its Repair phase is inefficient: to repair even one corrupt segment, the data owner has to retrieve all the n segments from the n servers, reconstruct the entire file, and then recompute the corrupted segment.

We inherit from HAIL the optimal storage cost and low communication cost during the Challenge phase. However, we redesign parts of HAIL to achieve an efficient Repair phase, in which the repair bandwidth is (asymptotically) equal to the optimal repair bandwidth. The design of our new scheme is motivated by two insights:

Insight 1. Server-side repair: We leverage server-side repair [13], a recently proposed concept which can minimize the load on the data owner during the Repair phase by allowing the storage servers to collaborate in order to generate a new segment whenever an existing segment has been corrupted. By incorporating server-side repair into RDC-EC, we obtain the following advantages:

− the repair bandwidth between the data owner and the storage servers is reduced considerably (only two segments are transmitted instead of n segments like in HAIL). The majority of the data transmission during Repair now happens between the storage servers.

This is beneficial since the data owner's connection may have limited bandwidth, whereas the storage servers are usually connected by a high bandwidth network.
− the computational burden during the Repair phase is shifted to the servers, allowing data owners to remain lightweight.

Insight 2. The elements of the encoding matrix are masked: To enable server-side repair, previous work reveals certain secrets to allow the servers to collaborate and repair the corrupted data. For example, when the distributed storage system relies on replication [13], the data owner reveals to the servers the secret key needed to differentiate the various replicas. A straightforward extension to the setting of erasure coding, would mean that the data owner must reveal the encoding matrix (*i.e.*, the matrix used to erasure code the original data). In all previous RDC schemes for erasure coding-based distributed systems (HAIL [7] and [31]), this encoding matrix needs to remain secret, otherwise the data can be corrupted unbeknownst to the data owner (the attack is described in Sec. 4.3).

To overcome this potential attack, the data owner does not reveal the encoding matrix to the storage servers. Instead, to repair a corrupt segment, the data owner engages in a two-round protocol with the storage system as follows. The data owner masks certain elements of the encoding matrix and provides them to the storage servers. These masked elements do not reveal anything about the original elements in the encoding matrix, but are used by the servers to collectively perform blind computations over the segments they store and to obtain two masked segments. The data owner receives the two masked segments and has enough information to unmask and combine them into one segment. This segment is sent to a new storage server to replace the corrupt segment.

This approach has the additional advantage of reducing the computational load on data owners. Instead of participating in an expensive decoding of n segments to reconstruct the entire data (like in HAIL), the data owner only processes two segments and lets the servers handle the bulk of the decoding and reconstruction.

What are the trade-offs? RDC-EC is able to reduce the load on the data owner during Repair (*i.e.*, lower bandwidth and computation) by shifting most of the burden from the data owner to the storage servers. Basically, RDC-EC incurs the following costs in order to achieve a more efficient Repair phase:
− increased load and more complex functionality at the storage servers (the servers are required to perform computations during Repair, as opposed to simply "serving" their data segments in HAIL; the servers are also required to perform additional interactions with the data owner and with the other servers during Repair).
− two rounds of interaction between the data owner and the storage system (as opposed to one round in HAIL).

We believe this trade-off between the resources of the data owner and those of the storage servers aligns well with the cloud computing model which assumes a resource-rich cloud data center.

1.2 Contributions

In this work, we propose RDC-EC, a remote data checking scheme for erasure code-based distributed storage systems that can function under an adversarial setting. With RDC-EC we offer a solution to an open problem posed in previous work and build the first such system that has an efficient Repair phase. The main insight is that RDC-EC is able to reduce the load on the data owner during Repair (i.e., lower bandwidth and computation) by shifting most of the burden from the data owner to the storage servers. Specifically, we make the following contributions:

- We provide an overview of the main methods to add redundancy in a distributed storage system. The previous main result that uses remote data checking (RDC) to ensure data remains retrievable over time in an erasure coding-based distributed storage system is HAIL [7]. Whereas HAIL is able to provide security guarantees against a strong adversary, it has an inefficient Repair phase.

- We propose RDC-EC, a remote data checking scheme for erasure code-based distributed storage systems that can function under an adversarial setting. With RDC-EC we offer a solution to an open problem posed in HAIL and build the first such system that has an efficient Repair phase. Similar with HAIL, RDC-EC inherits the advantages of systematic erasure coding: the storage overhead is optimal in order to achieve a certain reliability level, and sub-file access is possible (i.e., small portions of the coded data can be read without having to decode the entire data). Like HAIL, RDC-EC handles a strong mobile and Byzantine adversary which is allowed to corrupt b out of the n storage servers in any time interval (i.e., an epoch). However, unlike HAIL, RDC-EC is able to repair one corrupt segment by placing a minimal load on the data owner who only needs to download and process the equivalent of two segments (whereas HAIL requires n segments to be downloaded and processed).

  RDC-EC achieves efficient repair by incorporating *server-side repair*, which can minimize the load on the data owner during the Repair phase by allowing the storage servers to collaborate in order to generate a new segment whenever an existing segment has been corrupted. The main challenge is to leverage the resources of the storage servers while not revealing information that would allow the adversarial servers to attack the system and reduce its reliability over time. The data owner achieves this by requiring the servers to perform computation over a "masked" version of the data, which is then "un-masked" and used to recover the corrupted segment.

- We build a prototype for RDC-EC using the Jerasure [26] and OpenSSL [2] libraries. To achieve an appropriate security level, we extended Jerasure's coding functions to support 128-bit symbols. Experimental evaluations show that RDC-EC is efficient for encoding and repairing large files (less than 20 sec for a 1GB file). Due to space limitations, implementation and experimental details are presented in [10].

2. Distributed Storage Systems Redundancy

Data can be redundantly stored at multiple servers through *replication*, *erasure coding*, and *network coding*.

Replication. In replication, the data owner simply stores multiple copies of a file at multiple storage servers, such that the file is recoverable if at least one file copy remains intact. Although replication has the advantage of simplicity, it has a high storage cost. Today's storage systems usually handle "big data", which can be TBs or even PBs. Replicating multiple entire copies of the "big data" may become prohibitively expensive.

Erasure coding-based distributed storage systems. In erasure coding, given a file of k segments, the client encodes the file into n coded segments, such that any k out of n coded segments can be used to restore the original file. The client stores the n coded segments at n servers, one segment at each server. We provide details about the encoding/decoding process in [10].

Erasure coding was shown to be optimal in terms of redundancy-reliability tradeoff [34] and has been used extensively to ensure reliability for storage systems [9, 23, 26]. In addition, an erasure code is systematic, with its input embedded as part of its encoded output, e.g., in an (n, k) erasure code, the first k coded segments are the k original file segments. This has the advantage that any portion of the file can be read efficiently (we call this property "*sub-file access*"). Due to the aforementioned advantages, erasure coding was used broadly in storage systems which require frequent reads and can be categorized as read-frequently workloads, e.g., Microsoft Azure [1], HYDRAstor [19], etc.

Bowers et al. [7] introduced HAIL, a distributed cloud storage system which offers cloud users high reliability guarantees under a strong adversarial setting. Similar to RAID [25], which builds low-cost reliable storage from inexpensive drives, HAIL builds reliable cloud storage by combining cheap cloud storage providers. However, RAID has been designed to tolerate benign failures (e.g., hard drive crashes), whereas HAIL is able to deal with a strong (i.e., mobile and Byzantine) adversarial model, in which the adversary is allowed to perform progressive corruption of the storage providers over time. We provide an overview of HAIL in [10].

Unfortunately, erasure coding has an inefficient repair procedure. Repairing one corrupted segment requires to download k coded segments and reconstruct the whole file. This is exacerbated in an adversarial setting: to repair a corrupted segment, the client needs to download all the n coded segments (e.g., HAIL [7])).

Network coding-based distributed storage systems. Network coding can be used to encode and distribute a file to n servers, such that any k out of n servers have enough data to recover the file [17, 18]. Although network coding can achieve optimal repair bandwidth, it is not systematic. This makes it inefficient for read operations, because reading even a small portion of the file requires to reconstruct the whole file. Thus, applications of network coding to storage systems are limited to read-rarely workloads [15].

3. System and Adversarial Model

The client (i.e., data owner) divides the original file into k segments, and encodes them into n coded segments, such that: 1) the first k coded segments are the original file segments, and the remaining $n - k$ coded segments are the parity segments; 2) any k out of n segments can be used to restore the original file. The client stores the n coded segments at n storage servers (one segment per server) as follows: The k original segments are stored at k primary servers ($S_1, S_2, \ldots, S_k$), whereas the $n - k$ parity segments are stored at $n - k$ secondary servers ($S_{k+1}, \ldots, S_n$).

We consider a *mobile* and *Byzantine* adversary, similar to the one used in HAIL [7]. "Byzantine" means the adversary can behave arbitrarily. "Mobile" means that the adversary can corrupt any (and potentially all) of the servers over the lifetime of the storage system. However, it can only corrupt at most $(n - k - 1)/2$ out of the n servers within any given time interval. We refer to such a time interval as an *epoch*.

From an adversarial point of view, a storage server is seen as having two components, the *code* and the *storage*. The code refers to the software that runs on the server and defines the server's behavior in the interaction with the client, whereas the storage refers to the data stored by the server.

At the beginning of each epoch, the adversary picks a set of at most $(n - k - 1)/2$ servers, and corrupts both the code and the storage components on them. At the end of each epoch, the code component in each storage server will be restored to a correct state (*e.g.*, the data owner can simply remove the malware, and re-install a clean code component). However, the storage component may remain corrupted across epochs. Thus, in the absence of explicit defense mechanisms, the storage at more than $n - k$ servers may become corrupted over time and the original data may become unrecoverable. The client's goal is to detect and repair storage corruption before it renders the data unavailable. To this end, the client checks data possession with the servers in every epoch and if it detects any corrupted data in the faulty servers, it uses the redundancy at the remaining healthy servers to repair the corruption.

Each epoch consists of two phases:

— A *challenge phase* that contains two sub-phases:
(a) corruption sub-phase: The adversary corrupts up to b_1 servers.
(b) challenge sub-phase: The client checks data possession with all the servers. As a result, it may detect faulty servers with corrupted data (*i.e.*, faulty servers).

— A *repair phase* that contains two sub-phases and is triggered only if corruption is detected in the challenge phase:
(a) corruption sub-phase: The adversary corrupts up to b_2 servers.
(b) repair sub-phase: The client repairs the data at any faulty servers detected in the challenge phase.

The total number of servers that can be corrupted by the adversary during an epoch is at most $(n - k - 1)/2$ (*i.e.*, $b_1 + b_2 \leq (n - k - 1)/2$).

The structure of an epoch is similar with the one in HAIL [7], with one important modification: We explicitly allow the adversary to corrupt data after the challenge phase. This models attackers that act honestly during the challenge phase, but are malicious in the repair phase. Such behavior must be considered in any scheme that seeks to achieve a repair phase that is more efficient than simply retrieving all the n segments.

4. Remote Data Checking for Erasure Coding-based Distributed Storage Systems

In this section, we first introduce the key ideas in our design, and then present our main result, the RDC-EC scheme.

4.1 Key Ideas

A novel repair tag construction. We introduce a novel repair tag construction in which, to compute a repair tag for an erasure coded segment, we use a seed to generate a set of pseudorandom coefficients, and then use this set of coefficients to aggregate the symbols in the segment. A repair tag constructed in this way is *publicly computable*, but *privately verifiable*. Publicly computable means any party who knows the seed can generate the corresponding repair tag for the stored segment. Private verifiable means the correctness of the repair tags can be verified only by a party who knows some secret. During Repair, each storage server computes a repair tag for its stored segment based on a fresh seed sent by the client (publicly computable). The client can then verify the correctness of the repair tags from all the servers based on the seed and on a secret (privately verifiable), because all the repair tags together form a valid integrity-protected dispersal code that was constructed based on the client's secret (for details about the integrity-protected dispersal code, refer to HAIL [7]).

Enabling server-side repair for erasure coding to minimize the client's workload. In previous erasure coding-based distributed

storage systems such as HAIL, the original file of k segments is encoded into a code word of n segments which are outsourced to n storage servers. To repair a corrupted segment, the client first retrieves all the outsourced segments, decodes them to recover the original k file segments and then restores the corrupted segment. Our key idea is to leverage *server-side repair*, in which we allow the storage servers to collaborate in order to generate a new segment whenever an existing segment has been corrupted. As a result, the communication and computation load on the client during Repair is reduced considerably.

Enabling server-side repair to minimize the client's load in the setting of erasure coding-based distributed systems imposes several design decisions. During Repair, we require the client to verify the repair tags because this verification relies on secret keys and cannot be offloaded to the untrusted servers. The client needs to retrieve n small tags and perform a small amount of computation on them, which impose only a small burden on the client. In addition, to protect secret keys used to embed random values into the parity symbols (for the integrity-protected dispersal code), we require the client (rather than the servers) to perform the final step of restoring the corrupted segment. In this way, the client can remain lightweight because it only needs to perform a small amount of computation over a limited number of segments (*i.e.*, two in RDC-EC) in order to restore a corrupted segment. Most of the repair work (*e.g.*, aggregating a large number of segments to decode the original file) is offloaded to the servers.

Allowing untrusted servers to aggregate segments under an adversarial setting. In a benign setting, the information dispersal matrix used to erasure code the original file is needed to repair a corrupted segment. However, under an adversarial setting, this matrix needs to remain secret during the server-side repair process. Thus, the client has to leverage the computational power of the servers without revealing this matrix. For this, the client derives a set of intermediate coefficients from the dispersal matrix, masks them based on an algebraic function and sends them to the untrusted servers. Due to the algebraic properties of our masking function and of the erasure coding, the servers are able to perform useful computation over their stored segments based on the masked coefficients. This approach ensures the secrecy of the information dispersal matrix while allowing server-side repair.

4.2 The RDC-EC scheme

In the following, we present RDC-EC, the first erasure coding-based remote data checking scheme that allows server-side repair. This is the main result of the paper.

Let κ be a security parameter. The original file F is divided into k segments: $F = \{b_1, \ldots, b_k\}$. Each segment b_i can be viewed as a column vector: $b_i = (b_{i1}, b_{i2}, \ldots, b_{i\ell})$, where b_{ij} $(1 \leq j \leq \ell)$ is a symbol in $GF(2^w)$ and ℓ is the number of symbols in a segment. Throughout the paper, all the arithmetic operations are performed in $GF(2^w)$. We make use of a PRF g with the following parameters: $g : \{0, 1\}^* \times \{0, 1\}^\kappa \rightarrow GF(2^w)$. We use *file_handle* to uniquely identify the file to be encoded.

RDC-EC overview. Our RDC-EC scheme consists of three phases: Setup, Challenge, and Repair. During the Setup phase, the client preprocesses the original file F. The client first generates an $n \times k$ information dispersal matrix M and then uses M to encode the k segments of F, generating n coded segments such that: (a) the first k coded segments are the original file segments, (b) the remaining $n - k$ coded segments are the parity segments, and (c) any k out of n coded segments can be used to recover F. This part of the encoding process is described in more details in Sec. 2 and in [10].

The client further adds to each parity symbol a secret value, such that each parity symbol is converted into a message authentication code (MAC) of the corresponding file symbols [7]. The client then stores the n segments at n servers (one segment per server).

In the Challenge phase, the client challenges each of the n servers, requiring them to prove data possession of the stored segments. This integrity check can be achieved efficiently based on spot checking, in which the client only checks a random subset of symbols from each outsourced segment. Prior work shows that spot checking provides a probabilistic guarantee for corruption detection, but the detection probability can be made arbitrarily high by increasing the number of symbols being challenged [4]. In RDC-EC, the client challenges the same random subset of symbols from each of the n stored segments. Each server aggregates the challenged symbols based on the same set of random coefficients and sends back an aggregated response. After having received all the n aggregated responses, the client can check and localize the corrupted responses, because the n responses constitute a valid integrity-protected dispersal code. The Challenge phases in RDC-EC and HAIL [7] are similar.

The Repair phase is activated when the client detected at least one corrupted segment during Challenge. We do not differentiate between corruptions caused by malicious server behavior and natural faults because servers which allow natural faults to be visible to clients should be avoided just as well. To repair a corrupted segment, the client randomly picks a seed and sends it to the n servers. Each server computes and sends back a *repair tag*, which is generated based on the stored segment and the random seed. After receiving the n repair tags, the client verifies all the n repair tags, and is able to detect and localize any corrupted repair tags because the n repair tags constitute a valid integrity-protected dispersal code (see Sec. 4.1). The client then picks k repair servers, each of which will provide data for repairing the corrupted segment. Note that when picking the repair servers, the client will exclude the servers which were found corrupted either in the Challenge phase or in the aforementioned repair tag verification. From the remaining $n - k$ servers, the client randomly picks an *Aggregation Server (AS)*, who will be responsible for aggregating the data provided by the repair servers. The following steps occur next:

1. Based on the information dispersal matrix M, the client generates a set of intermediate coefficients. These coefficients are used to linearly combine the segments stored in the repair servers in order to recover the corrupted segment. To avoid leaking information about M, these coefficients are masked using secret random values before being sent to the repair servers.

2. Each repair server computes two partial segments based on its stored segment and the masked coefficients sent by the client. A *partial segment* is computed by multiplying the stored segment with a masked coefficient provided by the client.

3. The client restores AS's code component[1]. Since the AS's code component has been restored, we assume the AS acts honestly until the end of the Repair phase. The client sends to the AS both the masked intermediate coefficients and the k repair tags corresponding to the k repair servers.

4. Each repair server sends its two partial segments to the AS.

5. AS aggregates the partial segments, generating two intermediate segments. It verifies whether the intermediate segments are correctly computed based on the repair tags sent by the client. If the verification fails, it can further localize the faulty servers

---

We construct RDC-EC in three phases, Setup, Challenge, and Repair. All the arithmetic operations are performed over the finite field $GF(2^w)$. We use $file\_handle$ to identify the file to be encoded.

Setup: The client C runs sk $\leftarrow$ KeyGen(1^κ). C divides the file F into k segments, $b_1, \ldots, b_k$, then executes:

1. Generate the information dispersal matrix M by running
   $M \leftarrow$ GenInformationDispersalMatrix(sk, k, n)

2. For $k + 1 \leq i \leq n$:
   Generate the parity segment b_i: $(b_{i1}, \ldots, b_{i\ell})$ $\leftarrow$ ComputeParityHAIL($sk, b_1, \ldots, b_k, M, i$)

3. For $1 \leq i \leq n$: Send segment b_i to server S_i for storage

4. Delete the file F and store only the secret key sk

Challenge: Similar with the challenge phase in HAIL: The client cross-checks the n storage servers as described in [7].

Figure 1: The Setup and Challenge Phases of RDC-EC

KeyGen(1^κ):

1. Choose $2n - k + 2$ keys at random from $\{0, 1\}^\kappa$:
   $K_1, K_2, \ldots, K_n, K'_{k+1}, \ldots, K'_n, K_a, K_b$

2. Return $(K_1, K_2, \ldots, K_n, K'_{k+1}, \ldots, K'_n, K_a, K_b)$

GenInformationDispersalMatrix(sk, k, n):

1. Parse sk as $(K_1, K_2, \ldots, K_n, K'_{k+1}, \ldots, K'_n, K_a, K_b)$

2. For $1 \leq i \leq n$
   - For $1 \leq j \leq k$: $M_{ij} = K_i^j$ (that is, K_i raised to power j)

3. Transform M into a matrix in which the first k rows form an identity matrix

4. Return M

ComputeParityHAIL($sk, b_1, \ldots, b_k, M, i$):

1. Parse sk as $(K_1, K_2, \ldots, K_n, K'_{k+1}, \ldots, K'_n, K_a, K_b)$

2. For $1 \leq j \leq \ell$:
   $b_{ij} = \sum_{\alpha=1}^{k} M_{i\alpha} b_{\alpha j} + g_{K'_i}(file\_handle||i||j)$

3. Return $(b_{i1}, \ldots, b_{i\ell})$

Figure 3: Components of the RDC-EC scheme (1)

based on these repair tags. Ultimately, two correctly computed intermediate segments are sent back to the client.

6. The client uses the intermediate segments and some secret key material to recover the corrupted segment.

The client has to restore the code component on one of the servers (the AS) for a short period of time during the Repair phase. Although this requirement is not present in HAIL's Repair phase, we argue it is reasonable because code restoration is already required for all the servers at the end of each epoch in both HAIL and RDC-EC (see the adversarial model in Sec. 3).

The RDC-EC scheme. The details of the RDC-EC scheme are presented in Figures 1 (Setup and Challenge) and 2 (Repair), whereas Figures 3 and 4 contain components used in these phases.

The Setup phase. The client first generates keys $K_1, K_2, \ldots, K_n$, $K'_{k+1}, K'_{k+2}, \ldots, K'_n$ at random[2] and then an $n \times k$ information dispersal matrix M by running GenInformationDispersalMatrix. The client further computes n coded segments, in which the first k coded segments are the original file segments, and the remaining $n - k$ coded segments are computed by running ComputeParityHAIL. All the n coded segments are sent for stor-

---

[1]This can be achieved by removing the malware, and re-installing a clean code component. See the adversarial model in Sec. 3.

[2]Note that we can save storage by using a PRF and a master key to generate all these keys on the fly when needed.

Repair: Assume during Challenge the client C has detected a corrupted segment b_y and has identified the corresponding faulty server S_y.

1. C generates a key K at random from $\{0, 1\}^\kappa$. C sends K to each of the n servers.

2. Each of the n servers computes and sends back a repair tag:
   For $1 \leq i \leq n$: S_i runs $t_i \leftarrow \mathsf{ComputeRepairTag}(K, b_i)$, and sends t_i back to C

3. C verifies all the repair tags received from the n servers by running
   $(G, flag) \leftarrow \mathsf{VerifyAllRepairTag}(\mathrm{sk}, t_1, t_2, \ldots, t_n, K, M, n, k)$. If $flag = 0$, exit (the file cannot be repaired, too many servers are faulty).

4. C chooses k different repair servers $i_1, \ldots, i_k$, each of which is randomly picked from the healthy servers (*i.e.*, excluding server S_y and the servers in G which were found to have sent invalid repair tags). Note that $i_1, \ldots, i_k$ are in ascending order. C then computes the set of *intermediate coefficients* $z_{i_1}, \ldots, z_{i_k}$: $(z_{i_1}, \ldots, z_{i_k}) \leftarrow \mathsf{GenRepairServerCoefficient}(\mathrm{sk}, y, k, n, i_1, \ldots, i_k)$.

5. C generates $k + 2$ random numbers $a, r, x_1, \ldots, x_k$ by running $(a, r, x_1, \ldots, x_k) \leftarrow \mathsf{GenRandom}(\mathrm{sk}, y, i_1, i_2, \ldots, i_k)$, and masks $z_{i_1}, \ldots, z_{i_k}$: For $1 \leq j \leq k$: $Z_{i_j} = a z_{i_j} + r x_j$

6. C sends to the repair servers the *masked coefficients* $(Z_{i_1}, Z_{i_2}, \ldots, Z_{i_k}, x_1, x_2, \ldots, x_k)$

7. Each of the k repair servers computes two partial segments:
   For $1 \leq j \leq k$:
   (a) S_{i_j} computes a first partial segment $b'_{i_j} = (b'_{i_j 1}, \ldots, b'_{i_j \ell})$: For $1 \leq \alpha \leq \ell$: $b'_{i_j \alpha} = Z_{i_j} b_{i_j \alpha}$
   (b) S_{i_j} computes a second partial segment $b''_{i_j} = (b''_{i_j 1}, \ldots, b''_{i_j \ell})$: For $1 \leq \alpha \leq \ell$: $b''_{i_j \alpha} = x_j b_{i_j \alpha}$

8. C randomly picks an Aggregation Server (AS) from the remaining $n - k$ servers, and restores the code component at AS (*i.e.*, the AS will behave honestly up to the end of this epoch). C sends $(Z_{i_1}, Z_{i_2}, \ldots, Z_{i_k}, x_1, x_2, \ldots, x_k, t_{i_1}, t_{i_2}, \ldots, t_{i_k}, K)$ to the AS

9. Each of the k repair servers sends the computed partial segments to AS: For $1 \leq j \leq k$: S_{i_j} sends b'_{i_j} and b''_{i_j} to AS

10. AS aggregates the partial segments received from the k repair servers and generates two intermediate segments b'_y and b''_y:
    (a) AS computes the first intermediate segment $b'_y = (b'_{y1}, \ldots, b'_{y\ell})$: For $1 \leq \alpha \leq \ell$: $b'_{y\alpha} = \sum_{j=1}^k b'_{i_j \alpha}$
    (b) AS computes the second intermediate segment $b''_y = (b''_{y1}, \ldots, b''_{y\ell})$: For $1 \leq \alpha \leq \ell$: $b''_{y\alpha} = \sum_{j=1}^k b''_{i_j \alpha}$

11. AS computes the repair tags for the two intermediate segments by running $t' \leftarrow \mathsf{ComputeRepairTag}(K, b'_y)$ and $t'' \leftarrow \mathsf{ComputeRepairTag}(K, b''_y)$, and checks the correctness of t' and t'':
    (a) If $t' \neq \sum_{j=1}^k Z_{i_j} t_{i_j}$, AS localizes the corrupted partial segments among $b'_{i_1}, b'_{i_2}, \ldots, b'_{i_k}$ by running $G \leftarrow \mathsf{VerifyPartialRepairTag}(b'_{i_1}, b'_{i_2}, \ldots, b'_{i_k}, K, t_{i_1}, t_{i_2}, \ldots, t_{i_k}, Z_{i_1}, Z_{i_2}, \ldots, Z_{i_k})$. AS informs C to pick new repair servers to replace the faulty repair servers in G
    (b) Otherwise, if $t'' \neq \sum_{j=1}^k x_j t_{i_j}$, AS localizes the corrupted partial segments among $b''_{i_1}, b''_{i_2}, \ldots, b''_{i_k}$ by running $G \leftarrow \mathsf{VerifyPartialRepairTag}(b''_{i_1}, b''_{i_2}, \ldots, b''_{i_k}, K, t_{i_1}, t_{i_2}, \ldots, t_{i_k}, x_1, x_2, \ldots, x_k)$. AS informs C to pick new repair servers to replace the faulty repair servers in G
    (c) Otherwise, if $t' = \sum_{j=1}^k Z_{i_j} t_{i_j}$ and $t'' = \sum_{j=1}^k x_j t_{i_j}$, AS sends b'_y and b''_y back to C, and C uses them to restores b_y by running $(b_{y1}, \ldots, b_{y\ell}) \leftarrow \mathsf{RepairOneSegment}(\mathrm{sk}, b'_y, b''_y, i_1, \ldots, i_k, z_{i1}, \ldots, z_{ik}, y, a, r)$. C stores b_y at a new server S'.

Figure 2: The Repair **Phase of** RDC-EC

age at n storage servers, one segment per server. The client may now delete the original file F and only keep the key material.

In GenInformationDispersalMatrix, the client generates the information dispersal matrix M. It first computes an $n \times k$ Vandermonde matrix (as described in [10]), in which each element is computed as K_i^j, where i is the row index ($1 \leq i \leq n$) and j is the column index ($1 \leq j \leq k$). The client then transforms this matrix into a matrix whose first k rows form the identity matrix.

In ComputeParityHAIL, the client computes a parity segment with index i, where $k + 1 \leq i \leq n$, and embeds a MAC into each symbol of this segment. The client uses the set of elements in the i-th row of M to linearly combine the k original file segments, generating the corresponding parity segment. Each symbol in this parity segment is further converted into a MAC (for the k file symbols used to generate this parity symbol) by adding to it a secret random value, which is generated by applying PRF g keyed with K_i' over the concatenation of the unique file handle, the segment index i, and the location j of this symbol in the parity segment.

The Repair **phase.** To repair one corrupted segment, the client first generates a key K at random and sends it to the n servers. Each server S_i computes a repair tag by running ComputeRepairTag, and sends back the repair tag t_i, where $1 \leq i \leq n$. The client verifies the n repair tags $t_1, t_2, \ldots, t_n$ by running VerifyAllRepairTag.

If VerifyAllRepairTag returns successfully, the client picks k repair servers, excluding the servers being found corrupted in either the Challenge phase or the aforementioned repair tag verification. It then runs GenRepairServerCoefficient to generate a set of indices $i_1, \ldots, i_k$ and a set of *intermediate coefficients* $z_{i_1}, \ldots, z_{i_k}$. The indices $i_1, \ldots, i_k$ will be used to identify the k repair servers which will provide data for repairing the corrupted segment. The intermediate coefficients $z_{i_1}, \ldots, z_{i_k}$ will be used to linearly aggregate the segments stored in the repair servers to restore the corrupted segment. To prevent the intermediate coefficients from being leaked to the untrusted servers, the client masks each of the intermediate coefficients in the following way: $Z_{i_j} = a z_{i_j} + r x_j$, in which a, r, x_j (where $1 \leq j \leq k$) are random values generated by running GenRandom. It then sends the *masked coefficients* $Z_{i_1}, \ldots, Z_{i_k}$ and $x_1, \ldots, x_k$ to the k repair servers. Each repair server S_{i_j} computes two partial segments based on the stored segment b_{i_j} and the corresponding masked coefficients Z_{i_j} and x_j, where $1 \leq j \leq k$.

Meanwhile, the client picks an Aggregation Server (AS) randomly from the remaining $n - k$ servers. It restores the code component at the AS and discloses to the AS the values $Z_{i_1}, \ldots, Z_{i_k}$, $x_1, \ldots, x_k, t_{i_1}, t_{i_2}, \ldots, t_{i_k}$ and K. Each repair server then sends the computed partial segments to the AS and the AS aggregates the partial segments, generating two intermediate segments b'_y and b''_y. AS further computes the repair tags t' and t'' for the inter-

ComputeRepairTag(K, b_i):

1. Return $t = \sum_{j=1}^{\ell}(g_K(file\_handle||j))\mathsf{b}_{ij}$

VerifyAllRepairTag($\mathsf{sk}, t_1, t_2, \ldots, t_n, K, M, n, k$):

1. Parse sk as $(K_1, K_2, \ldots, K_n, K'_{k+1}, \ldots, K'_n, K_a, K_b)$

2. $G \leftarrow \emptyset$ (this is the set of servers that have sent invalid repair tags)

3. For $k + 1 \leq i \leq n$:
   $t'_i = t_i - \sum_{j=1}^{\ell} g_K(file\_handle||j) g_{K'_i}(file\_handle||i||j)$

4. Decode $(t_1, t_2, \ldots, t_k, t'_{k+1}, \ldots, t'_n)$ using the decoding algorithm of Reed-Solomon codes to obtain message $m = (m_1, m_2, \ldots, m_k)$

5. If the decoding algorithm fails, return $(G, 0)$

6. Otherwise, use M to encode $(m_1, m_2, \ldots, m_k)$, and generate the parity $(m_{k+1}, m_{k+2}, \ldots, m_n)$

7. If none of $m_{k+1}, m_{k+2}, \ldots, m_n$ matches $t'_{k+1}, \ldots, t'_n$, return $(G, 0)$

8. For $1 \leq i \leq k$: if $m_i \neq t_i$, $G = \{i\} \cup G$

9. For $k + 1 \leq i \leq n$: if $m_i \neq t'_i$, $G = \{i\} \cup G$

10. Return (G, 1)

GenRepairServerCoefficient($\mathsf{sk}, y, k, n, i_1, \ldots, i_k$):

1. Re-generate the information dispersal matrix M by running $M \leftarrow$ GenInformationDispersalMatrix(sk, k, n)

   (a) For $1 \leq j \leq k$: For $1 \leq \alpha \leq k$: $A_{j\alpha} = M_{i_j\alpha}$

   (b) Compute matrix B as the inverse of A: $B = A^{-1}$

2. If $y \notin \{1, \ldots, k\}$:
   - $C = M_y \times B$ /*M_y is a vector in the y-th row of M*/
   - For $1 \leq j \leq k$: $z_{i_j} = C_{1j}$

3. Otherwise:
   - For $1 \leq j \leq k$: $z_{i_j} = B_{yj}$

4. Return $(z_{i_1}, \ldots, z_{i_k})$

GenRandom($\mathsf{sk}, y, i_1, i_2, \ldots, i_k$):

1. Parse sk as $(K_1, K_2, \ldots, K_n, K'_{k+1}, \ldots, K'_n, K_a, K_b)$

2. $a = g_{K_a}(file\_handle||y||i_1||i_2||\ldots||i_k||1)$

3. $r = g_{K_a}(file\_handle||y||i_1||i_2||\ldots||i_k||2)$

4. For $1 \leq j \leq k$: $x_j = g_{K_b}(file\_handle||y||i_1||i_2||\ldots||i_k||j)$

5. Return $(a, r, x_1, \ldots, x_k)$

VerifyPartialRepairTag($\mathsf{b}_{i_1}, \mathsf{b}_{i_2}, \ldots, \mathsf{b}_{i_k}, K, t_{i_1}, t_{i_2}, \ldots, t_{i_k}, x_1, x_2, \ldots, x_k$):

1. $G \leftarrow \emptyset$

2. For $1 \leq j \leq k$:
   If $x_j t_{i_j} \neq \sum_{\alpha=1}^{\ell}(g_K(file\_handle||\alpha))\mathsf{b}_{i_j\alpha}$, $G = G \cup \{i_j\}$

3. Return G

RepairOneSegment($\mathsf{sk}, \mathsf{b}'_y, \mathsf{b}''_y, i_1, \ldots, i_k, z_{i_1}, \ldots, z_{i_k}, y, a, r$):

1. Parse sk as $(K_1, K_2, \ldots, K_n, K'_{k+1}, \ldots, K'_n, K_a, K_b)$

2. If $y \in \{1, \ldots, k\}$:
   - For $1 \leq j \leq \ell$:
     $\mathsf{b}_{yj} = a^{-1}(\mathsf{b}'_{yj} - r\mathsf{b}''_{yj}) - z_{i_k} g_{K'_{i_k}}(file\_handle||i_k||j)$

3. Otherwise:
   - For $1 \leq j \leq \ell$:
     $\mathsf{b}_{yj} = a^{-1}(\mathsf{b}'_{yj} - r\mathsf{b}''_{yj}) + g_{K'_y}(file\_handle||y||j)$

4. Return $(\mathsf{b}_{y1}, \ldots, \mathsf{b}_{y\ell})$

Figure 4: Components of the RDC-EC scheme (2)

mediate segments by running ComputeRepairTag, and verifies the correctness of t' and t'' using $t_{i_1}, t_{i_2}, \ldots, t_{i_k}$. If the verification succeeds, the AS will send back b'_y and b''_y to the client. Otherwise, it runs VerifyPartialRepairTag to localize the faulty repair servers, and informs the client to pick new repair servers to replace the faulty repair servers. After receiving b'_y and b''_y, the client calls RepairOneSegment to restore the corrupted segment.

In ComputeRepairTag, to generate the repair tag for segment b_i based on key K, we first generate ℓ random numbers and then use these numbers to linearly aggregate all the symbols in b_i.

In VerifyAllRepairTag, the client verifies the n repair tags sent back by the n servers based on the secret keys. The client can also localize the corrupted repair tags.

In GenRepairServerCoefficient, the client generates a set of intermediate coefficients, which will be used by the k repair servers to linearly combine their stored segments in order to restore the corrupted segment b_y. The intermediate coefficients are generated as follows: the client first constructs a $k \times k$ square matrix A, in which the elements in the j-th row are copied from the i_j-th row of the information dispersal matrix M, where $1 \leq j \leq k$. The client then computes B as the inverse of A. If b_y is a file segment, then the set of intermediate coefficients will be the set of elements in the y-th row of B. If b_y is a parity segment, then the set of intermediate coefficients will be the set of elements in the first row of $M_y \times B$, where M_y is a $1 \times k$ matrix formed by the elements from the y-th row of M.

In GenRandom, the client generates the random numbers used to mask the intermediate coefficients. To repair the same segment by using the same set of k other segments, the client will use the same set of the random numbers when masking the coefficients.

In VerifyPartialRepairTag, the AS relies on the repair tags $t_{i_1}, t_{i_2}, \ldots, t_{i_k}$ to localize the corrupted partial segments, which is feasible because: 1) the client has verified the correctness of $t_{i_1}, t_{i_2}, \ldots, t_{i_k}$, and 2) the repair tag for a partial segment can be derived from the repair tag of the corresponding stored segment. For example, if t_{i_j} is the repair tag for the stored segment b_{i_j}, then xt_{ij} will be the repair tag for its partial segment $x\mathsf{b}_{i_j}$, considering both repair tags are generated based on the same key.

In RepairOneSegment, the client uses intermediate segments b'_y and b''_y (received from the servers) to repair corrupted segment b_y.

4.3 Security Analysis for RDC-EC

A unique attack on erasure coding-based storage systems. By knowing the information dispersal matrix M, an adversary can successfully corrupt an erasure coding-based distributed storage system without being detected. The attack can be performed as follows: 1) re-compute the parity by applying M over the original file; 2) compute the secret random numbers embedded into the stored parity by using the stored parity to subtract the parity computed in step 1); 3) replace the original file with a bogus file (with the same size), and apply M over the bogus file, generating the forged parity; 4) embed the secret random numbers into the forged parity, and re-use the server codes as well as the parity for the server codes; 5) upon Challenge, the adversary answers a challenge request relying on the bogus file and the forged parity, and can pass the verification without being detected.

Our RDC-EC scheme can defend against the aforementioned attack, since the adversary cannot learn the information dispersal matrix (Theorem 4.1). In addition, RDC-EC can ensure data recoverability over time under an adversarial setting (Theorem 4.2). Due to space limitations, proofs are provided in [10].

THEOREM 4.1. *In RDC-EC, the probability that the adversary can learn the information dispersal matrix M is negligibly small.*

THEOREM 4.2. *RDC-EC can ensure data recoverability over time under an adversarial setting.*

5. Related Work

RDC for the single-server setting. Early remote data checking (RDC) protocols (PDP [4] and PoR [24, 27]) were designed for static data. Later, RDC protocols were designed to allow efficient updates on the outsourced data [5, 20, 32, 29, 36, 12, 11, 35, 28, 30]. Recently, several RDC schemes have been designed for version control systems [21, 14].

RDC for distributed setting. In a distributed RDC, the outsourced data is stored redundantly across multiple servers to achieve a certain reliability level. Distributed RDC protocols include MR-PDP [16], HAIL [7], WWRL [31], RDC-NC [15]. MR-PDP seeks to audit data that is replicated. Like RDC-EC, both HAIL and WWRL are built for erasure coding-based distributed storage systems. However, HAIL is expensive in Repair, because it requires to retrieve all the outsourced data in order to repair a single segment. WWRL is vulnerable to a mobile and Byzantine adversary, because it does not incorporate techniques to address small corruptions, and it only repairs the symbols in a segment being found corrupted during Challenge (spot checking-based). This will lead to a situation that un-checked corrupted symbols remain corrupt at the end of an epoch, and a mobile and Byzantine adversary can possibly corrupt the whole storage system by making a stripe (*i.e.*, the unit of an erasure code) unrecoverable in the following epochs.

New paradigms for RDC. Recently, RDC was applied in several other areas: (a) server-side repair [13], in which a data owner is able to outsource both the data and the management of the data, and thus can remain lightweight during both the challenge and repair phases; (b) proofs of fault tolerance [8], in which a data owner can obtain a proof that the outsourced file is distributed across an expected number of physical storage devices in a single datacenter; and (c) proofs of location (PoL) [6, 33, 22], in which a data owner is offered a guarantee that multiple replicas are stored in data centers located in different or specific geographic locations.

6. Conclusion

We have proposed RDC-EC, an RDC scheme for erasure coding-based distributed storage systems, which functions under an adversarial setting. Unlike previous schemes for this setting, RDC-EC achieves an efficient Repair phase by leveraging server-side repair to shift the burden from the data owner to the storage servers. In the future, we plan to explore mechanisms that can repair multiple data segments more efficiently, and to reduce some of the assumptions related to restoration of the code component at the storage servers.

Acknowledgements. This research was supported by the U.S. National Science Foundation under Grants No. CNS 1054754, CNS 1409523, and DUE 1241976. Bo Chen was also supported in part by NSF grants CNS 1161541, CNS 1318572, CNS 1223239, CCF 0937833, by US ARMY award W911NF-13-1-0142, and by gifts from Northrop Grumman Corporation, Parc/Xerox, and Microsoft Research.

7. References

[1] Microsoft azure. http://azure.microsoft.com.

[2] OpenSSL. http://www.openssl.org/.

[3] G. Ateniese, R. Burns, R. Curtmola, J. Herring, O. Khan, L. Kissner, Z. Peterson, and D. Song. Remote data checking using provable data possession. *ACM Trans. Inf. Syst. Secur.*, 14, June 2011.

[4] G. Ateniese, R. Burns, R. Curtmola, J. Herring, L. Kissner, Z. Peterson, and D. Song. Provable data possession at untrusted stores. In *Proc. of ACM Conference on Computer and Communications Security (CCS '07)*, 2007.

[5] G. Ateniese, R. D. Pietro, L. V. Mancini, and G. Tsudik. Scalable and efficient provable data possession. In *Proc. of International ICST Conference on Security and Privacy in Communication Networks (SecureComm '08)*, 2008.

[6] K. Benson, R. Dowsley, and H. Shacham. Do you know where your cloud files are? In *Proc. of ACM Cloud Computing Security Workshop (CCSW '11)*, 2011.

[7] K. Bowers, A. Oprea, and A. Juels. HAIL: A high-availability and integrity layer for cloud storage. In *Proc. of ACM CCS (CCS '09)*, 2009.

[8] K. D. Bowers, M. V. Dijk, A. Juels, A. Oprea, and R. L. Rivest. How to tell if your cloud files are vulnerable to drive crashes. In *Proc. of ACM CCS*, 2011.

[9] B. Calder, J. Wang, A. Ogus, N. Nilakantan, A. Skjolsvold, S. McKelvie, Y. Xu, S. Srivastav, J. Wu, H. Simitci, et al. Windows azure storage: a highly available cloud storage service with strong consistency. In *Proc. of the ACM Symposium on Operating Systems Principles (SOSP '11)*, pages 143–157. ACM, 2011.

[10] B. Chen, A. K. Ammula, and R. Curtmola. Towards server-side repair for erasure coding-based distributed storage systems. Technical report, NJIT, December 2014.

[11] B. Chen and R. Curtmola. Poster: Robust dynamic remote data checking for public clouds. In *Proc. of ACM CCS (CCS '12)*, 2012.

[12] B. Chen and R. Curtmola. Robust dynamic provable data possession. In *Proc. of International Workshop on Security and Privacy in Cloud Computing (ICDCS-SPCC '12)*, 2012.

[13] B. Chen and R. Curtmola. Towards self-repairing replication-based storage systems using untrusted clouds. In *Proceedings of the third ACM conference on Data and application security and privacy (CODASPY '13)*, 2013.

[14] B. Chen and R. Curtmola. Auditable version control systems. In *Proc. of the 21th Annual Network and Distrib. System Security Symp. (NDSS '14)*, 2014.

[15] B. Chen, R. Curtmola, G. Ateniese, and R. Burns. Remote data checking for network coding-based distributed storage systems. In *Proc. of ACM Cloud Computing Security Workshop (CCSW '10)*, 2010.

[16] R. Curtmola, O. Khan, R. Burns, and G. Ateniese. MR-PDP: Multiple-replica provable data possession. In *Proc. of International Conference on Distributed Computing Systems (ICDCS '08)*, 2008.

[17] A. G. Dimakis, B. Godfrey, M. J. Wainwright, and K. Ramchandran. Network coding for distributed storage systems. In *Proc. of IEEE INFOCOM*, 2007.

[18] A. G. Dimakis, P. B. Godfrey, Y. Wu, M. O. Wainwright, and K. Ramchandran. Network coding for distributed storage systems. *IEEE Trans. on Inf. Theory*, 56, Sept. 2010.

[19] C. Dubnicki, L. Gryz, L. Heldt, M. Kaczmarczyk, W. Kilian, P. Strzelczak, J. Szczepkowski, C. Ungureanu, and M. Welnicki. Hydrastor: A scalable secondary storage. In *FAST*, volume 9, pages 197–210, 2009.

[20] C. Erway, A. Kupcu, C. Papamanthou, and R. Tamassia. Dynamic provable data possession. In *Proc. of ACM CCS (CCS '09)*, 2009.

[21] M. Etemad and A. Kupcu. Transparent, distributed, and replicated dynamic provable data possession. In *Proc. of 11th International Conference on Applied Cryptography and Network Security (ACNS '13)*, 2013.

[22] M. Gondree and Z. N. Peterson. Geolocation of data in the cloud. In *Proceedings of ACM CODASPY (CODASPY '13)*, 2013.

[23] C. Huang, H. Simitci, Y. Xu, A. Ogus, B. Calder, P. Gopalan, J. Li, S. Yekhanin, et al. Erasure coding in windows azure storage. In *USENIX ATC*, 2012.

[24] A. Juels and B. S. Kaliski. PORs: Proofs of retrievability for large files. In *Proc. of ACM Conf. on Computer and Communications Security (CCS '07)*, 2007.

[25] D. A. Patterson, G. Gibson, and R. H. Katz. *A case for redundant arrays of inexpensive disks (RAID)*, volume 17. ACM, 1988.

[26] J. S. Plank and K. M. Greenan. Jerasure: A library in C facilitating erasure coding for storage applications – version 2.0. Technical Report UT-EECS-14-721, University of Tennessee, January 2014.

[27] H. Shacham and B. Waters. Compact proofs of retrievability. In *Proc. of ASIACRYPT (ASIACRYPT '08)*, 2008.

[28] E. Shi, E. Stefanov, and C. Papamanthou. Practical dynamic proofs of retrievability. In *Proc. of the 20th ACM CCS (CCS '13)*, 2013.

[29] E. Stefanov, M. van Dijk, A. Oprea, and A. Juels. Iris: A scalable cloud file system with efficient integrity checks. In *Proc. of ACSAC (ACSAC '12)*, 2012.

[30] S. R. Tate, R. Vishwanathan, and L. Everhart. Multi-user dynamic proofs of data possession using trusted hardware. In *Proc. of ACM CODASPY*, 2013.

[31] C. Wang, Q. Wang, K. Ren, and W. Lou. Ensuring data storage security in cloud computing. In *Proc. of IEEE IWQoS (IWQoS '09)*, 2009.

[32] Q. Wang, C. Wang, K. Ren, W. Lou, and J. Li. Enabling public auditability and data dynamics for storage security in cloud computing. *IEEE Trans. on Parallel and Distributed Syst.*, 22(5), May 2011.

[33] G. J. Watson, R. Safavi-Naini, M. Alimomeni, M. E. Locasto, and S. Narayan. LoSt: location based storage. In *Proc. of ACM CCSW (CCSW '12)*, 2012.

[34] H. Weatherspoon and J. D. Kubiatowicz. Erasure coding vs. replication: a quantitiative comparison. In *Proc. of IPTPS*, 2002.

[35] Y. Zhang and M. Blanton. Efficient dynamic provable possession of remote data via balanced update trees. In *Proc. of ACM ASIACCS (ASIACCS '13)*, 2013.

[36] Q. Zheng and S. Xu. Fair and dynamic proofs of retrievability. In *Proc. of ACM Conf. on Data and Application Security and Privacy (CODASPY '11)*, 2011.

Combining ORAM with PIR to Minimize Bandwidth Costs

Jonathan Dautrich
Google, Inc.
Irvine, California
jjldj@google.com

Chinya Ravishankar
Computer Science and Engineering
University of California, Riverside
ravi@cs.ucr.edu

ABSTRACT

Cloud computing allows customers to outsource the burden of data management and benefit from economy of scale, but privacy concerns limit its reach. Even if the stored data are encrypted, access patterns may leak valuable information. Oblivious RAM (ORAM) protocols guarantee full access pattern privacy, but even the most efficient ORAMs proposed to date incur large bandwidth costs.

We combine Private Information Retrieval (PIR) techniques with the most bandwidth-efficient existing ORAM scheme known to date (ObliviStore), to create OS+PIR, a new ORAM with bandwidth costs only half those of ObliviStore. For data block counts ranging from 2^{20} to 2^{30}, OS+PIR achieves a total bandwidth cost of only 11X–13X blocks transferred per client block read+write, down from ObliviStore's 18X–26X. OS+PIR introduces several enhancements in addition to PIR in order to achieve its lower costs, including mechanisms for eliminating unused dummy blocks.

Categories and Subject Descriptors

H.2.7 [**Database Management**]: Database Administration—*security, integrity, and protection*

Keywords

Data privacy; Oblivious RAM; private information retrieval

1. INTRODUCTION

Cloud computing allows customers to outsource the burden of data management and benefit from economy of scale, but privacy concerns limit its reach. Even if data blocks are encrypted by the client before being stored on the server, data access patterns may still leak valuable information [5, 11, 12]. *Private Information Retrieval* (PIR) [3] and *Oblivious RAM* (ORAM) [9] techniques both offer provable access pattern privacy for outsourced data, each with their own advantages and disadvantages. In this work, we combine the

strengths of existing ORAM and PIR constructs to create a new ORAM with reduced bandwidth costs.

In PIR, data on the server may be encrypted or unencrypted, and the client issues an encrypted query for a particular bit or block of B bits. The server evaluates each query *homomorphically* (without decryption), returning the desired block without learning which block was requested. In order to achieve this degree of security, the server must evaluate each query over all bits in the database, making PIR computationally prohibitive for most applications [16].

In ORAM, blocks of data are always encrypted by the client before being stored on the server. Informally, the ORAM defines a protocol that dictates how the client should fetch, permute (shuffle), re-encrypt, and store blocks from and to the server in order to prevent the server from learning any information about the pattern of plaintext block requests. The ORAM protocol guarantees that for any two same-length sequences of plaintext block requests, the resulting patterns of encrypted block accesses are computationally indistinguishable to all observers other than the client. ORAM requires negligible computation, but may incur substantial bandwidth or storage overheads.

Definition 1. The *bandwidth cost* W of an ORAM or PIR technique is the number of blocks transferred for every block requested. Equivalently, it is the total number of bits transferred in order to retrieve B bits, where B is the block size. If we upload and download 3 blocks for each request, $W = 6$X.

Bandwidth cost is particularly important when applying ORAM to mobile devices, where bandwidth costs are substantial. Existing ORAMs have bandwidth costs polylogarithmic in the total number of blocks N [7, 9, 10, 13, 18, 20, 23]. The ObliviStore (OS) ORAM [18] has the lowest bandwidth cost of any single-server ORAM proposed to date. OS's bandwidth cost is roughly $(\log_2 N)$X, with no hidden constants, though it requires extensive client storage. Other ORAMs require less storage [13, 14, 20] or reduce response times [2, 6, 22], but all incur higher total bandwidth costs.

1.1 Our Proposal: OS+PIR

In this work, we show how to drastically reduce ObliviStore's bandwidth costs by combining it with PIR. The combination yields a new ORAM that we call OS+PIR that offers reduced bandwidth costs and permits tradeoffs between bandwidth cost, client/server storage, and computation. Combining ORAM and PIR was proposed in [14], but their scheme uses a different ORAM [15] and emphasizes constant client storage instead of low bandwidth costs.

OS+PIR treats its PIR component largely as a black box, so any efficient PIR technique may be used. Section 4 discusses how we use the Trostle-Parrish PIR [21], also used in [14], to reduce online bandwidth costs in OS+PIR. In OS, for each request, the client retrieves and decrypts one block from each of $O(\log N)$ levels. At most one of the decrypted blocks is *real* and all others are *dummies* (Section 3.2) that can be discarded. We use PIR to retrieve only the real block without revealing which block was accessed. Since we use PIR for only a small number ($O(\log N)$) of blocks, it is computationally feasible.

We divide OS+PIR's total bandwidth cost W into an ORAM component W_O and a PIR component W_P, where $W = W_O + W_P$. W_O depends on the ORAM's behavior, and W_P depends on the specific PIR and parameters such as block size. Applying PIR reduces W_O by roughly 30%.

In Section 5 we show how to amplify this reduction by altering the number and relative sizes of partition levels, balancing the reduced bandwidth cost with the resulting increases in PIR computation and server storage.

We present experimental results in Section 6. For systems with 2^{20} to 2^{30} blocks of 2MiB each, OS+PIR reduces the total bandwidth cost from OS's 18X–26X to only 11X–13X.

In the full version of the paper, we present the previously undiscovered OS issue of *unused dummy blocks*, which is exacerbated in OS+PIR by the increased level sizes. Unused dummies occur because ObliviStore makes more evictions than requests, which causes unnecessary block downloads. We show how to mitigate this issue by securely altering OS+PIR's eviction pattern and creating fewer dummy blocks. We also analyze two previously proposed techniques that use available client space to reduce bandwidth cost, reducing the eviction rate [18] and applying level caching [6], and show how to strike a reasonable balance between them.

2. RELATED WORK

Oblivious RAM was first proposed in [9] and required a bandwidth cost of $O(\log^3 N)$X blocks transferred per block requested, where N is the number of data blocks in the ORAM. Subsequent works have reduced the bandwidth cost to $O(\log^2 N/\log\log N)$X using constant client-side storage [13]. While constant client storage is desirable, it is not always necessary in practical settings. Recent works have reduced bandwidth costs to $O(\log N)$X by allowing additional client storage, specifically: $O(BN^v)$ client storage for constant $v > 0$ in [10], $O(B\log N)$ for large $B \in O(log^2 N)$ in [20], and $O(N\log N + B\sqrt{N})$ in [6, 18, 19].

Not all ORAMs that achieve $O(\log N)$X bandwidth cost are equally practical. For block sizes on the order of kilobytes or larger, the ObliviStore (OS) family of ORAMs [6, 18, 19] has the lowest practical bandwidth cost of any single-server ORAM proposed to date. OS's bandwidth cost is roughly $(\log_2 N)$X, with no hidden constants, though it requires extensive client storage. In contrast, Path ORAM [20] requires closer to $(8\log_2 N)$X, and more if client space is reduced using recursion. The scheme in [10] requires roughly $\log_2 N$ round-trips per request, but each trip may include several block transfers, making the total bandwidth cost at least 3 to 4 times that of OS. Since OS has the lowest bandwidth cost, we compare with it when evaluating OS+PIR.

Prior work [14] combined PIR with the tree-based ORAM of [15]. While their construction achieves the desirable property of constant client memory, it still requires $O(\log^2 N)$X

Table 1: Notation

N	Total number of real (data) blocks in an ORAM
B	Size of each data block (in bits)
b	A specific plaintext data block
W	Total bandwidth cost
W_O	ORAM component of total bandwidth cost W
W_P	PIR component of total bandwidth cost W
ϵ	Eviction rate
p	A partition used in ObliviStore or OS+PIR
p_r	Request partition
p_a	Assignment partition
p_e	Eviction partition
k	Level size factor
K	Level configuration consisting of level size factors
r	Number of real blocks in a sub-level
L_M	Total number of main levels in a single partition
L_S	Total number of sub-levels in a single partition
D_i	Maximum number of dummies in main level i
s	Number of noise bits in PIR

bandwidth cost. In contrast, OS+PIR combines PIR with the partition-based OS [18] to achieve under $(1/2)(\log_2 N)$X bandwidth cost in practice. Multi-cloud oblivious storage [17] achieves very low bandwidth cost (under 3X), but makes the strong assumption of multiple non-colluding servers.

3. PRELIMINARIES

Key notation used throughout the paper is in Table 1.

3.1 Private Information Retrieval (PIR)

Private Information Retrieval (PIR) was first proposed in [3], and allows a client to retrieve specific bits from a server without revealing any information to the server, or any other observer, about which bits were accessed.

PIR comes in two flavors: *computational* and *information theoretic*. Computational PIR schemes are based on a hardness assumption, such that to retrieve information about a query, the adversary would need to solve a problem that is considered intractable. Information-theoretic PIR guarantees that query information remains secret, regardless of the adversary's computational resources, but generally requires an assumption of non-colluding servers [3]. The non-colluding server assumption is inconsistent with untrusted servers, so we use computational PIR in our work.

Each PIR query is encrypted by the client, sent to the server, and evaluated *homomorphically* (under encryption) by the server. The server returns the requested bit/block of bits but learns neither the plaintext contents of the query nor which bits were returned. PIR must perform a computational operation over every bit in the PIR database for every query in order to achieve its strong privacy guarantees.

Instead of using PIR for the entire database, we use it to reduce the bandwidth cost required to retrieve one of a small subset of a client's encrypted blocks that would otherwise all be returned as part of an ORAM protocol. In this scenario, the PIR database is small and the block size is relatively large, so the substantial bandwidth cost reduction can outweigh the small increase in computation. We discuss our use of PIR in more detail in Section 4.

3.2 Oblivious RAM (ORAM)

Oblivious RAM (ORAM) was first proposed in [9]. Like PIR, ORAM may be used to retrieve encrypted data from a server without revealing which data were accessed. ORAMs generally allow writes, while standard PIR is read-only.

Instead of evaluating queries homomorphically, ORAM defines a protocol for transferring and modifying encrypted blocks such that the underlying plaintext blocks accessed by different queries are unlinkable. ORAMs download encrypted blocks from the server to a trusted local client space, decrypt the desired data, then re-encrypt the blocks using a semantically secure encryption scheme to break correlations with previous encrypted *contents*. The ORAM then randomly permutes the blocks to break correlations with the previous block *position*, a process referred to as oblivious shuffling. Some ORAMs also use *dummy blocks*, which are indistinguishable from real blocks but contain irrelevant data, and download extra blocks, to break correlations.

ORAM security is defined as follows: For any two sequences of block requests of the same length, the resulting patterns of encrypted block accesses must be computationally indistinguishable to all observers other than the client [19]. Equivalently, the output of a simulator that has no access to any of the secret information (block contents and requested block addresses) should be able to produce a sequence of encrypted block transfers that is indistinguishable from that of the actual ORAM [13].

3.3 ObliviStore (OS)

OS+PIR builds on the ObliviStore (OS) ORAM [18]. A full description of OS and its underlying ORAM [19] is too extensive to include here, but we review the aspects most relevant to OS+PIR. For N blocks of B bits each, OS uses a relatively large amount of client storage, $O(B\sqrt{N}+N\log N)$ bits with small constants, in order to achieve a low bandwidth cost of $(\log_2 N)$X.

3.3.1 Partition and Level Structure

In OS, blocks stored on the server are arranged logically into $O(\sqrt{N})$ *partitions*, each of which contains $O(\sqrt{N})$ blocks. Each partition is a simplified hierarchical ORAM, similar to those of [9], with roughly $\log_2 \sqrt{N}$ levels. The lowest level in each partition (level 0) holds 1 real and 1 dummy block. Successive levels double in size, so level i has real-block capacity $r_i = 2^i$ and starts with 2^i dummy blocks. At any given time, each level may be occupied or empty, and only half the levels are occupied on average.

3.3.2 Requests and Evictions

Each block request involves three steps:

1) Partition Request When the client issues a request for block b, OS directs the request to the partition p_r containing b. The choice of p_r is deterministic, but appears random to an observer since b was previously assigned to a randomly chosen partition. OS then downloads exactly one block from every non-empty level in p. OS fetches b from whichever level contains it, and fetches a dummy block from every other level. Since levels were previously randomized, each fetched block appears randomly chosen from its level. After downloading the blocks, OS discards all dummies, returns b to the client then *assigns* b to a new partition.

2) Assignment: After reading and optionally updating b, OS encrypts it and assigns it to a partition p_a chosen uniformly at random. Each p_a maintains a local, hidden *eviction queue* of blocks assigned to p_a but not yet evicted to the server. OS assigns b to p_a by adding it to the end of p_a's eviction queue, but does not immediately evict it.

3) Eviction: After assigning b to p_a, OS independently chooses at least one partition p_e and evicts either the next block from p_e's eviction queue, or a dummy block if the queue is empty. We perform ϵ evictions after each request, where ϵ is the real-valued *eviction rate*.[1] If ϵ exceeds 1.0, OS adds the fractional component $\epsilon - 1.0$ into a global accumulator. When the accumulator reaches 1.0, OS makes another eviction and decrements the accumulator. Eviction partitions (p_e) may be chosen deterministically or randomly, as long as the choice is independent of p_a [19].

Choosing p_a randomly guarantees that future requests for b will appear to access a random partition. Choosing p_e independently of p_a prevents an observer from learning p_e and thus from tracking b between partitions. Thus, the independence of p_a and p_e is critical to OS's security.

Since p_a and p_e are chosen independently, blocks may accumulate in eviction queues. OS calls the space used by these assigned but not yet evicted blocks the *eviction cache*. Revealing the eviction cache size may leak information about prior choices of p_a, so a fixed amount of space sufficient for the eviction cache is reserved up-front. Statistically, the higher ϵ, the less space is required for the eviction cache.

3.3.3 Shuffling

Let level i in partition p initially contain r_i real and r_i dummy blocks. Once r_i evictions have been made to p since i was created, i is scheduled to be *re-shuffled*. Shuffling i consists of:

1. Downloading all blocks left in level i
2. Removing remaining dummies
3. Inserting any evicted blocks
4. Generating any additional dummies
5. Randomly permuting and re-encrypting all blocks
6. Uploading all blocks to a new level with $2r_i$ real and $2r_i$ dummy blocks

When two levels i and $i-1$ are both ready to be re-shuffled, the shuffle *cascades* upward. Level sizes increase by factors of 2, so every time level i is ready to be re-shuffled, all lower levels are also necessarily ready. When shuffling all levels up to i, we download all remaining blocks from levels $0-i$ and upload blocks to level $i+1$ with $2r_i$ real blocks, leaving levels $0-i$ empty to accommodate future evictions (see Figure 1).

3.3.4 Early Shuffle Reads

If level i has more than half its original $2r_i$ blocks remaining, then there is at least one dummy block in i to return. If instead i has at most r_i blocks remaining, it is possible that all the blocks are real, so to maintain obliviousness OS must *treat* such blocks as real. We call such blocks *early shuffle reads*, since they would eventually be downloaded as part of the upcoming shuffle. OS refers to such blocks as either *early cache-ins* or *real cache-ins* depending on the context.

Early shuffle reads are relatively rare, and are caused by delayed shuffles in OS. Since OS performs a constant amount of work per request, some levels to shuffle may have not yet been downloaded when a later request arrives, causing the

---

[1] OS uses slightly different notation, where v is the *background eviction rate*, equivalent to $1 - \epsilon$.

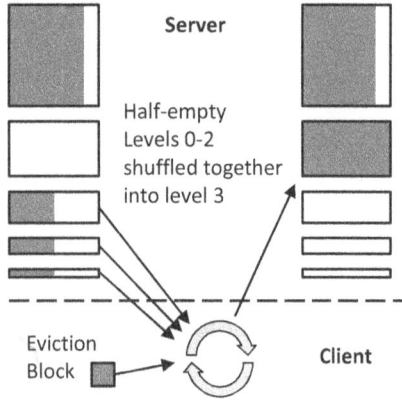

Figure 1: When shuffles cascade upward in OS, all levels to be re-shuffled are downloaded, shuffled with eviction blocks, and uploaded to a higher level.

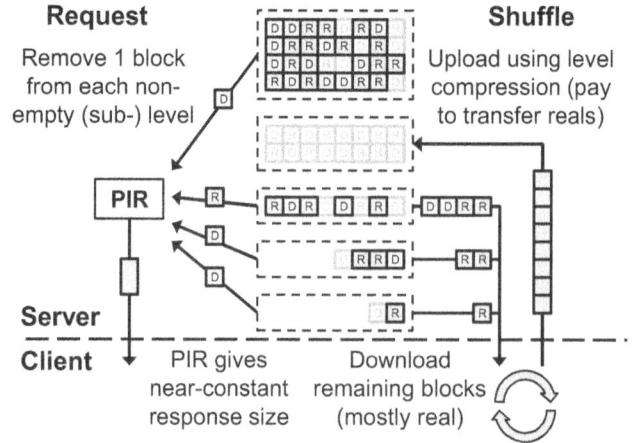

Figure 2: In OS+PIR, PIR reduces the response cost for each request to near-constant. During shuffling, only blocks remaining in each level (largely real) need be downloaded. With level compression, we need only transfer data of size equal to the uploaded reals. In all, dummy transfers are "free" — we effectively pay only to transfer real blocks.

early shuffle read. Other than early shuffle reads, all but one of the downloaded blocks are guaranteed to be dummies. Early shuffle reads are downloaded separately and stored.

3.3.5 Level Compression

OS's level compression algorithm [19] lets the client send k real and k dummy blocks to the server using only kB bits. The technique uses a pre-shared Vandermonde matrix $M_{2k \times k}$ to encode the k real blocks and their positions into a "compressed" kB-bit stream. The server decompresses the stream to get $2k$ blocks: k real and k dummies containing random data derived from the decompression. The dummy and real blocks are indistinguishable and intermixed.

We can alter the number of dummies generated by changing the number of rows in M from $2k$ to the desired total block count. This flexibility becomes important in Section 5 where we use it to reduce OS+PIR's bandwidth cost.

3.3.6 Bandwidth Costs

In OS, the client has enough space to store all $\sqrt{N}$ blocks from any given partition, and to store the location of all N blocks. Since every partition fits entirely in client memory, re-shuffling requires that each block be downloaded and uploaded only once. (Less client space we necessitate an expensive oblivious shuffling algorithm.) Thus, to shuffle r real blocks, we need only transfer $3r$ blocks: r real downloads, r dummy downloads, and r uploads for level compression.

The total bandwidth cost W of OS is determined by the number of times each block must be re-shuffled per request. Each partition has roughly $(\log_2 \sqrt{N})/2 = (\log_2 N)/4$ occupied levels at any time. Each of the $\sqrt{N}$ real blocks is shuffled once per occupied level per $\sqrt{N}$ evictions, for a total $(3/4) \log_2 N$ block transfers per eviction. Since ϵ is the number of evictions per request, we get an expected OS cost:

$$W \approx \frac{3\epsilon}{4} \log_2 N \qquad (1)$$

OS reports an actual cost $W \approx \log_2 N$ for $\epsilon = 1.3$ [18]. The slight discrepancy with Equation 1 can be accounted for by the problem of *unused dummies*, addressed in [4].

4. INTEGRATING PIR

In ObliviStore (OS), each request fetches one block from each level in a partition. At most one fetched block is real and all others are dummies, except in the case of *early shuffle reads*, which are returned individually. Since returned dummies are discarded, they are only transferred to mask the real block's identity. We want to retrieve the real block and hide its identity without paying to transfer dummies.

The recently-proposed Burst ORAM [6] combines these fetched blocks using XOR and returns a single block. The client reconstructs dummy blocks locally and subtracts them out of the combined block to recover the real. The XOR optimization is incompatible with OS's level compression, since level compression constructs dummies from reals during decompression, but XOR requires that dummies be generated by the client [6]. Thus, Burst ORAM avoids paying to *download* dummies, but overall savings are negated by the lack of level compression, which avoids paying to *upload* dummies.

In OS+PIR, we instead use PIR to retrieve the real block. Since PIR makes no stipulations on dummy block content, it can be used with level compression. PIR itself incurs a bandwidth cost W_P determined by block size B, number of blocks (levels) over which it queries, and the PIR scheme's properties. Other than W_P, dummy block transfers are essentially free (Figure 2), reducing W_O by roughly 30% up-front, and enabling additional cost-saving modifications (Section 5).

Given that the PIR's computational hardness assumption holds, the PIR operation leaks no information about which level's block was fetched. From a security standpoint, using PIR is therefore equivalent to OS's approach of downloading each level's block and discarding the dummies. Thus, OS+PIR's security guarantees are precisely those of OS except for the added PIR hardness assumption.

4.1 Choosing a PIR Technique

In OS+PIR, we execute the PIR protocol once per block request. Each PIR instance operates over a *PIR database* of $L_S \in O(\log N)$ blocks, one per level, and returns a single block. Since we query over $O(\log N)$ blocks, PIR is far more computationally feasible than when used over all N blocks.

PIR schemes often measure bandwidth in terms of the cost of returning the full PIR database. To remain consistent with Definition 1, we instead measure PIR bandwidth cost as W_P: the total amount of data transferred during each PIR operation, divided by B. We want a PIR scheme with low W_P (near the optimal 1X). Since OS's bandwidth cost is already low, even a W_P of 10X could negate any advantages of using PIR. Ideally, W_P should be constant: independent of L_S and B. In practice, we can use any PIR that offers low, nearly-constant W_P for small L_S and large B.

One candidate is the Gentry-Ramzan PIR [8], which offers a constant W_P with a theoretic 2X minimum (closer to 4X in practice), but incurs substantial computation costs. Another option is the more computationally-efficient Trostle-Parrish PIR [21], which offers low, but not constant, W_P when $B \gg L_S$. OS+PIR treats its PIR as a black box, so any PIR that meets our criteria can be used. For now, we use the Trostle-Parrish PIR [21] used in [14], due to its simplicity and low bandwidth and computation complexity.

Due to space constraints, we defer a detailed discussion of the Trostle-Parrish PIR to the full version of our paper [4].

5. ALTERING LEVEL SIZE FACTORS

Combining PIR with OS's level compression technique effectively gives OS+PIR free dummy block downloads and uploads, aside from PIR computation and bandwidth (W_P) costs. As noted in Section 3.3.5, we can modify level compression to produce additional dummy blocks at no extra cost. Similarly, given near-constant W_P, we can query over any number of additional levels at no extra bandwidth cost. We now show how to use these properties to reduce the bandwidth cost of OS+PIR's by altering level sizes.

In OS, successive levels increase in size by a factor of 2, yielding $\log_2 \sqrt{N}$ levels per partition. In OS+PIR, we allow successive levels to increase by any integer factor. Let k_i be the *level size factor* of main level i, which defines the sub-level real-block capacity ratio r_i/r_{i-1}. We must allow up to $k_i - 1$ instances or *sub-levels* of main level i, which when shuffled together with all lower levels become a single sub-level of main level $i + 1$. The real-block capacity of a sub-level in level i is given by $r_i = \prod_{j=0}^{i-1} k_j$.

To simplify the presentation of ideas throughout this Section, we assume that OS+PIR uses $\epsilon = 1.0$ (exactly one eviction per request). We address larger eviction rates in the full version of the paper [4].

5.1 Effects of Increasing Level Size Factors

We simplify our discussion of the high-level effects of increasing level size factors (k_i values), by assuming $k_i = k$ for all i, where $k = 2$ in OS. Figure 3 shows two level configurations ($k = 2$ and $k = 4$) for a partition with 15 real blocks. We discuss non-uniform level size factors and special handling of the top level later in this Section. Increasing k has the following effects:

It increases the total number of sub-levels L_S. For a partition of $\sqrt{N}$ blocks we need $L_M = \log_k \sqrt{N}$ main levels. With $k - 1$ sub-levels per main level, the total number of sub-levels is given by $L_S = (k-1)\log_k \sqrt{N}$, which increases almost linearly with k. To maintain obliviousness, we must

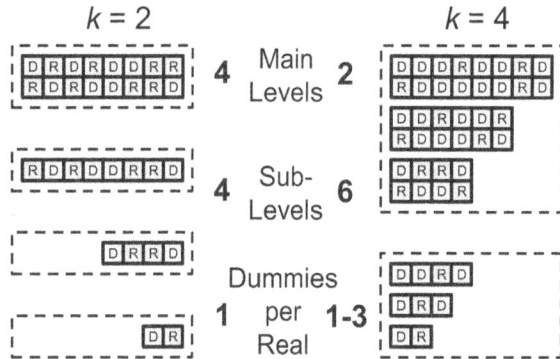

Figure 3: Level configurations with size factors $k = 2$ and $k = 4$, both with 15 real-block capacity. When shuffling, all sub-levels in a main level combine to form one new sub-level in next largest main level. $k = 4$ configuration has fewer main levels, thus lower shuffling costs. $k = 2$ has fewer dummies and sub-levels, thus lower disk and PIR costs.

fetch one block from every sub-level during each request. Thus, without PIR, the bandwidth cost W would increase almost linearly with k, which is why ObliviStore uses only $k = 2$. With near-constant W_P, the effect on W is negligible. Even with PIR, the number of blocks that must be read from disk to satisfy a request increases with k.

It increases level and sub-level lifetimes. The ith main level holds $k - 1$ sub-levels containing k^i real blocks each, and is re-shuffled after every k^{i+1} requests. Once the ith level is shuffled into a higher level, it stays empty for k^i requests before its first new sub-level is created. The first sub-level must live through $(k-1)k^i$ requests and still have k^i blocks left over to avoid early cache-ins. Thus we need $(k-1)k^i$ dummies in addition to the k^i reals, for a total of k^{i+1} blocks. The second sub-level lives for k^i fewer requests, so it needs only $(k-2)k^i$ dummies, and so on. The increased number of dummies also increases server storage to a factor of roughly k, which we address in Section 5.2.

It decreases the ORAM component bandwidth cost W_O. Between every shuffle (k^{i+1} requests), the ith level receives $k^{i+1}(k-1)/2$ dummy blocks and $(k-1)k^i$ real blocks in all. The number of shuffle *downloads* per request is only $((k-1)/k) \log_k \sqrt{N}$, since we only pay to download the remaining $(k-1)k^i$ blocks from each sub-level. With level compression, the number of shuffle *uploads* per request is the same, giving:

$$W_O \approx 2\frac{k-1}{k}(\log_k \sqrt{N})\text{X} \qquad (2)$$

Thus, for OS+PIR with $N = 2^{32}$ real blocks and $\epsilon = 1.0$, increasing k from 2 to either 4, 16, or 64 should reduce W_O from roughly 16X to either 12X, 7.5X, or 5.25X, resp.

5.2 Non-Uniform Level Size Factors

A major limitation of using a large fixed level size factor k is that it increases server storage cost. The ith level stores a total of k^{i+1} blocks, only k^i of which are real, for a server storage factor of roughly k. However, the bulk of the extra dummy blocks, at least $k - 1$ of each k, are stored in the largest level. With varying k_i, level $i \geq 1$ stores D_i dummy blocks in the worst case, given by:

$$D_i \approx \left(\frac{k_i}{2}\right)^2 \cdot \prod_{j=0}^{i-1} k_j \qquad (3)$$

By allowing level size factors to differ, specifically using smaller k_i for larger levels and vice-versa, we can mitigate the storage cost increase but keep the number of levels small.

For example, consider the two configurations $K_1 : (k_0 = 2^5, k_1 = 2^5, k_2 = 2^5)$ and $K_2 : (k_0 = 2^7, k_1 = 2^5, k_2 = 2^3)$. For both, the real-block capacity is roughly $\prod_{j=0}^{2} k_j = 2^{15}$. However, for K_1 we get $D_0 + D_1 + D_2 = 2^8 + 2^{13} + 2^{18} \approx 2^{18}$ dummy blocks total, while K_2 gives $D_0 + D_1 + D_2 = 2^{12} + 2^{15} + 2^{16} \approx 2^{16}$ dummies total, reducing the server storage factor from 8X to 2X.

By increasing level factors doubly-exponentially for a partition with $\sqrt{N}$ blocks, we can asymptotically reduce the main level count to $L_M \approx \log_2 \log_2 \sqrt{N}$, incurring only a L_M server storage cost factor. Consider the configuration:

$$K : (k_0 = 2^{(\log_2 \sqrt{N})/2}, k_1 = 2^{(\log_2 \sqrt{N})/4},$$
$$k_3 = 2^{(\log_2 \sqrt{N})/8}, \ldots, k_{L_M-3} = 2^8$$
$$k_{L_M-2} = 2^4, k_{L_M-1} = 2^2, k_{L_M} = 2^1).$$

Since the level factor exponents in K grow exponentially from 1 to $(\log_2 \sqrt{N})/2$, we have $L_M \approx \log_2 \log_2 \sqrt{N}$, and thus $W_O \approx (2 \log_2 \log_2 \sqrt{N})$X. Applying Equation 3, we see that $D_i \approx \sqrt{N}$ for all i. Since the real-block capacity is $\sqrt{N}$, the server storage overhead is just $(\log_2 \log_2 \sqrt{N})$X.

5.2.1 Practical Limits on Level Size Factor Growth

Unfortunately, increasing or skewing level size factors also increases the maximum total sub-level count L_S given by:

$$L_S \leq \sum_i (k_i - 1). \qquad (4)$$

For every request, we must fetch L_S blocks from disk and perform PIR over L_S blocks. Thus, disk read and PIR computation costs are at least proportional to the largest k_i, limiting growth in practice.

In the simple example above, K_2 suffers from $L_S \approx 165$, while K_1 has only $L_S \approx 93$. For such small skews, the difference is not dramatic, but in a comparable configuration with all $k_i = 2$, we have only $L_S \approx 15$. In the double-exponential growth example, $k_0 = 2^{(\log_2 \sqrt{N}/2)} = N^{1/4}$. For large databases with $N \geq 2^{32}$, we end up with $L_S \geq k_0 \geq 2^8$. Such large L_S values could easily make disk and PIR costs outweigh any benefit of reduced bandwidth cost in practice.

A more practical approach is to follow double-exponential growth only up to a maximum level factor determined by a fixed acceptable value of L_S that can be accommodated by the disk array and PIR computation hardware. In Section 6.2 we empirically evaluate the impact of different level size configurations on L_S.

6. EXPERIMENTS

We ran simulations to compare OS+PIR with OS [18]. OS+PIR is equipped with the additional bandwidth-saving enhancements discussed in the full version of the paper [4]: eliminating unused dummies, evicting to request partition, caching smallest levels, and shuffling largest jobs first. For

Table 2: Effects of changing the level configuration K for $N = 2^{28}$ block count, 512TiB capacity, 512GiB total client storage. Product of all level size factors for each K is 2^{16}.

K	Server Storage Factor	W_O	Avg L_S	Max L_S	W_P
$(2, \ldots, 2)$	2.9	16.1X	6.7	14	2.7X
$(4, \ldots, 4, 2, 2)$	3.1	13.1X	9.5	20	2.8X
$(4, 8, 8, 8, 8, 2, 2)$	3.5	11.2X	14.5	30	3.0X
$(4, 16, 8, 8, 4, 2, 2)$	3.2	11.3X	16.5	34	3.0X
$(4, 16, 16, 16, 2, 2)$	4.3	9.9X	23.0	47	3.2X
$(4, 32, 16, 16, 2)$	5.8	9.1X	30.5	62	3.4X
$(4, 128, 16, 4, 2)$	4.3	9.1X	72.5	146	4.1X
$(4, 128, 64, 2)$	15.7	7.6X	95.0	191	4.4X

fairness, we also compare with a modified OS equipped with these same enhancements (but not PIR).

In all our experiments, we assume a 2MiB block size ($B = 2^{24}$ bits). The large B is needed primarily to keep PIR bandwidth cost W_P low when using the Trostle-Parrish PIR. Changing B has little effect on the ORAM component bandwidth cost W_O. For the unmodified OS, we use $\epsilon = 1.3$ as in [18], and use $\epsilon = 1.1$ for the modified OS and for OS+PIR.

The full version [4] includes additional experiments evaluating the individual effects of each bandwidth enhancement and exploring the effects of changing eviction rates.

6.1 ORAM Simulator

We evaluated bandwidth costs for OS+PIR and ObliviStore using a simulator written in Java. Since ORAM behavior is oblivious, performance is independent of the specific sequence of blocks requested. Thus, for efficiency, the simulator uses counters to represent the number of remaining blocks in each level of each partition, and avoids storing block IDs and contents explicitly. Since we are primarily interested in bandwidth and computation costs, the simulator does not explicitly measure costs of permuting blocks, looking up IDs, or performing disk reads. Block encryption costs are also not logged, as they are dominated by PIR costs.

Each experiment includes a run-up and evaluation phase of $4N$ requests each. We count the total number of blocks transferred (uploads plus downloads) during the evaluation phase, and divide by $4N$ to get W_O. For OS+PIR we also record the number of sub-levels L_S accessed during each request. L_S varies across requests depending on the number of empty sub-levels in each partition.

6.2 Varying Level Size Configuration K

Table 2 shows the results of running $OS+PIR$ for various K given a fixed $N = 2^{28}$ and 512GiB of client storage. We use the same maximum real-block partition capacity for all K, so the product of all level factors in each K is fixed (2^{16}). As predicted in Section 5.2.1, using larger level factors, and thus fewer main levels $L_M = |K|$, greatly reduces ORAM bandwidth cost W_O, but also increases L_S, which in turn increases PIR and disk access costs. Server storage costs increase substantially when level factors for the highest levels are increased, even when bandwidth costs remain the same (see $K = (4, 32, 16, 16, 2)$ and $K = (4, 128, 16, 4, 2)$).

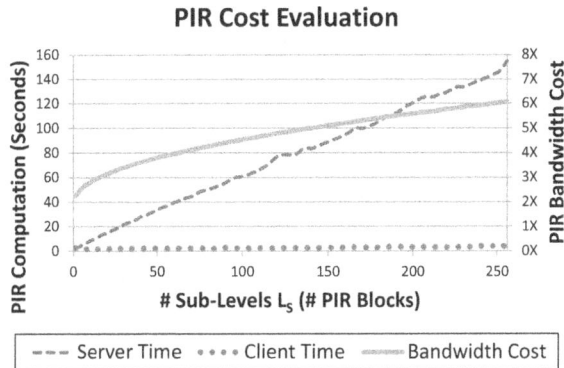

PIR Cost Evaluation

Figure 4: **Timing and bandwidth costs of Trostle-Parrish PIR implementation for varying numbers of blocks in PIR database, using** $s = 512$ **bits noise and 2MiB block size.**

6.3 PIR Implementation

We implemented the Trostle-Parrish PIR [21], as described in Section 4, using Java. Our implementation caches partial sums to avoid redundant computations, but is otherwise unoptimized. For all our experiments, we used $s = 2^9$ bits of extra noise in the PIR as discussed in the full version [4].

We measure wall-clock times running PIR on a single thread of a third generation Amazon Web Services (AWS) Elastic Compute Cloud [1] instance (half of a c3.large instance), equivalent to 3.5 AWS ECUs. As of May 2014, the cost for running the full c3.large instance was $0.105/hour, giving an approximate PIR cost of 1.46×10^{-5}/second on a single thread. Figure 4 gives PIR time and bandwidth costs for L_S up to 2^8, with a maximum server time under 160s, equivalent to $0.0023 per 2MiB block request.

We report times for a single thread to simplify cost analysis. However, server computation within each PIR operation can be trivially parallelized to at least $\sqrt{BL_S}$ threads. Since clients likely have less available parallelism, we expect the small reported client times, not the large server times, to correspond to real-world latencies.

6.4 Evaluating OS+PIR for Mobile Devices

We start by evaluating OS+PIR on parameters suitable to current mobile devices. We consider an OS+PIR with $N = 2^{22}$ of our 2MiB blocks, giving a server storage capacity of 8TiB. We allocate 64GiB total client storage, such that the ORAM increases effective storage capacity by a factor of 128. We can alter this factor by changing N (Section 6.5).

Table 3 shows our results. Comparing the modified and unmodified versions of OS, we see that our enhancements offer a slight improvement on their own, reducing total bandwidth cost W from 21.4X to 18.2X. Adding PIR offers another improvement, bringing W down to 16.2X. Finally, increasing the level factors reduces W to as little as 11.2X, but increases server storage and PIR computation costs.

We also give per-request costs in US cents (¢) for each scheme for two benchmark bandwidth costs. On one extreme we have the AWS [1] bandwidth cost of $0.12 per GB for the first 10TiB per month, for a cost of 0.025¢ per 2MiB block. On the other we have cellular data, which may cost as much as $10 per GB, for a cost of 2.10¢ per 2MiB block. At $0.12/GB, OS+PIR roughly breaks even, with its added

PIR computation cost canceling out the reduced bandwidth costs. At $10/GB, OS+PIR is a clear win, as the bandwidth cost savings far outweigh the PIR cost, cutting total cost down to nearly half that of OS. OS+PIR is clearly most cost-effective when bandwidth costs dominate, as would be the case for mobile devices.

6.5 Varying Block Count N

Table 4 shows client/server space consumption and total bandwidth cost W as N increases. We show results for the unmodified ObliviStore, OS+PIR with $K = (2, \dots, 2)$, and a custom K chosen to minimize L_M while keeping server storage costs low. Required client storage scales with $\sqrt{N}$, and for each N it is nearly the same for all three schemes. As N grows, the capacity/client space ratio grows as well, from 68 for $N = 2^{20}$ to 2189 for $N = 2^{30}$. For a large 2PiB database, the client needs 1TiB storage, and OS+PIR reduces W from 26.4X to 13.0X.

The bandwidth savings of OS+PIR depend on reducing the number of main levels $L_M = |K|$. However, to keep server storage costs low, we must use small level factors for the highest levels, limiting savings for small N. As N grows, our advantage increases, as L_M grows more slowly in OS+PIR than in OS due to OS+PIR's larger level factors.

7. CONCLUSION

We have presented OS+PIR, a new ORAM that combines the bandwidth-efficient ObliviStore (OS) ORAM [18] with PIR techniques to minimize total bandwidth costs. We have shown how to re-engineer OS to accommodate levels of varying relative sizes in order to fully exploit PIR, exposing a tradeoff between bandwidth cost, server computation, and server storage. OS+PIR also includes several enhancements that further reduce costs, including mechanisms for eliminating the unnecessary dummy blocks introduced in OS.

In all, OS+PIR achieves bandwidth costs at least 2 times lower than those of the already-efficient OS, making it especially advantageous for mobile devices, where bandwidth costs dominate. In other settings, OS+PIR's effectiveness is currently limited by its high PIR computation cost. However, since we can easily swap out the PIR protocol, OS+PIR can also be gainfully applied to less bandwidth-constrained settings as more efficient PIR schemes emerge.

8. ACKNOWLEDGEMENTS

This work was completed while the first author was a student at UC Riverside, and was supported by the National Physical Science Consortium Graduate Fellowship and by grant N00014-07-C-0311 from the Office of Naval Research.

9. REFERENCES

[1] Amazon web services. http://aws.amazon.com, May 2014.

[2] D. Boneh, D. Mazieres, and R. A. Popa. Remote oblivious storage: Making oblivious RAM practical. Manuscript, http://dspace.mit.edu/bitstream/handle/1721.1/62006/MIT-CSAIL-TR-2011-018.pdf, 2011.

[3] B. Chor, E. Kushilevitz, O. Goldreich, and M. Sudan. Private information retrieval. *Journal of the ACM (JACM)*, 45(6):965–981, 1998.

Table 3: Comparison of different bandwidth-efficient protocols given parameters tuned for current mobile devices with at least 64GiB storage. Common parameters: $N = 2^{22}$ data blocks, 2MiB block size, 64GiB total client storage. In practice, server latency will be much lower than reported single-thread times (Section 6.3).

Protocol	ϵ	Level Factors	Server Storage Factor	PIR Comp./Req.			Bandwidth Cost/Req.			Total Cost/Req.	
				Server Time (s)	Server Cost (¢)	Client Time (s)	PIR (W_P)	ORAM (W_O)	Total (W)	In ¢ at 12¢ / GB	In ¢ at \$10 / GB
ObliviStore	1.3	$(2,\dots,2)$	3.2	—	—	—	—	21.4X	21.4X	0.054	44.88
ObliviStore Mod.	1.1	$(2,\dots,2)$	2.9	—	—	—	—	18.2X	18.2X	0.046	38.17
OS+PIR	1.1	$(2,\dots,2)$	2.9	6.04s	0.009	0.78s	2.6X	13.6X	16.2X	0.050	33.98
OS+PIR	1.1	$(4,32,16,2,2)$	4.5	20.55s	0.030	0.92s	3.2X	8.5X	11.7X	0.059	24.56
OS+PIR	1.1	$(4,64,16,2)$	6.4	31.62s	0.046	0.99s	3.6X	7.6X	11.2X	0.074	23.53

Table 4: Effect of increasing N on client/server storage and bandwidth cost, with $\epsilon = 1.1$ for OS+PIR, $\epsilon = 1.3$ for ObliviStore.

N	Capacity (TiB)	ObliviStore			OS+PIR $K = (2,\dots,2)$			OS+PIR Custom K			
		Client (GiB)	Server (TiB)	W (X)	Client (GiB)	Server (TiB)	W (X)	K	Client (GiB)	Server (TiB)	W (X)
2^{20}	2	30	6.2	18.2	30	5.9	14.3	$(4,64,8,2)$	31	11.2	10.9
2^{22}	8	60	24.8	19.8	61	23.4	15.3	$(4,16,16,4,2)$	62	31.6	11.4
2^{24}	32	119	99.2	21.4	122	93.3	16.5	$(4,32,16,4,2)$	123	127.6	12.0
2^{26}	128	239	396.2	23.1	244	373.0	17.6	$(4,64,16,4,2)$	245	522.4	12.5
2^{28}	512	478	1584.6	24.7	488	1491.4	18.7	$(4,64,32,4,2)$	491	2452.4	12.7
2^{30}	2048	958	6335.8	26.4	980	5962.9	19.8	$(4,64,32,8,2)$	990	9756.0	13.0

[4] J. Dautrich. *Achieving Practical Access Pattern Privacy in Data Outsourcing.* PhD thesis, University of California, Riverside, 2014.

[5] J. Dautrich and C. Ravishankar. Compromising privacy in precise query protocols. In *Proc. EDBT*, 2013.

[6] J. Dautrich, E. Stefanov, and E. Shi. Burst ORAM: Minimizing ORAM response times for bursty access patterns. In *Proc. USENIX Security*, 2014.

[7] C. Gentry, K. Goldman, S. Halevi, C. Julta, M. Raykova, and D. Wichs. Optimizing ORAM and using it efficiently for secure computation. In *Proc. PETS*, 2013.

[8] C. Gentry and Z. Ramzan. Single-database private information retrieval with constant communication rate. In *Automata, Languages and Programming*, pages 803–815. Springer, 2005.

[9] O. Goldreich and R. Ostrovsky. Software protection and simulation on oblivious RAMs. *Journal of the ACM (JACM)*, 43(3):431–473, 1996.

[10] M. T. Goodrich, M. Mitzenmacher, O. Ohrimenko, and R. Tamassia. Privacy-preserving group data access via stateless oblivious RAM simulation. In *Proceedings of the Twenty-Third Annual ACM-SIAM Symposium on Discrete Algorithms*, pages 157–167. SIAM, 2012.

[11] M. Islam, M. Kuzu, and M. Kantarcioglu. Access pattern disclosure on searchable encryption: Ramification, attack and mitigation. In *Proc. NDSS*, 2012.

[12] M. S. Islam, M. Kuzu, and M. Kantarcioglu. Inference attack against encrypted range queries on outsourced databases. In *Proceedings of the 4th ACM conference on data and application security and privacy*, pages 235–246. ACM, 2014.

[13] E. Kushilevitz, S. Lu, and R. Ostrovsky. On the (in)security of hash-based oblivious RAM and a new balancing scheme. In *Proceedings of the Twenty-Third Annual ACM-SIAM Symposium on Discrete Algorithms*, pages 143–156. SIAM, 2012.

[14] T. Mayberry, E.-O. Blass, and A. H. Chan. Efficient private file retrieval by combining ORAM and PIR. In *Proc. NDSS*, 2014.

[15] E. Shi, H. Chan, E. Stefanov, and M. Li. Oblivious RAM with $O((\log N)^3)$ worst-case cost. In *Proc. ASIACRYPT*, 2011.

[16] R. Sion. On the computational practicality of private information retrieval. In *Proc. NDSS*, 2007.

[17] E. Stefanov and E. Shi. Multi-Cloud Oblivious Storage. In *Proc. ACM CCS*, 2013.

[18] E. Stefanov and E. Shi. ObliviStore: High performance oblivious cloud storage. In *Proc. IEEE Symposium on Security and Privacy*, 2013.

[19] E. Stefanov, E. Shi, and D. Song. Towards practical oblivious RAM. Proc. NDSS, 2012.

[20] E. Stefanov, M. van Dijk, E. Shi, C. Fletcher, L. Ren, X. Yu, and S. Devadas. Path ORAM: An extremely simple oblivious RAM protocol. In *Proc. ACM CCS*, 2013.

[21] J. Trostle and A. Parrish. Efficient computationally private information retrieval from anonymity or trapdoor groups. In *Information Security*, pages 114–128. Springer, 2011.

[22] P. Williams and R. Sion. Sr-oram: Single round-trip oblivious ram. *Proc. ACNS, industrial track*, pages 19–33, 2012.

[23] P. Williams, R. Sion, and A. Tomescu. PrivateFS: A parallel oblivious file system. In *Proc. ACM CCS*, 2012.

Can't You Hear Me Knocking: Identification of User Actions on Android Apps via Traffic Analysis

Mauro Conti
University of Padua
Padua, Italy
conti@math.unipd.it

Luigi V. Mancini
Sapienza University of Rome
Rome, Italy
lv.mancini@di.uniroma1.it

Riccardo Spolaor
University of Padua
Padua, Italy
rspolaor@math.unipd.it

Nino V. Verde
Sapienza University of Rome
Rome, Italy
verde@di.uniroma1.it

ABSTRACT

While smartphone usage become more and more pervasive, people start also asking to which extent such devices can be maliciously exploited as "tracking devices". The concern is not only related to an adversary taking physical or remote control of the device, but also to what a passive adversary without the above capabilities can observe from the device communications. Work in this latter direction aimed, for example, at inferring the apps a user has installed on his device, or identifying the presence of a specific user within a network.

In this paper, we move a step forward: we investigate to which extent it is feasible to identify the specific actions that a user is doing on mobile apps, by eavesdropping their encrypted network traffic. We design a system that achieves this goal by using advanced machine learning techniques. We did a complete implementation of this system and run a thorough set of experiments, which show that it can achieve accuracy and precision higher than 95% for most of the considered actions.

Categories and Subject Descriptors

C.2.0 [**Computer-Communication Networks**]: General - *Security and protection*

Keywords

Network traffic analysis; Machine learning; Privacy; Mobile security.

1. INTRODUCTION

People continuously carry smartphone devices with them and use them for daily communication activities, including not only voice calls and SMS but also emails and social network interaction. In the last years, several concerns have been raised about the capabilities of those portable devices to invade the privacy of the users and to become actual "tracking devices". Even when the adversary has no actual control of the phone (either physical or remote control via malicious apps) several attacks may violate the privacy of the communications. Indeed, if the network traffic is not encrypted, the task of an eavesdropper is simple: he can analyze the payload reading the content of each packet. However, many mobile apps use the Secure Sockets Layer (SSL) – and its successor Transport Layer Security (TLS) – as a building block for encrypted communications. Unfortunately there is often a gap between theory and practice, e.g., leveraging the SSL vulnerabilities of smartphone apps [15, 16] one might run an SSL man-in-the-middle attack to compromise the confidentiality of communications.

While people become more familiar with mobile technologies and their related privacy threats (also thanks to the attention raised by the media, e.g., see the recent attention on NSA for supposedly eavesdropping foreign governments leaders such as Angela Merkel [29]), users start adopting some good practices that better adapt to their privacy feeling and understanding. For examples, solutions to identify and isolate malware running on smartphones [27, 31, 36] as well as to protect against attacks coming from the network [3, 10] might significantly reduce current threats to user privacy. Unfortunately, we believe that even adopting such good practices would not close the door to malicious adversaries willing to trace people. In fact, the wireless and pervasive nature of mobile devices would still leave many practical options for adversarial tracing. In particular, even when such solutions are in place, the adversary can still infer a significant amount of information from the properly encrypted traffic. For example, work leveraging analysis of encrypted traffic already highlighted the possibility of understanding the apps a user has installed on his device [30], or identify the presence of a specific user within a network [32].

This work focuses on understanding whether the user profiling made through analyzing encrypted traffic can be pushed up to understand exactly what actions the user is doing on his phone: as concrete examples, we aim at identifying actions such as the user sending an email, receiving an email, browsing someone profile in a social network, rather than publishing a post or a tweet. The underlying issue we leverage in our work is that SSL and TLS protect the content of a packet, while they do not prevent the detection of networks packets patterns that instead may reveal some sensitive information about the user behavior.

An adversary may use our approach in several practical ways to threaten the privacy of the user. In the following, we report some possible scenarios:

- A censorship government may try to identify a dissident who spreads anti-government propaganda using an anonymous social network account. Comparing the time of the public posts with the time of the actions (inferred with our method), the government can guess the identity of that anonymous dissident.

- By tracing the actions performed by two users, and taking into account the communication latency, an adversary may guess (even if with some probability of error) whether there is a communication between them. Multiple observations could reduce the probability of errors.

- An adversary can build a behavioral profile of a target victim based on the habits of the latter one (e.g., wake up time, work time). For example, this could be used to improve user fingerprinting methods, to infer the presence of a particular user in a network [32], even when he accesses the network with different type of devices.

Contributions.

In this paper, we propose a framework to infer which particular actions the user executed on some app installed on his mobile-phone, by only looking at the network traffic that the phone generates. In particular, we assume the traffic is encrypted and the adversary eavesdrops (without modifying them) the messages exchanged between the user's device and the web services that he uses.

Our framework analyzes the network communications and leverages information available in TCP/IP packets (like IP addresses and ports), together with other information like the size, direction (incoming/outgoing), and timing. By using an approach based on machine learning, each app that is of interest is analyzed independently. To set up our system, for each app we first pre-process a dataset of network packets labeled with the user actions that originated them, we cluster them in flow typologies that represent recurrent network flows, and finally we analyze them in order to create a training set that will be used to feed a classifier. The trained classifier will be then able to classify new traffic traces that have never been seen before. We fully implemented our system, and we run a thorough set of experiments to evaluate our solution considering three very popular apps: Facebook, Gmail, and Twitter. The results shows that it can achieve accuracy and precision higher than 95%, for most of the considered actions.

Organization.

The rest of this paper is organized as follows. In Section 2, we revise the state of the art. In Section 3, we present our framework describing all its different components. We present the evaluation of our solution for identifying user actions in Section 4. We discuss about possible countermeasures against the proposed attack in Section 5. Finally, in Section 6 we draw some conclusions and point out ways in which this work can be further extended.

2. RELATED WORK

Our main claim in this paper is that network traffic analysis and machine learning can be used to infer private information about the user, i.e., the actions that he executes by using his mobile phone, even though the traffic is encrypted.

In the literature, several works proposed to track user activities on the web by analyzing unencrypted HTTP requests and responses [4, 5, 28]. With this analysis it was possible to understand user actions inferring interests and habits. However, in recent years, websites and social networks started to use SSL/TLS encryption protocol, both for web and mobile services. As a consequence, communications between endpoints are often encrypted and this type of analysis cannot be performed anymore.

Different works surveyed possible attacks that can be performed using traffic analysis assuming a very strong adversary (e.g., a national security agency) which is able to observe all communication links [6, 26]. In [21], Liberatore et al. evaluated the effectiveness of two traffic analysis techniques based on naive Bayes and on Jaccard's coefficient for identifying encrypted HTTP streams. Such an attack was outperformed by [19], where the authors presented a method that applies common text mining techniques to the normalized frequency distribution of observable IP packet sizes, obtaining a classifier that correctly identifies up to 97% of requests. Similarly, in [25] the authors presented a support vector machine classifier that was able to correctly identify web pages, even when the victim used both encryption and anonymization networks such as Tor. Finally, Cai et al. [8] presented a web pages fingerprinting attack and proved its effectiveness despite traffic analysis countermeasures, such as HTTPOS [22].

Unfortunately, none of the aforementioned works was designed for (or could easily be extended to) mobile devices. In fact, all of them focus on web pages identification in desktop environment (in particular, in desktop browsers), where the generated HTTP traffic strictly depends on how web pages are designed. Conversely, mobile users mostly access the contents through the apps installed on their devices [17]. These apps communicate with a service provider (e.g., Facebook) through a set of APIs. An example of such differences between desktop web browsers and mobile apps is the validation of SSL certificates [10, 16].

In [9], the authors show that despite encryption, also web applications suffer from side-channel leakages. The system model considered is different from our. In particular, their focus is on web applications. On the contrary, we focus on mobile applications.

Focusing on mobile devices, traffic analysis has been successfully used to detect information leaks [14], to profile users by their set of installed apps [30], and to automatically generating network profiles for identifying Android apps in the HTTP traffic [11]. Stober et al. [30] show that it is possible to identify the set of apps installed on an Android device, by eavesdropping the 3G/UMTS traffic that those apps generate. Similarly, Tongaonkar et al. in [11] introduce an automatic app profiler that creates the network fingerprint of an Android app relying on packet payload inspection. Unfortunately, their solution is viable only for apps that do not use encrypted traffic. In [37], Zhou et al. discovered three unexpected channels of information leaks on Android: per-app data-usage statistics, ARP information, and speaker status. Unfortunately, the authors focused only on a specific user action (i.e., send a tweet) without distinguish that action from the other ones a user could perform.

None of the works mentioned in this section aim at inferring and distinguish the potential user actions actions that a user can perform on mobile apps that rely on encrypted network traffic, which is the goal of our paper.

In the following, we briefly recall several machine learning and data mining concepts that we use in our paper: *Dynamic Time Warping*, *Hierarchical Clustering* and the *Random Forest classifier*. Furthermore, we point the reader to appropriate references for a complete introduction on those topics. *Dynamic Time Warping* (DTW) [24] is a useful method to find alignments between two time-dependent sequences (also referred as time series) which may vary in time or speed. This method is also used to measure the distance or similarity between time series. In particular, this method aims to find the alignment with minimum cost between two sequences X and Y. This cost is also called *optimal warping path* and it can be consider as a distance metric. In this paper, we will indicate the cost of an *optimal warping path* with $DTW(X, Y)$. *Hierarchical Clustering* is a cluster analysis method which seeks to build a hierarchy of clusters [18]. This clustering method has the distinct advantage that any valid measure of distance can be used. In fact, the observations themselves are not required: all that is used is a matrix of distances. *Random Forest* is an ensemble classifier [7] that combines a group of weak learners called "decision trees" to form a strong learner. In practice, it combines together the results of several decision trees trained with different portions of the training dataset and different subsets of features.

3. OUR FRAMEWORK

In this section we describe our framework. In particular, Section 3.1 introduces the pre-processing steps that allow us to model the network traffic. Section 3.2 describes the methodology used to build training and test datasets, and the procedure used to classify user actions.

3.1 Network Traffic Pre-Processing

Mobile apps generally rely on SSL/TLS to securely communicate with peers. These protocols are built on the top of the TCP/IP suite. The TCP layer receives encrypted data from the above layer, it divides data into chunks if the packets exceeds a given size. Then, for each chunk it adds a TCP header creating a TCP segment. Each TCP segment is encapsulated into an Internet Protocol (IP) datagram, and exchanged with peers. A fundamental entity considered in this paper is the traffic *flow*: with this term we indicate a time ordered sequence of TCP packets exchanged between two peers during a single TCP session. We model each network flow as a set of time series: (i) a time series is obtained by considering the bytes transported by incoming packets

only; (ii) another one is obtained by considering bytes transported by outgoing packets only; (iii) a third one is obtained by combining (ordered by time) bytes transported by both incoming and outgoing packets. Hence, we use this set of time series as an abstract representation of a connection between two peers.

Before generating for each flow the corresponding set of time series, a few pre-processing steps have to be performed. In particular: 1) we apply a domain filtering to select only flows belonging to the analyzed app; 2) we filter the remaining flows, in order to delete packets that may degrade the precision of our approach (i.e., we filter out ACK and retransmitted packets); 3) we limit the length of the generated time-series. In the following, we will detail these three pre-processing steps.

Domain filtering.

The network traffic generated by an app is generally directed toward a back-end infrastructure. The backend infrastructures might be composed by a single server, or a set of servers. The set of servers might even be behind a load balancer. Since we analyze each app independently, we need to make sure that traffic generated from apps other than the considered one (or traffic generated by the OS) do not interfere with the analysis. Different methods can be used in order to identify the app that generated each network flows. The destination IP address is a trivial discriminating parameter. However, in case of a load balanced back-end, we should know all the individual IP addresses that can be involved in the communication. The same happens when the back-end is composed by several components such as different web services, databases, etc. To overcome this problem we use another strategy: we take into consideration for further analysis only the flows which destination IP addresses owners have been clearly identified as related to the considered app. In the implementation of our framework, we leverage the WHOIS protocol for this purpose, but we want to highlight that this is only one of the possible way. Business and other context information may be used in order to perform the domain filtering. We also take into consideration the traffic related to third parties services (such as Akamai or Amazon) that are indeed used by several applications [33].

Packets filtering.

Due to network congestion, traffic load balancing, or other unpredictable network behavior, IP packets can be lost, duplicated, or delivered out of order. TCP detects these problems, hence requesting retransmission of lost data, and reordering out-of-order data. It comes out that several TCP packets that do not carry data, may hinder the analysis process. In the data exchange phase, for example, the receiver sends a packet with the ACK flag set to notify the correct reception of a chunk of data. These ACK packets are transmitted in asynchronous mode so they are affected by many factors related to round trip time of the connection link. The order of the received packets may hinder the evaluation of the similarity between two network flows. For this reason, we filter out all packets retransmissions, as well as packets marked with the ACK flag. Note that the metric that we will use in order to measure similarity between flows (see Section 3.2) will mitigate the consequences of missing packets. We filter out also other packets that do not bring any additional information helpful in characterize flows. In particular, we filter out the three way handshake executed to open a TCP connection.

Timeout and packets interval.

Two different techniques are used to limit the length of the generated time series: a *timeout* mechanism and the specification of a *packets interval*. The *timeout* mechanism is used to terminate the flows that did not receive any new packet since 4.5 seconds. Indeed, it has been proved experimentally that 95% of all packets arrive at most 4.43 seconds after their predecessors [30]. The *packets interval* specifies the first and the last packet to be considered. For example, considering a flow f composed by l packets, and the interval $[x, y]$ with $x \leq y$ and $y \leq l$, the corresponding time series will be composed by $y - x + 1$ values that report the bytes of the xth to the yth packet. This simple mechanism allows us to focus on particular portions of the flow. The first portion of a flow, for example, is often the more significant. In the experimental part, we report the results for different configurations of packets intervals, showing that the best configuration is app dependent.

3.2 Classification of User Action

Since we use a supervised learning approach, it is necessary to create a labeled dataset that describes the user actions that we want to classify. In order to build this dataset, we simulate a series of user actions, and for each one we identify the flows generated after the execution of the action itself. For each app that we analyze we focus on actions that are significant for that particular app.

In most cases, a single user action generates a set of different flows (i.e., not just a single one). Furthermore, different user actions may generate different sets of flows. Our classification method is based on the detection of the sets of flows that are distinctive of a particular user action. In order to elicit these distinctive sets of flows, we build clusters of flows by using an agglomerative Hierarchical Clustering method. Similar flows will be grouped together in the same cluster, while dissimilar flows will be assigned to different clusters. The average distance is used as linkage criterion, while the computation of the distance between two flows combines the distances of the corresponding time series.

Supposing that each flow f_i is decomposed into a set of n time series $\{T_1^i, \ldots, T_n^i\}$, the distance between f_i and f_j is defined as:

$$dist(f_i, f_j) = \sum_{k=1}^{n} w_k \times DTW(T_k^i, T_k^j),$$

where w_k is a weight assigned to the particular time series. Weights can be assigned in such a way to give more importance to some type of time series with respect to others. For example, it is possible to give more weight to the time series that represent incoming packets, and less weight to those that represent outgoing packets.

In order to reduce the computational burden of the subsequent classification, a leader is elected for each cluster. Leaders will be the representative flows of their clusters. Given a cluster C containing the flows $\{f_1, \ldots, f_n\}$, the leader is elected by selecting the flow f_i that has minimum overall distance from the other members of the cluster, that is:

$$\arg\min_{f_i \in C} \left(\sum_{j=1}^{n} dist(f_i, f_j) \right).$$

Clustering is executed on the set of flows that will be used to build the training dataset. In particular, after performing the clustering the training dataset will be composed as follow. The user actions will be the instances of the datasets, while the class of each instance is a label representing the action. We will have one integer feature for each cluster identified through the agglomerative clustering. The value of each feature is determined by analyzing the flows related to an action. Each flow f captured after the execution of an action will be assigned to the cluster that minimizes the distance between f and the leader of the cluster. The kth feature will therefore indicate the number of flows that have been assigned to the cluster C_k after the execution of that action. For example, for the action *send mail*, the kth feature will be equal to 2 if there are 2 flows labeled with *send mail* assigned to the cluster C_k.

Finally, we execute the classification with Random Forest algorithm. The main idea behind the overall approach is that different actions will "trigger" different sets of clusters. The classification algorithm will therefore learn which are these sets, and will be able to correctly determine the class labels for unseen instances.

4. EXPERIMENTAL RESULTS

In order to assess the performance of our proposal, we considered three widespread apps: Gmail, Facebook and Twitter. We select these apps because of their high popularity [1]. Indeed, Gmail is one of the largest email services and its Android app has over one billion downloads. On the other hand, Facebook and Twitter are not only the most popular Online Social Networks [2], but they also had a leading role in the Arab spring and the Istanbul's Taksim Gezi Park protests (when Turkish government blocked Twitter). We believe that the results of our analysis also hold for other apps that provide similar functionalities (e.g., Yahoo mail, WhatsApp or LinkedIn), while a thorough evaluation of this claim is left as future work. To collect the network traffic related to different user actions, we set up a controlled environment. In this section we present the elements that compose this environment (Section 4.1), the methodology used to collect the data (Section 4.2), and the results of the evaluation (Section 4.3).

4.1 Hardware and Network Configuration

For the evaluation of our solution, we used a Galaxy Nexus (GT-I9250) smartphone, running the Android 4.1.2 (Jelly bean) operative system. We enabled the *"Android Debug"* option in order to allow the usage of the ADB (Android Debug Bridge) interface via USB cable. We used a Wi-Fi access point (U.S. Robotics USR808054) to provide wireless connectivity to the mobile phone. Finally, we used a server (Intel Pentium Processor dual core E5400 2.7GHz with 4 GB DDR2 RAM) with two network cards running Ubuntu Server 11.04 LTS to route the traffic from the access point to the Internet, and vice versa.

To eavesdrop network packets flowing through the server, we used Wireshark software. From a Wireshark capture file, we created a comma separated file (csv), where each row describes a packet captured from the access point's interface. For every packet we reported source and destination IP addresses, ports, size in bytes and time in seconds from Unix epoch[1], protocol type and TCP/IP flags. Since the payload is not relevant to our analysis, it has been omitted. This data have been then used to generate the time series as explained in Section 3.1.

4.2 Dataset Collection and Analysis

For our study we considered three apps installed from the official Android market: Gmail v4.7.2 , Facebook v3.8, and Twitter v4.1.10. For each app, we created ten accounts that have been divided in two different categories of users: "*active*" and "*passive*" users. "*Active*" users simulated the behavior of users that actively use the app by sending posts, email, tweets, surfing the various menus, etc. "*Passive*" users simulated the behavior of users that passively use the app, just by receiving messages or posts. The accounts of both passive and active users have been configured in such a way to have several friends/followers within the group. We avoided to configure the accounts with actual friends or followers, in order to avoid interference due to notifications of external users activities that were not under our control.

A script submits the sequence of actions to the mobile phone through the ADB commands, and it captures the network traffic that is generated. The script records also the execution time of each action. By using the recorded execution time of each action, it is then possible to label the flows extracted from the network traffic with the user action that produced it. For each app, we choose a set of actions that are more sensitive than others from user privacy point of view (e.g., send an email or a message, for the reasons we report in Section 1). The list of these actions is reported in Table 1. We underline that we do not ignore other user actions, but we label them as *other*. In such a way we have several benefits [23]: we obtain a greater representation of data in terms of variety and variance of examples; we reduce the chances of overfitting; we improve the performance of the classifier on relevant user actions.

We collected and labeled the traffic generated by 220 sequences of actions for each app, where a sequence is composed by 50 types of actions (for a total of 11660 examples of actions for Gmail, 6600 for Twitter, and 10120 for Facebook). The user action examples in the dataset was divided in a training set and a test set. We use the training set to train the classifier, while we use the test set to evaluate its accuracy. We underline that to build the test set we used accounts that have not been used to create the training set. By using different accounts to generate the training and the test set, it is possible to assure that the results of the classification do not depend on the specific accounts that have been analyzed.

As explained in Section 3.1, each network flow is modeled as a set of time series. Table 2 reports the weights and the intervals for several configurations ("Conf." in the table) used to limit the length of the time series generated by each app. We used different weights configurations, and we selected the packets intervals by analyzing the statistical length of the flows. In particular, the median value and the third quartile have been used as thresholds to limit the maximum length of the generated time series.

[1]00:00:00 UTC, 01 January 1970

Facebook

Action	Description
send message	send a direct message to a friend
post user status	post a status on the user's wall
open user profile	select user profile page from menu
open message	select a conversation on messages page
status button	select "*write a post*" on user's wall
post on wall	post a message on a friend's wall
open facebook	open the Facebook app

Gmail

Action	Description
send mail	send a new mail
reply button	tap on the reply button
open chats	select chats page from menu
send reply	send a reply to a received mail

Twitter

Action	Description
refresh home	Refresh the home page
open contacts	select contacts page on menu
tweet/message	publish a tweet or send a message
open messages	select direct messages page
open twitter	open the Twitter app
open tweets	select tweets page

Table 1: Description of the relevant actions for each app.

Apps	Sets	Weights	In	Out	Complete
Gmail	Conf. 1	0.80	[1,4]	[1,2]	[1,6]
		0.20	[1,6]	[1,3]	[1,9]
	Conf. 2	0.66	[1,4]	[1,2]	[1,6]
		0.33	[1,6]	[1,3]	[1,9]
	Conf. 3	0.33	[1,4]	[1,2]	[1,6]
		0.66	[1,6]	[1,3]	[1,9]
Facebook	Conf. 1	0.66	[1,3]	[1,5]	[1,7]
		0.33	[1,6]	[1,7]	[1,12]
	Conf. 2	0.33	[1,3]	[1,5]	[1,7]
		0.66	[1,6]	[1,7]	[1,12]
	Conf. 3	0.20	[1,3]	[1,5]	[1,7]
		0.80	[1,6]	[1,7]	[1,12]
Twitter	Conf. 1	0.95	-	-	[7,10]
		0.05	-	-	[1,10]
	Conf. 2	0.95	-	-	[8,11]
		0.05	-	-	[1,11]
	Conf. 3	0.95	-	-	[8,10]
		0.05	-	-	[1,10]

Table 2: Weights set configurations and packets intervals for Gmail, Facebook and Twitter apps.

In our experiments, we used the Random forest classifier implemented by the Python library *scikit-learn*[2]. The classifier is trained using 40 estimators (or weak learners). Each estimator consists in a decision tree without any restrictions on its depth limit. The number of features for each estimator is equal to the the square root of the maximum number of available features.

4.3 Classification Performance

Before considering the classification of the user actions, it is worth discussing how to choose the number of clusters that should be used. In order to establish a reasonable value for this parameter, we used a validation dataset to study the accuracy of the classification when varying the number of clusters. Figure 1 reports the achieved results. For each app, we therefore considered the number of clusters that maximized the accuracy, in terms of averaged F-measure. In the following, we report the results of the classification

[2]http://scikit-learn.org/

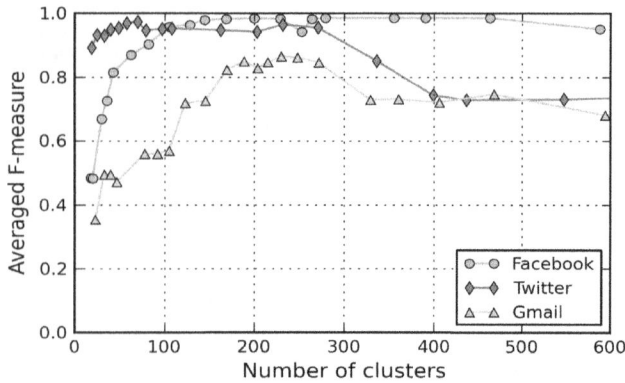

Figure 1: Classification accuracy over number of clusters.

Actions	Precision	Recall	F-measure
send message	1.00	1.00	1.00
post user status	1.00	0.95	0.97
open user profile	0.96	0.91	0.94
open message	0.98	1.00	0.99
status button	1.00	1.00	1.00
post on wall	1.00	0.98	0.99
open facebook	1.00	1.00	1.00
other	0.99	1.00	0.99
Average	0.99	0.98	0.99

Table 3: Classification results of Facebook actions by using Configuration 3.

app by app. In particular, we discuss the average accuracy reached when detecting each sensitive user action, we report detailed results for the precision, the recall and the F-measure metrics.

4.3.1 Facebook

We focused on seven different actions that may be sensitive when using the Facebook app. On average, the F-measure is equal to 99%, with a precision and a recall of 99% and 98% respectively. Performance reached with different configurations of weights and packets intervals constraints are reported in Figure 2a. For each action at least one of the configurations exceeds 94% of accuracy, while the worst performing is always higher than 74%.

Table 3 reports precision, recall and F-measure reached by using Configuration 3. We noticed that all the actions have a precision higher 96%. The recall is higher than 95% for all the actions but the *open user profile*, that reaches 91%.

4.3.2 Gmail

We analyzed four specific user actions of the Gmail app: *send mail*, *reply button*, *open chats* and *send reply*. Figure 2b shows the classification accuracy that has been reached. We observe that we are able to distinguish with high accuracy the action of sending of a new mail, from that of replying to a previously received message, as well as the tap over the reply button. The *open chats* action is instead more difficult to distinguish. Table 4 reports precision, recall and F-measure for different configurations of weights and packets intervals constraints. We can observe that the action *open chats* (that allows to read past chats) achieves a low precision but a high recall.

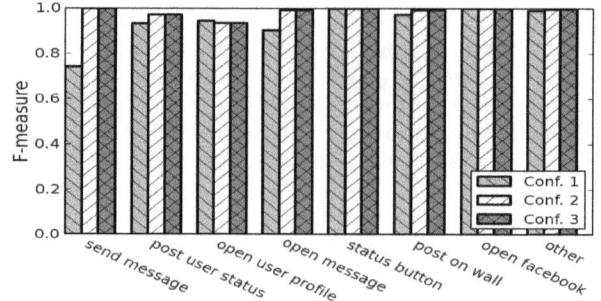

(a) Classification accuracy of the Facebook actions.

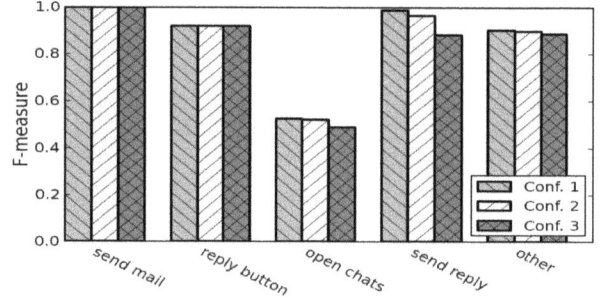

(b) Classification accuracy of the Gmail actions.

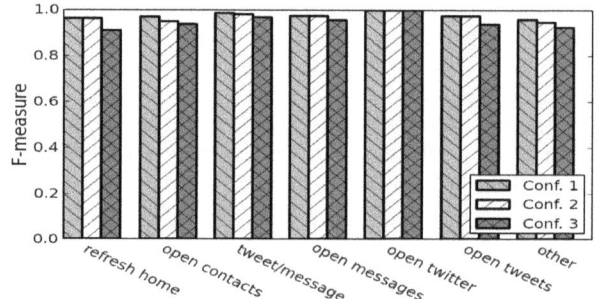

(c) Classification accuracy of the Twitter actions.

Figure 2: Classification accuracy of Facebook, Gmail and Twitter actions.

4.3.3 Twitter

During the analysis we noticed that Twitter actions may be more difficult to classify than Gmail and Facebook actions. Indeed, different Twitter actions generate similar time series that have in common a large portion. Only the last three or four packets of each time series show some difference. Nevertheless, we have been able to reach outstanding results also for this app. In particular, we focus on six specific user actions: *refresh home*, *open contacts*, *tweet/message*, *open messages*, *open twitter*, *open tweets*.

On average, the F-measure is equal to 97%, with a precision and a recall of 98% and 97% respectively (see Table 5). Performance reached are reported in Figure 2c. For each action at least one of the configurations exceeds 96% of accuracy, while the worst configuration has an accuracy in any case higher than 91%. The action *open twitter* has accuracy and recall equal to 100%, independently of the Configuration set used for the clustering phase. As a consequence, none of examples of the test set have been wrongly classified. Three of the six analyzed actions are correctly classified in more than the 99% of the cases. However, the other three actions,

Actions	Precision	Recall	F-measure
send mail	1.00	1.00	1.00
reply button	0.85	1.00	0.92
open chats	0.36	0.94	0.52
send reply	0.98	1.00	0.99
other	0.99	0.82	0.90
Average	0.83	0.85	0.86

Table 4: Classification results of Gmail actions reached by using Configuration 1.

Actions	Precision	Recall	F-measure
refresh home	0.94	0.99	0.96
open contacts	0.97	0.96	0.97
tweet/message	0.97	1.00	0.98
open messages	1.00	0.95	0.97
open twitter	1.00	1.00	1.00
open tweets	1.00	0.95	0.97
other	0.96	0.96	0.96
Average	0.98	0.97	0.97

Table 5: Classification results of Twitter actions reached by using the Configuration 1.

open contacts, *open messages* and *open tweets* are correctly classified in more than 95% of the cases.

5. POSSIBLE COUNTERMEASURES

Users and service providers might believe that their two parties communications are secure if they use the right encryption and authentication mechanisms. Unfortunately, current secure communication mechanisms limit their traffic encryption actions to the syntax of the transmitted data. The semantic of the communication is not protected in any way [20]. For this reason, it has been possible for example to develop classifiers for TLS/SSL encrypted traffic that are able to discriminate between applications.

The contribution of this paper was to investigate to which extent it is feasible to identify the specific actions that a user is doing on his mobile device, by simply eavesdropping the device's network traffic. While it is out of the scope of the paper to investigate possible countermeasure to the proposed attack, we discuss in the following some related issues.

One common belief is that simple padding techniques may be effective against traffic analysis approaches. However, it has to be considered that padding countermeasures are already standardized in TLS, explicitly to "frustrate attacks on a protocol that are based on analysis of the lengths of exchanged messages" [12]. Nevertheless, our attack worked against TLS encrypted traffic. More advanced techniques have been proposed in the literature, such as traffic morphing and direct target sampling [34, 35]. However, a recent result showed that none of the existing countermeasures are effective [13]. The intuition is that coarse information is unlikely to be hidden efficiently, and the analysis of these features may still allow an accurate analysis. On the light of these results, we believe it is not trivial to propose effective countermeasures to the attack we shown in this paper. Indeed, it is intention of the authors to highlight a problem that is becoming even more alarming after the revelation about the mass surveillance programs that are nowadays adopted by governments and nation states.

6. CONCLUSIONS

We proposed a framework to analyze encrypted network traffic and to infer which particular actions the user executed on some apps installed on his mobile-phone. We demonstrated that despite the use of SSL/TLS, our traffic analysis approach is an effective tool that an eavesdropper can leverage to undermine the privacy of mobile users. With this tool an adversary may easily learn habits of the target users. The adversary may aggregate data of thousand users in order to gain some commercial or intelligence advantage against some competitor. In addition, a powerful attacker such as a Government, could use these insights in order to de-anonimize user actions that may be of particular interest. We hope that this work will shed light on the possible attacks that may undermine the user privacy, and that it will stimulate researchers to work on efficient countermeasures that can be adopted also on mobile devices.

7. ACKNOWLEDGMENTS

Mauro Conti was supported by Marie Curie Fellowship PCIG11-GA-2012-321980, funded by the European Commission for the PRISM-CODE project. This work has been partially supported by the TENACE PRIN Project number 20103P34XC funded by the Italian MIUR, by the Project "Tackling Mobile Malware with Innovative Machine Learning Techniques" funded by the University of Padua, and by the European Commission Directorate General Home Affairs, under the GAINS project, HOME/2013/CIPS/AG/4000005057. We would like to thank Fabio Aiolli, Michele Donini, and Mauro Scanagatta for their insightful comments.

References

[1] Androidrank. http://www.androidrank.org/.

[2] Top 15 most popular social networking sites, May 2014. http://www.ebizmba.com/articles/social-networking-websites, May 2014.

[3] C. A. Ardagna, M. Conti, M. Leone, and J. Stefa. An anonymous end-to-end communication protocol for mobile cloud environments. *Services Computing, IEEE Transactions on*, 2014.

[4] R. Atterer, M. Wnuk, and A. Schmidt. Knowing the user's every move: User activity tracking for website usability evaluation and implicit interaction. In *Proceedings of ACM WWW*, 2006.

[5] F. Benevenuto, T. Rodrigues, M. Cha, and V. Almeida. Characterizing user navigation and interactions in online social networks. *Inf. Sci.*, July 2012.

[6] O. Berthold, H. Federrath, and M. Köhntopp. Project anonymity and unobservability in the internet. In *Proceedings of ACM CFP*, 2000.

[7] L. Breiman. Random forests. *Machine Learning*, 45, 2001.

[8] X. Cai, X. C. Zhang, B. Joshi, and R. Johnson. Touching from a distance: Website fingerprinting attacks and defenses. In *Proceedings of ACM CCS*, 2012.

[9] S. Chen, R. Wang, X. Wang, and K. Zhang. Side-channel leaks in web applications: A reality today, a challenge tomorrow. In *Proceedings of IEEE S&P*, 2010.

[10] M. Conti, N. Dragoni, and S. Gottardo. Mithys: Mind the hand you shake-protecting mobile devices from ssl usage vulnerabilities. In *Security and Trust Management*. Springer, 2013.

[11] S. Dai, A. Tongaonkar, X. Wang, A. Nucci, and D. Song. Networkprofiler: Towards automatic fingerprinting of android apps. In *Proceedings of IEEE INFOCOM*, 2013.

[12] T. Dierks and E. Rescorla. The Transport Layer Security (TLS) Protocol Version 1.2. RFC 5246 (Proposed Standard), August 2008.

[13] K. P. Dyer, S. E. Coull, T. Ristenpart, and T. Shrimpton. Peek-a-boo, I still see you: Why efficient traffic analysis countermeasures fail. In *Proceedings of IEEE S&P*, 2012.

[14] W. Enck, P. Gilbert, B.-G. Chun, L. P. Cox, J. Jung, P. McDaniel, and A. N. Sheth. Taintdroid: An information-flow tracking system for realtime privacy monitoring on smartphones. In *Proceedings of USENIX OSDI*, 2010.

[15] S. Fahl, M. Harbach, T. Muders, L. Baumgärtner, B. Freisleben, and M. Smith. Why eve and mallory love android: An analysis of android ssl (in)security. In *Proceedings of ACM CCS*, 2012.

[16] M. Georgiev, S. Iyengar, S. Jana, R. Anubhai, D. Boneh, and V. Shmatikov. The most dangerous code in the world: Validating ssl certificates in non-browser software. In *Proceedings of ACM CCS*, 2012.

[17] Y. Go, D. F. Kune, S. Woo, K. Park, and Y. Kim. Towards accurate accounting of cellular data for tcp retransmission. In *Proceedings of ACM HotMobile*, 2013.

[18] T. Hastie, R. Tibshirani, and J. Friedman. *The Elements of Statistical Learning (2nd ed.)*. Springer, 2009.

[19] D. Herrmann, R. Wendolsky, and H. Federrath. Website fingerprinting: Attacking popular privacy enhancing technologies with the multinomial naive-bayes classifier. In *Proceedings of ACM CCSW*, 2009.

[20] B. Krishnamurthy. Privacy and online social networks: Can colorless green ideas sleep furiously? *IEEE Security and Privacy*, 2013.

[21] M. Liberatore and B. N. Levine. Inferring the source of encrypted http connections. In *Proceedings of ACM CCS*, 2006.

[22] X. Luo, P. Zhou, E. W. W. Chan, W. Lee, R. K. C. Chang, and R. Perdisci. Httpos: Sealing information leaks with browser-side obfuscation of encrypted flows. In *Proceedings of NDSS*, 2011.

[23] T. M. Mitchell. *Machine learning*. 1997.

[24] M. Müller. *Information Retrieval for Music and Motion*. Springer, 2007.

[25] A. Panchenko, L. Niessen, A. Zinnen, and T. Engel. Website fingerprinting in onion routing based anonymization networks. In *Proceedings of ACM WPES*, 2011.

[26] J.-F. Raymond. Traffic analysis: Protocols, attacks, design issues, and open problems. In *Designing Privacy Enhancing Technologies*. Springer, 2001.

[27] B. P. Rocha, M. Conti, S. Etalle, and B. Crispo. Hybrid static-runtime information flow and declassification enforcement. *Information Forensics and Security, IEEE Transactions on*, 2013.

[28] F. Schneider, A. Feldmann, B. Krishnamurthy, and W. Willinger. Understanding online social network usage from a network perspective. In *Proceedings of ACM IMC*, 2009.

[29] C. Staff. Germany: U.s. might have monitored merkel's phone. http://edition.cnn.com/2013/10/23/world/europe/germany-us-merkel-phone-monitoring/, Oct. 2014.

[30] T. Stöber, M. Frank, J. Schmitt, and I. Martinovic. Who do you sync you are?: Smartphone fingerprinting via application behaviour. In *Proceedings of ACM WiSec*, 2013.

[31] G. Suarez-Tangil, J. E. Tapiador, P. Peris, and A. Ribagorda. Evolution, detection and analysis of malware for smart devices. *IEEE Communications Surveys & Tutorials*, 2013.

[32] N. V. Verde, G. Ateniese, E. Gabrielli, L. V. Mancini, and A. Spognardi. No nat'd user left behind: Fingerprinting users behind nat from netflow records alone. In *Proceedings of IEEE ICDCS*, 2014.

[33] X. Wei, L. Gomez, I. Neamtiu, and M. Faloutsos. Profiledroid: Multi-layer profiling of android applications. In *Proceedings of ACM Mobicom*, 2012.

[34] C. V. Wright, L. Ballard, S. E. Coull, F. Monrose, and G. M. Masson. Spot me if you can: Uncovering spoken phrases in encrypted voip conversations. In *Proceedings of IEEE S&P*, 2008.

[35] C. V. Wright, S. E. Coull, and F. Monrose. Traffic morphing: An efficient defense against statistical traffic analysis. In *Proceedings of NDSS*, 2009.

[36] Y. Zhauniarovich, G. Russello, M. Conti, B. Crispo, and E. Fernandes. Moses: Supporting and enforcing security profiles on smartphones. *Dependable and Secure Computing, IEEE Transactions on*, 2014.

[37] X. Zhou, S. Demetriou, D. He, M. Naveed, X. Pan, X. Wang, C. A. Gunter, and K. Nahrstedt. Identity, location, disease and more: Inferring your secrets from android public resources. In *Proceedings of ACM CCS*, 2013.

Securing ARP From the Ground Up

Jing (Dave) Tian
University of Florida
Gainesville, FL, USA
daveti@ufl.edu

Kevin R. B. Butler
University of Florida
Gainesville, FL, USA
butler@ufl.edu

Patrick D. McDaniel
The Pennsylvania State
University
University Park, PA, USA
mcdaniel@cse.psu.edu

Padma Krishnaswamy
Federal Communications
Commission
Washington, DC, USA
padma.krishnaswamy@gmail.com

ABSTRACT

The basis for all IPv4 network communication is the Address Resolution Protocol (ARP), which maps an IP address to a device's Media Access Control (MAC) identifier. ARP has long been recognized as vulnerable to spoofing and other attacks, and past proposals to secure the protocol have often involved modifying the basic protocol.

This paper introduces *arpsec*, a secure ARP/RARP protocol suite which a) does not require protocol modification, b) enables continual verification of the identity of the target (respondent) machine by introducing an address binding repository derived using a formal logic that bases additions to a host's ARP cache on a set of operational rules and properties, c) utilizes the TPM, a commodity component now present in the vast majority of modern computers, to augment the logic-prover-derived assurance when needed, with TPM-facilitated attestations of system state achieved at viably low processing cost. Using commodity TPMs as our attestation base, we show that *arpsec* incurs an overhead ranging from 7% to 15.4% over the standard Linux ARP implementation and provides a first step towards a formally secure and trustworthy networking stack.

1. INTRODUCTION

The Address Resolution Protocol (ARP) [20] is a fundamental part of IPv4 network connectivity. Operating below the network layer, ARP binds an IP address to the Media Access Control (MAC) identifier of a network device, e.g., an Ethernet card or a Wi-Fi adapter, which in turn completes the process of routing the packet to its intended destination. Such communication relies on the last hop for correct delivery. ARP is subject to a variety of attacks including spoofing and cache poisoning, as originally described by Bellovin [1]. Tools such as *dsniff* [26] and *nemesis* [14] can be used respectively to easily launch such attacks. An attack on ARP

can subsequently enable more sophisticated denial-of-service (DoS) and man-in-the-middle (MitM) [15] attacks.

While numerous methods have been proposed to secure ARP [35, 9, 18, 16, 30], they fall short of offering a comprehensive solution to these problems. First, a successful security solution must ensure that the basic ARP protocol itself remains unchanged. There is no "flag day" on which all ARP implementations embedded into the large variety of Internet-connected IPv4 devices will change. Second, the overhead of the implementation should be as small as possible in order to optimize system performance. Third, the ARP security mechanism should be flexible and reliable. Hard-coded security policies may not be applicable to varying network environments. Last, we need to know if the remote machine can be trusted. Trust here applies to both the authentication and the system integrity state of the remote machine, e.g., even if a binding is correct, we may not wish to add a remote host that cannot attest to the correctness of its operation. While past proposals have ranged from localized solutions to those involving public key infrastructures [2, 10, 5], they have not been widely deployed, either due to requiring specific network configurations, creating large system overheads, or requiring fundamental changes to ARP.

In this paper, we propose *arpsec*, an ARP security approach based on logic and the use of the Trusted Platform Module (TPM) [32], to implement security guarantees. *arpsec* does not change or extend the ARP itself. Instead of hard-coded security policies, *arpsec* formalizes the ARP system binding using logic. A logic prover then reasons about the validity of an ARP reply from the remote machine based on the codified logic rules and the previously stored binding history on the local system. A TPM attestation protocol is also implemented to challenge the remote machine if the logic layer fails to determine the trustworthiness of the remote machine. Using TPM hardware, we can authenticate (establish the identity) of the remote and discover whether the remote machine is in a good integrity state (i.e., not compromised). *arpsec* defends from most categories of ARP attacks by tethering address bindings to trusted hardware, establishing the basis for a trustworthy networking stack.

We have implemented *arpsec* in the Linux 3.2 kernel, using commodity TPMs and a Prolog engine. Our experiments show that *arpsec* only introduces a small system overhead, ranging from 7% to 15.4% compared to the original ARP and incurs the lowest overhead when compared to the two PKI-based ARP security proposals, S-ARP [2] and TARP [10].

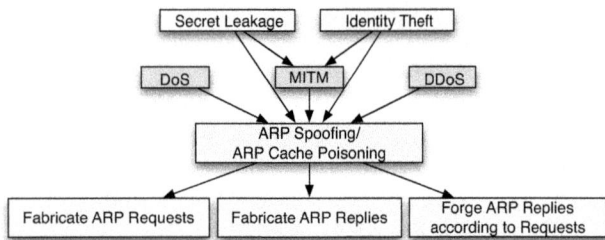

Figure 1: An attack tree for ARP.

The remainder of this paper is structured as follows. Section 2 outlines the background on ARP security issues and trusted computing. Section 3 details the design and architecture of *arpsec*. Section 4 shows details and tradeoffs during the implementation. Section 5 provides the performance evaluation. Section 6 discusses potential issues with *arpsec* and possible solutions. Section 7 reviews the past efforts on ARP security, and Section 8 concludes.

2. BACKGROUND

We first discuss ARP security issues based on the current ARP design and implementations, before explaining common attacks against ARP. As *arpsec* uses the TPM, a brief review of trusted computing is provided.

2.1 ARP Security Issues

ARP [20] is the glue between Layer 3 and Layer 2 in IPv4 networks, allowing for a binding between IP addresses and medium access control (MAC) addresses unique to a particular network interface card (NIC). [1] Before an IP packet is sent out from a NIC (e.g., an Ethernet card), the host's ARP cache is queried to find the MAC address assigned to the target IP address of the packet. If the MAC/IP binding is not found, an ARP *request* will be broadcast to the entire network segment (the *broadcast domain*). Only the host with the target IP address should send back an ARP *reply* containing its MAC address.

In reality, every machine in the network could send an ARP reply claiming that it has the requested MAC address, as there is no ARP reply authentication mechanism. In this case, most operating systems either accept the first reply or the latest one if multiple replies respond to the same request. They further optimize performance by processing ARP requests from other machines and adding MAC/IP bindings for future use. Though all bindings in the ARP cache have some Time-To-Live (TTL) control, the timer is usually large and designed for performance rather than security. As an example, Linux always accepts the first ARP reply to the request and ignores others. It also rejects ARP replies without a request while processing ARP requests from other machines. The TTL for each entry in the Linux ARP cache is around 20 minutes [2]. Solaris and Windows have similar optimizations and hence, similar security issues [27, 12].

One basic attack against ARP is message spoofing. The adversary could inject a new MAC/IP binding into the victim's ARP cache simply by sending a forged ARP request or reply to the victim. The other basic ARP attack is cache

poisoning [35], where the adversary generates the ARP reply using certain MAC address given the request from the victim. Both spoofing and poisoning attacks attempt to insert a malicious MAC/IP binding in the victim's ARP cache.

As shown in Figure 1, the attacks described above act as enablers for other adversary actions, such as man-in-the-middle (MitM) attacks [15] and denial of service (DoS) [35] attacks. For a DoS attack, the adversary can inject the victim's MAC address into a particular machine or substitute the victim's MAC address with another one. In the former case, all the IP traffic from that machine targeting a certain address will be redirected to the victim, while in the latter case, the victim would never receive the messages intended for it to provide the service. MitM attacks are particularly serious, since with the help of ARP spoofing/poisoning, the adversary can interpolate himself into the traffic between victims by injecting his MAC/IP binding into both victims' ARP cache. Both attacks are also quite simple to implement, with small usable scripts widely available, and these in turn can lead to attacks compromising user identity or allowing the leakage of secret information.

2.2 Trusted Platform Module (TPM)

A Trusted Platform Module (TPM) is a cryptographic chip embedded in motherboards. Though implemented by various vendors, all TPM chips follow the TPM specification [32] designed by the Trusted Computing Group (TCG). In conjunction with the system BIOS, TPMs can be used to form a root of trust in a system and to build the trust chain for the software along the software stack, including boot loaders, operating systems and applications [21, 6, 8, 17].

TPMs can help to determine the true identity of a remote host via the Attestation Identity Key (AIK) verification during the TPM attestation. After creating an AIK pair, the TPM hardware communicates with a Privacy Certification Authority (PCA) or Attestation Certification Authority (ACA) using the information embedded in itself to prove its identity and get the AIK credentials. A remote machine proves its integrity state by reporting the values of its Platform Configuration Registers (PCRs). If the *measurement* of PCR values during a TPM attestation different from what is expected, the remote may be compromised and thus not trustworthy. It is important to realize that the AIK private key and the measurement of PCRs are all stored in the TPM itself. Unless the TPM hardware is compromised [28], there is no disclosed method of hacking into the TPM through software and changing PCR values.

3. DESIGN

3.1 Threat Model

The hardware, BIOS, boot loader, operating system and the corresponding system libraries, as well as the *arpsecd* daemon, are trusted components in our local host. However, except for the TPM hardware in the remote machine, we do not trust anything generated by the remote machine. Moreover, the adversary may have compromised the remote machine and gained root permission, through which any ARP attacks can be launched, including ARP message spoofing and ARP cache poisoning. The adversary may also leak secret information he has gotten from the victim and use this information to impersonate the victim on another machine while taking the victim machine offline. In short, for the

---
[1] Reverse ARP [4] is generally obsolete in favor of other bootstrapping protocols such as DHCP and BOOTP.

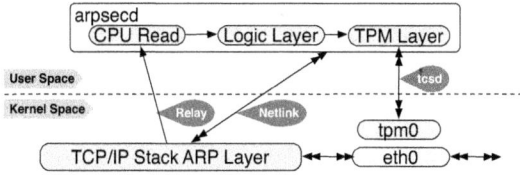

Figure 2: The architecture of *arpsec*.

```
while there is an ARP msg from the kernel do
    check the msg type;
    if msg.type == ARP request then
        if msg is for us then
            reply the request;
        else
            drop the request;
        end
    else if msg.type == ARP reply then
        if msg is for us then
            if msg passes the logic layer then
                add the MAC/IP binding into the ARP cache;
            else
                if msg passes the TPM layer then
                    add the MAC/IP binding into the ARP cache;
                else
                    drop the reply;
                end
            end
        else
            if msg passes the logic layer then
                add the MAC/IP binding into the ARP cache;
            else
                drop the reply;
            end
        end
    end
end
```

Algorithm 1: ARP message processing within *arpsec*

local *arpsec* host machine, the TCB includes all hardware and system software required to start *arpsecd*; the local host machine should also only trust the TPM hardware within the remote machine during the ARP processing.

It is important to note that the TPM hardware attacks, like TPM deconstructing [28] and TPM reset attack [8] are not considered in this paper, nor are potential TPM relay attacks, whose preferred solution is a special-purpose hardware interface [17]. Also, *arpsec* is not designed for DoS/DDoS attacks, though it has the ability to defend against simple DoS attacks, which we discuss further in Section 6.

3.2 System Design

Compared to proposals such as S-ARP and TARP, which take advantage of the PKI system to extend ARP, *arpsec* formalizes ARP address binding and validates ARP messages using both a logic prover and TPM attestations, all without requiring any changes to the original protocol. The architecture of *arpsec* is illustrated in Figure 2.

In the user space, *arpsecd* is the daemon process of *arpsec* that runs in the local machine and takes control of processing of all the ARP messages from the kernel. There are three major components in the *arpsecd* daemon: the CPU read, the logic layer and the TPM layer. The CPU read component retrieves all ARP request/reply messages from the kernel space and passes the preprocessed, logic-friendly messages to the logic layer component. The logic layer component then tries to handle these messages based on the message type, system state and the logic rules. We will detail the logic layer in the following section. For the ARP reply, if the logic layer is unable to validate the message, the TPM layer will then challenge the remote machine using the TPM attestation. Only the MAC/IP bindings (in the

ARP reply) validated by the logic layer or TPM attestation could be added into the local ARP cache. The pseudo code of *arpsecd* ARP processing is listed in Algorithm 1. Note that *arpsec* ignores ARP requests not for itself. These are usually processed by ARP implementations for performance but leave the ARP cache vulnerable.

3.3 Logic Formulation

The logic layer in *arpsec* is the first filter used to testify the trustiness of an ARP/RARP reply message. The logic layer imposes minimal performance costs when compared to the TPM layer, using a logic prover and a list of ARP logic rules. To leverage the power of the logic reasoning, firstly, we introduce an ARP system binding logic formulation.

Intuition: *The logic layer tracks statements (attestations) by systems that particular media addressed are mapped to network addresses. The timing of these statements are tracked such that the logic can "prove" exactly which binding is the most authoritative at a given time. The logic judges a binding to be authoritative if it is the most recent one received from a trusted system. At runtime, the system generates, if possible, the proof of a binding before using it for network communication.*

An instance of an ARP binding system is defined as $\mathcal{A} = \{\mathcal{N}, \mathcal{M}, \mathcal{T}, \mathcal{S}, \bar{\mathcal{S}}, \bar{\mathcal{R}}\}$, where

$$\mathcal{T} = \mathbb{P}$$
$$\mathcal{N} = (\epsilon, n_0, \ldots, n_a)$$
$$\mathcal{M} = (\epsilon, m_0, \ldots, m_b)$$
$$\mathcal{S} = (s_0, \ldots, s_c)$$
$$\bar{S} = \mathcal{S} \times \mathcal{T}$$
$$\bar{R} = \mathcal{S} \times \mathcal{N} \times \mathcal{M} \times \mathcal{T}$$

Intuitively, $\mathcal{T}$ is a set of all positive integers representing an infinite and totally ordered set of time epochs. $\mathcal{N}$ is the collection of network addresses and $\mathcal{M}$ is the collection of media addresses. For convenience, both address sets contain a special address ϵ representing the lack of binding assignment, described below. $\mathcal{S}$ is the set of systems that makes assertions about the address bindings within the network. $\bar{S}$ represents the timing of system trust validations (e.g., system attestations); $\bar{s}_{i,j} \in \bar{S}$ where system s_i was successfully vetted at time t_j. $\bar{\mathcal{R}}$ is the binding assertions made in the course of operation of the ARP protocol, where $\bar{R}_{i,j,k,l} \in \bar{\mathcal{R}}$ if system s_i asserts the binding (n_j, m_k) at time t_l. Lastly, for ease of exposition, we introduce the following derived binding and trust time-state elements within the system:

$$\mathcal{A} = (A_0, \ldots, A_{|\mathbb{P}|})$$
$$\mathcal{B} = (B_0, \ldots, B_{|\mathbb{P}|})$$

$\mathcal{R}$ is the key conceptual element here; each element of $\mathcal{R}$ captures the fact that system s_i stated (through an attestation) a binding of network address n_j to media address m_k at time t_l. The remainder of the logic simply reasons from the set of statements which binding should be considered authoritative at a given time.

Trust state : The trust state $\mathcal{A}$ of the system is a totally ordered set of subsets of $\mathcal{S}$ representing the instantaneous set of systems that have been determined to be in trusted state in each epoch (e.g., have been vetted through system attestations). The trust state of the A at time t_k, A_k is:

$$A_k^h = \{s \mid \exists j, (k-h) \leq j < k : (s, j) \in \bar{S}\}$$

Or simply, A_k is the set of all systems $s_i \in \mathcal{S}$ that have been vetted as trustworthy within the last h epochs. The security parameter h represents the durability of a system trust state. In the initial state of the system all systems are untrusted, e.g., $A_o = \{\emptyset\}$.

Binding state : We refer to the B_k as the binding state at time $\mathcal{T}_k$. The states of the binding system $\mathcal{B}$ are a totally ordered sequence of B_k, which is a relation over $\mathcal{N}$ and $\mathcal{M}$ representing the instantaneous binding of network to media addresses, where:

$$\forall B_k \in \mathcal{B} : B_k \subset \mathcal{N} \times \mathcal{M}$$

It is worth noting further that each B_k is constrained by a set of *coherency* properties that define correct operation of the binding protocol. Namely, $\forall B_k \in \mathcal{B}$:

(1) $\forall n_l \in \mathcal{N}$ $: \exists (n_l, m_o), m_o \in \mathcal{M}$
(2) $\forall m_o \in \mathcal{M}$ $: \exists (n_l, m_o), n_l \in \mathcal{N}$
(3) $\nexists (n_l, m_o), (n_p, m_q) : n_l = n_p \neq \epsilon$
(4) $\nexists (n_l, m_o), (n_p, m_q) : m_o = m_q \neq \epsilon$

That is, all network addresses (constraint 1) and media addresses (2) must have an assignment at each epoch. Further, the network address not bound to the unassigned element ϵ must be bound to exactly one media address (3), and the media address not bound to the unassigned element ϵ must be bound to exactly one network address (4).

We define the set of rules with operational properties for the binding set. We state that $(n_j, m_k) \in B_l$ if and only if:

(5) $\exists \bar{R}_{i,j,k,x} \in R, \ x \leq l, s_i \in A_x,$
      $\nexists \bar{R}_{v,j,p,y} \in R, p \neq k, y > x, s_v \in A_y,$
      $\nexists \bar{R}_{v,q,k,y} \in R, j \neq q, y > x, s_v \in A_y$

Constraint (5) indicates that any binding in B_l was asserted at or prior to time t_l by a trusted system, and no later assertion for that network or media address was subsequently received at or before t_l was asserted.

Finally, by definition, all network and media addresses are unassigned in the initial state B_0:

$$B_0 = \forall n_l \in \mathcal{N}, (n_l, \epsilon) \bigcup \forall m_o \in \mathcal{M}, (\epsilon, m_o)$$

In general, constraint (5) is the core property used by the logic prover to implement the ARP security. The logic layer stores all the verified bindings with the remote system identifiers and the time epochs. For any given MAC/IP binding in the ARP/RARP reply message from the remote, if there exists a binding record from the same (trusted) remote in the past that is no older than a pre-defined number of epochs (security parameter h) when compared to the current epoch. the logic layer would trust this binding, add the binding the to the local ARP cache and add this binding record into the logic prover for future reasoning. Security parameter h represents a tradeoff between reliability and performance, as it determines the time range of the past we would trust to validate the current event.

The Prolog engine continuously consumes assertions received at an end host and infers B_k at each time epoch using the above constraints. That generation thus provides a proof of authority; if a binding $(n_i, m_j) \in B_k$, then it is authoritative and can be used for communication at time t_i.

3.4 TPM Attestation

If an incoming ARP/RARP request or reply cannot be validated by the logic layer, *arpsec* turns to a TPM layer as a second line of defense. To establish trust in the remote host, we use a TPM attestation [32], whose general operation is described in Section 2. A *measurement* is taken based on the current state of the underlying hardware, BIOS, boot loader,

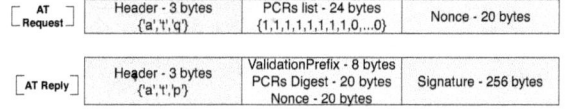

Figure 3: The AT Request/Reply

and operating system, with each value stored in a PCR. The TPM is tamper-resistant and access to PCRs is not possible except through expensive hardware attacks. The Attestation Identification Key (AIK) thus provides identity while the PCRs determine system integrity state.

We design the *arpsec* Attestation (AT) protocol for communication between the local machine (also known as the challenger) and the remote machine (also known as the attester), as shown in Figure 3. The request contains a header, a list of PCRs, and a nonce to prevent replay. The PCR list indicates which registers are of interest - for our purposes, these are registers 0 through 7. [2] When the host receives this challenge, it responds with a TPM *Quote*, which includes the nonce, PCR values and their corresponding digest, signed by the AIK private key, in the AT reply. If at this point any of these values fail and the signature cannot be validated, the address binding is purged from the ARP cache. Note that we do not put any MAC/IP binding into the AT reply. Comparing to the TPM, a MAC/IP binding is easy to fake and thus not trustworthy.

4. IMPLEMENTATION

We have implemented *arpsec* in Linux with the 3.2.0.55 kernel, using C and Prolog. The implementation details of the *arpsecd* daemon is shown in Figure 4. Our goals were high performance and *incremental deployment* to allow *arpsec* and standard ARP to coexist in the same network.

Depicted in Figure 4, the *relay* mechanism [36] transports ARP messages from kernel to user space, as it is designed to manage large amounts of asymmetric traffic. We also use a netlink socket to communicate from user to kernel space, in order to manipulate the ARP cache. This provides similar functionality to the `ioctl()` calls for cache management but uses the low-level kernel APIs to get rid of the extra locking in `ioctl()`. Using this netlink socket, we could also trigger the kernel to send the ARP reply given any request, at which point it is relayed to user space for efficient processing.

In user space, the logic formulation of the ARP binding system is implemented in GNU Prolog (GProlog) [3]. We integrate the GProlog-based logic prover into our C-based *arpsecd* using the GProlog-C interfaces, providing a 50X performance improvement compared to IPC between *arpsecd* and the GProlog interpreter. We set a 5-second security parameter, meaning that every 5 seconds we expect a new attestation of the ARP binding.

We also implemented a whitelist and two blacklists before logic processing occurs. The whitelist contains the MAC/IP bindings known to be good under all conditions. The two blacklists contain potentially malicious MAC addresses or IP addresses respectively. Currently, only the MAC/IP binding failed in the TPM attestation will be added into the black

---

[2] PCRs 0 through 7 cover the measurement for hardware, BIOS, boot loader and even OS [32] Other PCRs could be extended to cover system libraries and even applications.

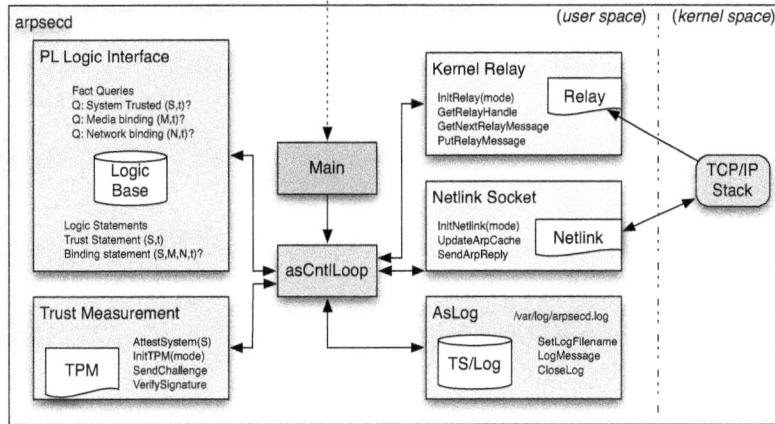

Figure 4: The implementation of *arpsec* daemon (*arpsecd*)

list . All entries in the blacklists have the same TTL of 200 seconds, at which point they are removed.

The *arpsec* TPM component is built on the top of the Trousers API [31] following the TPM 1.2 specification [32]. TPM information (PCRs and AIK public keys) of remote hosts is stored in an internal database.

arpsec relies on the knowledge of AIK and PCRs, which are built upon the TPM hardware. Compared to S-ARP and TARP, where keys are bound to a PKI, *arpsec* does not distinguish hosts through public keys. Instead, *arpsec* uses the MAC/AIK/PCRs binding to validate the trust to the remote host. To managing these bindings within an *arpsec* network, we introduce a *TPM Information Management Server* (TIMS) into the network. When a new machine wants to join the network, it creates the AIK pair to get the credential from the TIMS. The TIMS acts as a Privacy CA or an Attestation CA (ACA), and certifies the TPM within this new machine. The procedure follows the AIK certificate enrollment scheme defined by the TCG.

More information on the deployment of the TIMS and about the TPM Information Entry (TIE) bundles that we distribute from it can be found in our technical report [29].

5. PERFORMANCE EVALUATION

To fully understand the overhead of *arpsec*, we compare our implementation with standard ARP as well as the proposals that most closely mirror the security guarantees that we provide, S-ARP and TARP. We follow the experiment settings of TARP, providing macro- and microbenchmarks. Our testing environment involves 4 Dell Optiplex 7010 desktop PCs with quad-Core Intel i5-3470 3.20 GHz CPU, 8GB memory with Intel Pro/1000 full duplex Ethernet cards, running Ubuntu LTS 12.04 (x86-64) with Linux kernel version 3.2.0.55. All machines are equipped with TPM hardware from STM (version 1.2 and firmware 13.12), running Trousers API 1.2 rev 0.3. To eliminate the impact from exterior network traffic, all machines are isolated on a 1000-Mbps HP ProCurve switch. As S-ARP and TARP were written on Linux kernel 2.6, we have forward-ported the S-ARP and TARP implementations to our testing environment.

5.1 Macrobenchmark Testing

We benchmark performance based on the round-trip-time (RTT) using `ping` to provide overhead from an application's or user's perspective. This benchmark we used is also consistent with what was used by S-ARP and TARP. Like TARP, we also implemented a custom `ping` command: `ncping` (no-cache ping), which clears the local ARP cache before each ICMP echo request is sent. With `ncping`, we can get the performance evaluation in the worst case and reveal the true overhead of different methods.

We have performed three groups of experiments: (*a*) `ping` with the target MAC/IP binding in the ARP cache, (*b*) `ping` without the target MAC/IP binding in the ARP cache, and (*c*) `ncping`. Each test consists of 1000 ICMP echo requests or 10×1000 requests for the `ping` without caching.

Figure 5a shows the RTT average (mean), min ($mean - 2\sigma^2$) and max ($mean + 2\sigma^2$) from the `ping` command with the target binding in the ARP cache. In all experiments, internal caching of S-ARP and TARP is enabled to maximize performance. Once the target binding is in the ARP cache, RTT average values of all these methods look similar ranging from 0.210 to 0.240 *ms*. The max and min values among these methods are also comparable, which is intuitive given no ARP processing is occurring. We attribute *arpsec*'s slightly faster processing time to efficiency of processing in user space and of the relay system.

Figure 5b demonstrates the most common scenario, where the target binding is initially in the ARP cache. The first `ping` now takes much more time, as the ARP request will be broadcast and the corresponding reply will be handled before the binding can be added to the cache. Once the reply is processed and the binding is added, the performance is the same as in Figure 5a and the average RTTs converge to be similar to standard ARP.

To show the average time of the first-ARP-Reply processing, we repeated the 1000-run `ping` for 10 times. S-ARP, TARP and *arpsec* daemons were restarted each time to show the real processing time without caching. As shown in the figure, the left bar is the average over all 1000 pings and the right bar is the average of 10 first-time `ping`s. The left bars show the amortized costs are close to cached processing. From the right bars, we see that after standard ARP,

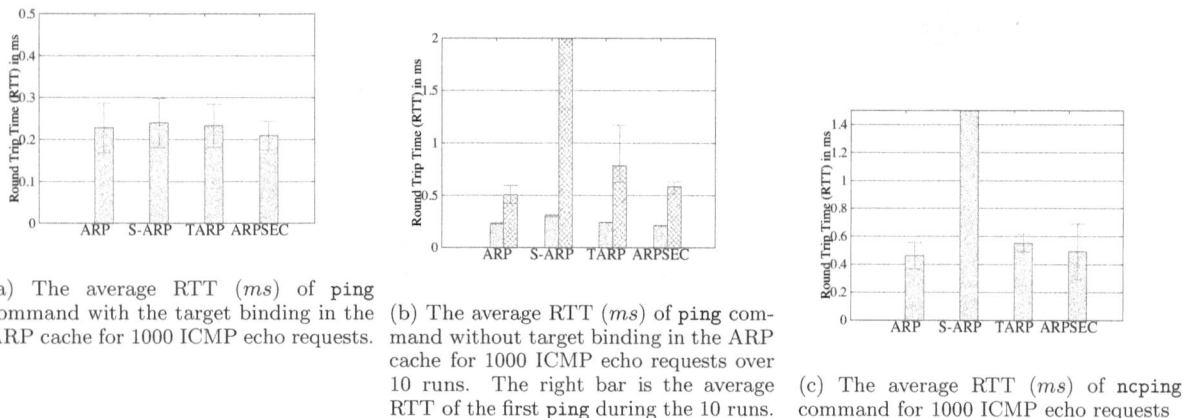

(a) The average RTT (*ms*) of `ping` command with the target binding in the ARP cache for 1000 ICMP echo requests.

(b) The average RTT (*ms*) of `ping` command without target binding in the ARP cache for 1000 ICMP echo requests over 10 runs. The right bar is the average RTT of the first `ping` during the 10 runs.

(c) The average RTT (*ms*) of `ncping` command for 1000 ICMP echo requests

Figure 5: The macro-benchmark of *arpsec*

arpsec has the smallest overhead by 15.4%. S-ARP, without the help of caching, introduces the biggest overhead, taking on average 64 *ms* for the new MAC/IP binding.

Figure 5c displays worst-case performance using the `ncping` command, where the ARP cache will be flushed before each ICMP echo request is sent. With the help of internal caching and one-setup signature validation, TARP introduces a small overhead of 19.9% comparing with the original ARP. Even with caching, S-ARP still shows the largest overhead with the RTT average value 8.4 *ms* (not shown in the figure) because of the time synchronization and communication with the AKD. Comparing with S-ARP and TARP, *arpsec* performs the best introducing a 7% overhead. Note that the TPM attestation is not triggered until the logic prover fails. The security parameter used by the prover is 5 seconds in our testing. Also, the RTT value of *arpsec* does not mean that TPM operation is fast, only that a quote can be amortized in the overhead. Because of the asynchronous operation of the TPM, the RTT value of *arpsec* is free from the degradation caused by the TPM attestation, but only limited by the user vs. kernel space communication and the logic prover.

5.2 Micro-benchmark

Using the GProlog-C interfaces, the logic prover can run as a pure C component without affecting performance of *arpsecd*. The prominent bottleneck in *arpsec* is then the TPM hardware, which is slow compared to a CPU [22].

Table 1 shows the key generation time of different methods. Here TARP* shows the ticket generation instead of the public/private key pair generation. *arpsec* is the cost of TPM AIK pair generation and the AIK public key certification. S-ARP has a mean key generation time of 90.364 *ms*. TARP is the fastest with the mean time 32.012 *ms* (public/private key pair + ticket). By contrast, *arpsec* is the slowest with the mean time 12.841 seconds, because we use the PrivacyCA to certify the AIK public key generated by the local TPM, following the complicated AIK certificate enrollment scheme described in the previous section. Fortunately, the AIK generation and certification is one-time effort. After this, the AIK private key is stored in the TPM and could be used in a secure manner. Moreover, both S-ARP and TARP have either the key expiration or the ticket expiration issue, which means after a certain time, either the key or the ticket has to be re-generated for each host within the network. In the long run, the time of *arpsec*'s one-time, offline key generation will be amortized by the key/ticket re-generation of S-ARP or TARP.

Table 2 profiles some TPM operations used by *arpsec*: AIK generation, cost of obtaining a random value, a TPM quote, signature verification, and TPM attestation verification, respectively. *AIKgen* is time consuming, as we saw from Table 1. Otherwise, the quote operation is the slowest with the mean time 336.109 *ms*. We summarize the comparison among S-ARP, TARP and *arpsec* in Table 3.

6. DISCUSSION

Arpsec is comprised of both a Logic Layer and a TPM Layer; we now discuss the implications of each of these layers. The logic formulation for the ARP binding system we have created is simple, straightforward and intuitive, due in part to the simple design of ARP. Even with these simple logic rules, we are able to record all ARP cache update events, which implicitly capture the provenance history of the ARP cache. This could potentially allow the logic prover to act as a forensic system identifying compromised hosts, and the logic system itself can be extended to formalize other network protocols that build on ARP.

To implement the TPM attestation protocol in *arpsec*, we introduce a TPM daemon (*tpmd*) and require each remote machine to install it. An extra TPM daemon is necessary based on the TPM specification and the TrouSerS API (the same reason why *arpsecd* is implemented in user space rather than a kernel module). TrouSerS provides a *tcsd* daemon process with RPC interfaces. These interfaces are for remote TPM management rather than TPM attestation from a challenger. Our *tpmd* communicates with the *tcsd* instead of calling the TPM directly as in `libtpm` [3]. Even if *tpmd* is compromised, the attacker would be unable to circumvent the TPM attestation protocol. This would require either a forged TPM Quote on known-good PCR values, or for the attacker to posses the AIK private key. An attacker would be unable to recover the AIK or edit the PCRs because they are stored on board the TPM.

By adding a host to the ARP cache and purging it if the attestation fails, we make a design trade-off. In the worst

---

[3]libtpm (http://ibmswtpm.sourceforge.net/) was developed before the TrouSerS API and the usage is deprecated.

Protocol	Min	Avg	Max	Mdev
ARP	36.16	90.36	330.7	34.79
TARP	5.17	31.01	69.48	10.83
TARP*	0.47	1.007	1.068	0.022
arpsec	3879	12841	46759	6062

Table 1: The key generation time (*ms*) with the key length 1024 bits averaged by 100 runs

TPM	Min	Avg	Max	Mdev
AIKgen	864	9385	43716	5932
Rand	10.92	11.40	11.47	0.035
Quote	324.5	336.1	336.5	0.698
SigVerify	0.120	0.199	0.213	0.006
AttVerify	0.208	0.307	0.344	0.009

Table 2: The TPM operation time (*ms*) averaged by 100 runs

Protocol	Mechanism	Formal Proofs	Remote Integrity	Change to ARP?	Change to Kernel?	Overhead
S-ARP	PKI	N	N	Y	Y	Large
TARP	Ticket-based PKI	N	N	Y	N	Small
arpsec	Logic+TPM	Y	Y	N	Y/N	Small

Table 3: General comparison among S-ARP, TARP and *arpsec*

case, we have made an incorrect binding for 300-500 *ms* until a TPM quote fails and a binding is removed from the cache. This can be exacerbated by TCP transmission delays. Currently, we set the TCP socket timeout to be 2 *s*. To optimize for security of the binding, we can purge it immediately after the challenge is sent and wait for the attestation before we update the cache again. This creates considerable overhead, however. Alternately, the ARP request could carry the challenge and the ARP reply could encapsulate the AT reply, at the cost of creating a protocol change to ARP.

Another limitation of using TPM attestation is that it only attests to what was loaded into the system at boot time (or load-time using integrity measurement). Runtime integrity checking provides more guarantees at the cost of requiring extra processors or significant overhead. Integrity systems such as IMA [21] or PRIMA [6] could be integrated with *arpsec*. To further reduce the TCB size, we could potentially run *arpsec* in an isolated root of trust environment with a dynamic root of trust as offered by Flicker [11] or TrustVisor [7]. A trusted path [38, 37] to the NIC could ensure IP and MAC identifiers are correctly retrieved.

Though not designed to defend against DoS attacks, *arpsec* could handle certain attacks against ARP. As mentioned before, once the TPM attestation fails, the malicious MAC address or IP address will be added into the corresponding black list. When the same MAC address or IP address is contained in the following ARP/RARP reply, the reply will be dropped without processing. However, if the malicious MAC address or IP address keeps changing, *arpsec* has to examine each message, as the black list does not help in this case. Moreover, if the DoS attack is triggered from a higher-level network protocol, this would be out of the scope of *arpsec*. Such protection could be helpful against spanning tree attacks and VLAN hopping, however [24].

The performance of *arpsec* is limited by the TPM hardware. The TPM chip is designed to be cheap - only a few dollars. While the low price helps embed a TPM chip into each machine even in mobile phones, it limits the scope of TPM usages. As shown in Table 2, TPM Quotes impose a 336 *ms* delay when TPM attestation is required. As the TPM 2.0 library specification is published for review now, new TPM implementations based on it could further reduce the cost of Quote operations.

While TPMs have been widely deployed in servers, desktops, laptops and even mobile devices, many legacy ma-

chines lack them. For these machines, software TPMs could be used as a replacement, such as `libtpm` mentioned above, or vTPMs [19] in cloud environments. However, as the TPM Quote command occurs in software rather than hardware, a secure, trusted and isolated execution path [38, 37] is needed to guarantee trustworthiness.

Currently, *arpsec* supports both ARP and RARP. Future work will support Gratuitous ARP and IPv6.

7. RELATED WORK

The security of address binding operations in IPv4 contexts, particularly ARP, has received considerable attention, focused on the problems summarized in previous sections. Although the threats are in a LAN context, as they impact correct packet delivery to destinations, it is critical that countermeasures to them be successfully employed.

Alternatives range from early suggestions for static bindings [1], which at normal scale on any type of network with frequent host additions/removals is intractable; to ARP modifications in S-ARP [2] and TARP [10] which introduce signed attestations, in the form of addresses bound to a public key or a ticket. S-ARP participants self-generate key pairs and register the public key in the central Authoritative Key Distributor (AKD). The AKD maintains the public key/MAC bindings and distributes these to all S-ARP hosts. TARP relies on Kerberos-style tickets and a central ticket-granting service to provide authentication, and is hence faster due to the use of symmetric keys. These approaches all require modifications to ARP itself, which limits adoption.

Another solution implements a Cache Poisoning Checker [30] to intercept ARP requests and responses and inspect them for correctness. It does not modify the ARP protocol itself. A more wide-ranging approach [23] aims at preventing IP address spoofing by using the IP address as an identity based key. However, address-based assertion has limited use in environments where IP address assignment is dynamic, and does not address binding of IP to MAC identifiers.

Other solutions use security policies to prevent ARP attacks. ArpON [18] defines different ARP binding policies for different networks, including static, dynamic, or hybrid networks. Instead of a centralized management server, hosts within the network all run the ArpON daemon and respect the same policies, thus adding complexity to defining and updating policies for different network environments.

Few proposals have considered a more holistic perspective of overall protocol design. Wang et al. consider secure networking from proposal design to formal verification [34] but focus on BGP and meta-routing rather than address binding. There has been little emphasis on approaches tying together system attestations grounded in hardware with formally verifiable operation of Internet protocols. While the Trusted Computing Group defines the TPM standard for roots of trust and standardizes its use network connect (network access control), protocol operations supporting Internet infrastructure have not been considered [33, 25].

The use of IPV4, and thus ARP, is relevant for the foreseeable future, but IPv6 deployment is increasing. The IPv6 Neighbor Discovery Protocol (NDP) [13] has capabilities beyond ARP, relying on autoconfiguration based on address binding. The concepts used to secure ARP are applicable to NDP as well, as we discuss in our technical report [29].

8. CONCLUSION

This work has proposed *arpsec*, a secure ARP protocol that provides a logic prover to reason about the validity of ARP/RARP replies and uses TPM attestation to guarantee the trust in remote hosts. Compared to the original ARP, *arpsec* introduces only $7\% - 15.4\%$ system overhead. While providing a formally secure and trustworthy networking stack will will remain an issue into the future, *arpsec* points the way to a new solution in this space through use of a logic prover and TPM hardware and minimizing the system overhead without impacting current implementations.

Acknowledgements

We wish to thank Stephen L. Squires and Jim Just for their helpful comments and discussion of the problem space. This work is funded in part by the US National Science Foundation under grant CNS-1254198. The views expressed in this paper are solely those of its authors and do not reflect the FCC position on the subject matter and related concepts.

9. REFERENCES

[1] S. M. Bellovin. Security problems in the ICP/IP protocol suite. *Comp. Comm. Review*, 2:32–48, April 1989.

[2] D. Bruschi, A. Ornaghi, and E. Rosti. S-ARP: a Secure Address Resolution Protocol. In *ACSAC*, 2003.

[3] D. Diaz et al. The GNU Prolog web site. http://gprolog.org/.

[4] R. Finlayson et al. A Reverse Address Resolution Protocol. http://tools.ietf.org/rfc/rfc903.txt, June 1984.

[5] B. Issac. Secure AP and Secure DHCP Protocols to Mitigate Security Attacks. *International Journal of Network Security*, 8:107–118, March 2009.

[6] T. Jaeger, R. Sailer, and U. Shankar. PRIMA: policy-reduced integrity measurement architecture. In *ACM SACMAT*, 2006.

[7] J. M. McCune et al. TrustVisor: Efficient TCB Reduction and Attestation. In *IEEE S&P*, 2010.

[8] B. Kauer. OSLO: Improving the security of Trusted Computing. In *USENIX Security Symposium*, 2007.

[9] LBNL Network Research Group. arpwatch: the ethernet monitor program. http://ee.lbl.gov/, 2006.

[10] W. Lootah, W. Enck, and P. McDaniel. TARP: Ticket-based Address Resolution Protocol. *ACSAC*, 2005.

[11] J. M. McCune et al. Flicker: An Execution Infrastructure for TCB Minimization. In *ACM EuroSys*, 2008.

[12] Microsoft Technet. Address Resolution Protocol. http://technet.microsoft.com/en-us/library/cc940021.aspx.

[13] T. Narten, E. Nordmark, W. Simpson, and H. Soliman. Neighbor Discovery for IP version 6 (IPv6). https://tools.ietf.org/html/rfc4861, September 2007.

[14] J. Nathan. Nemesis. http://nemesis.sourceforge.net/.

[15] A. Ornaghi and M. Valleri. Man in the middle attacks Demos. http://www.blackhat.com/presentations/bh-europe-03/bh-europe-03-valleri.pdf, Blackhat 2003.

[16] A. P. Ortega et al. Preventing ARP Cache Poisoning Attacks: A Proof of Concept using OpenWrt. In *Net. Ops. & Mgmt. Symp.*, 2009.

[17] B. Parno. Bootstrapping trust in a "trusted" platform. In *USENIX HotSec*, 2008.

[18] A. D. Pasquale. ArpOn: ARP Handler Inspection. http://arpon.sourceforge.net/index.html, 2008.

[19] Perez, Ronald, Reiner Sailer, and Leendert van Doorn and others. vTPM: Virtualizing the Trusted Platform Module. In *USENIX Security Symposium*, 2006.

[20] D. C. Plummer. An Ethernet Address Resolution Protocol or Converting Network Protocol Addresses to 48.bit Ethernet Address for Transmission on Ethernet Hardware. http://tools.ietf.org/search/rfc826, November 1982.

[21] R. Sailer, X. Zhang, T. Jaeger, and L. van Doorn. Design and Implementation of a TCG-based Integrity Measurement Architecture. In *USENIX Security*, 2004.

[22] J. Schmitz, J. Loew, J. Elwell, D. Ponomarev, and N. Abu-Ghazaleh. A Framework for Performance Evaluation of Trusted Platform Modules. In DAC, 2011.

[23] C. Schridde, M. Smith, and B. Freisleben. TureIP: Prevention of IP Spoofing Attacks Using Identity-Based Cryptography. In *SIN'09 Proc. 2nd Intl. Conf. on Security of information and networks*, pages 128–137, 2009.

[24] L. Senecal. Understanding and preventing attacks at layer 2 of the OSI reference model. In *Proc. 4th Comm. Networks & Services Research Conf*, 2006.

[25] S. Frankel, R. Graveman, J. Pearce, and Mark Rooks. Guidelines for the Secure Deployment of IPv6. http://csrc.nist.gov/publications/nistpubs/800-119/sp800-119.pdf, 2010. NIST.

[26] D. Song. dsniff. http://monkey.org/~dugsong/dsniff/, 2000.

[27] Symantec. Solaris Kernel Tuning for Security. http://www.symantec.com/connect/articles/solaris-kernel-tuning-security, Dec 20, 2000.

[28] C. Tarnovsky. Deconstructing a 'Secure' processor. *Black Hat DC*, 2010.

[29] J. Tian, K. Butler, P. McDaniel, and P. Krishnaswamy. Securing ARP From the Ground Up. Tech. Report REP-2015-573, Univ. of Florida, Jan. 2015.

[30] M. V. Tripunitara and P. Dutta. A middleware approach to asynchronous and backward compatible detection and prevention of ARP cache poisoning. In *ACSAC*, 1999.

[31] TrouSerS. The open-source TCG Software Stack. http://trousers.sourceforge.net/.

[32] Trusted Computing Group. TPM Main Specification. http://www.trustedcomputinggroup.org/resources/tpm_main_specification.

[33] Trusted Computing Group. Glossary. http://www.trustedcomputinggroup.org/developers/glossary.

[34] A. Wang, L. Jia, C. Liu, B. T. Loo, et al. Formally verifiable networking. In *ACM HotNets*, 2009.

[35] S. Whalen. An Introduction to ARP Spoofing. http://rootsecure.net/content/downloads/pdf/arp_spoofing_intro.pdf, 2001.

[36] T. Zanussi et al. relay (formerly relayfs). http://relayfs.sourceforge.net/.

[37] Z. Zhou, M. Yu, and V. Gligor. Dancing with Giants: Wimpy Kernels for On-demand Isolated I/O. In *IEEE S&P*, 2014.

[38] Z. Zhou, V. Gligor, J. Newsome, and J. M. McCune. Building Verifiable Trusted Path on Commodity x86 Computers. In *IEEE S&P*, 2012.

Tunably-Oblivious Memory: Generalizing ORAM to Enable Privacy-Efficiency Tradeoffs

Jonathan Dautrich
Google, Inc.
Irvine, California
jjldj@google.com

Chinya Ravishankar
Computer Science and Engineering
University of California, Riverside
ravi@cs.ucr.edu

ABSTRACT

We consider the challenge of providing privacy-preserving access to data outsourced to an untrusted cloud provider. Even if data blocks are encrypted, access patterns may leak valuable information. Oblivious RAM (ORAM) protocols guarantee full access pattern privacy, but even the most efficient ORAMs to date require roughly $\ell \log_2 N$ block transfers to satisfy an ℓ-block query, for block store capacity N.

We propose a generalized form of ORAM called Tunably-Oblivious Memory (λ-TOM) that allows a query's public access pattern to assume any of λ possible lengths. Increasing λ yields improved efficiency at the cost of weaker privacy guarantees. 1-TOM protocols are as secure as ORAM.

We also propose a novel, special-purpose TOM protocol called *Staggered-Bin TOM* (SBT), which efficiently handles large queries that are not cache-friendly. We also propose a read-only SBT variant called Multi-SBT that can satisfy such queries with only $O(\ell + \log N)$ block transfers in the best case, and only $O(\ell \log N)$ transfers in the worst case, while leaking only $O(\log \log \log N)$ bits of information per query. Our experiments show that for $N = 2^{24}$ blocks, Multi-SBT achieves practical bandwidth costs as low as 6X those of an unprotected protocol for large queries, while leaking at most 3 bits of information per query.

Categories and Subject Descriptors

H.2.7 [**Database Management**]: Database Administration—*security, integrity, and protection*

Keywords

Data privacy; Oblivious RAM; privacy tradeoff

1. INTRODUCTION

It has become common for resource-constrained clients to outsource data storage and management to *cloud* servers lying beyond their administrative control. Such outsourcing, however, raises data privacy concerns. Unfortunately,

merely encrypting data does not ensure privacy, since information is leaked by access patterns on encrypted data [4,11].

Oblivious RAM (ORAM) protocols [9] can guarantee full access pattern privacy in an outsourced block store. ORAM protocols use dummy block reads and periodic oblivious data block re-shufflings to guarantee that any two access patterns of the same length are computationally indistinguishable to any outside observer, including the server itself. The added costs incurred when using ORAM for data outsourcing are generally dominated by *bandwidth cost*, which we measure as the number of actual block transfers needed to satisfy a single block *access* (read or write).

ORAM bandwidth costs range from $O(\sqrt{N \log N})$ [1] to $O(\log N)$ [6, 10, 22, 23], where N is the ORAM block capacity. Recently, there has been a push to make ORAM practically, as well as asymptotically, efficient [14,22,24,25]. The most bandwidth-efficient ORAM construction known to date [22, 23] still incurs a bandwidth cost of roughly $\log_2 N$. Other protocols [8,13,16,24,25] use less client space than [22,23], but incur higher bandwidth costs. Some such protocols target use cases such as secure coprocessors [15], where bandwidth efficiency is less critical than client space.

This $\log_2 N$ cost is particularly disappointing for multiblock read-only queries, where we might expect better performance. To achieve full access pattern indistinguishability, ORAMs must ensure that all queries generate public access patterns of roughly the same length, regardless of access locality or ORAM state. As a result, all queries must incur the same, worst-case cost.

To avoid this limitation, we build special-purpose ORAM-like protocols that leak a strictly bounded amount of access pattern information in order to obtain a bandwidth cost under $\log_2 N$ for large queries. Existing schemes that partially protect access patterns (e.g. [7,18]) start with unprotected protocols and add obfuscation mechanisms to quantifiably limit the adversary's ability to make certain inferences. However, they do not consider all possible inferences, and thus cannot assess total information leakage. In contrast, we start with a fully protected protocol (ORAM) and carefully relax its privacy requirements in order to tightly bound the total access pattern information leaked.

1.1 Our Contributions

We propose Tunably-Oblivious Memory (TOM), a new model that relaxes and generalizes the traditional ORAM model, allowing controlled trade-offs between efficiency and information leakage. TOM permits variable-length public access patterns, allowing properties such as locality to be exploited to improve efficiency. Queries are distinguishable by access pattern length, so for each query λ-TOM generates an access pattern with one of λ pre-determined lengths, limiting information leaked per query to $\log_2 \lambda$ bits. λ-TOM protocols with large λ are more flexible and efficient, but leak more information. Protocols with small λ are more rigid, but offer better privacy. 1-TOM leaks no information, and has security equivalent to a traditional ORAM.

TOM can directly improve efficiency for queries showing locality by simply enhancing ORAM with a local block cache. However, we address the more challenging problem of building a TOM that efficiently handles workloads that are *not* cache-friendly. To this end, we propose a novel, special-purpose TOM called *Staggered-Bin TOM* (SBT). We prove that SBT achieves bandwidth cost $O(\log N / \log \log N)$ for large queries with blocks chosen uniformly at random, but has worst-case cost $O(\sqrt{N})$.

We also propose three read-only SBT variants, culminating in the Multi-SBT, which combines the SBT with a traditional ORAM, storing three copies of each block. The Multi-SBT achieves bandwidth cost $O(1)$ for large uniform random block queries, and $O(\log N)$ in the worst case, while leaking only $O(\log \log \log N)$ bits per query. Thus, Multi-SBT can satisfy any ℓ-block uniform random block query using only $O(\ell + \log N)$ block transfers.

We developed a simulator to evaluate SBT and its variants, and compare practical costs of the Multi-SBT with the ORAM in [23]. We show that Multi-SBT maintains a practical bandwidth cost of roughly 6X for queries of $4\sqrt{N}$ blocks, while [23] has substantially larger costs ranging from 22X to 29X for similar parameterizations (see Table 1).

The rest of this paper is organized as follows. Section 2 covers related work in protecting access pattern privacy. Section 3 presents the TOM model and its security definition. We describe the SBT in Section 4 and its variants in Section 5, with detailed performance analyses in the Appendix. Section 6 gives experimental results from our simulator comparing SBT and its variants.

2. RELATED WORK

2.1 ORAM and PIR Protocols

We focus on showing that the Multi-SBT outperforms the *Practical ORAM* in [22, 23] because it remains the most bandwidth-efficient single-server ORAM, and incurs a similar client space cost ($O(N)$ with low constant). Both Practical ORAM [22,23] and the SBT logically partition blocks on the server. In [22,23] each partition is itself an ORAM, so the bandwidth cost remains logarithmic. In Multi-SBT, every fetch retrieves a potentially-usable block, enabling constant bandwidth cost in the best case.

ORAMs that emphasize reduced client space incur even higher bandwidth costs. Assuming 64KB blocks, Practical ORAM [22, 23] requires $\log_2 N$ bandwidth cost. Path ORAM [24] requires closer to $8 \log_2 N$, and more if client space is reduced using recursion. The ORAMs in [13] and [8] both have asymptotic bandwidth cost $O(\log^2 N / \log \log N)$, and are outperformed in practice by Path ORAM [24]. Multi-cloud oblivious storage [21] achieves very low bandwidth cost (under 3X), but assumes multiple non-colluding servers.

Private Information Retrieval (PIR) techniques also support secure data outsourcing with full access pattern indistinguishability. PIR alone is generally computationally impractical [20], but progress has been made mixing ORAM with PIR to reduce bandwidth costs [5,16]. Due to the high latencies and drastic computation costs of such schemes, we do not compare the Multi-SBT with them here.

2.2 Partial Access Pattern Protection

Several efficient protocols have been proposed that *partially* protect access patterns. One example is the *Shuffle Index* [7], which uses an unchained B+ tree to store encrypted blocks. *Cover searches* provide access pattern privacy by making dummy block requests to obscure the true request. The authors quantify the adversary's ability to recognize that two given accesses correspond to the same block, but ignore other information leaks. For example, the protocol may run indefinitely without retrieving certain blocks. Since the adversary knows that such blocks are rarely requested, he can use their eventual request pattern to make additional inferences. In contrast, TOM's bounds on total information leakage hold for all inferences. Shuffle Index bandwidth cost is 16X, but drops to 4X with enough client space to store pointers to each block.

The protocol in [18] reads 2 blocks for every request, does no oblivious shuffling, and achieves a bandwidth cost as low as 4X even with limited client space. Like the Shuffle Index, it bounds the adversary's ability to correlate two accesses, but leaks even more unquantified information, via access patterns of rarely requested blocks, than the Shuffle Index.

Like TOM, the private computation protocol of [26] uses an ORAM and allows a bounded amount of access pattern information to leak in order to improve efficiency. However, the notions are otherwise fundamentally different. The protocol in [26] accesses main memory from trusted hardware via a black-box ORAM, using the additional space to enable more elaborate computations. Applications vary in the number of required ORAM fetches per computation. Leakage comes through each application's one-time maximum fetch rate choice. In contrast, TOM allows fetch counts to vary dynamically, letting the ORAM adjust fetch counts to match workloads, leaking information per query instead of per application setup. Thus, TOMs see efficiency improvements when the average number of fetches is small, even if the worst-case number is large.

3. TUNABLY-OBLIVIOUS MEMORY

3.1 ORAM Review

Oblivious RAM (ORAM) techniques [9] provide a mechanism for outsourcing encrypted data while ensuring that all possible access patterns are computationally indistinguishable to all observers other than the client, including the server itself. In an ORAM protocol, the client arranges his data in N fixed-size blocks of B bits each. Each block has a unique address $a \in \{0, 1, \ldots, N-1\}$. Each of the N blocks is encrypted using a semantically secure encryption scheme and then stored on the server. Every time a block a is written to the server, it is re-encrypted using a different nonce, and assigned a new server-side ID, preventing it from being directly linked to previous encrypted versions of a.

The goal of ORAM is to define an efficient protocol that re-shuffles and re-encrypts blocks to ensure that no information is leaked about the address or contents of each block, how frequently a given block is accessed, and whether the access is a read or write. The protocol may incorporate *dummy*

Table 1: Comparison of [23] with results based on proposed Multi-SBT using the ORAM component from [23], with the parameterizations and costs given below and in [23], with 64 KB block size. Multi-SBT average cost is for uniform random queries of length $\ell = 4\sqrt{N}, \lambda = 8$. Max. cost is three times ceiling of ORAM cost.

N	ORAM Capac-ity	ORAM [23]				Multi-SBT using ORAM from [23]				
		Client Storage	Server Storage	Cost		Client Storage	Server Storage	Avg. Cost	Cost Upper-Bound	Leaked Bits / Access
2^{20}	64 GB	204 MB	205 GB	22.5X		604 MB	333 GB	5.4X	69X	$3 \cdot 2^{-12}$
2^{22}	256 GB	415 MB	819 GB	24.1X		1.2 GB	1.3 TB	6.0X	75X	$3 \cdot 2^{-13}$
2^{24}	1 TB	858 MB	3.2 TB	25.9X		2.6 GB	5.2 TB	6.3X	78X	$3 \cdot 2^{-14}$
2^{28}	16 TB	4.2 GB	51 TB	29.5X		13.6 GB	83 TB	5.8X	90X	$3 \cdot 2^{-16}$

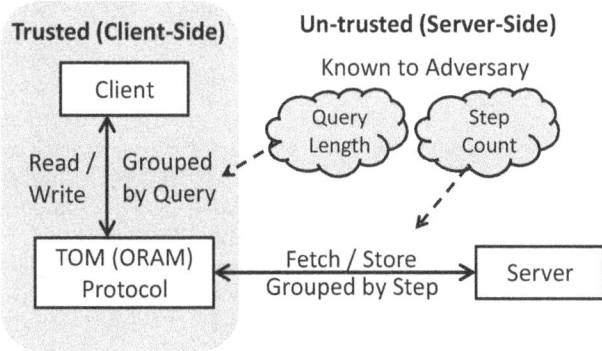

Figure 1: Client issues secret accesses (read/write) to ORAM/TOM protocol, which translates to a sequence of public accesses (store/fetch) to the server. Adversary knows query length (# requests in query) and step count (# steps needed to satisfy query).

blocks, which contain no data but are indistinguishable from encrypted data blocks.

A client interacts with the ORAM protocol as with a trusted block store (Figure 1), issuing a *secret access pattern* $\vec{S} = (s_1, \ldots, s_{|\vec{S}|})$ of block requests. Each secret access s is a triple $(type, a, data)$, where $type$ is the access type (*read* or *write*), a is the local address of the block to access, and $data$ is the plaintext data written to block a, if any.

The ORAM translates $\vec{S}$ into a *public access pattern* $P(\vec{S}) = (p_1, \ldots, p_{|P(\vec{S})|})$ that is generally much longer than $\vec{S}$. Each public access p is also a triple $(type, id, edata)$, where $type$ denotes the access type (*store* or *fetch*), id denotes the server-side ID of the accessed block, and $edata$ denotes the encrypted block data to be stored, if any. A fetch optionally removes the block from the server.

The term *access pattern* has been used in the literature ambiguously to refer to either $\vec{S}$ or $P(\vec{S})$. We disambiguate by calling $\vec{S}$ the *secret* access pattern and $P(\vec{S})$ the *public* access pattern. We now give the standard ORAM security definition of [23] in terms of our notation:

Definition 1. A protocol satisfies ORAM security if for every pair of secret access patterns $\vec{S_1}$ and $\vec{S_2}$ of the same length ($|\vec{S_1}| = |\vec{S_2}|$), $P(\vec{S_1})$ and $P(\vec{S_2})$ are computationally indistinguishable (to every observer other than the client).

If the ORAM block size B is reasonably large ($B \gg \log_2 N$), the communication cost is dominated by block transfers. The ORAM makes $|P(\vec{S})|$ block transfers to satisfy $\vec{S}$,

while an unprotected protocol needs only $|\vec{S}|$ transfers. Thus the *bandwidth cost* of using ORAM to obscure an access pattern is given by $\frac{|P(\vec{S})|}{|\vec{S}|}$. The more efficient an ORAM, the lower its bandwidth cost.

3.2 Trading Obliviousness for Efficiency

We introduce the term *step* to refer to a discrete unit of work performed by an ORAM or TOM. Informally, each step retrieves a single encrypted *target* block from the server. Each step may also fetch and store other blocks in order to obscure the target block's identity or prepare for future requests (e.g. shuffling).

In a traditional ORAM, each secret access yields exactly one such step, and the target block is simply the block associated with the secret access. Each ORAM step is powerful in that it can obliviously retrieve any given target block from the server, but this power also makes each step expensive. Informally, the *step count* is the total number of steps needed to satisfy a given secret access pattern. The step count must match the number of secret accesses in order to satisfy ORAM's perfect privacy guarantee, so such powerful, expensive steps are mandatory.

In contrast, the TOM generalization allows the step count to vary, creating the possibility for more efficient but less powerful steps, and thus for more efficient protocols. For example, the Staggered Bin TOM (Section 4) partitions the blocks on the server into k bins (Figure 2). Each step may only retrieve a target block from a single, pre-determined bin. Each such step is thus less powerful than an ORAM step, but it is also more efficient. In the worst case, k steps are needed to satisfy a single secret access, but by carefully scheduling secret accesses from the same multi-block query, we can obtain lower overall bandwidth cost than a comparable ORAM. Allowing the step count to vary inevitably leaks some access pattern information. We show how to tightly bound such information in Sections 3.4 and 3.5.

We now define the TOM model more precisely. For each secret access pattern $\vec{S}$, a TOM generates a public access pattern $P(\vec{S})$ divided into a sequence $\sigma(\vec{S})$ of discrete *steps*. We use $|\sigma(\vec{S})|$ to denote the *step count* of $P(\vec{S})$.

Definition 2. Each *step* is a series of stores and fetches used by the TOM protocol to retrieve a single *target* block from a subset of the blocks on the server. A step is complete when the TOM is ready to retrieve another target block.

Traditional ORAMs are special cases of TOM in which each secret access generates exactly one step ($|\sigma(\vec{S})| = |\vec{S}|$). Thus ORAM does not distinguish between *secret access* and *step*, necessitating our new terminology for TOM. In ORAM, the block subset accessible during a step includes all blocks on the server, while in Staggered Bin TOM (Section 4) it only includes blocks from one bin.

We say $\vec{S}$ is *satisfied* once all the steps in $\sigma(\vec{S})$ are complete. As in ORAM, if the TOM is *stateful*, some blocks updated by $\vec{S}$ may not be stored to the server immediately. Instead, even after the step completes, they are held locally as *dirty* blocks until they are written back to the server during a subsequent step.

Definition 3. A *query* is a secret access pattern $\vec{S}$ composed of a batch of secret accesses that may be satisfied in any order.

A TOM receives multi-block *queries* from the client. Queries are handled sequentially relative to each other, but accesses within a query may be processed in any order. For security, *query* and *secret access pattern* are interchangeable.

TOM decouples *steps* from *secret accesses*, allowing query length $|\vec{S}|$ to differ from step count $|\sigma(\vec{S})|$. This approach offers better efficiency than ORAM for two reasons. First, TOM need not generate steps for accesses to cached blocks. In ORAM, a repeat access to a recently cached block must still incur the overhead of a step, else the reduced step count would reveal the repeated access. Second, TOM need not require that each step be capable of accessing any block. By reducing the power of each step, TOM makes steps more efficient, potentially reducing a query's total bandwidth cost, even though the step count may increase. The SBT and its variants (Sections 4 and 5) exploit this second advantage.

3.3 TOM Security Definition

As in ORAM, we assume that query length $|\vec{S}|$ is public. We also make the worst-case assumption that the adversary can observe precisely when each query starts and ends, and thus knows the exact step count $|\sigma(\vec{S})|$ of each query.

In ORAM, $|\sigma(\vec{S})| = |\vec{S}|$, so $|\sigma(\vec{S})|$ reveals nothing new to the adversary. In TOM, $|\vec{S}|$ and $|\sigma(\vec{S})|$ may differ, so $|\sigma(\vec{S})|$ may leak information. For example, if $|\sigma(\vec{S})| < |\vec{S}|$, the adversary may infer that $\vec{S}$ contains repeated accesses. We limit such leakage by forcing $|\sigma(\vec{S})|$ to assume one of λ *milestone* values taken from a predefined set $\mathcal{M}_{|\vec{S}|}$. More milestones improve flexibility in generating $\sigma(\vec{S})$ and thus improve efficiency, but also leak more information about $\vec{S}$.

$\mathcal{M}_{|\vec{S}|}$ is defined up-front for each value of $|\vec{S}|$, so the milestones themselves do not leak information. Since the adversary knows $|\vec{S}|$, he already knows that $|\sigma(\vec{S})|$ will be one of the λ milestones. Thus, he only learns information through the specific choice of milestone used for $|\sigma(\vec{S})|$. Equivalently, he learns which of λ equivalence classes $\vec{S}$ belongs to, limiting information leakage by the size of λ.

We now define security for λ-TOM, which translates a secret access pattern $\vec{S}$ into a public access pattern with one of λ milestone step counts.

Definition 4. A protocol satisfies λ-TOM security if both of the following conditions hold for every possible pair of secret access patterns $\vec{S_1}$ and $\vec{S_2}$:

1. Let $\ell = |\vec{S_1}|$. If $|\vec{S_1}| = |\vec{S_2}|$ then $|\sigma(\vec{S_1})|, |\sigma(\vec{S_2})| \in \mathcal{M}_\ell$, where $\mathcal{M}_\ell$ is a set of *milestones* of cardinality $\leq \lambda$.

2. If $|\sigma(\vec{S_1})| = |\sigma(\vec{S_2})|$, then $P(\vec{S_1})$ and $P(\vec{S_2})$ are computationally indistinguishable (outside the client).

By ensuring that any two public access patterns with the same step count are indistinguishable, we guarantee that information about $\vec{S}$ only leaks through the observation of the step count $|\sigma(\vec{S})|$, which is in turn limited to one of λ milestones. We can bound the information leakage I_λ of a λ-TOM protocol by assuming the worst case, in which all milestones are equi-probable, giving:

Lemma 1. *A λ-TOM protocol leaks at most $I_\lambda \leq \log_2 \lambda$ bits per query in expectation.*

Proof. Let R be a random variable representing the choice of milestone. The expected information leaked by revealing the outcome of R is given by the entropy $H(R)$. $H(R)$ is maximized when each of the λ milestones is equi-probable, giving $H(R) = \log_2 \lambda$ bits. Thus we have that $I_\lambda \leq \log_2 \lambda$. $\square$

When $\lambda = 1$, the leakage is $I_\lambda = 0$, which indicates that 1-TOM is as strong as ORAM. In fact, for $\lambda = 1$, we have by Condition 1 of Definition 4 that $|\vec{S_1}| = |\vec{S_2}|$ implies $|\sigma(\vec{S_1})| = |\sigma(\vec{S_2})|$, and thus by Condition 2 that $|\vec{S_1}| = |\vec{S_2}|$ implies $P(\vec{S_1})$ and $P(\vec{S_2})$ are indistinguishable. Therefore any 1-TOM protocol satisfies ORAM security (Definition 1). The reverse is also true for any ORAM with a notion of steps. In any case, we make no claim that 1-TOM is substantively more secure than ORAM, so we treat 1-TOM and ORAM as equivalent.

Since each query leaks at most I_λ bits, larger queries leak less information per access. Combining small, independent queries would reduce leakage, but may also increase latency. It is critical that no query results be released to the client until the entire query is satisfied. If the client used partial results, the partial completion time might leak, revealing additional information. Thus, query size is limited by the size of the results cache allocated to the TOM, and excessively large queries may need to be broken up. In standard ORAM, $I_\lambda = 0$, so there is no motivation to make queries larger than a single block access.

What the adversary *gains* from leaked access pattern information depends heavily on what other information the adversary holds. Other schemes that obscure access patterns (e.g. [7]) focus on quantifying the adversary's inability to make particular inferences, but do not assess holistic information loss. In contrast, we upper-bound the total access pattern information leakage, and leave it to the client to decide how much leakage is acceptable given the application.

3.4 Paddable TOM Protocols

We now show how to construct a λ-TOM for any given λ from a *paddable* TOM. Intuitively, we start by choosing λ milestones, then delay each query's completion by silently padding it with dummy steps until its step count reaches a milestone. We use S_{MAX} to denote the worst-case per-access step count.

Definition 5. A protocol is a *Paddable TOM* if it satisfies:

1. Condition 2 of Definition 4 (indistinguishable patterns)

2. It has finite upper bound $\ell \cdot S_{\text{MAX}}$ on step count $|\sigma(\vec{S})|$ generated by a secret access pattern of length $\ell = |\vec{S}|$.

3. Any $P(\vec{S})$ may be *padded* by adding any number of *dummy* steps, increasing $|\sigma(\vec{S})|$ by any amount.

We can coerce any paddable TOM into satisfying λ-TOM for any given λ. We first define appropriate milestones for $\mathcal{M}_\ell$, then instruct the protocol to pad every public access pattern with dummy steps, increasing $|\sigma(\vec{S})|$ to the smallest milestone in $\mathcal{M}_\ell$ greater than or equal to the original step count. If we trivially set $\mathcal{M}_\ell = \{\ell \cdot S_{\mathrm{Max}}\}$, and translate every secret access pattern of length ℓ, with padding, into a public access pattern with step count $\ell \cdot S_{\mathrm{Max}}$, we satisfy 1-TOM and thus ORAM security.

Efficient paddable protocols will generate step counts much smaller than $\ell \cdot S_{\mathrm{Max}}$, so the padding required to reach $\ell \cdot S_{\mathrm{Max}}$ may incur substantial bandwidth cost. Increasing λ (adding milestones) can reduce cost, but also reduces privacy. To make the best possible tradeoffs, our strategy for choosing milestones should minimize cost due to padding for any λ.

3.5 Log-Spacing for Paddable Protocols

Let $m = |\sigma(\vec{S})|$ be the original step count generated from query $\vec{S}$ of length $\ell = |\vec{S}|$. We may have $m < \ell$ if most queried blocks are cached, but such cases are too rare to merit dedicated milestones, so we assume $\ell \leq m \leq \ell \cdot S_{\mathrm{Max}}$.

Let m' be the smallest milestone in $\mathcal{M}_\ell$ such that $m' \geq m$. In a paddable TOM, the fractional increase in step count, and thus bandwidth cost, is given by the *padding factor* m'/m. Let δ be the maximum padding factor (maximum possible value of m'/m). Given λ, we propose to minimize δ by log-spacing milestones as multiples of ℓ over $[\ell, \ell \cdot S_{\mathrm{Max}}]$:

$$\mathcal{M}_\ell = \left\{ \left\lceil \ell \left(S_{\mathrm{Max}} \right)^{i/\lambda} \right\rceil \mid i \in \mathbb{Z}, 1 \leq i \leq \lambda \right\}. \quad (1)$$

This spacing strategy minimizes the maximum padding factor δ, ensuring:

$$\delta \leq \left\lceil \left(S_{\mathrm{Max}} \right)^{1/\lambda} \right\rceil. \quad (2)$$

To minimize λ for given δ, we solve $\left(S_{\mathrm{Max}} \right)^{1/\lambda} \leq \delta$ for λ:

$$\lambda \geq \frac{\log S_{\mathrm{Max}}}{\log \delta} = \log_\delta S_{\mathrm{Max}}. \quad (3)$$

These expressions reveal a clear tradeoff between privacy (λ) and efficiency (δ). Smaller S_{Max} can improve privacy *and* efficiency, which is unsurprising since ORAMs fix privacy at $\lambda = 1$ and seek to reduce the worst-case per-access cost.

3.6 Assessing TOM Information Leakage

Since each query in a λ-TOM protocol leaks at most a fixed I_λ bits of information, smaller queries leak more information per access. Thus TOM is best applied in scenarios where queries are large or can be easily batched.

Consider a TOM with worst-case per-access step count $S_{\mathrm{Max}} \in O(polylog(N))$. The log-spacing strategy with $\delta = 2$ gives $\lambda \in O(\log \log N)$, and thus a leakage per query of only $I_\lambda \in O(\log \log \log N)$ bits per ℓ-block query. Even a less efficient TOM with $S_{\mathrm{Max}} \in O(\sqrt{N})$ leaks only $I_\lambda \in O(\log \log N)$ bits, which is still far better than the $O(\ell \log N)$ bits leaked by an unprotected protocol.

What the adversary actually *gains* from the leaked access pattern information depends heavily on when each step count was observed and what other information the adversary holds. Other schemes that obscure access patterns (e.g. [7]) focus on quantifying the adversary's inability to make particular types of inferences, but do not address all possible inferences, and thus do not assess holistic information loss. In contrast, we upper-bound the total access pat-

Table 2: SBT and TOM Notation

δ	Max. padding factor (padding cost increase)
H	Max. fetch queue length, before padding
All queries, strict upper bound:	
S_{Max}	Worst-case per-access step count, before padding
C_{Max}	Worst-case bandwidth cost, after padding
Large uniform rand. block queries, high-prob. bound:	
C_{HP}	High-prob. bandwidth cost, after padding

tern information leakage, and leave it to the client to decide how much leakage is acceptable given the application.

4. STAGGERED-BIN TOM

Here we present a novel λ-TOM protocol, called *Staggered-Bin TOM* (SBT), that reduces costs even for large queries that are not cache-friendly. In Section 5 we propose three read-only variants of SBT that store multiple copies of each block and reduce costs by choosing the most convenient copy to fetch. Table 2 gives some key notation, and Table 3 compares performance of SBT variants.

As noted in Section 3.3, an ORAM is simply a 1-TOM. TOM allows us to decouple steps from secret accesses, so we could improve on ORAM performance by simply increasing λ and adding a local block cache. We could then satisfy most cached block accesses without stepping the λ-TOM (without block transfers), while leaking only $\log_2 \lambda$ bits per multi-block query. However, caching only improves performance when secret access patterns exhibit temporal locality.

4.1 SBT Architecture

An SBT contains N blocks of B bits each placed in $n + 1$ logical *bins*, each with a maximum capacity of n blocks. We initialize the SBT by filling the bins with $n, n - 1, \ldots, 1, 0$ blocks, respectively, and storing them on the server. The SBT always keeps n more blocks locally, for $N = n(n+3)/2$ blocks total (Figure 2).

We choose n to be the smallest integer such that $N \leq n(n + 3)/2$, and add up to n extra data blocks to increase SBT capacity N to exactly $n(n+3)/2$. *No unusable dummy blocks of any kind are added*, keeping server storage overhead low. Bins are purely logical structures, so the server is free to use any physical configuration for storing blocks.

The SBT needs local (client-side) storage space for three purposes. First, it requires Bn bits for the n blocks always stored locally. Second, it needs $B\ell$ bits to cache the results of an ℓ-block query, so that all ℓ blocks can be simultaneously released to the client. Finally, as in [23], the SBT needs a small amount of space for each of the N blocks to record its server ID, containing bin's index, and a list of block addresses in each bin, for a total of roughly $2 \log_2 N$ bits per block.

In all, approximately $B(n + \ell) + 2N \log_2 N$ bits of client storage are required. Though these storage requirements may seem high, [23] and [22] note that B is large enough in practice that the space needed to store $n \approx \sqrt{2N}$ blocks is comparable to the space needed for the meta-data of all N blocks. For example, with $N = 2^{30}$ blocks, and block size $B = 64\text{KB}$, we need under 8GB for the meta-data, and up to 8GB local block storage for queries of $\ell = 3\sqrt{N}$ blocks.

Table 3: Comparison of our λ-TOM protocols, block size B. Numbers approximate; estimated average costs taken from Figures 5–7. Smaller C_{Max} improves privacy/efficiency tradeoff. $\lambda \leftarrow S_{\text{Max}}$ for constant δ. $\lg \equiv \log_2$

Protocol	Worst-Case C_{MAX}	Uniform Rand. Block C_{HP} for $\ell \approx 4\sqrt{N}$	Bits Leaked Per ℓ-Block Query	Efficient Write	Server Storage (Bits)	Client Storage (Bits)
Unprotected	1	1	$\ell \lg N$	Yes	NB	$O(1)$
ORAM [23]	$\lg N$	$\lg N$	0	Yes	$\leq 4NB$	$3B\sqrt{N} + 1.25N \lg N$
SBT	$2\sqrt{2N}$	$O\left(\frac{\log N}{\log \log N}\right)$	$\lg \lg(\sqrt{2N})$	Yes	NB	$(\ell + \sqrt{2N})B + 2N \lg N$
2-Choice SBT	$4\sqrt{N}$	$O(1), \approx (3\text{-}5)$	$\lg \lg(2\sqrt{N})$	No	$2NB$	$(\ell + 2\sqrt{N})B + 4N \lg N$
SBT+ORAM	$3 \lg N$	$O(\log \log N)$	$\lg \lg(3 \lg N)$	No	$\leq 5NB$	$(\ell + \sqrt{2N} + 3\sqrt{N})B + 3.25N \lg N$
Multi-SBT	$3 \lg N$	$O(1), \approx (4\text{-}7)$	$\lg \lg(3 \lg N)$	No	$\leq 6NB$	$(\ell + 5\sqrt{N})B + 5.25N \lg N$

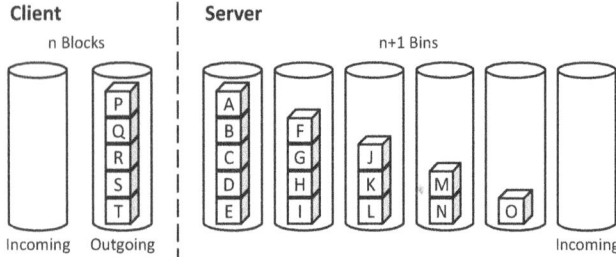

Figure 2: SBT in its initial state, with $n = 5$ blocks on the client, and $n(n+1)/2$ on the server. The empty server-side *incoming* bin will be filled in, one block at a time, by the n blocks from the client.

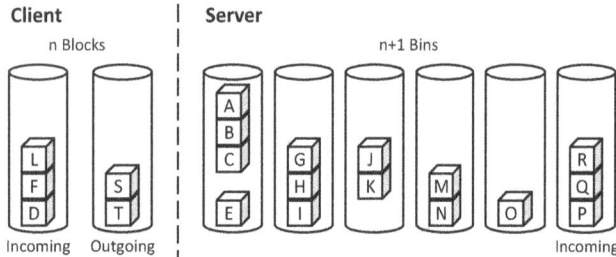

Figure 3: SBT after 3 steps. Server bins are accessed in a round-robin fashion. Blocks L, F, D have been fetched to the client-side *incoming* bin, and blocks R, Q, P stored to server-side *incoming* bin.

4.2 SBT Operation

Each step in the SBT fetches one block from and stores one block to the server. SBT operation is best described in terms of *passes* of n steps each. A pass fetches and removes one block from each of the n non-empty bins in order, and stores n blocks to the previously empty bin. After each pass, the bin load pattern rotates by 1 bin, and fetches continue round-robin (Figure 3). After each pass, the SBT re-encrypts the n fetched blocks, randomly permutes them, assigns them to the empty bin, and generates new server-side IDs to prevent linking to old copies.

Each query consists of ℓ secret accesses for distinct block addresses. A query may begin or end at any point during a pass. The SBT cannot change the one-per-bin round-robin fetch pattern, but may choose which block to fetch from each bin. Thus, a single-block query can always be satisfied in n steps, since we fetch at least one block from every non-empty bin. Similarly, any ℓ-block query takes at most ℓn

steps ($S_{\text{MAX}} = n$), since we always retrieve at least one target block per pass, even if all ℓ blocks are in one bin.

The SBT maintains a *fetch queue* for each bin. To start a query, we identify the bin containing each block to be accessed, and add an appropriate fetch to that bin's fetch queue. When the SBT is ready to issue a fetch for bin i, it first checks i's fetch queue. If the queue is non-empty, the next fetch is dequeued and dispatched to the server. Otherwise, a dummy fetch is generated for a randomly chosen block from the bin. Once all fetch queues are empty and all outstanding fetches finish, the query is satisfied and results are released to the client.

All fetches must proceed in order, as must all stores. Further, to maintain n blocks on the client, a given step's store cannot begin until its fetch completes. However, stores may trail their corresponding fetches as much as necessary to ensure full network bandwidth utilization. That is, we may initially let fetches get several steps ahead of stores, so that many stores and fetches run concurrently.

4.3 SBT Security

We now show that SBT meets the Paddable TOM criteria in Definition 5. We have shown that SBT has a finite step count upper bound ℓn, so it remains to show that public access patterns with the same step count are indistinguishable (Condition 2 of Definition 4), and that public access patterns may be padded.

Theorem 1. *In the SBT, for any two public access patterns $P(\vec{S_1}), P(\vec{S_2})$, if $|\sigma(\vec{S_1})| = |\sigma(\vec{S_2})|$, then $P(\vec{S_1})$ and $P(\vec{S_2})$ are computationally indistinguishable.*

Proof. First, the order in which the SBT fetches from and stores to bins is fixed. Hence, any two public access patterns with the same step count must make fetches and stores to and from exactly the same sequence of bins.

Store Patterns: After each pass, the locally-stored bin of blocks to be sent to the server is randomly permuted and re-encrypted using a semantically secure encryption scheme and a fresh nonce. Blocks are then stored to the server in their permuted order. Re-encryption ensures that the server cannot distinguish the blocks. Random permutation ensures that blocks are always stored in a uniformly random order, independent of fetch order. Thus any two *store* patterns of the same length are computationally indistinguishable.

Fetch Patterns: Since the blocks within each bin were randomly permuted, each block's location in the bin is independent of its data and any prior accesses. Thus each fetch is indistinguishable from a uniformly random choice from the bin's remaining blocks, and any two fetches from one bin are indistinguishable. Thus any two *fetch* patterns of the same length are indistinguishable.

Thus, since $P(\vec{S_1})$ and $P(\vec{S_2})$ have the same step count, and there is exactly one fetch and store per step, their fetch and store patterns each have the same length and are indistinguishable. Since both fetches and stores are indistinguishable, and the pattern of when to issue fetches and stores is predetermined, $P(\vec{S_1})$ and $P(\vec{S_2})$ are themselves computationally indistinguishable. □

Theorem 2. *Any public access pattern generated by SBT may be* padded *by adding any number of dummy steps.*

Proof. We can pad any public access pattern in SBT with any number d of additional steps by issuing d *dummy* fetches for randomly chosen blocks from each of the next d bins, along with their corresponding stores. □

Theorems 1 and 2 establish that SBT is a Paddable TOM, as per Definition 5. Thus we can coerce SBT into satisfying λ-TOM for any λ. In particular, we apply the log-spacing strategy of Section 3.5 to choose the λ milestones in $\mathcal{M}_\ell$. The smaller our choice of λ, the greater our privacy but the poorer our performance. By Equation 2, for a given λ, we have a maximum padding factor:

$$\delta \leq \left\lceil (S_{\text{Max}})^{1/\lambda} \right\rceil = \left\lceil n^{1/\lambda} \right\rceil \leq (2N)^{1/2\lambda}. \quad (4)$$

Similarly, by Equation 3, for a δ, we get a minimum milestone count λ given by:

$$\lambda \geq \log_\delta S_{\text{Max}} = \log_\delta n. \quad (5)$$

4.4 SBT Performance

The upper-bound on the SBT's per-access step count is given by $S_{\text{Max}} = n$, so the upper-bound bandwidth cost is given by $C_{\text{Max}} = 2n \leq 2\sqrt{2N}$. We now determine the bandwidth cost C_{HP} that holds with high probability for large, uniform random block queries, which are queries composed of ℓ block addresses chosen uniformly at random, without replacement.

The size of each fetch queue decreases by at most one during a given pass, so the number of passes needed to satisfy a query depends on the initial length of the longest fetch queue. We use H to denote the maximum length of the longest fetch queue. The query generates step count roughly nH without padding. In the best case, each fetch queue is nearly the same length, and in the worst case all fetches are in the same queue, so we know that $\lceil \ell/n \rceil \leq H \leq \ell$.

Theorem 3. *Let $\ell \geq n$ (large queries). With high probability for the SBT with uniform random block queries:*

$$H \in O\left(\frac{\ell}{n} \frac{\log n}{\log \log n} \right).$$

We prove this theorem in Appendix A, using the observation that we can bound H by bounding the maximum urn height in the well-known *balls and urns* problem [12, 19], where balls are thrown into urns uniformly at random, with replacement. Thus, for uniform random block queries with $\ell \geq n$, the bandwidth cost, with high probability, is:

$$C_{\text{HP}} \in O\left(\delta \frac{n}{\ell} \frac{\ell}{n} \frac{\log n}{\log \log n} \right) \subseteq O\left(\frac{\delta \log N}{\log \log N} \right), \quad (6)$$

with constant δ for at least $\lambda \in \Omega(\log N)$ milestones. Thus SBT is able to satisfy large queries that are not cache-friendly with a lower asymptotic cost than the best existing ORAM protocols (cost $O(\log N)$) while leaking only $I_\lambda \in O(\log \log N)$ bits per ℓ-block query.

5. SBT VARIANTS

We now propose three read-only SBT variants: *2-Choice SBT*, *SBT+ORAM*, and *Multi-SBT* (a combination of 2-Choice SBT and SBT+ORAM). These variants store multiple copies of each block and fetch the most convenient copy available, reducing bandwidth cost to as little as $C_{\text{Max}} = 3 \log_2 N$ in the worst case, and $C_{\text{HP}} \in O(1)$ for large uniform random block queries (see Table 3).

Read-only means that the client cannot update the contents of any of his blocks. However, blocks must still be re-encrypted and stored back to the server to preserve privacy. Writes *can* be supported, but would require all copies of a block to be updated, making writes substantially more expensive than reads.

5.1 The 2-Choice SBT Variant

We construct the 2-Choice SBT by creating two copies of each of the N data blocks, and adding them all to a single SBT with capacity $2N$, which treats both copies as independent blocks. The key difference from SBT is that when the 2-Choice SBT needs to read block a, it may choose to fetch the block from either of 2 bins. It is possible that both copies of a will be in the same bin, but this state is rare and transient, persisting only until either copy is fetched.

For a given query, each of the ℓ secret block accesses yields a fetch that is assigned to one of two bins' fetch queues. We want to optimize the assignment of fetches to bins, reducing the maximum queue length H. Since we know the entire query and the block-bin mapping, the optimization resembles the *optimal multi-choice allocation* [2], and *offline Cuckoo hashing* [17] problems.

5.1.1 Random Round Robin Algorithm

We optimize fetch assignments using the iterative *Random Round Robin (RRR)* algorithm proposed in [2]. We describe RRR briefly, replacing *balls* with block *fetches* and *bins* with fetch *queues*.

We first guess a target maximum queue length H', starting with the minimum $H' = \lceil \ell/n \rceil$. We then run RRR to try to find an assignment of fetches to queues with actual $H \leq H'$. If the attempt fails, we increment H' and repeat. In practice, we rarely expect more than two iterations [2], so we fix a maximum iteration count $r = 5$, after which we return the best available result. The iterative RRR runs efficiently, requiring time and space in $O(r(n + \ell))$.

For each RRR iteration, each fetch starts out *uncommitted*: assigned to the queues of both bins containing its block. When we *commit* a fetch to a queue, we irreversibly remove it from its other queue. We identify any queue q with length at most H', and commit to q all its uncommitted fetches. The intuition is that since q's length is at most H' and cannot increase, it should accept its current assignment, freeing as many fetches as possible from other queues. Any time we remove a fetch from a queue, we repeat this check.

We continue by stepping through all remaining queues with uncommitted fetches, for each queue randomly choosing one uncommitted fetch to commit to the queue, followed by the length check. We continue stepping through queues until all fetches are committed. If any queues still have more than H' fetches, the RRR iteration is declared a failure.

5.1.2 2-Choice SBT Security

To an observer, the 2-Choice SBT behaves just like the SBT, except for its higher capacity. Thus, 2-Choice SBT's security follows from the arguments for SBT security in Section 4.3. In particular, 2-Choice SBT meets the criteria of Definition 5 for a Paddable TOM Protocol with worst-case per-access step count $S_{\text{Max}} = n \leq 2\sqrt{N}$. Thus, it can be coerced to λ-TOM using the log-spacing strategy. By Equation 2, the maximum padding factor δ is given by $\delta \leq \lceil n^{1/\lambda} \rceil \leq (4N)^{1/(2\lambda)}$. For a given δ, Equation 3 gives $\lambda \geq \log_\delta n$.

5.1.3 2-Choice SBT Performance

Since $S_{\text{Max}} \leq 2\sqrt{N}$, we have $C_{\text{Max}} \leq 4\sqrt{N}$.

Conjecture 1. *With high probability, the 2-Choice SBT with uniform random block queries gives $H \in O(\ell/n + 1)$.*

For a related balls and urns problem, the authors in [2] show empirically that RRR yields maximum urn height in $O(\ell/n + 1)$, with performance nearly indistinguishable from the more complex *Selfless Algorithm*, which is proven to have maximum height $O(\ell/n + 1)$ with high probability. While we cannot provide a formal proof of Conjecture 1, we give a detailed argument supporting it in Appendix A, and show in Section 6 that it is borne out by our experiments.

Assuming Conjecture 1, the bandwidth cost of the 2-Choice SBT used on uniform random block queries with $\ell \geq n$ is, with high probability:

$$C_{\text{HP}} \in O\left(\delta \frac{n}{\ell} \left(\frac{\ell}{n} + 1\right)\right) \subseteq O(\delta), \qquad (7)$$

with constant δ for $\lambda \in \Omega(\log N)$. Thus, for large uniform random block queries, the 2-Choice SBT is highly efficient, and leaks only $I_\lambda \in O(\log \log N)$ bits/query.

Relative to SBT, the 2-Choice SBT doubles the storage space required for the server ($2N$), and increases required client block storage from $\sqrt{2N}$ to $2\sqrt{N}$ blocks and client index space from about $2N \log_2 N$ to nearly $4N \log_2 N$ bits.

5.2 The SBT+ORAM Variant

We construct the SBT+ORAM by merging a SBT with any efficient ORAM. We store one copy of each block in the SBT and in the ORAM, and run both protocols in parallel. To read a block, we either fetch it using the SBT, or read it using a single ORAM step. For now we use the practical ORAM of [23] due to its low bandwidth cost of roughly $\log_2 N$ block transfers per secret access.

For each query, we first assign all fetches to the SBT component's fetch queues and let it run normally. After every $\log_2 N$ SBT steps, we remove one fetch from the current longest fetch queue and re-assign it to the ORAM.

5.2.1 SBT+ORAM Security

The ORAM component advances one step for every $\log_2 N$ SBT steps. Thus, in the worst case where we rely strictly on the ORAM, we need $\ell(1 + \log_2 N)$ total steps to satisfy a query of length ℓ, so the per-access step count is bounded by $S_{\text{Max}} = 1 + \log_2 N$. We now show that SBT+ORAM

satisfies the indistinguishability and paddability conditions of a Paddable *TOM*.

Theorem 4. *In SBT+ORAM, for any public access patterns $P(\vec{S_1})$, $P(\vec{S_2})$, if $|\sigma(\vec{S_1})| = |\sigma(\vec{S_2})|$, then $P(\vec{S_1})$ and $P(\vec{S_2})$ are computationally indistinguishable.*

Proof. Since ORAM uses exactly one step per secret access, two public access patterns with the same step count have the same secret access pattern length. Thus, by Definition 1, any two public access patterns with the same step count generated by the ORAM are indistinguishable. By Theorem 2, any two public access patterns with the same step count generated by the SBT are also indistinguishable. Since the public access patterns generated by both protocols are indistinguishable, and the pattern of when to issue fetches from the SBT and the ORAM is predetermined, the SBT+ORAM's combined public access patterns $P(\vec{S_1})$ and $P(\vec{S_2})$ are indistinguishable. $\square$

Using the log-spacing strategy gives $\delta \leq \lceil (S_{\text{Max}})^{1/\lambda} \rceil = \lceil (1 + \log_2 N)^{1/\lambda} \rceil$ and $\lambda \geq \log_\delta S_{\text{Max}} = \log_\delta (1 + \log_2 N)$ (Equations 2, 3). Since S_{Max} is smaller for SBT+ORAM than SBT, the privacy/efficiency tradeoff is more favorable. In particular, to limit padding to $\delta = 2$, we need only $\lambda \approx \log_2 \log_2 N$ milestones.

5.2.2 SBT+ORAM Performance

We incur $\log_2 N$ block transfers for each ORAM step and 2 transfers for each SBT step. In the worst-case, we make ℓ ORAM steps and $\ell \log_2 N$ SBT steps for an ℓ-block query, giving $C_{\text{Max}} \leq 3 \log_2 N$.

We know from Theorem 3 that for large uniform random block queries, the SBT has maximum fetch queue length in $O(\ell \log N / n \log \log N)$. However, the expected queue length is only ℓ/n, so we rightly expect that relatively few queues have such large lengths. Though the ORAM runs slowly, focusing it on the largest queues first asymptotically reduces the final maximum queue length H.

Theorem 5. *Let $\ell \geq n$ and $N \geq 32$. With high probability for the SBT+ORAM with uniform random block queries we have:*

$$H \in O\left(\frac{\ell}{n} \log \log N\right).$$

In the full version of the paper [3] we present a proof for Theorem 5 based on a novel balls and urns analysis. By Theorem 5, the bandwidth cost of the SBT+ORAM used on uniform random block queries with $\ell \geq n, N \geq 32$ is, with high probability:

$$C_{\text{HP}} \in O\left(\delta \frac{n}{\ell} \frac{\ell}{n} \log \log N\right) \subseteq O(\delta \log \log N), \qquad (8)$$

with constant δ for only $\lambda \in \Omega(\log \log N)$ milestones. Thus, for large uniform random block queries, the SBT+ORAM is more efficient than the SBT. At the same time, it leaks only $I_\lambda \in O(\log \log \log N)$ bits per query, yielding better privacy than 2-Choice SBT, but slightly higher C_{HP}.

The server storage costs of [23] are reported at roughly $4BN$ bits, and we estimate that client storage is $1.25 \log_2 N + 3B\sqrt{N}$ bits, based on results in Table 2 of [23]. Thus, the SBT+ORAM has a total server storage cost of roughly $5BN$, and client storage $(\ell + \sqrt{2N} + 3\sqrt{N})B + 3.25N \log_2 N$ bits.

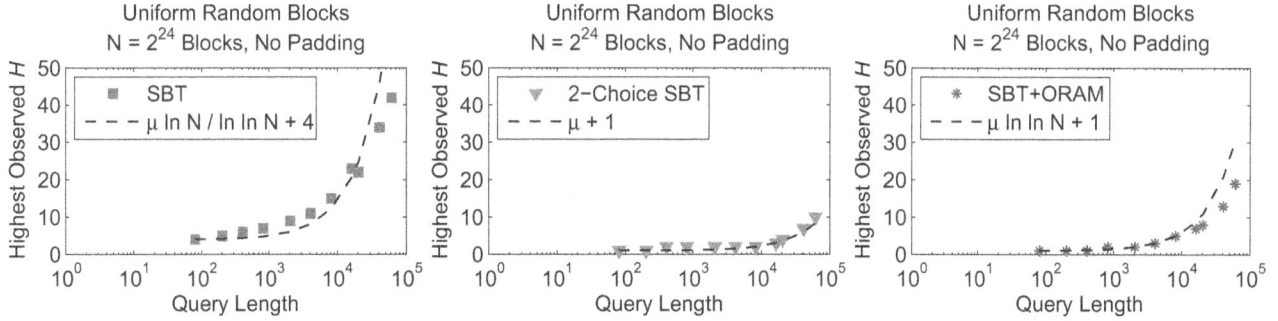

Figure 4: Analysis confirmation. Max. observed H asymptotically dominated by analytic predictions. $\mu = \ell/n$

5.3 The Multi-SBT Variant

The Multi-SBT replaces the SBT in a SBT+ORAM with a 2-Choice SBT. Thus, the Multi-SBT stores a total of three copies of each block. Its security follows directly from the security of 2-Choice SBT and SBT+ORAM.

The Multi-SBT inherits SBT+ORAM's excellent worst-case per-access step count $S_{\text{MAX}} = 1 + \log_2 N$ and bandwidth cost $C_{\text{MAX}} = 3 \log_2 N$. For large random block queries, it also inherits 2-Choice SBT's high-probability bandwidth cost:

$$C_{\text{HP}} \in O(\delta), \qquad (9)$$

while requiring only $\lambda \in \Omega(\log \log N)$ milestones for constant δ, and leaking only $I_\lambda \in O(\log \log \log N)$ bits per query. Thus, for uniform random block queries of any size, the Multi-SBT requires only $O(\ell + \log_2 N)$ block transfers!

Multi-SBT combines the best performance and privacy characteristics of 2-Choice SBT and SBT+ORAM, and can easily outperform both. Even in worst cases, the Multi-SBT incurs at most 3 times the bandwidth cost of SBT+ORAM, or 1.5 times the cost of SBT. Multi-SBT requires total server storage of roughly $6BN$, and client storage roughly $B\sqrt{N}(3 + \sqrt{2}) + 5.25N \log_2 N$ bits.

6. EVALUATION

We implemented prototypes for SBT and its variants to estimate actual bandwidth costs for various query types. The prototypes simulate secure transfers of blocks between the client and server, tracking each block's location at all times.

6.1 Maximum Queue Length Measurements

Theorems 3, 5 and Conjecture 1 give high-probability asymptotic bounds on H for large, uniform random block queries. We validated these bounds by running simulations for the corresponding SBT variants without padding, and measuring the highest observed H over $4N/\ell$ queries for various ℓ. Our results are shown in Figure 4 along with plots of concrete functions consistent with our bounds.

6.2 Simulator Details

We implemented our simulator in Java, fully modeling SBT behavior. The simulator accommodates padding, waiting to release query results until the step count reaches one of the milestones. Our simulator is synchronous, since asynchronous behavior is not needed to measure bandwidth cost.

On a single thread, the simulator requires 0.5 to 1.5μs per simulated block transfer, depending on the specific protocol and number of blocks. For the sake of speed, we do not

manipulate actual block contents. Thus, we're able to efficiently evaluate SBT bandwidth costs for larger block counts and longer runs without the expense of actually performing network transfers, disk IO, and encryption.

We assume a fully de-amortized black-box ORAM with $\log_2 N$ bandwidth cost per step, based on the ORAM in [23]. When simulating the protocols with ORAM components, we step the SBT component $\log_2 N$ times, then step the ORAM once, retrieving the previous step's result.

6.3 Bandwidth Cost Experiments

Figures 5–13 give our experimental results measuring bandwidth cost for three types of queries and varying three parameters (N, ℓ, λ). Recall that bandwidth cost is given by the total number of block transfers (fetches and stores counted individually), divided by the number of secret accesses (reads or writes) ℓ.

All the experiments used a 64KB block size and allow 8GB of client space, which includes the SBT's block-ID map, space for recently fetched blocks, and space for the ORAM component, if any. Any leftover client space is used as a local block cache. Different block sizes alter storage capacity and client space, but leave bandwidth costs largely unchanged. During a trial, we run $4N/\ell$ queries of fixed length ℓ, requesting each stored block four times on average.

Each experiment varies one of: block count N (Figures 5, 8, 11), query length ℓ (Figures 6, 9, 12), or milestone count λ (Figures 7, 10, 13). Our default block count $N = 2^{24}$ yields a 1TB TOM storage capacity. Our default query length $\ell = 4\sqrt{N}$ represents a 2^{14} block (1GB) query for the default N. Our default milestone count $\lambda = 8$ leaks at most $I_\lambda = 3$ bits per ℓ-block query.

6.3.1 Uniform Random Block Queries (Figures 5–7)

The *Uniform Random Block* queries are the best suited to the SBT protocols. For each query, we choose ℓ distinct blocks uniformly at random from all N blocks. We used the same type of query to derive our analytic bandwidth cost predictions. All SBT variants outperform ORAM for large uniform random block queries, with costs as low as 5X for the Multi-SBT (Figure 6).

6.3.2 Fixed Sequence Queries (Figures 8–13)

For fixed sequence queries, we divide the N blocks into $s = N/\ell$ non-overlapping fixed sequences of ℓ distinct blocks each before permuting the blocks and storing them on the server. Each query consists of exactly one of these fixed sequences, simulating a file system in which each query re-

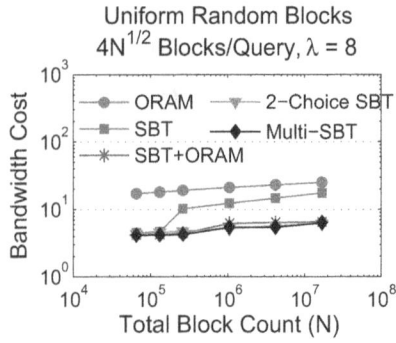

Figure 5: Uniform random block queries, varying N

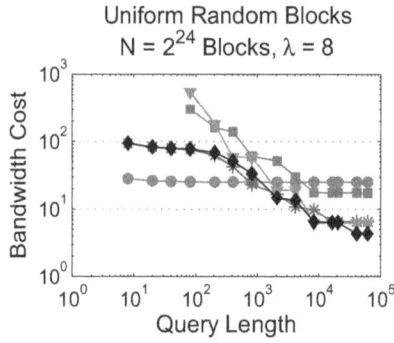

Figure 6: Uniform random block queries, varying ℓ

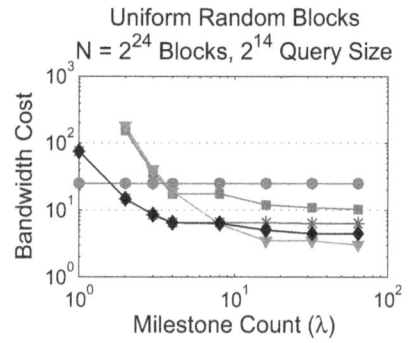

Figure 7: Uniform random block queries, varying λ

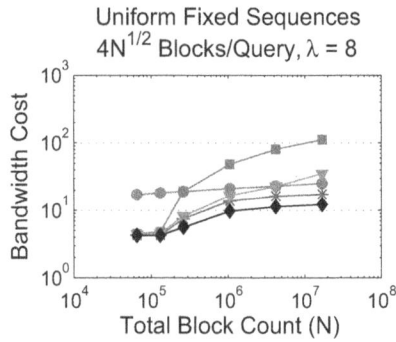

Figure 8: Uniform fixed sequence queries, varying N

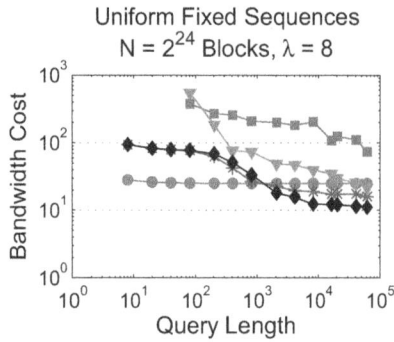

Figure 9: Uniform fixed sequence queries, varying ℓ

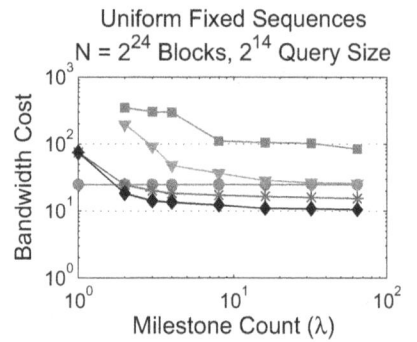

Figure 10: Uniform fixed sequence queries, varying λ

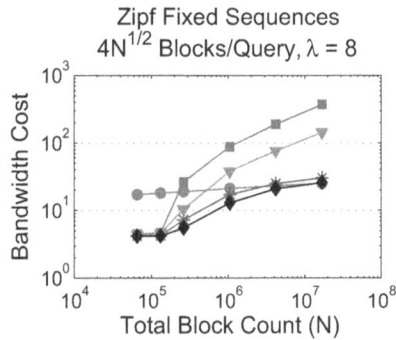

Figure 11: Zipf fixed sequence queries, varying N

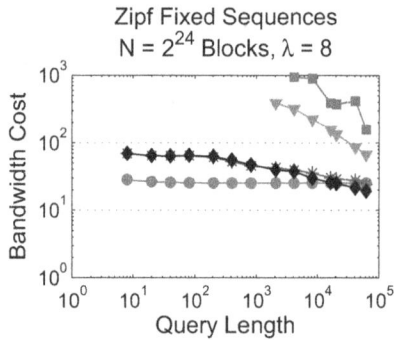

Figure 12: Zipf fixed sequence queries, varying ℓ

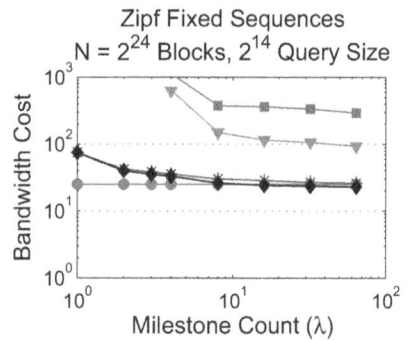

Figure 13: Zipf fixed sequence queries, varying λ

quests an entire file. *Uniform* fixed sequence experiments choose sequences uniformly at random, while *Zipf* experiments choose sequences from a power law distribution in which the ith most common sequence is chosen with probability H_s/i, where H_s is the sth harmonic number.

There are relatively few (N/ℓ) possible distinct fixed sequence queries, compared to the many (N choose ℓ) uniform random block queries. As a result, fixed sequence queries are far more likely to repeat, leading to poor SBT performance (Section 4.4). Zipf fixed sequence queries repeat frequently, so that ORAM nearly always outperforms the SBT variants (Figures 11–13). Uniform fixed sequence queries repeated less often, so several variants still outperform ORAM (Fig-

ures 8–10). We reiterate that SBT is a *special-purpose* TOM protocol. The more varied the query block distribution, the better SBT performs.

6.3.3 Other Observations

For small queries, SBTs with ORAMs converge to a worst-case cost $3\log_2 N$, while others converge to a much larger cost of n (Figures 6, 9, 12). Figures 7, 10, 13 show that we can improve performance by leaking more information (increasing λ) up to $\lambda \approx 32$ ($I_\lambda = 5$ bits). At this point padding costs become negligible, leaving the raw cost of the protocol. Since protocols with ORAM components have smaller worst-case costs, the milestones are packed more tightly, so padding effects become negligible sooner ($\lambda \approx 8$).

7. CONCLUSION

We presented a novel ORAM generalization called Tunably-Oblivious Memory (λ-TOM), which permits a privacy/efficiency tradeoff controlled via milestone count λ. We introduced the log-spacing strategy for choosing milestones to minimize padding costs, and strictly bounded the information leaked by each λ-TOM query. We also developed the special-purpose *Staggered-Bin TOM* protocol, and several read-only variants, including the Multi-SBT. We showed analytically and empirically that the Multi-SBT is highly efficient for large queries that are not cache-friendly, achieving bandwidth costs as low as 6X compared to the 22X-29X costs of the best existing ORAM protocols, while leaking at most 3 bits per query. We believe that the TOM model can be used in future work to build other highly secure special-purpose protocols, like SBT, that outperform current ORAM techniques on a variety of workloads.

8. ACKNOWLEDGEMENTS

This work was completed while the first author was a student at UC Riverside. The work was supported in part by the National Physical Science Consortium Graduate Fellowship and by grant N00014-07-C-0311 from the Office of Naval Research.

9. REFERENCES

[1] D. Boneh, D. Mazieres, and R. A. Popa. Remote oblivious storage: Making oblivious RAM practical. Manuscript, `http://dspace.mit.edu/bitstream/handle/1721.1/62006/MIT-CSAIL-TR-2011-018.pdf`, 2011.

[2] J. A. Cain, P. Sanders, and N. Wormald. The random graph threshold for k-orientiability and a fast algorithm for optimal multiple-choice allocation. In *Proc. SODA*, pages 469–476. Society for Industrial and Applied Mathematics, 2007.

[3] J. Dautrich. *Achieving Practical Access Pattern Privacy in Data Outsourcing*. PhD thesis, University of California, Riverside, 2014.

[4] J. Dautrich and C. Ravishankar. Compromising privacy in precise query protocols. In *Proc. EDBT*, 2013.

[5] J. Dautrich and C. Ravishankar. Combining oram with pir to minimize bandwidth costs. In *CODASPY*, 2015.

[6] J. Dautrich, E. Stefanov, and E. Shi. Burst ORAM: Minimizing ORAM response times for bursty access patterns. In *USENIX Security*, 2014.

[7] S. De Capitani di Vimercati, S. Foresti, S. Paraboschi, G. Pelosi, and P. Samarati. Efficient and private access to outsourced data. In *Proc. ICDCS*, 2011.

[8] C. Gentry, K. Goldman, S. Halevi, C. Julta, M. Raykova, and D. Wichs. Optimizing ORAM and using it efficiently for secure computation. In *PETS*, 2013.

[9] O. Goldreich and R. Ostrovsky. Software protection and simulation on oblivious RAMs. *Journal of the ACM (JACM)*, 43(3):431–473, 1996.

[10] M. T. Goodrich, M. Mitzenmacher, O. Ohrimenko, and R. Tamassia. Privacy-preserving group data access via stateless oblivious RAM simulation. In *Proc. SODA*, pages 157–167. SIAM, 2012.

[11] M. Islam, M. Kuzu, and M. Kantarcioglu. Access pattern disclosure on searchable encryption: Ramification, attack and mitigation. In *NDSS*, 2012.

[12] N. L. Johnson and S. Kotz. *Urn models and their application: an approach to modern discrete probability theory.* Wiley New York, 1977.

[13] E. Kushilevitz, S. Lu, and R. Ostrovsky. On the (in)security of hash-based oblivious RAM and a new balancing scheme. In *Proc. SODA*, pages 143–156. SIAM, 2012.

[14] J. R. Lorch, B. Parno, J. W. Mickens, M. Raykova, and J. Schiffman. Shroud: Ensuring private access to large-scale data in the data center. *FAST*, pages 199–213, 2013.

[15] M. Maas, E. Love, E. Stefanov, M. Tiwari, E. Shi, K. Asanovic, J. Kubiatowicz, and D. Song. PHANTOM: Practical oblivious computation in a secure processor. In *ACM CCS*, 2013.

[16] T. Mayberry, E.-O. Blass, and A. H. Chan. Efficient private file retrieval by combining ORAM and PIR. In *NDSS*, 2014.

[17] M. Mitzenmacher. Some open questions related to cuckoo hashing. In *Algorithms-ESA 2009*, pages 1–10. Springer, 2009.

[18] Y. Nakano, C. Cid, S. Kiyomoto, and Y. Miyake. Memory access pattern protection for resource-constrained devices. In *Smart Card Research and Advanced Applications*, pages 188–202. Springer, 2013.

[19] M. Raab and A. Steger. Balls into bins – a simple and tight analysis. In *Randomization and Approximation Techniques in Computer Science*, pages 159–170. Springer, 1998.

[20] R. Sion. On the computational practicality of private information retrieval. In *Proc. NDSS*, 2007.

[21] E. Stefanov and E. Shi. Multi-Cloud Oblivious Storage. In *CCS*, 2013.

[22] E. Stefanov and E. Shi. ObliviStore: High performance oblivious cloud storage. In *IEEE Symposium on Security and Privacy*, 2013.

[23] E. Stefanov, E. Shi, and D. Song. Towards practical oblivious RAM. NDSS, 2012.

[24] E. Stefanov, M. van Dijk, E. Shi, C. Fletcher, L. Ren, X. Yu, and S. Devadas. Path ORAM: An extremely simple oblivious RAM protocol. In *ACM CCS*, 2013.

[25] P. Williams, R. Sion, and A. Tomescu. PrivateFS: A parallel oblivious file system. In *CCS*, 2012.

[26] X. Yu, C. W. Fletcher, L. Ren, M. v. Dijk, and S. Devadas. Generalized external interaction with tamper-resistant hardware with bounded information leakage. In *Proc. ACM CCSW*, pages 23–34. ACM, 2013.

APPENDIX

A. PERFORMANCE ANALYSES / PROOFS

Here we prove Theorem 3 and argue for Conjecture 1. The proof of Theorem 5 is deferred to the extended version of the paper [3]. In each case, our goal is to upper-bound the maximum fetch queue length H — the maximum number of blocks that must be fetched from any one bin by the

SBT component to satisfy a query. Equivalently, H is the maximum number of SBT *passes* needed to satisfy a query.

For simplicity, we assume the SBT is at the start of a pass, so we are given n bins filled with $1, 2, \ldots, n$ blocks each.[1] Each query requests ℓ distinct blocks chosen uniformly at random, without replacement, from the set of all N blocks. We call such queries *uniform random block queries*. Every block has a unique *location*. Of the $N = n(n+3)/2$ blocks, n are located somewhere in the local cache, and the remaining $n(n+1)/2$ are located somewhere in one of the n bins. Requests for cached blocks are satisfied instantly.

We assign each queried block a unique index i between 1 and ℓ. Let $\Pr_B(i,j)$ be the maximum probability that block i will be in bin j, given any possible arrangement of the remaining queried blocks. The maximum $\Pr_B(i,j)$ occurs when j is the n-block bin, and the other $\ell - 1$ blocks are located in bins other than j. In this case, i has $N - \ell + 1$ possible locations, n of which are in bin j, giving:

$$\Pr_B(i,j) \leq \frac{n}{N - \ell + 1} \leq \frac{n}{N - \ell}. \tag{10}$$

A great deal of work has been done on the closely-related *balls and urns* problem (e.g. [12, 19]), in which balls are thrown independently into one of several urns chosen uniformly at random (with replacement).[2] There are well-known bounds on the resulting maximum urn occupancy. To use these bounds, we first reduce our blocks and bins problem to a larger balls and urns problem.

A.1 Problem Transformation

Consider the balls and urns problem with 3ℓ balls, where 3 distinct balls are given each index $1 \leq i \leq \ell$. We throw these 3ℓ balls independently and uniformly at random into n urns. Let $\Pr_U(i,j)$ be the probability that at least one ball with label i will appear in urn j, which is given by:

$$\Pr_U(i,j) = 1 - \left(\frac{n-1}{n}\right)^3 = \frac{3n^2 - 3n + 1}{n^3} \tag{11}$$

Intuitively, if $\Pr_B(i,j) \leq \Pr_U(i,j)$, then a ball labeled i is at least as likely to be placed in urn j as block i is to be located in bin j, and so the number of blocks found in bin j should be no larger than the number of balls in urn j. If we can show that $\Pr_B(i,j) \leq \Pr_U(i,j)$ for every i, j, then any upper-bound on the maximum urn occupancy in the balls and bins problem should hold for the maximum queue length H in the blocks and bins problem.

Lemma 2. $\Pr_B(i,j) \leq \Pr_U(i,j)$ holds for all $\ell \leq n^2/6$.

Proof. Substituting $N = n(n+3)/2$, we get:

$$\Pr_B(i,j) \leq \frac{n}{N - \ell} = \frac{2}{n + 3 - 2\ell/n}.$$

Thus we have

$$\Pr_B(i,j) \leq \Pr_U(i,j) \impliedby \frac{2}{n + 3 - 2\ell/n} \leq \frac{3n^2 - 3n + 1}{n^3}$$

$$\impliedby 2n^3 \leq 3n^3 + 6n^2 - 8n + 3 - \ell(6n - 6 + 2/n)$$

$$\impliedby \ell(6n - 6 + 2/n) \leq n^3 + 6n^2 - 4n + 3$$

$$\impliedby \ell \leq n^2/6$$

$\square$

A.2 SBT Analysis

We are now ready to prove Theorem 3.

Theorem 3. *Let $\ell \geq n$ (large queries). With high probability for the SBT with uniform random block queries, we have:*

$$H \in O\left(\frac{\ell}{n} \frac{\log n}{\log \log n}\right).$$

Proof. It is well known (e.g. [19]) that if we throw n balls independently and uniformly at random into n urns, we get a maximum urn occupancy in $O(\log n / \log \log n)$ with high probability. Thus, if we throw $m \geq n$ balls, we get a maximum height $O((m \log n)/n \log \log n)$. By Lemma 2, when $\ell \leq n^2/6$, an upper-bound on the maximum urn occupancy for $m = 3\ell$ balls and n urns applies to H, giving:

$$H \in O\left(\frac{3\ell \log n}{n \log \log n}\right) \subseteq O\left(\frac{\ell}{n} \frac{\log n}{\log \log n}\right), \text{ for } \frac{n}{3} \leq \ell \leq \frac{n^2}{6}$$

Further, since $H \leq n$, for $\ell > n^2/6$ we also have, trivially, that: $H \in O\left(\frac{\ell}{n}\right) \subseteq O\left(\frac{\ell}{n} \frac{\log n}{\log \log n}\right)$. $\square$

A.3 2-Choice SBT Analysis

Conjecture 1. *With high probability for the 2-Choice SBT with uniform random block queries, we have:*

$$H \in O\left(\ell/n + 1\right).$$

Authors in [2] analyze the *Selfless Algorithm* for allocating m balls to n urns, where each ball may be placed in either of two urns chosen uniformly at random. They show, analytically, that the Selfless Algorithm yields a maximum final urn occupancy $U' \in O(\lceil m/n \rceil) \subseteq O(m/n + 1)$ with high probability. They also show empirically that the simpler *Random Round Robin* algorithm, which we use for the 2-Choice SBT, has nearly equivalent performance.

As we did for SBT, we can think of the 2-Choice SBT's blocks and bins problem as a balls and urns problem where we throw $m = 3\ell$ balls into n urns. However, since each block now belongs to two bins, and can thus be added to either of two fetch queues, the corresponding ball may be placed in either of two urns, but need not be placed in both. Though Lemma 2 no longer holds, we appeal to the intuition that a bound on the maximum urn occupancy H' is likely to hold for the maximum fetch queue height H as well.

We therefore contend that $H \approx U' \in O(m/n + 1) \subseteq O(\ell/n + 1)$. Clearly, this argument is far from a proof, both because *Random Round Robin* has not been fully analyzed, and because of the different models used for the two-choice blocks and bins and two-choice balls and urns problems. However, we observe empirically that 2-Choice SBT does in fact appear to follow $H \in O(\ell/n + 1)$, as evidenced by Figure 4 in Section 6.

---

[1] We can force the SBT to the start of a pass for each query, which increases H by at most 1 and thus does not affect our asymptotic analysis.

[2] Such problems are commonly referred to as *balls and bins* problems, but since we use *bin* in our SBT construction, we use *urn* here for clarity.

HideM: Protecting the Contents of Userspace Memory in the Face of Disclosure Vulnerabilities *

Jason Gionta, William Enck, and Peng Ning
Dept. of Computer Science, North Carolina State University
Raleigh, NC, USA
jjgionta@ncsu.edu, enck@cs.ncsu.edu, pning@ncsu.edu

ABSTRACT

Memory disclosure vulnerabilities have become a common component for enabling reliable exploitation of systems by leaking the contents of executable data. Previous research towards protecting executable data from disclosure has failed to gain popularity due to large performance penalties and required architectural changes. Other research has focused on protecting application data but fails to consider a vulnerable application that leaks its own executable data.

In this paper we present HideM, a practical system for protecting against memory disclosures in contemporary commodity systems. HideM addresses limitations in existing advanced security protections (e.g., fine-grained ASLR, CFI) wherein an adversary discloses executable data from memory, reasons about protection weaknesses, and builds corresponding exploits. HideM uses the split-TLB architecture, commonly found in CPUs, to enable fine-grained execute and read permission on memory. HideM enforces fine-grained permission based on policy generated from binary structure thus enabling protection of Commercial-Off-The-Shelf (COTS) binaries. In our evaluation of HideM, we find application overhead ranges from a 6.5% increase to a 2% reduction in runtime and observe runtime memory overhead ranging from 0.04% to 25%. HideM requires adversaries to guess ROP gadget locations making exploitation unreliable. We find adversaries have less than a 16% chance of correctly guessing a single gadget across all 28 evaluated applications. Thus, HideM is a practical system for protecting vulnerable applications which leak executable data.

Categories and Subject Descriptors

K.6.5 [**Management of Computing and Information Systems**]: Security and Protection—*Unauthorized access*; D.4.6 [**Operating System**]: Security and Protection—*Information Flow Controls; Access Controls*

---

*This work is supported by U.S. National Science Foundation (NSF) under grant CNS-1330553.

General Terms

Security

Keywords

return-oriented programming; information leaks; memory disclosure exploits; code reuse attacks; memory protection

1. INTRODUCTION

Protecting memory is a critical component to ensuring the security of a system. Process memory contains many types of sensitive information including code, keys, and other secrets. Contemporary computer hardware contains page level memory protections preventing reads and writes. These protections provide isolation between address spaces (e.g. user and kernel-space).

Recent processor extensions seek to protect memory within an address space. For example, the no-execute (NX) protection bit prevents execution of specific memory pages (e.g., stacks). Unfortunately, techniques such as Return Oriented Programming (ROP) allow successful exploitation without executing these memory pages [23].

A common requirement for modern exploits to bypass system protections (e.g., ASLR, DEP) is reading memory. Specifically, a memory disclosure vulnerability is used to disclose code locations and values to ensure exploit reliability and correctness [17]. Memory disclosure vulnerabilities that leak code instructions are fundamentally possible because *execute permission always implies read permission* on commodity hardware. As a result, advanced protections such as fine-grained ASLR [14, 34] and Control Flow Integrity [2, 37] can be bypassed leading to exploitation [24, 10].

Execute-only memory is a well defined and understood technique for protecting the contents of memory. Multics, a classical secure system design and architecture, included an execute-only bit for memory pages [7]. XoM implemented execute-only memory by encrypting executable data and only decrypting on instruction loads. XoM required a custom processor architecture and suffered from poor performance making adoption difficult. Regardless, both approaches are too coarse grained in their protections.

We seek to broadly protect critical contents of userspace memory by leveraging a concept we call **code hiding**. Code hiding is inspired by PaX [28] for enabling no-execute memory without hardware extensions, as well as by advanced rootkit hiding that prevents forensic analysis [25]. We propose code hiding to protect userspace memory from being read by a malicious or vulnerable process. Code hiding is enabled using the unique features of the split Translation Lookaside Buffer (TLB) architecture to configure reads of executable pages on contemporary commodity hardware.

In this paper we propose HideM, a system that disallows userspace code from arbitrarily reading critical data in its own memory address space. HideM is built on code hiding to prevent reading executable data of existing legacy and COTS binaries. We observe the majority of code does not need to be read but only executed. We propose *code reading* policy as an approach to enforce fine grained read access on executable pages. Applications can also leverage HideM to protect sensitive data by encoding critical data in executable pages. The design of HideM allows integration with existing advanced security techniques (e.g., fine-grained ASLR [34, 14] and CFI approaches [37]). HideM ensures memory disclosure vulnerabilities cannot be used to find ROP gadgets to enable reliable exploitation, discover vulnerabilities in memory, and enable some forms of data leakage. Furthermore, HideM is generic and can be enabled on existing commercial hardware with minimal performance overhead to protect memory against disclosures.

Code reading policies are created based on data that may be legitimately read by code. For example, the GNU GCC compiler will embed exception handling data in code pages as an *.eh_frame* section. Policies are generated based on binary structure (e.g., read-only data in executable pages) and code/function symbols. To identify what code needs to be read as data, we perform binary analysis to recover code symbols from executable sections and identify data in code. We perform minimal manual analysis to verify the identification of data in code as correctly identifying all data in code is provably undecidable [35]

HideM uses *code reading* policies to divide read data from **executable data** (e.g., machine code) on executable pages. Shadow memory pages are created containing only required readable data or executable data. The OS kernel configures the hardware split-TLB to hide executable data from userspace read access. As a result, HideM can transparently apply *code reading* policies to commercial off-the-shelf (COTS) binaries.

In this paper, we make the following contributions:

- We design and implement HideM for protecting against the broader threat of information disclosure of process memory. HideM leverages *code hiding* as a new security mechanism to provide fine-grained userspace read access without changing current commodity hardware.

- We propose *code reading* policy to automatically configure userspace reads of binary executable pages. Policy is enforced at runtime and protects executable data vulnerable to memory disclosure.

- We evaluate compatibility, performance, and security impact of HideM. We find that HideM has limited impact on performance. The runtime increase ranges from 6.5% to a 2% reduction. We observe working memory increases ranging from 0.04% to 25%. Furthermore, HideM raises the level of security for protected binaries by reducing the probability of reliable exploit. We find an adversary has a less than 16% chance of guessing a single valid ROP gadget.

The remainder of this paper is as follows. Section 2 has a background on memory access and memory disclosures. Section 3 provides an overview, Section 4 discusses design, and Section 5 provides implementation details. Section 6 evaluates HideM. Section 7 discusses limitations and future work. Section 8 has related work. Section 9 concludes.

2. BACKGROUND AND MOTIVATION

We briefly provide background and motivation for HideM. First, we discuss memory accesses using hardware caching of virtual to physical mappings. Then, we motivate HideM looking at the threat of memory disclosure on existing security protections.

2.1 Memory Access via TLB

The Translation Lookaside Buffer (TLB) is a cache used by processors to reduce the cost of continuous memory accesses. The TLB stores mappings from page numbers (i.e., upper bits of a linear/virtual address) to physical frame (i.e., upper bits of physical address) along with page status and permissions. The TLB obviates the need for the system Memory Management Unit to walk page-tables for each memory access. The TLB also assists in MMU translations (i.e., walking pages-tables) by adding entries for intermediate page-table values (i.e., top level page directories).

Operations of TLB: TLB operations for managing entries are architecture specific. For example, SPARC implements TLB in software and thus the OS manages the TLB by adding and evicting entries [36]. On the other hand, x86 and ARM architectures use both hardware and software for TLB management [22, 13]. Specifically, entries are only added by hardware after the MMU walks page-tables. Entries are *flushed* (i.e., evicted) by both hardware events such as task-switch or using privileged CPU instructions.

Split-TLB Architecture: Processors commonly contain two TLBs, a DTLB to handle data accesses and an ITLB to handle instruction fetches. This split architecture allows for better locality of accessed memory [18]. In normal execution, the DTLB and ITLB are synchronized and contain the same values for a given address. TLB flushes of a specific address will remove associated entries from both the ITLB and DTLB. However, entries are added based on the type of CPU access. If an instruction is executed on a page, an ITLB entry is added. If memory is read, for example via a *mov* instruction, a DTLB entry is added.

2.2 Memory Disclosure

Memory disclosures are a subset of information leakage vulnerabilities in which an adversary gains unauthorized access to read raw memory. An adversary can then leak sensitive information such as encryption keys, passwords, or executable data. Using leaked executable code and associated addresses, an adversary can build reliable ROP based exploits in an automatic and just-in-time fashion [24]. Memory disclosures have also been used in bypassing CFI enforcement. Goktas et al. showed relaxed CFI code transfer enforcement can lead to ROP based exploitation [10]. The authors' exploit relied on a memory disclosure vulnerability to find function call and return stubs for trampolines.

There is a growing need to protect systems against memory disclosures; however existing research is limited. In independent work, Backes et al. [4] seek to provide "Execute Not Read" (XnR) permissions on code pages. Unfortunately, the proposed approach allows reading of the currently executing